Contemporary Authors

Bibliographical Series

American Dramatists

ISSN 0887-3070

Contemporary

Authors

Bibliographical Series

American Dramatists

Matthew C. Roudané
Georgia State University
Editor

volume 3

A Bruccoli Clark Layman Book
GALE RESEARCH, INC.
BOOK TOWER
DETROIT, MICHIGAN 48226

Editorial Directors

Matthew J. Bruccoli

Richard Layman

Copyright © 1989 by Gale Research, Inc.
ISBN 0-8103-2227-7
ISSN 0887-3070

Printed in the United States

To
Susan and Nickolas

Contents

Plan of the Work

Contemporary Authors Bibliographical Series (*CABS*) is a survey of writings by and about the most important writers since World War II in the United States and abroad. *CABS* is a new key to finding and evaluating information on the lives and writings of those authors who have attracted significant critical attention.

Purpose

Designed as a companion to the long-established *Contemporary Authors* bio-bibliographical series, *CABS* is dedicated to helping students, researchers, and librarians keep pace with the already massive and constantly growing body of literary scholarship that is available for modern authors of recognized stature. While this proliferation of literary criticism has provided a rich resource, it has also presented a perplexing problem: in the face of so much material, how does one efficiently find the required information, and how does one differentiate the good from the bad?

The purpose of *CABS* is to provide a guide to the best critical studies about major writers: to identify the uses and limitations of individual critiques, and to assist the user with the study of important writers' works.

Scope

CABS will include American as well as foreign authors, in volumes arranged by genre and nationality. Some of the subjects to be covered in the series include contemporary American dramatists, contemporary British poets, and contemporary American short story writers, to cite only a selection. While there will be a concentration of volumes on American and English writers, the scope of *CABS* is world literature, and volumes are also planned on contemporary European, South American, Asian, and African writers.

Format

Each volume of *CABS* provides primary and secondary bibliographies as well as an analytical bibliographical essay for approximately ten major writers. *CABS* entries consist of three parts:

1. A primary bibliography that lists works written by the author, divided for ease of use into:

–Books and Pamphlets

–Selected Other: translations, books edited by the subject of the entry, other material in books in which the subject had some role short of full authorship, and important short works that appeared in periodicals, all separated by rubrics.

–Editions, Collections

2. A secondary bibliography that lists works about the author, divided into:

–Bibliographies and Checklists

–Biographies

–Interviews

–Critical Studies, subdivided into:

  Books

  Collections of Essays

  Special Journals and Newsletters

  Articles and Book Sections

3. An analytical bibliographical essay in which the merits and the deficiencies of major critical and scholarly works are thoroughly discussed. This essay is divided into categories corresponding to those in the secondary bibliography.

Although every effort has been made to achieve consistency in the shaping of the checklists and essays included in this volume, each entry necessarily reflects the output of an author and his or her critics. Thus, if a writer has not published notebooks or translations, these rubrics or subrubrics are omitted from the primary checklist; similarly, if there is no biography or collection of essays on the author, these headings do not appear in the secondary checklist or in the essay.

CABS also contains a Critic Index, citing critics discussed in the biographical essays. For the convenience of researchers, this index will cumulate in all volumes after the first. Beginning with Volume 2, *CABS* will also include a cumulative Author Index, listing all the authors presented in the series.

Compilation Methods

Each *CABS* entry is written by an authority on his subject. The entries are reviewed by the volume editor–who is a specialist in the field–and the accuracy of the bibliographical details is verified at the Bruccoli Clark Layman editorial center. Each bibliographical entry is checked whenever possible against the actual publication cited in order to avoid repeating errors in other printed bibliographies. Full citations are provided for each item to facilitate location and the use of interlibrary loans.

Unlike other study guides, which are limited to a small selection of writers from earlier eras or which specialize in studies of individual authors, *CABS* is unique in providing comprehensive bibliographical information for the full spectrum of major modern authors. *CABS* is a map to the published critical appraisals of our most studied contemporary writers. It tells students and researchers what is available, and it advises them where they will find the information they seek about a writer and his works.

The publisher and the editors are pleased to provide researchers with this basic and essential service.

Preface

Represented in this volume are the major voices of contemporary drama as well as a selection of young writers whose plays and dramaturgic theories are as disparate, on ideological, theatrical, and metaphysical grounds, as the culture they dramatize. Readers will find a diverse assembly of dramatists who, collectively, represent the evolution of American drama since Eugene O'Neill, Susan Glaspell, and Thornton Wilder.

Each contributor was selected on the basis of his or her established reputation. In fact, no fewer than ten have published books either on his or her assigned author or on the field in general. Other contributors have published articles and, in some cases, directed productions of plays covered in these pages. Further, the contributors have engaged in meticulous research in a field that—because it involves producers, directors, theater troupes, acting versions of plays, revised text versions, unpublished plays, agents, and contradictory documentation—is as formidable as it is rewarding.

"There has been an explosion of scholarship and criticism on contemporary American novelists," observed James J. Martine in the preface for the volume on American novelists in this series, a remark that plainly applies to the drama as well. Nowhere is that contention more clearly confirmed than in the case of scholarship on Edward Albee, perhaps the most-discussed contemporary American playwright. Since *The Zoo Story* made its American premiere, some comment on his work—in books, essays, interviews, theater reviews—has appeared at the rate of once every four days, making the careful bibliography of Anne Paolucci and Henry Paolucci both a necessary and welcome addition to the scholarship.

Essays on the four black dramatists included in the volume capture the major influence blacks have exerted on American theater. Paul K. Jackson, Jr., traces critical reactions to Amiri Baraka's development from Greenwich Village poet to Black Nationalist playwright in the 1960s and early 1970s and follows his subsequent shift to Marxism. Sharon Friedman assesses the impact of another significant, if less controversial, dramatist: Lorraine Hansberry, whose

A Raisin in the Sun was the first play by a black woman staged on Broadway. Friedman discusses Hansberry's brief but influential impact on the American stage, focusing on Hansberry's exploration of racial and economic oppression and her struggle against political and human alienation. Lois More Overbeck argues that critics of Adrienne Kennedy's plays try to place her work in familiar critical categories but that her surreal personal vision jars against the realism of conventional black play writing as well as the message of political activism prevalent in the 1960s. Those who see parallels between Kennedy's work and the dramaturgy of expressionism, surrealism, and the absurd, contends Overbeck, do not account fully for the richness of poetic allusion in her work; this poeticism was illuminated in the 1970s by feminist criticism and a better understanding of traditional African dramaturgy. Many of the critical issues raised in Kennedy criticism are relevant to Ntozake Shange scholarship as well. Catherine Carr Lee writes on Shange, reporting on the intense biographical details that so shape Shange's theater images. Carr also covers Shange's use of nonstandard spelling and punctuation as well as her attitudes toward males as reflected in the plays.

Carson McCullers had a brief but important foray into the theater world, as Margaret B. McDowell reports, with uneven though engaging results. McDowell highlights McCullers's career as playwright and the critics' ambivalent response to her efforts. Linda L. Hubert surveys the critical work on Marsha Norman, which addresses such issues as her treatment of mother-daughter relationships, the curious connection between food and psychological power in her plays, her sardonic humor, and her realistically harsh character portrayals. Some, especially British reviewers, fault Norman for her emphasis on personal relationships rather than politics. Hubert observes that Norman attracts many feminist critical approaches, although Norman herself feels uncomfortable with such readings. Like Norman's, Beth Henley's career has been brief but, as Lisa J. McDonnell suggests, has already spurred important critical debates. Henley's exploration of death-as-theme, her position as a southern female dramatist, and her use of Gothic comedy bordering on tragedy are some of the issues McDonnell evaluates.

Doris Auerbach traces the critical discussion of Arthur Kopit's interest in the meaning of the American myth, the evaluation and betrayal of the artist, the question of self-identity, and the delight of language. Noting the central role the Vietnam War had in shaping David Rabe's dramatic vision, Rodney Simard points out the various ways in which critics are attracted to the playwright's fusion of realism, absurdism, and epic theater.

More than any of the other dramatists treated in this volume, Sam Shepard and David Mamet have been instrumental in rejuvenating American theater. Both have attracted an astonishing amount of recent critical attention. Lynda Hart analyzes Shepard criticism, which describes metatheatrical dimensions in Shepard's early works, modified forms of expressionism in the middle phase of his canon, and the more realistic forms of the later plays. June Schlueter evaluates critical discussion of Mamet's use of a poetic idiom and the way in which language defines, and entraps, his heroes.

Two titans of the 1940s and 1950s are most responsible for carrying on the American dramatic heritage established by O'Neill: Arthur Miller and Tennessee Williams. Miller has attracted a tremendous amount of scholarship. Schlueter reports on the state of Miller criticism, highlighting such issues as the American dream myth, the primal family unit, the father-son relationship, and the role tragedy and fate exert on what Miller calls "the common man." Many scholars identify Miller's dramatic innovations, his use of American speech, and his sense of history as hallmarks of his worldview. Schlueter carefully selects and evaluates the major critical statements, thus giving readers a healthy sampling of the most influential Miller studies available and a sense of Miller's emergence as the elder statesman of American drama. Pearl Amelia McHaney reports that the critical analyses of the work of Tennessee Williams focus on his themes of isolation, death, sexuality, and the South and discuss the diverse plays as examples of realistic, romantic, expressionistic, allegorical, and poetic drama. Scholarly studies investigate the influences of Chekhov, D. H. Lawrence, Hart Crane, and others, the development of poems and short stories into one-act and full-length plays, and the various revisions and productions of the major works. After singling out examples of the best of Williams criticism, McHaney calls for sensitive study of the later plays and for an objective critical examination of Williams's life in relation to his art.

Karen Laughlin addresses scholarship on Megan Terry's plays, which often centers on Terry's belief in the theater as a means for political change. Critics concentrate, Laughlin writes, on the nontraditional, nonlinear, transformational structures of Terry's plays, her interest in matriarchy and women's religion, and her contribution to feminist theater. Patricia R. Schroeder reports that, while critics have examined Wendy Wasserstein's comedy and wit, further scholarship is necessary before a critical consensus on her work is formed. Martin J. Jacobi's essay on Lanford Wilson brings the volume to a close by following the critical response to the playwright's movement from the bleak naturalistic vision of the early plays to the optimistic, even comic vision of the later works.

These essays outline the public issues and private tensions of a nation as dramatized by seventeen playwrights whose collective lover's quarrel with American history and thought crystallizes the civic as well as personal confrontations that inform contemporary American drama. The only traceable consistency in the scholarship concerns its rich diversity. A study of relevant books, articles, and theater reviews reveals a balkanization of criticism, the detractor's attack leavened by the supporter's defense. While many plays have attracted what Jonas Barish has called "unwelcome surgery" by scholars, there is an abundance of exemplary criticism available as well. The function of the essays in this volume is to sift through the great, the near-great, and the pseudo-great scholarship that has both bedeviled and enhanced our understanding of the genre.

–Matthew C. Roudané
Georgia State University

Acknowledgments

This book was produced by Bruccoli Clark Layman, Inc. Michael D. Senecal was the in-house editor.

Production coordinator is Kimberly Casey. Copyediting supervisor is Joan M. Prince. Typesetting supervisor is Kathleen M. Flanagan. William Adams and Laura Ingram are editorial associates. The production staff includes Brandy H. Barefoot, Rowena Betts, Charles D. Brower, Amanda Caulley, Teresa Chaney, Patricia Coate, Mary Colborn, Mary S. Dye, Sarah A. Estes, Cynthia Hallman, Judith K. Ingle, Kathy S. Merlette, Sheri Beckett Neal, and Virginia Smith. Penney L. Haughton did paste-up work for the volume.

Walter W. Ross and Jennifer Toth did the library research with the assistance of the reference staff at the Thomas Cooper Library of the University of South Carolina: Daniel Boice, Cathy Eckman, Gary Geer, Cathie Gottlieb, David L. Haggard, Jens Holley, Dennis Isbell, Jackie Kinder, Marcia Martin, Jean Rhyne, Beverly Steele, Ellen Tillett, Carol Tobin, and Virginia Weathers.

The editor wishes to thank Virginia Spencer Carr, Clyde W. Faulkner, and William J. Handy for their professional support over the years.

Contemporary Authors

Bibliographical Series

American Dramatists

Edward Albee

(1928-   )

Anne Paolucci
St. John's University
and
Henry Paolucci
St. John's University

PRIMARY BIBLIOGRAPHY

Books

The Zoo Story and The Sandbox; Two Short Plays. New York: Dramatists Play Service, 1960.

The Zoo Story and The American Dream. New York: Signet, 1960. Plays.

The Zoo Story, The Death of Bessie Smith, The Sandbox, Three Plays, Introduced by the Author. New York: Coward-McCann, 1960.

The American Dream; The Death of Bessie Smith; FAM and YAM. New York: Dramatists Play Service, 1960.

The Sandbox, The Death of Bessie Smith (with FAM and YAM). New York: New American Library, 1963.

Who's Afraid of Virginia Woolf?. New York: Atheneum, 1962; London: Cape, 1964. Play.

Tiny Alice. New York: Atheneum, 1965; London: Cape, 1966. Play.

A Delicate Balance. New York: Atheneum, 1966; London: Cape, 1968. Play.

Box and Quotations from Chairman Mao Tse-Tung, Two Inter-Related Plays. New York: Atheneum, 1969; London: Cape, 1970.

All Over. New York: Atheneum, 1971; London: Cape, 1972. Play.

Seascape. New York: Atheneum, 1975; London: Cape, 1976. Play.

Counting the Ways and Listening. New York: Atheneum, 1977. Plays.

The Lady from Dubuque, A Play. New York: Atheneum, 1980.

The Man Who Had Three Arms. New York: Atheneum, 1987. Play.

Adaptations

The Ballad of the Sad Cafe; the Play. Boston: Houghton Mifflin, 1963. From Carson McCullers's novella.

Malcolm. New York: Atheneum, 1966; London: Cape, 1967. From
    James Purdy's novel.
Everything in the Garden. New York: Atheneum, 1968. From Giles
    Cooper's play.
Lolita. New York: Dramatists Play Service, 1984. From Vladimir
    Nabokov's novel.

Premiere Productions

The Zoo Story. West Berlin, Germany, Schiller Theater Werkstaat, 28
    Sept. 1959; New York, Provincetown Playhouse, 14 Jan. 1960.
The Sandbox. New York, The Jazz Gallery, 15 Apr. 1960.
The Death of Bessie Smith. West Berlin, Germany, Schlosspark The-
    ater, 21 Apr. 1960; New York, York Playhouse, 1 Mar. 1961.
FAM and YAM. Westport, Connecticut, The White Barn, 27 Aug.
    1960.
The American Dream and *Bartleby.* New York, York Playhouse, 24 Jan.
    1961. [*Bartleby*, libretto adaptation of Herman Melville's short
    story, replaced by *The Death of Bessie Smith* on double bill, 1
    Mar. 1961.]
Who's Afraid of Virginia Woolf?. New York, Billy Rose Theater, 13
    Oct. 1962.
The Ballad of the Sad Cafe. New York, Martin Beck Theater, 30 Oct.
    1963.
Tiny Alice. New York, Billy Rose Theater, 29 Dec. 1964.
Malcolm. New York, Shubert Theater, 11 Jan. 1966.
A Delicate Balance. New York, Martin Beck Theater, 12 Sept. 1966.
Breakfast at Tiffany's. Music by Bob Merrill. Philadelphia, 1966. Musi-
    cal adaptation of Truman Capote's novel.
Everything in the Garden. New York, Plymouth Theater, 16 Nov.
    1967.
Box and *Quotations from Chairman Mao Tse-Tung* [*Box-Mao-Box*]. Buf-
    falo, New York, Studio Arena Theater, 6 Mar. 1968;
All Over. New York, Martin Beck Theater, 27 Mar. 1971.
Seascape. New York, Shubert Theater, 26 Jan. 1975.
Listening. Hartford, Connecticut, Hartford Stage Company, 28 Jan.
    1977.
Counting the Ways. London, National Theater, 6 Dec. 1976; Hart-
    ford, Connecticut, Hartford Stage Company, 28 Jan. 1977.
The Lady from Dubuque. New York, Morosco Theater, 31 Jan. 1980.
Lolita. New York, The Brooks Atkinson Theater, 19 Mar. 1981.

The Man Who Had Three Arms. Chicago, Goodman Theater, 4 Oct. 1982.
Finding the Sun. Colorado, 1983.
Envy. A part of *The Show of the Seven Deadly Sins* in Nagel Jackson's *Faustus in Hell*. Princeton, N.J., 1985.
The Marriage Play. Vienna, 1987.

Selected Other
"*L'Apres midi d'un faune*," *Choate Literary Magazine*, 31 (Nov. 1944), 43-44. Short story.
"Old Laughter," *Choate Literary Magazine*, 31 (Nov. 1944), 37-38. Poem.
"To a Gold Chain Philosopher at Luncheon," *Choate Literary Magazine*, 31 (Feb. 1945), 34. Poem.
"To Whom It May Concern," *Choate Literary Magazine*, 31 (Feb. 1945), 61. Poem.
"Associations," *Choate Literary Magazine*, 31 (May 1945), 15-16. Poem.
"Empty Tea," *Choate Literary Magazine*, 31 (May 1945), 53-59. Short story.
"Frustrations" and "Sonnet," *Choate Literary Magazine*, 31 (May 1945), 60. Poems.
"Question," *Choate Literary Magazine*, 31 (May 1945), 81. Poem.
"Richard Strauss," *Choate Literary Magazine*, 31 (May 1945), 87-93. Essay.
"Eighteen," *Kaleidograph*, 17 (Sept. 1945), 15. Poem.
"Monologue–The Atheist" and "Sonnet," *Choate Literary Magazine*, 32 (Nov. 1945), 10. Poems.
"Well, It's Like This," *Choate Literary Magazine*, 32 (Nov. 1945), 31-34. Short story.
"Reunion," *Choate Literary Magazine*, 32 (Nov. 1945), 71-72. Poem.
"Chopin," *Choate Literary Magazine*, 32 (Nov. 1945), 11. Poem.
"Chaucer: the Legend of Phyllis," *Choate Literary Magazine*, 32 (Nov. 1945), 59-63. Essay.
"A Place on the Water," *Choate Literary Magazine*, 32 (Feb. 1946), 15-18. Short story.
"Interlude," *Choate Literary Magazine*, 32 (Feb. 1946), 29. Poem.
"To a Maniac," *Choate Literary Magazine*, 32 (Feb. 1946), 71. Poem.
"Lady with an Umbrella," *Choate Literary Magazine*, 32 (May 1946), 5-10. Short story.

"Nihilist," *Choate Literary Magazine*, 32 (May 1946), 22. Poem.
"Schism," *Choate Literary Magazine*, 32 (May 1946), 87-110. Play.
"The Zoo Story," *Evergreen Review*, 4 (Mar.-Apr. 1960), 28-52. Play.
"Some First Plays Only Seem German," *New York Herald Tribune*, 15 May 1960, section 4, pp. 1, 3. Essay.
" 'What's It About?'–A Playwright Tries to Tell," *Lively Arts and Book Review* (*New York Herald-Tribune*), 22 Jan. 1961, p. 5. Essay.
"Which Theater is the Absurd One?," *New York Times Magazine*, 25 Feb. 1962, pp. 30-31, 64, 66. Essay.
"Some Notes on Nonconformity," *Harper's Bazaar*, 95 (Aug. 1962), 104. Essay.
"Carson McCullers–The Case of the Curious Magician," *Harper's Bazaar*, 96 (Jan. 1963), 98. Essay.
"*Vertical and Horizontal*, by Lillian Rose," *Village Voice*, 7 (11 July 1963), 7, 10. Review.
"A Novel Beginning," *Esquire*, 60 (July 1963), 59-60. Novel-in-progress.
"Who's Afraid of the Truth?," *New York Times*, 18 Aug. 1963, section 2, p. 1. Essay.
"Albee on Censorship," *Newsweek*, 62 (30 Sept. 1963), 4. Letter.
"Theater: *Icarus' Mother*," *Village Voice*, 11 (25 Nov. 1965), 19. Review.
"Notes for Noel about Coward." In *Three Plays by Noel Coward*. New York: Dell, 1965, 3-6. Essay.
"Who is James Purdy?," *New York Times*, 9 Jan. 1966, section 2, pp. 1, 3. Essay.
"The Writer as Independent Spirit: Creativity and Commitment," *Saturday Review*, 49 (4 June 1966), 26. Essay.
"Judy Garland." In *Double Exposure*, ed. Roddy McDowell. New York: Delacorte, 1966, 198-199. Essay.
"Apartheid in the Theater," *New York Times*, 30 July 1967, section 2, pp. 1, 6. Essay.
"Albee Says 'No Thanks' to John Simon," *New York Times*, 10 Sept. 1967, section 2, pp. 1, 8. Essay.
"The Decade of Engagement," *Saturday Review*, 53 (Jan. 24, 1970), 19-20. Essay.
"The Future Belongs to Youth," *New York Times*, 26 Nov. 1971, section 2, p. 1. Essay.
"Albeit." In *The Off-Broadway Experience*, ed. Howard Greenberger. Englewood Cliffs, N.J.: Prentice-Hall, 1971, 52-62. Essay.

"Peaceable Kingdom, France," *New Yorker*, 51 (29 Dec. 1975), 34. Poem.

"Edward Albee on Louise Nevelson: The World Is Beginning to Resemble Her Art," *Art News*, 79 (May 1980), 99-101. Essay.

"Foreword." In James Purdy, *Dream Palaces; Three Novels*. New York: Viking, 1980, vii-ix.

Collection

The Plays, 4 volumes. Volume 1, New York: Coward, McCann & Geoghegan, 1981; volumes 2, 3, and 4, New York: Atheneum, 1981-1983. Volume 1 comprises *The Zoo Story*, *The Death of Bessie Smith*, *The Sandbox*, and *The American Dream*; volume 2 comprises *Tiny Alice*, *A Delicate Balance*, and *Box* and *Quotations from Chairman Mao Tse-Tung*; volume 3 comprises *All Over*, *Seascape*, *Counting the Ways*, and *Listening*; volume 4 comprises *Everything in the Garden* (from the play by Giles Cooper), *Malcolm* (from the novel by James Purdy), and *The Ballad of the Sad Cafe* (from the novella by Carson McCullers).

SECONDARY BIBLIOGRAPHY

Bibliographies and Checklists

Amacher, Richard E., and Margaret Rule. *Edward Albee at Home and Abroad: A Bibliography*. New York: AMS, 1973. Primary and secondary.

Bigsby, C. W. E. *Edward Albee: Bibliography, Biography, Playography*. London: TQ Publications, 1980. Primary and secondary.

Giantvalley, Scott. *Edward Albee: A Reference Guide*. Boston: Hall, 1987. Secondary.

Green, Charles. *Edward Albee: An Annotated Bibliography, 1968-1977*. New York: AMS, 1980. Primary and secondary.

King, Kimball. *Ten Modern Playwrights: An Annotated Bibliography*. New York: Garland, 1982, 1-108. Primary and secondary.

Kolin, Philip C. "A Classified Edward Albee Checklist," *Serif*, 6 (Sept. 1969), 16-32. Secondary.

Kolin. "A Supplementary Edward Albee Checklist," *Serif*, 10 (Spring 1973): 28-39. Secondary.

Kolin and J. Madison Davis. "Introduction." In Kolin and Davis, 1-40. Primary and secondary bibliographical essay.

Owen, Lea Carol. "An Annotated Bibliography of Albee Interviews, with an Index to Names, Concepts, and Places." In Kolin and Davis, 193-218. Secondary.

Reed, Michael D., and James L. Evans. "Edward Albee: An Updated Checklist of Scholarship, 1977-1980." In De La Fuente, 121-129.

Rood, Karen. "Edward Albee." In *First Printings of American Authors: Contributions Toward Descriptive Checklists*, ed. Matthew J. Bruccoli, C. E. Frazer Clark, Jr., Richard Layman, and Benjamin Franklin V, volume 3. Detroit: Gale Research, 1978, 1-9.

Tyce, Richard. *Edward Albee: A Bibliography.* Metuchen, N.J.: Scarecrow, 1986. Primary and secondary.

Wilson, Robert A. "Edward Albee: A Bibliographical Checklist," *American Book Collector*, 4 (Mar./Apr. 1983), 37-44. Primary.

Interviews
Arnold, Christine. "Playwright Albee Gets Critical About Critics," *Miami Herald*, 16 Mar. 1986, pp. 1K, 3K.

Booth, John E. "Albee and Schneider Observe: 'Something's Stirring,'" *Theatre Arts*, 45 (Mar. 1961), 22-24, 78-79.

Brenner, Marie. "Tiny Montauk," *New York*, 16 (22 Aug. 1983), 13-15.

De La Fuente, Patricia. "Edward Albee: An Interview." In De La Fuente, 6-17.

Diehl, Digby. "Edward Albee Interviewed," *Transatlantic Review*, 13 (Summer 1963), 57-72.

Dommergues, Pierre. "Entretien avec Edward Albee," *Le Monde*, 22-23 Oct. 1967, p. 23.

Dommergues. "Rencontre avec Edward Albee." In his *Les U.S.A. à la recherche de leur identité: Rencontres avec 40 écrivains américains.* Paris: Grasset, 1967, 362-376, 401-403.

"Edward Albee: 'I Write to Unclutter My Mind,'" *New York Times*, 26 Jan. 1975, section 2, pp. 1, 7.

Flanagan, William. "The Art of the Theater IV: Edward Albee: An Interview," *Paris Review*, 10, no. 39 (1966), 92-121.

Flatley, Guy. "Edward Albee Fights Back," *New York Times*, 18 Apr. 1971, section 2, pp. 1, 10.

Glover, William. "Albee Not on a Soap Box, but . . . ," *New Orleans Times-Picayune*, 30 Jan. 1977, section 2, p. 11.

Gussow, Mel. "Albee: Odd Man In on Broadway," *Newsweek*, 61 (4 Feb. 1963), 49-52.

Kelly, Kevin. "Edward Albee on Albee: The Superstar of Drama," *Boston Globe*, 14 Mar. 1976, section A, pp. 9, 14.

Kolin, Philip C., ed. *Conversations with Edward Albee.* Jackson & London: University Press of Mississippi, 1988.

Krohn, Charles S., and Julian N. Wasserman. "An Interview with Edward Albee." In Wasserman, 1-27.

Lask, Thomas. "Dramatist in a Troubled World," *New York Times*, 22 Jan. 1961, section 2, pp. 1, 3.

McNally, Terrence. "Edward Albee in Conversation with Terrence McNally," *Dramatists Guild Quarterly*, 22 (Summer 1985), 12-23.

Meehan, Thomas. "Not Good Taste, Not Bad Taste–It's Camp," *New York Times Magazine*, 21 Mar. 1965, pp. 30-31, 113-115.

Oakes, Philip. "Goings On: Don't Shoot the Playwright," *Sunday Times* (London), 12 Dec. 1976, p. 35.

Roudané, Matthew C. "Albee on Albee," *RE: Artes Liberales*, 10 (Spring 1984), 1-8.

Roudané. "An Interview with Edward Albee," *Southern Humanities Review*, 16 (1982), 29-44.

Roudané. "A Playwright Speaks: An Interview with Edward Albee." In Kolin and Davis, 193-199.

Rutenberg, Michael E. "Two Interviews with Edward Albee." In his *Edward Albee: Playwright in Protest.* New York: Avon, 1969, 229-260.

Schechner, Richard. "Reality is Not Enough: An Interview with Alan Schneider," *Tulane Drama Review*, 9 (Spring 1965), 118-152. Excerpted in Bigsby, 69-75.

Schneider, Howard. "Albee: Hard Act for Himself to Follow," *Los Angeles Times*, 23 Mar. 1975, Calendar section, pp. 1, 50-51.

Stern, Daniel. "The Director's Approach–Two Views: Albee: 'I Want My Intent Clear,' " *New York Times*, 28 Mar. 1976, section 2, pp. 1, 5.

Stewart, R. S. "John Gielgud and Edward Albee Talk About the Theater," *Atlantic*, 215 (Apr. 1965), 61-68. Collected in Bigsby, 112-123.

Sullivan, Dan. "Edward Albee: Playwright with More Than One Act," *Los Angeles Times*, 15 Oct. 1978, Calendar section, p. 6.

"The Talk of the Town: Revisited," *New Yorker*, 56 (3 Mar. 1980), 29-31.

"The Talk of the Town: Theatre," *New Yorker*, 50 (3 June 1974), 28-30.

Wallach, Allan. "If the Play Can Be Described in One Sentence, That Should Be Its Length," *New Orleans Times-Picayune*, 19 Jan. 1979, Fanfare section, p. 4.

Wardle, Irving. "Albee Looks at Himself and at His Plays," *Times* (London), 18 Jan. 1969, pp. 17, 19.

Zindel, Paul, and Loree Yerby. "Interview with Edward Albee," *Wagner Literary Magazine*, no. 3 (1962), 1-10.

Zolotov, Sam. "Albee to Transplant a British Comedy," *New York Times*, 7 Mar. 1967, p. 45.

Critical Studies: Books

Amacher, Richard E. *Edward Albee.* New York: Twayne, 1969. Revised edition, Boston: Twayne, 1982.

Bigsby, C. W. E. *Albee.* Edinburgh, U.K.: Oliver & Boyd, 1969.

Braem, Helmut M. *Edward Albee.* Hanover: Velber, 1968. Revised edition, Munich: Deutscher Taschenbuch, 1977.

Cohn, Ruby. *Edward Albee.* Minneapolis: University of Minnesota Press, 1969.

Debusscher, Gilbert. *Edward Albee: Tradition and Renewal*, tr. Anne D. Williams. Brussels: American Studies Center, 1967.

Hayman, Ronald. *Edward Albee.* London: Heinemann, 1971.

Hirsch, Foster. *Who's Afraid of Edward Albee?.* Berkeley: Creative Arts, 1978.

Kerjan, Liliane. *Edward Albee: textes de Albee, points de vue critiques, témoignages, chronologie.* Paris: Seghers, 1971.

Kerjan. *Le théâtre d'Edward Albee.* Paris: Klincksieck, 1978.

McCarthy, Gerry. *Edward Albee.* London: Macmillan, 1985; New York: St. Martin's, 1987.

Paolucci, Anne. *From Tension to Tonic: The Plays of Edward Albee.* Carbondale: Southern Illinois University Press, 1972.

Roudané, Matthew C. *Necessary Fictions, Terrifying Realities: 'Who's Afraid of Virginia Woolf?.'* Boston: Twayne, forthcoming 1989.

Roudané. *Understanding Edward Albee.* Columbia: University of South Carolina Press, 1987.

Rutenberg, Michael. *Edward Albee: Playwright in Protest.* New York: Avon, 1969.

Schultz-Seitz, Ruth Eva. *Edward Albee, der Dichterphilosoph der Bühne.* Frankfurt am Main: Klostermann, 1966.

Stenz, Anita Maria. *Edward Albee: The Poet of Loss.* The Hague & New York: Mouton, 1978.

Treib, Manfred. *August Strindberg und Edward Albee: Eine vergleichende Analyse moderne Ehedramen (mit einem Exkurs über Friedrich Dürrenmatts "Play Strindberg")*. Frankfurt am Main: Lang, 1980.

Vos, Nelvin. *Eugene Ionesco and Edward Albee: A Critical Study*. Grand Rapids, Mich.: Eerdmans, 1968.

Critical Studies: Collections of Essays

Bigsby, C. W. E., ed. *Edward Albee: A Collection of Critical Essays*. Englewood Cliffs, N.J.: Prentice-Hall, 1975.

Bloom, Harold, ed. *Edward Albee*. New York: Chelsea House, 1987.

De La Fuente, Patricia, Donald E. Fritz, Jan Seale, and Dorey Schmidt, eds. *Edward Albee: Planned Wilderness: Interviews, Essays, and Bibliography*. Edinburg, Tex.: Pan American University School of Humanities, 1980.

Kolin, Philip C., and J. Madison Davis, eds. *Critical Essays on Edward Albee*. Boston: Hall, 1986.

Wassermann, Julian N., ed., J. L. Linsley and J. A. Kramer, assoc. eds., *Edward Albee: An Interview and Essays*. Houston, Tex.: University of St. Thomas, 1983.

Critical Studies: Major Reviews, Articles, and Book Sections

Adler, Thomas P., "Albee's *Seascape*: Humanity at the Second Threshold," *Renascence*, 31 (Winter 1979), 107-114. Collected in Kolin and Davis, 179-186.

Adler. "Albee's *Who's Afraid of Virginia Woolf ?*: A Long Night's Journey into Day," *Educational Theatre Journal*, 25 (Mar. 1973), 66-70.

Adler. "Art or Craft: Language in the Plays of Edward Albee's Second Decade." Collected in De La Fuente, 45-57.

Adler. "*Counting the Ways*," *Educational Theatre Journal*, 29 (Oct. 1977), 407-408. Collected in Kolin and Davis, 59-61.

Adler. "Edward Albee." In *Critical Survey of Drama: English Language Series*, ed. Frank McGill. Englewood Cliffs, N.J.: Salem Press, 1985, 11-23.

Adler. "*The Man Who Had Three Arms*," *Theatre Journal*, 35 (Mar. 1983), 124.

Adler. "The Pirandello in Albee: The Problem of Knowing in *The Lady From Dubuque*." In Wasserman, 109-119; in Bloom, 131-140.

"Albee Double Bill is Praised in Paris," *New York Times*, 13 Feb. 1965, p. 10.

"Albee Play Divides Stockholm Critics," *New York Times*, 6 Oct. 1963, p. 68.

"Albee-Barr to Film for Universal but Not New *Box-Mao-Box* Property," *Variety*, 13 Mar. 1968, p. 17.

Allen, Morse. "Plays of Worth," *Hartford Sunday Courant*, 20 Aug. 1961, Magazine section, p. 15.

Anderson, Mary Castiglie. "Ritual and Initiation in *The Zoo Story*." In Wasserman, 93-108.

Anderson. "Staging the Unconscious: Edward Albee's *Tiny Alice*," *Renascence*, 32 (Spring 1980), 178-192. Collected in Bloom, 83-96.

Anderson. "Theatre," *World Literature Today*, 56 (Summer 1982), 516-517.

Anderson. "Theatre," *World Literature Today*, 57 (Winter 1983), 108-109.

Atkinson, Brooks. "Theatre: A Double Off Broadway," *New York Times*, 15 Jan. 1960, p. 37.

Atkinson. "Village Vagrants," *New York Times*, 31 Jan. 1960, section 2, p. 1.

Ballew, Leighton M. "Who's Afraid of Tiny Alice?," *Georgia Review*, 20 (Fall 1966), 292-299.

Barnes, Clive. "Albee's *Seascape* Is a Major Event," *New York Times*, 27 Jan. 1975, p. 20. Collected in Kolin and Davis, 55-56.

Barnes. "*All Over*, Albee's Drama of Death Arrives," *New York Times*, 29 Mar. 1971, p. 41.

Barnes. "Double-Bill by Albee," *New York Times*, 4 Feb. 1977, p. C4.

Barnes. "*Krapp's Last Tape* and *Zoo Story*; Plays by Beckett and Albee Are Revived," *New York Times*, 11 Oct. 1968, p. 41.

Barnes. "*Lolita* is Humbug Humbug," *New York Post*, 20 Mar. 1981, p. 39.

Baxandall, Lee. "Theatre and Affliction," *Encore*, 10 (May/June 1963), 8-13.

Baxandall. "The Theatre of Edward Albee," *Tulane Drama Review*, 9 (Summer 1965), 19-40.

Bennett, Robert B. "Tragic Vision in *The Zoo Story*," *Modern Drama*, 20 (March 1977), 55-66. Collected in *Essays on Modern American Drama: Williams, Miller, Albee, and Shepard*, ed. Dorothy Parker. Toronto: University of Toronto Press, 1987, 109-120.

Ben-Zvi, Linda. "*Finding the Sun*," *Theater Journal*, 36 (Mar. 1984), 102-103.

Bermel, Albert. "Mud in the Plumbing," *New Leader*, 49 (10 Oct. 1966), 28-29.

Bernstein, Samuel J. "*Seascape*, Edward Albee." In his *The Strands Entwined: A New Direction in American Drama*. Boston: Northeastern University Press, 1980, 111-135.

Bigsby, C. W. E. "*Box* and *Quotations from Chairman Mao Tse-Tung*: Albee's Diptych." In Bigsby, 151-164.

Bigsby. "Curiouser and Curiouser: A Study of Albee's *Tiny Alice*," *Modern Drama*, 10 (Dec. 1967), 258-266.

Bigsby. "Edward Albee." In his *Confrontation and Committment: A Study of Contemporary American Drama, 1959-1966*. Columbia: University of Missouri Press, 1967, 71-92.

Bigsby. "Edward Albee." In his *A Critical Introduction to Twentieth-Century American Drama*, volume 2. New York: Cambridge University Press, 1984, 249-329.

Bigsby. "Edward Albee's Georgia Ballad," *Twentieth Century Literature*, 13 (Jan. 1968), 229-236.

Bigsby. "The Strategy of Madness: An Analysis of Edward Albee's *A Delicate Balance*," *Contemporary Literature*, 9 (Spring 1968), 223-235.

Bigsby. "*Tiny Alice*." In Bigsby, 124-134.

Bigsby. "To the Brink of the Grave: Edward Albee's *All Over*." In Bigsby, 168-174.

Bigsby. "*Who's Afraid of Virginia Woolf ?*: Edward Albee's Morality Play," *Journal of American Studies*, 1 (Oct. 1967), 257-268. Collected in Kolin and Davis, 80-87; collected in Bloom, 141-160.

Bolton, Whitney. "Provocative Double Bill at York Theatre," *New York Morning Telegraph*, 26 Jan. 1961, p. 2.

Bowers, Faubion. "Theatre of the Absurd: It's Here to Stay," *Theatre Arts*, 46 (Nov. 1962), 21, 23, 64-65.

Boyer, Mark. "Premiere Albee: Irresistable Rhythms, Unnatural Acts," *Hartford Courant*, 9 Feb. 1977, pp. 16, 19.

"Broadway: A Tale Within a Tail," *Time*, 85 (15 Jan. 1965), 68, 70.

Brown, Terrence. "Harmonia Discord and Stochastic Process: Edward Albee's *A Delicate Balance*," *Re: Arts and Letters*, 3 (Spring 1970), 54-60.

Brustein, Robert. "Albee and the Medusa's Head," *New Republic*, 147 (3 Nov. 1962), 29-30. Collected in his *Seasons of Discontent:*

Dramatic Opinions, 1959-1965. New York: Simon & Schuster, 1965, 145-148; collected in Kolin and Davis, 46-47.

Brustein. "Albee Decorates an Old House," *New Republic*, 155 (8 Oct. 1966), 35-36. Collected in his *The Third Theatre.* New York: Knopf, 1969, 83-86; collected in Bigsby, 135-137.

Brustein. "Albee's Allegory of Innocence," *New Republic*, 154 (29 Jan. 1966), 34, 36.

Brustein. "Death Rattles Down on Broadway," *Observer* (London), 25 Nov. 1962, p. 25.

Brustein. "Krapp and a Little Claptrap," *New Republic*, 142 (22 Feb. 1960), 21-22. Collected in his *Seasons of Discontent: Dramatic Opinions, 1959-1965*, 26-27.

Brustein. "Self-Parody and Self-Murder," *New Republic*, 182 (8 Mar. 1980), 26.

Brustein. "The Trashing of Edward Albee," *New Republic*, 184 (11 Apr. 1981), 27-28.

Bunce, Alan N. "*A Delicate Balance* Arrives on Broadway," *Christian Science Monitor*, 24 Sept. 1966, p. 4.

Byars, John A. "*Taming of the Shrew* and *Who's Afraid of Virginia Woolf ?*," *Cimarron Review*, 21 (Oct. 1972), 41-48.

Calta, Louis. "Albee Lectures Critics in Taste," *New York Times*, 23 Mar. 1965, p. 33.

Campbell, Mary Elizabeth. "The Statement of Edward Albee's *Tiny Alice*," *Papers on Language and Literature*, 4 (Winter 1968), 85-100.

Cappelletti, John. "Are You Afraid of Edward Albee?," *Drama Critique*, 6 (Spring 1963), 84-88.

Carr, Duane R. "St. George and the Snapdragons: The Influence of Unamuno on *Who's Afraid of Virginia Woolf ?*," *Arizona Quarterly*, 29 (Spring 1973), 5-13.

Casper, Leonard. "*Tiny Alice*: The Expense of Joy in the Persistence of Mystery." In Wasserman, 109-119.

Cau, Jean. "Virginia Woolf," *Les Nouvelle Litteraires* (26 Nov. 1964).

Chapman, John. "Albee's *Ballad of the Sad Cafe* Beautiful, Exciting, Enthralling," *New York Daily News*, 10 Nov. 1963, section 2, p. 3.

Chapman. "Albee's Play, *Delicate Balance*, a Shimmering Start for Season," *New York Daily News*, 23 Jan. 1966, p. 47.

Chapman. "Edward Albee's *Tiny Alice*, or the Temptation of John Gielgud," *New York Daily News*, 30 Dec. 1964, p. 36.

Chapman. "Revival of *Tiny Alice*: Still Metafuzzical Bore," *New York Daily News*, 30 Sept. 1969, p. 60.

Choudhuri, A. D. *"Who's Afraid of Virginia Woolf ?*: Death of an Illusion." In his *The Face of Illusion in American Drama*. Atlantic Highlands, N.J.: Humanities, 1979, 123-143.

Clarke, Gerald. "Theater: Night Games," *Time*, 11 Feb. 1980, p. 69.

Clurman, Harold. "Albee on Balance," *New York Times*, 13 Nov. 1966, section 2, pp. 1, 3.

Clurman. "Theater," *Nation*, 190 (13 Feb. 1960), 153-154. Collected in his *The Naked Image: Observations on the Modern Theater*. New York: Macmillan, 1966, 13-15.

Clurman. "Theater," *Nation*, 192 (11 Feb. 1961), 125-126. Collected in his *The Naked Image* and in his *The Divine Pastime*.

Clurman. "Theater," *Nation*, 195 (27 Oct. 1962), 273-274. Collected in Bigsby, 76-79.

Clurman. "Theater," *Nation*, 212 (11 Apr. 1971), 476-477.

Clurman. "Theater," *Nation*, 212 (3 May 1971), 571-572.

Cohn, Ruby. "Albee's Box and Ours," *Modern Drama*, 14 (Sept. 1971), 137-143.

Cohn. "Camp, Cruelty, Colloquialism." In *Comic Relief: Humor in Contemporary American Literature*, ed. S. B. Cohen. Urbana: University of Illinois Press, 1978, 12, 281-286, 303.

Cohn. *Currents in Contemporary Drama*. Bloomington: Indiana University Press, 1969, 4, 6, 8-10, 20-21, 71-74, 84, 182-186, 247-250.

Cohn. "The Verbal Murders of Edward Albee." In Kolin and Davis, 146-149.

Cohn and Bernard F. Dukore, eds., *Twentieth Century Drama: England, Ireland, and the United States*. New York: Random House, 1966, 605-652.

Cole, Douglas. "Albee's *Virginia Woolf* and Steele's *Tatler*," *American Literature*, 40 (Mar. 1968), 81-82.

Corona, Mario. "Edward Albee," *Studi americani*, 10 (1964), 369-394.

"Counting the Ways and *Listening*," *Kirkus Reviews*, 45 (1 Apr. 1977), 450.

Coy, Javier, and Juan José Coy. "El teatro de Edward Albee." In their *La anarquía y el orden: una clave interretativa de la literatura norteamericana*. Madrid: José Porrúa Turanzas, 1976, 91-187.

Coy, Juan José. "Albee, el hombre que perdio un premio," *Monteagudo* (Universidad de Murcia, Spain), 38 (1962), 4-27.

Cubeta, Paul. "Commentary." In *Modern Drama for Analysis*, third edition. New York: Holt, Rinehart & Winston, 1962, 598-602.

Davison, Richard A. "Edward Albee's *Tiny Alice*: A Note of Re-Examination," *Modern Drama*, 11 (May 1968), 54-60.

Debusscher, Gilbert. "*The Death of Bessie Smith*." In Bigsby, 54-61.

Debusscher. "The Playwright in the Making." In Kolin and Davis, 74-80.

Deutsch, Robert H. "Writers Maturing in the Theater of the Absurd," *Discourse*, 7 (Spring 1964), 181-187.

Dommergues. "Le Cannibalisme dynamique d'Edward Albee." In his *Les écrivains américains d'aujourd-hui*. Paris: Presses Universitaires de France, 1967, pp. 96, 99-101.

Dommergues, Pierre. "La Conscience magique d'Edward Albee," *Cahiers de la Compagnie Madelaine Renaud–Jean-Louis Barrault*, no. 63 (Oct. 1967), 18-22.

Driver, Tom F. "Drama: Bucketful of Dregs," *Christian Century*, 77 (17 Feb. 1960), 193-194. Excerpted in Kolin and Davis, 44.

Driver. "What's the Matter with Edward Albee?," *Reporter*, 30 (2 Jan. 1964), 38-39.

Ducker, Dan. " 'Pow!,' 'Snap!' 'Pouf!': The Modes of Communication in *Who's Afraid of Virginia Woolf ?*," *CLA Journal*, 26 (June 1983), 465-477.

Dukore, Bernard F. "*Tiny Alice*," *Drama Survey*, 5 (Spring 1966), 60-66.

Dukore. "A Warp in Albee's *Woolf*," *Southern Speech Journal*, 30 (Spring 1965), 261-268. Collected in Kolin and Davis, 95-101.

Egri, Peter. "European Origins and American Originality: The Case of Drama," *Zeitschrift für Anglistik und Amerikanistik*, 29, no. 2 (1981), 179-206.

Esslin, Martin. "*Counting the Ways*," *Plays and Players*, 24 (Feb. 1977), 33.

Esslin. "The Theater of the Absurd: Edward Albee." In Bigsby, 23-25; in Kolin and Davis, 63-65.

Falb, Lewis W. "New Playwrights of the Sixties: Edward Albee." In his *American Drama in Paris, 1945-1970: A Study of Its Critical Reception*. Chapel Hill: University of North Carolina Press, 1973, 69-76.

Finkelstein, Sidney. "The Existentialist Trap: Norman Mailer and Edward Albee," *American Dialog*, 2 (Feb./Mar. 1965), 23-28.

Fischer, Gretl Kraus. "Albee and Virginia Woolf," *Dalhousie Review*, 49 (Summer 1969), 196-207.

Flasch, Joy. "Games People Play in *Who's Afraid of Virginia Woolf ?*," *Modern Drama*, 10 (Dec. 1967), 280-288.

Force, William. "The *What* Story? or Who's Who at the Zoo?," *Studies in the Humanities*, 1 (Winter 1969/1970), 47-53.

Franzblau, Abraham. "A Psychiatrist Looks at *Tiny Alice*," *Saturday Review*, 48 (30 Jan. 1965), 39. Collected in Bigsby, 110-111.

Fumerton, M. Patricia. "Verbal Prisons: The Language of Edward Albee's *A Delicate Balance*," *English Studies in Canada*, 7 (Summer 1981), 201-211.

Gabbard, Lucina P. "Albee's *Seascape*: An Adult Fairy Tale," *Modern Drama*, 21 (Sept. 1978), 307-317.

Gabbard. "Edward Albee's Triptych on Abandonment," *Twentieth Century Literature*, 28 (Spring 1982), 14-33.

Gabbard. "The Enigmatic *Tiny Alice*," *Journal of Evolutionary Psychology*, 6 (1985), 73-86.

Gabbard. "From O'Neill to Albee," *Modern Drama*, 19 (Dec. 1976), 365-373.

Gabbard. "Unity in the Albee Vision." In De La Fuente, pp. 18-32.

Galbraith, John Kenneth. "The Mystique of Failure: A Latter-Day Reflection of *Who's Afraid of Virginia Woolf?*," *Show*, 4 (May 1964), 112. Collected in Kolin and Davis, 149-151.

Galey, Matthieu. "Albee sur le chemin de la gloire," *Nouvelles littéraires*, 11 Feb. 1965, p. 13.

Galey. "Un Auteur modeste," *Avant-Scene*, 334 (15 May 1965), 6.

Gassner, John. "Broadway in Review," *Educational Theatre Journal*, 15 (Mar. 1963), 78-84. Collected in Kolin and Davis, 48-49.

Gautier, Jean-Jacques. "Qui a peur. . . . ," *Figaro*, 3 Dec. 1964, p. 30.

Gill, Brendan. "Who Died?," *New Yorker*, 47 (3 Apr. 1971), 95. Collected in Kolin and Davis, 56-58.

Gilman, Richard. "Here We Go Round the Albee Bush," *Commonweal*, 77 (9 Nov. 1962), 175-176. Collected in his *Common and Uncommon Masks: Writings on Theatre, 1961-1970*. New York: Random House, 1971, 133-136.

Glenn, Jules. "The Adoption Theme in Edward Albee's *Tiny Alice* and *The American Dream*," *Psychoanalytic Study of the Child*, 29 (1974), 413-429. Collected in *Lives, Events, and Other Players: Directions in Psychobiography*, ed. Joseph T. Coltrera. New York: Aronson, 1981, 255-269.

Gottfried, Martin. "*Everything in the Garden*," *Women's Wear Daily*, 30 Nov. 1967, p. 36.

Gottfried. "Theatre: Albee's *All Over*. . . . Talked to Death," *Women's Wear Daily*, 29 Mar. 1971, p. 12.

Guernsey, Otis L., Jr. *The Best Plays of 1979-80*. New York: Dodd, Mead, 1980, pp. 4, 15.

Gussow, Mel. "Stage: A New Look at 7 Deadly Sins," *New York Times*, 3 Feb. 1985, section 1, p. 55.

Hankiss, Elemér. "Who's Afraid of Edward Albee?," *New Hungarian Quarterly*, 5 (Autumn 1964), 168-174.

Harris, James Neil. "Edward Albee and Maurice Maeterlinck: *All Over* as Symbolism," *Theatre Research International*, 3 (May 1978), 200-208. Collected in Kolin and Davis, 107-115.

Harris, Wendell V. "Morality, Absurdity, and Albee," *Southwest Review*, 49 (Summer 1964), 249-256. Excerpted in Kolin and Davis, 117-122.

Hayman, Ronald. "*All Over*." In Bloom, 67-74.

Hewes, Henry. "Broadway Postscript: Benchmanship," *Saturday Review*, 43 (6 Feb. 1960), 32. Excerpted in Kolin and Davis, 42-43.

Hewes. "Broadway Postscript: The *Tiny Alice* Caper," *Saturday Review*, 48 (30 Jan. 1965), 38-39. Collected in Bigsby, 99-104.

Hewes. "The Theater: Death Prattle," *Saturday Review*, 54 (17 Apr. 1971), 54. Collected in Bigsby, 165-167.

Hirsch, Foster. "Evasions of Sex: The Closet Dramas." In Kolin and Davis, 125-135.

Hopkins, Anthony. "Conventional Albee: *Box* and *Chairman Mao*," *Modern Drama*, 16 (Sept. 1973), 141-147. Collected in Bloom, 75-82.

Hopper, Stanley Romaine. "How People Live Without Gods: Albee's *Tiny Alice*," *American Poetry Review*, 2 (Mar./Apr. 1973), 35-38.

Hughes, Catharine. "Edward Albee: Who's Afraid of What?," *Critic*, 21 (Feb./Mar. 1963), 16-19.

Hurley, Paul J. "France and America: Versions of the Absurd," *College English*, 26 (May 1965), 634-640.

Johnson, Timothy W. "*Who's Afraid of Virginia Woolf ?*," In *Magill's Survey of Cinema: English Language Films*, ed. Frank N. Magill, volume 4. Englewood Cliffs, N.J.: Salem Press, 1980, 1842-1844.

Jones, David Richard. "Albee's *All Over*." In De La Fuente, 87-98.

Julier, Laura. "Faces of the Dawn: Female Characters in the Albee Plays." In De La Fuente, 34-41.

Kane, Leslie. "Albee." In her *The Language of Silence: On the Unspoken and the Unspeakable in Modern Drama*. Rutherford, N.J.: Fairleigh Dickinson University Press, 1984, 158-178.

Kaplan, Donald H. "Homosexuality and American Theatre: A Psychoanalytic Comment," *Tulane Drama Review*, 9 (Spring 1965), 25-55.

Kauffmann, Stanley. "*All Over*; *The Proposition*," *New Republic*, 164 (17 Apr. 1971), 24, 38-39.

Kauffmann. "Stanley Kauffmann on Theater: *Seascape*," *New Republic*, 172 (22 Feb. 1975), 22, 33-34. Collected in his *Persons of the Drama: Theater Criticism and Comment*. New York: Harper & Row, 1976, 222-224.

Kauffmann. "Theater: Edward Albee's *Malcolm*," *New York Times*, 12 Jan. 1966, p. 29.

Kauffmann. "Theater: *Lolita* Undone," *Saturday Review*, 8 (May 1981), 78-79.

Kelly, Kevin. "Albee Suffers Deja Vu," *Boston Evening Globe*, 10 Feb. 1977, p. 32.

Kelly. "Calling Dr. Albee; *Holly* Under Scalper," *Boston Globe*, 20 Nov. 1966, pp. A11, A17.

Kemper, Robert Graham, "A Weekend with the 'Can Do' Family," *Christian Century*, 83 (23 Nov. 1966), 1447. Collected in Kolin and Davis, 54-55.

Kerr, Walter. "Albee vs. Albee," *Herald-Tribune Sunday Magazine*, 30 Jan. 1966, p. 17.

Kerr. "Albee's *Tiny Alice*–Walter Kerr's Review," *New York Herald-Tribune*, 30 Dec. 1964, p. 10.

Kerr. "Kerr Reviews *Malcolm*," *New York Herald-Tribune*, 22 Jan. 1966, p. 10.

Kerr. "Making a Cult of Confusion," *Horizon*, 5 (Sept. 1962), 33-41.

Kerr. "Non-Sense and Nonsense," *New York Times*, 13 Oct. 1968, section 2, p. 5.

Kerr. "Off Broadway: Two One-Act Plays Given at the Provincetown Playhouse," *New York Herald-Tribune*, 15 Jan. 1960, p. 8.

Kerr. "Only Time Really Happens to People," *New York Times*, 2 Oct. 1966, section 2, p. 1. Collected in Kolin and Davis, 52-54.

Kerr. "Stage: Albee's *Lady From Dubuque*," *New York Times*, 1 Feb. 1980, p. C5.

Kerr. "Three One-Act Plays Presented at Jazz Gallery," *New York Herald-Tribune*, 17 May 1960, p. 22.

Kesting, Marianne. "Edward Albee." In her *Panoramam des zeitgenössischen Theaters*. Munich: R. Piper, 1962, 196-198. Enlarged, 1969, 222-227.

Kolin, Philip C. "Bawdy Uses of *Et Cetera*," *American Speech*, 58 (Spring 1983), 75-78.

Kolin. "Edward Albee's *Counting the Ways*: The Ways of Losing Heart." In Wasserman, 121-140.

Kolin. "Two Early Poems by Edward Albee," *Resources for American Literary Study*, 5 (Spring 1975), 95-97.

Kostelanetz, Richard. "The Art of Total No," *Contact*, 4 (Oct./Nov. 1963), 62-70.

Kroll, Jack. "Albee's Humbug Humbug," *Newsweek*, 97 (30 Mar. 1981), 85.

Kroll. "Going to Hell with Albee," *Newsweek*, 94 (11 Feb. 1980), 102-103. Collected in Kolin and Davis, 58-59.

La Fontaine, Barbara. "Triple Threat On, Off and Off-Off Broadway," *New York Times Magazine*, 25 Feb. 1968, pp. 36-37, 39, 41-42, 44, 46.

Lahr, John. "The Adaptable Mr. Albee," *Evergreen Review*, 12 (May 1968), 37-39, 82, 84-87.

Lester, Bill. "*This Property Is Condemned* and *The Zoo Story*," *Plays and Players*, 7 (Oct. 1960), 13.

Levine, Mordecai. "Albee's Liebestod," *CLA Journal*, 10 (Mar. 1967), 252-255.

Lewis, Allan. "The Fun and Games of Edward Albee," *Educational Theater Journal*, 16 (Mar. 1964), 29-39.

Loney, Glenn M. "Theatre of the Absurd: It's Only a Fad," *Theatre Arts*, 46 (Nov. 1962), 20, 67-68.

Lucey, William F. "Albee's *Tiny Alice*: Truth and Appearance," *Renascence*, 21 (Winter 1969), 76-80, 110.

Luere, Jeanne. "*The Marriage Play*," *Theatre Journal*, 40 (Mar. 1988), 108-110.

Luft, Friedrich. "*The Death of Bessie Smith*: The German Premiere." Translated from the German in Kolin and Davis, 45.

Luft. "Review of *The Zoo Story*." Translated from the German in Kolin and Davis, 41.

Macklin, Anthony. "The Flagrant Albatross," *College English*, 28 (Oct. 1966), 58-59.

Malcolm, Donald. "Off Broadway: And Moreover. . . ," *New Yorker*, 35 (23 Jan. 1960), 72, 74-76.

Mandanis, Alice. "Symbol and Substance in *Tiny Alice*," *Modern Drama*, 12 (May 1969), 92-98.

Marker, Lise-Lone, and Frederick J. Marker. *Ingmar Bergman: Four Decades in the Theater*. Cambridge: Cambridge University Press,

1982, 15-16, 45, 47-48, 242-243.

Markus, Thomas B. *"Tiny Alice* and Tragic Catharsis," *Educational Theatre Journal*, 17 (Oct. 1965), 225-233.

Mayberry, Robert. "Dissonance in a Chinese Box: Edward Albee's *Box* and *Quotations from Chairman Mao Tse-Tung.*" In De La Fuente, pp. 70-85.

Mayberry. "A Theater of Discord: Some Plays of Beckett, Albee, and Pinter," *Kansas Quarterly*, 12 (1980), 7-16.

McClain, John. "Albee's Secret is Safe," *New York Journal-American*, 30 Dec. 1964, p. 13.

McDonald, Daniel. "Truth and Illusion in *Who's Afraid of Virginia Woolf?*," *Renascence*, 17 (Winter 1964), 63-69.

Michaelis, Rolf. "Albees Spiel in den Tod," *Theater heute*, 5 (June 1964), 12-20.

Morgan, Thomas B. "Angry Playwright in a Soft Spell," *Life*, 67 (26 May 1967), 90-99.

Moses, Robbie Odom. "Death as a Mirror of Life: Edward Albee's *All Over*," *Modern Drama*, 19 (Mar. 1976), 67-77.

Norton, Rictor. "Folklore and Myth in *Who's Afraid of Virginia Woolf?*," *Renascence*, 23 (Spring 1971), 159-167.

Otten, Terry. *After Innocence: Visions of the Fall of Modern Literature.* Pittsburgh: Pittsburgh University Press, 1982, 174-191.

Paolucci, Anne. "Albee and the Restructuring of the Modern Stage," *Studies in American Drama, 1945-Present*, 1 (1986), 3-23.

Paolucci. "Albee come Pirandello." *America/Oggi*, 16 Nov. 1988, p. 5b.

Paolucci. "Edward Albee and the Theater of Arrogance," *Barnard Alumnae Magazine*, 18 (Fall 1968), 22-24.

Paolucci. "Exorcisms: *Who's Afraid of Virginia Woolf?*." In Kolin and Davis, 151-162.

Paolucci. "Pirandello and the Waiting Stage of the Absurd (with Some Observations on a New 'Critical Language')," *Modern Drama*, 23 (Mar. 1980), 102-111.

Paolucci. "Shakespeare and the Genius of the Absurd," *Comparative Drama*, 7 (Fall 1973), 237-246.

Paolucci. "Those Wonderful Lizards of Ooze," *Literary Tabloid*, 5 (Oct. 1975), 19-20.

Paolucci. "A Vision of Baal: *A Delicate Balance*." In Bigsby, 138-150.

Parone, Edward. Introduction to *New Theater in America*, ed. Parone. New York: Dell, 1965, 2-3, 6, 9-10.

Perry, Virginia I. "Disturbing Our Sense of Well-Being: The 'Uninvited' in *A Delicate Balance*." In Wasserman, 55-64.

Popkin, Henry. "Theatre Chronicle," *Sewanee Review*, 69 (Spring 1961), 333-345.

Porter, M. Gilbert. "Toby's Last Stand: The Evanescence of Commitment in *A Delicate Balance*," *Educational Theatre Journal*, 31 (Oct. 1979), 398-408. Collected in Kolin and Davis, 167-179.

Post, Robert M. "Cognitive Dissonance in the Plays of Edward Albee," *Quarterly Journal of Speech*, 55 (Feb. 1969), 54-60.

Post. "Fear Itself: Edward Albee's *A Delicate Balance*," *CLA Journal*, 13 (Dec. 1969), 162-171.

Purdon, Liam O. "The Limits of Reason: *Seascape* as Psychic Metaphor." In Wasserman, 141-153; in Bloom, 119-130.

Quackenbush, L. Howard. "The Legacy of Edward Albee's *Who's Afraid of Virginia Woolf?* in Spanish-American Absurdist Theatre," *Revista/Review InterAmericana*, 9 (1979), 51-71.

Richards, Stanley. "On and Off Broadway," *Players Magazine*, 37 (Oct. 1960), 9-10.

Richards. "Theatre in New York," *Players Magazine*, 39 (Dec. 1962), 85.

Richmond, Hugh M. "Shakespeare and Modern Sexuality: Albee's *Virginia Woolf* and *Much Ado*." In his *Shakespeare's Sexual Comedy: A Mirror for Lovers*. Indianapolis: Bobbs-Merrill, 1971, 177-196.

Rocha Filho, Rubem. "Albee, processo e tentativa," *Tempo brasileiro: Revista de cultura*, no. 3 (Mar. 1963), 167-172.

Rogoff, Gordon. "Albee and Mamet: The War of the Words," *Saturday Review*, 4 (2 Apr. 1977), 36-37.

Roth, Philip. "The Play that Dare Not Speak Its Name," *New York Review of Books*, 4 (25 Feb. 1965), 4. Collected in Bigsby, 105-109.

Roudané, Matthew C. "Animal Nature, Human Nature, and the Existentialist Imperative: Edward Albee's *Seascape*," *Theatre Annual*, 38 (1983), 31-47.

Roudané. "Communication as Therapy in the Theater of Edward Albee," *Journal of Evolutionary Psychology*, 6 (1985), 302-317.

Roudané. "A Monologue of Cruelty: Edward Albee's *The Man Who Had Three Arms*." In Kolin and Davis, 187-192; in Bloom, 161-164.

Roudané. "On Death, Dying, and the Manner of Living: Waste as Theme in Edward Albee's *The Lady From Dubuque*." In Wassermann, 65-81.

Roy, Emil. *"Who's Afraid of Virginia Woolf?* and the Tradition," *Bucknell Review*, 13 (Mar. 1965), 27-36. Collected in Kolin and Davis, pp. 87-94.

Rutenberg, Michael. "Albee in Protest." In Kolin and Davis, 122-125.

Rutenberg. *"The Ballad of the Sad Cafe."* In Bigsby, 89-98.

Saurel, Rénee. "Paris production of *Virginia Woolf,"* *Temps modernes,* 20 (Jan. 1965), 1318-1322.

Schechner, Richard. "Who's Afraid of Edward Albee?," *Tulane Drama Review*, 7 (Spring 1963), 7-10. Collected in Bigsby, 62-65.

Schlueter, June. "Albee's Martha and George." In her *Metafictional Characters in Modern Drama.* New York: Columbia University Press, 1979, 79-87.

Schlueter. "Is It 'All Over' for Edward Albee?: *The Lady From Dubuque."* In De La Fuente, 112-119.

Schneider, Alan. "Why So Afraid?," *Tulane Drama Review,* 7 (Spring 1963), 10-13. Collected in Bigsby, 66-68.

Sheed, Wilfred. "A Bunch of Drunks," *Jubilee,* 10 (Feb. 1963), 55-56.

Simard, Rodney. "Harold Pinter and Edward Albee: The First Postmoderns." In his *Postmodern Drama: Contemporary Playwrights in America and Britain.* Lanham, Md.: University Press of America, 1984, 25-47.

Simon, John. "Evolution Made Queasy," *New York,* 8 (10 Feb. 1975), 52.

Simon. "From Hunger, Not Dubuque," *New York,* 13 (11 Feb. 1980), 74-75.

Simon. "Of Nothing and Something," *New York,* 4 (5 Apr. 1971), 58-59.

Simon. "Theater Chronicle," *Hudson Review,* 21 (Winter 1968/1969), 703-712.

Skloot, Robert. "The Failure of *Tiny Alice,"* *Players Magazine,* 43 (Feb./ Mar. 1968), 79-81.

Smilgis, Martha. "Edward Albee Blames His Newest Flop on the Critics—and Casts for *Lolita* on the Subways," *People,* 13 (25 Feb. 1980), 70, 73.

Smith, Kitty Harris. "A Dream of Dragons: Albee Starthrower in *Seascape."* In De La Fuente, 99-110.

Spencer, Sharon D. "Edward Albee–the Anger Artist," *Forum* (Houston), 4 (Winter/Spring 1967), 25-30. Collected in Kolin and Davis, 135-141.

Spielberg, Peter. "The Albatross in Albee's Zoo," *College English*, 27 (Apr. 1966), 562-565.

Spielberg. "Reply: The Albatross Strikes Again!," *College English*, 28 (Oct. 1966), 59.

Stark, John. "Camping Out: *Tiny Alice* and Susan Sontag," *Players Magazine*, 47 (Apr./May 1972), 166-169. Collected in Kolin and Davis, 162-166.

Stayton, Richard. "Students Run with Albee Rebellion," *Los Angeles Herald Examiner*, 25 May 1984, Weekend section, p. 29.

Sullivan, Dan. "Albee's One-Acters Pitched in Sand," *Los Angeles Times*, 26 May 1984, section 5, p. 2.

Sullivan. "A Double Bill of Pale Albee," *Los Angeles Times*, 3 Feb. 1977, section 4, pp. 1, 13.

Sullivan. "Ill-Fated *Breakfast at Tiffany's*," *New York Times*, 15 Dec. 1966, p. 60.

Sullivan. "Radio Drama and the Way We Sound Now," *Los Angeles Times*, 31 Oct. 1976, p. 50.

Sullivan. "Stage Wire," *Los Angeles Times*, 14 Feb. 1987, section 6, p. 5.

Sykes, Carol A. "Albee's Beast Fables: *The Zoo Story* and *A Delicate Balance*," *Educational Theatre Journal*, 25 (Dec. 1973), 448-455.

Szilassy, Zoltan. "Edward Albee: First Among Equals." In his *American Theater of the 1960s*. Carbondale: Southern Illinois University Press, 1986, 11-23.

Taubman, Howard. "Theater: Albee's *Tiny Alice* Opens," *New York Times*, 30 Dec. 1964, p. 14. Excerpted in Kolin and Davis, 51-52.

Taylor, Marion A. "Edward Albee and August Strindberg: Some Parallels Between *The Dance of Death* and *Who's Afraid of Virginia Woolf?*," *Papers on English Language and Literature*, 1 (Winter 1965), 59-71.

"Tinny Alegory," *Time*, 85 (8 Jan. 1965), 32.

Tolpegin, Dorothy Dunlap. "The Two-Petaled Flower: A Commentary on Edward Albee's Play, *Tiny Alice*," *Cimarron Review*, 14 (Jan. 1971), 17-30.

Trewin, J. C. "Nights with the Ripsaw," *Illustrated London News*, 22 Feb. 1964, p. 288. Excerpted in Kolin and Davis, 50-51.

Trilling, Diana. "The Riddle of Albee's *Who's Afraid of Virginia Woolf ?*." In her *Claremont Essays*. New York: Harcourt, Brace & World, 1964, 203-207; in Bigsby, 80-88.

Trilling. "Who's Afraid of the Culture Elite?," *Esquire*, 60 (Dec. 1963), 69, 72, 74, 76, 78, 80, 82-84, 86, 88.

Trotta, Geri. "On Stage: Edward Albee," *Horizon*, 4 (Sept. 1961), 78-79. Excerpted in Kolin and Davis, 44.

Turner, W. L. "Absurdist, Go Home!," *Players Magazine*, 40 (Feb. 1964), 139-140.

Valgemae, Mardi. "Albee's Great God Alice," *Modern Drama*, 10 (Dec. 1967), 267-273. Collected in Kolin and Davis, 101-106.

Wallace, Robert S. "*The Zoo Story:* Albee's Attack on Fiction," *Modern Drama*, 16 (June 1973): 49-54.

Wardle, Irving. "Nabokov's *Lolita* by Edward Albee," *Times* (London), 23 Mar. 1981, p. 7.

Wardle. "New Plays in London," *Observer* (London), 28 Aug. 1960, p. 24.

Wardle. "Sixty-minute, Second-rate Doodle," *Times* (London), 7 Dec. 1976, p. 11.

Wasserman, Julian N. " 'The Pitfalls of Drama': The Idea of Language in the Plays of Edward Albee." In Wasserman, 29-53; in Bloom, 97-118.

Watt, Douglas. "Albee's *Lolita* a Script-Tease," *New York Daily News*, 20 Mar. 1981, Friday section, pp. 3-4.

Watts, Richard. "Edward Albee has a Catastrophe," *New York Post*, 12 Jan. 1966, p. 38.

Way, Brian. "Albee and the Absurd: *The American Dream* and *The Zoo Story*." In Bigsby, 26-44; in Kolin and Davis, 65-73; in Bloom, 9-28.

Weales, Gerald. "Edward Albee: Don't Make Waves." In his *Jumping Off Place: American Drama in the 1960s*. New York: Macmillan, 1969, 24-53; collected in Bigsby, 10-22; collected in Bloom, 29-50.

Weales. Review of *The Man Who Had Three Arms*. *Georgia Review*, 37 (Fall 1983), 605-606.

Weales. "Stop the Balance, I Want to Get Off," *Reporter*, 35 (20 Oct. 1966), 52-53.

Weiner, Leslie. "Dissent on *Virginia Woolf*," *New York Times*, 3 July 1966, section 2, p. 5.

White, Fred D. "Albee's Hunger Artist: *The Zoo Story* as a Parable of the Writer vs. Society," *Arizona Quarterly*, 39 (Spring 1983), 15-22.
White, James E. "An Early Play of Edward Albee," *American Literature*, 42 (Mar. 1970), 98-99.
Wilson, Raymond J. "The Dynamics of *Who's Afraid of Virginia Woolf ?*," In De La Fuente, 58-69.
Witherington, Paul. "Albee's Gothic: The Resonance of Cliche," *Comparative Drama*, 4 (Fall 1970), 151-165. Collected in Bloom, 51-74.
Witherington. "Language of Movement in Albee's *The Death of Bessie Smith*," *Twentieth Century Literature*, 13 (July 1967), 84-88. Collected in Kolin and Davis, 142-146.
Zimbardo, Rose A. "Symbolism and Naturalism in Edward Albee's *The Zoo Story*," *Twentieth Century Literature*, 8 (Apr. 1962), 10-17. Collected in Bigsby, 45-53.

BIBLIOGRAPHICAL ESSAY

Bibliographies and Checklists

The bibliographical essay by Philip C. Kolin and J. Madison Davis that introduces their 1986 collection of critical essays, interviews, and reviews provides a richly annotated discussion of the most important critical materials available on the plays of Edward Albee. The essay includes sections on reference material, criticism of the individual plays, and critical themes. Kolin and Davis exclude consideration of adaptations by Albee and conclude with a general comment on his dramatic work in its entirety.

Primary Albee bibliographies completed before 1986 provide a complete list only if they are considered as a group. Robert A. Wilson's "Edward Albee: A Bibliographical Checklist" (Mar./Apr. 1983) represents a good beginning provided the studies by James E. White (1970) and Kolin (Spring 1975) are also consulted. Karen Rood's descriptive checklist (1978) is authoritative for the years covered. Richard Tyce (1986) and Scott Giantvalley (1987) provide superseding updates.

The two major book-length secondary bibliographies are by Tyce and Giantvalley. Tyce calls his work the "most detailed bibliography to date" (2,711 citations); it gives a complete list of English-language criticism on Albee through 1984 and extending into 1985 and a limited number of foreign-language citations, supported by references to book reviews, many cross-references, and a long index of authors and play titles. Tyce divides the criticism into three sections: the first limited to items discussing more than three works; the second to theses and dissertations; and the third to criticism and reviews of individual plays. Of the items in the first section, many are full-length books or collections of essays on Albee, and many more are Albee interviews. Giantvalley's bibliography of secondary sources, including interviews, is, unlike Tyce's, extensively and ably annotated. The entries are arranged alphabetically by year. There is a long analytical index that permits Albee students to approach the main bibliography from diverse perspectives. Giantvalley's book very ably supplements the Kolin and Davis essay and the Tyce bibliography as a major aid to Albee studies.

Interviews

Albee has been a much-interviewed playwright. Philip C. Kolin's *Conversations with Edward Albee* (1988) comprises twenty-seven examples and is a sensible addition to Albee scholarship. Lea Carol Owen's annotated bibliography of seventy-five interviews, included in Kolin and Davis, notes that Albee's "frequent interviews . . . provide a remarkable commentary on his career, elucidating not only his writings and development, but also his aesthetic theories and views on the theater world." Charles Green (1980) provides a similarly arranged annotated list of twenty-six interviews, many of them not cited by Owen. In Tyce an index entry for interviews lists over one hundred items. Many book-length works on Albee include interviews. There are two in Rutenberg (1969); Bigsby (1975) includes R. S. Stewart's interview with John Gielgud and Albee; De La Fuente (1980) and Wasserman (1983) include interviews by the editors; and Kolin and Davis (1986) includes the latest of Matthew Roudané's.

One of the Rutenberg interviews is interesting for its revelation of Albee's attitude toward hostile critics. Albee says wittily that it would certainly "help" the American theater community to "rid ourselves from what Harold Clurman refers to as the Jewish Mafia, this group made up of [John] Simon, [Robert] Brustein, and that very sick man [Martin Gottfried] from *Women's Wear Daily*." But in a 1976 London *Sunday Times* interview with Philip Oakes, he explains, "I never mind a bad review if it has something to do with what I intended to write." Albee repeatedly chides critics for dwelling on "biographical details" in interpreting his plays. In the Krohn and Wasserman interview Albee was asked if biography was important in understanding his work. He replied, "Biography and me? Oh, I think totally unimportant. . . . There is very little in my life that is of such great apparent significance or earth shaking importance that would lead to this or that play. And I'd rather people judge the work for itself. . . . No worthwhile piece of literature is any good if it has to be related to some biographical factor in the author's life."

Albee insists, rather, on discussing the content of his work, because his "true life" is that of a literary person completely wrapped up in his art. Since he has started directing his own plays he has been frequently asked for "personal" explanations of the relationship of his directing to his writing. His characteristic response—summed up in the title of his 1976 interview with Daniel Stern, "Albee: 'I Want My Intent Clear,' "—is: "If you can remember what you intended when you wrote the play . . . you can probably, if you're somewhat objective, end up with a fair representation of what you intended": though, of course, you "won't necessarily end up with the most effective production."

The subject of the intent of Albee's directing is the central theme of his 1977 interview with William Glover. He insists that a "first-rate play can only be proved, not improved, by production"; that the author's intent must somehow be realized in the written text; and that, if the author is able to direct his own work reasonably well, he ought to do so in order to make its intent thoroughly clear. In the Roudané interview in Kolin and Davis he adds, "When I write a play, I see it and hear it on a stage. I therefore have the closest vision of what I the author want the play to hear and sound like. Why not share that with an audience? No other director can come as close to my original intention; whether that's the best for the play or not doesn't matter."

Albee also addresses the issue of drama as social criticism in the 1986 Roudané interview. He declares that the playwright, at his best, is a "demonic" critic, "concerned with altering people's perceptions, altering the status quo." In an introduction to the interview Roudané commented that "consciousness" is Albee's "most compelling subject" as a critical playwright. Repeatedly, Albee suggests in his work that "self-awareness . . . not only produces better social, economic, political, and aesthetic choices, but seems essential if the individual is to remain alive." Albee told Roudané that he follows Sartre and Camus in writing to encourage people to live their lives as "fully conscious . . . no matter how dangerous or cruel or terror-filled" such living may be. Albee thus applies to contemporary play writing what Eliot says of contemporary poetry: in our age of criticism, our best playwrights must write critical plays.

Critical Studies: Books

The most important early critical study of Albee's work is the 1969 volume by C. W. E. Bigsby. Kolin and Davis state that the work established Bigsby "as one of the most perceptive Albee scholars." Matthew Roudané, in his *Understanding Edward Albee* (1987), calls Bigsby "one of the world's leading Albee scholars." Bigsby acknowledges the power of Albee's dramatic focus on societal alienation in the "spiritually and morally deformed" condition of American life. Nevertheless, Bigsby correctly locates in Albee's early plays a tentative sense of redemptive hope. He also shows that Albee draws upon a rich mix of European and American traditions and influences, none of which ought to be treated as dominant. Bigsby felt in 1969 that Albee had not succumbed to the absurdist dramatic vision: his protagonists were not antiheroes crushed "by environment and heredity," or by the "sheer weight of an indifferent universe," as in many of the plays of Samuel Beckett.

Bigsby's work was preceded by the Belgian critic Gilbert Debusscher's *Edward Albee: Tradition and Renewal* (1967)–translated from the French by Anne D. Williams–which traces the relationship of Albee's pre-1967 plays and adaptations to the works of such playwrights as Jean Genet, Tennessee Williams, Samuel Beckett, and Eugene Ionesco. The term "tradition" in the subtitle refers to the "larger stage" of European, American, and world drama. Unlike Bigsby, Debusscher found "no positive philosophy or social message" in Albee's work; in his view, Albee's theater belonged to "the pessimistic, defeatist or nihilistic current which characterizes the entire contemporary theatrical scene," and offered "no exit" except death from the burden of "our conscious life."

Anne Paolucci's *From Tension to Tonic: The Plays of Edward Albee* (1972), a useful overview of Albee's work to that date, is primarily concerned with Albee's use of language. The book traces Albee's linguistic development in an effort to show that Albee "has done more than any other recent writer to revive the glorious tradition of polysemous writing, in a modern vein." Paolucci finds the key to Albee's stylistic achievement in a mastery of dialogue that permits him to realize a strikingly original "integration of realism and abstract symbolism"; she views Albee as the "best product of the theater of the absurd, with Pirandello rather than O'Neill as his master."

Albee's "language," his "talent for dialogue," is likewise stressed in Ruby Cohn's *Edward Albee* (1969). Cohn analyzes Albee's treatment of dialogue through all the plays to the time of *Box* and *Quotations from Chairman Mao Tse-Tung*, and she judges that he has proved himself "the most skillful composer of dialogue that America has produced." Her central judgment on Albee's American connections is that he draws upon "O'Neill's repetitions, Miller's inflections, and Williams's atmospheric imagery," yet always with his own "idiomatic pungency and studied rhythms." Albee's dramatic approach to the "reality of the human condition" is compared to that of major European contemporary playwrights such as Sartre, Camus, Beckett, Genet, Ionesco, and Pinter, who "represent that reality in all its allegorical absurdity." Albee, Cohn declares, is "preoccupied with illusions that screen man from reality"; but, while such illusions are "still present" in Albee's plays, his art serves to dramatize "the process of collapse" of those illusions. Cohn suggests that Albee's verbal ingenuity and craft often threatens to obscure what might be called the "genuineness of his artistic search," making us long, sometimes–particularly in such plays as *Tiny Alice, Box* and *Quotations from Chairman Mao Tse-Tung*, or *The Lady from Dubuque*–for a more genuine "groping" toward art. Albee, she fears, may be providing more surface than substance.

Michael Rutenberg's *Edward Albee: Playwright in Protest* (1969) contends that Albee is above all an "engaged" writer. Arguing that Albee "writes reformist plays which unflinchingly reveal the pustulous sores of a society plagued with social ills," Rutenberg chides critics for failing to plumb the many-layered depths of protest beneath the "strangely beautiful" surface of *A Delicate Balance,* for example, because it is, in Rutenberg's view, Albee's best play.

Foster Hirsch's *Who's Afraid of Edward Albee?* (1978) suggests that, with the passing years, the one person really afraid of Albee seems to be Albee himself. Hirsch blames Albee's insecurity on his failure to confront squarely the central facts about his life, starting with his homosexuality.

Anita Maria Stenz's *Edward Albee: The Poet of Loss* (1978) focuses on characterization in Albee's major plays (through *Seascape*). The plays are viewed solely as stage performances. She tries to interpret the performances outside of conventional contextual references, assuming a critical stance that emphasizes the crucial function of performance in dramatic interpretation in a way that is at least partially free of conventional dependence on purely literary elements.

Of further value to Albee scholars are Richard E. Amacher's *Edward Albee* (1969; revised, 1982), Liliane Kerjan's *Le théâtre d'Edward Albee* (1978), and Nelvin Vos's brief *Eugene Ionesco and Edward Albee: A Critical Study* (1968). Vos's book focuses on Ionesco's philosophical "absurdism" and the way in which Ionesco's absurdism differs from Albee's. He treats the two playwrights separately, thus denying the reader a full comparative analysis. Kerjan's book treats Albee as a social critic, considering him within a European and, indeed, a global context. Amacher's book is rich in biographical detail, draws parallels between Albee's plays and Greek tragedy, and identifies major themes; yet its interpretations often seem forced.

The most important recent full-length study of Albee's theater is Roudané's *Understanding Edward Albee*. There are, throughout the book, extensive references to previous secondary studies. Little that is insightful in earlier Albee criticism is neglected. Roudané's primary concern "centers on tracing Albee's artistic vision," which, he claims, "is essentially an affirmative existentialist world view." Although Albee's plays "typically address such issues as betrayal, abandonment, [and] withdrawal into death-in-life existence," Roudané writes, careful study reveals that "underneath the external action, aggressive texts, and obvious preoccupation with death lies an inner drama that discloses the playwright's compassion for his fellow human beings." Roudané also recognizes that Albee has made specific contributions to the drama genre. Much of the book focuses on Albee's "ongoing efforts to reinvent dramatic language and contexts," thereby demonstrating, as Roudané explains in an allusion to T. S. Eliot, "his awareness of the modern dramatic tradition, and his individual talents."

Roudané frames his judgments about the individual plays with remarkable verbal compression—despite Albee's well-known statement, made in a 1979 interview with Allan Wallach, that "if a play can be described in one sentence, that should be its length." The chapter on *The Zoo Story* and *The American Dream* is called "Beginnings"; the title "Toward the Marrow" is used to stress the central importance of *Who's Afraid of Virginia Woolf?*; the obscure plays *Tiny Alice* and *A Delicate Balance* are called "Betrayals"; "Death and Life" sums up the focus of *All Over* and *Seascape*; and *The Lady From Du-*

buque and *The Man Who Had Three Arms* are presented as illustrations of Albee's preoccupation with "Public Issues, Private Tensions." Roudané closes by crediting Albee with "reinventing the American stage at a time when its originality and quality seemed to be fading. He continues to be a major spokesperson for the moral seriousness of American theater. Above all, he has the artistic instinct, even arrogance, to stage significant, universal public issues and private tensions of the individual and a culture thinking in front of themselves."

Roudané's *Necessary Fictions, Terrifying Realities: 'Who's Afraid of Virginia Woolf?'* (1989) is the first full-length analysis of Albee's best-known play. The book sets the play in historical and cultural context, reports on its critical reception, details its set and setting, and analyzes the characters and Albee's theatrical strategy.

Critical Studies: Collections of Essays
The earliest collection of critical studies on Albee was edited by C. W. E. Bigsby (1975). The book offers nineteen previously published essays, reviews, and interviews and provides new studies on *Tiny Alice* and *Box* and *Quotations from Chairman Mao Tse-Tung* by the editor. Studies by Gerald Weales and Martin Esslin begin the collection. Weales's essay stresses the intentional ambiguities and ambivalences of Albee's art, while Esslin's details Albee's links with Anglo-European theater of the absurd. The early "short plays" come under scrutiny in essays by Brian Way, Rose Zimbardo, and Gilbert Debusscher. The critiques of *Who's Afraid of Virginia Woolf?* that Bigsby chose–by Howard Clurman, Richard Schechner, Alan Schneider, and Diana Trilling–characterize the general current of all subsequent criticism of the play. Clurman's 1962 essay argues that, while the play is apt to appear as but a minor work in comparison to what Albee was bound to write later, there is no denying that at the time it was written the play occupied a "major position in our scene." Schechner's 1963 essay introduces the view that the play lacks "intellectual size" and "dramatic electricity," and that its hints of "morbidity and sexual perversity" serve only to titillate an "impotent and homosexual theater and audience." Alan Schneider replies that same year with a director's defense of Albee's "honesty," but Diana Trilling counters with an essay in which she characterizes Albee's attitude as manifested in *Who's Afraid of Virginia Woolf?* as inverted snobbery.

Philip Roth's essay on *Tiny Alice* argues that the seriousness of the play's theme, which involves the deluded quest of a religious man for unity with God, "trapped" Albee "in a lie," because the material used to express the theme amounted to little more than "ghastly pansy rhetoric and repartee." In another essay, Abraham Franzblau does Albee the counterservice of subjecting *Tiny Alice* to a Freudian analysis to show that the work was far from being a "sly in-joke on straight audiences." *Tiny Alice* "reaches the citadels of private certainties and shoots them full of question marks." Robert Brustein calls *A Delicate Balance* a "very bad play" with no "internal validity"; but, by way of compensation, Bigsby provides an excerpt from Anne Paolucci's 1972 book, in which the same play is celebrated as a masterpiece. Brendan Gill finds Albee's *All Over* "disappointing," though he is quick to declare that Albee "has been characteristically precise, ironic, prankish, and gallant" in naming the play as he has.

The next two collections, one edited by Patricia De La Fuente, Donald E. Fritz, Jan Seale, and Dorey Schmidt (1980) and the other by Julian N. Wassermann with the assistance of J. L. Linsley and J. A. Kramer (1983), consist of introductory interviews and specially commissioned essays. De La Fuente presents three essays on general themes: the "unity" of Albee's artistic vision is discussed by Lucina P. Gabbard; Albee's female characters are analyzed by Laura Julier; and language in Albee's later plays is described by Thomas P. Adler. Five studies of individual plays follow: Raymond J. Wilson on *Who's Afraid of Virginia Woolf ?*; Robert Mayberry on *Box* and *Quotations from Chairman Mao Tse-Tung*; David Richard Jones on *All Over*; Kitty Harris Smith on *Seascape*; and June Schlueter on *The Lady from Dubuque*. Adler's judgment that Albee's later plays are primarily about the contemporary debasement of language is notable, as is Albee's statement, in an introductory interview, that serious art has generally shown itself to be "an attempt to modify and change people's perception of themselves, to bring them into larger contact with the fact of being alive." The Wasserman volume presents seven studies of individual plays: Virginia I. Perry on the "uninvited" in *A Delicate Balance*; Matthew Roudané on "waste" in *The Lady From Dubuque*; Leonard Casper on the abiding "mystery" and "expense" of joy in *Tiny Alice*; Mary Castiglie Anderson on biblical language and ritual in *The Zoo Story*; Thomas P. Adler on the Pirandello influence in *The Lady From Dubuque*; Philip C. Kolin on what "shocks rather than soothes" in *Counting the Ways*; and Liam O.

Purdon on *Seascape* as a "psychic metaphor" on the "limits of reason."

The collection edited by Philip C. Kolin and J. Madison Davis presents thirty-nine essays and reviews, several of which are published for the first time. The scope of the work perhaps makes it the best Albee collection published to date. Many prominent critics and scholars make appearances: Adler, Brustein, Esslin, Kohn. Roudané supplies the first published essay on one of Albee's most recent plays, *The Man Who Had Three Arms*.

The collection edited by Harold Bloom (1987) likewise gathers together much of the most prominent Albee criticism. Contributors include Brian Way, Gerald Weales, Paul Witherington, Ronald Hayman, Anthony Hopkins, Mary C. Anderson, Wasserman, Purdon, Alder, Bigsby, and Roudané. Bloom's introduction sets the tone of the book. In it he defines Albee as "the crucial American dramatist of his generation, standing as the decisive link between our principal older dramatists—Eugene O'Neill, Thornton Wilder, Tennessee Williams, Arthur Miller—and the best of the younger ones—Sam Shepard and David Mamet, among others." But Bloom also suggests that the essays he has collected confirm his overall judgment that Albee's plays lack a certain dramatic character. Way, writes Bloom, finds Albee "to be far more deeply contaminated by a theater of naturalist reality" than are Beckett and Harold Pinter. Weales finds in Albee's writings a consistent lack of what he calls "the dramatic image upon the stage."

Critical Studies: Major Reviews, Articles, and Book Sections

The reception of Albee's plays in Europe is still a largely neglected area of study—although the introduction to Giantvalley's bibliography offers hope of a change for the better. Albee has repeatedly called attention to the fact that *The Zoo Story* had its world premiere in Europe and in a language—German—of which he "knew not a word." Kolin and Davis have done us the service of publishing translated excerpts of the first German reviews, not only of *The Zoo Story* but also of the second Albee play that premiered in a German version, *The Death of Bessie Smith*. The German critic Friedrich Luft, who reviewed *The Zoo Story* (1959), recalled in his review of *Bessie Smith* (1960) that Albee had indeed "been discovered a year ago" by an "experimental group" in Berlin. "Now," he added, "the whole world is playing his Zoo story"; but the fact is that Albee had to "go through" a Berlin suburb to "get to New York."

Critical reaction to the American premiere of *The Zoo Story* was mixed. Even at this early stage in Albee's career there were examples of the extreme positive and negative reactions that were eventually to establish themselves as the norms of Albee criticism. Brooks Atkinson, in two *New York Times* reviews (15 Jan. 1960 and 31 Jan. 1960), reflected the emerging critical extremes, observing that "nothing of enduring value is said" in *The Zoo Story*, though Albee is "an excellent writer and designer of dialogue." The character of Jerry is "searching and caustic," but the violence of the conclusion "drops the level of the play as a whole."

In Robert Brustein's review of *The Zoo Story* for the *New Republic* (22 Feb. 1960), critical extremes are even more clearly delineated. Albee, wrote Brustein, has "a powerful dramatic talent"; but the play's "Beat ideology," which suggests that "the psychotic, the criminal and the invert are closer to God than anyone else," is objectionable. The play's conclusion, with its "masochistic-homosexual perfume," yields "more readily to clinical than to theological analysis." Harold Clurman (13 Feb. 1960) wrote perhaps with greater accuracy when he commented that Albee "brilliantly" dramatized Jerry, the Beat character, with "rude humor," "splendid eloquence," and "keen intuition." Mordecai Levine (Mar. 1967) called *The Zoo Story* "Albee's Liebestod," pointing to the use of "traditional" religious love-death symbolism.

In the short plays that followed *The Zoo Story*, Albee revealed how determined he was to dramatize recognizably American themes. Critics have repeatedly asked whether the "matter" of *The Death of Bessie Smith, The Sandbox, The American Dream*, and *FAM and YAM* is authentically American, or only superficially so. But not one of the short plays is presented by Albee as a reflection of American life. Each is something "crafted" to embody Albee's view of American matters more intensely than particular real-life situations could. In his review of *The Sandbox*, Walter Kerr (17 May 1960) said that Albee, showing his quality, remains strongly promising; and he concluded that while the little play gives the immediate impression of a random collage, one gets the sense, before it is over, of its being held together by a "nearly invisible strand of intelligence and sentiment." In a later review (Sept. 1962) Kerr observed that while *The American Dream* ran the risk of belaboring its theme, *The Sandbox* was not only touching but also among "the most attractive avant-garde plays." John Cappelletti (Spring 1963) also considers the two short plays together, as does Kathleen R. Shull (1983), who stresses the absurdist exaggerations and contrasts the treatments of the shared characters, noting, as Giantvalley puts it, "the similarities of Mrs. Barker and Mommy and the differences of Mommy and Daddy from Martha and George."

A serious account of the first phase of the American critical reception of Albee should properly begin with consideration of the reviews of the double bill of 24 January 1961 at the York Playhouse in New York, featuring *Bartleby* with *The American Dream*. Whitney Bolton's review (26 Jan. 1961) noted that *The American Dream* was not as taut as *The Zoo Story*, but was nevertheless spirited and "theatrically engaging," while the libretto of *Bartleby* had "moments of penetrative wisdom." Harold Clurman (11 Feb. 1961) compared *The American Dream* with Ionesco, concluding that French influence on Albee was "not altogether helpful" and that Albee ought to stick closer to the "realism" that had worked so well in *The Zoo Story*; *Bartleby* was waved aside as an "honorable failure." But one should here also notice Morse Allen's early book review (1961) of *The Zoo Story, The Death of Bessie Smith, The Sandbox* (1960). Allen hails Albee as the most promising contemporary American playwright, giving high praise to *The Zoo Story* and comparing the "less important" *The Sandbox* to Wilder and the not fully coherent *The Death of Bessie Smith* to Tennessee Williams.

The body of critical writing on Albee was enlarged and enriched with the performance and publication of *Who's Afraid of Virginia Woolf?* in 1962. The success of the play stimulated debate over the value of absurdist drama. In the November 1962 issue of *Theater Arts*, Faubion Bowers and Glenn M. Loney skillfully summarized both sides of the argument. Loney held that Albee was the most skillful contemporary user of absurdist dramatic techniques, but that the success of his plays depended mostly on the extent to which he curbed their use. *Who's Afraid of Virginia Woolf?* was his least absurdist play, and hence his most successful. Bowers held that absurdism was by 1962 a permanent feature in American drama and that to depart from it meant only diminished success.

The confusion over Albee's faithfulness to absurdist tenets only heightened interest in the play. Walter Kerr (Sept. 1962) wrote that it "need not be liked, but it must be seen." Stanley Richards (Dec. 1962) declared that the play "may not be everyone's bowl of 'Wheaties,' but I challenge anyone to dismiss it." Richard Gilman (9 Nov. 1962) thought that it made "Lillian Hellman seem like the recording secretary of a garden club." Both Wendell V. Harris (Summer 1964) and Elemér Hankiss (Autumn 1964) argued that, despite undeniable links with Albee's earlier absurdist plays, *Who's Afraid of Virginia Woolf?* had a distinctly positive effect. It transformed oppressive human events into an inspiring vision, so that, despite its gloom, the play was full of light.

Some work has been done to trace the influence of Albee's masterpiece on later playwrights. A section of Foster Hirsch's 1978 study argues that, while the "anti-realistic revolution" that produced "today's New Theater" clearly started with playwrights such as Alfred Jarry, Antonin Artaud, Samuel Beckett, Eugene Ionesco, Jean Genet, and Harold Pinter, "its social commitment was influenced by Edward Albee and his English counterpart, John Osborne." Hirsch considers *Who's Afraid of Virginia Woolf?* to be Albee's earliest statement of true social commitment, as distinct from the realism and surrealism of his earlier plays. "Young American playwrights such as Rochelle Owens, Sam Shepard, Paul Foster, Megan Terry, Leonard Melfi, Lanford Wilson, Jean-Claude van Itallie, LeRoi Jones, Rosalyn Drexler, and many, many others," Hirsch concludes, "came out of Albee's Playwrights Unit and other Off-Off Broadway hostels." Studies by Edward Parone (1965) and Allan Lewis (Mar. 1964) mention the play's influence on subsequent American plays, and L. Howard Quackenbush's 1979 study of the influence of *Virginia Woolf* on the Spanish-American Absurdist Theater makes use of plays by four Spanish-American writers–Rene Marques, Jose de Jesus Martinez, Virgilio Pinera, and Maruxa Vilalta–to show the extent of Albee's influence.

The amount of foreign-language material on *Who's Afraid of Virginia Woolf?* testifies to its wide influence. Rolf Michaelis's "Albees Spiel in den Tod" (June 1964) compares German productions of the play in Berlin, Hamburg, Munich, Stuttgart, and Vienna. French productions are reviewed in a section of Lewis W. Falb's *American Drama in Paris, 1945-1970* (1973). An essay by Jean Cau (26 Nov. 1964), celebrated French translator of *Who's Afraid of Virginia Woolf?*, contrasted Albee's techniques with those of leading French playwrights and called Albee's masterpiece the "most important" postwar play. In a January 1965 review of Cau's version, Rénee Saurel strongly disagreed. Spanish critic Juan José Coy (1962) considered *The Zoo Story*, *The American Dream*, and *Who's Afraid of Virginia Woolf?* to be Albee's better plays and in a review of his career emphasized the hostile critical reception of his work and its essentially hopeful content. Mario Corona (1964) covered the same ground in Italian, taking note of foreign productions and critical responses and observing that *Who's Afraid of Virginia Woolf?* seemed to have been "written as a sonata would be by a composer."

Much has been written of the highly successful film version of Albee's play, which was directed by Mike Nichols from a screenplay by Ernest Lehman and features actors Richard Burton and Elizabeth Taylor. Leslie Weiner's "Dissent on *Virginia Woolf*" (3 July 1966) declares that the film is inferior to the play, that Taylor is miscast as Martha, and that Burton's George is so dominant throughout the proceedings that the ending is weakened.

In a suggestive summation designed to determine what Albee might be "up to" after his great success, Richard Kostelanetz (Oct./Nov. 1963) examined his early work and concluded that Albee had rejected the "sexual-psychological drama" of Tennessee Williams as well as the "social realism-tragedy" of Arthur Miller. Kostelanetz preferred to compare him to Genet and Nathanael West. Allan Lewis's "The Fun and Games of Edward Albee" (Mar. 1964) predicted that Albee was likely to be rated the best dramatist of the 1960s. Lewis wrote that his plays were "paeans to impotence" that laughed a "popular demonic laughter at the grave of man." Albee, Lewis concluded, had the capacity to "express the human condition dramatically and metaphorically" in its profoundest truth.

Highly controversial was Tom F. Driver's "What's the Matter with Edward Albee?" (2 Jan. 1964). Driver wrote that *Who's Afraid of Virginia Woolf?* was the "most pretentious" American play since Eugene O'Neill's *Mourning Becomes Electra*. Even so, because of his barbed dialogue, Albee had become a "cultural hero." Pointing to homosexual "overtones and undercurrents," Driver concluded that Albee was not aware of what he was saying, or, worse, was "afraid to say what he means."

But many of Albee's early American critics compared his work to that of the French absurdists, usually in Albee's favor. W. L. Turner (Feb. 1964) considered both *The Zoo Story* and *The American Dream* to be superior to the work of Ionesco, but he then made himself notorious for writing of the character of George in *Who's Afraid of Virginia Woolf?*: "If college professors behave that way, I've been sadly out of touch with my colleagues." However, what Albee put on stage in *Who's Afraid of Virginia Woolf?* was crafted reality, more real than anything he could actually have witnessed. Albee's George and Martha were, of course, not copies of anything; they were dramatic originals crafted by the high art of a first-rate American play-wright.

More typical of American critics who traced the French influ-ence on Albee was Paul J. Hurley, who, in "France and America: Ver-sions of the Absurd" (May 1965), contrasted Albee's *The American Dream* with Ionesco's *Jack or the Submission*, noting that while Ionesco merely revealed absurdities, Albee preached about them, and moved beyond them in *The Death of Bessie Smith* and *Who's Afraid of Vir-ginia Woolf ?*. C. W. E. Bigsby (Oct. 1967) said the same thing in his study of the play. Notable, too, is Lee Baxandall's frequently cited article (Summer 1965), which, in assessing the plays through *Tiny Alice*, supplied a suggestive grouping of Albee characters spread over three generations.

Harold Clurman (13 Nov. 1966) wrote that to determine Albee's true place in American drama, students ought to be willing to wait until he had been on the scene for at least twenty years. Sens-ing that book-length studies would soon be appearing, Clurman briefly "weighed and measured" the Albee writing that existed. Link-ing realistic and absurdist tendencies in the plays, he pointed out that Albee constantly pressed his realism in the direction of "allegori-cal stylization" and "outright symbolism" in a way that has made him the American theater's "most incisive voice."

A deservedly praised reevaluation of the early short plays is Lu-cina P. Gabbard's "Edward Albee's Triptych on Abandonment" (Spring 1982). She writes that *The Zoo Story, The Death of Bessie Smith*, and *The Sandbox* reflect the period of the early 1960s through representations of "rage at society's disregard for its out-casts"; they also explore the depths of psychological anxiety through their shared "themes of ambivalence, escape into phantasy, and preoccupation with death." Mary Castiglie Anderson has also supplied valuable retrospective criticism in reviews (Summer 1982, Winter 1983) of the first three volumes of the collected original plays. She thinks that Albee's early works testify to his talent for dia-logue and theatrical craftsmanship. She also notes that the more ex-perimental later plays contain themes no less disturbing, developed in a way that makes the plays "serious, thought-provoking reflec-tions of contemporary life." Rodney Simard's "Harold Pinter and Edward Albee: The First Postmoderns" (1984) is interesting be-cause it traces much in Albee back to earlier modern playwrights and forward to other "postmoderns." Zoltan Szilassy's "Edward

Albee: First Among Equals" (1986) ably covers much the same ground.

Albee's next play, *Tiny Alice*, had, by 1986, garnered even more attention than *Who's Afraid of Virginia Woolf?*. It has been charged that in *Tiny Alice* Albee abandoned himself to the worst tendencies displayed in the earlier plays. John McClain (30 Dec. 1964) confessed in a review that he could not begin to decipher what was supposed to be going on. Leonard Casper's essay on *Tiny Alice* (1983) speaks of the "bafflement" otherwise friendly critics–such as Howard Taubman, Walter Kerr, Richard Watts, and John Chapman– felt in dealing with the new play. But, in his review of the premiere, Taubman (30 Dec. 1964) began by praising Albee for his "refusal to stand still or repeat himself " and for moving boldly on "into the difficult, mysterious, even tantalizing realm of faith." Albee, wrote Taubman, "has attempted nothing less than a large, modern allegory on a theme that . . . is essentially timeless . . . the passion of a Christ-like figure, if not a Christ himself." The play's conclusion, where the allegory becomes transparent, is disappointing to Taubman; nevertheless, he concludes that "one does not forget the boldness and wonder of the journey Mr. Albee has dared to undertake."

Kerr (30 Dec. 1964) was less patient than Taubman with what he considered to be the artificiality of Albee's mystery story. Its "rigid and self-indulgent language" sounded to him like a translation from "euphuistic Latin." Chapman (30 Dec. 1964) wrote that the premiere, which reminded him of T. S. Eliot's *The Cocktail Party*, was obscure, but certainly not boring. It offered its audience some "splendid writing and acting." Four years later (30 Sept. 1969), however, Chapman changed his mind. In a reexamination of the play prompted by its onstage revival, he wrote that, "except for its brilliant opening scene," the play was too full of tiresome chatter. Philip Roth (25 Feb. 1965) thought that *Tiny Alice* had a "simple-minded homosexual theme" over which Albee spread a disguising veil, a transparent "sham." But there have been other critics, like Martin Gottfried (30 Nov. 1967), who praised the transparency of that "sham" as the play's foremost virtue.

Other important critical studies of *Tiny Alice* are by Mardi Valgemae (Dec. 1967), John Stark (Apr./May 1972), Mary Elizabeth Campbell (Winter 1968), and Abraham Franzblau (30 Jan. 1965).

Critical responses to Albee's next play, *A Delicate Balance*, were widely varied. Albert Bermel (10 Oct. 1966) called it "the most besotted script since *Virginia Woolf* "; Robert Brustein (1966) called it "boring and trivial"; and Alan N. Bunce (24 Sept. 1966) contented himself with the declaration that it was simply "too long." On the other hand, John Chapman (23 Jan. 1966) thought *A Delicate Balance* was Albee's "best and most mature" play. It was beautiful, gentle, and probing in its characterizations, but the "terror" in it was relentless; and Harold Clurman (13 Nov. 1966) praised Albee as the contemporary theater's "most incisive" voice. He thought the play was "brilliant," superior to *Who's Afraid of Virginia Woolf ?*.

A *Delicate Balance* shows Albee at his most critical: it is a play written for a critical age, to be appreciated by thoroughly *critical* minds. Recognizing that tendency, Walter Kerr (2 Oct. 1966) felt obliged to draw an unfavorable conclusion. Given Albee's view of life's unreality, of its being made up of language and nothing else, it follows that a play about life must be about language. The play is "more interesting to contend with," Kerr writes, "than any of the author's last three plays"; but for Kerr there was no escaping the conclusion that it was a mere "exercise when it might have been an experience." Still, Kerr gives high praise when compared to the judgment of Robert Kemper (23 Nov. 1966). Kemper writes that unless Albee's purpose is to "needle" a world that knows giant moral evils like "Hiroshima, Selma, Wall Street, Vietnam," the play is unworthy of him. "It would be too bad," he continues, "for a major American dramatist to spend his talents on problems better handled by Ann Landers." Perhaps Albee had declined to identify the "terror" that knocked on the door of his can-do suburban family precisely to avoid identifying with newspaper headlines in those days of radical chic.

C. W. E. Bigsby's essay on *Box* and *Quotations from Chairman Mao-Tse-Tung* is outstanding. He stresses the plays' visual spectacle, derived from constrasting dramatic effects, and the almost musical quality of the dialogue. Kerr (13 Oct. 1968) thought that the plays were "gratifying" because they accurately echoed "where we are" and because their "discontinuous techniques" displayed Albee's "natural affinity for the stage." In his review Kerr agreed with Albee's claim that in the paired plays he was using a musical rather than a narrative structure. John Simon (Winter 1968/1969) identified in the plays the same "artificial, circumlocutory prose Albee keeps elaborating in his later sterile works," and finally dismisses the plays as "pseudoliterate monologues." In contrast, Anne Paolucci (1972) characterized *Box* and *Quotations from Chairman Mao* as, together, the "most ingenious product of Albee's fertile imagination . . . a leap into the unexplored . . . an experience altogether new and–characteristically–curiously reminiscent of earlier works of Albee's." With *Box*, Albee students "seem to be inside the replica of *Tiny Alice*, in the great memory of history"; the characters are drawn like "Dantesque figures caught in their everlasting virtue or vice."

Despite the four-year interval that separated the premieres of *All Over* and *Seascape*, the two plays are often paired for critical appraisal. *All Over* quickly proved itself to be one of the most controversial of Albee's plays. Clive Barnes (29 Mar. 1971) greeted it with sophisticated praise, stressing its musical qualities. He called it a "poignant and deeply felt" performance, less written than orchestrated: a "consciously operatic, or at least string-quartetish" piece, with a "preternaturally precise" language the very "artifice" of which made the total effect all the more poignant. Harold Clurman (11 Apr. 1971) first hailed it as "the best play of several seasons," conveying a powerful "existential shudder"; and then (3 May 1971) defended it as drama against critics who had called it a bore that would probably come off better if read rather than staged.

Negative reviews pullulated. Among the harshest was Martin Gottfried's (29 Mar. 1971). He praised the "abstracted realism" of Albee's earlier plays and complained that it had been completely abandoned in favor of the "surrealism" of *All Over*, thus betraying Albee's "inability to feel for other people" and canceling whatever hopes critics may have had that Albee would someday reach a kind of artistic maturity. Henry Hewes called his review "The Theater: Death Prattle"; Stanley Kauffmann (17 Apr. 1971) wrote that the play was "bastard Chekhov"–an "arrogant display piece, puffed up with sophomoric diction"; and John Simon (5 Apr. 1971) dismissed it as plotless and characterless, a work clearly "descended from the plays of Eliot and Fry, the progeny of eunuchs," totally deficient in real language "as opposed to snide or lacerating repartee."

In his review of *Seascape* Clive Barnes (27 Jan. 1975) noted that Albee had identified it as a companion piece to *All Over*; he added that it showed Albee in full maturity, "leaner, sparer, and simpler" in his art than ever before. In *Seascape* Albee accomplished his ends as a writer and director with "strong theatrical strokes" and compassion. Barnes called the play a major event. Thomas P. Adler's extended appraisal of *Seascape* (Winter 1979) took as its point of departure Barnes's observation that, by contrast with its companion piece, "this is an optimistic play, a rose play rather than a black play." But Adler then argued that, to find a true "companion piece" for *Seascape*, "one needs to go back farther than *All Over* . . . to Albee's other Pulitzer Prize-winning drama, *A Delicate Balance*"; he proceeds, then, to show in detail that the "most fruitful way to approach *Seascape*" is indeed "to examine it as a reverse image of the earlier play." In her early appraisal, titled "Those Wonderful Lizards of Ooze" (Oct. 1975), Anne Paolucci also took Clive Barnes's review as a point of departure, noting that where Barnes praised Albee for having "become leaner, sparer, and simpler," other critics tended to agree with John Simon (10 Feb. 1975), who dismissed the play as a "simple-minded allegory" about men and salamanders. Simon went on to dismiss Albee as "a playwright of ideas," but only "for people who have never had an idea." For Paolucci, too, *Seascape* and *A Delicate Balance* made a better pair than *Seascape* and *All Over*. Like Adler, she stressed the fact that Albee had, in his new play, given us "paired characters in parallel but reversible situations."

Adler noted that, while the *Seascape* lizards serve as recollections for the human couple in the play, their counterparts in *A Delicate Balance*, Harry and Edna, are identified before the play begins—in the list of players—"as very much like Agnes and Tobias," mirror images in which Agnes and Tobias are constrained to "see themselves as they never have before," hollowed out by the same piercing plague which their friends, as uninvited guests, have just brought into their home. In *A Delicate Balance* both the paired couples know that they cannot touch souls across that chasm of terror, which is a terror of death. In *Seascape*, on the contrary, when the terror of mirrored recollection and anticipation seizes the paired couples, there is an instinctive "reaching out" on the part of the human couple that at once reconciles them to their past and enables them to extend an apparently irresistible, gracious invitation to their fearful visitors to "join them" for a new "beginning."

Seascape has had much adverse criticism, to be sure. Stanley Kauffmann's review (22 Feb. 1975) can be taken as a fair example of the worst that can be said with intelligence. Kauffmann held that *Seascape* depicted contemporary sterility through banalities but apparently without satirical purpose, offering "a trite anatomy of middle-class marriage and spiritual menopause." What Kauffmann thought to be undistinguished dialogue was at least not Albee's recent "fake manderinese" but instead followed "his pseudo-Chekhovian mode" of reminiscence. The play was "nothing more than . . . an echoingly hollow statement of bankruptcy." What makes such criticism intelligent is Kauffmann's implied recognition that Albee is a critical playwright, writing plays that are essentially critical in substance, for a critical age.

Albee's *Listening* was commissioned by BBC Radio 3 and broadcast on 28 March 1976. Reviewer Dan Sullivan (31 Oct. 1976) quoted from the play's program, which indicated that the play was about "people who don't listen to each other." Later, when he reviewed the American premiere pairing *Listening* with Albee's *Counting the Ways*, Sullivan (3 Feb. 1977) wrote that the two plays were "finger exercises." He called *Counting the Ways* a theme with variations: "something like a set of piano pieces by Satie." Its London premiere, not directed by Albee—as the later American premiere in Hartford would be—got an initial very bad review by Irving Wardle (7 Dec. 1976), titled "Sixty-Minute, Second-rate Doodle." A later review by Adler (Oct. 1977) supplied what is likely to remain a more abiding critical perspective. "The work's subtitle, 'A Vaudeville,' " Adler wrote, "indicates what the audience should expect: a series of skits, or turns, twenty or so in the seventy-minute evening, each punctuated by a blackout and the sound of a whipcrack." Clive Barnes (4 Feb. 1977) was equally approving, characterizing Albee's direction as "meticulous." In the only full-scale critical study of the play, Philip Kolin (Spring 1983) stressed Albee's wordplay and drew a comparison with *The Glass Menagerie*, contrasting Tennessee Williams's "theater of the heart" with Albee's "absurd arena of love."

Adler noted in 1983 that *The Lady From Dubuque*, with its insistence "on the necessity to perceive life as essentially multi-leveled," was "Albee's most Pirandellian play to date." Before drawing that conclusion Adler had reviewed the evidence of Pirandellian influence in earlier Albee plays, beginning with *The Sandbox*, and continuing with *The American Dream, Box* and *Quotations from Chairman Mao Tse-Tung*, and *Counting the Ways*. In all those plays, in differing measures and ways, Alder found that "Pirandellian motives—illusion/reality, play-acting, life/art—become a concern," though it was in *The Lady from Dubuque*, to be sure, that Pirandello's most characteristic trait—the "Modernist convention of making the audience conscious of themselves as audience"—was most effectively applied.

The real-world origins of the "Lady from Dubuque" moniker also stimulated the interest of critics. Adler pointed out that she was a "mythical creation of *New Yorker* editor Harold Ross." Jack Kroll (11 Feb. 1980) had helped break the news: " 'The Lady from

Dubuque' is the famous phrase of Harold Ross . . . , who defined his sophisticated magazine by saying that it wasn't for her." Gerald Clarke (11 Feb. 1980) wrote that the title was "derived from Harold Ross's famous statement that he was not editing *The New Yorker* for 'the little old lady from Dubuque.' " Albee's genius lies in his subjection of such a little old lady to the Pirandellian treatment, making her another Signora Ponza, the mystery lady of Pirandello's *It Is So! (If You Think So!)*, to which Albee clearly alludes when Elizabeth–his lady–is made to say: "You have a woman upstairs. You say she is your wife; I say she is my daughter." The early reviews of *The Lady from Dubuque* were mostly hostile. Brustein (8 Mar. 1980) charged that it was "an awful piece." Simon (11 Feb. 1980) complained that it was "one of the worst plays about anything, ever." Still, as Thomas P. Adler observes, Otis Guernsey, Jr., "rightly includes it among *The Best Plays of 1979-80*, predicting with some justification, I suspect, that 'this distinguished and durable play . . . will surely be heard in time, globally.' "

The Man Who Had Three Arms, which has been seen all too briefly on stage and not much read, is nevertheless destined to be one of Albee's most controversial plays. In 1985, Albee said that it was already by then the play "for which I have received the most enthusiastic and favorable response from people in the arts–my peers"; and more recently, in his preface to *Selected Plays* (1987), he has said not only that it is "greatly admired by my fellow playwrights" but also that it is "greatly loathed by the tastemakers who were–oddly enough–its subjects." In a review of the first galleys, later revised for publication, Roudané (1986) observed that the "largely negative reception of the play may be understandable," for it has struck some critics as "not a play at all, but a nasty and embarrassing display of bad manner." Roudané stresses the obvious Pirandellian parallel, noting that, "like the unnamed hero in Pirandello's *When One Is Somebody*," Albee's protagonist, Himself, "becomes a prisoner completely trapped within his (post)celebrityhood." Finally, Roudané admonishes himself and the rest of us not to draw hasty conclusions about a play that needs more time than it has had to shape a responsive audience for what so far stands before us as an experimental tour de force, as much for its author as for its protagonist-performer. Whatever the critical response, this play has all the earmarks of Albee's extraordinary use of the stage as a *focusing* telescopic medium through which the audience, in heightened Pirandellian fashion, is brought into the drama both as critic and spectator.

Albee directed the premiere of *Finding the Sun* in Colorado in early 1983. Linda Ben-Zvi (Mar. 1984) observed that in its contrast of youth and old age it recalled the earlier *The American Dream*, but that the relations of its two married couples (whose husbands have been lovers) were too ambiguous and complicated to be brought into sharp dramatic focus. Ben-Zvi concluded that the performance was vivid and well paced. Later the play was paired with another Albee play, *Walking*, for student performance under Albee's direction in California. In a review of the performance, Richard Stayton (25 May 1984) considered *Walking* to be too personal, a "beautiful maze of symbolism" that was impressive more as "a post-modernist painting than a play." Summing up, he called it "an obsessive metaphor of seduction and the sexual war between men and women," that was "permeated by homosexual conflicts," and that struggled "to communicate, in primordial imagery and fundamental sounds, Albee's sexual isolation."

Sullivan (26 May 1984) titled his review of the same production "Albee's One-Acters Pitched in Sand." Albee, working with student actors, proved himself to be a good director, but Sullivan thought that the plays were all talk, in what he called Albee's "neo-Jamesian idiom." *Walking*, which has "de-evolution" as its theme, stood "as naked a statement of Albee's view of the sexes as we have had," animating an "all-devouring female" and a "frozen, potentially murderous male." Sullivan (14 Feb. 1987) also reviewed a reading of Albee's most recent work, *The Marriage Play*, given by Albee in Washington, D.C., in anticipation of the play's premiere in Vienna, Austria. Sullivan paraphrased Albee's description of the piece as a study of "a profound relationship between two intelligent people who are engaged in the battle to end that which they know will never end." Jeanne Luere likened *The Marriage Play* to *Who's Afraid of Virginia Woolf?* in her favorable review (Mar. 1988).

The first order of future scholarly/critical business is to reexamine carefully the foreign reception of Albee's plays. Giantvalley provides a beginning and the Kolin and Davis bibliographical essay also makes an important contribution, with its section on "Albee and World Theater." More needs to be done to keep up with the record of Albee translations and performances in foreign lands, and, more important, with the record of foreign critical appreciation by foreign critics mainly interested in their own national literatures.

Albee's links with modern Anglo-European existentialists and playwrights of the Absurd, as well as with the great playwrights of the Western tradition, make such a study feasible and necessary. That sort of study is only part of what is needed to supply us with a critical sense of Albee's significance in world theater. Albee seems destined to fare better than most modern American playwrights in the world's estimate of what a distinctively American playwright ought to be writing. He has long been mirroring the grand tradition of Western drama in a characteristically American way—with strong local flavor and unconscious universality. It is likely that foreign appreciation of Albee's talent will prod more and more of us at home to value, according to their due, both his dramatically insightful statements about the "condition of man" and the mastery of stage technique and dialogue that he has brought to our American drama.

Amiri Baraka (LeRoi Jones)
(1934-)

Paul K. Jackson, Jr.
Spelman College

PRIMARY BIBLIOGRAPHY

Books and Pamphlets

Preface to a Twenty Volume Suicide Note, as Jones. New York: Totem/ Corinth, 1961. Poems.

Blues People. . . . Negro Music in White America, as Jones. New York: Morrow, 1963; London: MacGibbon & Kee, 1965. Music history.

The Dead Lecturer, as Jones. New York: Grove, 1964. Poems.

Dutchman and The Slave: Two Plays, as Jones. New York: Morrow, 1964; London: Faber & Faber, 1965.

The System of Dante's Hell, as Jones. New York: Grove, 1965; London: MacGibbon & Kee, 1966. Novel.

Black Art, as Jones. Newark, N.J.: Jihad, 1966. Poems.

Home: Social Essays, as Jones. New York: Morrow, 1966; London: MacGibbon & Kee, 1968.

Arm Yourself, or Harm Yourself! A One Act Play, as Jones. Newark, N.J.: Jihad, 1967.

The Baptism and The Toilet, as Jones. New York: Grove, 1967. Plays.

Slave Ship, as Jones. Newark, N.J.: Jihad, 1967. Play.

Tales, as Jones. New York: Grove, 1967; London: MacGibbon & Kee, 1969. Short stories.

Black Music, as Jones. New York: Morrow, 1967; London: Mac-Gibbon & Kee, 1969. Essays.

Black Magic: Sabotage, Target Study, Black Art: Collected Poetry 1961-1967, as Jones. Indianapolis & New York: Bobbs-Merrill, 1969; London: Calder & Boyars, 1971.

Four Black Revolutionary Plays: All Praises to the Black Man. Indianapolis & New York: Bobbs-Merrill, 1969; London: Calder & Boyars, 1971. Comprises *Experimental Death Unit #1, A Black Mass, Great Goodness of Life: A Coon Show,* and *Madheart.*

A Black Value System. Newark, N.J.: Jihad, 1970. Essay.
J-E-L-L-O. Chicago: Third World, 1970. Play. Includes the essay "Negro Theatre Pimps Get Big Off Nationalism."
In Our Terribleness (Some Elements and Meaning in Black Style), by Baraka and Fundi (Billy Abernathy). Indianapolis & New York: Bobbs-Merrill, 1970.
It's Nation Time. Chicago: Third World, 1970. Poems.
Raise Race Rays Raze: Essays Since 1965. New York: Random House, 1971.
The New Nationalism. Chicago: Third World, 1972. Essays.
Spirit Reach. Newark, N.J.: Jihad, 1972. Poems.
Crisis in Boston. Newark, N.J.: Vita Wa Watu-People's War Publishing, 1974. Essay.
Hard Facts. Newark, N.J.: People's War Publishing, 1975. Essays.
The Motion of History and Other Plays. New York: Morrow, 1978. Comprises *The Motion of History, Slave Ship,* and *S-1.*
The Sidnee Poet Heroical, in 29 Scenes. New York: Reed, 1979. Play.
Reggae or Not! Poems. New York: Contact II, 1979.
The Autobiography of LeRoi Jones. New York: Freundlich, 1984.
Daggers and Javelins: Essays, 1974-1979. New York: Morrow, 1984.
The Music: Reflections on Jazz and Blues, by Amiri Baraka and Amina Baraka. New York: Morrow, 1987.

Premiere Productions
A Good Girl Is Hard To Find. Montclair, N.J., Sterington House, 28 Aug. 1958.
Dante. New York, Off Bowery Theatre, Oct. 1961. Produced again as *The Eighth Ditch,* New York, New Bowery Theatre, 1964.
Dutchman. New York, Village South Theatre, 12 Jan. 1964.
The Baptism. New York, Writers' Stage Theatre, 23 Mar. 1964.
The Slave and *The Toilet.* New York, St. Marks Playhouse, 16 Dec. 1964.
J-E-L-L-O. New York, Black Arts Repertory Theatre, 1965.
Experimental Death Unit #1. New York, St. Marks Playhouse, 1 Mar. 1965.
A Black Mass. Newark, N.J., Proctor's Theatre, May 1966.
Slave Ship: A Historical Pageant. Newark, N.J., Spirit House, Mar. 1967.
Madheart. San Francisco, San Francisco State College, May 1967.
Arm Yourself, or Harm Yourself! Newark, N.J., Spirit House, 1967.

Great Goodness of Life (A Coon Show). Newark, N.J., Spirit House, Nov. 1967.

Black Power Chant. Newark, N.J., Spirit House, 1968.

Board of Education. Newark, N.J., Spirit House, 1968.

Home on the Range. Newark, N.J., Spirit House, Mar. 1968.

Resurrection in Life. Harlem, N.Y., Afro-American Studio for Acting and Speech, 24 Aug. 1969.

Junkies Are Full of (SHH . . .) and *Bloodrites*. New York, New Federal Theatre, 21 Nov. 1970.

Columbia, The Gem of the Ocean. Washington, D.C., Howard University Spirit House Movers, 1973.

A Recent Killing. New York, New Federal Theatre, 26 Jan. 1973.

The New Ark's a Moverin'. Newark, N.J., Spirit House, Feb. 1974.

Sidnee Poet Heroical or If in Danger of Suit, The Kid Poet Heroical. New York, New Federal Theatre, 15 May 1975.

S-1. New York, Afro-American Studio, 23 July 1976.

The Motion of History. New York, New York City Theatre Ensemble, 27 May 1977.

What Was the Relationship of the Lone Ranger to the Means of Production? New York, Ladies Fort, May 1979.

Dim'Crackr Party Convention. New York, Columbia University, July 1980.

Boy & Tarzan Appear in a Clearing. New York, New Federal Theatre, Oct. 1981.

Money. New York, La Mama Experimental Theatre Club, Jan. 1982.

Selected Periodical Publications

"Communications Project," as Jones, *Drama Review*, 12 (Summer 1968), 53-57. Essay.

Home on the Range, as Jones, *Drama Review*, 12 (Summer 1968), 106-111. Play.

Police, as Jones, *Drama Review*, 12 (Summer 1968), 112-116. Play.

"The Black Aesthetic," *Negro Digest*, 18 (Sept. 1969), 5-6. Essay.

"The Coronation of the Black Queen," *Black Scholar*, 1 (June 1970), 46-48. Scenario.

Columbia, The Gem of the Ocean, Black World, 23 (Apr. 1974). Play.

" 'Why I Changed My Ideology': Black Nationalism and Socialist Revolution," *Black World*, 24 (July 1975), 30-43. Essay.

Selected Other

The Moderns: An Anthology of New Writing in America, ed., with an intro-
` duction, by Jones. New York: Corinth, 1963; London: May-
flower, 1967.
"Philistinism and the Negro Writer," as Jones. In *Anger and Beyond:
The Negro Writer in the United States,* ed. Herbert Hill. New
York: Harper & Row, 1966. Essay.
Black Fire: An Anthology of Afro-American Writing, ed., with contribu-
tions, by Jones and Larry Neal. New York: Morrow, 1968.
Junkies are Full of (SHHH. . . .) and *Bloodrites.* In *Black Drama Anthol-
ogy,* ed. Woodie King and Ron Milner. New York & London: Co-
lumbia University Press, 1972, 11-24, 25-32.
Ba-Ra-Ka. In *Spontaneous Combustion: Eight New American Plays,* ed. Ro-
chelle Owens. New York: Winter House, 1972, 175-182.

Collections

Selected Plays and Prose of Amiri Baraka-LeRoi Jones. New York: Morrow, 1979.
Selected Poetry of Amiri Baraka-LeRoi Jones. New York: Morrow, 1979.

SECONDARY BIBLIOGRAPHY

Bibliographies and Checklists

Arata, Esther Spring, and Nicholas John Rotoli. *Black American Playwrights, 1800 to the Present: A Bibliography.* Metuchen, N.J.: Scarecrow, 1976, 11-20.
Arata, Marlene J. Erickson, Sandra Dewitz, and Mary Linse Alexan-
der. *More Black American Playwrights: A Bibliography.* Metuchen,
N.J. & London: Scarecrow, 1978, 9-23.
Dace, Letita. *LeRoi Jones (Imamu Amiri Baraka): A Checklist of Works by
and about Him.* London: Nether, 1971.
Eddleman, Floyd Eugene. *American Drama Criticism: Interpretations
1890-1977.* 2nd ed., rev. Hamden, Conn.: Shoe String, 1979,
177-180.
Eddleman. *American Drama Criticism: Supplement to the Second Edition.*
Hamden, Conn.: Shoe String, 1984, 83-84.
French, William P., Michel J. Fabre, Amritjit Singh, and Geneviève
E. Fabre. *Afro-American Poetry and Drama, 1760-1975.* Detroit:
Gale Research, 1979, 331-338.

Hatch, James V., and OMANii Abdullah. *Black Playwrights, 1823-1977: An Annotated Bibliography of Plays.* New York & London: Bowker, 1977, 12-15.

Hudson, Theodore R. *A LeRoi Jones (Amiri Baraka) Bibliography: A Keyed Research Guide to Works by LeRoi Jones and to Writing About Him and his Works.* Washington, D.C.: Privately printed, 1971.

King, Kimball. *Ten Modern American Playwrights.* New York & London: Garland, 1982, 108-135.

Peavy, Charles D. *Afro-American Literature and Culture Since World War II.* Detroit: Gale Research, 1979, 200-217.

Rush, Theressa Gunnels, Carol Fairbanks Myers, and Esther Spring Arata. *Black American Writers Past and Present: A Biographical and Bibliographical Dictionary,* 2 volumes. Metuchen, N.J.: Scarecrow, 1975, I: 50-56.

Schatt, Stanley. "LeRoi Jones: A Checklist to Primary and Secondary Sources," *Bulletin of Bibliography and Magazine Notes,* 28 (Apr.-June 1971), 55-57.

Turner, Darwin T. *Afro American Writers.* New York: Appleton-Century-Crofts, 1970, 63-64.

Interviews

Allen, Robert L., and Astrid Sengstacke. "Problems of Black Power: An Interview," *Guardian,* 23 Mar. 1968, 3.

Allen. "Art, Artist and Revolution: Part II of the Interview," *Guardian,* 30 Mar. 1968, 6.

Benston, Kimberly W. "Amiri Baraka: An Interview," *Boundary 2,* 6 (Winter 1978), 303-316.

Coleman, Michael. "What is Black Theatre?: An Interview with Imamu Amiri Baraka," *Black World,* 20 (Apr. 1971), 32-36.

Faruk, and Marvin X. "Islam and Black Art; An Interview with LeRoi Jones," *Negro Digest,* 18 (Jan. 1969), 4-10, 77-80.

Gottlieb, Saul. "They Think You're an Airplane and You're Really a Bird!," *Evergreen Review,* 11 (Dec. 1967), 51-53, 96-97.

Melhelm, D. H. "Revolution: The Constancy of Change: An Interview with Amiri Baraka," *Black American Literature Forum,* 16 (Fall 1982), 87-103.

Ossman, David. *The Sullen Art: Interviews with Modern American Poets.* New York: Corinth, 1963, 77-86.

Sollors, Werner. *Amiri Baraka/Leroi Jones: The Quest for a "Populist Modernism."* New York: Columbia University Press, 1978, 247-262.

Stone, Judy. "If It's Anger . . . Maybe That's Good," *San Francisco Chronicle*, 23 Aug. 1964, pp. 39-42.

X, Marvin. "Everything's Cool . . . An Interview," *Black Theatre*, 1 (1968), 16-23.

Critical Studies: Books

Benston, Kimberly W. *Baraka: The Renegade and The Mask.* New Haven & London: Yale University Press, 1976.

Brown, Lloyd W. *Amiri Baraka.* Boston: Twayne, 1980.

Harris, William J. *The Poetry and Poetics of Amiri Baraka: The Jazz Aesthetic.* Columbia: University of Missouri Press, 1985.

Hudson, Theodore R. *From LeRoi Jones to Amiri Baraka: The Literary Works.* Durham: Duke University Press, 1973.

Lacey, Henry C. *To Raise, Destroy and Create: The Poetry, Drama, and Fiction of Imamu Amiri Baraka (LeRoi Jones).* Troy, N.Y.: Whitston, 1981.

Ricard, Alain. *Théâtre et nationalisme: Wole Soyinka et LeRoi Jones.* Paris: Présence Africaine, 1972.

Sollors, Werner. *Amiri Baraka/Leroi Jones: The Quest for a "Populist Modernism."* New York: Columbia University Press, 1978.

Critical Studies: Collection of Essays

Benston, Kimberly W., ed. *Imamu Amiri Baraka (LeRoi Jones): A Collection of Critical Essays.* Englewood Cliffs, N.J.: Prentice-Hall, 1978.

Critical Studies: Articles and Book Sections

Adams, George R. "Black Militant Drama," *American Imago*, 28 (Summer 1972), 107-128.

Adams. " 'My Christ' in *Dutchman*," *CLA Journal*, 15 (Sept. 1971), 54-58.

Andrews, W. D. E. "The Marxist Theatre of Amiri Baraka," *Comparative Drama*, 18 (Summer 1984), 137-161.

Benston, Kimberly W. "Vision and Form in *The Slave Ship*." In Benston, 174-185.

Bermel, Albert. "*Dutchman* or the Black Stranger in America," *American Society*, 9 (Winter 1972), 423-444.

Bigsby, C. W. E. *Confrontation and Commitment: A Study of Contemporary American Drama 1959-1966.* Columbia: University of Missouri Press, 1967, 138-155.

Billingsley, R. G. "LeRoi Jones's *The Slave*: Right Ideas Stink a Lotta Times," *Umoja*, 2 (1975), 72-81.

Brady, Owen E. "Baraka's *Experimental Death Unit #1*: Plan for (R)evolution," *Negro American Literature Forum*, 9 (Summer 1975), 59-61.

Brady. "Cultural Conflict and Cult Ritual in LeRoi Jones's *The Toilet*," *Educational Theatre Journal*, 28 (Mar. 1976), 69-77.

Brady. "*Great Goodness of Life*: Baraka's Black Bourgeoisie Blues." In Benston, 157-166.

Brady. "LeRoi Jones's *The Slave*: A Ritual of Purgation," *Obsidian*, 4 (Spring 1978), 5-18.

Brecht, Stefan. "LeRoi Jones's *Slave Ship*," *Drama Review*, 14 (Winter 1970), 212-219.

Brown, Lloyd W. "The Cultural Revolution in Black Theatre," *Negro American Literature Forum*, 8 (Spring 1974), 159-174.

Brown. "High and Crazy Niggers: Anti-Rationalism in LeRoi Jones," *Journal of Ethnic Studies*, 2 (Spring 1974), 1-9.

Burford, W. W. "Leroi Jones: From Existentialism to Apostle of Black Nationalism," *Players*, 47 (Dec. 1972), 60-64.

Burns, Glen. "How the Devil Helped LeRoi Jones Turn into Imamu Amiri Baraka." In *Amerikanisches Drama und Theater um 20. Jahrhundert*. Göttingen: Vandenhoeck, 1975, 261-288.

Casimir, Louis J. "*Dutchman*: The Price of Culture is a Lie." In *Binding of Proteus: Perspectives on Myth and the Literary Process*, ed. Marjorie W. McCune and T. Tucker Orbison. Lewisburg, Pa.: Bucknell University Press, 1980, 298-310.

Costello, Donald P. "Black Man as Victim," *Commonweal*, 88 (14 June 1968), 436-440.

Dennison, George. "The Demagogy of LeRoi Jones," *Commentary*, 39 (Feb. 1965), 67-70.

Early, Gerald. "The Case of LeRoi Jones/Amiri Baraka," *Salmagundi*, no. 70-71 (Spring/Summer 1986), 343-352.

Feuser, Willfried. Review of Alain Ricard, *Théâtre et nationalisme: Wole Soyinka et LeRoi Jones*, *African Literature Today*, no. 8 (1976), 124-130.

Fischer, William C. "The Pre-Revolutionary Writings of Imamu Amiri Baraka," *Massachusetts Review*, 14 (Spring 1973), 259-305.

Freydberg, Elizabeth Hadley. "The Concealed Dependence Upon White Culture in Baraka's 1969 Aesthetic," *Black American Literature Forum*, 17 (1983), 27-29.

Gaffney, Floyd. "Black Theatre: The Moral Function of Imamu Amiri Baraka," *Players*, 50 (Summer 1975), 122-131.

Grabes, Herbert. "LeRoi Jones (Imamu Amiri Baraka), *Dutchman*." In *Das Amerikanische Drama der 4 Gegenwart*. Krönberg: Athenäum, 1976, 185-200.

Hagopian, John V. "Another Ride on Jones's Subway," *CLA Journal*, 21 (Dec. 1979), 269-274.

Iannarella, Michael J. "Black and White," *Massachusetts Studies in English*, 3 (Spring 1971), 1-6.

Jackson, Esther M. "LeRoi Jones (Imamu Amiri Baraka): Form and the Progression of Consciousness," *CLA Journal*, 17 (Sept. 1973), 33-56. Collected in Benston, 36-48.

Jackson, Kathryn. "LeRoi Jones and New Black Writers of the Sixties," *Freedomways*, 9 (Summer 1969), 232-246.

Jouffroy, Alain. "Leroi Jones, Théâtre de la revolution noire," *Cahier de la Compagnie Madeleine Renaud-Jean Louis Barrault*, no. 63 (Oct. 1967), 44-53.

Klinkowitz, Jerome. "LeRoi Jones [Imamu Amiri Baraka]: *Dutchman* As Drama," *Negro American Literature Forum*, 7 (Winter 1973), 123-126.

Knox, George. "The 'Mythology' of LeRoi Jones's *Dutchman*." In *Interculture*, ed. Sy M. Khan and Martha Raetz. Vienna: Braumauller, 1975, 243-251.

Köhler, Klaus. "Das Underground theatre." In *Studien zum amerikanischen Drama nach dem zweiten Weltkrieg*, ed. Eberhard Brüning, Köhler, and Berhard Scheller. Berlin: Rütten & Loening, 1977.

Lederer, Richard. "The Language of LeRoi Jones' *The Slave*," *Studies in Black Literature*, 4 (Spring 1973), 14-16.

Lhamon, W. T. "Baraka and the Bourgeoisie Figure," *Studies in Black Literature*, 6 (Spring 1975), 18-21.

Lindberg, John. "*Dutchman* and *The Slave*: Companions in Revolution," *Black Academy Review: Quarterly of the Black World*, 21 (1972), 101-107. Collected in Benston, 141-147.

Lindenberg, Daniel. "Un Théâtre militant," *Temps Modernes*, 21 (Apr. 1966), 1918-1920.

Margolies, Edward. *Native Sons: A Critical Study of Twentieth-Century Negro American Authors*. Philadelphia: Lippincott, 1968.

Menchise, Don N. "LeRoi Jones and a Case of Shifting Identities," *CLA Journal*, 8 (Dec. 1976), 232-234.

Miller, Jeanne-Marie A. "The Plays of LeRoi Jones," *CLA Journal*, 14 (Mar. 1971), 331-339.

Mitchell, Loften. *Black Drama: The Story of The American Negro in the Theatre*. New York: Hawthorn, 1965.

Mootry, Maria K. "Theme and Symbols in Two Plays by LeRoi Jones," *Negro Digest*, 21 (1969), 42-47.

Nadin, Mihai. "A Semiotic Procedural Approach to Dramatic Literature." In *Empirical Studies: A Collection of New Approaches in the Field*, ed. Burghard B. Rieger. Bochum: Brockmeyer, 1981.

Neal, Lawrence P. "The Development of LeRoi Jones," *Liberator*, 6 (Jan. 1966), 4-5; (Feb. 1966), 18-19. Collected in Benston, 23-28.

Nelson, Hugh. "LeRoi Jones' *Dutchman*: A Brief Ride on a Doomed Ship," *Educational Theatre Journal*, 20 (Mar. 1968), 53-59.

Peavey, Charles D. "Myth, Magic and Manhood in LeRoi Jones's *Madheart*," *Studies in Black Literature*, 1 (Summer 1970), 12-20. Collected in Benston, 167-173.

Phillips, Louis. "LeRoi Jones and Contemporary Black Drama." In *The Black American Writer*, ed. C. W. E. Bigsby. De Land, Fla.: Everett/Edwards, 1969, 203-217.

Ralph, George. "Jones's *Dutchman*," *Explicator*, 43 (Winter 1985), 58-59.

Reck, Tom S. "Archetypes in LeRoi Jones's *Dutchman*," *Studies in Black Literature*, 1 (1970), 66-68.

Reed, Daphne S. "LeRoi Jones: High Priest of the Black Arts Movement," *Educational Theatre Journal*, 22 (Mar. 1970), 53-59.

Rice, Julian C. "LeRoi Jones' *Dutchman*: A Reading," *Contemporary Literature*, 12 (Winter 1971), 42-59.

Rich, Cynthia Jo. "Where's Baraka's Jones?," *Black Times* (Palo Alto, Calif.), 4 (1972), 6-7.

Richards, Sandra L. "Negative Forces and Positive Non-Entities: Images of Women in the Dramas of Amiri Baraka," *Theatre Journal*, 34 (May 1982), 233-240.

Russell, Charlie. "LeRoi Jones Will Get Us all in Trouble," *Liberator*, 4 (Aug. 1964), 18.

Savory, Jerold J. "Descent and Baptism in *Native Son, Invisible Man*, and *Dutchman*," *Christian Scholar's Review*, 3 (1972), 33-37.

Sollors, Werner. "Amiri Baraka (LeRoi Jones)." In *Essays on Contemporary American Drama*, ed. Hedwig Bock and Albert Wertheim. Munich: Hueber, 1981, 105-122.

Sollors. "LeRoi Jones (Imamu Amiri Baraka)." In *Amerikanische Literatur der Gegenwart*, ed. Martin Christadler. Stuttgart: Kroner, 1973.

Taylor, Willene P. "The Fall of Man Theme in Imamu Amiri Baraka's (LeRoi Jones's) *Dutchman*," *Negro American Literature Forum*, 7 (Winter 1973), 127-130.

Tener, Robert L. "The Corrupted Warrior Heroes: Amiri Baraka's *The Toilet*," *Modern Drama*, 17 (June 1974), 207-215. Collected in Benston, 148-156.

Tener. "Role Playing as a Dutchman," *Studies in Black Literature*, 3 (Fall 1972), 17-21.

Velde, Paul. "Pursued by the Furies," *Commonweal*, 88 (14 June 1968), 440-441.

Weisgram, Dianne H. "LeRoi Jones' *Dutchman*: Inter-racial Ritual of Sexual Violence," *American Imago*, 29 (Fall 1972), 215-232.

Werner, Craig. "Brer Rabbit Meets the Underground Man: Simplification of Consciousness in Baraka's *Dutchman* and *Slave Ship*," *Obsidian*, 5 (1979), 35-40.

Williams, Sherley Anne. "The Search for Identity in Baraka's *Dutchman*." In her *Give Birth to Brightness*. New York: Dial, 1972. Collected in Benston, 135-140.

Willis, Robert J. "Anger and the Contemporary Black Theatre," *Negro American Literature Forum*, 8 (Summer 1974), 213-215.

Witherington, Paul. "Exorcism and Baptism in LeRoi Jones's *The Toilet*," *Modern Drama*, 15 (Sept. 1972), 159-163.

Zatlin, Linda G. "Paying His Dues: Ritual in LeRoi Jones's Early Dramas," *Obsidian*, 2 (Spring 1976), 21-31.

BIBLIOGRAPHICAL ESSAY

Bibliographies and Checklists

Though they are now out of date and occasional discrepancies exist among them, the bibliographies of works by and about Amiri Baraka, when taken together, provide a substantial list of materials published by the late 1970s. The bibliography in this volume updates the list of Baraka's publications through 1987 and provides the most comprehensive listing of criticism on Baraka published to date.

Esther Spring Arata and Nicholas John Rotoli's *Black American Playwrights, 1800 to the Present* (1976) lists the Baraka plays published separately, in anthologies, and in periodicals through 1972.

The volume also provides a partial list of Baraka's critical essays. A substantial list of criticism on Baraka–including overviews, analyses of individual plays, and reviews–concludes the bibliography. Theressa Gunnels Rush, Carol Fairbanks Myers, and Arata provide essentially the same material in *Black American Writers Past and Present* (1975). Arata, Marlene J. Erickson, Sandra Dewitz, and Mary Linse Alexander update the primary bibliography through 1977 and expand and update the list of criticism in *More Black American Playwrights: A Bibliography* (1978).

Charles D. Peavy's *Afro-American Literature and Culture Since World War II* (1979) gives an annotated list of Baraka criticism and primary publications through 1973. The annotations, especially of the criticism, suggest useful topical guidelines. William P. French, Michel J. Fabre, Amritjit Singh, and Geneviève E. Fabre provide annotated primary and secondary lists through 1975 in *Afro-American Poetry and Drama, 1760-1975* (1979). James V. Hatch and OMANii Abdullah's *Black Playwrights, 1823-1977: An Annotated Bibliography of Plays* (1977) lists the Baraka plays produced through 1976 with information on the casts and premiere dates.

Floyd Eugene Eddleman's *American Drama Criticism* (1979) lists criticism and reviews of individual Baraka plays through 1975. Eddleman's 1984 update extends the list through 1981. Kimball King's *Ten Modern American Playwrights* (1982) is probably the best previously published bibliography. The Baraka chapter includes a short biographical and critical introduction; a substantially annotated list of plays, poetry, nonfiction, and books edited; an annotated list of four interviews; and annotated lists of selected criticism through 1980, dissertations, and reviews.

Interviews

The art and politics of Amiri Baraka have inspired curiosity, concern, and condemnation from the beginning of his career. As a result he has been a frequent subject for interviewers. Three interviews in particular capture strategic stages of Baraka's development. These interviews–by David Ossman (1963), Saul Gottlieb (Dec. 1967), and Kimberly W. Benston (Winter 1978)–not only probe Baraka's writings but also, in Gottlieb and Benston, the complexities of his continually developing political ideology. Baraka frequently discusses drama in reference to its political ends, and the interviews naturally reflect the playwright's then-current beliefs.

The Ossman interview captures the early LeRoi Jones, the bohemian Greenwich Village poet, at a point when he was fascinated by the creative process and nurtured by Village culture and by a newly invigorated Afro-American consciousness among artists there. He saw a close connection between art and life: "I believe that the poet–someone with a tempered sensibility–is able, or should be able, to take almost any piece of matter, idea, or whatever, and convert it if he can, into something really beautiful. I don't mean 'beautiful' the way Bernard Berenson means it–but something moving at least. And I don't think that there are any kind of standard ideas or sentiments or emotions or anything that have to be in a poem. A poem can be made up of anything so long as it is well made. It can be made up out of any feeling. And if I tried to cut anything out of life–if there was something in my life that I couldn't talk about . . . it seems monstrous that you can tell almost anything about your life except those things that are most intimate or mean the most to you. That seems a severe paradox."

Jones also addresses the question of literary influences in the Ossman interview. His early reading was of the poetic establishment, but he quickly moved into more novel territory: "I was very much influenced by Eliot, and reading Lorca helped to bring me out of my Eliot period." More important, however, were the Afro-American aspects of his heritage: "There are certain influences on me as a Negro person, that certainly wouldn't apply to a poet like Allen Ginsberg. . . . And I'm sure he couldn't write certain things that have to deal with, say, Southern Baptist church rhythms. Everything applies–everything in your life." Jones also speaks about his relationship with Langston Hughes and their aesthetic differences.

By the time Saul Gottlieb interviewed Jones in December 1967 he was an enfant terrible of the Off Broadway theater scene and a committed black nationalist increasingly involved in the political struggles of the day. He moved back to his birthplace, Newark, New Jersey, in late 1966 and was arrested on charges of unlawfully carrying firearms and resisting arrest during the riots there the next summer. Jones's strained relationship with the political establishment is vividly articulated in the interview. His arrest reinforced his negative view of political authority: "I was standing there very composed while they were beating me up with guns and clubs and handcuffs, trying to obey all the laws. That's what really happened. Then I spent the next four or five days in jail. The first night they put some stitches in my head. They pulled my tooth out–somebody hit me in the mouth and loosened my tooth."

Spirit House Movers and Players, a black community theater and political organization that Jones helped found in Newark in 1966, was the focus of much of his attention in 1967. As he explained to Gottlieb: "We have a repertory system–we not only change the plays but we have films or poetry readings or lectures as well. Anything the community wants–sports, music, parties, meetings, classes–something is going on every night. The plays are only on weekends. We have an ensemble of actors; they're in most of the plays, and of course, we use a lot of kids. We do a lot of children plays, too. We don't use Actor's Equity members; we don't have anything to do with that; that's another world."

Kimberly W. Benston interviewed a more subdued, contemplative Baraka in 1978. His nationalism, manifested most explicitly in his adoption of the Islamic name Imamu Amiri Baraka in 1968, had been gradually incorporated into a Marxist worldview in which racial subjugation became a component of an oppressive class structure. Baraka called it "a development . . . from a lower to a higher stage of awareness." He dropped the title Imamu (spiritual leader) from his name in 1974.

Baraka told Benston that he had been "always, from the first poem that I had ever printed . . . concerned with national oppression." His nationalist viewpoint of the 1960s had led him to condemn what he called "middle-class" black writing (such as that by Lorraine Hansberry) on the grounds that middle-class black writers "wanted to style themselves after the white bourgeoisie. I felt that what they wrote wasn't actually *black* writing in the first place." He incorporated elements of ritual and idiom in his nationalist plays (*Slave Ship, Home on the Range, Resurrection in Life*) in part as an attack on traditional literary modes. But as a historical materialist he came to see these elements of nationalism as ahistorical. In *Slave Ship* ritual elements had helped define blackness in a way that defied "time, space, and economic conditions." Black-nationalist literature had been an attempt "to make African culture a static, unchanging artifact." The Marxist view held that life was a process of "continual and progressive struggle," so that "now [in 1977] to use ritual you would have to use it in a critical way."

Critical Studies: Books

The book-length studies of Amiri Baraka's work invariably discuss the connection between his continually developing political ideology and his literary style. Theodore R. Hudson, whose *From LeRoi Jones to Amiri Baraka* (1973) is the first such study written in English, stresses this linkage throughout his survey. Hudson feels that Baraka "all along" has been using the theater "as a device for edification and motivation," citing Baraka's 1966 article "Revolutionary Theatre" (published in *Home: Social Essays*, 1966) as evidence of Baraka's political intent. By 1970 Baraka was at the height of his nationalist period, and his rhetoric was at its most strident. He wrote in "Negro Theatre Pimps Get Big Off Nationalism" (published as an introduction to the play *J-E-L-L-O*, 1970) that "Black Theatre has gotta raise the dead, and move the living. Otherwise it is a teacup in a cracker mansion."

Hudson feels that Baraka's drama "has changed drastically in structure and technique but not basically in theme since his early success in *Dutchman*." His later dramas are more "impulsive, pageantlike, and ritualistic," and more obviously mediums for "teaching, evangelizing, and motivating." But in spite of changes in emphasis, Hudson declares that throughout, Baraka's writing attempts to conform to principles of a black aesthetic "as they apply to literature." These principles include "utilitarianism; strong ethnocentric content; black nationalistic content; identification with the black masses; collective or communal black, as opposed to an individualistic or private, attitude; cynicism about or rejection of Euro-American culture values; disregard for the type of universality which black aestheticians claim the American literary establishment wrongly equates with Westernism (Euro-Americanism) rather than with worldism; usefulness for social, political, and economic change; ethnic pride and celebration of a hitherto sometimes avoided or disdained black culture (life style and value system); urban and rural black folk elements; 'black language'; energetic diction; experimentation in search of new, or black, forms and techniques."

Hudson acknowledges that Baraka's writing is, ironically, too esoteric to be read by most of the people to whom it is directed: "The majority of his readers still are white intellectuals, the black college students, and the relatively small 'in group' of black cultural nationalists and Afro-Americans not identified as part of the bulk of the black masses." Hudson credits Baraka with making a "conscious attempt to get his writing directly to the black masses in comprehensible form" but in the end recognizes the relative inaccessibility of this "supreme writer" to be one small area of failure.

Kimberly Benston's *Baraka: The Renegade and The Mask* (1976) is most significant for its refusal to view Baraka "primarily as a politician and only incidentally as an artist." To cite Baraka's own statements in support of this view "confuses aesthetic investigation with aestheticism and actually verges on disrespect for the artist." Benston treats Baraka as "a serious artist"; critical preoccupation with his political views, Benston thinks, has resulted in a lack of attention to the "subtle processes by which Baraka has given expression to his perception of the Afro-American experience."

Benston chronicles Baraka's "movement from the avant-garde of the white, Euro-American tradition to the vanguard of black revolutionary art" as a conscious act of redemption. The young Jones, a black man educated in a white world, found that the inward process of artistic creation, what Benston calls "the contemporary poet's relentless retreat into the self," brought him "sharply upon the dialectical junctures of his own moral and existential duplicities where decision *must* be reacted." Thus Baraka embraced blackness.

Thus, Baraka's mature work, as playwright and critic Larry Neal puts it in the foreword to Benston's book, "strives for a non-Western symbology and ethos." Particularly important to Benston is the connection between Baraka's writing and Afro-American music. "The music has never had to explain itself; it simply exists in all of its glory. . . . It has forged a character all its own, and it apologized to no one," writes Neal. Benston shows that the emulation of the Afro-American musical ethos in literature was the most direct path Baraka could take toward the establishment of a personal ethos independent from the white culture in which he came to consciousness.

Werner Sollors, in *Amiri Baraka/Leroi Jones: The Quest for a "Populist Modernism"* (1978), attempts a kind of synthesis of Baraka's political and artistic selves. He sees in Baraka's development an attempt to merge his "committed" side with his "literary" side to form a "populist modernism, a unity of life and art, literature and society." He provides a schematic diagram, which, while "helpful to an understanding of the magnitude of Baraka's changes in art and politics, . . . of course does not 'fit' each and every work he wrote":

	1958-61	1960-65	1964-74	1974-
COMMITMENT	aesthetic	political/	Black	Marxism
	protest	ethnic	Cultural	Leninism
		protest	Nationalism	Mao-Tse-
				Tung-
	Beat			
	Bohemianism	New Left	Kawaida	Thought
AESTHETIC	expressive	mimetic	pragmatic	pragmatic

Sollors's synthetic approach is "located somewhere between American/Black Studies and Comparative Literature: the latter discipline helps to establish and take seriously the literary voice of Baraka in the international context of the 'Isms' of 19th- and 20th-century literature, from Symbolism to Dadaism, Surrealism, and Absurdism, while the former interdisciplinary orientation sheds light on the social dimensions of a Black writer in confrontation with the political and ethnic reality of America and helps us to conceptualize Black bourgeois socialization, 'Crow-Jimism,' and different models of Black Nationalism."

Lloyd W. Brown's *Amiri Baraka* (1980), a volume in Twayne's United States Authors Series, is a brief, accessible synthesis of scholarship drawing heavily on the investigations of Hudson, Benston, and Sollors. Brown attempts to provide "a comprehensive analysis, one that surveys Baraka's achievement in the various genres represented by his writings as a whole." Like Sollors, Brown sees in Baraka's writings a continuous reaction to traditional modes of expression and the political status quo. The book also includes useful biographical material. Like most of the books in the Twayne series, it is a convenient introduction to its subject's life and writings.

Like Benston, Henry C. Lacey, in *To Raise, Destroy and Create: The Poetry, Drama, and Fiction of Imamu Amiri Baraka (LeRoi Jones)* (1981), attempts to "present the writer as an artist at all stages of his development." According to Lacey, Baraka's best writing displays "two powerful and rich possessions of an otherwise weak and impoverished people." Especially in his later works, Lacey holds, Baraka shows a great appreciation for the rhythms of black speech, while his poetry echoes "the sounds of modern jazz, the most important artistic creation of black America."

Lacey's study is most important for its characterization of the stages of Baraka's literary and political development as a "microcosmic presentation of the black American's crisis of identity, purpose, and direction, the crisis of the '60's." In passing through periods of self-hatred, new nationalism, and synthesis, Baraka was consciously groping "for a rapport with black America" at the same time the culture as a whole was seeking its own positive identity. So, while the most fruitful way to understand Baraka's writing is to understand it primarily as art, the critical content of that art not only enriches the student's understanding of Baraka, but also of a recent epoch in the history of black America.

The most recent book-length study of Baraka, William J. Harris's *The Poetry and Poetics of Amiri Baraka: The Jazz Aesthetic* (1985) is about "Baraka's transformations: of avant-garde poetics into ethnic poetics, of white liberal politics into black nationalist and Marxist politics, of jazz forms into literary forms." Harris uses the term "jazz aesthetic" to refer to "both a theory of beauty and a theory of action and of the political" that uses "jazz variations as paradigms for the conversion of white poetic and social ideas into black ones." Harris thus adopts essentially the same synthetic view of Baraka's writing as Sollors. Creation itself is a political act: Baraka "wants to take weak Western forms, rip them asunder, and create something new out of rubble," much in the same manner that saxophonist John Coltrane "murders" popular song in his improvisations. The relationship between literary creation and improvisation is parallel: "from the white avant-garde Baraka learned how to write and think . . . , but from jazz he learned how to reject, invert, and transform what the white avant-garde had taught him."

Critical Studies: Collection of Essays

The only published collection of essays on Amiri Baraka was edited by Kimberly W. Benston (1978). The collection consists of eighteen essays and excerpts, most of which were previously published by leading Baraka scholars and literary compatriots. A brief introductory tribute by Langston Hughes opens the section on general assessments; essays by Lawrence P. (Larry) Neal, Cecil M. Brown, and Esther M. Jackson place Baraka in critical context. Neal's 1966 piece stresses Baraka's political side during a time when the writer's nationalist stance was becoming explicit. Brown's 1970 article declares Baraka to be the progenitor of a new black literary tradition to which many subsequent black writers, including himself, declare allegiance. Jackson's 1973 work places Baraka in the mainstream of modern American drama, which, she thinks, is preoccupied with "consciousness in crisis." What makes Baraka singularly significant is his use of motifs from black life to record his search for meaning, his "passage from despair to the tranquility of ethical totality."

An excerpt from Theodore R. Hudson's *From LeRoi Jones to Amiri Baraka*, which chronicles Baraka's 1967 arrest in Newark, New Jersey, is the sole biographical piece in Benston's book. A section on Baraka's music criticism, comprising pieces by Ralph Ellison and William C. Fischer, follows. Both Ellison and Fischer discuss Baraka's 1963 work, *Blues People*. Ellison accuses Baraka of ignoring the aesthetic nature of the blues in order to make an ideological point on the separateness of black culture; Fischer describes that aesthetic as ideological: the "delimitation of a sharp dichotomy between the African/Afro-American and the Western/European-American culture families." Lloyd W. Brown and Larry G. Coleman discuss Baraka's prose in the next section of Benston's book. Brown traces the many allusions to great works of Western literature in Baraka's 1965 novel, *The System of Dante's Hell*. Coleman chronicles Baraka's move "toward a blacker art" in his 1967 story collection, *Tales*. Lee A. Jacobus, Clyde Taylor, and Nate Mackey provide general overviews of Baraka's poetry in the penultimate section of the book. Jacobus's 1973 essay describes Baraka's quest for moral order in his poetry. Baraka, declares Jacobus, progressed from an Eliot-inspired vision of a wasteland in the early 1960s to a revolutionary vision of black apotheosis as the 1970s dawned. Taylor writes in 1973 about Baraka's poetry as an extension of Baraka's personality. Mackey's 1978 essay locates jazz-music forms in the verse.

Benston includes six articles on Baraka's drama in the book's final section. Sherley Anne Williams's 1972 piece discusses the play *Dutchman* as an encapsulation of the black man's quest for survival in the West. Survival depends upon the black man's "ability to keep his thoughts and his true identity hidden." John Lindberg's 1972 essay finds in *The Slave* a victory over white dominance, accomplished through dislocation from history and other cultural accoutrements. Robert L. Tener's 1974 piece reveals the tense and dehumanizing struggle for black identity in *The Toilet*. Owen E. Brady's previously unpublished study describes the positive use of parody in *Great Goodness of Life*. Charles D. Peavy describes the mythical, magical, and masculine elements in *Madheart*. Benston's contribution, on "Vision and Form in *Slave Ship*," closes the book.

Critical Studies: Articles and Book Sections

Several important essays supplement the book-length work on Amiri Baraka. Daphne S. Reed, in "LeRoi Jones: High Priest of the Black Arts Movement" (Mar. 1970), gives a laudatory overview of Baraka's dramatic development through *Great Goodness of Life*. The early plays–*Dutchman, The Slave, The Baptism, The Toilet*–are called cathartic (from the perspective of black audiences). Later plays, such as *J-E-L-L-O* and *Home on the Range*, are praised for their ridiculous and satiric antiwhite elements. Reed predicts that Baraka's future plays (after 1970) "may become increasingly foreign to the white world as time goes on, but the work of a major writer will always be subject to appreciation by way of translation."

Lloyd W. Brown's "The Cultural Revolution in Black Theatre" (Spring 1974) attempts to come to terms with the new theater in which Baraka was playing so great a part. This forum was "a militantly anti-bourgeois theatre that emphasizes the need for a cultural revolution and underscores the probabilities of physical rebellion." Baraka's plays expressed an "anti-integrationist ethic" that was, according to white critics (particularly C. W. E. Bigsby), as systematic as those white systems the new black writers so consciously tried to reject. But Brown accuses the critical "establishment" (circa 1974) of cultural "myopia": "shallow literalism that interprets his [the black playwright's] materials as narrowly conceived stereotypes and gratuitous violence, as vicarious forms of revenge." True insight into the motives of Baraka and others, Brown concludes, depends on "the extent to which the critic first discards white ethnocentricity and fearful literalism, and then recognizes the symbolic structures and psychological insights of the materials before him."

Owen E. Brady's "Cultural Conflict and Cult Ritual in LeRoi Jones's *The Toilet*" (Mar. 1976) shows that the Baraka play is a dramatic expression of black duality of the kind W. E. B. Du Bois described in his *The Souls of Black Folk* (1903): Du Bois wrote that the black American "ever feels his twoness–an American, a Negro; two souls, two thoughts, two unreconciled strivings, two warring ideals in one dark body . . . with . . . this longing to attain self-conscious manhood, to merge his double self into a better and truer self." The character of Footes in *The Toilet* is Brady's archetype of the conflict between individual expression and communal pressure of consciousness entrapped.

Unlike Lloyd Brown, Elizabeth Hadley Freydberg sees Baraka's nationalist plays as failures. In "The Concealed Dependence

Upon White Culture in Baraka's 1969 Aesthetic" (1983), she reasons that plays such as *Slave Ship* "simply do not last." Early,
prenationalist plays such as *Dutchman*, which do not conform to the
aesthetic, are more successful in the long run. Freydberg views the
aesthetic in two ways, "in terms of the actual criteria it insists upon
and in terms of the spirit it attempts to capture." She insists that it
is in the latter that the aesthetic finds its artistic merit.

W. D. E. Andrews's "The Marxist Theatre of Amiri Baraka"
(Summer 1984) traces the development of Baraka's Marxist ideology and sees precedent for his liberal-national-Marxist progression
in the writings of Frantz Fanon and Jean-Paul Sartre. Throughout
Baraka's aesthetic and polemic development Andrews observes one
constant: the denouncement of bourgeois art. Andrews also observes that many of Baraka's peers came to view nationalism as politically incorrect in the early 1970s and that Baraka ran the risk of
being perceived as dogmatically fascist as it became clear that racial
rapprochement was the most viable social goal in America.

Andrews sees a potential conflict between the successful nationalist play, such as *Slave Ship*, and the more recent Marxist-inspired
plays such as *The Motion of History* and *S-1*: "As a Marxist playwright, Baraka is . . . contemplating a kind of theater that will in-
volve the forfeiture of those very qualities that had elevated his racial statements to the level of significant drama. In his experiment
with a black theater, he had been struggling to transcend the pro-
fane limitations of his political message in order to link it with values, laws, and forces more powerful than those of human existence. His aim had been to impart the highest possible associations
to political objectives by postulating conversion as not just political
but, at its most fundamental level, spiritual–hence, the usefulness to
him of the Afro-American mystique of 'soul.' "

Baraka's nationalist plays, Andrews continues, employ elements of myth and ritual in order to arouse audiences, to instill in
them support for a "conviction" that is "no longer . . . shackled to
earthly argument." But in the Marxist theater the urge to arouse
must be coupled with the portrayal of Marxist dialectical materialism. The full-length Marxist plays *The Motion of History* and *S-1* suffer because of the necessary difficulty "of resolving the conflict between individual creative temperament and the claims of abstract
dogma."

Lorraine Hansberry
(1930-1965)

Sharon Friedman
New York University

PRIMARY BIBLIOGRAPHY

Books

A Raisin in the Sun. New York: Random House, 1959; London: Methuen, 1960. Republished in *A Raisin in the Sun and The Sign in Sidney Brustein's Window.* New York: New American Library, 1987. Play. 1987 edition restores scenes from the original version of *A Raisin in the Sun.*

The Movement: Documentary of a Struggle for Equality. New York: Simon & Schuster, 1964. Republished as *A Matter of Colour: Documentary of the Struggle for Racial Equality.* Harmondsworth, U.K.: Penguin, 1965. Photohistory.

The Sign in Sidney Brustein's Window. New York: Random House, 1965. Republished in *A Raisin in the Sun and The Sign in Sidney Brustein's Window.* New York: New American Library, 1987. Play.

To Be Young, Gifted and Black. Lorraine Hansberry in Her Own Words, adapted by Robert Nemiroff. Englewood Cliffs, N.J.: Prentice-Hall, 1969. Autobiographical collage assembled from her works. Includes a foreword by Robert Nemiroff.

To Be Young, Gifted and Black, ed. Nemiroff. New York: French, 1971. Play.

Les Blancs & The Last Plays of Lorraine Hansberry, ed. Nemiroff. New York: Random House, 1972. Comprises *Les Blancs, The Drinking Gourd,* and *What Use Are Flowers?* Republished as *Lorraine Hansberry: The Collected Last Plays.* New York: New American Library, 1983. Contains an enlarged version of *Les Blancs.*

Premiere Productions

A Raisin in the Sun. New York, Ethel Barrymore Theatre, 11 Mar. 1959.

The Sign in Sidney Brustein's Window. New York, Longacre Theatre, 15 Oct. 1964.
To Be Young, Gifted and Black, adapted by Robert Nemiroff. New York, Cherry Lane Theatre, 2 Jan. 1969.
Les Blancs, adapted by Nemiroff. New York, Longacre Theatre, 15 Nov. 1970.

Selected Other

"On Summer," *Playbill,* 29 June 1960, pp. 3, 25-27. Collected in *Short Essays,* ed. Gerald Levin. New York: Harcourt Brace Jovanovich, 1977, 52-56. Essay.
"This Complex of Womanhood," *Ebony,* 15 (Aug. 1960), 40. Essay.
"Me Tink Me Hear Sounds in De Night," *Theatre Arts,* 44 (Oct. 1960), 9-11. Collected as "The Negro in American Theatre," in *American Playwrights on Drama,* ed. Horst Frenz. New York: Hill & Wang, 1960, 160-167. Essay.
"Genet, Mailer and the New Paternalism," *Village Voice,* 1 June 1961, pp. 10, 14-15. Essay.
"The Negro in American Culture." In *The New Negro,* ed. Matthew H. Ahmann. Notre Dame, Ind.: Fides, 1961, 109-145. Reprinted in *The Black American Writer,* ed. C. W. E. Bigsby, volume 1. De Land, Fla.: Everett/Edwards, 1969, 79-108.
A Raisin in the Sun. Columbia Pictures, 1961. Screenplay.
"A Challenge to Artists," *Freedomways,* 3 (Winter 1963), 33-35. Collected in *Harlem, USA,* ed. John Henrik Clarke. New York: Macmillan/Collier, 1971, 129-135. Collected again in *The Voice of Black America: Major Speeches by Negroes in the U.S. 1797-1971,* ed. Philip S. Foner. New York: Simon & Schuster, 1972, 954-959.
"The Legacy of W. E. B. DuBois," *Freedomways,* 5 (Winter 1965), 19-20. Collected in *Black Titan: W. E. B. DuBois: An Anthology,* ed. by the editors of *Freedomways.* Boston: Beacon, 1970, 17. Tribute.
"The Black Revolution and the White Backlash." In *Black Protest: History, Documents and Analyses, 1619 to the Present,* ed. Joanne Grant. New York: Fawcett, 1968, 442-448. Essay.
"Original Prospectus for the John Brown Memorial Theatre of Harlem," *Black Scholar,* 10 (July/Aug. 1979), 14-15. Essay.
"The Negro Writer and His Roots: Toward a New Romanticism," *Black Scholar,* 12 (Mar./Apr. 1981), 2-12. Essay.

"Willie Loman, Walter Younger, and He Who Must Live." Article. "On Strindberg and Sexism" and "Arthur Miller, Marilyn Monroe, and 'Guilt' ". Letters. In *Women in Theatre: Compassion and Hope*, ed. Karen Malpede. New York: Drama Book Publishers, 1983, 166-176.

"All the Dark and Beautiful Warriors," *Village Voice*, 16 Aug. 1983, pp. 1, 11-19. Novel excerpt.

"Three Songs for the 'New World,' " *Black Collegian*, 14 (Mar./Apr. 1984), 48. Poems.

"All the Dark and Beautiful Warriors," *Triquarterly*, no. 60 (Spring/Summer 1984), 35-60. Novel excerpt.

"The Buck Williams Tennessee Memorial Association," *Southern Exposure*, 12 (Sept./Oct. 1984), 28-31. Novel excerpt.

"In Defense of the Equality of Men." In *The Norton Anthology of Literature by Women*, ed. Sandra M. Gilbert and Susan Gubar. New York: Norton, 1985, 2055-2066. Essay.

"Toussaint: Excerpt from a Work in Progress." In *Nine Plays by Black Women*, ed. Margaret B. Wilkerson. New York: New American Library, 1986, 41-68.

Recording

Lorraine Hansberry Speaks Out: Art and the Black Revolution. Caedmon TC 1352, 1972.

SECONDARY BIBLIOGRAPHY

Bibliography

Kaiser, Ernest, and Robert Nemiroff. "A Lorraine Hansberry Bibliography," *Freedomways*, 19 (Fourth quarter 1979), 287-304.

Interviews

Isaacs, Harold R. "Five Writers and their Ancestors: 'Lorraine Hansberry.' " In his *The New World of Negro Americans*. New York: Day, 1963, 277-287.

Poston, Ted. "We Have So Much to Say," *New York Post*, 22 Mar. 1959, p. 2.

Robertson, Nan. "Dramatist Against Odds," *New York Times*, 8 Mar. 1959, section 2, p. 3.

"Talk of the Town: Playwright," *New Yorker*, 35 (9 May 1959), 33-35.

Terkel, Studs. "Make New Sounds," *American Theatre*, 1 (Nov. 1984), 5-7.

Critical Studies: Book
Cheney, Anne. *Lorraine Hansberry*. Boston: Twayne, 1984.

Critical Studies: Collection of Essays
Bond, Jean Carey, ed. *Lorraine Hansberry: Art of Thunder, Vision of Light*. Special issue of *Freedomways*, 19 (Fourth quarter 1979).

Critical Studies: Major Reviews, Articles, and Book Sections
Abramson, Doris E. *Negro Playwrights in the American Theatre, 1925-1959*. New York & London: Columbia University Press, 1969, 239-254, 263-266.

Anderson, Mary Louise. "Black Matriarchy: Portrayals of Women in Three Plays," *Negro American Literature Forum*, 10 (Spring 1976), 93-95.

Aufderheide, Pat. "*Les Blancs* Rekindles Racial Controversies," *These Times*, 9-15 Mar. 1988, p. 18.

Baldwin, James. "Lorraine Hansberry at the Summit," *Freedomways*, 19 (Fourth quarter 1979), 269-272.

Baldwin. "Sweet Lorraine." In Hansberry, *To Be Young, Gifted and Black: Lorraine Hansberry in Her Own Words*, 1969, ix-xii.

Baraka, Amiri. "*A Raisin in the Sun's* Enduring Passion." In Hansberry, *A Raisin in the Sun and The Sign in Sidney Brustein's Window*, 1987, 9-20.

Barthelemy, Anthony. "Brother, Sister, Wife: A Dramatic Perspective," *Southern Review*, new series 21 (Summer 1985), 770-789.

Bennett, Lerone, Jr., and Margaret G. Burroughs. "Lorraine Hansberry Rap," *Freedomways*, 19 (Fourth quarter 1979), 226-233.

Bigsby, C. W. E. "Lorraine Hansberry." In his *Confrontation and Commitment: A Study of Contemporary American Drama, 1959-66*. Columbia: University of Missouri Press, 1968, 156-173.

Bond, Jean Carey. "Lorraine Hansberry: To Reclaim her Legacy," *Freedomways*, 19 (Fourth quarter 1979), 183-185.

Braine, John. "An Appreciation: Sidney Brustein—A 'Great' Play—No Other Word is Possible." In Hansberry, *A Raisin in the Sun and The Sign in Sidney Brustein's Window*, 1987, 155-159.

Brown, Lloyd W. "Lorraine Hansberry as Ironist: A Reappraisal of 'A Raisin in the Sun,'" *Journal of Black Studies,* 4 (Mar. 1974), 237-247.

Bruckner, D. J. R. "Stage: At Roundabout, 'A Raisin in the Sun,'" *New York Times,* 15 Aug. 1986, p. C3.

Carter, Steven R. "Commitment Amid Complexity: Lorraine Hansberry's Life-in-Action," *Melus,* 7 (Fall 1980), 39-53.

Carter. "Images of Men in Lorraine Hansberry's Writing," *Black American Literature Forum,* 19 (Winter 1985), 160-162.

Carter. "The John Brown Theatre: Lorraine Hansberry's Cultural Views and Dramatic Goals," *Freedomways,* 19 (Fourth quarter 1979), 186-191.

Clurman, Harold. "Theatre," *Nation,* 211 (7 Dec. 1970), 605-606.

Cruse, Harold. *The Crisis of the Negro Intellectual.* New York: Morrow, 1967, 267-284.

Elder, Lonne, III. "Lorraine Hansberry: Social Consciousness and the Will," *Freedomways,* 19 (Fourth quarter 1979), 213-218.

Erstein, Hap. " 'Les Blancs' at Arena: Perceptive Black Drama," *Washington Times,* 12 Feb. 1988, p. E3.

Farrison, W. Edward. "Lorraine Hansberry's Last Dramas," *CLA Journal,* 16 (Dec. 1972), 188-197.

Friedman, Sharon. "Feminism as Theme in Twentieth-Century American Women's Drama," *American Studies,* 21 (Spring 1984), 69-89.

Fuchs, Elinor. "Rethinking Lorraine Hansberry," *Village Voice,* 15 Mar. 1988, pp. 93, 98, 105.

Gill, Glenda. "Techniques of Teaching Lorraine Hansberry: Liberation from Boredom," *Negro American Literature Forum,* 8 (Summer 1974), 226-228.

Giovanni, Nikki. "An Emotional View of Lorraine Hansberry," *Freedomways,* 19 (Fourth quarter 1979), 281-282.

Gresham, Jewell Handy. "Lorraine Hansberry as Prose Stylist," *Freedomways,* 19 (Fourth quarter 1979), 192-204.

Gussow, Mel. "Stage: 'A Raisin in the Sun' at Yale," *New York Times,* 9 Nov. 1983, p. C23.

Haley, Alex. "The Once and Future Vision of Lorraine Hansberry," *Freedomways,* 19 (Fourth quarter 1979), 277-280.

Hays, Peter L. "*Raisin in the Sun* and *Juno and the Paycock,*" *Phylon,* 33 (Summer 1972), 175-176.

Holtan, Orley I. "Sidney Brustein and the Plight of the American Intellectual," *Players,* 46 (June/July 1971), 222-225.

Kerr, Walter. "Theatre: 'Raisin in the Sun,' " *New York Herald-Tribune*, 22 Mar. 1959, Lively Arts section, pp. 1-2.

Keyssar, Helene. *Feminist Theatre: An Introduction to Plays of Contemporary British and American Women.* London: Macmillan, 1984, 32-36.

Killens, John Oliver. "Lorraine Hansberry: On Time!," *Freedomways*, 19 (Fourth quarter 1979), 273-276.

King, Woodie, Jr. "Lorraine Hansberry's Children: Black Artists and *A Raisin in the Sun*," *Freedomways*, 19 (Fourth quarter 1979), 219-221.

Lester, Julius. "Afterword." In Hansberry, *Lorraine Hansberry: The Collected Last Plays*, 1983, 262-275.

Lester. "Foreword." In Hansberry, *Lorraine Hansberry: The Collected Last Plays*, 1983, 1-2.

Malpede, Karen. "Lorraine Hansberry." In her *Women in Theatre: Compassion and Hope.* New York: Drama Book Publishers, 1983, 163-176.

Mayfield, Julian. "Lorraine Hansberry: A Woman for All Seasons," *Freedomways*, 19 (Fourth quarter 1979), 263-268.

Miller, Jeanne-Marie A. "Images of Black Women in Plays by Black Playwrights," *CLA Journal*, 20 (June 1977), 494-507.

Miller, Jordan Y. "Lorraine Hansberry." In *The Black American Writer*, ed. C. W. E. Bigsby, 2 volumes. Baltimore, Md.: Penguin, 1969, II: 157-170.

Mitchell, Loften. *Black Drama: The Story of the American Negro in the Theatre.* New York: Hawthorn, 1967, 180-182, 202-204.

Nemiroff, Robert. "A Critical Background to *Les Blancs*." In Hansberry, *Lorraine Hansberry: The Collected Last Plays*, 1983, 27-35.

Nemiroff. "A Critical Background to *The Drinking Gourd*." In Hansberry, *Lorraine Hansberry: The Collected Last Plays*, 1983, 143-162.

Nemiroff. "A Critical Background to *What Use Are Flowers?*." In Hansberry, *Lorraine Hansberry: The Collected Last Plays*, 1983, 223-226.

Nemiroff. "The 101 'Final' Performances of *Sidney Brustein*." In Hansberry, *A Raisin in the Sun and The Sign in Sidney Brustein's Window*, 1987, 160-205.

Potter, Vilma R. "New Politics, New Mothers," *CLA Journal*, 16 (Dec. 1972), 247-255.

Powell, Bertie J. "The Black Experience in Margaret Walker's *Jubilee* and Lorraine Hansberry's *The Drinking Gourd*," *CLA Journal*, 21 (Dec. 1977), 304-311.

Rahman, Aishah. "To Be Black, Female and a Playwright," *Freedomways*, 19 (Fourth quarter 1979), 256-260.

Rich, Adrienne. "The Problem with Lorraine Hansberry," *Freedomways*, 19 (Fourth quarter 1979), 247-255.

Rich, Frank. *"A Raisin in the Sun, The 25th Anniversary."* In Hansberry, *A Raisin in the Sun and The Sign in Sidney Brustein's Window*, 1987, 7-8.

Richards, David. "Shining 'Raisin in the Sun,'" *Washington Post*, 17 Nov. 1986, p. D1.

Riley, Clayton. "Lorraine Hansberry: A Melody in a Different Key," *Freedomways*, 19 (Fourth quarter 1979), 205-212.

Royals, Demetria Brendan. "The Me Lorraine Hansberry Knew," *Freedomways*, 19 (Fourth quarter 1979), 261-262.

Salaam, Kalamu ya. "What Use Is Writing? Re-Reading Lorraine Hansberry," *Black Collegian*, 14 (Mar./Apr. 1984), 45-46.

Schiff, Ellen. *From Stereotype to Metaphor: The Jew in Contemporary Drama*. Albany, N.Y.: State University of New York Press, 1982, 155-160.

Tynan, Kenneth. *Curtains*. New York: Atheneum, 1961, 306-309.

Ward, Douglas Turner. "Lorraine Hansberry and the Passion of Walter Lee," *Freedomways*, 19 (Fourth quarter 1979), 223-225.

Weales, Gerald. *The Jumping-Off Place: American Drama in the 1960's*. New York & London: Macmillan, 1969, 117-122.

Wilkerson, Margaret B. "Introduction." In Hansberry, *Lorraine Hansberry: The Collected Last Plays*, 1983, 3-23.

Wilkerson. "Lorraine Hansberry: Artist, Activist, Feminist." In Helen Crich Chinoy and Linda Walsh Jenkins, *Women in American Theatre*, revised and enlarged edition. New York: Theatre Communications Group, 1987, 180-185.

Wilkerson. "Lorraine Hansberry: The Complete Feminist," *Freedomways*, 19 (Fourth quarter 1979), 235-245.

Wilkerson. "The Sighted Eyes and Feeling Heart of Lorraine Hansberry," *Black American Literature Forum*, 17 (Spring 1983), 8-13.

Wright, Sarah E. "Lorraine Hansberry on Film," *Freedomways*, 19 (Fourth quarter 1979), 283-284.

BIBLIOGRAPHICAL ESSAY

Bibliographies

The Lorraine Hansberry bibliography compiled by Ernest Kaiser and Robert Nemiroff (Fourth quarter 1979) is the most comprehensive on the playwright to date. It was published as part of a special issue of *Freedomways* that sought to encourage the study of Hansberry's life and works. The 251 entries in the bibliography encompass both writings by Hansberry (including recordings and films), and writings about Hansberry and her work (journal and newspaper articles, theses, and sections of books). Some entries have brief annotations.

The bibliography is prefaced by separate introductory notes by each author. Ernest Kaiser, member of the Schomburg Center for Research in Black Culture and an associate editor of *Freedomways*, asserts that "Hansberry's artistic handling of political issues and societal problems makes her plays models for black playwrights and novelists of today that should be studied extensively." Robert Nemiroff, Hansberry's former husband and the executor of her literary estate, warns readers of "misinformation" and "misstatements" concerning the facts of Hansberry's life and the philosophy and intention of her art. Nemiroff singles out one misquoted statement in an early *New York Times* interview ("Dramatist Against Odds," by Nan Robertson, 8 Mar. 1959) that "spread like a prairie fire" and influenced interpretations of the playwright's work for years to come. In the *Times* interview Hansberry is quoted as saying that her first play, *A Raisin in the Sun,* was not a "Negro play" but a play about "believable, many-sided people who happen to be Negroes." Whatever Hansberry said about the universal dimensions of her play, the statement that was printed obscured her concern with the oppression of black people in America, which was always at the center of her art and politics.

Robert Nemiroff, Hansberry's creative partner in life, continues to assiduously collect and catalog material related to her. He generously provided an updated "selected bibliography" (as yet unpublished) which proved essential to this bibliographic essay.

Interviews

In the years following the success of *A Raisin in the Sun* Hansberry granted numerous interviews to newspapers and magazines. Studs Terkel's conversation with Hansberry, originally broadcast on his "Almanac" radio show and published under the title "Make New Sounds" (Nov. 1984), is among the most noteworthy in terms of understanding her artistic intentions. The ideas Hansberry expresses in the Terkel interview–the creation of the universal in the specific, the differences between realism and naturalism, the truth of the affirmative heroic stance, the particular oppression of women in oppressed groups–appear frequently in Hansberry's writing and in her commentary.

Responding to the critical misinterpretation of *A Raisin in the Sun* as a play "that could be about anybody," Hansberry states directly that it is about "a Negro family, specifically and culturally, but it's not even a New York family or southern Negro family–it is specifically Southside Chicago. To the extent we accept them and believe them as who they're supposed to be . . . they can become everybody." Alluding to the universal as well as the specifically "Negro" character of the play, she continues, "I believe that one of the soundest ideas in dramatic writing is that in order to create the universal, you must pay very great attention to the specific. Universality, I think, emerges from truthful identity of what it is."

Hansberry goes on to describe Walter Lee Younger, the protagonist in *A Raisin in the Sun,* as an affirmative and realistic hero. For Hansberry a realistic work is one which "shows not only what *is* but what is possible–which is part of reality, too."

In the interview with Terkel, Hansberry also acknowledges her respect for the Irish playwright Sean O'Casey and suggests certain parallels between the characters Mother Younger in *A Raisin in the Sun* and Juno in O'Casey's *Juno and the Paycock.* These comments are interesting because they indicate Hansberry's feminist perspective, which has been recognized in recent Hansberry criticism but was ignored by earlier critics: "No doubt there was a necessity among oppressed peoples, black or Irish or otherwise, for the mother to assume a certain kind of role. Obviously the most oppressed group of any oppressed group will be its women, who are twice oppressed. . . . As oppression makes people more militant, women become twice militant."

A *New Yorker* "Talk of the Town" interview (9 May 1959) reveals autobiographical detail that sheds considerable light on the thematic material of Hansberry's *A Raisin in the Sun.* Hansberry chronicles her relatively young life (she was twenty-nine at the time), focusing on her childhood on the South Side of Chicago. Her family was comparatively well-off financially, but hardly insulated from

the racism that pervaded life in Chicago. Her father was a successful businessman, a U.S. marshal, and the founder of one of the
first Negro banks in Chicago. Moreover, he had triumphed in a key
civil rights case on restricted covenants that went all the way to the
U.S. Supreme Court. But he had become so depressed by the fact
"that this country was hopeless in its treatment of Negroes," that he
became an expatriate to Mexico. He was making plans for his family to join him there when he died. Thus, it makes little sense to pin
the label "middle-class" on Hansberry. Indeed, Hansberry recounts
how she lived in a ghetto and went to Jim Crow schools. When her
family attempted to move to a white neighborhood she was almost
killed when "a brick came crashing through the window with such
force it embedded itself in the opposite wall." In this way she implicitly answers critics who claimed that she had lived outside the experience she renders in *A Raisin in the Sun,* which deals with the
dreams and frustrations of a poor black family determined to leave
the ghetto. However, Hansberry's personal response to racism was
different from her father's, largely because she identified with the rising tide of black protest in the United States and abroad: "I'm
afraid I have to agree with Daddy's assessment of this country. But
I don't agree with the leaving part. I don't feel defensive.... One
of the reasons I feel so free is that I belong to a world majority and
a very assertive one."

   In an interview with Harold Isaacs, which appears as part of a
chapter entitled "Five Writers and their Ancestors" in his *The New
World of Negro Americans* (1963), Hansberry elaborates on the links
she perceives between the Negro American and the black African.
Isaacs characterizes Hansberry's work as completing "a circle"
begun by Langston Hughes, in that the reunion between Negro
Americans and black Africans appears in a "new, much more realistic setting." (He alludes here to scenes from *A Raisin in the Sun.*) According to Isaacs, "it is no longer a wispy literary yearning after a
lost primitivism.... Nor is it any longer a matter of going back to Africa as the ultimate option of despair in America. In Lorraine
Hansberry's time it has become a matter of choice between new freedoms now in the grasp of black men, both African and American."

   In the Isaacs interview Hansberry also recounts her rebellion
as a child against "the shame about Africa among Negroes" and recalls her identification with people of color in other parts of the
world: "Little as I was, I remember the newsreels of the Ethiopian
war and the feeling of outrage in our Negro Community." She had

never heard of Marcus Garvey, but had read Negro poets–
Langston Hughes, Countee Cullen, Warren Cuney. "I was deeply influenced by them and their images of Africa were marvelous and
beautiful." Although Hansberry identifies herself as part of a
"world majority" of oppressed people who are claiming their freedoms, Isaacs paraphrases her as saying, "Africans have their own national identities, and American Negroes have–or must now shape–
their own."

These dual concerns–the international struggle against colonial-
ism and the shaping of a strong Negro nationalist identity–were evident in a *New York Post* interview with Ted Poston published on 22
March 1959. Here she discusses her plans for two never-completed
projects: an opera based on the life of Toussaint L'Ouverture, the
slave who liberated Haiti from the France of Napoleon; and a dramatic adaptation of *The Marrow of Tradition*, by the early black novelist Charles Chesnutt, which deals with the postreconstruction "re-
enslavement" of the new freedmen in South Carolina.

Critical Studies: Book

Lorraine Hansberry, by Anne Cheney (1984), a volume in
Twayne publishers' United States Authors Series, is the only published book-length study of Hansberry's life and work. The book includes a chronology as well as a selected bibliography. In almost story-
book fashion Cheney recounts key stages of Hansberry's life: her
childhood in Chicago; her years at the University of Wisconsin; her
move to New York City; her marriage to Robert Nemiroff, with
whom she shared artistic and political concerns; and, finally, her premature death from cancer at the age of thirty-four. Cheney
sketches Hansberry's developing interests and practical education in
politics, African culture, and the theater. Leaving the University of
Wisconsin for New York, Hansberry enrolled in classes at the New
School for Social Research and joined the staff of Paul Robeson's *Freedom,* a radical journal to which she contributed reviews of works by
black artists, reports on conferences, and articles on social inequity,
events in Africa, and life in Harlem. Cheney also touches on some
of Hansberry's political activities in the 1950s. For example, she represented Paul Robeson at the International Peace Congress in Montevi-
deo, Uruguay, in 1952, after the State Department revoked his pass-
port.

Cheney presents a rather skeptical view of Hansberry's men-
tors, W. E. B. Du Bois and Robeson, men who Cheney believes "advo-

cated theories out of sync with the black working class." However, she credits them as having provided Hansberry with "exemplary models of black artists."

Cheney's book also presents an analysis of Hansberry's plays, drawing on her speeches, articles, and interviews to interpret the texts. Labeling the form of Hansberry's plays "conventional twentieth-century social drama," Cheney asserts that in their content "the plays break new ground," representing black as well as white struggles on the American stage.

Cheney regards Hansberry as an "outsider" who never fully resolved the "duality of her life and works—upper-middle-class affluence and black heritage and revolution." For Cheney, this outsider perspective and unresolved duality is an asset: "All artists must distance themselves from their worlds: they observe the status quo, reject the dross and create new, valuable works of art." This interpretation, however, seems curiously at odds with Hansberry's powerful sense of group identification, as is evident in the interviews cited above. It is also at odds with the thrust of recent scholarship, which characterizes her as the quintessentially committed and engaged artist.

Margaret B. Wilkerson is currently writing an extensive critical biography of Hansberry. She has full access to Hansberry's papers.

Critical Studies: Collection of Essays

A special issue of *Freedomways*, entitled *Lorraine Hansberry: Art of Thunder, Vision of Light* (1979), is an unusual and invaluable resource. In addition to the extensive bibliography by Ernest Kaiser and Robert Nemiroff it contains eighteen articles ranging in subject from stylistic analyses to thematic and contextual discussions of individual plays to personal reminiscences by key figures in the black cultural community who knew or admired Hansberry (Woody King, Jr., Clayton Riley, Lonne Elder III, Douglas Turner Ward, Julian Mayfield, James Baldwin, John Oliver Killens, Alex Haley, and Nikki Giovanni). Published fourteen years after Hansberry's death, this collection marks the beginning of a reevaluation of her work.

The introductory article by issue editor Jean Carey Bond outlines the two primary objectives of the issue: to introduce Hansberry to those who are unfamiliar with the range of her work; and to encourage the study of an artist whose work entitles her to inclusion among the best of modern American writers. Carey argues that as a black, female writer, Hansberry's vision was not "tangentially, but quintessentially of this place." *A Raisin in the Sun* "prophetically embodied the Afro-American spirit that was soon to engulf the nation in a historic movement for social change."

The diversity of critical approaches found in the *Freedomways* collection almost ensures a full, balanced presentation of Hansberry's life and work. Jewell Handy Gresham examines the "classical artistry" of the playwright's prose. Particularly interesting is Gresham's discussion of the near exclusion of Hansberry from the formal American literary canon. Woody King, Jr., explains why his documentary film on the black theater movement begins with *A Raisin in the Sun*. Charles Clayton Riley analyzes the rejection of Hansberry's work in the 1960s, when her "consistent refusal to legitimize hatred of whites" did not correspond to certain "racialist precepts." James Baldwin provides a poignant memoir of his and Hansberry's historic meeting with Robert Kennedy to discuss the failure of the FBI to provide protection for civil rights activists in the American South.

Critical Studies: Major Reviews, Articles, and Book Sections
In the years following Hansberry's untimely death she was essentially remembered as the successful black playwright of *A Raisin in the Sun* but ignored in the wake of the militant black arts movement. In the past decade, however, scholars have come to appreciate the complexity of her art and thought. Some have gone so far as to suggest that Hansberry was the major catalyst of the black theater movement.

In a brief article entitled "What Use Is Writing? Re-Reading Lorraine Hansberry" (Mar./Apr. 1984), Kalamu ya Salaam examines personal and political reasons that explain why Hansberry is "missed or overlooked" in certain critical views. She not only died young and at the beginning of the black arts movement, but the bulk of her work was in drama, "a form which is seldom widely read." Moreover, because her drama was first presented on Broadway and not in the black community, critics characterized her work as "commercial" or "white"-oriented. Against the background of surging black nationalism, some critics used her relatively affluent background and her marriage to a white man to dismiss her as an inauthentic voice of black America. Salaam cautions his readers against ignoring this critical talent, one of the first black playwrights to speak out about the "nexus of alienation, the responsibilities and freedom of the Black middle class vis-a-vis the Black working class and vis-a-vis the world."

Salaam alludes to LeRoi Jones's *Dutchman* as the play often cited as the beginning of the black theater movement of the 1960s. Thus it is interesting to consider Baraka's critical reevaluation of Hansberry, which appears in the expanded twenty-fifth anniversary edition of *A Raisin in the Sun* (1987). He reflects on his earlier, unfavorable assessment of her work in terms of his own drama and the political climate of the 1960s. Then, characterizing Hansberry as a "critical realist" in the tradition of Langston Hughes, Richard Wright, and Margaret Walker, Baraka extols her work while explaining his own earlier misreading: "We thought Hansberry's play [*A Raisin in the Sun*] was part of the 'passive resistance' phase of the movement. . . . We missed the essence of the work–that Hansberry had created a family on the cutting edge of the same class and ideological struggles as existed in the movement itself and among the people." Suggesting that his own play, *Dutchman*, "is too concerned with white people," he argues that Hansberry's characters are of the "black majority," and their concerns for moving out of the ghetto are "reflections of the essence of black people's striving and the will to defeat segregation, discrimination, and national oppression."

The controversy surrounding the portrayal of these themes is certainly evident in earlier criticism of Hansberry's work. Writing in 1967, Harold Cruse dismisses *A Raisin in the Sun* as a dated, integrationist play, essentially about real estate. Cruse attributes what he construes as integrationist philosophy to Hansberry's middle-class origins and left-wing literary ethos, which seeks the integration of the Negro literary image in the mainstream. Jordan Y. Miller (1969) likewise speculates that the Youngers are attempting to assimilate themselves into white society. In the end Miller refuses to discuss the merits of the play "on the basis of any form of racial consciousness" or in terms of its "social significance," but only as "dramatic literature, quite apart from other factors."

On the other hand, Lloyd W. Brown (Mar. 1974) objects to the discussion of the "structure or technique" of *A Raisin in the Sun* apart from its social significance. He perceives Hansberry's message in the irony he believes is intentional in the play. The play's title, an image from Langston Hughes's poem, "Harlem," is Hansberry's response to the poet's question: "What happens to a dream deferred/ Does it dry up/Like a raisin in the sun?" Brown maintains that in this image lies the key to Hansberry's irony and her political acumen: "Given the pervasive connotations of dried up hopes and deferred dreams, then the very notion of choice . . . has been restricted to a set of ironically balanced alternatives. . . . The integration which is eventually realized at the end of the play has been severely, and realistically, limited by Hansberry's awareness of the contradiction between the dream ideals of reconciliation and equality and the social realities of hatred and unresolved conflict."

Similarly, in his foreword to the expanded edition of *A Raisin in the Sun* (1987), Robert Nemiroff scoffs at the idea that the play has a happy ending. In discussing the significance of scenes and lines that were restored to the 1987 edition he shows that the new material "makes plain the realities that await the Youngers at the curtain." Furthermore, he maintains that the previously excised passages are pertinent to the concerns of a play that "presaged" a revolution in black consciousness concerning family values, generational and class conflicts, and the pertinence of ongoing revolutionary ferment in Black Africa.

A full recognition of these themes and their enduring significance in Hansberry's plays is at the heart of the overall critical reevaluation of her work taking place in the 1980s. Indeed, Nemiroff calls our attention to theater reviews of revivals of *A Raisin in the Sun* that acclaim it as an American classic, belonging to an "inner circle" with such dramas as Arthur Miller's *Death of a Salesman*, Eugene O'Neill's *Long Day's Journey Into Night,* and Tennessee Williams's *The Glass Menagerie.*

Lorraine Hansberry's second play, *The Sign in Sidney Brustein's Window,* is about intellectuals in New York's Greenwich Village and their retreat from emotional and political involvement. Julius Lester (1983) characterizes the play's dominant theme as "Man's relationship to his time"–specifically, the civil rights movement, the black power movement, and the "call to arms" to white liberals and intellectuals in the early 1960s. Noting that it was a "risk of the highest order" for an eminent black playwright to follow *A Raisin in the Sun* with a drama about white liberal intellectuals, he suggests that, despite superficial appearances to the contrary, the play is an important and logical successor. Lester argues that there is "prognostication" in Hansberry's plays, and interprets *The Sign in Sidney Brustein's Window* as a "warning" and a "plea" to Hansberry's white intellectual counterparts to meet the challenge of a society about to explode with racial riots and protests against the Vietnam War.

Lester also stresses the idea that Hansberry's politics were infused with "caring" and that this sensibility precluded her from stereotyping her black characters. Other critics have likewise noted the attention she pays to each character, dramatizing the ways in which their lives intersect and illuminate each other's experiences. As novelist John Braine notes (1987), the characters in *The Sign in Sidney Brustein's Window* are "larger than expectation has permitted either them or us. There are no merely supporting actors, the equivalents of the spearman and the butler and the maid. All are real . . . gloriously diverse, illuminatingly contradictory, heart-breakingly alive." Jordan Miller (1969) found this quality in the "beautifully executed patterns of interrelationships. No character is a foil for another." What Sidney and Iris Brustein are and "what they become are parts of what Mavis, Alton, David and Gloria are."

Focusing on the character of the Jew in contemporary drama, Ellen Schiff (1982) argues that the character of Sidney Brustein is effective on two levels: he is "one of the most successful characterizations of the Jew on the post-1945 stage," and at the same time he emerges as "a metaphor for the unaccommodated man determined to shape his world to more human proportions." He represents "a veteran of the battle against the quota."

In "The 101 'Final' Performances of *Sidney Brustein*" (1987), Robert Nemiroff presents a cogent analysis of the reviews that followed the opening of the play and identifies qualities that may have confounded previous critics. The play was not "neat, simple, 'well-made.' " It was not "easily classifiable." It was "too hopeful" and too "readily accessible" to seem serious. Finally, it was "stylistically unorthodox." Nemiroff, always an invaluable source for understanding the circumstances of Hansberry's productions and an astute guide to their critical reception, reveals in graphic detail how the theatrical community kept the play running during the time its author lay critically ill.

Hansberry's last three plays were edited by Nemiroff and published posthumously. Only *Les Blancs* has been performed professionally in its entirety. (See the reviews of its current revival by Aufderheide [Mar. 1988], Erstein [Feb. 1988], Fuchs [Mar. 1988], and Clurman's review of the original production [Dec. 1970].) Although Nemiroff made editorial changes in *Les Blancs* and *What Use Are Flowers?*, he has indicated that Hansberry is the author of them from beginning to end.

Nemiroff's critical introductions to each play (1983) are important documents since they provide information about the playwright's intentions, gleaned from Nemiroff and Hansberry's discussions and from her notebook jottings. Furthermore, Nemiroff was directly involved with the experiences that shaped Hansberry's thinking and influenced her creative decisions.

In the introduction to *Les Blancs* Nemiroff traces Hansberry's education in African history and political movements, which was initiated by her uncle William Leo Hansberry, a scholar of African antiquity, and continued by W. E. B. Du Bois, "father of Pan-Africanism," leading to friendships with black exiles from South Africa and Rhodesia. The influence African studies had on her work is evident in *Les Blancs,* which dramatizes a rebellion in a mythical African colony. Perhaps like the exiles Hansberry knew, the play's protagonist—an African educated in Europe—struggles with his commitment to Africa and his desire to transcend historical circumstances. Nemiroff also discusses her intentions in the context of her critical response to Jean Genet's *Les Negres.* In the introduction to *The Drinking Gourd,* a television drama originally commissioned by NBC in 1960 to commemorate the Civil War, Nemiroff reveals the circumstances surrounding NBC's decision to cancel the production. In doing so, he presents his analysis of the originality of the work: the play "depicted, as never before in a television script, the crimes of American slavery . . . not merely to set the record straight . . . but to focus on the system that required the crimes, the culture that shaped the Southern white personality in its countless variations." According to Nemiroff, there are a number of factors that made *The Drinking Gourd* an explosive play, the most significant of which was the myth-shattering character Rissa, a jolting variation of the prototypical black mammy. Hansberry's fantasy depicts a "post-atomic" world in which a hermit, emerging from seclusion, attempts to teach a group of children who survive the destruction of the earth the "remnants of civilization" which might yet provide the hope necessary to continue. Nemiroff's introductory remarks to *What Use Are Flowers?* take a literary approach, as he discusses Hansberry's fantasy as a response to the "questions of life and death, survival and absurdity" she saw addressed in Samuel Beckett's *Waiting for Godot.*

In "The 101 'Final' Performances of *Sidney Brustein*" (1987), Nemiroff admits that he cannot "pretend to objectivity about Hansberry" and urges critics to pay closer attention to her work.

The two most significant scholars to give her work close scrutiny in the period of reevaluation are Steven R. Carter and Margaret B. Wilkerson. Expanding on Julius Lester's thesis of "the politics of caring" (1983), they view Hansberry as a fully engaged artist.

Carter's article, "Commitment Amid Complexity" (Fall 1980), elucidates Hansberry's political and social concerns—black liberation, feminism, Pan-Africanism, socialism, and world peace. With considerable subtlety he sorts out Hansberry's beliefs. His thesis is that Hansberry "made great efforts to understand all sides of a conflict and that she felt compassion for everyone involved [evident in her ability to create sympathetic characters across the social and political spectrum] while firmly deciding where justice lay—and acting on that decision [apparent in the moral choices that her characters make]." Carter includes a chronology to indicate the relationship between Hansberry's life and her ideas. His discussion also places her ideas in a socio-literary context; specifically, he discusses her reaction to the theater of the absurd and the values embodied in that theatrical form. Carter explains that Hansberry agreed with the absurdists in their view that the modern world offered "no gods and no values extrinsic to human beings" in the face of complex and often overwhelming forces. However, Hansberry rejected their attitude of despair and the abandonment of hope. She argued that humans could do " 'what the apes never will—impose the reason for life on life' " and in her drama focused on the "social question of how we should live" rather than the metaphysical debate about "why we are here on earth."

In an article focusing on Hansberry's perspectives for a community theater in Harlem, the John Brown Theatre, Carter (Fourth quarter 1979) explores the links between Hansberry's cultural views and her dramatic goals. He outlines the "consciously paradoxical nature of Hansberry's world view and art": she was a black dramatist who frequently adopted and adapted techniques and materials from non-black writers; she was a Pan-Africanist who wished to portray the western heritage of Afro-Americans alongside the African heritage; she was a "revolutionary dramatist" who aspired to be an artist as well as a propagandist. Artistically, all of her plays draw on classic European dramatic forms while they also incorporate elements of both Afro-American and African culture.

In an equally compelling article Margaret B. Wilkerson (Spring 1983) succinctly analyzes the social statements in all of Hansberry's plays. Wilkerson claims that these statements are a product of an acute consciousness of the life that surrounded her–"the struggles and the anger of poor people" and the social events of the 1950s and 1960s that would have had to spark the conscience of a black woman with her sensibilities. Incorporating Hansberry's special language, Wilkerson's thesis is as follows: "Hansberry's 'sighted eyes' forced her to confront . . . the depravity, cruelty, and . . . foolishness of men's actions, but her 'feeling heart' would not allow her to lose faith in humanity's potential for overcoming its own barbarity."

Both Wilkerson and Carter address Hansberry's feminist concerns, which, they believe, have been largely ignored in the critical literature. Drawing on her explicit statements about women in her writing and discerning feminist themes in her plays, these critics illuminate yet another dimension of Hansberry's social and political analysis.

Steven Carter's article, "Images of Men in Lorraine Hansberry's Writing" (Winter 1985)–consistent with his thesis on the complexity of her art and politics–claims that Hansberry's feminist analysis identifies "ideology" rather than "man" as the enemy. Paralleling her portrayal of the ways in which the ideology of white racism acts on individuals and distorts relations between the races, Hansberry's feminism prompted her to create "convincing and sympathetic male characters" who are "caught in the web of . . . conditioning in male supremacy," ultimately harming themselves as well as women.

Margaret Wilkerson's articles on Hansberry's feminism, "Lorraine Hansberry: The Complete Feminist" (Fourth quarter 1979) and "Lorraine Hansberry: Artist, Activist, Feminist" (1987), are also consistent with her overall thesis that Hansberry's social statements are rooted in her life experience: "Her consciousness of both ethnicity and gender from the very beginning brought awareness of two key forces of conflict and oppression in the contemporary world." Wilkerson argues that Hansberry understood the "hidden alliance between racism and sexism long before it was popular to do so."

Other critics with a feminist perspective have recognized Hansberry's contribution to understanding the condition of women in her insightful portrayals of women's experiences. Helene Keyssar (1984) maintains that although most of the theater experiments of the 1950s and 1960s were "dominated by and identified with particular men," Hansberry emerged, along with other black women playwrights, to draw "female characters with sharp and bold lines." She cites *A Raisin in the Sun* as the drama that "raises the curtain on the complex interaction between racism and sexism."

In her anthology of women in the theater, Karen Malpede (1983) includes two letters by Hansberry that demonstrate her acute observations of the relationship between the sexes as it has been portrayed by two revered playwrights ("On Strindberg and Sexism" and "Arthur Miller, Marilyn Monroe and 'Guilt' "). Malpede also observes Hansberry's ability to create a drama in which "not one central character but a network of . . . compelling personalities" gives a vision of "freedom and hope" and sees this quality in Hansberry's drama as foreshadowing the aesthetic of contemporary feminist theater.

In her article "Feminism as Theme in Twentieth-Century American Women's Drama" (Spring 1984), Sharon Friedman shows how Hansberry's feminist concerns are woven into her exploration of racial and economic oppression. In contrast to critics who regard Hansberry's mother figures as passive, inhibiting, and/or destructive (for example, Vilma Potter [Dec. 1972]), Friedman sees a portrayal of women who "contribute not only to the survival of their families and communities but also the active resistance often necessary to that survival." Furthermore, Hansberry depicts the realities underlying the stereotype of the black matriarch and suggests that the perception of her as "emasculating" is a function of patriarchy. (For a comparative analysis of the image of black women in plays by black playwrights—Hansberry, Childress, Franklin, Milner, Amiri Baraka, and Adrienne Kennedy—see Jeanne-Marie Miller [June 1977]).

The critical evaluations of Lorraine Hansberry have in part been shaped by the mixed blessing of early success. She was the first black woman to have a play staged on Broadway, and with *A Raisin in the Sun* she became the youngest American playwright, the fifth woman, and the first black writer ever to win the New York Drama Critics Circle Award. In his tribute, "Sweet Lorraine" (1969), James Baldwin observes that "her fame was to cause her to be criticized very harshly, very boldly, and very often by both black and white people." Assuming certain limitations of the American psyche, he feels that her work demands the assessment of a "far less guilty and constricted people." Still his own judgment resounds in the claim that "never before in the entire history of the American theater, had so much of the truth of black people's lives been seen on the stage."

The "truth" to which Baldwin bears witness no doubt inspires the recent revivals of Hansberry's plays as well as the resurgence of scholarship of her life and works. In addition to the much anticipated critical biography by Margaret B. Wilkerson, the work of Steven R. Carter promises to bring a close analysis to the plays, interpreting her social and political themes in the context of the dramatic and cultural forms that were her legacy.

Beth Henley
(1952-)

Lisa J. McDonnell
Denison University

PRIMARY BIBLIOGRAPHY

Books

The Miss Firecracker Contest. New York: Theater Communications Group, 1979; New York: Doubleday, 1985. Play.

Crimes of the Heart. New York: Viking/Penguin, 1982. Play.

Am I Blue. New York: Dramatists Play Service, 1982. Play.

The Wake of Jamey Foster. New York: Dramatists Play Service, 1983. Play.

The Lucky Spot. New York: Dramatists Play Service, 1987. Play.

Premiere Productions

Am I Blue. Dallas, Texas, Margo Jones Theater, Southern Methodist University, Fall 1973.

Crimes of the Heart. Louisville, Kentucky, Actors Theatre, 18 Feb. 1979.

The Miss Firecracker Contest. Los Angeles, California, Victory Theatre, Spring 1980.

The Wake of Jamey Foster. Hartford, Connecticut, Hartford Stage Theatre, 1 Jan. 1982.

The Debutante Ball. Costa Mesa, California, South Coast Repertory, 9 Apr. 1985.

The Lucky Spot. Williamstown, Massachusetts, Williamstown Theatre Festival, Summer 1986.

Selected Other

Hymn in the Attic. In *Twenty-Four Hours*, ed. Robert Hurwitt. Berkeley: California Theater Council, 1985. Play.

Nobody's Fool. Island Pictures, 1986. Screenplay.

True Stories, by Henley, David Byrne, and Stephen Tobolowsky. Warner Brothers, 1986. Screenplay.

"A Family Tree," by Henley and Budge Threlkeld. *Trying Times,* PBS, Oct. 1987. Television script.
Crimes of the Heart. De Laurentis Entertainment Group, 1986. Screenplay.

SECONDARY BIBLIOGRAPHY

Bibliography
Coven, Brenda. "Beth Henley." In her *American Women Dramatists of the Twentieth Century: A Bibliography.* Metuchen & London: Scarecrow, 1982, 111-112.

Interviews
Berkvist, Robert. "Act I: the Pulitzer, Act II: Broadway," *New York Times,* 25 Oct. 1981, section 2, pp. 4, 22.
DeVries, Hilary. "Beth Henley Talks about Her Way of Writing Plays," *Christian Science Monitor,* 26 Oct. 1983, pp. 23, 26.
Drake, Sylvie. "Henley's Heart is in the Theater," *Los Angeles Times,* 16 Apr. 1983, section 5, pp. 1, 8.
Freedman, Samuel G. "Beth Henley Writes a 'Real, Real Personal' Movie," *New York Times,* 2 Nov. 1986, section 2, pp. 1, 26.
Jones, John Griffin. "Beth Henley." In *Mississippi Writers Talking,* volume 1, ed. Jones. Jackson, Miss.: University Press of Mississippi, 1982, 169-190.
Lawson, Carol. "Beth Henley's New Offbeat Play Is in Rehearsal," *New York Times,* 14 Sept. 1982, p. C9.
Rochlin, Margy. "The Eccentric Genius of *Crimes of the Heart,*" *Ms.,* 15 (Feb. 1987), 12, 14.
Sessums, Kevin. "Beth Henley," *Interview,* 17 (Feb. 1987), 85.
Walker, Beverly. "Beth Henley," *American Film,* 12 (Dec. 1986), 30-31.

Critical Studies: Major Reviews, Articles and Book Sections
Baskin, Geoffrey. "*The Debutante Ball,*" *Variety,* 318 (17 Apr. 1985), 228.
Beaufort, John. " 'Miss Firecracker Contest': Beth Henley's Latest is Lush, Wacky Drama," *Christian Science Monitor,* 6 June 1984, p. 22.
Beaufort. "A Play That Proves There's No Explaining Awards," *Christian Science Monitor,* 9 Nov. 1981, p. 20. Review of *Crimes of the Heart.*

Beaufort. "Sensitive One-Act Plays at the Circle Rep," *Christian Science Monitor*, 19 Jan. 1982, p. 19. Review of *Am I Blue*.

Blau, Eleanor. "Broadway: Of Jamey Foster, Who Isn't in New Beth Henley Play," *New York Times*, 13 Aug. 1982, p. C2. Review of *The Wake of Jamey Foster*.

Brustein, Robert. "Broadway Inches Forward," *New Republic*, 185 (23 Dec. 1981), 25-27. Review of *Crimes of the Heart*.

Buckley, Peter. "Beating the Odds," *Horizon*, 25 (Dec. 1982), 49-55.

Canby, Vincent. "Henley's 'Crimes of the Heart,' " *New York Times*, 12 Dec. 1986, p. C19.

Colodner, Joel. *"The Miss Firecracker Contest,"* *Theater Journal*, 34 (May 1982), 260-261.

Corliss, Richard. "I Go with What I'm Feeling," *Time*, 119 (8 Feb. 1982), 80.

Cunliffe, Simon. "A Confederacy of Dunces," *New Statesman*, 113 (24 Apr. 1987), 23. Review of *Crimes of the Heart*.

Current Biography Yearbook: 1983, ed. Charles Moritz. New York: Wilson, 1983, 185-188.

Durham, Ayne C. "Beth Henley." In *Critical Survey of Drama [Supplement]*, ed. Frank N. Magill. Englewood Cliffs, N.J.: Salem Press, 1987, 192-197.

Gill, Brendan. "Backstage," *New Yorker*, 57 (16 Nov. 1981), 182-183. Review of *Crimes of the Heart*.

Gill. "Steps Going Down," *New Yorker*, 58 (25 Oct. 1982), 160-161. Review of *The Wake of Jamey Foster*.

Gold, Sylviane. "A Fondness for Freaks," *Wall Street Journal*, 20 June 1984, p. 28. Review of *The Miss Firecracker Contest*.

Goldberg, Robert. "A Mutant Sitcom on PBS," *Wall Street Journal*, 26 Oct. 1987, p. 25. Review of *A Family Tree*.

Gussow, Mel. "Critics' Awards to 'Aloes' and 'Crimes of the Heart,' " *New York Times*, 11 June 1981, p. C17.

Gussow. "Louisville Again Mines Rich Ore of Stage Talent," *New York Times*, 20 Feb. 1979, p. C7. Review of *Crimes of the Heart*.

Haller, Scot. "Her First Play, Her First Pulitzer Prize," *Saturday Review*, 8 (Nov. 1981), 40, 42, 44. Review of *Crimes of the Heart*.

Harbin, Billy J. "Familial Bonds in the Plays of Beth Henley," *Southern Quarterly*, 25 (Spring 1987), 81-94.

Hargrove, Nancy D. "The Tragicomic Vision of Beth Henley's Drama," *Southern Quarterly*, 22 (Summer 1984), 54-70.

Hummler, Richard. *"Confluence,"* *Variety*, 305 (27 Jan. 1982), 88. Review of *Am I Blue*.

Hummler. "*The Wake of Jamey Foster,*" *Variety,* 308 (20 Oct. 1982), 331.

Kael, Pauline. "Families," *New Yorker,* 62 (15 Dec. 1986), 81-82, 85. Review of *Crimes of the Heart.*

Kalem, T. E. "Southern Sibs," *Time,* 118 (16 Nov. 1981), 122. Review of *Crimes of the Heart.*

Kauffmann, Stanley. "Dark Sides," *New Republic,* 195 (15 Dec. 1986), 22-23. Review of *Nobody's Fool.*

Kauffmann. "Lone Stars," *New Republic,* 195 (10 Nov. 1986), 26. Review of *True Stories.*

Kauffmann. "The Three Sisters," *New Republic,* 196 (2 Feb. 1987), 26-27. Review of *Crimes of the Heart.*

Kauffmann. "Two Cheers for Two Plays," *Saturday Review,* 9 (Jan. 1982), 54-55. Review of *Crimes of the Heart.*

Kerr, Walter. "Stage View: Offbeat—But a Beat Too Far," *New York Times,* 15 Nov. 1981, section 2, pp. 3, 31. Review of *Crimes of the Heart.*

Kerr. "Stage View: Two Parts Gimmickry, One Part Discretion," *New York Times,* 24 Jan. 1982, pp. D3, D10. Review of *Am I Blue.*

Kroll, Jack. "The Best of Off-Broadway," *Newsweek,* 99 (25 Jan. 1982), 71, 73. Review of *Am I Blue.*

Kroll. "Birthday in Manhattan," *Newsweek,* 98 (16 Nov. 1981), 123. Review of *Crimes of the Heart.*

Kroll. "New Blood in Louisville," *Newsweek,* 93 (19 Mar. 1979), 92, 96. Review of *Crimes of the Heart.*

Leonard, John. "Something Mild," *New York,* 20 (26 Oct. 1987), 165. Review of *A Family Tree.*

Maslin, Janet. "David Byrne in 'True Stories,'" *New York Times,* 4 Oct. 1986, p. 7.

McDonnell, Lisa J. "Diverse Similitude: Beth Henley and Marsha Norman," *Southern Quarterly,* 25 (Spring 1987), 95-104.

Morrison, Hobe. "*Crimes of the Heart,*" *Variety,* 305 (11 Nov. 1981), 84.

Nightingale, Benedict. "Asking for Trouble," *New Statesman,* 103 (14 May 1982), 30-31. Review of *The Miss Firecracker Contest.*

Nightingale. "Low-powered," *New Statesman,* 105 (27 May 1983), pp. 25-26. Review of *Crimes of the Heart.*

Nightingale. "Stage View: A Landscape That Is Unmistakably by Henley," *New York Times,* 3 June 1984, pp. 3, 7. Review of *The Miss Firecracker Contest.*

Oliver, Edith. "*L'Amour Francais,*" *New Yorker,* 63 (11 May 1987), 80-81. Review of *The Lucky Spot.*

Oliver. "Off Broadway," *New Yorker,* 56 (12 Jan. 1981), 81. Review of *Crimes of the Heart.*

Oliver. "Off Broadway," *New Yorker,* 60 (11 June 1984), 112. Review of *The Miss Firecracker Contest.*

Rich, Frank. "Critic's Notebook: The Varied Use of History in 'Good' and 'Plenty,' " *New York Times,* 11 Nov. 1982, p. C21. Review of *The Wake of Jamey Foster.*

Rich. "Stage: 'Confluence', 3 One-Acters, at Circle Rep," *New York Times,* 11 Jan. 1982, p. C14. Review of *Am I Blue.*

Rich. "Stage: 'Crimes of the Heart', Comedy about 3 Sisters," *New York Times,* 22 Dec. 1980, p. C16.

Rich. "Stage: 'Lucky Spot' by Beth Henley," *New York Times,* 29 Apr. 1987, p. C22.

Rich. "Theater: Beth Henley, 'Wake of Jamey Foster,' " *New York Times,* 132, 15 Oct. 1982, p. C3.

Rich. "The Theater: Beth Henley's 'Crimes of the Heart,' " *New York Times,* 5 Nov. 1981, p. C21.

Rich. "Theater: 'Firecracker', A Beth Henley Comedy," *New York Times,* 28 May 1984, p. 11.

Richards, David. "Olney's Crazy *Contest:* Beth Henley's Comic Visions of the South," *Washington Post,* 8 Aug. 1985, pp. 1B, 10B.

Richards. "Southern Eccentric," *Washington Post,* 2 June 1984, p. 5C. Review of *The Wake of Jamey Foster.*

Richards. "Where's the Drama: Off Broadway, Three Plays and New Life for U.S. Playwrights," *Washington Post,* 8 July 1984, pp. 1H, 5H. Review of *The Miss Firecracker Contest.*

Rosenfeld, Megan. "At Olney, The Best of *Crimes,*" *Washington Post,* 8 June 1984, pp. 1B, 6B.

Sauvage, Leo. "Dark and Shallow Visions," *New Leader,* 65 (15 Nov. 1982), 19-20. Review of *The Wake of Jamey Foster.*

Sauvage. "Reaching for Laughter," *New Leader,* 64 (30 Nov. 1981), 19-20. Review of *Crimes of the Heart.*

Schickel, Richard. "Jagged Flashes of Inspiration," *Time,* 123 (11 June 1984), 80. Review of *The Miss Firecracker Contest.*

Simon, John. "All's Well That Ends *Good,*" *New York,* 15 (25 Oct. 1982), 77-79. Review of *The Wake of Jamey Foster.*

Simon. "Bad Quirks, Good Quirks," *New York,* 20 (11 May 1987), 82-84. Review of *The Lucky Spot.*

Simon. "Living Beings, Cardboard Symbols," *New York*, 14 (16 Nov. 1981), 125-126. Review of *Crimes of the Heart*.

Simon. "Repeaters," *New York*, 17 (4 June 1984), 79-80. Review of *The Miss Firecracker Contest*.

Simon. "Sisterhood is Beautiful," *New York*, 14 (12 Jan. 1981), 42, 44. Review of *Crimes of the Heart*.

Simon. "Slow Flow," *New York*, 15 (25 Jan. 1982), 56-57. Review of *Am I Blue*.

Smith, Douglas. *"The Miss Firecracker Contest,"* *Variety*, 304 (4 Nov. 1981), 84.

Sullivan, Dan. "All Odds, No Evens at the *Ball*," *Los Angeles Times*, 11 Apr. 1985, section 6, pp. 1, 4. Review of *The Debutante Ball*.

Sullivan. "A Glow in the Heart of *Crimes*," *Los Angeles Times*, 19 Apr. 1983, section 6, pp. 1, 4.

Tarbox, Lucia. "Beth Henley." In *Dictionary of Literary Biography Yearbook: 1986*, ed. J. M. Brook. Detroit: Gale Research, 1987, 302-305.

Taylor, Markland. *"The Wake of Jamey Foster,"* *Variety*, 305 (27 Jan. 1982), 90.

Wilson, Edwin. "Beth Henley: Aiming for the Heart," *Wall Street Journal*, 6 Nov. 1981, p. 35.

Wilson. "On Becoming a Nazi; Beth Henley's New Play," *Wall Street Journal*, 20 Oct. 1982, p. 32. Review of *The Wake of Jamey Foster*.

BIBLIOGRAPHICAL ESSAY

Bibliographies and Checklists

Before the publication of this volume the only bibliography of Beth Henley was in Brenda Coven's *American Women Dramatists of the Twentieth Century: A Bibliography* (1982). It contains citations for four plays, two biographical articles, and six reviews. This bibliography is considerably more extensive, containing all primary and secondary listings of Henley material except minor reviews.

Interviews

Because there is as yet no formal biography of Henley, interviews and essays must serve as the main sources of biographical data.

Although published early in Henley's career, John Griffin Jones's 1982 interview with the young playwright remains the most informative. The interview supplies basic data on the dramatist's fam-

Bibliographical Series, Volume 3

ily circumstances and education, explores her limited play-writing experience before the phenomenal success of *Crimes of the Heart,* and provides valuable information on the genesis of that play. Henley declares the major sources of her inspiration to be her family life in Mississippi and the southern oral tradition. She also comments at length upon her literary influences, debunking the then-common opinion that Flannery O'Connor had been of great importance in the development of her style: "I hadn't read Flannery O'Connor. Like, in my first review in Louisville they compared me to her. I hadn't read her. Now I love her. I think she's great." She instead credits Chekhov and Shakespeare as the two major influences on her writing: "Chekhov and Shakespeare, of course, are my favorite playwrights. Chekhov, I feel he influenced me more than anyone else, just with getting lots of people on stage. I don't do anything close to what he does with orchestration. That fascinates me. I also like how he doesn't judge people as much as just shows them in the comic and tragic parts of people. Everything's done with such ease, but it hits so deep."

The most valuable aspect of the interview is its exploration of Henley's attitudes toward her play writing. Henley says that she did not consciously set out to write in the southern grotesque or Gothic mode, but that southern stories interest her because they are always "more vivid and violent" than other stories. She feels that living in the South helps a writer to understand character: "I think that in a small Southern town there's not that much to detract from looking at characters. If you live in Los Angeles there's so much going on that you can't write about it. But here things are small and Southern and insular, and you get a bird's-eye view of people's emotions." She also likes to write about the South for stylistic reasons, "because you can get away with making things more poetic. The style can just be stronger."

Kevin Sessums's February 1987 interview offers the fascinating insight that Henley writes "to survive." In the interview the playwright admits that when she first sat down to write, she "did it out of desperation. It was a lifeline to me." She talks of the importance of taking positive action in life so that one can be in control. She agrees with the character of Jessie Cates in Marsha Norman's play *'night, Mother* that even suicide can be a positive act because it can catapult one out of pain, and she confesses that "I'm always thinking about killing myself. Aren't you? Sometimes I just sit with a knife and wonder if this is the time I'm going to stab myself—you know, when I'm in the kitchen or something." She frequently transfers variations on this scenario to her plays; for example, suicide is an important theme in *Crimes of the Heart.* "The fact that you have the choice to live or die is a triumph, in a way," Henley says. "When my characters try to kill themselves, it's always like, 'Okay, I know how to solve this problem—I'll kill myself! That's what I'll do! I'm in control!' And it's an exhilarating feeling."

Henley's interest in death as a theme is also discussed in a 1982 interview with Carol Lawson of the *New York Times,* "Beth Henley's New Offbeat Play Is in Rehearsal." In discussing *The Wake of Jamey Foster* she reveals that the problem of how people deal with the death of a loved one had been on her mind for a long time, precipitated by her father's death in 1978: "Someone suddenly drops out of your life and you can't talk to him. How do you deal with something that bizarre? And if you have something unresolved with that person, how do you resolve it by yourself? I thought it would be interesting to write about that." She admits that she likes to write about people in stressful situations, because "they make people act bigger than life. They intensify the family situation, which is always volatile anyway." Stressful situations also offer a showcase for the black comedy for which Henley is justly famous.

Two interviews take up the interesting question of Henley's view of herself as a female playwright. Hilary DeVries, in "Beth Henley Talks about Her Way of Writing Plays" (26 Oct. 1983), comments that "sparks are . . . in evidence" when Henley is pressed about why women were slow to gain recognition in creative fields: "Well, picture not going to college. Picture tons of kids. No way to earn a livin' . . . not being able to vote. Think about that. People pretend that life is like the commercials. And it's not." Robert Berkvist, in "Act I: the Pulitzer, Act II: Broadway" (25 Oct. 1981), records a similar reaction. Henley, he tells us, is impatient with those who accuse female playwrights of writing plays that do not have universal appeal: "Women's problems are people's problems . . . I don't think being a woman limits my concerns."

Margy Rochlin, in "The Eccentric Genius of *Crimes of the Heart*" (Feb. 1987), and Sylvie Drake, in "Henley's Heart is in the Theater" (16 Apr. 1983), take up the matter of character creation with the playwright. A key query concerns the extent to which Henley's plays are autobiographical. Henley tells Rochlin that they are only "middling autobiographical. My sisters were very disappointed when they saw *Crimes.* They thought it would be about them." Nevertheless, Henley is acutely aware of how influential her southern up-bringing has been on her characterizations: "Individuality or inde-pendence is applauded in the South much more so than other places. There is a wildness in us that we are always trying to sub-due. It's important to have the ability to tell stories and do outra-geous things like throw steaks out of your plate glass window." Both interviewers also question Henley about the criticism she has re-ceived for creating characters perceived as "too off the wall, too kooky to be believed as real." Henley tells Drake that "my plays aren't realistic. They're born of images of real events. I really can't write reality. . . . They're real because they come from somethin' real." When Rochlin interviews Henley four years later, the play-wright is still trying to counter the charge that she feels only con-tempt for her small-town characters, but her views have undergone a slight shift: "I think it offends some people that I don't cast a blind eye. It's about looking at people for who they are. I don't talk down to them. To say that all small towns are quaint and darling would be like saying, 'All women are sweet, cute, and well be-haved.' "

Samuel G. Freedman's 1986 interview, "Beth Henley Writes a 'Real, Real Personal' Movie," provides a forthright discussion of the themes that dominate both Henley's life and her art: " '*Nobody's Fool* was real, real personal to me. . . . It's about someone who's in de-spair and has made mistakes and is looking for salvation. Theater is a world that understands magic and imagination. Also, there's the sense in theater of the family, an immediate sense of belonging. But a belonging where you can be different.' Or as Cassie in *Nobody's Fool* puts it when she explains why she wants to take an act-ing class: 'Watching that Shakespeare show got me thinking how good it would be to be someone other than me. Even if it was for an hour or a half hour.' "

Now that Henley has established herself the time has come for some in-depth, analytical interviews. The lengthy Jones interview, while full of basic data, was conducted when the playwright was in the earliest stages of her career. Briefer, more recent interviews have revealed her developing consciousness of her own literary style, her themes, and her place in the theater as a woman and as a southerner.

Critical Studies: Major Reviews, Articles, and Book Sections
The most valuable background article on Henley is Scot
Haller's "Her First Play, Her First Pulitzer Prize" (Nov. 1981).
Haller gives good coverage of Henley's life, her development as a
playwright, and the narrative line of *Crimes of the Heart*. He finds
Crimes of the Heart to be an unusual hybrid of naturalism and
absurdism: "She has chosen the family drama as her framework–
the play takes place entirely in the MaGrath kitchen–but she has populated the household with bizarre characters. In effect, she has
mated the conventions of the naturalistic play with the unconventional protagonists of absurdist comedy." He also notes that Henley
is one of a growing number of author/actors in contemporary theater; the group also includes Christopher Durang, Sam Shepard,
and Bill C. Davis. Playwright Frederick Bailey, an old friend of
Henley's, remarks that the combination of authorship and acting allows her to approach a play "from the point of view of theater, not literature." Melvin Bernhardt, director of the Broadway production
of *Crimes of the Heart,* observes that Henley the playwright "hears
the fun in what people say. And as an actress, she then knows how
to make it stageworthy." Henley herself explains the phenomenon
at its most basic level: "I think of things *I'd* like to do on stage," she
says.
     Haller also delves fascinatingly into Henley's handling of her
unconventional characters: "Like Flannery O'Connor, Henley creates ridiculous characters but doesn't ridicule them. Like Lanford
Wilson, she examines ordinary people with extraordinary compassion. Treating the eccentricities of her characters with empathy, she
manages to render strange turns of events not only believable but af-
fecting." Jon Jory, the director who staged the first production of
Crimes of the Heart at Actors Theater in Louisville, Kentucky, observes in the piece that "most American playwrights want to expose
human beings. Beth Henley embraces them." He also notes that
what initially impressed him when he selected her play as a co-
winner of the Great American Playwrighting Contest was "this immensely sensitive and complex view of relationships. And the comedy didn't come from one character but from between characters.
That's very unusual for a young writer."
     Haller also takes up the question of whether Henley would de-
velop into an enduring playwright or become a one-hit wonder.
After reviewing the latter phenomenon in recent theater history, exemplified by the experiences of Robert Marasco (*Child's Play*), Jason

Miller (*That Championship Season*), and D. L. Coburn (*The Gin Game*), Haller concludes that Henley is in for the long haul, quoting director Jory once again: "When a writer portrays relationships as accurately as Beth does, you've got to assume she's a long distance runner."

With the exception of scholarly articles, the best source of critical analysis of Henley's plays is a series of reviews in *New York* by John Simon. An incisive (and frequently scathing) critic, Simon expresses such admiration for Henley's talent in his reviews of *Crimes of the Heart* that scholar/critic/director Robert Brustein feels compelled to comment upon it in his own critique, "Broadway Inches Forward" (23 Dec. 1981): "Only 29 years old, Miss Henley already displays enough winning theatrical manners to melt the stoniest heart (John Simon's, for example)." Indeed, precious few of Simon's reviews for his *New York* audience employ words as kind as those he uses to open a 12 January 1981 review of *Crimes of the Heart:* "From time to time a play comes along that restores one's faith in the theater, that justifies endless evenings spent, like some unfortunate Beckett character, chin-deep in trash." In his several reviews of the play Simon demonstrates a sensitivity to the characters of the three sisters and an understanding of the dynamic that operates among them that has been surprisingly rare in critical judgments of the play. In "Sisterhood is Beautiful" Simon asserts that "the three sisters are wonderful creations: Lenny out of Chekhov, Babe out of Flannery O'Connor, and Meg out of Tennessee Williams in one of his more benign moods. But 'out of' must not be taken to mean imitation; it is just a legitimate literary genealogy. Ultimately, the sisters belong to Miss Henley and themselves. Their lives are lavish with incident, their idiosyncrasies insidiously compelling, their mutual loyalty and help (though often frazzled) able to nudge heartbreak toward heartlift." In "Living Beings, Cardboard Symbols" (16 Nov. 1981), Simon further develops the dynamic of the sisterly bond: "For this is one of those rare plays about a family love that you can believe and participate in, because that love is never sappy or piously cloying, but rather irreverently prankish and often even acerb. Warmhearted Lenny is also an irritating fussbudget and martyr; Meg is selfish and irresponsible as well as sensible and ultimately generous; Babe, though blessed with the queer wisdom of the unreconstructed child, is also obtuse and infuriating. It is the ties of sympathy–or, if you will, the bloodline–among these three that

101

form the play's crazy, convoluted, but finally exhilarating tracery: sisterly trajectories that diverge, waver, and explosively reunite."

Simon is not as laudatory in his reviews of Henley's subsequent plays; he finds her too frequently yielding to a proclivity toward "bizarre cuteness" (25 Jan. 1982) and comments ruefully in "All's Well That Ends *Good*" (25 Oct. 1982) that "it may be that this tragicomic whimsicality has become an incipient cliché, or it may be that Miss Henley has become too prodigiously adept at conjuring it up without anchoring it in solid, universal humanity . . . there is too much head on too small beer." His recommendations to Henley in his reviews of *The Miss Firecracker Contest*, *Am I Blue*, and *The Wake of Jamey Foster* are pithily summed up in the conclusion to his review of the last: "A little more human ballast, please, Miss Henley, and a bit more plain, earthbound purpose, and all should be well again." Henley's most recent stage play, *The Lucky Spot*, restores Simon's faith; although he finds it (11 May 1987) less successful than *Crimes of the Heart*, he feels that it is by far the best play she has written since and commends it for having "the same offhand energy, the same unwitting wit with which the characters confront their predicaments, the same pathos that gets drowned in humor rather than tears, and (something that *Crimes* hasn't) the tremendous interplay of the two warring spouses with its two rousing climaxes." He is delighted that Henley's gift for "redeeming the *un*lucky spots in her writing with a splendidly sudden throwaway line remains sovereign," and he finds the play, while "small and not unflawed," one that "breathes, palpitates, and pleases."

Another critic who has written an estimable series of Henley reviews is Frank Rich of the *New York Times*. Simon and Rich tend to agree in their evaluation of the plays, but Rich contributes a useful discussion (5 Nov. 1981) of Henley's comic technique: "She builds from a foundation of wacky but consistent logic until she's constructed a funhouse of perfect-pitch language and ever-accelerating misfortune. By Act III, we're so at home in the crazy geography of the characters' lives that we're laughing at the slightest prick of blood. At that point Miss Henley starts kindling comic eruptions on the most unlikely lines–'Old Grandaddy's in a coma!'–without even trying. That's what happens when a playwright creates a world and lets the audience inhabit it." Rich, like Simon, eschews the popular critical notion that Henley resorts to sick humor to garner cheap laughs, and he accurately delineates the true source of her comedy: "The playwright gets her laughs not because she tells sick jokes, but because she refuses to tell jokes at all. Her characters always stick to the unvarnished truth, at any price, never holding back a single gory detail. And the truth–when captured like lightning in a bottle–is far funnier than any invented wisecracks."

Stanley Kauffmann moves away from the usual critical emphasis on Henley's comedy to explore the darker elements of her work. He is dismayed that reviewers perceive Henley not as a serious dramatist but as a parodist, while he sees her as a "quietly tenacious pursuer of horror, a writer shaken into pitch-black comedy by the buried terrors in the superficially smooth, tabby-cat lives she has seen" (Jan. 1982). He feels that Henley has struck a rich dramatic lode in "the tension between the fierce lurking lunacy underlying the small-town life she knows so well and the sunny surface that tries to accommodate it." She provides no resolution for the tension but instead offers a microcosmic view of human chaos with a "ludicrously horrifying honesty" that Kauffmann applauds. He draws similar conclusions in "Dark Sides" (15 Dec. 1986), his review of Henley's screenplay, *Nobody's Fool,* which he calls a film about "helplessness and its counterfeit armor, about a young woman in the grip of a destructive sexual attraction who is ultimately saved by another lover–who may or may not turn out to be equally hurtful. Henley even underscores the dark basic threats in the story–in the world–with such touches as Cassie's visits to a friend who is now gravely disturbed mentally."

In the wide field of film reviews of *Crimes of the Heart,* only Pauline Kael's is valuable; the others are shallow, standard fare. Even Kael's critique (15 Dec. 1986) is disappointingly thin in its analysis of *Crimes of the Heart* in its screenplay incarnation, but it does an excellent job of exploring the characters of the three sisters as interpreted by actresses Diane Keaton, Jessica Lange, and Sissy Spacek.

For the reader who wants a general overview of Henley and her work, there are a number of good book sections available, containing various mixtures of biographical data, general literary analysis, and selections from contemporary criticism. The best overview is Lucia Tarbox's essay in the *Dictionary of Literary Biography Yearbook: 1986* (1987) which gives chronological listing of Henley's published plays, play productions, screenplays, and television scripts; an interesting and clearly drawn biography of the playwright; and analyses of *Crimes of the Heart* and *Nobody's Fool.* The single drawback is the dearth of references for further research. For more detailed biographical data, the unsigned essay in *Current Biography Yearbook:*

1983 (1983) traces Henley's personal history up to the New York staging of *Am I Blue* in January 1982; additional material of interest includes eight references for further research and the address of
Henley's literary agent. A briefer but still valuable tool is Ayne C.
Durham's "Beth Henley" in *Critical Survey of Drama* (1987). The
piece has the advantage of being the most recent of the overviews
and includes general analytical discussions of *The Miss Firecracker Contest* and *The Wake of Jamey Foster* in addition to *Crimes of the Heart*. It
lists five of the best critical articles on Henley and gives an incomplete listing of her screenplays and teleplays through 1986.

Only three scholarly articles on Henley's work have been published as of this writing, all in *Southern Quarterly*. This suggests that,
despite Henley's success on the New York stage, scholars still view
her primarily as a regional writer. The lack of scholarly attention
may also have something to do with the fact that Henley is a
woman. As Billy J. Harbin indicates in his Spring 1987 article, "Familial Bonds in the Plays of Beth Henley," it has taken female playwrights some time to "get out of the small spaces to which they had
largely been relegated and into the main houses," so they may be experiencing similar difficulties getting notice in scholarly journals.
Harbin's article is valuable because it places Henley in the context
of the women writers movement of the 1960s, 1970s, and 1980s.
He explains how female playwrights have had to "turn from the radical experimentation of their predecessors and [seek] ways to make
use of traditional structures and modes without sacrificing the integrity of what they [have] to say" in order to achieve commercial and
critical acceptance. While the awarding of Pulitzer Prizes to Henley
for *Crimes of the Heart* (1981) and to Marsha Norman for *'night,
Mother* (1983) "helped consolidate the phenomenon of a women writers movement and the emergence of a southern writers contingent," and while "feminists applauded the breakthrough that the Pulitzer awards represented, they also noted that both plays were in a
conventional realistic mode, and that neither challenged custom, either aesthetically or politically. They [feminists] pointed out that
the innovative work of earlier risk-taking dramatists, such as Megan
Terry, Rochelle Owens and Maria Irene Fornes, had been ignored
as influences in favor of the 'safer' tradition of male realists."

Harbin comments that the success of *Crimes of the Heart* "seems
to underscore the notion that the marketable play cannot stray off
convention's beaten path"; he also agrees with Tina Howe's assertion that "the serious [female] writer [must] cover her scent" and

holds that "Beth Henley's grave vision in *Crimes of the Heart* is both masked by and realized through a depiction of the ludicrous." Harbin then notes significantly that "Henley's southern roots . . . regional settings and comic emphasis upon the peculiar in ordinary situations [has] led many critics to admire her whimsical imagination and to underestimate the significant implications of her humor. Furthermore, in productions of the play, the comic clues in the script, of which there are many, have not only been seized but enlarged upon, especially in regional dialect and eccentric behavior, all but engulfing the serious terrain that lies beneath the ludicrous gesture." Harbin sets out to redress this wrong by exploring the more serious themes of Henley's plays through the unpublished *The Debutante Ball*. He finds that in all of her plays, "Henley takes up themes related to the disintegration of traditional ideals, such as the breakup of families, the quest for emotional and spiritual fulfillment, and the repressive social forces within a small southern community." Along the way he deals with a number of key themes in great detail, including a fascinating discussion of "the metaphoric use of food and drink as narcotics . . . to numb the pain of loneliness, familial disintegration and spiritual emptiness." Although the themes he discusses recur in all of Henley's plays, his treatment of *Crimes of the Heart* is particularly fine.

The first scholarly article to appear on Henley's work was Nancy D. Hargrove's "The Tragicomic Vision of Beth Henley's Drama" (Summer 1984). Hargrove, like Harbin three years later, is obviously concerned by the critical overemphasis on the comic elements of the plays and neglect of the more serious aspects. She notes that the plots of *Crimes of the Heart, The Miss Firecracker Contest,* and *The Wake of Jamey Foster* express similar negative themes: "Life is portrayed as painful and lonely, full of cruelty, suffering, shattered dreams, and unattained ambitions. . . . Human beings [are depicted] as unhappy, defeated, isolated, and cruel. . . . Many of the human relationships based on romantic love cause pain and anguish, rather than furnishing support and warmth." To reinforce this pessimistic view of humanity Henley employs several groups of symbols, among them a "staggering number of physical deformities and diseases" and "animal symbolism . . . emphasizing the bestial qualities of humanity and the universe." However, Hargrove concedes that "Henley's drama is not entirely negative in its vision of the human condition. In fact, one of the dominant themes in all three works is the value of love, of human solidarity, especially through the family. Love not only sustains the characters but occasionally lends meaning and even joy to their otherwise bleak lives." She also notes that "a final positive element is that the major characters do learn something in the process of the plays. . . . That each play ends with two or more characters joined together in a bond of human solidarity . . . suggests an affirmation of humanity's ability to persevere and to endure, if not achieve some kind of victory or success. Her portrayal of the human condition seems . . . realistic, painfully honest, and yet consistently compassionate." Also notable in Hargrove's article is her discussion of the "nightmare" structure of the three plays.

Lisa J. McDonnell's spring 1987 article "Diverse Similitude: Beth Henley and Marsha Norman" appeared with Harbin's in a special issue of *Southern Quarterly* devoted to southern women playwrights. McDonnell compares the work of the two most prominent New Wave women dramatists who are "coupled in the public consciousness as Southern, female, Pulitzer Prize winners," yet are deemed the "most dissimilar" of the New Wave group by *New York Times* critic Mel Gussow. Using Henley's *Crimes of the Heart, The Miss Firecracker Contest,* and *The Wake of Jamey Foster* and Norman's *Getting Out* and *'night, Mother* as the basis for comparison, McDonnell finds that Henley and Norman "share their remarkable gift for storytelling, their use of family drama as a framework, their sensitive delineation of character and relationships, their employment of a bizarre Gothic humor and their use of the southern vernacular to demonstrate the poetic lyricism of the commonplace." She also finds that the two playwrights differ in a number of significant ways: "While both focus on their protagonists' quests for self-determination, they view very differently the important familial role in these quests. While both portray characters and relationships insightfully, Henley is affectionate, if mildly ridiculing in her depictions; Norman, realistic and frequently harsh. While both employ Gothic humor in their plays, Henley's predominant mode is wild and outrageous, Norman's, dry and sardonic. They even approach their craft from different perspectives: Henley writes comedy with serious dimensions, Norman, serious drama with comic overtones; Henley's plays [written by an actress] demonstrate a more 'theatrical' orientation, Norman's [written by a teacher], a more 'literary' bent." McDonnell asserts that while Henley and Norman may be currently "coupled in the public consciousness," it is obvious "that with all their similarities, they have already, relatively early in their careers, set themselves on paths that are likely to become increasingly divergent." Other points of interest in the article are its discussion of the southern aspects of the plays: southern oral tradition, Gothic humor, and emphasis on the importance of family ties; and its examination of "storytelling" as a key narrative technique.

While the themes and techniques identified by the three scholars in *Southern Quarterly* encompass most of Henley's still relatively narrow range, reviews of the plays indicate the need for additional study, especially in the area of feminist criticism. For example, almost without exception reviewers have passed over Babe's explanation (in *Crimes of the Heart*) that she had an affair with Willie Jay because she "was so lonely," and that she shot Zackery after a history of severe physical abuse that spanned "the past four years"—and then only after Zackery assaulted Willie Jay. The reviewers concentrated on her earlier flip and evasive comment, "I didn't like his looks! I just didn't like his stinking looks!" and ignored the more serious factors involved. Scholars have begun to treat such issues, but much more work is needed.

Adrienne Kennedy

(1931-)

Lois More Overbeck
Atlanta, Georgia

PRIMARY BIBLIOGRAPHY

Books

Cities in Bezique. New York: French, 1969. Comprises *The Owl Answers* and *A Beast Story*. Plays.

Funnyhouse of a Negro. New York: French, 1969. Play.

The Lennon Play: In His Own Write, by Kennedy, John Lennon, and Victor Spinetti. New York: Simon & Schuster, 1969. Adapted from Lennon's books, *In His Own Write* and *A Spaniard in the Works*.

People Who Led to My Plays. New York: Knopf, 1987. Autobiography.

Premiere Productions

Funnyhouse of a Negro. New York, Circle-in-the-Square Theatre, workshop production, 1962.

The Owl Answers. Westport, Conn., White Barn Theatre, 1963.

A Rat's Mass. Boston, Theatre Company of Boston, 12 Apr. 1966.

The Lennon Play: In His Own Write. London, National Theatre Workshop, Dec. 1967; Albany, N.Y., Summer Theatre, Aug. 1969.

A Lesson in a Dead Language. London, Royal Court Theatre, 28 Apr. 1968; New York, Theatre Genesis, 1970.

Sun: A Poem for Malcolm X Inspired By His Murder. London, Royal Court Theatre, 1968; New York, La Mama Experimental Theatre Club, 1970.

A Beast Story. New York, Public Theatre, 12 Jan. 1969.

Boats. Los Angeles, The Forum, 1969.

Evening with Dead Essex. New York, American Place Theatre Workshop, 1973.

A Movie Star Has to Star in Black and White, New York, Public Theatre Workshop, 1976.
A Lancashire Lad. Albany, N.Y., Empire State Plaza Performing Center, May 1980.
Orestes and Electra. New York, Juilliard School of Music, 1980.
Black Children's Day. Providence, R.I., Brown University, Nov. 1980.

Selected Periodical Publications
Sun: A Poem for Malcolm X Inspired by His Murder, Scripts, 1 (Nov. 1971), 51-56. Play.
"Becoming a Playwright," *American Theatre*, 4 (Feb. 1988), 26-27. Autobiographical essay.

Selected Other
A Lesson in a Dead Language. In *Collision Course*, ed. Edward Parone. New York: Random House, 1968, 33-40. Play.
A Rat's Mass. In *New Black Playwrights*, ed. William Couch. Baton Rouge: Louisiana State University Press, 1968, 61-70. Play.
A Movie Star Has to Star in Black and White. In *Wordplays 3*. New York: Performing Arts Journal Publications, 1984. Play.

Collection
Adrienne Kennedy in One Act. Minneapolis: University of Minnesota Press, 1988. Comprises *Funnyhouse of a Negro, The Owl Answers, A Lesson in a Dead Language, A Rat's Mass, Sun, A Movie Star Has to Star in Black and White, Greek Adaptations: Electra; Orestes*. Plays.

SECONDARY BIBLIOGRAPHY

Bibliographies
Arata, Esther Spring, and Nicholas John Rotoli. *Black American Playwrights, 1800 to the Present: A Bibliography*. Metuchen, N.J.: Scarecrow, 1976, 127-129.
Arata, Marlene J. Erickson, Sandra Dewitz, and Mary Linse Alexander. *More Black American Playwrights: A Bibliography*. Metuchen, N.J. & London: Scarecrow, 1978, 130-132.
French, William P., Michel J. Fabre, Amritjit Singh, and Geneviève E. Fabre. *Afro-American Poetry and Drama, 1760-1975*. Detroit: Gale Research, 1979, 389-390.

Hatch, James V., and OMANii Abdullah. *Black Playwrights, 1823-1977: An Annotated Bibliography of Plays.* New York & London: Bowker, 1977, 137-138.

Interviews
Betsko, Kathleen, and Rachel Koenig. "Adrienne Kennedy." In their *Interviews with Contemporary Women Playwrights.* New York: Morrow, 1987, 246-258.

Dunning, Jennifer. "Adrienne Kennedy Decides That the Classroom's the Thing," *New York Times,* 29 Dec. 1977, p. C13.

Hals, Hilton. "Stardust Memories: Adrienne Kennedy Shows and Tells," *Village Voice,* 3 Nov. 1987, p. 61.

Lehman, Lisa. "A Growth of Images," *Drama Review,* 21 (Dec. 1977), 41-48.

"Where are the Women Playwrights?," *New York Times,* 20 May 1973, section 2, pp. 1, 3. Brief interviews with Gretchen Cryer, Rosalyn Drexler, Lillian Hellman, Kennedy, Jean Kerr, Clare Boothe Luce, Rochelle Owens, and Renee Taylor.

Critical Studies: Major Reviews, Articles, and Book Sections
Abramson, Doris E. *Negro Playwrights in the American Theatre 1925-1950.* New York & London: Columbia University Press, 1969, 279, 281, 293.

Barnes, Clive. " 'A Rat's Mass' Weaves Drama of Poetic Fabric," *New York Times,* 1 Nov. 1960, p. 39.

Barnes. "Theater: 'Cities in Bezique' Arrives at the Public," *New York Times,* 13 Jan. 1969, p. 26.

Benston, Kimberly W. "*Cities in Bezique*: Adrienne Kennedy's Expressionistic Vision," *CLA Journal,* 20 (Dec. 1976), 235-244.

Blau, Herbert. "The American Dream in American Gothic." In his *The Eye of Prey: Subversions of the Postmodern.* Bloomington & Indianapolis: Indiana University Press, 1987, 42-64.

Brown, Lorraine A. " 'For the Characters are Myself ': Adrienne Kennedy's *Funnyhouse of A Negro,*" *Negro American Literature Forum,* 9 (Fall 1975), 86-88.

Case, Sue-Ellen. *Feminism and Theatre.* New York: Methuen, 1988, 100-102, 129.

Clurman, Harold. Review of *Funnyhouse of a Negro, Nation,* 198 (10 Feb. 1964), 154.

Cohn, Ruby. *New American Dramatists 1960-1980.* New York: Grove Press, 1982, 108-115.

Curb, Rosemary K. "Fragmented Selves in Adrienne Kennedy's *Funnyhouse of a Negro* and *The Owl Answers*," *Theatre Journal*, 32 (May 1980), 180-195.

Curb. " 'Lesson I Bleed.' " In *Women in American Theatre*, ed. Helen Krich Chinoy and Linda Walsh Jenkins. New York: Crown, 1981, 50-56.

Curb. "Re/cognition, Re/presentation, Re/creation in Woman-Conscious Drama: The Seer, The Seen, The Scene, The Obscene," *Theatre Journal*, 37 (Oct. 1985), 302-316.

Duberman, Martin. "Theater 69," *Partisan Review*, 36, no. 3 (1969), 483-500.

Fabre, Geneviève. *Le Théâtre Noir aux Etats-Unis*. Paris: Centre National de la Recherche Scientifique, 1982. Translated and abridged by Melvin Dixon as *Drumbeats, Masks, and Metaphor: Contemporary Afro-American Theater*. Cambridge, Mass. & London: Harvard University Press, 1983, 14, 110-111, 119-122, 218.

Fletcher, Winona L. "Who Put the 'Tragic' in the Tragic Mulatto?" In *Women in American Theatre*, ed. Chinoy and Jenkins. New York: Crown, 1981, 260-266.

Harrison, Paul Carter. *The Drama of Nommo*. New York: Grove, 1972, 216-220.

Hatch, James. "Speak to Me in Those Old Words, You Know, Those La-La Words, Those Tung-Tung Sounds (Some African Influences on the Afro-American Theatre)," *Yale/Theatre*, 8 (Fall 1976), 25-34.

Hay, Samuel A. "African-American Drama, 1950-1970," *Negro History Bulletin*, 36 (Jan. 1973), 5-8.

Houghton, Norris. *The Exploding Stage: An Introduction to Twentieth Century Drama*. New York: Weybright & Talley, 1971, 198.

Jackson, Oliver. Introduction to *Kuntu Drama: Plays of the African Continuum*, ed. Paul Carter Harrison. New York: Grove, 1974.

Kerr, Walter. "Some Day Adrienne Kennedy Will . . . ," *New York Times*, 19 Jan. 1969, section 2, p. 3.

Keyssar, Helene. *Feminist Theatre: An Introduction to Plays of Contemporary British and American Women*. London: Macmillan, 1984; New York: Grove, 1985, 12, 20, 71, 102, 109-112, 120, 152.

Lewis, Allan. *American Plays and Playwrights of the Contemporary Theatre*. New York: Crown, 1965. Revised edition, 1970, 236, 253.

Miller, Jeanne-Marie A. "Images of Black Women in Plays by Black Playwrights," *CLA Journal*, 20 (June 1977), 494-507. Collected as "Black Women in Plays by Black Playwrights" in *Women in American Theatre*, ed. Chinoy and Jenkins. New York: Crown, 1981, 254-259.

Mitchell, Loften. *Black Drama: The Story of the American Negro in Theatre*. New York: Hawthorn, 1967, 198-199, 216-217.

Oliver, Clinton F. Introduction to *Contemporary Black Drama: From "A Raisin in the Sun" to "No Place to Be Somebody,"* ed. Oliver and Stephanie Sills. New York: Scribners, 1971.

Oliver, Edith. Review of *Cities in Bezique*, *New Yorker*, 44 (25 Jan. 1969), 77.

Oliver, Edith. Review of *Funnyhouse of a Negro*, *New Yorker*, 39 (25 Jan. 1964), 76-78.

Poland, Albert, and Bruce Mailman, eds. *The Off Off Broadway Book: The Plays, People, Theatre*. Indianapolis: Bobbs-Merrill, 1972, xi-xiv.

Rich, Frank. "Stage: 'Lancashire Lad' for Children," *New York Times*, 21 May 1980, section 2, p. 30.

Rudin, Seymour. "Theatre Chronicle: Winter-Spring 1969," *Massachusetts Review*, 10 (Summer 1969), 586-587.

Simon, John. *Uneasy Stages: A Chronicle of the New York Theater, 1963-1973*. New York: Random House, 1975, 181, 185-187.

Sontag, Susan. "Going to the Theater (and the Movies)," *Partisan Review*, 31 (Spring 1964), 284-294.

Talbot, William. "Every Negro in His Place," *Drama Critique*, 7 (Spring 1964), 92-95.

Taubman, Howard. *The Making of the American Theatre*. New York: Coward McCann, 1965, 334-335.

Tener, Robert L. "Theatre of Identity: Adrienne Kennedy's Portrait of the Black Woman," *Studies in Black Literature*, 6 (Summer 1975), 1-5.

Turner, Darwin T. "Negro Playwrights and the Urban Negro," *CLA Journal*, 12 (Sept. 1968), 19-25.

Wilkerson, Margaret B. "Adrienne Kennedy." In *Dictionary of Literary Biography*, volume 38: *Afro-American Writers After 1955: Dramatists and Prose Writers*, ed. Thadious M. Davis and Trudier Harris. Detroit: Gale, 1985, 162-169.

Wilkerson. "Diverse Angles of Vision: Two Black Women Playwrights," *Theatre Annual*, 40 (1985), 91-114.

Williams, Mance. *Black Theatre in the 1960's and 1970's: A Historical-Critical Analysis of the Movement*. Westport, Conn. & London: Greenwood, 1985, 7, 133, 142-148.

BIBLIOGRAPHICAL ESSAY

Bibliographies

While no book or essay devoted solely to the writings of Adrienne Kennedy has been published, several bibliographies on Afro-American drama published in the late 1970s include useful sections on her work. Esther Spring Arata and Nicholas John Rotoli's *Black American Playwrights, 1800 to the Present* (1976) presents a listing of Kennedy plays published separately and in anthologies through 1975. Arata and Rotoli also cite five critical analyses of Kennedy's work, ten articles on individual plays, and ten reviews. Arata, Marlene J. Erickson, Sandra Dewitz, and Mary Linse Alexander's 1978 volume increases the number of critical citations but deletes all but one review. James V. Hatch and OMANii Abdullah's *Black Playwrights, 1823-1977* (1977) lists Kennedy's published work through 1976 with brief annotations. William P. French, Michel J. Fabre, Amritjit Singh, and Geneviève E. Fabre's *Afro-American Poetry and Drama, 1760-1975* (1979) gives an annotated list of Kennedy's published and unpublished plays through 1975. The volume also contains informative lists of general studies about Afro-American drama, periodicals devoted to Afro-American drama, anthologies, and critical monographs.

Interviews and Autobiography

No biography or book-length critical study of Adrienne Kennedy has been published, but her 1987 autobiography, *People Who Led to My Plays*, and her published interviews together provide much useful biographical and critical information. "Autobiographical work is the only thing that interests me," Kennedy declared in a 1977 interview with Lisa Lehman. Writing was a "figuring out of the 'why' of things" and "an outlet for inner, psychological confusion and questions stemming from childhood." In the interview Kennedy explained the creative process as "a growth of images," recounting how the idea for her play *A Rat's Mass* originated in a haunting dream and took shape in response to real-life events such as her brother's death. The great rush of plays that "exploded" from Kennedy after her first, *Funnyhouse of a Negro*, premiered in 1962, came from ideas she had been pondering for years.

In her autobiography the young Kennedy is steeped in varied and sometimes conflicting cultural influences. A close student of English literature, she was raised in a middle-class black family and felt white oppression. Her childhood—Snow White, *Jane Eyre*, her mother's miscarriage, the bombing of Pearl Harbor, games of Old Maid—continually echoes in her plays. Being well educated helped her to be creative. Giotto's emotive use of color in paintings stimulated her own feelings of pain and conflict; Plato's concept of anamnesis, or recollection as a source of knowledge, and such "pop" events as the Wolf Man's movie metamorphosis influenced her use of remembrances to create multi-layered characters; the rhythms of biblical Psalms found their way into her monologues; an understanding of the power of repetition was learned from Poe; and Aristotle explained to her that the use of metaphor was a "sign of genius" because it implied an "intuitive perception of the similarity in dissimilars." She considered her 1960-1961 journey to West Africa to be a turning point in her literary life, when the conflict between her exterior and interior lives became clear. In Ghana (Lumumba's death happened "just when I had discovered the place of my ancestors") during the time it became a republic, she read Chinua Achebe, Amos Tutuola, Wole Soyinka, and Efna Sutherland and began *Funnyhouse of a Negro*.

In a brief autobiographical essay, "Becoming a Playwright" (Feb. 1988), Kennedy tells the story of the 1962 development of *Funnyhouse of a Negro* from the Edward Albee drama workshop. Her impulse had been to excise material in the play that she considered to be too dark and violent, but Albee talked her out of withdrawing it by saying, " 'A playwright is someone who lets his guts out on the stage.' " She was reluctant but let the anguish of earlier drafts back into the play for its workshop premiere at the Circle-in-the-Square Theatre in New York.

In a 1987 interview with Kathleen Betsko and Rachel Koenig, Kennedy expounds further upon her literary development. The African experience gave her time to write; she discovered "a sense of power and strength" in her connection to West Africa. There were other developments: "A huge breakthrough" came when "my main characters began to have other personas," unlike her own. Another came when she gave up the notion that she had to write full-length plays. Also, Kennedy discovered from literary models (Edward Albee, Federico Garcia Lorca, Tennessee Williams) that she had "an affinity for symbolism as a way of surviving." She found that her notes on dreams "had a vitality that my writing did not." Although art became for her a kind of refuge, she is nonetheless disturbed by interpretations of her work that "dissect my psyche." To early charges that she was an "irrelevant black writer" she countered, "I knew my alliances" (her father, a Morehouse College graduate, was a spokesman for the NAACP). She claims not to have been affected by the women's movement ("I hate groups") and instead claims that her work has been influenced by Picasso, Cocteau and French film, the monologues of Eugene O'Neill, the plays of Alice Childress, and the choreography of Martha Graham ("everything seemed to come out of darkness. People played many parts, she used a lot of black and white, [and there was] . . . fluidity and a deemphasis on the narrative").

Critical Studies: Major Reviews, Articles, and Book Sections
Early reviews of Adrienne Kennedy's *Funnyhouse of a Negro* were very favorable. Edith Oliver (25 Jan. 1964) describes the play as a series of "hallucinations" in which the character of Sarah impersonates four eminent people who "materialize onstage, and seem to turn on her, mimicking and mocking her, and at times speaking her disordered mind." Sarah is an unreliable narrator, obsessed with her hair as an image of Negro identity and consumed with grief and guilt over her treatment of her father. Oliver calls the play "strong and original." Harold Clurman (10 Feb. 1964) considers the play to be a universal statement that speaks to "all people who suffer the pathology of minorities. Their number extends far beyond the boundaries of race."

Kennedy's early work also warranted mention in major critical overviews of the time. In *The Making of the American Theatre* (1965) Howard Taubman briefly comments on the emergence of black dramatists from Edward Albee's Playwrights' Unit, linking Adrienne Kennedy and LeRoi Jones (Amiri Baraka) as "young Negroes with a scorching report on the agony of being a Negro and an alien in one's own land." Loften Mitchell, in *Black Drama: The Story of the American Negro in Theatre* (1967), defends Kennedy's work from the criticism that it is too personal to represent accurately the black condition, writing that it is "unrealistic to expect a Negro writer" to solve social problems in creative work.

On the other hand, Darwin T. Turner, in "Negro Playwrights and the Urban Negro" (Sept. 1968), is less appreciative of the personal aspects of *Funnyhouse of a Negro*. He writes, "She dramatizes the psychoses of a Negro woman" who "in delusions. . . . voices her hate for the dark-skinned man who, by marrying her white mother, made her Negro." The epilogue to Doris E. Abramson's *Negro Play-*

wrights in the American Theatre 1925-1950 (1969) places *Funnyhouse of a Negro* within the absurdist tradition as described by critic Martin Esslin. She remarks that Kennedy's "move from outer to inner reality" was "working in a genre very new to Negro playwrights, that of . . . somber interior fantasy."

Allan Lewis, in *American Plays and Playwrights of the Contemporary Theatre* (1965; revised, 1970), declares that the production of plays by Kennedy and LeRoi Jones in the mid 1960s signaled "a literary awakening and a source of untapped talent." He calls *Funnyhouse of a Negro* "less a play than a visualized nightmare." But Lewis adds that *Cities in Bezique*, the title given to the 1969 publication of two of Kennedy's one-act plays, *The Owl Answers* and *A Beast Story*, displays a "continuing power with words, a poetic flair, and a preoccupation with the inner disturbances that beset the black in his search for identity."

Martin Duberman (1969) claims that Kennedy's *Cities in Bezique* demonstrates private fantasies, fuzzy images, and "self-enclosed" language that mark her distance from the more traditional black theater of Lorraine Hansberry, Ed Bullins, and Lonne Elder III. Seymour Rudin's "Theatre Chronicle: Winter-Spring 1969" (Summer 1969) also compares Kennedy's style with Elder's, but Rudin claims that "poetic sensibility" is inadequately displayed in her plays. John Simon writes in *Uneasy Stages: A Chronicle of the New York Theater, 1963-1973* (1975) that *Cities in Bezique* is a "Negro masochist play." Linking the work with Kennedy's earlier "psychodrama," *Funnyhouse of a Negro*, Simon notes the similar use of multiple identities, "desperate pseudopoetry," and a harried, self-accusatory tone.

Clinton F. Oliver, in his introduction to the anthology *Contemporary Black Drama* (1971), calls *Funnyhouse of a Negro* "sheer theater in which the mind and spiritual conflicts of a young black woman are brilliantly and painfully explored." Kennedy "overlays" images (birds, flowers, hair) to create an "ornate tapestry." The play is a kind of symbolic dream, about "externally induced self-hatred and a resultant will to self-destruction."

In *The Off Off Broadway Book: The Plays, People, Theatre* (1972), editors Albert Poland and Bruce Mailman suggest that Adrienne Kennedy's plays are similar to many written in the late 1950s and 1960s that promote no manifesto but share "a new syntax." They claim that playwrights such as Megan Terry, Maria Fornes, Julie Bovasso, Jones (Baraka), Sam Shepard, David Rabe, and Israel

Horovitz work in a "similar way: syntactically, contextually, and theatrically." The new form depends on the "vigor of the production to make it work," and results in a "new acting and directing style." Together, impressionism, expressionism, and "Brecht's alienation theories, in combination with Artaud's horrors," create in these plays "a rich collage" that brings "a new strength to . . . drama."

Paul Carter Harrison's *The Drama of Nommo* (1972) analyzes Kennedy's *A Rat's Mass* as it relates to African traditions. He notes that Kennedy's style has a tendency to obscure content, but the "ambiguity of too many voices talking at once" that characterizes her fragmented characters reinforces her "sensibility of the African continuum." Kennedy's rhythmic fusion of time and space suggests a unity of "nightmares and visions" that evokes the reality of Negro oppression. In the introduction to Harrison's collection, *Kuntu Drama: Plays of the African Continuum* (1974), Oliver Jackson addresses issues raised by the critical reception of Kennedy's plays by the white majority. Theater critics who applaud sociological representations of the black community often have little appreciation of "modes of theater" like Kennedy's, that reflect the "African continuum." The Kuntu forces—song, dance, and drum—capture the "total engagement of body/spirit"; they provide a frame for Kennedy's dramaturgy. The Kennedy play in the anthology, *A Beast Story*, "comes at us in fragments," creating a "polyrhythm of language," so that the play is "an active matrix of forces" comparable to "light passing through a prism."

In "African-American Drama, 1950-1970" (Jan. 1973) Samuel A. Hay notes that while African-American plays written in these decades display common themes of social injustice, they can be classified into three groups: dramas of accusation; dramas of self; and dramas of cultural nationalism. Kennedy's *Funnyhouse of a Negro* is a drama of self-celebration that explores the "direct white influence on Afro-American life" and "uses the surreal to show how and why a mulatto 'hates her black father.' "

In "Theatre of Identity: Adrienne Kennedy's Portrait of the Black Woman" (Summer 1975) Robert L. Tener offers a penetrating study of the mythic resonance of the owl as a metaphor of evil and darkness, which anchors the heroine's "problem of identity" to her origins and her self-image in Kennedy's play *The Owl Answers*. Tener sees the owl in the play as a reflection of the main character, SHE, a black woman whose "identity is fragmented because half of her physical roots are black but almost all of her intellectual heritage is white." Using the owl is Kennedy's way of pointing out "that the black in America has no historical or literary heroes to identify with and to achieve personal unity through." Further, Tener suggests that Kennedy's association of the fig tree with the owl is her way of referring to traditional images of woman, the knowledge of good and evil, and sterility. Fusing these images, Kennedy makes "bitter and satirical comment on the American black female," who is "trapped by the conflict of cultures and sexual roles"; the owl and the fig tree together "emphasize the gulf between the physical self and the spiritual center."

Kennedy's kinship with the dramatic traditions of Samuel Beckett and Jean Genet are noted by Lorraine A. Brown in " 'For the Characters are Myself ': Adrienne Kennedy's *Funnyhouse of A Negro*" (Fall 1975). Citing the montage of images in the play, Brown observes that Kennedy "projects a world . . . where Blackness, femaleness, and education are equally important isolating factors." She points out that powerful political and spiritual dimensions in the play's split characters uncover tension, in "Sarah's strenuous efforts to achieve wholeness and identity, and her concurrent contest with paranoia, self-hatred, and the will to self-destruction."

In his discussion of Kennedy's *Cities in Bezique*, Kimberly W. Benston (Dec. 1976) considers the expressionism of the plays to be of crucial relevance to the racial issues they raise. As long as naturalism was the dominant mode of black drama, blacks were depicted as "controlled and absorbed" by their environments. Naturalism could thus do little more than express the plight of black people. Amiri Baraka's *Four Black Revolutionary Plays* (1969) had begun the move toward a new dramatic form, but Kennedy's work took "the first steps toward a complete departure from naturalism." Rapidly changing scenes and role fragmentation—constant shifting between realistic and symbolic modes—create feelings of "dislocation" in the audience. Benston suggests that this calls for a "conscious process of readjustment" which accounts for the sense of menace felt in Kennedy's work. But the menace is a "threat of meaning," not "violence"; it is the fear that "what lurks in the inner self and the collective past will emerge . . . useless." Paradoxically, Benston declares that "the further the plays move into the symbolic realm, the nearer they come to the world of the audience." But Kennedy's dramatic dislocations finally produce a sense of triumph. Caught in "webs of congenital horrors," Kennedy's heroines "still pass through crisis to epiphany, shattering though this process may be."

Jeanne-Marie A. Miller, in "Images of Black Women in Plays by Black Playwrights" (June 1977), provides several illustrations of "intimate inside visions," of positive black characters, spawned by the civil rights and black consciousness movements of the 1950s and 1960s, that thwart traditional stereotypes. Discussing Kennedy along with Alice Childress, Lorraine Hansberry, J. E. Franklin, Ron Milner, Ed Bullins, and Baraka, Miller clearly separates Kennedy. She is seen as an "avant-gardist" because of her "experiments with expressionism and surrealism." Still, the material in Kennedy's plays is of the real black experience; it deals with the "pressures of being Black in America." Kennedy's visions of black women are, however, apparently less optimistic than those of other black playwrights, as her plays are marked by patterns of madness and self-doubt.

Elaborating on Kennedy's expressionism, Rosemary K. Curb, in "Fragmented Selves in Adrienne Kennedy's *Funnyhouse of a Negro* and *The Owl Answers*" (May 1980), suggests that fragmentation of character and antiphonal monologue create "alternate visions of the same divided consciousness." Tension between real black selves and dream white selves and white culture and black culture govern the plays. Although doubling marks the dramaturgy of both plays, scenes shift in *Funnyhouse of a Negro* (indicated by "discordant sounds and light changes") but are simultaneous in *The Owl Answers*. Both plays employ an external framing character where the conflict is played out. Curb understands Kennedy's imagistic dramaturgy as flowing "outward from an impenetrable core" so that there is "no single point in the play when the image/symbol manifests its full meaning." She claims Kennedy's central images convey the "perversion of vital female powers." Themes of confinement, powerlessness (linked with feminine passivity), the desire for power, and death (seen in color imagery) link the two plays.

Curb's " 'Lesson I Bleed' " (1981) focuses on blood imagery in *A Lesson in a Dead Language*, but notes that an interest in blood or bleeding is displayed in other Kennedy plays as well. Kennedy uses menstruation to signify budding womanhood, as a mark of the female's passage from child to childbearer. But the loss of blood is also associated with death, so the symbol is ambiguous. The onset of menstruation is, in a sense, educational, a life-and-death experience, and adolescence is thus a "painful passage."

In "Who Put the 'Tragic' in the Tragic Mulatto?" (1981) Winona L. Fletcher examines the image of miscegenation as a sentimental stage convention; the traditional mulatto was virtuous, noble, and resigned to alienation. Fletcher notes that Kennedy's "tragic mulatto is developed with horrifying intensity," for the mulatto is trapped in stereotypes, "torn by paradoxes," and in search of identity. Sarah, in *Funnyhouse of a Negro*, and Clara, in *The Owl Answers*, struggle "to resolve their love/hate for Black/white," while caught in a never-ending "attraction/rejection syndrome."

Ruby Cohn's survey of *New American Dramatists 1960-1980* (1982) offers a retrospective of Kennedy's plays from *Funnyhouse of a Negro* to the unpublished *A Movie Star Has to Star in Black and White* (produced in 1976). Although Kennedy has described her plays as states of mind, Cohn refines the phrase to suggest that they are "*acts* of mind—tremulous or masterful, but always highly imaged and eloquent." By blending surrealism ("strong visual images" derived from dreams) and expressionism ("inner conflicts externalized as different characters"), the plays become both original in their imagery and mythic in their "incantatory repetitions." Conversely, Cohn praises the realism of *Evening with Dead Essex*, which is based on the assassination of black sniper Mark James Essex; the play directs that " 'actors use their real names and the director should get the actors to play themselves.' " It is a play within a play; as the actors rehearse, the story is pieced together. The more-usual Kennedy method is employed in *A Movie Star Has to Star in Black and White*, which reprises the character Clara from *The Owl Answers* and embeds her in the white culture of the American film tradition. Clara's fragmented self includes roles as writer, daughter, wife, mother, and "*alter ego* to any of the film actresses." This fragmentation is what makes Kennedy's plays so distinctively evocative. Cohn writes, "Her plays are contemporary renderings of the myth of the Double. Seeking an identity under schizophrenic splits, a catharsis through tragic events, the plays brim with lovely gravity."

Placing Kennedy within a broad Afro-American tradition, Geneviève Fabre (1982; translated, 1983) writes that Kennedy's plays explore "the surrealistic side of the ethnic consciousness." Among others who use metaphors of degradation (such as the rats in *A Rat's Mass*) and the prison of a dominant language mandating that blacks stay in their places (in *A Lesson in a Dead Language*), Kennedy evokes "inseparable yet irreconcilable black and white worlds." Her "theatre unfolds in a closed world" where character is the "prisoner" of divided selves in confrontation. For example, the bastard type "symbolizes an aborted identity"; to reclaim it is to "avenge the shame" of bastardy. *Sun*, dedicated to Malcolm X, depicts the mutilation of a man, a broken hope, and the universe. Fabre says that Kennedy uses fantasy in the play to "reveal a hidden truth."

As the one black woman among the founders of New York's Women's Theater Council in 1972, Kennedy joined Maria Irene Fornés, Rosalyn Drexler, Julie Bovasso, Rochelle Owens, and Megan Terry in building support for women playwrights; their original proposal was to stage a season of plays by each of the founders of the group in hopes of soliciting work by other women writers. In 1973 the Women's Theater Council became the Theater Strategy and included male playwrights. Though this group later disbanded, the commitment to supporting women's drama was established. Helene Keyssar, in *Feminist Theatre* (1984), notes that Kennedy emerged in the 1960s as a black playwright and was "rediscovered" in the 1970s as a feminist; Kennedy's work admits the fusion.

Keyssar's book examines the fortress that Sarah of *Funnyhouse of a Negro* claims to build around herself. It is a fortress that cannot "protect her from the 'beasts' inside." *Funnyhouse of a Negro* is not a story of a woman's madness; rather, it is an "enacted metaphor . . . of cultural structures that make self-deceit and mendacity viable alternatives to self-hatred for a person who is black and female." Understanding, as did Tennessee Williams, the "destructive power of the lie," Adrienne Kennedy addresses the vulnerability of black women who are hemmed in by the lies of both black and white culture.

In a broad theoretical essay about feminism and feminist drama, Rosemary K. Curb (Oct. 1985) posits that "Woman-conscious theatre presents a multi-dimensional unraveling of women's collective imagination in a psychic replay of myth and history" and demands a new language of theatrical form. Curb establishes a spectrum which is useful in understanding the web of conflicting selves that is a dominant feature of Kennedy's dramaturgy. *Funnyhouse of a Negro* exemplifies "re/cognition," the psychic mirroring of the seeing subject and the object seen. The locus is Sarah's "split-second consciousness at the moment of death"; the multi-faceted mirror-images of self that "replay past psychic lives" can only be destroyed in the "annihilation of the seer."

In "Diverse Angles of Vision: Two Black Women Playwrights" (1985) Margaret B. Wilkerson compares the work of Lorraine Hansberry and Adrienne Kennedy in a piece that reflects Wilkerson's biographical interest in both playwrights. She details Kennedy's formative travels to Africa and Europe in 1960-1961. In defining the differing visions and styles of the two playwrights,

Wilkerson concludes that Kennedy's imagistic and surrealistic drama reveals submerged violence in her characters. She writes from "the inside out," presenting a "terrifying relationship between the private self and public history."

Mance Williams, in *Black Theatre in the 1960's and 1970's* (1985) declares that Kennedy's work demands a structuralist approach; critical questions should weigh formalist against polemical preoccupations, explore mythic implications, and address the tensions between play and audience as layers of consciousness revealed in the drama. Williams compares Kennedy with Edgar White, indicating that both "use the Black Experience as a convenient frame . . . to explore the dilemma of the individual in a hostile environment" and to evoke a universalistic concern for oppression. Kennedy's themes reflect concern for "collective consciousness" as well as "emotions of fear and guilt." Called "choreopoetry" by Williams, Kennedy's *Sun* is described as "movement built around, or into, a single poem," a play of movement, sound, and light, without character, dialogue, or narrative; he sees the play as precursor of Ntozake Shange's *For Colored Girls Who Have Considered Suicide When the Rainbow is Enuf* (1975).

Herbert Blau writes about Sam Shepard and Adrienne Kennedy in a chapter of his *The Eye of Prey: Subversions of the Postmodern* (1987). Blau cites Eugene O'Neill's claim that "this nation is the greatest failure because it has betrayed the greatest promise" and sees in Kennedy's writing "the persistence of desire in language to overcome the failed promise." Her characters' inner divisions, guilts, and phobias illustrate the "racial pathology . . . of self-contempt nurtured by the long shameful history" of the United States. But her language and contexts are more literary than revolutionary. Tautologically locked in a circular nightmare, the figures of Kennedy's divided selves split, elude, and fade; surreal dramaturgy similarly animates objects and ideas. Kennedy's dramaturgy also displaces space; the narratives "move in and out of focus in a memory flux"; and "monologic, semichoral, autistic" speeches have "the effect of ritual and incantation." Of *A Rat's Mass*, Blau comments, "It is not African roots, then, that constitute their [the characters of the play] image of redemption, *at-one*ment, but the archaic romance of Western tradition." In conclusion, Blau writes, "What one may object to in all these transformative visions of Adrienne Kennedy is that her politics exist almost entirely in the unconscious, with its cannibalistic operations of dismembered being."

The publication of Kennedy's collected works, *Adrienne Kennedy in One Act* (1988), lends a long-needed accessibility to her writing. Critical approaches that have already been fruitful should serve as guidelines for deeper study. Furthermore, a closer comparison of Kennedy's work and that of Williams, Lorca, Albee, Baraka, Shange, and others is warranted. Further work by feminist critics, particularly the black feminists, should blend the suggestiveness of the analysis by Curb with the need to view Kennedy on her own terms. The publication of her autobiography makes feasible greater study of Kennedy's use of life experiences as literary sources; such study would help readers appreciate the nuances of her richly connotative writing. Critics should continue to analyze the plays to uncover their evocative power and then attempt to understand Kennedy's contribution to contemporary drama and the expression of the American and Afro-American experience.

Arthur L. Kopit

(1937-)

Doris Auerbach
Fairleigh Dickinson University

Books

Oh Dad, Poor Dad, Mama's Hung You in the Closet and I'm Feelin' So Sad: A Pseudoclassical Tragifarce in a Bastard French Tradition. New York: Hill & Wang, 1960; London: Methuen, 1962. Play.

The Day the Whores Came Out to Play Tennis and Other Plays. New York: Hill & Wang, 1965; London: Methuen, 1969. Comprises *The Day the Whores Came Out to Play Tennis, The Questioning of Nick, Sing to Me through Open Windows, Chamber Music, The Conquest of Everest,* and *The Hero.*

Indians. New York: Hill & Wang, 1969; London: Methuen, 1970. Play.

Wings. New York: Hill & Wang, 1978; London: Methuen, 1979. Play. Includes a preface by Kopit.

Nine: The Musical. Garden City, N.Y.: Doubleday, 1982. Adapted by Kopit from the Fellini film *81/2.*

End of the World. New York: Hill & Wang, 1984. Play.

Premiere Productions

The Questioning of Nick. Cambridge, Mass., Harvard University Drama Workshop, Oct. 1957.

Gemini. Cambridge, Mass., Harvard University Drama Workshop, Nov. 1957.

Don Juan in Texas, by Kopit and Wally Lawrence. Cambridge, Mass., Harvard University Drama Workshop, Dec. 1957.

On the Runway of Life You Never Know What's Coming Off Next. Cambridge, Mass., Harvard University Drama Workshop, Apr. 1958.

Across the River and Into the Jungle. Cambridge, Mass., Harvard University Drama Workshop, Dec. 1958.

Aubade. Cambridge, Mass., Harvard University Drama Workshop, Apr. 1959.

Sing to Me Through Open Windows. Cambridge, Mass., Harvard University Drama Workshop, Apr. 1959.

Oh Dad, Poor Dad, Mama's Hung You in the Closet and I'm Feelin' So Sad. Cambridge, Mass., Agassiz Theatre, Jan. 1960.

Chamber Music. Philadelphia, Society Hill Playhouse, 1965.

The Day the Whores Came Out to Play Tennis. New York, Players Theatre, 15 Mar. 1965. With *Sing to Me Through Open Windows.*

Indians. London, Aldwych Theatre, 4 July 1968; Washington, D.C., Arena Stage, 6 May 1969.

The Hero. New York, Play Box, 3 Oct. 1970.

The Conquest of Everest. New York, Assembly Theatre, 20 Nov. 1970.

Wings. New Haven, Yale Repertory Theatre, 3 March 1978.

End of the World. Washington, D.C., Kennedy Center, 28 Mar. 1984.

Selected Other

The Questioning of Nick. WNHC, 1 June 1959. Teleplay.

"The Vital Matter of Environment," *Theatre Arts,* 45 (Apr. 1961), 12-13. Essay.

The Conquest of Television, NETV, 1966. Teleplay.

Oh Dad, Poor Dad, Mama's Hung You in the Closet and I'm Feelin' So Sad. Paramount, 1967. Screenplay.

"An Incident in the Park." In *Pardon Me, Sir, But Is My Eye Hurting Your Elbow?,* ed. Bob Booker and George Foster. New York: Geis, 1967.

Wings. "Earplay," NPR, 1978. Radio play.

Hands of a Stranger. NBC, 1987. Teleplay.

SECONDARY BIBLIOGRAPHY

Interviews

Funke, Lewis. "Origin of 'Indians' Recalled by Kopit," *New York Times,* 15 Oct. 1969, p. 37.

Guttman, Melinda. "Interview with Kopit," *Soho News,* 2 Feb. 1979.

Lahr, Anthea, ed. "A Dialogue Between Arthur Kopit and John Lahr." In *Indians.* New York, Toronto & London: Bantam, 1971.

Parker, Judith. "A Play Has to Breathe," *Harvard Magazine* (Mar./ Apr. 1979).

Secrest, Meryle. "Out West with Kopit," *Washington Post*, 20 Apr. 1969, section K, p. 1.

Shewey, Don. "Arthur Kopit: A Life on Broadway," *New York Times Magazine*, 29 Apr. 1984, pp. 88-90, 104-105.

Topor, Tom. "Interview with Kopit," *New York Post*, 1 Feb. 1979.

Critical Studies: Book

Auerbach, Doris. *Sam Shepard, Arthur Kopit, and the Off Broadway Theater*. Boston: Twayne, 1982.

Critical Studies: Major Reviews, Articles, and Book Sections

Adler, Thomas P. "Public Faces, Private Graces: Apocalypse Postponed in Arthur Kopit's *End of the World*," *Studies in the Literary Imagination*, 22 (Fall 1988), 107-118.

Barnes, Clive. "Indians," *New York Times*, 9 July 1968.

Barnes. "Laughing All the Way to the End of the World," *New York Post*, 7 May 1984.

Billman, Carol. "Illusions of Grandeur: Altman, Kopit and the Legends of the Wild West," *Literature/Film Quarterly*, 6 (Summer 1978), 253-261.

Bolton, Whitney. Review of *Oh Dad, Poor Dad*, *Morning Telegraph*, 3 Mar. 1961.

Bradish, Gaynor F. Introduction to *Oh Dad, Poor Dad*. New York: Hill & Wang, 1960, 9-12.

Brustein, Robert. "Bagatelles and Jacks," *New Republic*, 152 (10 Apr. 1965), 23-24.

Brustein. "The Great Artistic Director Burn-Out," *New Republic*, 186 (9 June 1982), 24-26.

Brustein. "The Theater of Metaphor," *Partisan Review*, 51, no. 4 (1984), 650-662.

Clurman, Harold. "The Kopit Plays," *Nation*, 200 (5 Apr. 1965), 373-374.

Cohen, R. "Spoken Dialogue in Written Drama," *Essays in Theatre*, 4, no. 2 (1986), 85-97.

Copeland, Roger. "The Theatre in the 'Me Decade'," *New York Times*, 3 June 1979, section 2, p. 1.

Curtis, Bruce. "The Use and the Abuse of the Past in American Studies: Arthur Kopit's *Indians*, a Case Study," *American Examiner*, 1 (1973), 4-5.

Dasgupta, Gautam. "Arthur Kopit." In *American Playwrights : A Critical Survey*, by Bonnie Marranca and Dasgupta. New York: Drama Book Specialists, 1981, I: 15-25.

Dieckman, Suzanne and Richard Brayshaw. "Wings, Watchers, and Windows: Imprisonment in the Plays of Arthur Kopit," *Theatre Journal*, 35 (May 1983), 195-211.

Duclow, Donald F. "Dying on Broadway: Contemporary Drama and Mortality," *Soundings*, 64 (Summer 1981), 197-216.

Eder, Richard. "Wings Comes to Broadway: Memories of Flying," *New York Times*, 29 Jan. 1979, p. C13.

Edgerton, Gary. "Wings: Radio Play Adapted to Experimental Stage," *Journal of Popular Culture*, 16 (Spring 1983), 152-158.

Gassner, John. "Broadway in Review," *Educational Theatre Journal*, 14 (May 1962), 169-177.

Gill, Brendan. "Women as Things," *New Yorker*, 58 (24 May 1982), 100-102.

Harley, Carol. "Arthur Kopit." In *Dictionary of Literary Biography*, volume 7: *Twentieth-Century American Dramatists*, part 2, ed. John MacNicholas. Detroit: Gale, 1981, 41-49.

Hewes, Henry. "The Square Fellow," *Saturday Review*, 45 (17 Mar. 1962), 35.

Hurrell, Barbara. "Oh Say, Can You See?" *American Examiner*, 1 (1973), 1-3.

Jiji, Vera. "*Indians*: A Mosaic of Memories and Methodologies," *Players*, 47 (June/July 1972), 230-236.

Jones, John Bush. "Impersonation and Authenticity: The Theatre as Metaphor in Kopit's *Indians*," *Quarterly Journal of Speech*, 59 (Dec. 1973), 443-457.

Kroll, Jack. "Nuclear Jabberwocky," *Newsweek*, 103 (28 May 1984), 87.

Lahr, John. "Arthur Kopit's *Indians*: Dramatizing National Amnesia." In his *Up Against the Fourth Wall: Essays on Modern Theater*. New York: Grove, 1970.

Levett, Karl. "*Ghosts* by Ibsen, Adaptation by Kopit," *Drama*, no. 147 (1983), 40-41.

Levett. "New York: The Salesman and the Artist," *Drama*, no. 153 (1984), 42-43.

Murch, Anne C. "Genet-Triana-Kopit: Ritual as 'Danse Macabre'," *Modern Drama*, 15 (Mar. 1973), 369-381.

Nathanson, Arthur Nicholas. "Wings–A Play," *World Literature Today*, 54 (Winter 1980), 109.

Oestreicher, Pamela. "On *Indians*," *American Examiner*, 1 (1973), 3-5.

Oliver, Edith. "Off Broadway: And Lies and Lies and Lies," *New Yorker*, 41 (27 Mar. 1965), 144-147.

O'Neill, Michael C. "History as Dramatic Presence: Arthur L. Kopit's *Indians*," *Theatre Journal*, 34 (Dec. 1982), 493-504.

Rich, Frank. "New Kopit Play: Mystery of Motive," *New York Times*, 7 May 1984, p. C15.

Rinear, David. *"The Day the Whores Came Out to Play Tennis*: Kopit's Debt to Chekhov," *Today's Speech*, 22 (Spring 1974), 19-23.

Rutledge, Frank. "Kopit's *Indians*," *American Examiner*, 1 (1973), 5-6.

Schwenger, Peter. "Writing the Unthinkable," *Critical Inquiry*, 13, no. 1 (1986), 31-48.

Simon, John. "Bangs and Whimpers," *New York Magazine*, 17 (21 May 1984), 104-106.

Simon. "Pieces of '8 1/2,' " *New York Magazine*, 15 (24 May 1982), 88-90.

Simon. "Theater Chronicle: Kopit, Norman, and Shepard," *Hudson Review*, 32 (Spring 1979), 77-88.

Smith, S. "Ironic Distance and the Theatre of Feigned Madness," *Theatre Journal*, 39 (Mar. 1987), 57-64.

Szilassy, Zoltan. "Yankee Burlesque or Metaphysical Farce?" *Hungarian Studies in English*, 11 (1977), 143-147.

Taubman, Howard. "One Work at a Time: Each Avant-Garde Play Stands on Own Merits," *New York Times*, 11 Mar. 1962, section 2, p. 1.

Valentine, Dean. "Kopit Earns His Wings," *New Leader*, 62 (26 Feb. 1979), 19-20.

Weales, Gerald. "American Theater Watch, 1983-1984," *Georgia Review*, 38 (Fall 1984), 594-609.

Wellwarth, George. "Arthur Kopit." In his *The Theater of Protest and Paradox*. Revised edition. New York: New York University Press, 1971, 345-347.

Westarp, Karl-Heinz. "Myth in Peter Shaffer's *The Royal Hunt of the Sun* and in Arthur Kopit's *Indians*," *English Studies*, 65 (Apr. 1984), 120-128.

Wolter, Jürgen. "Arthur Kopit: Dreams and Nightmares." In *Essays on Contemporary American Drama*, ed. Hedwick Bock and Albert Werthrim. Rochester, N.Y.: Adler, 1981, 55-74.

BIBLIOGRAPHICAL ESSAY

Interviews

Although few first plays have received as much critical attention and caused such great controversy as did *Oh Dad, Poor Dad, Mama's Hung You in the Closet and I'm Feelin' So Sad* (hereafter referred to as *Oh Dad, Poor Dad*), interviews with Arthur Kopit began appearing with frequency only after *Indians*, his second major play, was produced in America in 1969. In a 20 April 1969 interview with Meryle Secrest of the *Washington Post* Kopit emphasized his interest in the nature of language and the role it plays in his plays: "I think the theater must have language at its core. I want to discover new ways of seeing things." At a time when nonverbal aspects of theater were often emphasized, Kopit was a defender of the power of the word. Kopit also used the interview to explain that his plays were cultural commentaries and that the artist's role in such creations must necessarily be muted: "The suppression of the 'I' has always been a concern. When you write plays, you the author don't appear. You are impersonal. I'm very comfortable in this role."

Critic John Lahr was the most enthusiastic champion of *Indians*. In a conversation with Lahr included in the 1971 Bantam edition of the play, Kopit said that he wrote it "to explore the Western conflict, particularly the way in which a myth had evolved about the [American] West to justify what we had done to the Indians." Writing about the West was a way to "put the Vietnamese situation into the context of American history." He explained, "The white man was dealing with a totally alien culture. This struck me as a great similarity to Vietnam. . . . they [our soldiers] regard the Vietnamese as Gooks and feel the killing of Vietnamese is very easy because they are subhuman. . . . It was hard for the white man to consider the Indian a human being." Such a connection, Kopit stressed, could never have been made "if there hadn't been Western films which glorified and romanticized a history of white violence and thievery." And although most playgoers were first introduced to Kopit's depiction of the tradition in *Indians*, myths of glorification had long fascinated him. The unpublished *Don Juan in Texas*, written by Kopit and Wally Lawrence in 1957 when they were Harvard University students, is a humorous account of a traveling soap salesman who is mistaken for Billy the Kid. The reactions of the townspeople to their new hero are displays of the "communal imagination."

After Kopit's next major play, *Wings*, was produced and published in 1978, he was widely regarded as a major but obscure voice in American theater. The play is a curious study of a former stunt pilot's attempts to recover after suffering a debilitating stroke. In a 2 February 1979 interview with Melinda Guttman of *Soho News* he commented that even though his plays seemed to have little in common, they were holistic: "I've been dealing with related issues for a long time: airplanes, flying, crashing, women pilots and women heroines." *Wings* was not a departure but, rather, a progression: "I've always seen my plays as adventure stories and explorations of the unknown–that is, going into forbidden territories, into the Netherworld." One continually fascinating theme is human language and "our mysterious ability or inability to take command of it." Much of *Wings* consists of the stroke victim's struggle to communicate with her attendants.

In the spring of 1979 Kopit spoke at great length to Judith Parker, as reported in *Harvard Magazine*. He attempted to explain why such long periods of time elapsed between the production of new plays. During the Harvard years he had seven plays produced before the phenomenal success of *Oh Dad, Poor Dad*: "Suddenly I was a successful playwright at 23. And there didn't seem much left to say." The money he earned from *Oh Dad, Poor Dad* and *Indians* gave him time to go on exploring, which he needed "because all my plays are–explorations." But he was puzzled why "I shouldn't be able to turn out a play every two years" and concluded that "a play has to–wait. It takes time. A play has to breathe." About those prolific years at Harvard, he remarked that "the best thing for a writer is to know whom he's writing for, to have his own company of actors, and to have to turn out a play a year."

That *Wings* was having a successful New York run pleased Kopit because he thought it was his best play. He told Parker, "I wouldn't change a line." He thought it successful because it stood as commentary, as a statement of human perseverance: "A play has to *mean* something. To me and, I hope, to others. Especially now, when so much is produced for pure entertainment." Being able to entertain was important, but he wanted to do more: "Plays have to be–important."

Parker wondered if the frequent surfacing of dark elements in Kopit's plays made him a pessimist: "I don't think so. I'm not an optimist either. I'm neither. I think the world will survive. I think we'll all survive. I don't see how we can. But I think we will." Human survival, of course, was the main concern in his next and most recent drama, *End of the World*. However, in a conversation with Kopit published in the *New York Times Magazine* (29 Apr. 1984) Don Shewey suggested that the theme of the play was "not only the survival of the human race, but the survival of a serious playwright on Broadway." While Kopit never gained the success of such dramatists as Jack Gelber (*The Connection*, 1960) and Edward Albee (*Who's Afraid of Virginia Woolf?*, 1962), only he "has survived more than 20 years on Broadway artistically sound and financially solvent." Kopit wondered what a Broadway playwright was, and Shewey answered that a Broadway playwright is one who is produced on Broadway. Kopit characterized himself as being fond of the glamour of Broadway, but he disagreed with Shewey's assessment. He considered Robert Anderson and Neil Simon to the best examples of Broadway writers.

End of the World was more serious than Broadway and almost entirely autobiographical. In 1980, while teaching a play writing course at City College in New York, Kopit met an insurance millionaire who had written a "futuristic" four-page "scenario about a Soviet-American military showdown" and wanted someone to write a play based on it. Kopit initially laughed at the idea of "writing someone else's play," but the offer of thirty thousand dollars for researching and writing it was too tempting to reject. Kopit was horrified at what his research revealed and came to realize that what should be dramatized, instead of the scenario, "was his own inability to come to terms emotionally with the horrifying reality of nuclear weapons." Kopit's playfulness with language manifests itself in *End of the World* in passages that display the "Pentagon's genius for inventing euphemisms." These kinds of devices, however, are always used strategically: "In the theater you must feel and think. It has to do with why theater has always existed in civilization. Theater *matters*."

Critical Studies: Book

No book-length study devoted solely to Arthur Kopit has been published to date. However, Doris Auerbach's *Sam Shepard, Arthur Kopit, and the Off Broadway Theater* (1982) provides abbreviated but still-useful readings of his major plays in a way that places them in a larger context. Auerbach argues that despite obvious differences between Kopit and Sam Shepard–the former writes sparingly in the "literate idiom of an urbane eastern intellectual," while the latter writes prolifically in a kind of 1960s mode, in the language of "television, science fiction, cool jazz, rock, and drugs"–the two "share a communality of concerns for the meaning of the American myth, the evaluation and betrayal of the American dream, the fate of the American family, the precarious situation of the artist, the problems of identity, and . . . a fascination with the nature of language." In turn, these two major playwrights share the perspective of many Off-Broadway playwrights, who were spawned and are supported by the existence of "alternative, noncommercial" theater.

Auerbach emphasizes the parodistic nature of *Oh Dad, Poor Dad*, Kopit's comedy on the efforts of a man-hating widow to maintain her repressed son's chastity while her dead husband lies preserved in a closet. The French tradition referred to in Kopit's subtitle is absurdism. Auerbach uses an early Kopit critical essay, "The Vital Matter of Environment," to explain his theories on the relation of the artist to his milieu. "One can never wholly dissociate a work of art from its creative environment any more than one can separate its style from the tradition around it," wrote Kopit. "Tradition has always been the basis of all innovation. . . . Style is related to tradition to the extent that it is representative of a cultural or social characteristic of its creative environment, and is itself characteristic to the extent that it has evolved from or rebelled" against tradition. Lacking a traditional tradition against which to rebel, Auerbach argues, Kopit turned to the absurd and bastardized it.

Auerbach's chapter on *Indians* synthesizes criticism of the controversial play, but it relies perhaps too heavily on John Lahr's work. Auerbach points out that Kopit's interest in the role of the Vietnam War in the creation of American myth was in the structuralist tradition, which views the function of myth primarily as a way of validating the existing social order. To reinforce the point she quotes a leading French anthropologist, Claude Levi-Strauss: " 'In our own [Western] societies, history has replaced mythology and fulfills the same functions . . . to ensure that as closely as possible, the future will remain faithful to the present and the past.' "

The *Wings* material draws on Kopit's preface to the 1978 Hill and Wang edition of the play. Auerbach emphasizes that the theme of the difficulty of human communication can be traced through all of Kopit's plays. She makes use of tenets of structuralism and semiotics to explain Kopit's use of the damaged mind of a stroke victim to draw attention to the function of language. Indeed, the play's themes are "the exploration of the nature and structure of language as the particularly human way of experiencing the world" and the use of the stroke victim as a metaphor "for the human cour-age which can overcome existential human isolation."

Critical Studies: Major Reviews, Articles, and Book Sections

Until more book-length material on Arthur Kopit and his work appears, reviews and essays must serve as the main sources of critical information. In his introduction to the 1960 Hill and Wang version of *Oh Dad, Poor Dad*, Gaynor F. Bradish, Kopit's tutor at the Harvard Drama Workshop, remarks that the play is "the logical fu-sion of the comic and the serious facets of Kopit's imagination." Bradish sees his young protégé's work as "an attack" on realism and an attempt to reclaim for the theater "the domain of imaginary forces." He places Kopit's student plays, culminating with *Oh Dad, Poor Dad*, in a "kingdom of the extraordinary," where theater al-ways reigns in "its time of ascendance."

The audiences that kept the play running for nearly a year in New York and who flocked to see it in several road tours, undoubt-edly enjoyed its burlesque aspects as well as the numerous literary al-lusions in this parodistic joke. In a 3 March 1961 review Whitney Bol-ton noted that the play might have been written in collaboration with "Samuel Beckett, Sophocles, Ronald Firbank, Edgar Allan Poe, Salvador Dali, and Robert Benchley." Howard Taubman of the *New York Times* (11 Mar. 1962) appreciated Kopit's "affinity for the bi-zarre" and his ability to "translate it into theatrical terms." He charac-terized *Oh Dad, Poor Dad* as "partly diverting and partly obnoxious" and held out the hope of Kopit becoming an "important" play-wright.

In March 1965 a double bill of Kopit plays opened in New York. The fact that one of the plays, *The Day the Whores Came Out to Play Tennis*, had a catchier title may have been the reason why crit-ics gave it more attention than the other play, *Sing to Me Through Open Windows*. Harold Clurman (5 Apr. 1965) thought the former possessed "a somewhat vicious extravagance that surprises one into risibility," and he considered it a metaphorical representation of the "rootless urban middle class," but in the final analysis he found it to be little better than "fraternity-house" Ionesco. Edith Oliver (27 Mar. 1965) compared the two plays to *Oh Dad, Poor Dad*, which she thought benefited from its "undertones of horror." But in the plays of the double bill, wrote the *New Yorker* reviewer, there "were no un-dertones of anything." Robert Brustein (10 Apr. 1965) agreed with

Clurman and Oliver's negative assessments of the two short plays, finding them little more than "sophomoric exercises." He also faulted Kopit's titles, which he dubbed "attention-getting mechanisms, full of simpers and winks."

A 1970 essay by John Lahr, which was partially based on a series of lengthy interviews with the playwright (excerpted in a 1971 edition of *Indians*), provides a good example of the new seriousness with which Kopit was regarded after the production of *Indians*. The article draws a thematic parallel between *Indians* and the trauma of the Vietnam War. Kopit told Lahr that the "provocation" for the play was a statement by American General William C. Westmoreland made after a particularly massive slaughter of Vietnamese civilians during the War: "Our hearts go out to the innocent victims." Westmoreland's statement made Kopit go "beserk," for Kopit "didn't think Vietnam was the real problem but a symptom of something which went back much further" into American history, which was a struggle against "people . . . spiritually, morally, economically and intellectually our inferiors." Lahr characterized *Indians* not as a "protest play, but a process play," a dramatization of the "creation of mythology," a successful attempt to confront Americans with the self-delusion of American history. He quoted Kopit: "The way we took the country was not what we want to know. Our dream of glory wasn't the nightmare of destruction, of willfullness, of greed, of perjury, of murder which it became." Americans in the Vietnam era, Kopit continued, displayed a "capacity for 'built-in' amnesia . . . and the danger of changing what happened into a fable."

Vera Jiji (June/July 1972) continued the vein of serious criticism of *Indians*. Her close reading of the play revealed its debt to several theatrical conventions: Brechtian alienation, expressionism, and naturalism. Jiji interpreted the play as an attempt "to teach the audience a lesson from history." While voicing "great admiration" for it she shied away from calling it completely successful: "With all the brilliance with which Kopit has manipulated the manifold conflicts and conventions of the play, it fails to develop an organic forward motion until the split personality of Cody coalesces into one struggling human being." She faulted Kopit's close ties to Brecht, which kept the play from being "completely authentic on its own terms." Kopit's earlier plays had displayed the same "imitative" element that now threatened to "overwhelm" *Indians*, which deemphasized "its own structural autonomy in favor of schematic imitation."

John Bush Jones (Dec. 1973) gave a more positive appraisal of the play. In a scene-by-scene analysis he attributed its success to the fact that its "structure and theme are inseparable." He showed how varieties of "mythic theatrical impersonation constitute the basic dramatic materials out of which Kopit shaped a play whose main idea also concerns impersonation, theatricality, [and] myth creation." He concluded his valuable analysis by delineating the differences between mythmaking, in which "the myth becomes reality," and playmaking, where "the line between fact and fiction is always maintained."

In a brief 1973 essay Barbara Hurrell interpreted *Indians* through what she called its imagery of seeing: "The play was about how the white man 'saw' the Indian as an animal, or a stubborn child, and how this white man's vision came to be accepted in varying degrees by the Indian himself." She related this image of seeing to existential works such as Jean Paul Sartre's *Huis clos* (*No Exit*, 1945): "To deprive a people of their ability to 'see' is to take their freedom."

The seldom performed *Chamber Music* was related by Anne C. Murch (Mar. 1973) to the plays of Jean Genet, which deal with "man's estrangement from himself, about his fears, his flights from an unbearable reality, his groping toward identity, and his failure to achieve it." Murch identified the theme of *Chamber Music* as the co-option of the sane by the insane. The fight for individual survival in the play is turned inward and ritually enacted.

David Rinear (Spring 1974) traces the influence of Chekhov's *The Cherry Orchard* (1904) on *The Day the Whores Came Out to Play Tennis*. The country club in the Kopit play serves the same purpose as the estate in Chekhov's; it "is the home of the degenerate aristocracy." Rinear shows that the characters in both plays remain "passive" toward a force that seeks to destroy them and are drawn in the same "comic-pathetic vein." He applauds the playwright's skill in employing literary allusions from sources as diverse as the Bible and Hemingway. The play is "both enlightening and amusing."

After the New Haven, Connecticut, opening of *Wings* on 3 March 1978, Kopit was very favorably reviewed. Richard Eder (29 Jan. 1979) called the play a brilliant work and praised not only the sensitivity of its writing but the excitement that Kopit brought to the viewers' "voyage of discovery." He noted that Kopit had previously gotten attention because of the controversies his plays had raised, but with *Wings* it would be his craftsmanship that garnered praise. John Simon (Spring 1979) applauded the significance of the play's title, a symbol for life "which comes to us on wings, and we leave on the pinions of death." He emphasized the theme of language in the play. *Wings* "addresses itself to the question of how, why, and when we comprehend something and can translate it into understandable utterance."

Kopit's growing reputation as a major American playwright is evidenced by two sizable articles that appeared in reference books on theater in 1981. In *American Playwrights* Gautam Dasgupta summarizes Kopit's work, which, although "small in output, . . . reflects a more comprehensive world view than many of his prolific contemporaries." He commends Kopit's willingness to act as "America's social conscience" through *Indians* and applauds his ability to devise "provocative theatrical forms to argue his perceptive social vision." Carol Harley's *Dictionary of Literary Biography* article (1981) gives biographical data on Kopit and an expansive treatment of each major play. Both Dasgupta and Harley somewhat inaccurately characterize Kopit as an absurdist; in fact, he tried to mock absurdism in *Oh Dad, Poor Dad*. Harley, however, praises Kopit for extending the "use of language, bearing testimony to the value of the theatre as the domain of imaginative power."

Kopit assumed another role in 1982, that of the author of the book for the musical *Nine*, which was adapted from the Fellini film *8 1/2*. While the musical was a box-office hit, it was not a critical success for Kopit. Simon (24 May 1982) found the musical's book "an impoverishment" of the film. Brustein (9 June 1982) faulted Kopit for losing "interest in his book" after establishing the protagonists' personalities and for sacrificing "his plotting to camp effects."

An excellent study of *Indians*, by Michael O'Neill, was also published in 1982 (Dec.). Thirteen years after the New York opening, O'Neill thought that "*Indians* has emerged as one of the best plays of the Vietnam era." He compared it to other war plays of the time and praised Kopit profusely: "It is a measure of achievement of *Indians* that in seeking to develop a new dramatic form, Kopit managed to avoid the excesses of the avant garde of the period, shaping a play which is neither historical drama or representational in the traditional way." The play was "exclusively about Indians as much as Ibsen's *Ghosts* is about venereal disease." The plight of the Red Man in *Indians* indicates "a larger, more destructive force embedded in the entire social structure."

Suzanne Dieckman and Richard Brayshaw (May 1983) characterized Kopit's writing as "a mirror of modern culture and the way in which it imprisons us." They chart his literary progression "from imprisonment to fragmentation, violence and paralysis," but find that *Wings* reverses the process and faces "the unknown head-on" in a "search for freedom." Even *Nine: The Musical* was integrated into their view of Kopit. Although it was an adaptation they saw it as a "further step in the new direction" begun by *Wings*.

End of the World opened on Broadway to mixed reviews on 28 March 1984. Clive Barnes (7 May 1984) stressed Kopit's versatility: "He never writes the same play twice." He thought the play was "funny, clever, thoughtful, not always thought-out" with a dialectic reminiscent of George Bernard Shaw. The play was about "the deadly glitter of destruction," and its faults were "windiness and hysteria," compensated for by "logic and humor." In a more negative review Frank Rich faulted Kopit for "bungling" the "red-hot subject of the spectre of nuclear holocaust" so completely that he might have been writing "about toad stools rather than mushroom clouds." He considered the play to be an "aberration" in the career of a "talented writer."

Gerald Weales (Fall 1984) thought the play dealt with "coming to terms with the possibility of a nuclear holocaust" but that it was primarily about a playwright's efforts to write a play about the possibility. The result is an "odd mixture of parody, satire, lecture, and character study," both "funny and frightening." Kopit's use of the playwright character as detective was a "workable metaphor for the playwright's creative process."

In a scholarly article on the metaphoric aspect of modern theater Brustein (1984) cited *End of the World* as an example of the works of those dramatists, who, "while unable to solve problems, present them correctly." The play was like a film noir that dealt with the writing of the play about doom. The protagonist of *End of the World* concluded that the writing of such a play was impossible, and he abandoned the project and all hope. Brustein quoted at length the scene where Kopit dramatized the "seductive lure" of destruction, a scene that is "all metaphor" and which owed its power to the power of that metaphor: "Without evading his responsibilities as a citizen under nuclear threat, indeed by frontally facing these responsibilities, Kopit has managed to understand our terrors and form them into art," he concluded.

Thomas P. Adler also discussed *End of the World* in a volume of *Studies in the Literary Imagination* (Fall 1988) devoted to contemporary American drama. Adler wrote that in Kopit's plays he "both criticizes the habit of mind that feeds on the inevitability of nuclear Armageddon and also asserts the possibility of breaking through the existence of evil, morally as well as aesthetically." Adler ably refers to a number of Kopit plays and brings his essay to a close with a discussion of the audience response to *End of the World*.

Future scholarship on Arthur Kopit will depend on the future his career takes. With every full-length play produced, interest in his work as a whole has been stimulated. The greatest present need in Kopit studies is for a book-length synthesis that makes Kopit's diverse body of work a sensible whole.

David Mamet

(1947-)

June Schlueter
Lafayette College

PRIMARY BIBLIOGRAPHY

Books

American Buffalo. New York: Grove, 1977. Play.

A Life in the Theater. New York: French, 1977. Play.

Sexual Perversity in Chicago and Duck Variations: Two Plays. New York: French, 1977.

American Buffalo, Sexual Perversity in Chicago, and Duck Variations: Three Plays. London: Methuen, 1978.

The Revenge of the Space Pandas, or Binky Rudich and the Two-Speed Clock. Chicago: Dramatic Publishing, 1978. Play.

The Water Engine and Mr. Happiness: Two Plays. New York: Grove, 1978.

Reunion and Dark Pony: Two Plays. New York: Grove, 1979.

The Woods. New York: Grove, 1979. Play.

Lakeboat. New York: Grove, 1981. Play.

The Poet and the Rent: A Play for Kids from Seven to 8:15. New York: French, 1981.

Short Plays and Monologues. New York: Dramatists Play Service, 1981. Comprises *The Blue Hour: City Sketches, Prairie du Chien, A Sermon, Shoeshine, Litko: A Dramatic Monologue, In Old Vermont,* and *All Men Are Whores: An Inquiry.*

Squirrels. New York: French, 1982. Play.

Edmond. New York: Grove, 1983. Play.

The Frog Prince. New York: French, 1983. Play.

Glengarry Glen Ross. New York: Grove, 1984; London: Methuen, 1984. Play.

A Collection of Dramatic Sketches and Monologues. New York: French, 1985. Comprises *Two Conversations, The Power Outage, The Dog, Film Crew, Four A.M., Food, Pint's a Pound The World Around, Deer Dogs, Columbus Avenue, Two Scenes, Conversations with the*

Spirit World, Maple Sugaring, Morris and Joe, Steve McQueen, Yes, Downing, In the Mall, Yes But So What, Cross Patch, and *Goldberg Street.*

Goldberg Street: Short Plays and Monologues. New York: Grove, 1985. Includes *Goldberg Street, Cross Patch, The Spanish Prisoner, Two Conversations, Two Scenes, Yes But So What, Vermont Sketches, The Blue Hour: City Sketches, A Sermon, Shoeshine, Litko: A Dramatic Monologue, In Old Vermont,* and *All Men Are Whores: An Inquiry.*

The Shawl and Prairie du Chien: Two Plays. New York: Grove, 1985.

Three Children's Plays. New York: Grove, 1986. Comprises *The Poet and the Rent, The Frog Prince,* and *The Revenge of the Space Pandas, or Binky Rudich and the Two-Speed Clock.*

Warm and Cold. New York: Fawbush/Solo, 1985. Poem.

Writing in Restaurants. New York: Viking, 1986. Addresses and essays.

House of Games. New York: Grove, 1987. Screenplay.

Three Jewish Plays. New York: French, 1987. Comprises *The Disappearance of the Jews, Goldberg Street,* and *The Luftmensch.*

The Woods, Lakeboat, Edmond: Three Plays. New York: Grove, 1987.

The Cherry Orchard: An Adaptation of Chekhov's Play. New York: Grove, 1988. Adapted from Peter Nelles's translation.

Speed-the-Plow. New York: Grove, 1988. Play.

Premiere Productions

Camel. Plainfield, Vermont, Goddard College, 1968.

Lakeboat. Marlboro, Vermont, Theater Workshop, Marlboro College, 1970.

Duck Variations. Plainfield, Vermont, St. Nicholas Theater Company, Goddard College, 1972.

Litko: A Dramatic Monologue. Chicago, Body Politic, 1972.

Sexual Perversity in Chicago. Chicago, Organic Theater Company, summer 1974.

The Poet and the Rent. Chicago, St. Nicholas Theater Company, Oct. 1974.

Squirrels. Chicago, St. Nicholas Theater Company, Oct. 1974.

Mackinac. New York, Center Youth Theater at the Bernard Horwich Jewish Community Center, 1975.

Marranos. New York, Center Youth Theater at the Bernard Horwich Jewish Community Center, 1975.

American Buffalo. Chicago, Goodman Theater, Stage Two, 23 Nov. 1975.

Reunion. Chicago, St. Nicholas Theater Company, 9 Jan. 1976.
All Men Are Whores: An Inquiry. New Haven, Conn., Yale Cabaret, Feb. 1977.
A Life in the Theater. Chicago, Goodman Theater, Stage Two, 3 Feb. 1977.
The Water Engine: An American Fable. Chicago, St. Nicholas Theater Company, 11 May 1977.
Dark Pony. New Haven, Conn., Yale Repertory Theater, 14 Oct. 1977.
The Woods. Chicago, St. Nicholas Theater Company, 11 Nov. 1977.
The Revenge of the Space Pandas, or Binky Rudich and the Two-Speed Clock. Chicago, St. Nicholas Theater Company, Children's Theater, 19 Nov. 1977.
Mr. Happiness. New York, Plymouth Theater, 6 Mar. 1978.
A Sermon. Chicago, Apollo Theater Center, 1979.
The Blue Hour: City Sketches. New York, New York Shakespeare Festival, Public Theater, Feb. 1979.
Lone Canoe, or The Explorer. Chicago, Goodman Theater, 18 May 1979.
The Sanctity of Marriage. New York, Circle Repertory, 18 Oct. 1979.
Shoeshine. New York, Ensemble Studio Theater, Nov. 1979.
Edmond. Chicago, Goodman Theater, 4 June 1982.
The Disappearance of the Jews. Chicago, Goodman Theater, 1983.
Red River, translated and adapted by Mamet from Pierre Laville's *Le Fleuve rouge*. Chicago, Goodman Theater, 2 May 1983.
Five Unrelated Pieces. New York, Ensemble Studio Theater, May 1983.
The Dog. New York, Jason's Park Royal, 14 July 1983.
Film Crew. New York, Jason's Park Royal, 14 July 1983.
Four A. M. New York, Jason's Park Royal, 14 July 1983.
Glengarry Glen Ross. London, Cottesloe Theater at the National Theater, 21 Sept. 1983; Chicago, Goodman Theater, 27 Jan. 1984.
The Frog Prince. Milwaukee, Wis., Milwaukee Repertory Theater, 19 Apr. 1984.
Vermont Sketches (Conversations with the Spirit World, Pint's a Pound the World Around, Downing, Deer Dogs). New York: Ensemble Studio Theater, 24 May 1984.
Cross Patch. Evanston, Illinois, WNUR Radio, Northwestern University, 4 Mar. 1985.

Goldberg Street. Evanston, Illinois, WNUR Radio, Northwestern University, 4 Mar. 1985.

The Shawl. Chicago, Goodman Theater, New Theater Company, 19 Apr. 1985.

The Spanish Prisoner. Chicago, Goodman Theater, New Theater Company, 19 Apr. 1985.

Prairie du Chien. New York, Lincoln Center Theater, 23 Dec. 1985.

Vint, adapted by Mamet from Avrahm Yarmolinsky's translation of Anton Chekhov's story. New York, Ensemble Studio Theater, 22 Apr. 1986.

The Cherry Orchard: An Adaptation of Chekhov's Play. Chicago, Goodman Theater, New Theater Company, Mar. 1988.

Speed-the-Plow. New York, Mitzi E. Newhouse Theater at Lincoln Center, 29 Mar. 1988.

Screenplays

The Postman Always Rings Twice. Paramount, 1981.

The Verdict. Columbia, 1982.

House of Games. Orion, 1987.

The Untouchables. Paramount, 1987.

Things Change. Columbia, 1988.

Selected Other

"The Power Outage: A Short Play," *New York Times,* 6 Aug. 1977, p. 17.

"A 'Sad Comedy' About Actors," *New York Times,* 16 Oct. 1977, section 2, p. 7.

"Learn to Love the Theater," *Horizon,* 21 (Oct. 1978), 96.

"Playwrights on Resident Theaters: What Is To Be Done?" *Theater,* 10 (Summer 1979), 82.

"A Tradition of the Theater as Art," *New York Theater Review,* 3 (Feb. 1979), 24.

"A Playwright Learns from Film," *New York Times,* 20 July 1980, section 2, p. 6.

"Columbus Avenue," *Village Voice,* 10 Sept. 1980, p. 23. Play.

"My Kind of Town," *Horizon,* 24 (Nov. 1981), 56-57.

"Air Plays," *Horizon,* 25 (May/June 1982), 20-23.

"Conventional Warfare," *Esquire,* 105 (Mar. 1985), 110-114.

SECONDARY BIBLIOGRAPHY

Bibliographies

Carroll, Dennis. *David Mamet.* New York: St. Martin's, 1987, 162-165.

Davis, J. Madison, and John Coleman. "David Mamet: A Classifed Bibliography," *Studies in American Drama, 1945-Present,* 1 (1986), 83-101. Primary and secondary.

King, Kimball. *Ten Modern American Playwrights: An Annotated Bibliography.* New York: Garland, 1982, 179-186. Primary and secondary.

Interviews

Allen, Jennifer. "David Mamet's Hard Sell," *New York,* 9 (9 Apr. 1984), 38-41.

Becker, Robert. "Donald Sultan with David Mamet," *Interview,* 13 (Mar. 1983), 56, 58.

Cantwell, Mary. "David Mamet: Bulldog of the Middle Class," *Vogue,* 174 (July 1984), 216-217, 281.

Case, Brian. "The Hot Property Man," *Times Magazine* (London), 18 Sept. 1983, pp. 72-73.

Chase, Chris. "At the Movies," *New York Times,* 20 Mar. 1981, p. C6.

Christiansen, Richard. "Master of the Game," *Arts Guardian,* 16 Nov. 1987, p. 18.

Christiansen. *"Postman* Script: David Mamet's Special Delivery," *Chicago Tribune,* 15 Mar. 1981, section 6, pp. 5, 16.

Christy, Desmond. "A Man for the Forgotten Frontier," *Guardian,* 16 Sept. 1983, p. 15.

DeVries, Hilary. "In David Mamet's Hands a Pen Becomes a Whip," *Christian Science Monitor,* 21 Mar. 1984, pp. 21-22.

Drake, Sylvie. "The Lunching of a Playwright," *Los Angeles Times,* 5 Feb. 1978, Calendar section, p. 54.

Dullea, Georgia. "For Mamet and Crouse, a Movie Is a Family Matter," *New York Times,* 11 Oct. 1987, section 2, pp. 25, 30.

Earley, Michael. "Playwrights Making Movies," *Performing Arts Journal,* 5, no. 3 (1981), 36-40.

Fraser, C. Gerald. "Mamet's Plays Shed Masculinity Myth," *New York Times,* 5 July 1976, p. 7.

Gottlieb, Richard. "The 'Engine' That Drives Playwright David Mamet," *New York Times,* 15 Jan. 1978, section 2, pp. 1, 4.

Gussow, Mel. "Real Estate World a Model for Mamet," *New York Times*, 28 Mar. 1984, p. C19.

Kissel, Howard. "David Mamet: A Voice from the Side Pocket," *W*, 11-18 Nov. 1977, p. 24.

Lahr, John. "Winners and Losers," *New Society*, 29 Sept. 1983, pp. 476-477.

Leahey, Mimi. "David Mamet: The American Dream Gone Bad," *Other Stages*, 5 (4-17 Nov. 1982), 3.

Leogrande, Ernest. "A Man of Few Words Moves On to Sentences," *New York Sunday News*, 13 Feb. 1977, Leisure section, p. 3.

Nuwer, Hank. "Two Gentlemen of Chicago: David Mamet and Stuart Gordon," *South Carolina Review*, 17 (Spring 1985), 9-20.

Roudané, Matthew C. "An Interview with David Mamet," *Studies in American Drama, 1945-Present*, 1 (1986), 73-81.

Savran, David. "Trading in the American Dream," *American Theater*, 4 (Sept. 1987), 13-18.

Sessums, Kevin. "Dammit Mamet!," *Interview*, 18 (Oct. 1987), 140-141.

Shewey, Don. "David Mamet Puts a Dark New Urban Drama on Stage," *New York Times*, 24 Oct. 1982, section 2, pp. 1, 4.

Taylor, Clarke. "Mamet and the Hollywood Wringer," *Los Angeles Times*, 28 Mar. 1981, section 2, p. 10.

Terry, Clifford. "At Work and Plays with David Mamet," *Chicago Tribune Magazine*, 8 May 1977, pp. 16, 17, 21, 23, 26, 28.

Winer, Linda. "David Mamet Embarks on a 'Lone Canoe' Trip," *Chicago Tribune*, 20 May 1979, section 6, pp. 3, 15.

Winer. "David Stages a Victory over a Village Goliath," *Chicago Tribune*, 15 Aug. 1976, section 6, p. 2.

Yakir, Don. "The Postman's Words," *Film Comment*, 17 (Mar./Apr. 1981), pp. 21-24.

Zweigler, Mark. "David Mamet: The Solace of a Playwright's Ideals," *After Dark*, 20 (Aug. 1976), 42-45.

Critical Studies: Books

Bigsby, C. W. E. *David Mamet*. London & New York: Methuen, 1985.

Carroll, Dennis. *David Mamet*. New York: St. Martin's, 1987.

Critical Studies: Major Reviews, Articles, and Book Sections

Almansi, Guido. "David Mamet, a Virtuoso of Invective." In *Critical Angles: European Views of Contemporary American Literature*, ed.

Marc Chénetier. Carbondale: Southern Illinois University Press, 1986, 191-207, 241-242.

Barbera, Jack V. "Ethical Perversity in America: Some Observations on David Mamet's *American Buffalo*," *Modern Drama*, 24 (Sept. 1981), 270-275.

Berkowitz, Gerald M. *New Broadways: Theatre Across America 1950-1980*. Totowa, N.J.: Rowman & Allanheld, 1982, 136-137.

Bigsby, C. W. E. *A Critical Introduction to Twentieth-Century American Drama*, volume 3: *Beyond Broadway*. Cambridge & New York: Cambridge University Press, 1985, 251-290.

Billington, Michael. "Theater in London: Mamet Turns to the World of Salesmen," *New York Times*, 9 Oct. 1983, section 2, pp. 6, 19.

Blumenthal, Eileen, Michael Feingold, and Terry Curtis Fox. "Mamet à Trois," *Village Voice*, 7 May 1979, p. 103.

Cardullo, Bert. "Comedy and *Sexual Perversity in Chicago*," *Notes on Contemporary Literature*, 12 (Jan. 1982), 6.

Christiansen, Richard. "The Young Lion of Chicago Theater," *Chicago Tribune Magazine*, 11 July 1982, pp. 8-9, 11-14.

Clay, Carolyn. "Will Mamet Make It?: America's Hottest Young Playwright Moves from *American Buffalo* to Smaller Game," *Boston Phoenix*, 28 Feb. 1978, section 3, pp. 1, 12.

Clurman, Harold. "Theater," *Nation*, 225 (12 Nov. 1977), 504-506.

Clurman. "Theater," *Nation*, 226 (28 Jan. 1978), 92.

Clurman. "Theater," *Nation*, 228 (19 May 1979), 581-582.

Cohn, Ruby. "Narrower Straits: Ribman, Rabe, Guare, Mamet." In her *New American Dramatists: 1960-1980*. New York: Grove, 1982, 41-46.

Ditsky, John. " 'He Lets You See the Thought There': The Theater of David Mamet," *Kansas Quarterly*, 12 (Fall 1980), 25-34.

Duberman, Martin. "The Great Gray Way," *Harper's*, 256 (May 1978), 79-87.

Eder, Richard. "David Mamet's New Realism," *New York Times Magazine*, 12 Mar. 1978, pp. 40, 42, 45, 47.

Eder. "Stage: Mamet Reinvents Radio," *New York Times*, 6 Jan. 1978, p. C3.

Eder. "Stage: Mamet's *Perversity*, Mosaic on Modern Mores, Moves," *New York Times*, 17 June 1976, p. 29.

Eder. "Stage: *Water Engine* Is Uptown," *New York Times*, 7 Mar. 1978, p. 42.

Feingold, Michael. "The Way We Are," *Village Voice*, 9 Nov. 1982, pp. 81-82.

Fleckenstein, Joan. "*Dark Pony* and *Reunion*," *Educational Theatre Journal*, 30 (Oct. 1978), 417-419.

Forbes, Daniel. "Dirty Dealing," *American Theatre*, 4 (Feb. 1988), 13-18.

Freedman, Samuel G. "The Gritty Eloquence of David Mamet," *New York Times Magazine*, 21 Apr. 1985, pp. 32, 40, 42, 46, 50, 51, 64.

Gale, Steven H. "David Mamet: The Plays, 1972-1980." In *Essays on Contemporary American Drama*, ed. Hedwig Bock and Albert Wertheim. Munich: Hueber, 1981, 207-223.

Gill, Brendan. "No News from Lake Michigan," *New Yorker*, 53 (28 Feb. 1977), 54-56.

Gill. "The Theater: The Lower Depths," *New Yorker*, 60 (2 Apr. 1984), 114.

Gottfried, Martin, "Cult of the Second-rate," *Saturday Review*, 5 (4 Mar. 1978), 41.

Gussow, Mel. "*American Buffalo* in London—The Accent's OK, but the Music's Off," *New York Times*, 23 July 1978, section 2, pp. 4, 31.

Gussow. "A Rich Crop of Writing Talent Brings New Life to the American Theater," *New York Times*, 21 Aug. 1977, section 2, pp. 1, 16.

Gussow. "David Mamet's Latest Microcosm," *New York Times*, 4 Dec. 1977, section 3, pp. 3, 34.

Gussow. "Mamet Wins with *Life in Theater*," *New York Times*, 5 Feb. 1977, p. 10.

Gussow. "Stage: Illusion Within an Illusion," *New York Times*, 21 Oct. 1977, p. C3.

Gussow. "Stage: *Lakeboat*, Mamet's First, at Long Wharf," *New York Times*, 17 Feb. 1982, p. C23.

Gussow. "Stage: Mamet Explores the Fall of *Edmond*," *New York Times*, 17 June 1982, p. C17.

Gussow. "Stage: *Reunion*, 3 Mamet Plays," *New York Times*, 19 Oct. 1979, p. C3.

Gussow. "Stage: Two Pungent Comedies by New Playwright," *New York Times*, 1 Nov. 1975, p. 15.

Gussow. "Theater: Mamet's *American Buffalo*," *New York Times*, 28 Jan. 1976, p. 30.

Gussow. "The Daring Visions of Four New, Young Playwrights," *New York Times*, 13 Feb. 1977, section 2, pp. 1, 9, 13-14.

Hayman, Ronald. "Following the Lead: David Mamet, *Glengarry Glen Ross*, Cottesloe Theater," *Times Literary Supplement*, 30 Sept. 1983, p. 1042.

Hoffman, Jan. "Barking Up the Wrong Tree," *Village Voice*, 25 May 1982, pp. 94, 96.

Jacobs, Dorothy H. "Working Worlds in David Mamet's Dramas," *Midwestern Miscellany*, 14 (1986), 47-57.

Kerr, Walter. "Al Pacino's Supercharged *Buffalo*," *New York Times*, 14 June 1981, section 2, p. 3.

Kerr. "Off Broadway This Week, a Trio of Openings," *New York Times*, 15 Jan. 1978, pp. D3, D25.

Kerr. "Two New Plays That Focus on the Male Loner," *New York Times*, 7 Nov. 1982, section 2, pp. 3, 24.

Kolin, Philip C. "Revealing Illusions in David Mamet's *The Shawl*," *Notes on Contemporary Literature*, 16 (Mar. 1986), 9-10.

Lawson, Steve. "Language Equals Action," *Horizon*, 20 (Nov. 1977), 40-45.

Lieberson, Jonathan. "The Prophet of Broadway," *New York Review of Books*, 21 July 1988, pp. 3-4, 6.

Miner, Michael D. "Grotesque Drama in the '70s," *Kansas Quarterly*, 12, no. 4 (1980), 99-109.

Nightingale, Benedict. "Is Mamet the Bard of Modern Immorality?" *New York Times*, 1 Apr. 1984, section 2, pp. 5, 23.

Novick, Julius. "The Mamet Show," *Village Voice*, 16 Jan. 1978, p. 89.

Oliver, Edith. "Off Broadway: David Mamet of Illinois," *New Yorker*, 51 (10 Nov. 1975), 135-136.

Oliver. "The Theater: Off Broadway," *New Yorker*, 55 (29 Oct. 1979), 81-82.

Oliver. "Watered Down," *New Yorker*, 54 (19 Jan. 1978), 69.

Rich, Frank. "Mamet's Dark View of Hollywood as a Heaven for the Virtueless," *New York Times*, 4 May 1988, p. C17.

Rich. "Theater: Al Pacino in *American Buffalo*," *New York Times*, 5 June 1981, p. C3.

Rich. "Theater: Mamet's *Edmond* at the Provincetown," *New York Times*, 28 Oct. 1982, p. 23.

Rich. "Theater: Patti LuPone in Mamet's *The Woods*," *New York Times*, 17 May 1982, p. C12.

Rogoff, Gordon. "Albee and Mamet: The War of the Words," *Saturday Review*, 4 (2 Apr. 1977), 36-37.

Rogoff. "The Seductions of Cynicism," *Village Voice*, 17 May 1988, pp. 105-106.

Roudané, Matthew C. "Public Issues, Private Tensions: David Mamet's *Glengarry Glen Ross*," *South Carolina Review*, 19 (Fall 1986), 35-47.

Salmon, Eric. "Three American Plays." In his *Is the Theater Still Dying?*, Westport, Conn.: Greenwood, 1985, 223-239.

Schlueter, June, and Elizabeth Forsyth. "America as Junkshop: The Business Ethic in David Mamet's *American Buffalo*," *Modern Drama*, 26 (Dec. 1983), 492-500.

Simon, John. "Bluffalo," *New York*, 14 (15 June 1981), 66.

Simon. "Permanents and Transients," *New York*, 12 (14 May 1979), 75-76.

Simon. "Queasy Quartet," *New York*, 12 (5 Nov. 1979), 87-88.

Simon. "Theater Chronicle," *Hudson Review*, 30 (Summer 1977), 259-260.

Simon. "Theater Chronicle," *Hudson Review*, 31 (Spring 1978), 154-155.

Solomon, Alisa. "The Goodman, the Organic and the St. Nicholas: Resident Theaters in Chicago," *Theater*, 10 (Summer 1979), 75-81.

Storey, Robert. "The Making of David Mamet," *Hollins Critic*, 16-17 (Oct. 1979), 1-11.

Stothard, Peter. "*Sexual Perversity in Chicago* and *Duck Variations*," *Plays and Players*, 25 (Feb. 1978), 30-31.

Sullivan, Dan. "Stage: Waiting for Mamet," *Los Angeles Times*, 27 Nov. 1977, Calendar section, p. 72.

Sultanik, Aaron. "Death and David Mamet," *Midstream: A Monthly Jewish Review*, 24 (May 1978), 56-57.

Sweet, Jeffrey. "Living Playwrights in the Living Theater: David Mamet," *Dramatics*, 53 (Nov. 1981), 40-41.

Ventimiglia, Peter James. "Recent Trends in American Drama: Michael Cristofer, David Mamet, and Albert Innaurato," *Journal of American Culture*, 1 (Spring 1978), 195-204.

Weales, Gerald. "American Theater Watch, 1977-1978," *Georgia Review*, 32 (Fall 1978), 518-519.

Weales. "The Mamet Variations, or A New Life in the Theater," *Decade–Promotional Issue*, 1978, pp. 10-13.

Weales. "The Stage," *Commonweal*, 105 (14 Apr. 1978), 244-245.

Wetzsteon, Ross. "David Mamet: Remember That Name," *Village Voice*, 5 July 1976, pp. 101, 103.

Wetzsteon. "New York Letter: Ross Wetzsteon Introduces an Exciting New Writer, David Mamet," *Plays and Players*, 23 (Sept. 1976), 37-38.

Witt, Linda. "Playwright David Mamet Fashions a Life in the Theater Out of Scavenged Speech," *People*, 12 (12 Nov. 1979), 58-63.

BIBLIOGRAPHICAL ESSAY

Bibliographies and Checklists

The most comprehensive bibliography on David Mamet is J. Madison Davis and John Coleman's, in *Studies in American Drama, 1945-Present* (1986). The primary bibliography includes forty-two items: plays, screenplays, and essays. The secondary bibliography lists more than four hundred interviews, critical articles, reviews, and biographical essays garnered from American and Canadian scholarly and popular publications.

The Mamet bibliography in Kimball King's *Ten Modern American Playwrights* (1982) has been superseded by Davis and Coleman, not only because King's was compiled six years earlier but also because it is spottier. King lists Mamet's primary works, two interviews, thirteen critical essays, and fifty reviews. The interviews and critical essays, as well as an occasional review, are annotated.

Special notice should be taken of the bibliography in Dennis Carroll's critical study, *David Mamet* (1987). Though slender, it includes a valuable listing of three archival collections and nine videocassettes (primarily of performances of Mamet's plays) which are held at the New York Public Library at Lincoln Center.

Interviews

Mamet gave four important interviews in 1976, in the wake of the premiere of *American Buffalo*. Ross Wetzsteon conducted one of the earliest interviews with Mamet and included comments from it (on the attenuated goodbye scene in *American Buffalo*, for example) in his *Village Voice* article, "David Mamet: Remember That Name" (5 July 1976). Mark Zweigler's *After Dark* interview, "David Mamet: The Solace of a Playwright's Ideals" (Aug. 1976), covers Mamet's early career and provides information on his creative habits, his reactions to critics, and his views on the state of American theater.

Linda Winer interviewed the playwright in New York during the Cherry Lane Theater production of *Sexual Perversity in Chicago* and *Duck Variations*. In "David Stages a Victory over a Village Goliath" (15 Aug. 1976) Winer and Mamet review Mamet's playwriting career and discuss Chicago and New York theater. C. Gerald Fraser's 5 July 1976 *New York Times* interview, "Mamet's Plays Shed Masculinity Myth," contains candid comments by the playwright concerning his attitudes toward women. Mamet confesses a reluctance to write parts for women because he feels his personal experience enables him to create "fleshier parts" for men.

In 1977 Mamet was interviewed by Ernest Leogrande and Clifford Terry. Leogrande's "A Man of Few Words Moves On to Sentences" (13 Feb. 1977) is an unusually unified interview that focuses on Mamet's language. Mamet speaks of his interest in musical rhythms, his compulsion to rewrite, the one play–*Duck Variations*–in which he changed only two sentences, and his language patterns. Terry's feature article in the *Chicago Tribune Magazine*, "At Work and Plays with David Mamet" (8 May 1977), covers familiar ground and adds a number of original comments concerning Mamet's attitude toward critics, who, he wishes, had more than a "visceral understanding" of the theater.

Two interviews in 1978 focused on Mamet's plays *The Water Engine* and *American Buffalo*. In Sylvie Drake's *Los Angeles Times* interview, "The Lunching of a Playwright" (5 Feb. 1978), Mamet discusses his favorite writers and gives a probing analysis of *The Water Engine*. Richard Gottlieb, during a break in rehearsals for *The Water Engine*, talked with Mamet about his experiences as a playwright. In his "The 'Engine' That Drives Playwright David Mamet" (15 Jan. 1978) Mamet speaks of plays as "dope," of *American Buffalo* as an expression of his anger about business, of his satisfaction with his plays, of the theater's recognition of an American identity, of the value of healthy criticism, and of the effects of his success on his life and art.

Linda Winer's 20 May 1979 *Chicago Tribune* interview, "David Mamet Embarks on a 'Lone Canoe' Trip," deals exclusively with Mamet's *Lone Canoe*, which opened in Chicago that week. Mamet describes the play as one with a classical structure, an adventure story that brings together nineteenth-century drama and fairy tales.

Michael Earley, Chris Chase, Richard Christiansen, Clarke Taylor, and Don Yakir were among the many to interview Mamet in 1981. Most of the interviews focused on Mamet's screenplay for the

1981 Paramount film *The Postman Always Rings Twice*. In the interview with Earley, "Playwrights Making Movies" (1981), Mamet
speaks of the differences in working on stage plays and screenplays,
registering his preference for the stage.

Two interviews in 1982 examined Mamet's play *Edmond*, which
opened that year. Don Shewey's *New York Times* interview, "David
Mamet Puts a Dark New Urban Drama on Stage" (24 Oct. 1982), contains much commentary on the playwright's view of his new play.
Mamet calls it a fairy tale about modern life, a play about an
"unintegrated personality," which was inspired in part by Georg
Büchner's *Woyzeck* (1879). He also speaks of his frustration with the
New York theater world, a frustration which, he claims, is reflected
in *Edmond*. An interview in *Other Stages* by Mimi Leahey, "David
Mamet: The American Dream Gone Bad" (4-17 Nov. 1982), is excellent because Mamet is exceptionally candid. He is impassioned in
his analysis of the American dream, which, he claims, cannot work
anymore, there being no one left to be exploited. His passion car-
ries over into his assessment of theater critics.

Desmond Christy, Brian Case, and John Lahr interviewed
Mamet on the occasion of the staging of his *Glengarry Glen Ross* in
London in 1983. A 1983 interview by Robert Becker pairs Mamet
with his best friend, artist Donald Sultan. Mamet and Sultan discuss
their collaboration and their views on the visual arts and theater. In
Hilary DeVries's "In David Mamet's Hands a Pen Becomes a Whip"
(21 Mar. 1984) Mamet talks about the need for spiritual security. Jennifer Allen's "David Mamet's Hard Sell" (9 Apr. 1984), an interview
conducted just before the Broadway opening of *Glengarry Glen Ross*,
records the playwright's preproduction anxiety. Mamet speaks of
the play's business theme, his own experiences with real estate salesmen, and the circumstances of the play's composition; he also offers general comments about his life in the theater. Mary Cantwell
also talks with Mamet about *Glengarry Glen Ross* in her July 1984
Vogue essay, "David Mamet: Bulldog of the Middle Class." In it
Mamet comments on Arthur Miller's *Death of a Salesman* and his
own *All Men Are Whores: An Inquiry*. Hank Nuwer, in his "Two Gentlemen of Chicago: David Mamet and Stuart Gordon" (Spring 1985),
compels Mamet to speak of the theater as a celebration of the myster-
ies of life; he also discusses his reading, editing, and rewriting habits, growing up in the Midwest, and Chicago and New York theater
audiences.

Matthew C. Roudané conducted an important interview with Mamet in 1986. Mamet tells Roudané of his fascination with the myth of the American dream, a dream he thinks can only be realized at the expense of others; of how business corrupts and legitimizes unethical behavior; and of the influence of Thorstein Veblen on his work. Mamet said he considers himself an honest writer. For him, the purpose of theater is to explore the "paradox between the fact that everyone tries to do well but that few, if any, succeed." When asked to explain his dependence on Ibsenite dramatic form, Mamet claimed that he was indeed trying to write the well-made play, a form which, in its insistence on a beginning, a middle, and an end, imitates human perception. He also speaks of the difference in structure between *Glengarry Glen Ross* and *American Buffalo* and of the ways that structure affects characters and endings. He says the protagonist of *American Buffalo*, Danny Dunbrow, exemplifies an unassailable moral position and is in a position similar to that of Levene in *Glengarry Glen Ross*. Mamet calls his idiom poetic, claiming he does not capture language but creates it. In the creative process, form and content coalesce. Mamet sees himself as a storyteller and admits that the clarity demanded in writing for the screen has helped his writing for the stage. The playwright discusses the role of the media, the artist, and the audience: Hollywood and mass media have dulled the artistic palate of their audiences, who crave theatrical experience; an artist has to get better every year, and an audience needs to grow as it experiences plays; acting has nothing to do with emotion, everything to do with action; a writer must continue to do his job.

David Savran precedes his September 1987 interview with Mamet, "Trading in the American Dream," with a brief account of the playwright's background and an overview of his thematic concerns, particularly the demystification of the American dream. For Mamet, who often writes about the business world, the capitalist dream authorizes pillage and encourages destructive competitiveness. Mamet's plays, which deal with estrangement of various kinds, are concerned with the division between character and action and with ways that characters attempt to use language as a mediator. While Mamet's work is connected with Eugene O'Neill's and Miller's, his view is unsentimental, without nostalgia for a time when the business world respected human values. Mamet sees theater as a place of "ethical interchange," a place where "society can debate its future."

154

Throughout the conversation with Savran it is evident that Mamet values his directing and acting experiences, and that his writing for the stage is informed by that substantial knowledge. Mamet identifies as influences Bertolt Brecht, Lanford Wilson, Sanford Meisner, and Samuel Beckett's *Waiting for Godot*. He distinguishes himself from Miller, whom he calls a playwright of social conscience– his own plays try to bring to the stage "the life of the soul." Mamet identifies acting and writing as having to do with two people who want something different: we are all trying to "achieve our wishes from each other." But the point is "not to speak the desire but to speak that which is most likely going to bring about the desire." In response to questions concerning the process of writing, Mamet talks about his attempts to break down the barriers between the subconscious and the conscious mind. He writes expansively, then cuts. He attends rehearsals, often rewriting in response to them. His favorite productions are Gregory Mosher's of *Edmond* and John Dillon's of *Lakeboat*. Mamet describes his style as one informed by "honesty, simplicity and directness." His plays are not confrontational: he feels that theater should deal with what cannot be dealt with rationally. The playwright also speaks of his work in film and of his 1988 play *Speed-the-Plow*.

There were two good interviews looking at Mamet as a writer for the screen in 1987. Richard Christiansen interviewed Mamet about his screenplay for the film *House of Games* in his "Master of the Game" (16 Nov. 1987). Georgia Dullea spoke with both Mamet and his wife, Lindsay Crouse, who starred in *House of Games*, in "For Mamet and Crouse, a Movie Is a Family Matter" (11 Oct. 1987).

Critical Studies: Books

Two full-length studies of Mamet's work have appeared to date. C. W. E. Bigsby's *David Mamet* (1985), in Methuen's Contemporary Writers series, covers thirteen plays, from *Lakeboat* and *Duck Variations* through *Glengarry Glen Ross* and *The Shawl*. Intelligently analytic, Bigsby surveys Mamet's work with emphasis on the playwright's creation of a poetic idiom that both defines and entraps his characters. Concerned with American values, especially business values, Mamet examines the ethical and moral assumptions of a variety of characters. Bigsby thinks that Mamet, though committed to a kind of surface realism, redefines language, character, and action, offering a radical revisioning of theater.

Dennis Carroll's *David Mamet* (1987), in the St. Martin's Press Modern Dramatists series, also covers the plays from *Duck Variations* through *The Shawl*, grouping them in four thematic categories: business, sex, learning, and communion. In an especially helpful chapter on the plays in the theater, Carroll reviews productions, with emphasis on *The Water Engine*, which, he claims, illustrates "that special elusive 'dimension' " that informs the staging of Mamet's work. Like other books in the Modern Dramatists series, this is an introductory book designed for both scholarly and general readers. Its analyses include plot summaries and thematic motifs as well as commentary on the critical reception of the plays in production. An early chapter, "A Sense of Moral Dismay," identifies the vision that informs Mamet's major work and provides the basis for Carroll's analysis. A final chapter reviews Mamet's other writing, including his essays, adaptations, and his less significant or less ambitious dramas.

Critical Studies: Major Reviews, Articles, and Book Sections
C. W. E. Bigsby discusses Mamet's work in *A Critical Introduction to Twentieth-Century American Drama*, volume 3: *Beyond Broadway* (1985), in what may well be the most valuable essay on Mamet written to date. The essay covers the plays from *Duck Variations* through *Edmond*. It places Mamet in the context of the modern theater, noting his influence in shifting theater away from a New York–dominated enterprise to a decentralized national one and productively comparing qualities of his writing to work by Edward Albee, O'Neill, Harold Pinter, Beckett, and others. Bigsby also discusses the relationship between Mamet's work and dramatic realism, suggesting that the power of Mamet's plays rests in the moments "when language becomes attenuated and when the surface realism is stretched to the point of translucency." Mamet's world, he remarks, is a world of collapse in which characters live provisionally. Bigsby sees Mamet's vision as one that at once reflects both the modernist impulse and liberal humanism.

Two important essays on Mamet's book appeared in 1982. Ruby Cohn's *New American Dramatists: 1960-1980* includes a discussion of Mamet in a chapter entitled "Narrower Straits: Ribman, Rabe, Guare, Mamet." An introductory overview, Cohn's discussion covers the plays from *Duck Variations* through *The Woods*. She praises Mamet for his economical dialogue and his mastery of authentic idioms but deprecates the absence of ideas in his work. Gerald M. Berkowitz's survey, *New Broadways: Theatre Across America 1950-*

1980, includes passing references to Mamet as well as two paragraphs on several Mamet plays.

A substantial account of Mamet's work may be found in Steven H. Gale's essay, "David Mamet: The Plays, 1972-1980," which is part of Hedwig Bock and Albert Wertheim's edited collection *Essays on Contemporary American Drama* (1981). Treating each of the plays Mamet wrote in the first eight years of his career in turn, Gale gives plot summaries and offers information on staging. His thematic analysis focuses on Mamet's growing ability to render accurately a variety of relationships: friendships, sexual relations, business relations, private-public relations. Gale judges the early Mamet as a promising playwright, his work "likely to become a standard against which his contemporaries will be measured."

Guido Almansi's essay, "David Mamet, a Virtuoso of Invective," in *Critical Angles: European Views of Contemporary American Literature* (1986), edited by Marc Chénetier, provides lively insights into the world of Mamet's plays through *Glengarry Glen Ross*. Mamet, notes Almansi, is a "chronicler and parodist of the stag party." Even as he notices the dominance of a male culture in Mamet's plays, Almansi argues that Mamet is at his strongest when his primary characters are male. Dubbing him an "artist of invectives" and "a virtuoso of obscene expressions," Almansi proposes that for Mamet's characters vulgar language authenticates existence. Though his best plays are informed with a comic spirit, so also are they chronicles of American values, particularly of family and business, in decline. *Glengarry Glen Ross* provides an accurate view of the contemporary salesman, divorced from moral scruples and required professionally to be aggressive and shameless. The play, Almansi claims, prompted a reevaluation of the contemporary American theater to make a place for Mamet.

One writer who refuses to call Mamet's *American Buffalo* any more than a "modest little achievement" is Eric Salmon. In "Three American Plays," a chapter in his *Is the Theater Still Dying?* (1985), Salmon reacts to a New York revival of the Mamet play, noticing theatrically brilliant moments but generally disparaging the play and, in particular, the play's idiom, which for him is mocking.

In the 1970s, essays on Mamet were largely in general readership publications rather than scholarly journals. Ross Wetzsteon, recognizing Mamet's talent, admonishes his readership to take notice of the playwright in his article "David Mamet: Remember That Name" (5 July 1976) in the *Village Voice.* Other playwrights have attempted to create an authentic American idiom, he says, but only Mamet has succeeded. His extraordinary promise rests in the "exhilarating perfection" of his dramatic language. Wetzsteon, an Obie Award judge, notes that, of all in the new generation of playwrights, the committee felt Mamet was the one deserving major critical recognition. Mamet was introduced to readers of the British publication *Plays and Players* in Wetzsteon's "New York Letter: Ross Wetzsteon Introduces an Exciting New Writer, David Mamet" (Sept. 1976), essentially a revision of the article in the *Village Voice*.

In 1977 Mel Gussow wrote two features on Mamet's place in contemporary theater in the *New York Times*. In "The Daring Visions of Four New, Young Playwrights" (13 Feb. 1977) Gussow explores the dramatic worlds of Albert Innaurato, Christopher Durang, Michael Cristofer, and Mamet, as four writers who gained visibility in New York in the 1970s. Mamet came to New York by way of regional theater, in Chicago, as did Cristofer, who premiered in Los Angeles. The article provides an introduction to the work of these four playwrights, remarking that they represent the "broad spectrum of the post-Albee American theater." They share an irrespressible comic impulse, musical training, facility with language, and acting backgrounds. In "A Rich Crop of Writing Talent Brings New Life to the American Theater" (21 Aug. 1977) Gussow provides an encouraging overview of the American theater in the 1970s, a decade of considerable Off-Off-Broadway (and some Broadway) theatrical activity by new playwrights. Included in his survey are Mamet, Cristofer, Innaurato, Durang, Ntozake Shange, David Rabe, Richard Wesley, Ronald Ribman, and others, such as Sam Shepard and Wilson, who established themselves in the 1960s. Gussow notes that the emergence of these new dramatists is coincident with a fragmented and diversified American theater, which has moved its center away from Broadway. The consequence is greater opportunity, not only in New York but across the nation. Gussow claims no "group profile" for these new writers (beyond a sense of humor) but finds strength in their diversity. Mamet is mentioned with high praise several times.

Written following the production of Mamet's *The Water Engine*, Richard Eder's *New York Times Magazine* essay, "David Mamet's New Realism" (12 Mar. 1978), offers an assessment of the playwright's career through his first nine plays. Mamet, Eder claims, clearly has a style and a voice of his own, and the development of his work through nine plays staged in two and a half years can be traced.

Eder sees Mamet's work as moving modern theater away from a dramatization of the meaninglessness of life toward a celebration of a damaged but vital humanity. From Eder's analysis surfaces a definition of Mamet's "new realism": its language is "grotesquely realistic," authentic yet lyrical; its action is an action of language and emotion; its impact is emotional. Mamet has an ear both for speech and for heartbeat. His work through *The Water Engine* suggests that the later plays combine his "extraordinary command of mood, character and language" with a more fully realized plot.

Dan Sullivan's "Stage: Waiting for Mamet" (27 Nov. 1977), which appeared in the *Los Angeles Times,* acknowledged Mamet's considerable success in Chicago and New York and registered impatience for West Coast productions. (Until then, there had been only one: *Duck Variations* by the Acting Company performing at the University of California at Los Angeles.) Sullivan, having seen *A Life in the Theater* in New York and *Reunion* in New Haven, praises Mamet's dialogue as well as the "disconnections" in it.

The *Boston Phoenix* carried a major piece on Mamet on 28 February 1978 in its Arts and Leisure section. In "Will Mamet Make It?: America's Hottest Young Playwright Moves from *American Buffalo* to Smaller Game" Carolyn Clay cautions that extravagant press coverage could have a negative impact on his career. Like Albee, who was praised inordinately for *Who's Afraid of Virginia Woolf?,* Mamet might have trouble following his own *American Buffalo.* The piece provides information on Mamet's rise to recognition, discussing his 1976 Obie and 1977 New York Drama Critics awards. Written on the occasion of two productions of *American Buffalo* in New England— at the Off Broadway Theater in Cambridge, Massachusetts, and at Trinity Square Repertory in Providence, Rhode Island—the piece discusses the play and the two mountings, then moves to a consideration of "minor Mamet," *The Water Engine* and *A Life in the Theater.*

Linda Witt's *People* magazine piece, "Playwright David Mamet Fashions a Life in the Theater Out of Scavenged Speech" (12 Nov. 1979), provides anecdotal information about Mamet's childhood and marriage to Lindsay Crouse that should interest the general reader. The piece creates a portrait of a moderately successful young playwright who, despite his attraction to intimate theater, is still striving for the big play.

Scholarly articles on Mamet's work from the late 1970s include Steve Lawson's "Language Equals Action" (Nov. 1977); Martin Duberman's "The Great Gray Way" (May 1978); Peter James

Ventimiglia's "Recent Trends in American Drama: Michael Cristofer, David Mamet, and Albert Innaurato" (Spring 1978); Gerald Weales's "The Mamet Variations, or A New Life in the Theater" (1978); and Robert Storey's "The Making of David Mamet" (Oct. 1979). Lawson's piece is an intelligently written analysis of Mamet's plays with special reference to *American Buffalo, A Life in the Theater,* and *The Water Engine.* He sees Mamet's distinctiveness in his exploration and use of language. For Mamet, language is a source of power, a function of survival, and the dramatic action in nearly plotless plays. Lawson defines Mamet's cadenced profanity, punctuated frequently by silence, as "new eloquence" and says the term defines Mamet's theatrical voice and his contribution to the American stage. Duberman's essay surveys American drama of the 1960s and 1970s, discussing the trio of new male playwrights—Thomas Babe, Innaurato, and Mamet—who received considerable critical acclaim during 1978. Judging Mamet "the most technically proficient" of the trinity, Duberman offers comments on three plays: *American Buffalo, A Life in the Theater,* and *The Water Engine.* Ventimiglia's essay provides perceptive insights into the work of Cristofer, Innaurato, and Mamet through focusing on their most recent work—*American Buffalo* in the case of Mamet. The essay explores how these playwrights are both responding to and defining the needs of the American theater. They tend toward the realistic play in order to understand important American concerns like the failure of capitalism, for example, in Mamet's *American Buffalo.* All three write in the distinctive idiom of modern America, and all three are helping the American theater to meet once again the demands of a changing society.

Weales speaks perceptively of Mamet as an emerging playwright, collecting comments from interviews and reviews to suggest his distinctiveness and his promise. Most of the piece deals with *American Buffalo,* which Weales calls an "invasion play," that is, a play in which an "outsider enters a closed circle and disrupts the delicate balance." He sees *A Life in the Theater* and *The Water Engine* as lesser works but suggestive as well of Mamet's inventiveness and talent. Storey explores the "verbal busyness" of Mamet's early plays, noting how, for Mamet, language determines behavior, rather than the other way around. For example, in his first three plays—*Duck Variations, Sexual Perversity in Chicago,* and *American Buffalo*—Mamet enters into "mocking complicity" with his characters, filling the dramatic space with the energy of language. In *The Water Engine, Mr. Happi-*

ness, and *A Life in the Theater,* Mamet explores the relationship between the language of the media and the language of experience.
Storey concludes that, in these six plays, Mamet's characters are
their language; it is language that allows them to exist; in the later
plays, instincts "that transcend both the values and imperatives of
their language" surface more insistently. In Mamet's 1977 play, *The
Woods,* Storey sees a new direction in his writing, toward drama that
offers "nakedly human contact."

Alisa Solomon's "The Goodman, the Organic and the St. Nicholas: Resident Theaters in Chicago" (Summer 1979) provides information on these Chicago theaters and their artistic directors, with particular attention to Mamet. Each of the theaters claims him as its own,
since his plays have been staged in all three, but Mamet helped
found the St. Nicholas.

Scholarly attention to Mamet grew in the 1980s, as the playwright gained greater recognition and formal acknowledgment of
his achievement through two Obies, a Pulitzer Prize, and a New
York Drama Critics Circle Award, not to mention two Tony nomina-
tions in one year (1984). In " 'He Lets You See the Thought
There': The Theater of David Mamet" (Fall 1980) John Ditsky proposes that, while British theater has been a theater of articulation,
American theater has been one of inarticulation. Mamet's plays, he
suggests, reflecting as they do an idiom that is "Chicagoan-
Pinteresque" and distinctly Mamet's own, represent the most important embodiment of this theater of inarticulation. Using *American Buffalo, A Life in the Theater,* and *The Woods* as examples, Ditsky
examines various recurring devices such as parenthetical dialogue,
musicality of form, banality, and humor. He concludes that Mamet
represents American drama's best hope for the survival of a theater
of language.

Michael D. Miner included a discussion of *Duck Variations* in
his article "Grotesque Drama in the '70s" (1980). Miner discusses
the conversation between George and Emil in Mamet's play, evaluating the discussion concerning ducks as an exercise not in absurd
logic but in absurd imagery and the discussion concerning the an-
cient Greeks as a grotesque intellectual caricature.

Written for an educational theater audience, Jeffrey Sweet's November 1981 *Dramatics* piece on Mamet ("Living Playwrights in the
Living Theater: David Mamet") provides an introduction to his career and work. Sweet notes the relationship between the plays and
Mamet's home city, Chicago. While endorsing the critical enthusi-

asm for Mamet's dialogue, Sweet argues that Mamet's primary strength is in his respect for the actor as collaborator. He singles out *The Water Engine* and *A Life in the Theater* as being of special interest to schools.

In "Ethical Perversity in America: Some Observations on David Mamet's *American Buffalo*" (Sept. 1981) Jack V. Barbera establishes the locale of the play as Chicago but registers his belief that specific location is less important than identifying an urban American subculture. He acknowledges the play's coarse vocabulary and praises Mamet's verbal rhythms, which include frequent elliptical expression. Taking issue with reviewers who do not see much substance in the play, he proposes that the relationship between the play's major motifs—friendship, self-interest, business, and being knowledgeable—and the relationships, tensions, and contradictions in the language of Don and Teach constitute the play's concerns. Barbera ends by suggesting the title might have a double meaning, one referring to a marginal class of society, the other to the act of intimidation, that is, to "buffalo" someone.

Bert Cardullo's "Comedy and *Sexual Perversity in Chicago*" (Jan. 1982) is a brief essay that suggests that bonding is the focus of *Sexual Perversity in Chicago*. Much of the play shows two couples failing at sexual relationships, resorting to bonding with a member of the same sex. The effort and the failure to find partners is comic, as is the disparity between the characters' perception of their circumstances and the audience's.

In "America as Junkshop: The Business Ethic in David Mamet's *American Buffalo*" (Dec. 1983) June Schlueter and Elizabeth Forsyth examine the prevailing business ethic in *American Buffalo*, an ethic that informs the robbery plans of the petty criminals. Noting Teach's commitment to free enterprise, his reliance on the rhetoric of business, and his distortions of the work ethic defining the American dream, Schlueter and Forsyth propose that, for Mamet, the decadence of American values is related to the dominance of the American business ethic. In *American Buffalo* the junkshop becomes an image of the pile of cast-off values that is the consequence of the business ethic's having penetrated the national consciousness and the national language.

In "Public Issues, Private Tensions: David Mamet's *Glengarry Glen Ross*" (Fall 1986) Matthew Roudané speaks of the Tocquevillean dialect present in many of Mamet's plays. Mamet is especially concerned with how public issues—particularly business issues—

affect the individual's private world. Collisions between these two worlds create the dramatic interest in Mamet's plays, which reflect the playwright's belief in the power of art to create a liberal humanism. Even as Mamet's ethically corrupt characters struggle to avoid confrontations and assure their own lack of self-awareness, Mamet's audiences evaluate those characters' ethical and moral balancing acts. Roudané looks closely at the world of *Glengarry Glen Ross,* in which business is presented as "sacrament." The play's characters, Roudané argues, accept the American drama as a "talismanic cultural force." As in Tocqueville's early nineteenth-century America, self-interest is wrongly understood by Mamet's characters.

In "Working Worlds in David Mamet's Dramas" (1986) Dorothy H. Jacobs examines the importance of place in Mamet's plays, noting that much of his work is set not in the domestic sphere of much of American drama but in a working world. Exploring in particular the working worlds of *Glengarry Glen Ross, American Buffalo, Lakeboat,* and *A Life in the Theater,* Jacobs proposes a constant and distinctive preoccupation with laboring men—as real estate salesmen, junkshop owners, petty thieves, seamen, actors—all "vitally engaged in their work." In these and other plays, Mamet shifts the identifying world of American drama from family to workplace. His concern with the working class links him thematically to a Chicago literary tradition that includes James T. Farrell, Saul Bellow, Hamlin Garland, and a host of novelists who "presented harrowing accounts of men confronting the solid materialism of Chicago."

Philip C. Kolin's brief essay, "Revealing Illusions in David Mamet's *The Shawl*" (Mar. 1986), proposes that Mamet's play is a significant postmodern attack on the place illusion occupies in our internal and external reality. Through tricks of magic he at once exposes illusion and demonstrates his audience's need for it. "See" and "know" are frequently used verbs, and the shawl, ultimately, is a cover for the protagonist's tricks.

Popular publications continued to include Mamet in their pages in the 1980s. The *Chicago Tribune Magazine* carried a feature by Richard Christiansen, "The Young Lion of Chicago Theater," on 11 July 1982. The essay is based on a number of interviews conducted with people who knew Mamet in his early years of work in the Chicago theater and with Mamet himself. It is a carefully researched, exceptionally valuable piece that traces the cycle of Mamet's career in Chicago from its beginnings to *Lone Canoe.*

A 21 April 1985 *New York Times Magazine* feature, Samuel G. Freedman's "The Gritty Eloquence of David Mamet," is packed with information and insights, and, as such, is probably the best piece for the nonscholar interested in learning about Mamet quickly. Freedman ranges freely throughout the Mamet canon, noticing qualities of his writing. He includes considerable biographical detail from Mamet's childhood, his Chicago theater days, and his present life with Crouse. Based on interviews with Mamet and others as well as solid research, the piece includes comments by drama critic Robert Brustein on the moral underpinnings of Mamet's plays and on his dramatic style: Brustein calls Mamet a "behavioristic poet." It includes as well a discussion of the relationship between Mamet and director Gregory Mosher, some discussion of Mamet's methods of research for material for his plays, and commentary on his highly disciplined writing practices. Freedman compares Mamet's unfashionable machismo with that of Ernest Hemingway, calling Mamet a traditionalist in both process and product.

A recent piece in *American Theatre*, "Dirty Dealing," by Daniel Forbes (Feb. 1988), includes Mamet's *Glengarry Glen Ross* in its discussion of six recent plays about business corruption.

Nearly fifteen years after the mounting of his first play in Chicago, Mamet is well established as an important American playwright. There have been many reviews of his plays by reviewers who recognize Mamet's special idiom as a distinctive voice in American theater. But so also have there been less enthusiastic reviews, disparaging that same language for its vulgarity, criticizing the nearly plotless action of Mamet's plays, and complaining about the playwright's consistent economy; his plays, in short, do not follow the recipe for Broadway success. The one major reviewer who has been most consistently supportive of Mamet has been *New York Times* critic Mel Gussow. The following overview of the reception of Mamet's plays on stage will suggest the extent of Gussow's support and, despite its selectiveness both with respect to critics cited and plays reviewed, will provide insight into other critics' reactions as well.

Mamet's New York career began in 1975, with the Off-Off-Broadway staging of *Sexual Perversity in Chicago* and *Duck Variations* at St. Clement's and a revival the following year at the Cherry Lane Theater. In "Stage: Two Pungent Comedies by New Playwright," Gussow's 1 November 1975 review of the premiere, he calls Mamet's plays a "welcome gust of laughter from Chicago"; Edith Oliver, in "Off Broadway: David Mamet of Illinois" (10 Nov. 1975), calls Mamet a "remarkable writer." In "Stage: Mamet's *Perversity*, Mosaic on Modern Mores, Moves" (17 June 1976), his review of a 1976 production, Richard Eder calls *Sexual Perversity* a "glittering mosaic of tiny, deadly muzzle-flashes from the war between men and women."

Mamet's best-known play to date remains *American Buffalo*, staged in New York in 1976 at St. Clement's and favorably received by Gussow in "Theater: Mamet's *American Buffalo*" (28 Jan. 1976). Gordon Rogoff, reviewing a 1977 production of *American Buffalo* at the Ethel Barrymore Theater with Robert Duvall as Teach in "Albee and Mamet: The War of the Words" (2 Apr. 1977), concentrates on Mamet's dialogue, noting its derivation from the film dialogue used by Humphrey Bogart, James Cagney, Edward G. Robinson, and Marlon Brando. Rogoff registers distaste for Mamet's patronizing attitude toward his trio of petty criminals. In "No News from Lake Michigan" (28 Feb. 1977) Brendan Gill calls *American Buffalo* a "curiously offensive piece of writing" not because of its language but because it offers no intellectual stimulation. John Simon's *Hudson Review* article "Theater Chronicle" (Summer 1977) similarly finds little to praise in the play. Though gutter poetry is possible, Simon suggests, Mamet has not achieved it, and the play, in its inaction and its failure to move its audience, simply "marks time." In "Bluffalo," a review of the 1981 New York Circle in the Square revival featuring Al Pacino, Simon acknowledges that the play offers "a field day for actors." *New York Times* reviewer Frank Rich, in "Theater: Al Pacino in *American Buffalo*" (5 June 1981), liked not only the play but the production, praising playwright and actors for their success in creating a "nonliterate comic beat." The play, he remarks, has the "power to explode the largest of American myths." Walter Kerr, also writing for the *New York Times* in an article called "Al Pacino's Supercharged *Buffalo*" (14 June 1981), praised Pacino's wildly energetic performance, comparing his rendering favorably to that of the more subdued Duvall in 1977. Gussow's review of the London production of *American Buffalo* in 1978, at the National Theater's Cottesloe Theater, is notable in that it speaks of the failure of British actors to capture the American idiom. In *"American Buffalo* in London–The Accent's OK, but the Music's Off " (23 July 1978) Gussow uses a production of the Mamet play to speak to a perennial problem involved in British imitations of American speech and behavior. Two of the three actors play their roles like "English punks" rather than "small-time American hoodlums," and they do not get the rhythms and cadences right. Gussow also records British reviewers' reactions to the play.

Gussow's reaction to *A Life in the Theater* staged at the Goodman Theater in Chicago (5 Feb. 1977) is that it is a slight play, though not lacking in consequence. With his previous work, however, it establishes Mamet as "one of the brightest and most original young playwrights." In "Stage: Illusion Within an Illusion" (21 Oct. 1977) Gussow calls Mamet a "master of two-part harmony," an "abundantly gifted playwright" who "brings new life to the theater." Reviewers generally echoed Gussow's praise, but Harold Clurman, in his *Nation* coverage "Theater" (12 Nov. 1977), judges the play "a trifle" and expresses surprise at the warm reception given it by other theater critics.

Gussow reviewed *The Water Engine* twice, first at its New York premiere directed by Joseph Papp at the Public Theater in January 1978 and then after it moved to Broadway in March of the same year. His praise for Mamet was shared by some critics. Many reviewers of the opening production were celebratory–Richard Eder ("Stage: Mamet Reinvents Radio," 6 Jan. 1978), Walter Kerr ("Off Broadway This Week, a Trio of Openings," 15 Jan. 1978), Martin Gottfried ("Cult of the Second-rate," 4 Mar. 1978), and Gerald Weales ("The Stage," 14 Apr. 1978), for example. Julius Novick's *Village Voice* remarks ("The Mamet Show," 16 Jan. 1978) are respectful. Harold Clurman ("Theater," 28 Jan. 1978) and Edith Oliver ("Watered Down," 19 Jan. 1978) argue that the play does not work, Clurman because its audiences assent without caring, Oliver because its "ponderous irony" and "its foolishness" are no replacements for Mamet's usual humor and subtle tensions. Eder's review of the production at the Plymouth Theater ("Stage: *Water Engine* Is Uptown," 7 Mar. 1978) is highly enthusiastic, but the *New York Times* reviewer thought the addition of Mamet's *Mr. Happiness* as a curtain raiser was a mistake.

Gussow's high regard for Mamet is apparent in his review of *The Woods* at the St. Nicholas Theater in Chicago in 1977; his *New York Times* assessment of the play ("David Mamet's Latest Microcosm," 4 Dec. 1977) was not shared by reviewers of the first New York production at the Public Theater two years later. Clurman ("Theater," 19 May 1979) and Simon ("Permanents and Transients," 14 May 1979) found little to like, and Eileen Blumenthal

("Mamet à Trois," 7 May 1979) was especially offended by the misogyny that, she claimed, infested the play.

The Woods had a New York revival at the Second Stage in 1982, but the play–"dull," "flat," unimaginative, without humor–left *Village Voice* critic Jan Hoffman ("Barking Up the Wrong Tree," 25 May 1982) feeling "insulted." Frank Rich, in a *New York Times* review ("Theater: Patti LuPone in Mamet's *The Woods*," 17 May 1982), said the play was a "pseudo-abstract, frationalized, monosyllabic surface spread over an emotional vacuum."

Reviews for *Reunion, Dark Pony*, and *The Sanctity of Marriage* were positive. *Reunion* and *Dark Pony* came to New York in 1979 in a Circle Repertory Theater production, after playing at the Yale Repertory Company two years earlier–now with *The Sanctity of Marriage* as well. Joan Fleckenstein's *Educational Theatre Journal* review of the double bill in New Haven (Oct. 1978) is sensitive to Mamet's "magnificently turned ear for dialogue," apparent in both pieces. Gussow, evaluating the triple bill in New York ("Stage: *Reunion*, 3 Mamet Plays," 19 Oct. 1979), directed by Mamet and starring Crouse, liked the "small, quiet pleasures" of *Reunion* but was less taken with the two curtain raisers. Edith Oliver, writing for *New Yorker* ("The Theater: Off Broadway," 29 Oct. 1979), thought *Reunion* a "distinguished and remarkable" "poem for two voices," *Dark Pony* a "charmer," and *The Sanctity of Marriage* elusive. Simon ("Queasy Quartet," 5 Nov. 1979) found the two curtain raisers "wretched," *Reunion* "appreciably better."

Reviews for Mamet's *Edmond* were mixed. *Edmond* opened in 1982, first at the Goodman Theater in Chicago and then at the Provincetown Playhouse in New York. Gussow's review of the Goodman production, "Stage: Mamet Explores the Fall of *Edmond*," (17 June 1982), while registering his preference for Mamet's earlier plays, respectfully notes that this "New York-by-nightmare" play–which he compares to Büchner's *Woyzeck*–is "not an easy play to like, but it will be a difficult one to forget." In "Two New Plays That Focus on the Male Loner" (7 Nov. 1982) Kerr offers a detailed plot summary of the episodes in the seventy-five minute Provincetown production but expresses disappointment that Edmond's motives remain vague. The play, he concludes, is "overly ambitious." Rich, reviewing the production in "Theater: Mamet's *Edmond* at the Provincetown," (28 Oct. 1982), felt that Mamet was neglecting his gifts: *Edmond* is filled with clichés, and Mamet has become "tone-deaf." Michael Feingold, by contrast, found the play Mamet's "strongest and deepest to date." In a substantial *Village Voice* review, "The Way We Are" (9 Nov. 1982), Feingold praises this drama of the radicalization of the middle-class businessman as "harrowing and laughable, breathtaking and dismaying, thought-and-ire-provoking," concluding that its power comes from Mamet's "willingness to cross-breed his art with life." Reviewers of the London production at the Royal Court in 1985 generally agreed with Feingold's assessment.

Reviews of *Glengarry Glen Ross* were laudatory. The play had a British rather than American premiere, at the National Theater's Cottesloe Theater in 1983. Ronald Hayman's review in the *Times Literary Supplement*, "Following the Lead" (30 Sept. 1983), praises the play (and the production), which convincingly portrays the near-hysteria of real estate salesman confronting the pressures of a grueling and greedy business world. Hayman and *Guardian* critic Michael Billington, writing for the *New York Times* ("Theater in London: Mamet Turns to the World of Salesmen," 9 Oct. 1983), applaud the lively dialogue. Billington identifies the salesman as a classic figure in American drama; unlike Arthur Miller's *Death of a Salesman*, however, *Glengarry Glen Ross* maintains a tone of "moral neutrality," presenting the salesman as both con man and victim. Benedict Nightingale, asking "Is Mamet the Bard of Modern Immorality?" in his *New York Times* review (1 Apr. 1984) of the Broadway production, is celebratory. He calls the play a "scabrous, seamy, charmless, funny, brilliant and unmissable play." While he registers doubts about its Broadway success, he expresses high confidence in the play as a durable property. Brendan Gill's *New Yorker* review, "The Theater: The Lower Depths" (2 Apr. 1984), is also appreciative, calling Mamet's "howl of protest" both funny and convincing.

Frank Rich's *New York Times* review of the Broadway production of *Speed-the-Plow*, "Mamet's Dark View of Hollywood as a Heaven for the Virtueless" (4 May 1988), provides a full account of another Mamet dramatic attack on the business world. The Hollywood film industry and the public that keeps it running are his target. Rich praises this "cynical and exciting" play, which interweaves plots and repeatedly alludes to an anonymously authored apocalyptic script, *The Bridge*, as it relentlessly plows through its revealing material. Rich especially applauds Mamet for refusing to imagine that art might eventually win the competition with commerce.

Clearly Mamet has commanded considerable scholarly and critical attention and has gained the respect of theatrical communities in Chicago, New York, London, and many regional theaters. Of his plays, *American Buffalo* has received the most scholarly attention, and it, along with *Glengarry Glen Ross*, has garnered the most consistent theatrical acclaim. But scholars have not exhausted the study of either of these plays, and there is much material in the Mamet canon that has not yet entered scholarly discourse. Recently, British television filmmakers produced a documentary on the playwright, called *Mamet: Profile of a Writer*. The fifty-five-minute video, produced and directed by Alan Benson and available from Home Vision, includes interviews with Mamet, British director Bill Bryden, and actor Jack Shepherd, as well as scenes from *American Buffalo*, *Glengarry Glen Ross*, and *Edmond*.

Carson McCullers
(1917-1967)

Margaret B. McDowell
University of Iowa

PRIMARY BIBLIOGRAPHY

Books

The Heart Is a Lonely Hunter. Boston: Houghton Mifflin, 1940; London: Cresset, 1943. Novel.

Reflections in a Golden Eye. Boston: Houghton Mifflin, 1941; London: Cresset, 1942. Novel.

The Member of the Wedding. Boston: Houghton Mifflin, 1946; London: Cresset, 1946. Novel.

The Member of the Wedding: A Play. New York: New Directions, 1951.

The Ballad of the Sad Café: The Novels and Stories of Carson McCullers. Boston: Houghton Mifflin, 1951. Comprises *The Ballad of the Sad Café,* "Wunderkind," "The Jockey," "Madame Zilensky and the King of Finland," "The Sojourner," "A Domestic Dilemma" (published for first time), "A Tree. A Rock. A Cloud," *The Heart Is a Lonely Hunter, Reflections in a Golden Eye, The Member of the Wedding.* Republished as *The Shorter Novels and Stories of Carson McCullers.* London: Cresset, 1952. *The Heart Is a Lonely Hunter* omitted.

The Square Root of Wonderful. Boston: Houghton Mifflin, 1958; London: Cresset, 1958. Play. Includes a preface by McCullers.

Clock Without Hands. Boston: Houghton Mifflin, 1961; London: Cresset, 1961. Novel.

As Sweet as a Pickle and Clean as a Pig. Boston: Houghton Mifflin, 1964; London: Cape, 1965. Children's poems.

The Mortgaged Heart, ed. Margarita G. Smith. Boston: Houghton Mifflin, 1971; London: Barrie & Jenkins, 1972. Selected short pieces, some previously unpublished.

Premiere Productions
The Member of the Wedding. New York, Empire Theater, 5 Jan. 1950.
The Square Root of Wonderful. New York, National Theater, 30 Oct. 1957.

Selected Periodical Publications
"How I Began to Write," *Mademoiselle,* 27 (Sept. 1948), 256-257. Collected in *The Mortgaged Heart.* Essay.
"Loneliness . . . An American Malady," *This Week* (*New York Herald-Tribune*), 19 Dec. 1949, pp. 18-19. Collected in *The Mortgaged Heart.* Essay.
"The Vision Shared," *Theatre Arts,* 34 (Apr. 1950), 23-30. Collected in *The Mortgaged Heart.* Essay.
"The Flowering Dream: Notes on Writing," *Esquire,* 52 (Dec. 1959), 162-164. Collected in *The Mortgaged Heart.* Essay.

Television
The Invisible Wall, Omnibus, CBS, 27 Dec. 1953.
The Sojourner, NBC, 25 May 1964.

Recording
Carson McCullers Reads from The Member of the Wedding and Other Works. MGM E3619ARC, 1958.

Papers
Humanities Research Center, University of Texas, Austin, Texas.
Robert Flowers Collections, Perkins Library, Duke University, Durham, North Carolina.

SECONDARY BIBLIOGRAPHY

Bibliographies and Checklists
Bixby, George. "Carson McCullers: A Bibliographical Checklist," *American Book Collector,* new series 5 (Jan./Feb. 1984), 38-43.
Carr, Virginia Spencer. "Carson McCullers." In *Contemporary Authors Bibliographical Series,* volume 1: *American Novelists,* ed. James Martine. Detroit: Gale, 1986, 293-345.
Carr, and Joseph P. Millichap. "Carson McCullers." In *American Women Writers: Bibliographical Essays,* ed. Maurice Duke, Jackson R. Bryer, and Thomas Inge. Westport, Conn.: Greenwood, 1981, 297-319.

Kiernan, Robert F. *Carson McCullers and Katherine Anne Porter: A Reference Guide.* Boston: G. K. Hall, 1976. Secondary.

Phillips, Robert S. "Carson McCullers: 1956-1964–A Selected Checklist," *Bulletin of Bibliography,* 24 (Sept./Dec. 1964), 113-116. Primary and secondary.

Shapiro, Adrian, Jackson R. Bryer, and Kathleen Field. *Carson McCullers, A Descriptive Listing and Annotated Bibliography of Criticism.* New York & London: Garland, 1980. Primary and secondary.

Stanley, William T. "Carson McCullers: 1965-1969, A Selected Checklist," *Bulletin of Bibliography,* 27 (Jan./Apr. 1970), 91-93. Primary and secondary.

Stewart, Stanley. "Carson McCullers, 1940-1956: A Selected Checklist," *Bulletin of Bibliography,* 22 (Jan./Apr. 1959), 182-185. Primary and secondary.

Biographies

Carr, Virginia Spencer. *The Lonely Hunter: A Biography of Carson McCullers.* Garden City, N.Y.: Doubleday, 1975.

Evans, Oliver. *Carson McCullers: Her Life and Work.* London: Owen, 1965. Republished as *The Ballad of Carson McCullers.* New York: Coward-McCann, 1966.

Interviews

Balakian, Nona. "Carson McCullers Completes New Novel Despite Adversity," *New York Times,* 3 Sept. 1961, p. 46.

Breit, Harvey. "Behind the Wedding," *New York Times,* 1 Jan. 1950, section 4, p. 3.

"Call on the Author," *Newsweek,* 58 (18 Sept. 1961), 106-107.

Doar, Harriet. "Love Is At the Heart–Battling Ill Health, Carson McCullers Writes On," *Charlotte Observer,* 5 May 1963, p. C10.

Gordy, Mary. "*Ledger* Reporter Finds Former Columbus Girl, Now Celebrated Author, Unspoiled by Fame," *Columbus* (Ga.) *Ledger,* 16 Dec. 1940, p. 7.

Hutchens, John K. "Carson McCullers," *New York Herald-Tribune Book Review,* 17 June 1951, p. 2.

"An Interview with Carson McCullers," *Literary Cavalcade,* 9 (Feb. 1957), 5.

Kelly, Frank K. " 'Lonely' Miss McCullers Coming Home to Write," *Atlanta Journal,* 16 Nov. 1941, p. 13.

Lee, Harry. "Columbus Girl Thinks South Is Sick," *Atlanta Constitution,* 6 Mar. 1941, p. 4.

MacDougall, Sally. "Author, 22, Urges Aid to Refugees," *New York World-Telegram,* 1 July 1940, p. 12.

Morehouse, Ward. "Broadway After Dark–Carson McCullers Cuts Her Own Hair," *New York World-Telegram,* 31 Mar. 1950, p. 36.

Morgan, Nonie. "Carson McCullers, Distinguished Novelist, and Her Mother Visiting Here," *Macon* (Ga.) *News,* 18 Mar. 1949, p. 11.

Pollock, Arthur. "Theatre Time–Carson McCullers Talks About Self and First Play," *New York Daily Compass,* 7 Oct. 1949, p. 18.

"Quarrels and Cussing–Playwright Tells of Pangs," *Philadelphia Inquirer,* 13 Oct. 1957, Amusement and Arts section, pp. 1, 5.

Reed, Rex. " 'Frankie Addams' at 50," *New York Times,* 16 Apr. 1967, section 2, p. 15.

Rice, Vernon. "A Little Southern Girl Speaks from a Well of Despair," *New York Post,* 29 Jan. 1950, p. M8.

Rutherford, Marjory. "New Broadway Hit for Carson McCullers?," *Atlanta Journal and Constitution Magazine,* 29 Sept. 1963, pp. 10, 12.

Selby, John. "Mrs. McCullers of Carolina Puzzles Gotham Lit'ry Set," *Charlotte Observer,* 10 July 1940, section 2, p. 1.

"The *Marquis* Interviews Carson McCullers," *Marquis,* Lafayette College, Easton, Pa., 1964, pp. 5-6, 20-23.

Watson, Latimer. "Carson McCullers Gets Guggenheim Fellowship," *Columbus* (Ga.) *Enquirer,* 6 Apr. 1942, pp. 1, 3.

White, Terence de Vere. "With Carson McCullers: Terence de Vere White Interviews the American Novelist at the Home of Her Host, John Huston," *Irish Times* (Dublin), 10 Apr. 1967.

Critical Studies: Books

Cook, Richard M. *Carson McCullers.* New York: Ungar, 1975.

Edmonds, Dale. *Carson McCullers.* Austin: Steck-Vaughn, 1969.

Graver, Lawrence. *Carson McCullers.* Minneapolis: University of Minnesota Press, 1969.

McDowell, Margaret B. *Carson McCullers.* Boston: Twayne, 1980.

Critical Studies: Major Reviews, Articles, and Book Sections

Aldridge, Robert. "Two Planetary Systems: 'The Heart Is A Lonely Hunter.' " In *The Modern American Novel and the Movies,* ed. Gerald Perry and Roger Shatzkin. New York: Ungar, 1978.

Alvarez, A. "Circling the Squares," *London Observer,* 15 Mar. 1959, p. 23.

Aston, Frank. "Theatre: A Story of Love–*Square Root* Is Like Magic," *New York World-Telegram*, 31 Oct. 1957, p. 32.

Atkinson, Brooks. "At the Theatre," *New York Times*, 6 Jan. 1950, p. 26.

Atkinson. "Poetry in a Drama–*The Member of the Wedding* Remains Constant and Unimpaired," *New York Times*, 17 Sept. 1950, section 2, p. 1.

Atkinson. "Theatre: Square Root," *New York Times*, 31 Oct. 1957, p. 40.

Atkinson. "Three People–The Member of the Wedding Superbly Acted by an Excellent Company," *New York Times*, 15 Jan. 1950, section 2, p. 1.

Barnes, Howard. "Fine Acting in *Member of the Wedding*," *New York Herald-Tribune*, 15 Jan. 1950, section 5, pp. 1, 2.

Barnes. Review of *The Member of the Wedding*, *New York Herald-Tribune*, 6 Jan. 1950, p. 12.

Beaufort, John. "*The Member of the Wedding* on Broadway Stage– Simplicity and Composure Fused to Gain Rare Effect," *Christian Science Monitor*, 14 Jan. 1950, p. 4.

Bentley, Eric. "The American Drama, 1944-54." In *American Drama and Its Critics: A Collection of Critical Essays*, ed. Alan S. Downer. Chicago: University of Chicago Press, 1965, 188-202.

Beyer, William. "The State of the Theatre: Actors Take Honors," *School and Society*, 66 (8 Apr. 1950), 213-214.

Bolton, Whitney. "Stage–*Member of the Wedding* Just What Theatre Needs," *New York Morning Telegraph*, 7 Jan. 1950, pp. 2, 3.

Bolton. "Stage Review–Square Root: Odd, Rambling, Verbose," *New York Morning Telegraph*, 2 Nov. 1957, p. 2.

Brown, John Mason. "Plot Me No Plots," *Saturday Review*, 33 (28 Jan. 1950), 27-29.

Callaway, Joe A. "New York Plays . . . Deplorable Dependence on Broadway," *Player's Magazine*, 26 (Mar. 1950), 126.

Chapman, John. "Great Met Performances–Theatre Lagging," *New York Sunday News*, 10 Nov. 1957, section 2, p. 3.

Chapman. "An Interesting Member of the Race," *New York Sunday News*, 15 Jan. 1950, section 2, p. 3.

Chapman. "*Member of the Wedding* and Its Cast Earn Cheers," *New York Daily News*, 6 Jan. 1950, p. 55.

Chapman. " 'The Square Root of ' Scatters Neuroses Along the Psychopath," *New York Daily News*, 31 Oct. 1957, p. 65.

Clurman, Harold. "American Playwrights: Carson McCullers." In his *Lies Like Truth: Theatre Reviews and Essays.* New York: Macmillan, 1958, 62-64.

Clurman. "The Kind of Theatre We Have." In *Let's Meet the Theatre,* ed. Dorothy and Joseph Samachson. New York: Abelard-Schuman, 1954, 73-79.

Clurman. "*Member of the Wedding* Upsets a Theory," *New York Herald-Tribune,* 29 Jan. 1950, section 5, p. 3.

Clurman. *The Naked Image: Observations on the Modern Theatre.* New York: Macmillan, 1966, 297-298.

Clurman. *On Directing.* New York: Macmillan, 1972, 17-19, 49, 136-139, 189-196.

Clurman. "Theatre," *Nation,* 185 (23 Nov. 1957), 394.

Clurman. "Theatre: From a Member," *New Republic,* 122 (30 Jan. 1950), 28-29.

Colby, Ethel. "Entertainment: Julie Harris Makes Touching Ingenue," *Journal of Commerce and Commercial* (New York), 6 Jan. 1950, p. 9.

Coleman, Robert. " 'Square Root of Wonderful' Ain't," *New York Mirror,* 1 Nov. 1957, pp. 32-33.

Coleman. "The Theatre—*Member of the Wedding* Is a Stirring Hit," *New York Daily Mirror,* 6 Jan. 1950, p. 34.

Cooke, Richard P. "Adolescent Problem," *Wall Street Journal,* 9 Jan. 1950, p. 12.

Cooke. "The Theatre—McCullers' Second Best," *Wall Street Journal,* 1 Nov. 1957, p. 8.

Dash, Thomas R. "The Member of the Wedding," *Women's Wear Daily* (6 Jan. 1950), 57.

Dedmond, Francis. "Doing Her Own Thing: Carson McCullers' Dramatization of *The Member of the Wedding,*" *South Atlantic Bulletin,* 40 (May 1975), 47-52.

Dusenberry, Winifred. *The Theme of Loneliness in Modern American Drama.* Gainesville: University of Florida Press, 1960, 57-67, 200, 202.

Dwyer, Rebecca. "McCullers in Baltimore," *Drama Critique,* 11 (Winter 1968), 47-48.

Eaton, Hal. "First Night—*Member of Wedding* Is First Hit of 1950," *Long Island Daily Press,* 6 Jan. 1950, section 5-C, p. 8.

Feibleman, Peter S. "A Play Is Born from Novel," *Boston Sunday Globe,* 8 July 1962, p. A3.

Field, Rowland. "Broadway: Twisted Tale . . . Tedious Social Exercise," *Newark Evening News*, 31 Oct. 1957, p. 53.

Field. "Member of the Wedding," *Newark Evening News*, 6 Jan. 1950, p. 20.

Freedly, George. "The Theatre," *Library Journal*, 83 (1 June 1958), 1800.

Gabriel, Gilbert W. "New Plays on Broadway–Wend Your Way Westward to the Empire," *Cue*, 19 (14 Jan. 1950), 20.

Gaghan, Jerry. "Anne Baxter Stars at Walnut," *Philadelphia Daily News*, 15 Oct. 1957, p. 43.

Garland, Robert. "The Member of the Wedding–Something Special But Not Quite A Play," *New York Journal-American*, 6 Jan. 1950, p. 18.

Gassner, John. *Directions in Modern Theatre and Drama*. New York: Holt, Rinehart & Winston, 1966, 85-86.

Gianetti, Louis D. "The Member of the Wedding," *Literature/Film Quarterly*, 4 (Winter 1976), 28-38.

Gibbs, Wolcott. "The Theatre: Brook and River," *New Yorker*, 25 (14 Jan. 1950), 46-49.

Gibbs. "The Theatre: Music and Words," *New Yorker*, 33 (9 Nov. 1957), 100-103.

Hawkins, William. "Novice Calmly Steals the Show," *New York World-Telegram*, 14 Jan. 1950, p. 9.

Hawkins. "Theatre–Waters, Harris; Roles Spark *Wedding*," *New York World-Telegram*, 6 Jan. 1950, p. 32.

Hayes, Richard. "Private Worlds," *Commonweal*, 67 (13 Dec. 1957), 288-289.

Herron, Ima Honaker. *The Small Town in American Drama*. Dallas: Southern Methodist University Press, 1969, 398-401.

Hipp, Edward Southern. "A Most Precocious Little Girl–Frankie Addams . . . Is A Fantastic Heroine," *Newark Sunday News*, 15 Jan. 1950, section 2, p. 38.

Kazin, Alfred. "We Who Sit in Darkness: The Broadway Audience at the Play." In his *The Inmost Leaf: A Selection of Essays*. New York: Harcourt, Brace, 1955, 127-135.

Kerr, Walter. "First Night Report," *New York Herald-Tribune*, 31 Oct. 1957, p. 22.

Kronenberger, Louis, "The Season on Broadway." In *The Best Plays of 1957-1958*, ed. Kronenberger. New York & Toronto: Dodd, Mead, 1958, 3-38.

Lewis, Emory. "The Theatre–Elementary Math," *Cue*, 26 (9 Nov. 1957), 9.

Mace, Louise. "Here and There in the Theatre–The Member of the Wedding," *Springfield* (Mass.) *Sunday Republican*, 5 Feb. 1950, p. A16.

Marshall, Margaret. "Drama," *Nation*, 170 (14 Jan. 1950), 44.

Martin, Linton. "The Call Boy's Chat-Able Acting Aids Illusion; Theatre Half Century Ago," *Philadelphia Inquirer*, 1 Jan. 1950, Society section, p. 13.

McClain, John. "Diffuse Doubletalk Adds Up to a Big 0," *New York Journal-American*, 31 Oct. 1957, p. 22.

"The Member of the Wedding," *Theatre Arts*, 34 (Mar. 1950), 13.

"*Member of the Wedding* Is Praised by New York Critics," *Columbus* (Ga.) *Ledger*, 30 Jan. 1950, p. 6.

Miller, Jordan Y. "*The Member of the Wedding*." In his *American Dramatic Literature: Ten Modern Plays in Historical Perspective*. New York, Toronto & London: McGraw-Hill, 1961, 426-428.

Morgan, Nonie. " 'Talkin' It Over," *Macon* (Ga.) *News*, 16 Jan. 1950, p. 6.

Morrison, Hobe. "The Square Root of Wonderful," *Variety*, 6 Nov. 1957, p. 72.

Murdock, Henry T. "McCullers' Love Mathematics Doesn't Quite Add Up," *Philadelphia Inquirer*, 15 Oct. 1957, p. 17.

Murdock. "McCullers' *Member of the Wedding* Bows At Walnut," *Philadelphia Inquirer*, 23 Dec. 1949, p. 20.

Nathan, George Jean. *The Theatre Book of the Year 1949-1950*. New York: Knopf, 1950, 164-166.

"New Play in Manhattan," *Time*, 55 (16 Jan. 1950), 45.

"New Plays," *Newsweek*, 35 (16 Jan. 1950), 74.

"New Plays in Manhattan," *Time*, 70 (11 Nov. 1957), 93-94.

Olauson, Judith. *The American Woman Playwright: A View of Criticism and Characterization*. Troy, N.Y.: Whitson, 1981, 67-71, 147-148, 154-159, 178.

Phelan, Kappo. "The Stage–*The Member of the Wedding*," *Commonweal*, 51 (27 Jan. 1950), 437-438.

Phillips, Louis. "The Novelist as Playwright: Baldwin, McCullers, and Bellow." In *Modern American Drama: Essays in Criticism*, ed. William E. Taylor. De Land, Fla.: Everett/Edwards, 1968, 145-157.

Phillips. " 'The Sun Shines for Julie Harris': Playing a tomboy half her own age, a new actress triumphs in a new Broadway hit, 'The Member of the Wedding,' " *Life*, 28 (23 Jan. 1950), 63-66.

Pollock, Arthur. "Theatre Time–*Member of the Wedding* Poignant and Sensitive," *New York Daily Compass*, 6 Jan. 1950, p. 18.

Sensenderfer, R.E.P. "*The Member of the Wedding* Opens at the Walnut," *Philadelphia Evening Bulletin*, 23 Dec. 1949, p. 14.

Sheaffer, Louis. "Curtain Time–About *Member of the Wedding* and Whether It Really Is a Play," *Brooklyn Eagle*, 15 Jan. 1950, p. 25.

Sheaffer. "Curtain Time–*Member of the Wedding*," *Brooklyn Eagle*, 6 Jan. 1950, p. 10.

Sievers, Wieder David. *Freud on Broadway: A History of Psychoanalysis and the American Drama*. New York: Hermitage House, 1955, 431-433.

"*The Square Root of Wonderful*," *Theatre Arts*, 42 (Jan. 1958), 24.

Van Druten, John. *Playwrights at Work*. New York: Harper, 1953, 35-36, 174-175, 181-183, 187, 189-190.

Watson, Latimer. "Ovation Greets Opening Of Carson's Play In New York," *Columbus* (Ga.) *Ledger*, 6 Jan. 1950, pp. 1-2.

Watts, Richard. "Two on the Aisle–The New McCullers Play," *New York Post*, 31 Oct. 1957, p. 30.

Watts. "Two on the Aisle–The Stage Has a New Playwright," *New York Post*, 15 Jan. 1950, p. M4.

Weales, Gerald. "The Vagaries of Adaptation." In his *American Drama Since World War II*. New York: Harcourt, Brace & World, 1962, 154-181.

Worsley, T. C. "Growing Up," *New Statesman*, new series 53 (16 Feb. 1957), 201-202.

Wyatt, Euphemia Van Rensseler. "Theatre," *Catholic World*, 170 (Mar. 1950), 467-468.

Wyatt. "Theatre," *Catholic World*, 186-187 (Jan. 1958), 304-308.

BIBLIOGRAPHICAL ESSAY

In her short career Carson McCullers produced a remarkable variety of works in fiction, discursive prose, poetry, and drama, and attracted attention both from professional critics and general readers. Her first four novels and her best short stories–all preceding the three catastrophic strokes she suffered before the age of thirty–are her most influential writings and represent her greatest achievement, but they have also overshadowed the excellence of her work in other genres. Although her essays are generally brief and intermingle comment on literature and philosophy with references to her childhood, youth, and region, they are frequently original and provocative. Her poems, though few in number and written primarily in her late years, deserve more attention than they have attracted. Her work in the drama, though she wrote only two plays, extends her achievement.

Bibliographies and Checklists

None of the previously published bibliographies on Carson McCullers focuses specifically on her dramatic work. A series of primary and secondary checklists published in the *Bulletin of Bibliography*, by Stanley Stewart (Jan./Apr. 1959), Robert S. Phillips (Sept./Dec. 1964), and William T. Stanley (Jan./Apr. 1970), includes critical work on her two plays through 1969. These lists have been substantially updated and corrected in recent years, first by Robert F. Kiernan (1976), whose annotated list of secondary books and articles cites many reviews of premiere performances and a smaller number of critical essays devoted to McCullers's drama. Kiernan arranges the citations alphabetically by year and avoids evaluative statements in the annotations, concentrating instead on brief summaries of the major critical points made in each selection.

The 1980 bibliography by Adrian Shapiro, Jackson R. Bryer, and Kathleen Field contains descriptive lists and identifying photographs of all of McCullers's book publications, including reprints. The secondary bibliography includes citations through 1978; its alphabetically arranged and annotated lists appear in six divisions: books and sections of books; periodical articles; reviews of books; reviews of plays; dissertations; and foreign-language materials. A distinctive feature of the Shapiro volume is its inclusion of many local newspaper and magazine pieces, which give the student of McCullers an idea of the importance of the South in her own outlook and of the response of her own region to her literary accomplishments.

The most up-to-date previously published bibliography is by Virginia Spencer Carr, for the volume on American novelists in *Contemporary Authors Bibliographical Series* (1986). Carr provides a complete list of McCullers's book-length publications; selected listings of her fiction, essays, and poetry published in periodicals; and an extensive secondary bibliography emphasizing criticism of McCullers's fiction. The accompanying essay focuses on the most important examples of that criticism. The bibliography in this volume follows the same format as Carr's but emphasizes criticism of McCullers's drama.

Biographies

Oliver Evans's *Carson McCullers: Her Life and Work* (1965; republished as *The Ballad of Carson McCullers,* 1966), the first published McCullers biography, makes use of critical and biographical materials and published and unpublished interviews and letters to account for the relationship between McCullers's life and her writings. Evans summarizes and evaluates McCullers's work, recounts the circumstances of its composition, and evenhandedly reports on the critical response. Sections of the book that attempt to explain the author's personal experiences as thematic sources are speculative, but it remains a usable biocritical introduction to McCullers. Evans had the advantage of knowing McCullers and visiting her in the latter part of her life.

Virginia Spencer Carr's *The Lonely Hunter* (1975) is the standard full-length McCullers biography. It centers less on critical analysis of McCullers's work than on an exhaustive attempt to discover and explain the details of McCullers's life; to re-create her personality. To do this Carr not only utilized published accounts and interviews in the manner of Evans, but also conducted many interviews with McCullers and with family and friends of McCullers. These make it possible for Carr to correct certain misstatements of fact in Evans's earlier work. The book also includes an introduction by Tennessee Williams and some seventy-five photographs.

Interviews

Because McCullers was more a novelist than a dramatist, she gave only a few interviews focusing primarily on her plays, and they are all brief newspaper notices. For example, Arthur Pollock interviewed McCullers for the *New York Daily Compass* of 7 October 1949, and Harvey Breit did the same for the *New York Times* of 1 January 1950. In these pieces McCullers gives a bit of the history of the composition of the dramatic version of *The Member of the Wedding* and discusses the play's theme of adolescent loneliness. Tennessee Williams wrote *Summer and Smoke* across a table from McCullers while the pair spent the summer of 1946 together on Nantucket Island. She was working on her own play at the time. Vernon Rice interviewed McCullers for the *New York Post* of 29 January 1950, and Ward Morehouse did the same for the *New York World-Telegram* of

31 March 1950. In these postpremiere articles McCullers concentrates more on her favorable impression of the production itself.

A series of personal essays written during the same period gives deeper insight into the circumstances of the composition of *The Member of the Wedding* and the creative motives of a novelist-turned-playwright. In "How I Began to Write" (Sept. 1948) McCullers recalls that some of her formative creative experiences were related to drama. She writes of her participation in at-home family productions for which she wrote the scripts, acted (with her brother and sister), and directed. By the time she was fifteen the entertainments had evolved into full-fledged play-writing ventures, partly inspired by her admiration for the work of Eugene O'Neill. These early efforts included what she called "a three-acter about revenge and incest," and something entitled "The Fire of Life," which featured a rhymed dialogue between Jesus and Friedrich Nietzsche. Another personal essay deals more with the intellectual foundations of the play. In "Loneliness . . . An American Malady" (19 Dec. 1949), written after the novel was converted into a play, she discusses the moral context of both versions, commenting on the intolerable nature of "moral isolation," on fear as the primary source of evil, and on love as the agent that casts out fear. One sees reflected in the essay not only the internal conflicts of the characters of Frankie and Berenice in *The Member of the Wedding* but also the broader sensibility that McCullers later expressed in the equation forming the imagistic core of her second play, *The Square Root of Wonderful*. In that work, the square root of sin is humiliation and the square root of wonderful is love.

In "The Vision Shared" (Apr. 1950) McCullers writes about practical aspects of the drama, emphasizing, in the wake of the first series of reviews of *The Member of the Wedding*, the pressures upon "professional writers to adapt to the expectations of publishers, directors, or audiences, rather than to see themselves as artists who must follow a vision and communicate it." She insisted that her writing must be the result of a combination of labor and intuition, even if that meant that critics' charges that the play was diffuse and weak in plot would continue to surface. Part of the problem, she thought, was that the theater was the "most pragmatic" (and commercialized) of art media, and therefore somewhat resistant to unconventional drama such as *The Member of the Wedding*. She defended herself against charges of unconventionality by contending that she used "inner conflict" as an antagonist, producing the kind of onstage struggle often associated with classical drama. It was difficult for reviewers to evaluate such a "lyric tragi-comedy," in which grief and laughter were often concentered in a single line. She believed that the director and cast showed great expertise in rendering such juxtapositions. The actors, in their "fugue-like parts," produced, she thought, an effect of "dazzling precision and harmony."

Critical Studies: Books

All four critical studies of Carson McCullers published to date are to an extent limited by page restrictions imposed by the editors of the series of which they are parts, but each makes useful contributions to the body of critical work on McCullers. However, as might be expected, the books concentrate more on the author's novels than they do on her plays. No book-length study of McCullers as a dramatist has seen publication.

Two 1969 volumes provide brief critical evaluations of McCullers's major works. Dale Edmonds's *Carson McCullers*, in Steck-Vaughn publishers' Southern Writers Series, concentrates on the theme of love in the novels and plays and describes their "Southern" qualities. Lawrence Graver's *Carson McCullers*, in the University of Minnesota's Pamphlets on American Writers Series, analyzes only the novels. Graver focuses on McCullers's symbolism, imagery, and style more fully than do the other authors of book-length studies. Both books are preceded by a brief biographical sketch and attempt to relate details of McCullers's life to her writing.

Richard M. Cook's 1975 study is likewise preceded by a biographical sketch, and it includes chapters on each of the five novels. Part of a series of Modern Literature Monographs published by Ungar, Cook's book praises McCullers's first novel, *The Heart Is a Lonely Hunter*, for its convincing, tender treatment of the theme of loneliness. The next novel, *Reflections In a Golden Eye*, is considered less riveting, and the next, *The Member of the Wedding*, is viewed as her most internalized. *The Ballad of the Sad Café* garners high praise for its magical, tragicomic quality; and the last novel, *Clock Without Hands*, is dismissed as structureless. Cook makes only passing reference to the plays in a concluding chapter.

Margaret B. McDowell's 1980 study is the most extensive on McCullers published to date. In Twayne's United States Authors Series, the book concentrates primarily on the diversity in McCullers's work—in genre, style, and philosophy. It includes discussion of most of the stories and all of the poems. Though her poetry has been somewhat ignored by critics, it is linked to an understanding of her drama, in which she once said she sought to create a poetic precision, balance, and harmony.

Critical Studies: Major Reviews, Articles, and Book Sections

McCullers's first dramatic work provides an excellent example of what can be gained in the conversion of a work of fiction to the stage. Her second play has raised questions about the difficulty for an artist of being both a novelist and a playwright. Important work on the subject of movement between genres includes Louis Phillips's comparative study, "The Novelist as Playwright: Baldwin, McCullers, and Bellow," in William E. Taylor's *Modern American Drama: Essays in Criticism* (1968), and Gerald Weales's *American Drama Since World War II* (1962), which offers an entire chapter on the difficulties of doing such adaptations.

Among books on the drama of the 1950s and thoughtful reviews of McCullers's plays, the writings by Harold Clurman are most pertinent to an understanding of her achievement. He directed the successful premiere production of *The Member of the Wedding* and believes that *The Square Root of Wonderful* failed, in large part, because directors and actors did not grasp the playwright's intent as he and the actors in *The Member of the Wedding* had been able to do.

In *Lies Like Truth* (1958) Clurman tells what he learned from directing *The Member of the Wedding*—that to be successful a play must have some sort of central focus, but that directors and actors must sometimes search for that center. He recounts that in rehearsing McCullers's play, he and actresses Julie Harris and Ethel Waters ("a great natural force"), after some effort, realized that the play should revolve around Frankie's need to "connect" with a world beyond the kitchen. It was an "inward motion" that was intense enough to provide a kinetic center. To emphasize the sweeping motion of this inner action, Clurman supplied visual "emotional equivalents," such as the excited hopping of John Henry during Frankie's fantasy that she will fly around the world in order to become a "member of the whole world."

In a 23 November 1957 essay for *Nation* Clurman compared McCullers's plays in a way no other critic had, emphasizing basic similarities, rather than the differences, between the two. He declared that the theatrical "dud"—*The Square Root of Wonderful*— was the product of a gifted designer, talented actors, and a superior playwright.

He criticized McCullers, however, for passively following her advisors and for attempting to make the play simple and straightforward, when she was best at improvising around strong characters and a single situation to weave a poetic web of imagery and feeling.

In the script for *The Square Root of Wonderful* Clurman saw "lyric writing" and "wonderfully intuitive character sense," but both were lost in the stage performance. He saw Mollie Lovejoy in the script as an innocent young woman, frank about her sexuality; but on stage she became a "spiritual" or unreal figure who always spoke in breathy lines. He saw Phillip in the script as a "lost soul" who was trying to find a cocoon for himself, but he became on stage a sadistic and aggressive monster. Only the whispering librarian—the visiting sister-in-law—became on the stage what Clurman thought McCullers had meant the character to be.

In *The Naked Image* (1966) Clurman encouraged the commercial theater to take risks on innovative art and pointed to the financial success of *The Member of the Wedding* as an example of the prudent nature of the policy, but he also declared that if the play had failed, as most had expected, his own "appreciation of its quality would have remained undiminished." He continued this line of thought in his *On Directing* (1972). He gave credit in that book to Robert Whitehead, the producer of *The Member of the Wedding*, for his early faith in McCullers's script. Clurman tells that he assumed the director's job after earlier directors found the play awkward and repetitive. He made only a few changes—primarily the deletion of two scenes between the time of the Philadelphia premiere and the Broadway opening, occasioned by the visit of two high-school youths who had been moved by the play and asked whether the bar scene with the lustful soldier was necessary. Clurman believed that the play's excellence came from its similarity to the novel. In a 29 January 1950 newspaper article he had declared that if *The Member of the Wedding* was not a play, he wanted to direct more nonplays, and he pointed out that the success of this play on the stage indicated that "the boundaries of our artistic conceptions must always be subject to extension."

In a similar plea for flexibility across genre lines, Louis Phillips, in "The Novelist as Playwright," defended the novelists McCullers, James Baldwin, and Saul Bellow for turning to the theater to broaden the scope of their art: "It is somewhat of a paradox that in a time of immense diversity we do not expect our artists to be diverse." Yet Phillips concedes that few artists are equally competent in both genres. He also points out that, despite McCullers's strong interest in the social problems that impinge on her characters, Baldwin's plays dissect "an entire community or social evil," but McCullers's center merely on the family unit and are "far more intimate and closely-knit in their concern."

While critics of *The Member of the Wedding* looked askance at its supposed plotlessness and its lack of conventional form and polish, almost all agreed that it was charming, had a kind of magical quality, and cast a poetic spell. However, they were still ambivalent. Richard Watts, in the *New York Post* (15 Jan. 1950), described *The Member of the Wedding* as beautiful, but then wrote that the vague quality of its "mood, suggestion, and implications" was not distinct enough for "our literal theater." John Mason Brown (28 Jan. 1950), with even more ambivalence, praised the play as "an illustration of the differences between plot and story." He defended McCullers against charges of plotlessness by reminding readers of Galsworthy's contention that "a human being is the best plot there is" and that a bad plot impales characters on a row of stakes instead of giving them life. But then he criticized the lack of movement or "inward progression" in the play. He expressed particular disappointment with the insubstantial third act and the overall lack of character development.

Francis Dedmond's May 1975 critical article expresses a similar view of the third act—a view that seems to question McCullers's integrity in presenting Frankie's easy accommodation to the world of the high-school girls bent on popularity as an ironic regression rather than a progression. In another reflection on the play's third act, Gerald Weales, in "The Vagaries of Adaptation" (1962), notes specific differences in the closing of the book and the closing of the play. He questions the changes made in the character of T. T. Williams, the middle-class businessman, who becomes in the play a handyman-helper. He questions also the outburst of Mr. Addams, who yells about "biggety, worthless niggers" because Honey Camden Brown declines to help serve guests at the wedding. On the other hand, Weales applauds the director's excision of the violence and sexual allusions that had been implicit in the novel's presentation of Frankie's evening at the bar with the soldier. Weales understands the childish talk of the newly mature Frances as she tells of meeting her new best friend at the cosmetic counter at Woolworth's, but he does not defend the conclusion, which suggests to him that the action of the play has not been "formative, but only incidents on the edge of a process that will take place without them."

The problem for many critics may lie in their unfamiliarity with McCullers's consistent ironic juxtaposition of joy and tragedy. Thus they are critical of what appears to be an overly easy happy ending for Frances.

Alfred Kazin, in "We Who Sit in Darkness: The Broadway Audience at the Play" (1955), writes of the emotional separation he perceives between Broadway audiences and the plays they view. The audience goes to see a certain actor or actress and focuses on that individual, separating him or her from the other characters on the stage and from the play itself. He praises Ethel Waters's performance in the play, but criticizes her symbolic utilization as the great Negro mother, which makes him feel "as if even the performer whom we love for herself alone, especially when we cannot love the play, were, still, only the embodiment of a race or class or type." Kazin concludes that the play provides no situation for the audience to enter into; there are only characters suffering passively within themselves. He does not recognize that McCullers's theme is expressed in the attempts of the characters to understand their isolation, their identities, and their awkward and sometimes tragic efforts to become members "of the whole world."

Another interesting later essay on *The Member of the Wedding* is Jordan Miller's, in his *American Dramatic Literature: Ten Modern Plays in Historical Perspective* (1961). He sees the play as representative of the comedy of sensibility, a "pleasant play" that mingles and balances comedy and reality. He thinks the casual treatment of the off-stage tragedies in the play "helps keep the play within the bounds of comedy." He stresses that *The Member of the Wedding* is never allowed to become a "sentimental play," and he concludes that its warm comic quality arouses sensitivities by "refinement of taste and by gentle play on our emotions, while asking us to laugh in sympathy and understanding."

Some commentaries on McCullers's first play discuss it in certain thematic contexts. Winifred Dusenberry discusses the theme of isolation in *The Member of the Wedding* in her 1960 book. Judith Olauson (1981) analyzes the woman author's treatment of the female character in her discussion of the play. Ima Honaker Herron discusses its cultural setting in *The Small Town in American Drama* (1969).

Reviews of *The Square Root of Wonderful* (dated October to December 1957) are notable for their similarity. Many of these writers had praised *The Member of the Wedding*, and most of them express regret that a playwright who gained fame in the theater seven years before should have produced such an unattractive play. Generally, the play was judged to be sentimental, and the comic aspects unentertaining. Frank Aston's 31 October 1957 review is notable because it is one of the few positive statements among major magazine and newspaper reviews of the play.

Arthur Miller

(1915-)

June Schlueter
Lafayette College

PRIMARY BIBLIOGRAPHY

Books

Situation Normal. New York: Reynal & Hitchcock, 1944. Reportage. Contains an unfinished screenplay, *The Story of G.I. Joe.*

Focus. New York: Reynal & Hitchcock, 1945; London: Gollancz, 1949. Novel.

All My Sons. New York: Reynal & Hitchcock, 1947; Harmondsworth, U.K.: Penguin, 1961. Play.

Death of a Salesman. New York: Viking, 1949; London: Cresset, 1949. Play.

An Enemy of the People, adapted from Henrik Ibsen's play. New York: Viking, 1951; Harmondsworth, U.K.: Penguin, 1977. Play. Contains a preface by Miller.

The Crucible. New York: Viking, 1953; London: Cresset, 1956. Play.

A View from the Bridge: Two One-Act Plays. New York: Viking, 1955; London: Cresset, 1957. Comprises *A View from the Bridge* and *A Memory of Two Mondays.* Contains "On Social Plays," preface by Miller.

A View from the Bridge: A Play in Two Acts. New York: Dramatists Play Service, 1957; London: Cresset, 1957. Contains an introduction by Miller.

The Misfits. New York: Viking, 1961; London: Secker & Warburg, 1961. Screenplay.

Jane's Blanket. New York: Crowell/Collier, 1963; London: Collier/Macmillan, 1963. Children's book.

After the Fall. New York: Viking, 1964; London: Secker & Warburg, 1965. Play. Contains a foreword by Miller.

Incident at Vichy. New York: Viking, 1965; London: Secker & Warburg, 1966. Play.

189

I Don't Need You Any More: Stories. New York: Viking, 1967; London: Secker & Warburg, 1967.

The Price. New York: Viking, 1968; London: Secker & Warburg, 1968. Play.

In Russia, by Miller and Inge Morath. New York: Viking, 1969; London: Secker & Warburg, 1969. Prose, photographs.

The Creation of the World and Other Business. New York: Viking, 1973. Play.

In the Country, by Miller and Morath. New York: Viking, 1977. Prose, photographs.

Chinese Encounters, by Miller and Morath. New York: Farrar, Straus & Giroux, 1979. Prose, photographs.

Playing for Time. New York: Bantam, 1981. Teleplay.

Some Kind of Love Story. New York: Dramatists Play Service, 1982. Play.

Elegy for a Lady. New York: Dramatists Play Service, 1982. Play.

The American Clock. New York: Dramatists Play Service, 1982. Play.

The Archbishop's Ceiling. London: Methuen, 1984. Play.

"Salesman" in Beijing. New York: Viking, 1984; London: Methuen, 1984. Prose, photographs.

Two-Way Mirror: A Double Bill. London: Methuen, 1984. Comprises *Elegy for a Lady* and *Some Kind of Love Story.*

Playing for Time (acting edition). Chicago: Dramatic Publishing, 1985.

Danger: Memory! London: Methuen, 1986; New York: Grove, 1987. Comprises *I Can't Remember Anything* and *Clara.*

Timebends: A Life. New York: Grove, 1987. Autobiography.

Premiere Productions

No Villain. Ann Arbor, Mich. University of Michigan, 1936.

They Too Arise. Ann Arbor, Mich. Lydia Mendelssohn Theater, 12 Mar. 1937.

That They May Win. Victory Committee of Welfare Center 67 at Albemarle Road, Brooklyn, New York, mounted by Stage for Action, 1943-1944.

The Man Who Had All the Luck. New York, Forrest Theater, 23 Nov. 1944.

All My Sons. New York, Coronet Theater, 29 Jan. 1947.

Death of a Salesman. New York, Morosco Theater, 10 Feb. 1949.

An Enemy of the People. New York, Broadhurst Theater, 28 Dec. 1950.

The Crucible. New York, Martin Beck Theater, 22 Jan. 1953.

A View from the Bridge (one-act version) and *A Memory of Two Mondays.* New York, Coronet Theater, 29 Sept. 1955.

A View from the Bridge (two-act version). London, Comedy Theater, 11 Oct. 1956.

After the Fall. New York, Lincoln Center Repertory Company at ANTA-Washington Square Theater, 23 Jan. 1964.

Incident at Vichy. New York, Lincoln Center Repertory Company at ANTA-Washington Square Theater, 3 Dec. 1964.

The Price. New York, Morosco Theater, 7 Feb. 1968.

Fame. New York, New Theater Workshop, Nov. 1970.

The Reason Why. New York, New Theater Workshop, Nov. 1970.

The Creation of the World and Other Business. New York, Shubert Theater, 30 Nov. 1972.

Up from Paradise (musical version of *The Creation of the World and Other Business*). Ann Arbor, Mich., Power Center for the Performing Arts, University of Michigan, 23 Apr. 1974.

The Archbishop's Ceiling. Washington, D.C., Eisenhower Theater, John F. Kennedy Center for the Performing Arts, 30 Apr. 1977.

The American Clock. Charleston, S.C., Dock Street Theater, Spoleto USA Festival, 24 May 1980.

Elegy for a Lady and *Some Kind of Love Story.* New Haven, Conn., Long Wharf Theater, Oct. 1982.

Playing for Time. Washington, D.C., Studio Theater, 22 Sept. 1985.

Danger: Memory! New York, Mitzi E. Newhouse Theater, Lincoln Center, Feb. 1987.

Selected Periodical Publications

"Should Ezra Pound Be Shot?," *New Masses*, 57 (25 Dec. 1945), 6. Essay.

"The Plaster Masks," *Encore*, 9 (Apr. 1946), 424-432. Essay.

"It Takes a Thief," *Collier's*, 119 (8 Feb. 1947), 23, 75-76. Story.

"Subsidized Theater," *New York Times*, 22 June 1947, section 2, p. 1. Essay.

"Tragedy and the Common Man," *New York Times*, 27 Feb. 1949, section 2, pp. 1, 3. Collected in Weales, 1967, 143-147; collected in Hurrell, 38-40; collected in *The Theater Essays of Arthur Miller*, 3-7.

"Arthur Miller on 'The Nature of Tragedy,' " *New York Herald-Tribune*, 27 Mar. 1949, section 5, pp. 1, 2. Collected in *The Theater Essays of Arthur Miller*, 8-11.

"The *Salesman* Has a Birthday," *New York Times*, 5 Feb. 1950, section 2, pp. 1, 3. Collected in Weales, 1967, 147-151; collected in *The Theater Essays of Arthur Miller*, 12-15.

"Monte Saint Angelo," *Harper's*, 202 (Mar. 1951), 39-47. Story.

"An American Reaction," *World Theater*, 1 (1951), 21-22. Essay.

"Many Writers: Few Plays," *New York Times*, 10 Aug. 1952, section 2, p. 1. Collected in Weales, 1971, 157-161; collected in *The Theater Essays of Arthur Miller*, 22-26.

"Journey to *The Crucible*," *New York Times*, 8 Feb. 1953, section 2, p. 3. Collected in *The Theater Essays of Arthur Miller*, 27-30.

"University of Michigan," *Holiday*, 14 (Dec. 1953), 68-71, 128-132, 136-137, 140-143. Essay.

"A Modest Proposal for Pacification of the Public Temper," *Nation*, 179 (3 July 1954), 5-8. Essay.

"The American Theater," *Holiday*, 17 (Jan. 1955), 90-98, 101-102, 104. Collected in Weales, 1967, 151-155; collected in *The Theater Essays of Arthur Miller*, 31-50.

"A Boy Grew in Brooklyn," *Holiday*, 17 (Mar. 1955), 54-55, 117, 119-120, 122-124. Essay.

"Picking a Cast," *New York Times*, 21 Aug. 1955, section 2, p. 1. Essay.

"The Family in Modern Drama," *Atlantic*, 197 (Apr. 1956), 35-41. Collected in *The Theater Essays of Arthur Miller*, 69-85.

"The Playwright and the Atomic World," *Colorado Quarterly*, 5 (Autumn 1956), 117-137. Collected as "1956 and All This" in *The Theater Essays of Arthur Miller*, 86-109.

"The Writer in America," *Mainstream*, 10 (July 1957), 43-46. Essay.

"Global Dramatist," *New York Times*, 21 July 1957, section 2, p. 1. Essay.

"The Misfits," *Esquire*, 48 (Oct. 1957), 158-166. Story.

"The Writer's Position in America," *Coastlines*, 7 (Autumn 1957), 38-40. Essay.

"Brewed in *The Crucible*," *New York Times*, 9 Mar. 1958, section 2, p. 3. Collected in Weales, 1971, 169-173; collected in *The Theater Essays of Arthur Miller*, 171-174.

"The Shadows of the Gods: A Critical View of the American Theater," *Harper's*, 217 (Aug. 1958), 35-43. Collected in *The Theater Essays of Arthur Miller*, 175-194.

Bridge to a Savage World, *Esquire*, 50 (Oct. 1958), 185-190. Unfinished screenplay.

"My Wife Marilyn," *Life*, 50 (22 Dec. 1958), 146-147. Essay.

"On Adaptations," *New York Times*, 29 Nov. 1959, section 2, p. 13. Collected in *The Theater Essays of Arthur Miller*, 215-217.

"I Don't Need You Any More," *Esquire*, 52 (Dec. 1959), 270-309. Story.

"Please Don't Kill Anything," *Noble Savage*, no. 1 (Mar. 1960), 126-131. Story.

"Art and Commitment," *Anvil and Student Partisan*, 11 (Winter 1960), 5. Essay.

"The Prophecy," *Esquire*, 56 (Dec. 1961), 140-141, 268-287. Story.

"Glimpse at a Jockey," *Noble Savage*, no. 5 (Oct. 1962), 138-250. Story.

"The Bored and the Violent," *Harper's*, 225 (Nov. 1962), 50-52, 55-56. Essay.

"A New Era in American Theater?," *Drama Survey*, 3 (Spring 1963), 70-71. Essay.

"On Recognition," *Michigan Quarterly Review*, 2 (Autumn 1963), 213-220. Collected in *The Theater Essays of Arthur Miller*, 237-251.

"Lincoln Repertory Theater–Challenge and Hope," *New York Times*, 19 Jan. 1964, section 2, pp. 1, 3.

"Foreword to *After the Fall*," *Saturday Evening Post*, 237 (1 Feb. 1964), 32. Collected in *The Theater Essays of Arthur Miller*, 255-257.

"With Respect for Her Agony–But with Love," *Life*, 56 (7 Feb. 1964), 66. Essay.

"How the Nazi Trials Search the Hearts of All Germans," *New York Herald-Tribune*, 15 Mar. 1964, p. 24. Essay.

"Our Guilt for the World's Evil," *New York Times Magazine*, 3 Jan. 1965, pp. 10-11, 48.

"*After the Fall:* An Author's View," *New Haven Register*, 25 Apr. 1965, Features section, p. 9.

"What Makes Plays Endure?," *New York Times*, 15 Aug. 1965, section 2, pp. 1, 3. Collected in *The Theater Essays of Arthur Miller*, 258-263.

"The Writer as Independent Spirit: The Role of P.E.N.," *Saturday Review*, 49 (4 June 1966), 16-17. Essay.

"Arthur Miller: P.E.N., Politics and Literature," *Publisher's Weekly*, 190 (18 July 1966), 32-33. Essay.

"Literature and Mass Communication," *World Theater*, 15 (1966), 164-167. Essay.

"The Recognitions," *Esquire*, 56 (July 1966), 76, 118. Story.

"A Search for the Future," *Saturday Evening Post*, 239 (13 Aug. 1966), 64-68, 70. Essay.

"It Could Happen Here—and Did," *New York Times*, 30 Apr. 1967, section 2, p. 17. Collected in *The Theater Essays of Arthur Miller*, 294-300.

"The Age of Abdication," *New York Times*, 23 Dec. 1967, p. 40. Essay.

"The New Insurgency," *Nation*, 206 (3 June 1968), 717. Essay.

"On the Shooting of Robert Kennedy," *New York Times*, 8 June 1968, p. 30. Essay.

"Writers in Prison," *Encounter*, 30 (June 1968), 60-61. Essay.

"The Battle of Chicago: From the Delegates' Side," *New York Times Magazine*, 15 Sept. 1968, pp. 29-31, 122, 124, 126, 128. Essay.

"Kidnapped?," *Saturday Evening Post*, 242 (25 Jan. 1969), 40-42, 78-82. Essay.

"Are We Interested in Stopping the Killing?," *New York Times*, 8 June 1969, section 2, p. 21. Essay.

"Broadway, From O'Neill to Now," *New York Times*, 21 Dec. 1969, section 2, pp. 3, 7. Collected in *The Theater Essays of Arthur Miller*, 347-353.

"The Bangkok Prince," *Harper's*, 241 (July 1970), 32-33. Essay.

"The War between Young and Old, or Why Willy Loman Can't Understand What's Happening," *McCall's*, 97 (July 1970), 32. Essay.

"Banned in Russia," *New York Times*, 10 Dec. 1970, p. 47. Essay.

"When Life Had at Least a Form," *New York Times*, 16 Oct. 1971, p. 29. Essay.

"In Hiding: The Life of Manuel Cortes, by Ronald Fraser," *New York Times*, 9 July 1972, section 7, p. 34. Book review.

"Arthur Miller on *The Crucible*," *Audience*, 2 (July-Aug. 1972), 46-47. Essay.

"Arthur Miller vs. Lincoln Center," *Dramatists Guild Quarterly*, 8 (Winter 1972), 6-11. Collected in *The Theater Essays of Arthur Miller*, 354-361.

"Politics as Theater," *New York Times*, 4 Nov. 1972, p. 33. Essay.

"Making Crowds," *Esquire*, 78 (Nov. 1972), 160-161, 216, 218, 220, 222, 224, 226, 228. Essay.

"Miracles," *Esquire*, 80 (Sept. 1973), 112-115, 202-204. Essay.

"Sakharov, Detente and Liberty," *New York Times*, 5 July 1974, p. 21. Essay.

"What's Wrong with This Picture?," *Esquire*, 82 (July 1974), 124-125, 170. Essay.

"The Limited Hang-Out: The Dialogues of Richard Nixon as a Drama of the Antihero," *Harper's*, 249 (Sept. 1974), 13-14, 16, 18-20. Essay.

"Rain in a Strange City," *Travel and Leisure*, 4 (Sept. 1974), 8. Essay.

Introduction to *Kesey's Garage Sale*, ed. Ken Kesey. New York: Viking, 1974, xiii-xviii.

"Authors on Translators," by Miller and others, *Translation*, 2, nos. 1-2 (1974), 5-8. Essay.

"On True Identity," *New York Times Magazine*, 13 Apr. 1975, p. 111. Essay.

"The Prague Winter," *New York Times*, 16 July 1975, p. 37. Essay.

"U.S. Urged to Guarantee Freedom of All Writers," *New York Times*, 19 Nov. 1975, p. 25. Essay.

"Ham Sandwich," *Boston University Journal*, 24, no. 2 (1976), 5-6. Essay.

"Toward a New Foreign Policy," *Society*, 13 (Mar.-Apr. 1976), 10, 15, 16. Essay.

"Our Most Widespread Dramatic Art is Our Most Unfree," *New York Times*, 26 Nov. 1978, section 2, p. 33. Essay.

"The American Writer: The American Theater," *Michigan Quarterly Review*, 21 (Winter 1982), 4-20. Essay.

Motion Pictures

The Witches of Salem. Kingsley-International, 1958.

The Misfits. United Artists, 1961.

Television

Playing for Time. CBS, Sept. 1980.

Selected Other

The Pussycat and the Expert Plumber Who Was a Man and *William Ireland's Confession*. In *One Hundred Non-Royalty Plays*, ed. William Kozlenko. New York: Greenberg, 1941, 20-30, 512-521. Radio plays.

The Man Who Had All the Luck. In *Cross-Section: A Collection of New American Writing*, ed. Edwin Seaver. New York: Fischer, 1944, 486-552. Play.

Grandpa and the Statue. In *Radio Drama in Action*, ed. Erik Barnouw. New York: Farrar & Rinehart, 1945, 267-281. Radio play.
That They May Win. In *The Best One-Act Plays of 1944*, ed. Margaret Mayorga. New York: Dodd, Mead, 1945, 45-59.
The Story of Gus. In *Radio's Best Plays*, ed. Joseph Liss. New York: Greenberg, 1947, 303-320. Radio play.
"Concerning the Boom." In *International Theater Annual*, no. 1, ed. Harold Hobson. New York: Citadel, 1956; London: Calder, 1956, 85-88. Essay.

Collections
Collected Plays, 2 volumes. Volume 1, New York: Viking, 1957; London: Cresset, 1958. Comprises *All My Sons, Death of a Salesman, The Crucible, A Memory of Two Mondays*, and *A View from the Bridge* (two-act version). Contains an introduction by Miller. Volume 2, New York: Viking, 1981; London: Secker & Warburg, 1981. Comprises *The Misfits, After the Fall, Incident at Vichy, The Price, The Creation of the World and Other Business*, and *Playing for Time*. Contains an introduction by Miller.
The Theater Essays of Arthur Miller, ed. Robert A. Martin. New York: Viking, 1978; London: Secker & Warburg, 1979.

SECONDARY BIBLIOGRAPHY

Bibliographies and Checklists
Bigsby, C.W.E. *File on Miller*. London & New York: Methuen, 1987.
Carpenter, Charles A. "Studies of Arthur Miller's Drama: A Selective International Bibliography, 1966-1979." In *Arthur Miller: New Perspectives*, ed. Robert A. Martin, 205-219. Secondary. See Collections of Essays.
Eissenstat, Martha Turnquist. "Arthur Miller: A Bibliography," *Modern Drama*, 5 (May 1962), 93-106. Primary and secondary.
Ferres, John H. *Arthur Miller: A Reference Guide*. Boston: G. K. Hall, 1979. Primary and secondary.
Hayashi, Tetsumaro. *Arthur Miller and Tennessee Williams: Research Opportunities and Dissertation Abstracts*. Jefferson, N.C. & London: McFarland, 1983.
Hayashi. *Arthur Miller Criticism*. Metuchen, N.J.: Scarecrow, 1969. Revised as *An Index to Arthur Miller Criticism*. Metuchen, N.J.: Scarecrow, 1976. Primary and secondary.

Hayashi. "Arthur Miller: The Dimension of His Art and a Checklist of His Published Works," *Serif*, 4 (June 1967), 26-32. Primary.

Jensen, George H. *Arthur Miller: A Bibliographical Checklist.* Columbia, S.C.: Faust, 1976. Primary.

Martin, Robert A. "Bibliography of Works (1936-1977) by Arthur Miller." In *The Theater Essays of Arthur Miller*, 379-392. Primary.

Ungar, Harriet. "The Writings of and about Arthur Miller: A Check List 1936-1967," *Bulletin of the New York Public Library*, 74 (Feb. 1970), 107-134. Primary and secondary.

Interviews

Allsop, Kenneth. "A Conversation with Arthur Miller," *Encounter*, 13 (July 1959), 58-60. Collected in *Conversations with Arthur Miller*, ed. Matthew C. Roudané, 52-55.

"Arthur Miller Ad-Libs on Elia Kazan," *Show* (Jan. 1964), 55-56, 97-98. Collected in Roudané, 68-77.

"Arthur Miller on *The Crucible*" (film version), *Audience*, 2 (July-Aug. 1972), 46-47.

"Arthur Miller Talks," *Michigan Quarterly Review*, 6 (Summer 1967), 153-184. Collected in Roudané, 128-136.

Barthel, Joan. "Arthur Miller Ponders *The Price*," *New York Times*, 28 Jan. 1968, section 2, pp. 1, 5.

Bigsby, Christopher. "Miller's Odyssey to a Brutal Decade," *Guardian*, 4 Aug. 1986, p. 9.

Brandon, Henry. "The State of the Theater: A Conversation with Arthur Miller and Marilyn Monroe," *Harper's*, 221 (Nov. 1960), 63-69. Collected in *The Theater Essays of Arthur Miller*, 223-237; collected in Roudané, 56-67.

Buckley, Tom. "Miller Takes His Comedy Seriously," *New York Times*, 29 Aug. 1972, p. 22. Collected in Roudané, 249-252.

Calta, Louis. "Miller Defends Theme of *Price*," *New York Times*, 5 Mar. 1968, p. 32.

Carlisle, Olga, and Rose Styron. "The Art of the Theater II: Arthur Miller, An Interview" *Paris Review*, 10 (Summer 1966), 61-98. Collected as "Arthur Miller: An Interview" in *The Theater Essays of Arthur Miller*, 264-293; collected in Roudané, 85-111.

Centola, Steven R. " 'The Will to Live': An Interview with Arthur Miller," *Modern Drama*, 27 (Sept. 1984), 345-360. Collected in Roudané, 343-359.

"The Contemporary Theater," *Michigan Quarterly Review*, 6 (Summer 1967), 153-163. Collected in *The Theater Essays of Arthur Miller*, 301-318; collected in Roudané, 112-127.

"Conversation at St. Clerans between Arthur Miller and John Huston," *Guardian*, 25 Feb. 1960, p. 6.

Cook, Jim. "Their Thirteenth Year Was Most Significant," *Washington Post and Times Herald*, 10 July 1956, p. 24.

Corrigan, Robert W. "Arthur Miller: Interview," *Michigan Quarterly Review*, 13 (Autumn 1974), 401-405. Collected in Roudané, 253-257.

Downer, Alan S. "Mr. Williams and Mr. Miller," *Furioso*, 4 (Summer 1949), 66-70.

Evans, Richard I. *Psychology and Arthur Miller*. New York: Dutton, 1969. Republished as *Dialogue with Arthur Miller*. New York: Praeger, 1981. Excerpt collected as "The Writer and Society" in Roudané, 152-172.

Fallaci, Oriana. "A Propos of *After the Fall*," *World Theatre*, 14 (Jan. 1965), 79, 81.

Feron, James. "Miller in London to See *Crucible*," *New York Times*, 24 Jan. 1965, p. 82. Collected in Roudané, 83-84.

Frank, Stanley. "A Playwright Ponders a New Outline for TV," *TV Guide*, 14 (8 Oct. 1966), 7-8, 10-11.

"Freedom in the Mass Media," *Michigan Quarterly Review*, 6 (Summer 1967), 163-178. Panel with Mike Wallace, Arnold Gingrich, and Arthur Miller.

Funke, Lewis. "Thoughts on a Train Bound for Wilmington," *New York Times*, 18 Jan. 1953, pp. 1, 3.

Gelb, Barbara. "Question: 'Am I My Brother's Keeper?,' " *New York Times*, 29 Nov. 1964, section 2, pp. 1, 3. Collected in Roudané, 78-82.

Gelb, Phillip. "Morality and Modern Drama," *Educational Theatre Journal*, 10 (Oct. 1958), 190-202. Collected in *The Theater Essays of Arthur Miller*, 195-214; collected in Roudané, 35-51.

Gelb, Arthur Miller, Gore Vidal, Richard Watts, John Beaufort, Martin Dworkin, and David W. Thompson. "*Death of a Salesman*: A Symposium," *Tulane Drama Review*, 2 (May 1958), 63-69. Collected as "A Matter of Hopelessness in *Death of a Salesman*" in Hurrell, 76-81; collected in Roudané, 27-34.

Gollub, Christian-Albrecht. "Interview with Arthur Miller," *Michigan Quarterly Review*, 16 (Spring 1977), 121-141. Collected in Roudané, 273-290.

Goyen, William. "Arthur Miller's Quest for Truth," *New York Herald-Tribune Magazine*, 19 Jan. 1964, p. 35.

Greenfield, Josh. " 'Writing Plays is Absolutely Senseless,' Arthur Miller Says, 'But I Love It. I Just Love It,' " *New York Times Magazine*, 13 Feb. 1972, pp. 16-17, 34-39. Collected in Roudané, 233-248.

Griffin, John and Alice. "Arthur Miller Discusses *The Crucible*," *Theater Arts*, 37 (Oct. 1953), 33-34. Collected in Roudané, 24-26.

Gruen, Joseph. "Portrait of the Playwright at Fifty," *New York*, 24 Oct. 1965, 12-13. Collected in his *Close Up*. New York: Viking, 1968, 58-63.

Gussow, Mel. "Arthur Miller Returns to Genesis for First Musical," *New York Times*, 17 Apr. 1974, p. 37.

Halberstam, David. "Polish Students Question Miller," *New York Times*, 17 Feb. 1965, p. 36.

Hayman, Ronald. "Arthur Miller." In his *Playback II*. London: Davis-Poynter, 1973, 7-22.

Hayman. "Arthur Miller Talks About His Play," *Times* (London), 15 Feb. 1969, p. 19. Enlarged as "Interview with Arthur Miller" in his *Arthur Miller*. London: Heinemann, 1970, 1-14; collected in Roudané, 187-199.

Heaton, C. P. "Arthur Miller on *Death of a Salesman*," *Notes on Contemporary Literature*, 1. no. 1 (1971), 5.

Hewes, Henry. "Broadway Postscript: Arthur Miller and How He Went to the Devil," *Saturday Review*, 36 (31 Jan. 1953), 24-26. Collected in *"The Crucible": Text and Criticism*, ed. Gerald Weales, 1971, 182-188; collected in Roudané, 19-23. See Collections of Essays.

Hewes. "Death of a Longshoreman," *Saturday Review*, 38 (15 Oct. 1955), 25-26.

Hills, Rust. "Conversation: Arthur Miller and William Styron," *Audience*, 1 (Nov./Dec. 1971), 4-21. Collected in Roudané, 206-232.

Hughes, Catharine. "The Crucible." In her *Plays, Politics, and Polemics*. New York: Drama Book Specialists, 1973, 15-25.

Hutchens, John K. "Mr. Miller Has a Change of Luck," *New York Times*, 23 Feb. 1947, section 2, pp. 1, 3. Collected in Roudané, 3-5.

Hyams, Barry. "A Theater: Heart and Mind," *Theater: The Annual of the Repertory Theater of Lincoln Center*, 1 (1964), 56-61.

James, Caryn. "On Film Credits List, That Miller is Arthur," *New York Times*, 22 Nov. 1988, p. C17.

Lamos, Mark. "An Afternoon with Arthur Miller," *American Theatre*, 3 (May 1986), 18-23, 44. Collected in Roudané, 376-388.

Lardner, James. "Arthur Miller–Back in Control at 65," *Washington Post*, 26 Oct. 1980, Show section, pp. L1, L5.

"Learning from a Performer: A Conversation with Arthur Miller," *Gamut*, 1 (1982), 9-23.

Lenz, Harold. "At Sixes and Sevens–A Modern Theater Structure," *Forum*, 11, no. 3 (1973-1974), 73-79.

Mailer, Norman. "The Jewish Princess." In his *Marilyn*. New York: Grosset & Dunlap, 1973, 157-206.

Martin, Robert A. "Arthur Miller and the Meaning of Tragedy," *Modern Drama*, 13 (May 1970), 34-39. Collected in Roudané, 200-205.

Martin. "Arthur Miller–Tragedy and Commitment," *Michigan Quarterly Review*, 8 (Summer 1969), 176-178. Collected in Roudané, 173-176.

Martin. "The Creative Experience of Arthur Miller: An Interview," *Educational Theatre Journal*, 21 (Oct. 1969), 310-317. Collected in Roudané, 177-186.

Martin, and Richard D. Meyer. "Arthur Miller on Plays and Playwriting," *Modern Drama*, 19 (Dec. 1976), 375-384. Collected in Roudané, 262-272.

Martine, James J. " 'All in a Boiling Soup': An Interview with Arthur Miller." In *Critical Essays on Arthur Miller*, ed. Martine, 177-188; collected in Roudané, 291-306. See Collections of Essays.

"Morality and Modern Drama," *Educational Theatre Journal*, 10 (Oct. 1958), 190-202. Collected in *"Death of a Salesman": Text and Criticism*, ed. Gerald Weales, 1967, 172-186; collected in *The Theater Essays of Arthur Miller*, 195-214. See Collections of Essays.

Morley, Sheridan. "Miller on Miller," *Theatre World* (London), 61 (Mar. 1965), 4, 8.

Moss, Leonard. " 'The Absence of the Tension': A Conversation with Arthur Miller." In his *Arthur Miller*. Revised edition, New York: Twayne, 1980, 107-122. Collected in Roudané, 315-331.

Rajakrishnan, V. "After Commitment: An Interview with Arthur Miller," *Theatre Journal*, 32 (May 1980), 196-204. Collected in Roudané, 332-342.

Ratcliffe, Michael. "Miller's Russian Tale," *Observer*, 26 Oct. 1986, p. 23.

Roudané, Matthew C. "An Interview with Arthur Miller," *Michigan Quarterly Review*, 24, no. 3 (1985), 373-389. Collected in Roudané, 360-375.

Roudané, ed. *Conversations with Arthur Miller*. Jackson: University Press of Mississippi, 1987.

Samachson, Dorothy and Joseph. Untitled interview. In their *Let's Meet the Theater*. New York: Abelard-Schuman, 1954, 15-20.

Schumach, Murray. "Arthur Miller Grew in Brooklyn," *New York Times*, 6 Feb. 1949, section 2, pp. 1, 3. Collected in Roudané, 6-8.

Schumach. "Miller Still a 'Salesman' for a Changing Theater," *New York Times*, 26 June 1975, p. 32. Collected in Roudané, 258-261.

Shenker, Israel. "Jewish Cultural Arts: The Big Debate," *New York Times*, 13 Jan. 1976, p. 42.

Sylvester, Robert. "Brooklyn Boy Makes Good," *Saturday Evening Post*, 222 (16 July 1949), 26-27, 97-98, 100. Collected in Roudané, 9-18.

"Symposium: Playwriting in America: Joyce Carol Oates, Arthur Miller, Eric Bentley," *Yale/Theater*, 4, no. 1 (1973), 8-27.

Terkel, Studs. "Studs Terkel Talks with Arthur Miller," *Saturday Review* (Sept. 1980), 24-27. Collected in Roudané, 307-314.

Vajda, Miklos. "Playwriting in America Today: A Telephone Interview with Arthur Miller," *New Hungarian Quarterly*, 77 (1980), 123-124.

Wager, Walter. "Arthur Miller." In *The Playwrights Speak*, ed. Wager. New York: Delta, 1967, 1-24. Collected in Roudané, 137-151.

Wain, John. "Arthur Miller," *Observer*, 8 Sept. 1957, p. 5.

Weatherby, W. J. "Making *The Misfits*," *Manchester Guardian*, 3 Nov. 1961, p. 8.

Wertham, Frederic. "Let the Salesman Beware," *New York Times Book Review*, 15 May 1949, pp. 4, 12.

Whitcomb, J. "Marilyn Monroe: The Sex Symbol versus the Good Wife," *Cosmopolitan*, 149 (Dec. 1961), 53-57.

Wolfert, Ira. "Arthur Miller, Playwright in Search of His Identity," *New York Herald-Tribune*, 25 Jan. 1953, section 4, p. 3.

Critical Studies: Books

Bhatia, Santosh K. *Arthur Miller: Social Drama as Tragedy.* New York: Humanities Press, 1985; New Delhi: Arnold-Heinemann, 1985.

Carson, Neil. *Arthur Miller.* New York: Grove, 1982.

Goode, James. *The Story of "The Misfits."* Indianapolis: Bobbs-Merrill, 1963.

Harshbarger, Karl. *The Burning Jungle: An Analysis of Arthur Miller's "Death of a Salesman."* Washington, D.C.: University Press of America, 1979.

Hayman, Ronald. *Arthur Miller.* London: Heinemann, 1970; New York: Ungar, 1972.

Hogan, Robert. *Arthur Miller.* Minneapolis: University of Minnesota Press, 1964.

Huftel, Sheila. *Arthur Miller: The Burning Glass.* New York: Citadel, 1965; London: Allen, 1965.

Moss, Leonard. *Arthur Miller.* New York: Twayne, 1967. Revised and enlarged, 1980.

Murray, Edward. *Arthur Miller: Dramatist.* New York: Ungar, 1967.

Nelson, Benjamin. *Arthur Miller: Portrait of a Playwright.* London: Owen, 1970; New York: McKay, 1970.

Panikkar, N. Bhaskara. *Individual Morality and Social Happiness in Arthur Miller.* New Delhi: Milind Publications Private Limited, 1982; Atlantic Highlands, N.J.: Humanities Press, 1982.

Partridge, C. J. *Death of a Salesman.* Oxford: Blackwell, 1969.

Schlueter, June, and James K. Flanagan. *Arthur Miller.* New York: Ungar, 1987.

Welland, Dennis. *Arthur Miller.* Edinburgh: Oliver & Boyd, 1961; New York: Grove, 1961.

Welland. *Miller: A Study of His Plays.* London: Eyre/Methuen, 1979. Revised and enlarged as *Miller: The Playwright.* London & New York: Methuen, 1983.

White, Sidney H. *Guide to Arthur Miller.* Columbus, Ohio: Merrill, 1970.

Critical Studies: Collections of Essays

Bloom, Harold, ed. *Arthur Miller.* New York: Chelsea House, 1987.

Bloom, ed. *Arthur Miller's "All My Sons."* New York: Chelsea House, 1988.

Bloom, ed. *Arthur Miller's "Death of a Salesman."* New York: Chelsea House, 1988.

Corrigan, Robert W., ed. *Arthur Miller: A Collection of Critical Essays.* Englewood Cliffs, N.J.: Prentice-Hall, 1969.

Ferres, John H., ed. *Twentieth Century Interpretations of "The Crucible."* Englewood Cliffs, N.J.: Prentice-Hall, 1972.

Hurrell, John D., ed. *Two Modern American Tragedies: Reviews and Criticism of "Death of a Salesman" and "A Streetcar Named Desire."* New York: Scribners, 1961.

Koon, Helene Wickham, ed. *Twentieth Century Interpretations of "Death of a Salesman."* Englewood Cliffs, N.J.: Prentice-Hall, 1983.

Martin, Robert A., ed. *Arthur Miller: New Perspectives.* Englewood Cliffs, N.J.: Prentice-Hall, 1982.

Martine, James J., ed. *Critical Essays on Arthur Miller.* Boston: G. K. Hall, 1979.

Meserve, Walter J., ed. *The Merrill Studies in "Death of a Salesman."* Columbus, Ohio: Merrill, 1972.

Parker, Dorothy, ed. *Essays on Modern American Drama: Williams, Miller, Albee, and Shepard.* Toronto: University of Toronto Press, 1987, 53-106.

Weales, Gerald, ed. *"The Crucible": Text and Criticism.* New York: Viking, 1971; Harmondsworth, U.K.: Penguin, 1977.

Weales, ed. *"Death of a Salesman": Text and Criticism.* New York: Viking, 1967; Harmondsworth, U.K.: Penguin, 1977.

Critical Studies: Major Reviews, Articles, and Book Sections

Aarnes, William. "Tragic Form and the Possibility of Meaning in *Death of a Salesman*," *Furman Studies*, 29 (Dec. 1983), 57-80. Collected in Bloom, *Arthur Miller's "Death of a Salesman,"* 1988, 95-111.

Abirached, Robert. "Allez à Aubervilliers," *Nouvel Observateur*, no. 27 (20 May 1965), 32-33. Collected in Meserve, 17-19.

Adamczewski, Zygmunt. "The Tragic Loss–Loman the Salesman." In his *The Tragic Protest.* The Hague: Martinus Nijhoff, 1963; London: Heinemann, 1964, 172-193.

Adler, Henry. "To Hell with Society," *Tulane Drama Review*, 4 (May 1960), 53-76. Collected in *Theater in the Twentieth Century*, ed. Robert W. Corrigan. New York: Grove, 1963, 245-272.

Allen, Jennifer. "Miller's Tale: America's Premier Playwright is Still on the Job," *New York*, 24 (Jan. 1983), 33-37.

Anderson, M. C. *"Death of a Salesman*: A Consideration of Willy Loman's Role in Twentieth-Century Tragedy," *CRUX: A Journal on the Teaching of English*, 20, no. 2 (1986), 25-29.

Angelico da Costa, Luiz. "The Role of Language in *Death of a Salesman*," *Estudos Anglo-Americanos*, 2, no. 1 (1978), 21-31.

Atkinson, Brooks. "At the Theater," *New York Times*, 23 Jan. 1953, p. 15. Collected in Weales, 1971, 192-196.

Atkinson. *"Death of a Salesman*, A New Drama by Arthur Miller, Has Premiere at the Morosco," *New York Times*, 11 Feb. 1949, p. 27. Collected in Martine, 21-22.

Atkinson. *"Death of a Salesman*: Arthur Miller's Tragedy of an Ordinary Man," *New York Times*, 20 Feb. 1949, section 2, p. 1. Collected in Hurrell, 54-56.

Atkinson. "Fredric March in *An Enemy of the People*, Adapted by Arthur Miller," *New York Times*, 29 Dec. 1950, p. 14. Collected in Martine, 52-54.

August, Eugene R. *"Death of a Salesman*: A Men's Studies Approach," *Western Ohio Journal*, 7 (Spring 1986), 53-71.

Aylen, Leo. "Miller." In his *Greek Tragedy and the Modern World*. London: Methuen, 1964, 248-257.

Aymé, Marcel. "I Want to be Hanged Like a Witch," *Arts*, 15-21 Dec. 1954, pp. 1, 3. Collected in Weales, 1971, 239-241.

Banerjee, Chinmoy. "Arthur Miller: The Prospect of Tragedy," *An English Miscellany*, 3 (1965), 66-76.

Barksdale, Richard K. "Social Background in the Plays of Miller and Williams," *CLA Journal*, 6 (Mar. 1963), 161-169.

Bates, Barclay W. "The Lost Past in *Death of a Salesman*," *Modern Drama*, 11 (Sept. 1968), 164-172. Collected in Koon, 60-69.

Baxandall, Lee. "Arthur Miller: Still the Innocent," *Encore*, 11 (May/June 1964), 16-19. Collected in Weales, 1971, 352-358.

Bell, Robert F. "Perspectives on Witch Hunts: Lion Feuchtwanger and Arthur Miller." In *Deutsches Exildrama und Exiltheater: Akten des Exilliteratur-Symposiums der University of South Carolina 1976*, ed. Wolfgang Elfe, James Hardin, and Günther Holst. Frankfurt: Lang, 1977, 113-118.

Bentley, Eric. "Arthur Miller." In *Thirty Years of Treason: Excerpts from Hearings Before the House Committee on Un-American Activities*, ed. Bentley. New York: Viking, 1971, 791-825.

Bentley. "Back to Broadway," *Theater Arts*, 33 (Nov. 1949), 10-19.

Bentley. "Miller's Innocence," *New Republic*, 128 (16 Feb. 1953),

22-23. Collected as "The Innocence of Arthur Miller" in Weales, 1971, 204-209.

Bergeron, David M. "Arthur Miller's *The Crucible* and Nathaniel Hawthorne: Some Parallels," *English Journal*, 58 (Jan. 1969), 47-55.

Bergman, Herbert. "The Interior of the Heart: *The Crucible* and *The Scarlet Letter*," *University College Quarterly*, 15, no. 4 (1970), 27-32.

Bermel, Albert. "Right, Wrong and Mr. Miller," *New York Times*, 14 Apr. 1968, section 2, pp. 1, 7.

Bertin, Michael. " 'Riding on a Smile and a Shoeshine': The Broadway Salesman." In *Before His Eyes: Essays in Honor of Stanley Kauffmann*, ed. Bert Cardullo. Lanham, Md.: University Press of America, 1986, 103-107.

Bettina, Sister M. "Willy Loman's Brother Ben: Tragic Insight in *Death of a Salesman*," *Modern Drama*, 4 (Feb. 1962), 409-412. Collected in Meserve, 80-83.

Beyer, William. "The State of the Theater: The Season Opens," *School and Society*, 70 (3 Dec. 1949), 363-364. Collected in Weales, 1967, 228-230.

Bhatia, S. K. "*Death of a Salesman* as a Social Document," *Banasthali Patrika*, 20 (1976), 45-49.

Bierman, Judah, James Hart, and Stanley Johnson. "Arthur Miller: *Death of a Salesman*." In *The Dramatic Experience*, ed. Bierman and others. Englewood Cliffs, N.J.: Prentice-Hall, 1958, 490-493. Collected in Weales, 1967, 265-271.

Bigsby, C. W. E. "Arthur Miller." In his *Confrontation and Commitment*. London: MacGibbon & Kee/Columbia: University of Missouri Press, 1968, 26-49.

Bigsby. *A Critical Introduction to Twentieth-Century American Drama*, volume 2: *Williams, Miller, Albee*. Cambridge: Cambridge University Press, 1984, 135-248; collected as "*Death of a Salesman*: In Memoriam" in Bloom, Arthur Miller's "*Death of a Salesman*," 1988, 113-128.

Bigsby. *A Critical Introduction to Twentieth-Century American Drama*, volume 3: *Beyond Broadway*. Cambridge: Cambridge University Press, 1985, 251-290.

Bigsby. "Drama from a Living Center." In Bloom, 1987, 103-125.

Bigsby. "The Fall and After: Arthur Miller's Confession," *Modern Drama*, 10 (Sept. 1967), 124-136. Collected in Parker, 68-79.

Bigsby. "Realism and Idealism." In Bloom, *Arthur Miller's "All My Sons,"* 1988, 107-112.

Bigsby. "What Price Arthur Miller? An Analysis of *The Price*," *Twentieth Century Literature*, 16, no. 1 (1970), 16-25. Collected in Martine, 161-170.

Blau, Herbert. "Counterforce I: The Social Drama." In his *The Impossible Theater*. New York: Macmillan, 1964, 186-192. Collected as "The Whole Man and the Real Witch" in Corrigan, 122-130; collected in Weales, 1971, 231-238; collected as "No Play Is Deeper Than Its Witches" in Ferres, 61-66.

Bliquez, Guerin. "Linda's Role in *Death of a Salesman*," *Modern Drama*, 10 (Feb. 1968), 383-386. Collected in Meserve, 77-79.

Blumberg, Paul. "Sociology and Social Literature: Work Alienation in the Plays of Arthur Miller," *American Quarterly*, 21 (Summer 1969), 291-310. Collected as "Work as Alienation in the Plays of Arthur Miller" in Martin, 48-64.

Bly, Robert. "The Dead World and the Live World," *Sixties*, 8 (Spring 1966), 2-7.

Boggs, W. Arthur. "*Oedipus* and *All My Sons*," *Personalist*, 42 (Autumn 1961), 555-560.

Bonnet, Jean-Marie. "Society vs. the Individual in Arthur Miller's *The Crucible*," *English Studies*, 63 (Feb. 1982), 32-36.

Bordewyk, Gordon. "Saul Bellow's *Death of a Salesman*," *Saul Bellow Journal*, 1 (Fall 1981), 18-21.

Boruch, Marianne. "Miller and Things," *Literary Review*, 24 (Summer 1981), 548-561.

Brashear, William R. "The Empty Bench: Morality, Tragedy, and Arthur Miller," *Michigan Quarterly Review*, 5 (Fall 1966), 270-278.

Brater, Enoch. "Ethics and Ethnicity in the Plays of Arthur Miller." In *From Hester Street to Hollywood: The Jewish-American Stage and Screen*, ed. Sarah Blacher Cohen. Bloomington: Indiana University Press, 1983, 123-136.

Brater. "Miller's Realism and *Death of a Salesman*." In Martin, 115-126.

Bronson, David. "*An Enemy of the People*: A Key to Arthur Miller's Art and Ethics," *Comparative Drama*, 2 (Winter 1968-1969), 229-247. Collected in Martine, 55-71.

Broussard, Louis. "Everyman at Mid-Century." In his *American Drama: Contemporary Allegory from Eugene O'Neill to Tennessee Williams*. Norman: University of Oklahoma Press, 1962, 116-121.

Brown, Frances. "Miller Opens P.E.N. Congress in France," *New York Times*, 16 Sept. 1969, p. 43.

Brown, Ivor. "As London Sees Willy Loman," *New York Times Magazine*, 28 Aug. 1949, pp. 11, 59. Collected in Weales, 1967, 244-249.

Brown, John Mason. "*Death of a Salesman.*" In his *Dramatis Personae.* New York: Viking, 1963, 94-100. Collected as "Even As You and I" in Weales, 1967, 205-211.

Brucher, Richard T. "Willy Loman and *The Soul of a New Machine*: Technology and the Common Man," *Journal of American Studies*, 17 (Dec. 1983), 325-336. Collected in Bloom, *Arthur Miller's "Death of a Salesman,"* 1988, 83-94.

Brustein, Robert. "Arthur Miller's Mea Culpa," *New Republic*, 150 (8 Feb. 1964), 26-28, 30. Collected in his *Seasons of Discontent.* New York: Simon & Schuster, 1965, 243-247.

Brustein. "Drama in the Age of Einstein," *New York Times*, 7 Aug. 1977, section 2, pp. 1, 22.

Brustein. "The Memory of Heroism," *Drama Review*, 4 (Mar. 1960), 5-7. Collected in his *The Third Theater.* New York: Knopf, 1969, 242-244.

Brustein. "The Unseriousness of Arthur Miller," *New Republic*, 158 (24 Feb. 1968), 39-41. Collected in his *The Third Theater*, 103-106.

Brustein. "Why American Plays are Not Literature," *Harper's*, 219 (Oct. 1959), 167-172.

Budick, E. Miller. "History and Other Spectres in Arthur Miller's *The Crucible,*" *Modern Drama*, 28 (Dec. 1985), 535-552. Collected in Bloom, 1987, 127-144.

Buitenhuis, Peter. "Arthur Miller: The Fall from the Bridge," *Canadian Association for American Studies Bulletin*, 3 (Spring/Summer 1967), 55-71.

Burhans, Clinton S., Jr. "Eden and the Idiot Child: Arthur Miller's *After the Fall,*" *Ball State University Forum*, 20, no. 1 (1979), 3-16.

Calarco, N. Joseph. "Production as Criticism: Miller's *The Crucible,*" *Educational Theatre Journal*, 29 (Oct. 1977), 354-361.

Callahan, Elizabeth Amidon. "The Tragic Hero in Contemporary Secular and Religious Drama," *Literary Half-Yearly*, 8 (Jan./July 1967), 42-49.

Carson, Neil. "*A View from the Bridge* and the Expansion of Vision." Collected in Bloom, 1987, 93-102.

Cassell, Richard A. "Arthur Miller's 'Rage of Conscience,'" *Ball State University Forum*, 1 (Winter 1960), 31-36.

Casty, Alan. "Post-Loverly Love: A Comparative Report," *Antioch Review*, 26 (Fall 1966), 399-411.

Centola, Steven R. "Bad Faith in *All My Sons*." In Bloom, *Arthur Miller's "All My Sons,"* 1988, 123-133.

Centola. "Compromise as Bad Faith: Arthur Miller's *A View from the Bridge* and William Inge's *Come Back, Little Sheba,*" *Midwest Quarterly*, 28 (Autumn 1986), 100-113.

Centola. "The Monomyth and Arthur Miller's *After the Fall,*" *Studies in American Drama 1945-Present*, 1 (1986), 49-60.

Centola. "Unblessed Rage for Order: Arthur Miller's *After the Fall,*" *Arizona Quarterly*, 39 (Spring 1983), 62-70.

Centola. "What Price Freedom? The Fall Revisited: Arthur Miller's *The Creation of the World and Other Business,*" *Studies in the Humanities*, 12 (June 1985), 3-10.

Chaikin, Milton. "The Ending of Arthur Miller's *The Price,*" *Studies in the Humanities*, 8 (Mar. 1981), 40-44.

Chapman, John. "*The Man Who Had All the Luck*: A Good Try, But Is Out of Luck," *New York Daily News*, 24 Nov. 1944. Collected in Martine, 3-4.

Chapman. "Miller's *View from the Bridge* is Splendid, Stunning Theater," *New York Daily News*, 30 Sept. 1955. Collected in Martine, 105-106.

Chatterji, Ruby. "Existentialist Approach to Modern American Drama." In *Existentialism in American Literature*, ed. Chatterji. Atlantic Highlands, N.J.: Humanities Press, 1983, 80-98.

Chiari, Joseph. "Drama in the U.S.A." In his *Landmarks of Contemporary Drama*. London: Jenkins, 1965, 146-157.

Cismaru, Alfred. "Before and *After the Fall,*" *Forum*, 11, no. 3 (1973), 67-71.

Clark, Eleanor. Review of *Death of a Salesman*. *Partisan Review*, 16 (June 1949), 631-635. Collected in Hurrell, 61-64; collected as "Old Glamour, New Gloom" in Weales, 1967, 217-223.

Clurman, Harold. "Arthur Miller: Theme and Variations," *Theater: The Annual of the Repertory Theater of Lincoln Center*, 1 (1964), 31-40. Enlarged as "Editor's Introduction" in *The Portable Arthur Miller*, ed. Clurman. New York: Viking, 1971, xi-xxv; collected as a section in "Arthur Miller's Later Plays" in Corrigan, 143-168.

Clurman. *"Death of a Salesman," Tomorrow*, 8 (May 1949), 48-51. Collected in his *Lies Like Truth: Theater Reviews and Essays*, 68-72; collected in Hurrell, 65-67; collected as "The Success Dream on the American Stage" in Weales, 1967, 212-216.

Clurman. "Director's Notes: *Incident at Vichy*," *Drama Review*, 9 (Summer 1965), 77-90. Collected as a section in "Arthur Miller's Later Plays" in Corrigan, 143-168.

Clurman. *Lies Like Truth: Theater Reviews and Essays*. New York: Macmillan, 1958, 64-68. Collected as "Thesis and Drama" in Bloom, *Arthur Miller's "All My Sons,"* 1988, 15-18.

Clurman. "The Merits of Mr. Miller," *New York Times*, 21 Apr. 1968, section 2, pp. 1, 3. Collected as a section in "Arthur Miller's Later Plays" in Corrigan, 143-168.

Clurman. "Theater: Attention!," *New Republic*, 120 (28 Feb. 1949), 26-28. Collected in Meserve, 6-8.

Cohn, Ruby. "The Articulate Victims of Arthur Miller." In her *Dialogue in American Drama*. Bloomington: Indiana University Press, 1971, 68-96. Collected in Martin, 65-74; collected in Bloom, *Arthur Miller's "Death of a Salesman,"* 1988, 39-46.

Collins, Anthony R. "Arthur Miller and the Judgment of God," *South Central Bulletin*, 42 (Winter 1984), 120-124.

Collins. "Confrontation with the Other: Alienation in the Works of Arthur Miller and Jean-Paul Sartre," *Journal of Evolutionary Psychology*, 5 (Mar. 1984), 1-11.

Cook, Larry W. "The Function of Ben and Dave Singleman in *Death of a Salesman*," *Notes on Contemporary Literature*, 5, no. 1 (1975), 7-9.

Corrigan, Robert W. "The Achievement of Arthur Miller," *Comparative Drama*, 2 (Fall 1968), 141-160. Collected in *The Theater in Search of a Fix*, ed. Corrigan. New York: Delacorte, 1972, 325-347.

Couchman, Gordon W. "Arthur Miller's Tragedy of Babbitt," *Educational Theatre Journal*, 7 (Oct. 1955), 206-211. Collected in Meserve, 68-75.

Curtis, Penelope. *"The Crucible," Critical Review*, 8 (1965), 45-58. Collected in Weales, 1971, 255-271; collected as "Setting, Language, and the Force of Evil in *The Crucible*" in Ferres, 67-76.

Deedy, John. "Critics and the Bible," *Commonweal*, 97 (5 Jan. 1973), 290.

Dillingham, William B. "Arthur Miller and the Loss of Conscience," *Emory University Quarterly*, 16 (Spring 1960), 40-50. Collected in Weales, 1967, 339-349.

Ditsky, John. "Stone, Fire and Light: Approaches to *The Crucible*," *North Dakota Quarterly*, 46, no. 2 (1978), 65-72.

Donoghue, Denis. "The Human Image in Modern Drama," *Lugano Review*, 1 (Summer 1965), 167-168.

Douglass, James W. "Miller's *The Crucible*: Which Witch is Which?," *Renascence*, 15 (Spring 1963), 145-151. Excerpted as "Which Witch is Witch?" in Ferres, 101-103.

Downer, Alan S. "Mr. Williams and Mr. Miller," *Furioso*, 4 (Summer 1949), 66-70.

Downer. "Old, New, Borrowed, and (a Trifle) Blue: Notes on the New York Theater, 1967-68," *Quarterly Journal of Speech*, 54 (Oct. 1968), 203-211. Excerpted as "Review of *The Price*" in Martine, 155-157.

Driver, Tom F. "Strength and Weakness in Arthur Miller," *Tulane Drama Review*, 4 (May 1960), 45-52. Collected in Corrigan, 59-68; collected in Bloom, 1987, 17-25.

Dusenbury, Winifred L. "Personal Failure." In her *The Theme of Loneliness in Modern American Drama*. Gainesville: University of Florida Press, 1960, 16-26.

Dworkin, Martin. "Miller and Ibsen," *Humanist*, 11 (1951), 110-115.

Edwards, John. "Arthur Miller: An Appraisal," *Time and Tide*, 42 (4 May 1961), 740-741.

Eisinger, Chester E. "Focus on Arthur Miller's *Death of a Salesman*: The Wrong Dreams." In *American Dreams, American Nightmares*, ed. David Madden. Carbondale: Southern Illinois University Press, 1970, 165-174.

Engle, John D. "The Metaphor of Law in *After the Fall*," *Notes on Contemporary Literature*, 9, no. 3 (1979), 11-12.

Epstein, Arthur D. "A Look at *A View from the Bridge*," *Texas Studies in Literature and Language*, 7 (Spring 1965), 109-122. Collected in Martine, 107-118.

Epstein, Leslie. "The Unhappiness of Arthur Miller," *Tri-Quarterly*, 1 (Spring 1965), 165-173.

Falb, Lewis W. "Arthur Miller." In his *American Drama in Paris, 1945-1970*. Chapel Hill: University of North Carolina Press, 1973, 37-50.

Feldman, Robert Lee. "Tragedy and the Common Man: Existential

Analysis and Arthur Miller," *Family Therapy: Journal of California Institute for Family, Marital and Individual Therapy,* 7, no. 1 (1980), 1-71.

Fender, Stephen. "Precision and Pseudo Precision in *The Crucible,*" *Journal of American Studies,* 1 (Apr. 1967), 87-98. Collected in Weales, 1971, 272-289.

Ferguson, Alfred R. "The Tragedy of the American Dream in *Death of a Salesman,*" *Thought: A Review of Culture and Ideas,* 53 (Mar. 1978), 83-98.

Ferres, John H. "Still in the Present Tense: *The Crucible* Today," *University College Quarterly,* 17 (May 1972), 8-18.

Field, B. S., Jr. "Hamartia in *Death of a Salesman,*" *Twentieth Century Literature,* 18 (Jan. 1972), 19-24. Collected in Koon, 79-84.

Fisher, Walter R., and Richard A. Filloy. "Argument in Drama and Literature: An Exploration." In *Advances in Argumentation Theory and Research,* ed. J. Robert Cox and Charles Arthur Willard. Carbondale: Southern Illinois University Press, 1982, 343-362.

Flaxman, Seymour L. "The Debt of Williams and Miller to Ibsen and Strindberg," *Comparative Literature Studies,* 1 (Special Advance Number, 1963), 51-60.

Foster, Richard J. "Confusion and Tragedy: The Failure of Miller's *Salesman.*" In Hurrell, 82-88.

Foulkes, A. P. "Demystifying the Witch Hunt (Arthur Miller)." In his *Literature and Propaganda.* London & New York: Methuen, 1983, 83-104.

Freedman, Morris. "Bertolt Brecht and American Social Drama." In his *The Moral Impulse: Modern Drama from Ibsen to the Present.* Carbondale: Southern Illinois University Press, 1967, 99-114.

Freedman. "The Jewishness of Arthur Miller: His Family Epic." In his *American Drama in Social Context.* Carbondale: Southern Illinois University Press, 1971, 43-58.

Fuller, A. Howard. "A Salesman is Everybody," *Fortune,* 39 (May 1949), 79-80. Collected in Weales, 1967, 240-243.

Ganz, Arthur. "Arthur Miller: After the Silence," *Drama Survey,* 3 (Fall 1964), 520-530.

Ganz. "The Silence of Arthur Miller," *Drama Survey,* 3 (Fall 1963), 224-237. Excerpted in Ferres, 107-108.

Gardner, R. H. "Tragedy of the Lowest Man." In his *The Splintered Stage.* New York: Macmillan, 1965, 122-134.

Garland, Robert. "Audience Spellbound by Prize Play of 1949," *New York Journal-American*, 11 Feb. 1949, p. 24. Collected in Weales, 1967, 199-201.

Gascoigne, Bamber. "Arthur Miller." In his *Twentieth-Century Drama*. London: Hutchinson, 1962, 49-50, 72-73, 174-183.

Gassner, John. "Affirmations?" In his *Theater at the Crossroads*. New York: Holt, Rinehart & Winston, 1960, 274-278. Collected as "Miller's *The Crucible* as Event and Play" in Ferres, 27-31.

Gassner. "Aspects of the Broadway Theatre," *Quarterly Journal of Speech*, 35 (Feb. 1949), 289-294. Collected as "*Death of a Salesman*: First Impressions, 1949" in his *The Theater in Our Times*. New York: Crown, 1954, 368-373; collected in Weales, 1967, 231-239.

Gassner. "The Theater Arts," *Forum*, 111 (Apr. 1949), 219-222. Collected in Meserve, 2-6.

Gassner. "Tragic Perspectives: A Sequence of Queries," *Tulane Drama Review*, 2 (May 1958), 20-22.

Gianakaris, C. J. "Theater of the Mind in Miller, Osborne, and Shaffer," *Renascence*, 30 (Fall 1978), 33-42.

Gilroy, Harry. "A Million Sales for Willy Loman," *New York Times*, 8 Mar. 1968, p. 36.

Goetsch, Paul. "Arthur Miller's *Zeitkritik* in *Death of a Salesman*," *Die Neueren Sprachen*, 16 (1967), 105-117.

Gomwalk, Philemon V. "The Tragic Element in Arthur Miller's *Death of a Salesman*," *Kuka: Journal of Creative and Critical Writing* (1980-1981), 34-40.

Goodman, Walter. "Miller's *Salesman*, Created in 1949, May Mean More to 1975," *New York Times*, 15 June 1975, section 2, pp. 1, 5.

Gordon, Andrew. "Richard Brautigan's Parody of Arthur Miller," *Notes on Modern American Literature*, 6 (Spring/Summer 1982), item 8.

Gordon, Lois. "*Death of a Salesman*: An Appreciation." In *The Forties: Fiction, Poetry, Drama*, ed. Warren French. De Land, Fla.: Everett/Edwards, 1969, 273-283. Collected in Koon, 98-108.

Graybill, Robert V. "Why Does Biff Boff Bimbos? Innocence as Evil in *Death of a Salesman*," *Publications of the Arkansas Philological Association*, 13 (Fall 1987), 46-53.

Gross, Barry. "*All My Sons* and the Larger Context," *Modern Drama*, 18 (Mar. 1975), 15-27. Collected in Martine, 10-20; collected in Parker, 55-67; collected in Bloom, *Arthur Miller's "All My Sons,"* 1988, 63-76.

Gross. "Peddler and Pioneer in *Death of a Salesman*," *Modern Drama*, 7 (Feb. 1965), 405-410. Collected in Meserve, 29-34.

Gupta, R. "*Death of a Salesman* and Miller's Concept of Tragedy," *Kyushu American Literature*, 15 (1974), 10-19.

Hagopian, John V. "*Death of a Salesman*," *Insight*, 1 (1962), 174-186. Republished as "Arthur Miller: The Salesman's Two Cases," *Modern Drama*, 6 (Sept. 1963), 117-125. Collected in Meserve, 34-42.

Hansen, Chadwick. "The Metamorphosis of Tituba, or Why American Intellectuals Can't Tell an Indian Witch from a Negro," *New England Quarterly*, 47 (Mar. 1974), 3-12.

Hark, Ina Rae. "A Frontier Closes in Brooklyn: *Death of a Salesman* and the Turner Thesis," *Postscript*, 3 (1986), 1-6.

Haugen, Einar. "Ibsen as Fellow Traveler: Arthur Miller's Adaptation of *An Enemy of the People*," *Scandinavian Studies*, 51 (Autumn 1979), 343-353.

Hawkins, William. "*Death of a Salesman* Powerful Tragedy," *New York World-Telegram*, 11 Feb. 1949, p. 16. Collected in Weales, 1967, 202-204.

Hayashi, Tetsumaro. "Arthur Miller: The Dimension of His Art and a Checklist of His Published Works," *Serif*, 4, no. 2 (1967), 26-32.

Hayes, Richard. "The Stage: *The Crucible*," *Commonweal*, 57 (Feb. 1953), 498. Excerpted as "Hysteria and Ideology in *The Crucible*" in Ferres, 32-34.

Hayman, Ronald. "Arthur Miller: Between Sartre and Society," *Encounter*, 37 (Nov. 1971), 73-79.

Hays, Peter L. "Arthur Miller and Tennessee Williams," *Essays in Literature*, 4 (1977), 239-249.

Heilman, Robert B. "Arthur Miller." In his *The Iceman, the Arsonist, and the Troubled Agent: Tragedy and Melodrama on the Modern Stage*. Seattle: University of Washington Press, 1973, 142-161.

Heilman. "Salesmen's Deaths: Documentary and Myth," *Shenandoah*, 20 (Spring 1969), 20-28.

Heyen, William. "Arthur Miller's *Death of a Salesman* and the American Dream." In *Amerikanisches Drama und Theater im 20. Jahrhundert*, ed. Alfred Weber and Siegfried Neuweiler. Göttingen: Vandenhoech & Ruprecht, 1975, 190-210. Collected in Bloom, *Arthur Miller's "Death of a Salesman*," 1988, 47-58.

Higgins, David. "Arthur Miller's *The Price*: The Wisdom of Solomon." In *Itinerary 3: Criticism*, ed. Frank Baldanza. Bowling Green, Ohio: Bowling Green University Press, 1977, 85-94.

Hill, Phillip G. "*The Crucible*: A Structural View," *Modern Drama*, 10 (Dec. 1967), 312-317. Collected in Ferres, 86-92.

Hobson, Harold. "Fair Play," *Sunday Times* (London), 14 Nov. 1954, p. 11. Collected in Weales, 1971, 227-230.

Hoeveler, Diane Long. "*Death of a Salesman* as Psychomachia," *Journal of American Culture*, 1 (Fall 1978), 632-637. Collected in Bloom, *Arthur Miller's "Death of a Salesman*," 1988, 77-82.

Hogan, Robert. "Action and Theme in *The Crucible*." In Ferres, 95-97.

Högel, Rolf K. "The Manipulation of Time in Miller's *After the Fall*," *Literatur in Wissenschaft und Unterricht*, 7 (1974), 115-121.

Huftel, Sheila. "Miller, Ibsen, and Organic Drama." In Bloom, *Arthur Miller's "All My Sons*," 1988, 33-45.

Huftel. "Subjectivism and Self-Awareness." In Ferres, 104-106.

Hughes, Catharine. "Arthur Miller." In her *American Playwrights 1945-75*. London: Pitman, 1976, 32-43.

Hume, Beverly. "Linda Loman as 'the Woman' in Miller's *Death of a Salesman*," *Notes on Modern American Literature*, 9 (Winter 1985), item 14.

Hunt, Arthur. "Realism and Intelligence: Some Notes on Arthur Miller," *Encore*, 7 (May/June 1960), 12-17, 41. Collected in Weales, 1971, 324-332.

Hunter, Frederick J. "The Value of Time in Modern Drama," *Journal of Aesthetics and Art Criticism*, 16 (Dec. 1957), 199-200.

Hurd, Myles R. "Angels and Anxieties in Miller's *A View from the Bridge*," *Notes on Contemporary Literature*, 13 (Sept. 1983), 4-6.

Hynes, Joseph A. "Arthur Miller and the Impasse of Naturalism," *South Atlantic Quarterly*, 62 (Summer 1963), 327-334.

Hynes. "'Attention Must Be Paid...,'" *College English*, 23 (Apr. 1962), 574-578. Collected in Weales, 1967, 280-289.

Innes, Christopher. "The Salesman on the Stage: A Study in the Social Influence of Drama," *English Studies in Canada*, 3 (Fall 1977), 336-350. Collected in Bloom, *Arthur Miller's "Death of a Salesman*," 1988, 59-75.

Inserillo, Charles R. "Wish and Desire: Two Poles of the Imagination in the Drama of Arthur Miller and T. S. Eliot," *Xavier Uni-*

versity Studies, 1 (Summer/Fall 1962), 247-258.

Ishizuka, Koji. "Two Memory Plays: Williams and Miller." In *American Literature in the 1940's*. Tokyo: Tokyo Chapter, American Literature Society of Japan, 1976, 208-212.

Ito, Akira. "The Contrast between the City and the Country in *Death of a Salesman*," *Essays in Foreign Languages and Literatures*, 25 (1979), 89-116.

Jackson, Esther Merle. "*Death of a Salesman*: Tragic Myth in the Modern Theater," *CLA Journal*, 7 (Sept. 1963), 63-76. Collected in Bloom, 1987, 27-38; collected in Meserve, 57-68; collected in Bloom, *Arthur Miller's "Death of a Salesman,"* 1988, 7-18.

Jacobson, Irving. "The Child as Guilty Witness," *Literature and Psychology*, 24, no. 1 (1974), 12-23.

Jacobson. "Christ, Pygmalion, and Hitler in *After the Fall*," *Essays in Literature*, 2 (Aug. 1974), 12-27.

Jacobson. "Family Dreams in *Death of a Salesman*," *American Literature*, 47 (May 1975), 247-258. Collected in Martine, 44-52.

Jacobson. "The Vestigial Jews on Monte Sant' Angelo," *Studies in Short Fiction*, 13 (Fall 1976), 507-512. Collected in Martine, 206-211.

James, Stuart B. "Pastoral Dreamer in an Urban World," *University of Denver Quarterly*, 1 (Autumn 1966), 45-57.

John, S. B., and C. A. Burns. "The Mirror of the Stage: Vichy France and Foreign Drama." In *Literature and Society: Studies in Nineteenth and Twentieth Century French Literature Presented to R. J. North*, ed. Burns. Birmingham: Goodman for University of Birmingham, 1980, 200-213.

Johnson, Kenneth E. "Memory Plays in American Drama." In *Within the Dramatic Spectrum*, ed. Karalisa V. Hartigan. Lanham, Md.: University Press of America, 1986.

Kalven, Harry, Jr. "A View from the Law," *New Republic*, 136 (27 May 1957), 8-13.

Kanamaru, Tosao. "McCarthyism and Arthur Miller." In *American Literature in the 1950's*. Tokyo: Tokyo Chapter, American Literature Society of Japan, 1977, 140-146.

Kazan, Elia. Excerpts from Kazan's notebooks for *Death of a Salesman*. In *A Theater in Your Head*, ed. Kenneth Thorpe Rowe. New York: Funk & Wagnalls, 1960, 44-59.

Keck, Marilyn. "Symposium: *Death of a Salesman*," *Folio* (Indiana University), 17 (Mar. 1952), 22-26.

Kennedy, C. E. "*After the Fall*: One Man's Look at His Human Nature," *Journal of Counseling Psychology*, 12 (Summer 1965), 215-217.

Kennedy, Sighle. "Who Killed the Salesman?," *Catholic World*, 171 (May 1970), 110-116. Collected in Koon, 33-40.

Kernodle, George R. "The Death of the Little Man," *Tulane Drama Review*, 1 (1955-1956), 47-60.

Kerr, Walter. "*The Crucible*," *New York Herald-Tribune*, 23 Jan. 1953, p. 12. Excerpted in Weales, 1971, 189-191; excerpted as "A Problem Playwright" in Ferres, 35-36.

Kerr. "Miller's *After the Fall*," *New York Herald-Tribune*, 24 Jan. 1964, pp. 1, 11. Collected in Martine, 122-124.

Kerr. "Mr. Miller's Two New Faces," *New York Times*, 18 Feb. 1968, section 2, pp. 1, 3. Collected in Martine, 158-160.

Kerr. "This *Salesman* is More Man Than Myth," *New York Times*, 29 June 1975, section 2, pp. 1, 5.

Kitchin, Laurence. "The Potent Intruder." In his *Mid-Century Drama*, second edition, revised. London: Faber & Faber, 1962, 56-63.

Koppenhaver, Allen J. "*The Fall* and After: Albert Camus and Arthur Miller," *Modern Drama*, 9 (Sept. 1966), 206-209.

Kracht, Fritz Andre. "Rise and Decline of U.S. Theater on German Stages," *American-German Review*, 32 (June/July 1966), 13-15.

Langer, Lawrence. "The Americanization of the Holocaust on Stage and Screen." In *From Hester Street to Hollywood: The Jewish-American Stage and Screen*, ed. Sarah Blacher Cohen. Bloomington: Indiana University Press, 1983, 213-230.

Lannon, William W. "The Rise and Rationale of Post World War II American Confessional Theater," *Connecticut Review*, 8 (Apr. 1975), 73-81.

Lawrence, Stephen A. "The Right Dream in Miller's *Death of a Salesman*," *College English*, 25 (Oct./May 1963-1964), 547-549. Collected in Koon, 56-59.

Lawson, John Howard. "The Dilemma of Arthur Miller." In his *Theory and Technique of Playwriting*. New York: Hill & Wang, 1960, xxvi-xxxii.

Leaska, Mitchell A. "Miller." In his *The Voice of Tragedy*. New York: Speller, 1963, 273-278.

Levin, David. "Salem Witchcraft in Recent Fiction and Drama," *New England Quarterly*, 28 (Dec. 1955), 537-546. Collected in Weales, 1971, 248-254.

Lewis, Allan. "The American Scene: Williams and Miller." In his *The Contemporary Theater: The Significant Playwrights of Our Time*. New York: Crown, 1962, 286-288, 293-301.

Lewis. "Arthur Miller–Return to the Self." *American Plays and Playwrights of the Contemporary Theater*, revised edition. New York: Crown, 1970, 35-52.

Leyburn, Ellen Douglas. "Comedy and Tragedy Transposed," *Yale Review*, 53 (Summer 1964), 555-557.

Liston, William T. "John Proctor's Playing in *The Crucible*," *Midwest Quarterly*, 20 (Summer 1979), 394-403.

Loughlin, Richard L. "Tradition and Tragedy in *All My Sons*," *English Record*, 14 (Feb. 1964), 23-27.

Lowenthal, Lawrence D. "Arthur Miller's *Incident at Vichy*: A Sartrean Interpretation," *Modern Drama*, 18 (Mar. 1975), 29-41. Collected in Martine, 143-154; collected in Martin, 173-187; collected in Parker, 94-106.

Luft, Friedrich. "Arthur Miller's *Death of a Salesman*: Hebbel-Theater [Berlin]." In his *Stimme der Kritik–Berliner Theater seit 1945*. Velber bei Hannover: Friedrich, 1965, 82-85. Collected in Meserve, 19-22.

Macey, Samuel L. "Non-heroic Tragedy: A Pedigree for American Tragic Drama," *Comparative Literature Studies*, 6 (Mar. 1969), 1-19.

Maini, Darshan Singh. "The Moral Vision of Arthur Miller." In *Indian Essays in American Literature: Papers in Honour of Robert E. Spiller*, ed. Sujit Mukherjee and D. V. K. Raghavacharyulu. Bombay: Popular Prakashan, 1969, 85-96.

Maloff, Saul. "Symposium: *Death of a Salesman*," *Folio* (Indiana University), 17 (Mar. 1952), 9-18.

Mander, John. "Arthur Miller's *Death of a Salesman*." In his *The Writer and Commitment*. London: Secker & Warburg, 1962; Philadelphia: Dufour, 1962, 138-152.

Manocchio, Tony, and Patrick Roberts. "The Loman Family." In their *Families Under Stress: A Psychological Interpretation*. London & Boston: Routledge & Kegan Paul, 1975, 129-168.

Martin, Robert A. "Arthur Miller–Tragedy and Commitment," *Michigan Quarterly Review*, 8 (Summer 1969), 176-178.

Martin. "Arthur Miller's *The Crucible*: Background and Sources," *Modern Drama*, 20 (Sept. 1977), 279-292. Collected in Martine, 93-104; collected in Parker, 80-93.

McAnany, Emile G. "The Tragic Commitment: Some Notes on Arthur Miller," *Modern Drama*, 5 (May 1962), 11-20.

McCarthy, Mary. "Americans, Realists, Playwrights," *Encounter*, 17 (July 1961), 24-31.

McCarthy. "Naming Names: The Arthur Miller Case," *Encounter*, 8 (May 1957), 23-25. Collected in her *On the Contrary*. New York: Farrar, Straus & Cudahy, 1961, 147-154.

McGill, William J., Jr. "The Crucible of History: Arthur Miller's John Proctor," *New England Quarterly*, 54 (June 1981), 258-264.

McIntyre, Alice T. "Making *The Misfits* or Waiting for Monroe or Notes from Olympus," *Esquire*, 45 (Mar. 1961), 74-81.

McLean, Lydia. "A View from the Country: A Weekend with the Arthur Millers," *Vogue*, 159 (15 Mar. 1972), 102-109, 114.

McMahon, Helen. "Arthur Miller's Common Man: The Problem of the Realistic and the Mythic," *Drama and Theater*, 10 (Spring 1972), 128-133.

Meserve, Walter J. "*The Crucible*: 'This Fool and I.' " In Martin, 127-138.

Meserve. "Who Killed Willy Loman?," In Meserve, v-ix.

Mesher, David R. "Arthur Miller's *Focus*: The First American Novel of the Holocaust?," *Judaism*, 29, no. 4 (1980), 469-478.

Meyer, Richard D. and Nancy Meyer. "*After the Fall*: A View from the Director's Notebook," *Theater* (Lincoln Center), 2 (1965), 43-73.

Meyer, and Nancy Meyer. "Setting the Stage for Lincoln Center," *Theater Arts*, 48 (Jan. 1964), 12-16.

Mielziner, Jo. "Designing a Play: *Death of a Salesman*." In her *Designing for the Theater*. New York: Atheneum, 1965, 23-63. Excerpted in Weales, 1967, 187-198.

Miles, O. Thomas. "Three Authors in Search of a Character," *Personalist*, 46 (Winter 1965), 65-72.

Miller, E. S. "Perceiving and Imagining at Plays," *Annali Instituto Universitario Orientale*, 5 (1967), 5-11.

Miller, Jeanne-Marie A. "Odets, Miller, and Communism," *CLA Journal*, 19 (June 1976), 484-493.

Miller, Jordon Y. "Myth and the American Dream: O'Neill to Albee," *Modern Drama*, 7 (Sept. 1964), 190-198.

Morgan, Edmund S. "Arthur Miller's *The Crucible* and the Salem Witch Trials: A Historian's View." In *The Golden and the Brazen World: Papers in Literature and History, 1650-1900*, ed. John M.

Wallace. Berkeley: University of California Press, 1985, 171-186.

Morgan, Frederick. "Notes on the Theater," *Hudson Review,* 2 (1949), 270-276. Collected in Martine, 23.

Moss, Leonard. "*All My Sons.*" In Bloom, *Arthur Miller's "All My Sons,*" 1988, 101-106.

Moss. "Arthur Miller and the Common Man's Language," *Modern Drama,* 7 (May 1964), 52-59. Collected in Meserve, 85-92.

Moss. "Biographical and Literary Allusion in *After the Fall,*" *Educational Theatre Journal,* 18 (Mar. 1966), 34-40.

Moss. "Colloquial Language in *All My Sons.*" In Martin, 107-114.

Moss. "The Perspective of a Playwright." In Bloom, 1987, 79-92.

Moss. "A 'Social Play.' " In Ferres, 37-45.

Mottram, Eric. "Arthur Miller: The Development of a Political Dramatist in America." In *American Theater,* ed. John Russell Brown and Bernard Harris. New York: St. Martin's Press, 1967; London: Arnold, 1967, 126-161. Collected in Corrigan, 23-58; excerpted as "Jean-Paul Sartre's *Les Sorcières de Salem*" in Ferres, 93-94.

Murray, Edward. "Arthur Miller–*Death of a Salesman, The Misfits,* and *After the Fall.*" In his *The Cinematic Imagination.* New York: Ungar, 1972, 69-85.

Murray. "Dramatic Technique in *The Crucible.*" In Ferres, 46-53.

Murray. "Point of View in *After the Fall,*" *CLA Journal,* 10 (Dec. 1966), 135-142.

Nathan, George Jean. "*Death of a Salesman.*" In *Theater Book of the Year, 1948-1949.* New York: Knopf, 1949, 279-285. Collected in his *The Magic Mirror.* New York: Knopf, 1960, 243-250; collected in Hurrell, 57-60.

Nathan. "Henrik Miller," *Theater Arts,* 37 (Apr. 1953), 24.

Nelson, Benjamin. "Avant-Garde Dramatics from Ibsen to Ionesco," *Psychoanalytic Review,* 55 (1968), 505-512.

Nelson. "*A Memory of Two Mondays*: Remembrance and Reflection in Arthur Miller." In his *Arthur Miller: Portrait of a Playwright.* New York: McKay, 1970; London: Owen, 1970. Collected in Martin, 149-158.

Newman, William J. "Arthur Miller's *Collected Plays,*" *Twentieth Century,* 164 (Nov. 1958), 491-496. Collected in Hurrell, 68-71.

Nichols, Lewis. "The Philosophy of Work Against Chance Makes Up *The Man Who Had All the Luck,*" *New York Times,* 24 Nov. 1944, p. 18. Collected in Martine, 1-2.

Noevels, Diane Long. *"Death of a Salesman* as Psychomachics," *Journal of American Culture*, 1 (1978), 632-637.

Nolan, Paul T. "Two Memory Plays: *The Glass Menagerie* and *After the Fall*," *McNeese Review*, 17 (1966), 27-38.

Oberg, Arthur K. *"Death of a Salesman* and Arthur Miller's Search for Style," *Criticism*, 9 (Fall 1967), 303-311. Collected in Meserve, 92-99; collected in Koon, 70-78.

O'Connor, Frank. "The Most American Playwright," *Holiday*, 19 (Feb. 1956), 65, 68, 70.

O'Neal, Michael J. "History, Myth, and Name Magic in Arthur Miller's *The Crucible*," *Clio*, 12 (Winter 1983), 111-122.

Otten, Charlotte F. "Who Am I? . . . A Re-investigation of Arthur Miller's *Death of a Salesman*," *Cresset*, 26 (Feb. 1963), 11-13. Collected in Koon, 85-91.

Overland, Orm. "The Action and Its Significance: Arthur Miller's Struggle with Dramatic Form," *Modern Drama*, 18 (Mar. 1975), 1-14. Collected in Martin, 33-47; collected in Bloom, 1987, 51-64; collected in Bloom, *Arthur Miller's "All My Sons,"* 1988, 77-89.

Parker, Brian. "Point of View in Arthur Miller's *Death of a Salesman*," *University of Toronto Quarterly*, 35 (Jan. 1966), 144-157. Collected in Corrigan, 95-110; collected in Koon, 41-55; collected in Bloom, *Arthur Miller's "Death of a Salesman,"* 1988, 25-38.

Popkin, Henry. "Arthur Miller Out West," *Commentary*, 31 (May 1961), 433-436.

Popkin. "Arthur Miller: The Strange Encounter," *Sewanee Review*, 68 (Winter 1960), 34-60. Collected in *American Drama and Its Critics*, ed. Alan S. Downer. Chicago: University of Chicago Press, 1965, 218-239.

Popkin. "Arthur Miller's *The Crucible*," *College English*, 26 (Nov. 1964), 139-146. Excerpted as "Historical Analogy and *The Crucible*" in Ferres, 77-85.

Porter, Thomas E. "Acres of Diamonds: *Death of a Salesman*." In his *Myth and Modern American Drama*. Detroit: Wayne State University Press, 1969, 127-152. Collected in Martine, 24-43.

Porter. "The Long Shadow of the Law: *The Crucible*." In his *Myth and Modern American Drama*, 177-199. Collected in Martine, 75-92.

Porter. "The Mills of the Gods: Economics and Law in the Plays of Arthur Miller." In Martin, 75-96.

Pradhan, Narindar Singh. "Arthur Miller and the Pursuit of Guilt." In *Studies in American Literature: Essays in Honour of William Mulder*, ed. Jagdish Chander and Pradhan. Delhi: Oxford University Press, 1976, 28-42.

Press, David P. "Arthur Miller's *The Misfits*: The Western Gunned Down," *Studies in the Humanities*, 8, no. 1 (1980), 41-44.

Price, Jonathan R. "Arthur Miller: Fall or Rise?," *Drama*, 73 (Summer 1964), 39-40.

Prudhoe, John. "Arthur Miller and the Tradition of Tragedy," *English Studies*, 43 (Oct. 1962), 430-439.

Rahv, Philip. "Arthur Miller and the Fallacy of Profundity," *New York Review*, 14 Jan. 1965, p. 3. Collected in his *The Myth and the Powerhouse*. New York: Farrar, Straus & Giroux, 1965, 225-233; collected in his *Literature and the Sixth Sense*. Boston: Houghton Mifflin, 1969, 385-391.

Rajinder, Paul. "*Death of a Salesman* in India." In Meserve, 23-27.

Ranald, Margaret Loftus. "*Death of a Salesman*: Fifteen Years After," *Comment: A New Zealand Quarterly*, 6 (Aug. 1965), 28-35.

Raymont, Henry. "Miller Refuses Greek Book Plan," *New York Times*, 3 July 1969, p. 29.

Reno, Raymond H. "Arthur Miller and the Death of God," *Texas Studies in Literature and Language*, 11 (Summer 1969), 1069-1087.

Rosinger, Lawrence. "Miller's *Death of a Salesman*," *Explicator*, 45 (Winter 1987), 55-56.

Ross, George. "*Death of a Salesman* in the Original," *Commentary*, 11 (Feb. 1951), 184-186. Collected in Weales, 1967, 259-264.

Roth, Martin. "Sept-d'un-coup," *Chicago Review*, 19, no. 1 (1966), 108-111. Collected in Martine, 139-142.

Rothenberg, Albert, and Eugene D. Shapiro. "The Defense of Psychoanalysis in Literature: *Long Day's Journey into Night* and *A View from the Bridge*," *Comparative Drama*, 7 (Spring 1973), 51-67.

Rovere, Richard H. "Arthur Miller's Conscience," *New Republic*, 136 (17 June 1957), 13-15. Collected in *Contemporary Moral Issues*, ed. Harry K. Girvetz. Belmont, Cal.: Wadsworth, 1963, 75-79; collected as "The Conscience of Arthur Miller" in his *The American Establishment, and Other Reports, Opinions and Speculations*. New York: Harcourt, Brace & World, 1962, 276-284; collected in Corrigan, 315-323.

Rowe, Kenneth. "Shadows Cast Before." In Martin, 13-32.

Rusch, Frederick L. "Approach Literature through the Social Psychology of Erich Fromm." In *Psychological Perspectives on Literature: Freudian Dissidents and Non-Freudians: A Casebook*, ed. Joseph Natoli. Hamden, Conn.: Archon, 1984, 79-99.

Saisselin, Remy G. "Is Tragic Drama Possible in the Twentieth Century?," *Theater Annual*, 17 (1960), 12-21. Collected in Meserve, 44-51.

Samachson, Dorothy and Joseph. "Why Write a Play? In their *Let's Meet the Theater*. New York: Abelard-Schumann, 1955, 15-20.

Sata, Masanori. "American Realism and Arthur Miller's Struggle." In *The Traditional and the Anti-Traditional: Studies in Contemporary American Literature*, ed. Kenzaburo Ohashi. Tokyo: Tokyo Chapter, American Literature Society of Japan, 1980, 174-190.

Sata. "Arthur Miller to the Great Depression: *The American Clock* no Igri," *English Literature and Language*, 18 (1982), 82-91.

Sata. "Arthur Miller's Warning Concerning the American Dream." In *American Literature in the 1940s*. Tokyo: Tokyo Chapter, American Literature Society of Japan, 1976, 219-225.

Sato, Susumu. "The 'Awakening' Theme in Clifford Odets and Arthur Miller." In *American Literature in the 1940s*, 180-185.

Scanlan, Tom. "Reactions I: Family and Society in Arthur Miller." In his *Family, Drama, and American Dreams*. Westport, Conn.: Greenwood, 1978, 126-155.

Schechner, Richard, and Theodore Hoffman. "Look, There's the American Theater," *Tulane Drama Review*, 9 (Winter 1964), 61-83.

Schlueter, June. "The Dramatic Strategy of *All My Sons*. In *Arthur Miller*, by Schlueter and James K. Flanagan. New York: Ungar, 1987. Collected in Bloom, *Arthur Miller's "All My Sons,"* 1988, 113-122.

Schlueter. "Power Play: Arthur Miller's *The Archbishop's Ceiling*," *CEA Critic*, 49 (Winter/Summer 1986-1987), 134-138.

Schneider, Daniel E. "Play of Dreams," *Theater Arts*, 33 (Oct. 1949), 18-21. Collected as "A Modern Playwright" in his *The Psychoanalyst and the Artist*. New York: Farrar, Straus, 1950, 246-255; collected in Weales, 1967, 250-258.

Schraepen, Edmond. "Arthur Miller's Constancy: A Note on Miller as a Short Story Writer," *Revue des Langues Vivantes*, 36 (1970), 62-71.

Schumach, Murray. "Arthur Miller Grew in Brooklyn," *New York Times*, 6 Feb. 1949, section 2, pp. 1, 3.
Schumach. "Miller Still a 'Salesman' for a Changing Theater," *New York Times*, 26 June 1975, p. 32.
de Schweinitz, George. "*Death of a Salesman*: A Note on Epic and Tragedy," *Western Humanities Review*, 14 (Winter 1960), 91-96. Collected in Meserve, 52-57; collected in Weales, 1967, 272-279.
Seager, Allan. "The Creative Agony of Arthur Miller," *Esquire*, 52 (Oct. 1959), 123-126. Collected in Weales, 1967, 326-338.
Seiger, Marvin L. "Symposium: *Death of a Salesman*," *Folio* (Indiana University), 17 (Mar. 1952), 3-9.
Selz, Jean. "Raymond Rouleau among the Witches," trans. Gerald Weales, *Lettres Nouvelles*, 3 (Mar. 1955), 422-426. Collected in Weales, 1971, 242-247.
Sharma, P. P. "Making the World a Home: Arthur Miller's Major Thematic Concern," *Rajasthan University Studies in English*, 8 (1975), 62-71.
Sharma. "Realism in Arthur Miller's Plays," *Punjab University Research Bulletin (Arts)*, 6, no. 2 (1975), 1-11.
Sharma. "Search for Self-Identity in *Death of a Salesman*," *Literary Criterion*, 11, no. 2 (1974), 74-79.
Sharpe, Robert Boies. "Modern Trends in Tragedy." In his *Irony in the Drama*. Chapel Hill: University of North Carolina Press, 1959, 194-203.
Shatzky, Joel. "Arthur Miller's 'Jewish' Salesman," *Studies in American Jewish Literature*, 2, no. 1 (1976), 1-9.
Shatzky. "The 'Reactive Image' and Miller's *Death of a Salesman*," *Players*, 48 (Feb./Mar. 1973), 104-110.
Shaw, Patrick W. "The Ironic Characterization of Bernard in *Death of a Salesman*," *Notes on Contemporary Literature*, 11 (May 1981), 12.
Shelton, Frank W. "Sports and the Competitive Ethic: *Death of a Salesman* and *That Championship Season*," *Ball State University Forum*, 20, no. 2 (1979), 17-21.
Shepherd, Allen. " 'What Comes Easier–': The Short Stories of Arthur Miller," *Illinois Quarterly*, 34 (Feb. 1972), 37-49. Collected in Martine, 197-205.
Shipley, Joseph T. "Arthur Miller's New Melodrama is Not What It Seems To Be," *New Leader*, 36 (9 Feb. 1953), 25-26. Collected in Weales, 1971, 201-203.

Siegel, Paul N. "The Drama and the Thwarted American Dream," *Lock Haven Review*, 7 (1965), 52-62.

Siegel. "Willy Loman and King Lear," *College English*, 17 (Mar. 1956), 341-345. Collected in Koon, 92-97.

Sievers, W. David. "Tennessee Williams and Arthur Miller." In his *Freud on Broadway: A History of Psychoanalysis and the American Drama.* New York: Hermitage, 1955, 376-380; collected in Hurrell.

Simon, John. "Theater Chronicle," *Hudson Review*, 17 (Summer 1964), 234-236. Excerpted in Martine, 119-121.

Sinha, Prashant K. "The Disoriented Self and the Oppressive Society: A Study of Some Major American Plays of the 1950s and Early 1960s," *Indian Journal of American Studies*, 14 (July 1984), 67-72.

Stallknecht, Newton, P., and others. "Symposium: *Death of a Salesman,*" *Folio* (Indiana University), 17 (Mar. 1952), 3-26.

Stambusky, Alan. "Arthur Miller: Aristotelian Canons in the Twentieth Century Drama." In *Modern American Drama: Essays in Criticism*, ed. William E. Taylor. De Land, Fla.: Everett/Edwards, 1968, 91-115.

Standley, Fred L. "An Echo of Milton in *The Crucible,*" *Notes and Queries*, 15 (Aug. 1968), 303.

Stanton, Stephen S. "Pessimism in *After the Fall.*" In Martin, 159-172.

Steene, Birgitta. "Arthur Miller's *After the Fall,*" *Moderna Språk*, 58 (1964), 446-452.

Steene. "The Critical Reception of American Drama in Sweden," *Modern Drama*, 5 (May 1962), 71-82.

Steinbeck, John. "The Trial of Arthur Miller," *Esquire*, 47 (June 1957), 86. Collected in *Contemporary Moral Issues*, ed. Harry K. Girvetz. Belmont, Cal.: Wadsworth, 1963, 72-74.

Steinberg, M. W. "Arthur Miller and the Idea of Modern Tragedy," *Dalhousie Review*, 40 (Autumn 1960), 329-340. Collected in Corrigan, 81-94; collected in Ferres, 98-100.

Steppat, Michael P. "Self-Choice and Aesthetic Despair in Arthur Miller and Tennessee Williams," *Literary Criterion*, 20, no. 3 (1985), 49-59.

Stevens, Virginia. "Seven Young Broadway Artists," *Theater Arts*, 31 (June 1947), 56.

Stinson, John J. "Structure in *After the Fall*: The Relevance of the Maggie Episodes to the Main Theme and the Christian Symbolism," *Modern Drama*, 10 (Dec. 1967), 233-240.

Styan, J. L. "A View from the Crucible; or, The Compleat Playwright," *Michigan Quarterly Review*, 18 (1979), 509-515.

Styan. "Why *A View from the Bridge* Went Down Well in London: The Story of a Revision." In Martin, 139-148.

Szondi, Peter. "Memory and Dramatic Form in *Death of a Salesman*." In his *Theory of the Modern Drama*. Minneapolis: University of Minnesota Press, 1987. Collected in Bloom, *Arthur Miller's "Death of a Salesman*," 1988, 19-23.

Thompson, Alan. "Professor's Debauch," *Theater Arts*, 35 (Mar. 1951), 25-27.

Trócsányi, Miklós. "Two Views of American Puritanism: Hawthorne's *The Scarlet Letter* and Miller's *The Crucible*." In *The Origins and Originality of American Culture*, ed. Tibor Frank. Budapest: Akadémiai Kradó, 1984, 63-71.

Trowbridge, Clinton W. "Arthur Miller: Between Pathos and Tragedy," *Modern Drama*, 10 (Dec. 1967), 221-232. Collected in Martine, 125-135; collected in Bloom, 1987, 39-50.

Tyler, Ralph. "Arthur Miller Says the Time is Right for *The Price*," *New York Times*, 17 June 1979, section 2, pp. 1, 6.

Tynan, Kenneth. "American Blues: The Plays of Arthur Miller and Tennessee Williams," *Encounter*, 2 (May 1954), 13-19. Collected in his *Curtains: Selections from the Drama Criticism and Related Writings*. New York: Atheneum, 1961; London: Longmans, 1961, 257-266; excerpted in *The Modern American Theater*, ed. Alvin B. Kernan. Englewood Cliffs, N.J.: Prentice-Hall, 1967, 34-44.

Vogel, Dan. "Willy Tyrannos." In his *The Three Masks of American Tragedy*. Baton Rouge: Louisiana State University Press, 1974, 91-102.

Vos, Nelvin. "The American Dream Turned to Nightmare: Recent American Drama," *Christian Scholar's Review*, 1 (Spring 1971), 200-201.

Walden, Daniel. "Miller's Roots and His Moral Dilemma: or, Continuity from Brooklyn to Salesman." In Martine, 189-196.

Walker, Philip. "Arthur Miller's *The Crucible*: Tragedy or Allegory?," *Western Speech*, 20 (Fall 1956), 222-224.

Warshow, Robert. "The Liberal Conscience in *The Crucible*," *Commentary*, 15 (Mar. 1953), 265-271. Collected in *The Immediate Experi-

ence: Movies, Comics, Theatre, and Other Aspects of Popular Culture. Garden City, N.Y.: Doubleday, 1962, 189-203; collected in *The Scene Before You: A New Approach to American Culture,* ed. Chandler Brossard. New York: Rinehart, 1955, 191-203; collected in Corrigan, 111-121; collected in Weales, 1971, 210-226.

Waterstradt, Jean Anne. "Making the World a Home: The Family Portrait in Drama," *Brigham Young University Studies,* 19 (Summer 1979), 501-521.

Watt, Douglas. "Miller's *Creation of the World* is a Plodding Comedy-Drama," *New York Daily News,* 1 Dec. 1972. Collected in Martine, 175-176.

Wattenberg, Richard. "Staging William James's 'World of Pure Experience': Arthur Miller's *Death of a Salesman,*" *Theater Annual,* 38 (1983), 49-64.

Watts, Richard, Jr. "Arthur Miller Looks at the Nazis," *New York Post,* 4 Dec. 1964. Collected in Martine, 137-138.

Watts. "Arthur Miller's *Creation* Opens at Shubert Theater," *New York Post,* 1 Dec. 1972. Collected in Martine, 173-176.

Watts. "Mr. Miller Looks at Witch-Hunting," *New York Post,* 23 Jan. 1953. Collected in Martine, 73-74.

Weales, Gerald. "All About Talk: Arthur Miller's *The Price,*" *Ohio Review,* 13 (Winter 1972), 74-84. Collected in Martin, 188-199.

Weales. "Arthur Miller: Man and His Image," *Tulane Drama Review,* 7 (Fall 1962), 165-180. Collected in his *American Drama Since World War II.* New York: Harcourt, Brace & World, 1962, 3-17; collected as "Arthur Miller's Shifting Image of Man" in *The American Theater Today,* ed. Alan S. Downer. New York: Basic Books, 1967, 85-98; collected in Weales, 1967, 350-366; revised as "Arthur Miller's Shifting Image of Man" in Corrigan, 131-142; collected in Weales, 1971, 333-351.

Weales. "Plays and Analysis," *Commonweal,* 66 (12 July 1957), 382-383.

Weales. "Williams and Miller." In his *The Jumping-Off Place: American Drama in the 1960's.* New York: Macmillan, 1969; London: Macmillan, 1969, 1-23. Excerpted as "Arthur Miller in the 1960s" in Martin, 97-105.

Welland, Dennis. "*Death of a Salesman.*" In Koon, 15-32.

Welland. "*Death of a Salesman* in England." In Meserve, 8-17.

Welland. "The Devil in Salem." In Ferres, 54-60.

Welland. "The Drama of Forgiveness." In Bloom, 1987, 65-77.

Welland. "Two Early Plays." In Bloom, *Arthur Miller's "All My Sons,"* 1988, 91-99.

Wells, Arvin R. "The Living and the Dead in *All My Sons*," *Insight*, 1 (1962), 165-174. Collected in Martine, 5-9; collected in Bloom, *Arthur Miller's "All My Sons,"* 1988, 27-32.

Wertheim, Albert. "Arthur Miller: *After the Fall* and After." In *Essays on Contemporary American Drama*, ed. Hedwig Bock and Wertheim. Munich: Hueber, 1981, 19-32.

West, Paul. "Arthur Miller and the Human Mice," *Hibbert Journal*, 61 (Jan. 1963), 84-86.

Whitley, Alvin. "Arthur Miller: An Attempt at Modern Tragedy," *Transactions of the Wisconsin Academy of Sciences, Arts and Letters*, 42 (1953), 257-262.

Wiegand, William. "Arthur Miller and the Man Who Knows," *Western Review*, 21 (Winter 1957), 85-102. Collected in Weales, 1967, 290-312; collected in Weales, 1971, 290-314.

Willett, Ralph. "The Ideas of Miller and Williams," *Theater Annual*, 22 (1966), 31-40.

Willett. "A Note on Arthur Miller's *The Price*," *Journal of American Studies*, 5 (1971), 307-310.

Williams, Raymond. "Arthur Miller." In his *Drama from Ibsen to Brecht*, second edition, revised. London: Chatto & Windus, 1968, 267-276. Collected as "Arthur Miller: An Overview" in Bloom, 1987, 7-16.

Williams. *Modern Tragedy*. Stanford: Stanford University Press, 1966; London: Chatto & Windus, 1966, 103-105.

Williams. "The Realism of Arthur Miller," *Critical Quarterly*, 1 (Summer 1959), 140-149. Collected in Corrigan, 69-80; collected in Weales, 1967, 313-325.

Willis, Robert J. "Arthur Miller's *The Crucible*: Relevant for All Time," *Faculty Journal*, 1 (1970), 5-14.

Winegarten, Renee. "The World of Arthur Miller," *Jewish Quarterly*, 17 (Summer 1969), 48-53.

"Witchcraft and Stagecraft," unsigned review of *The Crucible*, *New York Post*, 1 Feb. 1953, p. M9. Collected in Weales, 1971, 197-200.

Wolfert, Ira. "Arthur Miller, Playwright in Search of His Identity," *New York Herald-Tribune*, 25 Jan. 1953, section 4, p. 3.

Worsley, T. C. "American Tragedy," *New Statesman*, 56 (23 Aug. 1958), 220.

Worsley. "Poetry Without Words," *New Statesman*, 38 (6 Aug. 1949), 146-147. Collected in Weales, 1967, 224-227.

Yorks, Samuel A. "Joe Keller and His Sons," *Western Humanities Review*, 13 (Autumn 1959), 401-407. Collected in Bloom, *Arthur Miller's "All My Sons,"* 1988, 19-26.

Yuan, Henian. "*Death of a Salesman* in Beijing," *Chinese Literature*, 10 (Oct. 1983), 103-109.

BIBLIOGRAPHICAL ESSAY

Bibliographies and Checklists
The most comprehensive bibliography on Arthur Miller is John H. Ferres's *Arthur Miller: A Reference Guide* (1979), which lists both primary and secondary sources from 1944 through 1978. On secondary material the bibliography supersedes all previous bibliographies (Martha Turnquist Eissenstat [May 1962], Tetsumaro Hayashi [1969; revised, 1976], Harriet Ungar [1970], and Charles A. Carpenter [1982]); it lists critical books and essays, dissertations, theater and book reviews, bibliographies, interviews, and (selective) accounts of Miller's public involvement. Ferres lists and annotates virtually all items published in English and translated into English in the United States and abroad. The entries are arranged alphabetically by year. Bibliographical information on works by and about Miller produced since 1979 is found in the annual bibliographies in *Modern Drama* (prepared, since March 1974, by Carpenter) and *MLA*, the latter of which is now on-line. Bibliographies may also be found in many of the full-length critical studies of Miller's work. No one has yet attempted a bibliography of journalistic writing about Miller, who has often been in the public eye; but James J. Martine, in *Critical Essays on Arthur Miller* (1979), notes that he has personally cataloged over 950 items.

The primary bibliography that begins this entry may be considered definitive. Some may also wish to refer to George H. Jensen, *Arthur Miller: A Bibliographical Checklist* (1976); that primary bibliography (books, essays, published speeches, interviews, recordings) includes the publishing history of all of Miller's books through 1975 and provides illustrations of title pages.

An especially useful guide is C. W. E. Bigsby's *File on Miller* (1987), in Methuen's Writer-Files series. Following a brief chronology, the volume proceeds, play by play, through the dramatic writing (including stage, radio, and television plays; and films and operas) and then through the nondramatic writing. Bigsby offers dates of publication and (where appropriate) production, a summary, and a selection of excerpts of critical responses to the work at the time of its publication or production. A section on "The Writer on His Works" excerpts comments by Miller from various sources. The volume ends with a select bibliography of primary and secondary materials.

Interviews

Though no biography of Miller appeared until the playwright's own, *Timebends: A Life*, in 1987, the playwright has been hospitable to interviewers throughout the more than four decades of his career. Taken together with the many essays on theater and on social and political issues that Miller has authored, the interviews provide an informative context in which to read the plays. The interviews are rich not only in biographical detail and personal insights, but in commentary on the playwright's ideas about dramatic art, his intentions with respect to specific plays, and his reaction to critics' assessments of those plays. As might be expected with any writer as receptive to conversation as Miller has been, the original material in each interview often shares space with familiar material as well. Yet such repetition, spread out over a playwright's career, reinforces the consistency of the writer's commitments. Many of the interviews annotated below are collected in Matthew C. Roudané's *Conversations with Arthur Miller* (1987), an enormously useful volume in the University Press of Mississippi's "Literary Conversations" series that provides a convenient means of surveying Miller's comments on his life and work.

The earliest interviews with Miller, not surprisingly, took place in 1947 and 1949, the years *All My Sons* and *Death of a Salesman*, respectively, were staged. John K. Hutchens's "Mr. Miller Has a Change of Luck" (23 Feb. 1947) offered the *New York Times* readership an introduction to the man whose first Broadway play, *The Man Who Had All the Luck*, failed but whose second, *All My Sons*, was a success. The interview contains information on Miller's background, his writing habits, and his preference for the kind of drama represented by Sidney Howard's *The Silver Cord* (1927) and Eugene O'Neill's *Anna Christie* (1922).

With the production of *Death of a Salesman* Miller rose to celebrity status. Murray Schumach's *New York Times* interview, "Arthur Miller Grew in Brooklyn" (6 Feb. 1949), provides an engaging account of Miller's development as a writer, his attitude toward play writing, his fondness for manual labor. Robert Sylvester's piece in the *Saturday Evening Post* (16 July 1949), the most thorough of the early interviews, gave even wider circulation to the emerging story of the playwright. In the interview, "Brooklyn Boy Makes Good," Sylvester speculates first on the financial rewards *Death of a Salesman* will bring, then reviews the humble beginnings of the man who, despite success, was still a subway straphanger. Miller comments on the scenery in *Death of a Salesman*, on early attempts by others to change the title, on opening night, and on the Requiem bouquet that audiences, though in a position to claim it as a souvenir, always let lie.

Frederic Wertham published an interview with Miller in the *New York Times Book Review* of 15 May 1949. Focusing on *Death of a Salesman*, the interview records Miller's thoughts on the character of Willy Loman (a man in need of an "efficient, successful, praiseworthy personality") and on the social significance of the play.

The production of *The Crucible* in 1953 brought another round of interviews, chief among them those with Lewis Funke (18 Jan. 1953), Henry Hewes (31 Jan. 1953), and John and Alice Griffin (Oct. 1953). Funke's "Thoughts on a Train Bound for Wilmington" is a conversation with both Miller and Jed Harris, director of *The Crucible*, in which the two defend the play not as social commentary, but as theatrical experience. Two weeks later, Hewes, in effect, continues the conversation, at a rehearsal of *The Crucible*. Here Miller speaks of the Puritan ideology turned orthodoxy, of the liberties he took with historical fact, and of the play's political or allegorical intent. Hewes records Miller's responsiveness to actors' suggestions and his respect for Harris as director. He also reports Miller's responses to a questionnaire and reveals the playwright's respect for Bertolt Brecht and Miller's feeling that a new theater can arise only through new social and psychological insights.

The interview with the Griffins also concerns *The Crucible*. Miller claims that the idea for the play was in his mind since his University of Michigan days. He was attracted to the articulateness and moral force of the people of Salem. He saw in them the potential for a drama that, in reflecting the insight of its characters, did not yield to pathos. Miller also notes that *The Crucible*, in his opinion, is more theatrical than *Death of a Salesman*.

The mid 1950s brought a spate of more general interviews: with Dorothy and Joseph Samachson (1954), in which Miller offers opinions on critics and the theater scene, including community theater and noncommercial productions; with Jim Cook (10 July 1956), who publishes biographical portraits of both Miller and Marilyn Monroe and an interview with Miller and his sister Joan Copeland on their early lives; and with John Wain (8 Sept. 1957), who discusses the social commitment of the writer, "social realism" as a form, and Miller's criteria for good plays.

Three interviews late in the decade are particularly informative. The first, *"Death of a Salesman*: A Symposium" (May 1958), records a panel discussion on Miller's best-known play, moderated by Phillip Gelb. Following opening remarks by several panelists, Miller responds with comments concerning questions of values and of Willy Loman as an American Everyman.

Gelb interviewed Miller separately in 1958 as well, publishing the dialogue in the October 1958 issue of *Educational Theatre Journal*. Although Roudané's collection reprints only the recycled portions of the panel discussion, the interview, in its original version, ranges over a variety of topics, including Miller's concept of dramatic realism, the relationship of the artist to society, the reactions of conservatives to Miller's social liberalism, and the importance of the right of dissent. The interview is a portrait of a playwright of social conscience.

Kenneth Allsop's July 1959 conversation with Miller records the playwright's perceptions of American society and theater in that decade. It registers Miller's view of the Beat Generation as a "recurrence of a kind of bohemianism." Miller sees protest drama of the 1950s as "anti-dramatic drama," evasive drama with no concern for the future. Plays about the generational conflict, for example, speak of the collapse of authority but ignore the fact that authority is more rigorously asserting itself. Miller gives his capsule vision of social and cultural history before and after the Korean War: by 1959 the country had arrived at a point of predictability, having lost "friction with the future"; its drama had become private rather than social.

Henry Brandon's November 1960 interview continues the Allsop conversation, recording Miller's extensive and insightful assessment of American drama of the 1950s. Miller sees the typical American play of the era as "preeminently active" but "unreflective," recording only the surface of American life. For him theater is neither sensationalism nor sentimental idealism, but a place in which the audience's awareness of what "living in our times involves" may be heightened. Miller also comments on McCarthyism, Chekhov's social commitment, Britain's angry young men (in whose work he finds American resonance), and American playwrights who preceded him.

Other interviews in the 1960s concerned themselves with *The Misfits* (Weatherby [3 Nov. 1961], Whitcomb [Dec. 1961]) and included Marilyn Monroe, for whom Miller wrote the film script and who starred in the film.

When *After the Fall* appeared in 1964, several interviews ensued. In discussions with William Goyen (19 Jan. 1964) and Joseph Gruen (24 Oct. 1965) Miller speaks of the process of writing and the play's themes; with Goyen he also comments on the Lincoln Center Repertory Company, and with Gruen he offers remarks on his opposition to American involvement in the Vietnam conflict.

The most valuable interview on *After the Fall*, published in *Show* in January 1964, took place during the rehearsal period for that play. Miller's enthusiasm for the play and his optimism for the forthcoming production, to be directed by Elia Kazan, is abundantly expressed. The unsigned interview, "Arthur Miller Ad-Libs on Elia Kazan," discusses the genesis of *After the Fall* (5,000 pages, reduced to 180), its unorthodox form, and his confidence in Lincoln Center—as opposed to Broadway—as the production forum. He speaks of ways in which Kazan, with whom he had worked previously, pursues commitments and approaches that complement his own.

Despite Miller's enthusiasm, however, *After the Fall* was not well received. In a January 1965 interview with Oriana Fallaci, Miller reacts to critics' unfavorable remarks, defending the play as the "story of a man trying to find out why he is alive."

In a 29 November 1964 interview with Barbara Gelb, Miller claimed that he no longer cared what critics said about his plays. Conducted on the eve of the opening of *Incident at Vichy*, Miller expressed his satisfaction with that play as having "a shape, a form, a truth."

In an extensive and highly informative interview with Miller, Olga Carlisle and Rose Styron (Summer 1966) engage the playwright in a wide-ranging discussion. He speaks of his early attraction to tragedy, which seemed to him "the only form there was," and of the two plays he had seen before he began writing plays: one about a cannibal with a time bomb on board a ship, the other about a Chinatown dope ring. His comments on modern tragedy note the presence of an "inconsolable universe" and the absence of a "reassertion of community." He speaks as well of his own father and of the father figures in his plays, who cast an "immense shadow" over the sons. He comments on Russian and French theater audiences and on the American version of Method acting, which he considers a perversion of the European. He gives a lengthy assessment of O'Neill's work and comments on the differences between stage plays and movies and on the suitability of television as a medium for drama. Of his own work he says he feels closest to *The Crucible*, though he expresses a fondness for his radio plays as well, including *William Ireland's Confession*, which features a character who rewrites *King Lear*. There are comments on the personal and the political, on dramatic critics (academics "seem to feel that the theater is an intrusion on literature"), on Franco Zeffirelli's Italian production of *After the Fall*, on the genesis of *The Crucible*, and, finally, an extended section on his experience with the United States House Un-American Activities Committee.

Miller's return to the University of Michigan in 1967 resulted in the publication of unsigned pieces, as "Arthur Miller Talks," in the *Michigan Quarterly Review* (Summer 1967), including his informal remarks before a large audience and his conversations with classes. Miller speaks freely about the state of American theater: a New York stage that is inhospitable to serious plays; the extraordinary influence of a small number of theater critics; the high price of commercial theater tickets; an audience interested only in a "musical or a quick laugh." Miller discusses the advantages and disadvantages of subsidized theater and the role of Lincoln Center in the dissemination of dramatic art. His defense of the theater is impassioned: "it can't die," for we must have "some kind of symbolization of our lives." The discussion period prompted a mélange of questions related to Miller's remarks, as did his conversations with a stage-directing class, in which students were interested in knowing about the relationship of the director to the playwright and the play.

Walter Wager's 1967 interview divides its attention between Miller's process of writing and his *Incident at Vichy*. In the first part Wager asks questions about Miller's writing habits and his goals. In the second Miller speaks of the "Nazi mechanism," his attendance at the German war-crime trials, and the problem of finding an appropriate dramatic form to present a particular theme.

The production of *The Price* in 1968 brought more interviews: with Joan Barthel (28 Jan. 1968), in which Miller speaks of the relationship of *The Price* to *Death of a Salesman* and of casting and staging the play; with Louis Calta (5 Mar. 1968), in which Miller defends the play's relevance to contemporary life; and with Ronald Hayman (15 Feb. 1969), in which the playwright identifies his interest in *The Price* not in the father/son relationship, but in a character's refusal to yield to society's success motives. Hayman's interview, expanded in his 1973 book on Miller, also asks a variety of questions unrelated to *The Price*.

The most extensive interview with Miller is actually composed of three interviews, published in Dutton's "The Dialogue Format" project and also filmed and distributed by Association Instructional Films of New York. The publication, Richard I. Evans's *Psychology and Arthur Miller* (1969), is justified by the belief that Miller's drama "reflects a profound contribution to personality psychology." In "The Writer as Creator" Miller speaks of the task of creating "real" people, of establishing characters' motives, of the subjectivity of the artist, of the communicative relationship between the writer and the audience. In "The Writer and Psychology" Evans queries the playwright on creativity and personality theory, the subjectivity of the scientist, the message in the play, the growth of character, and role conflict. In "The Writer and Society" he moves to questions of predicting human behavior, conformity and the loss of identity, personality and social function, personality and cultural determinism, and psychological versus technological growth. The volume ends with an appendix that discusses the three kinds of determinism that occupy psychologists: biological, cultural, and self.

Robert A. Martin published three interviews in 1969 and 1970. In "Arthur Miller–Tragedy and Commitment" (Summer 1969) he explores with Miller the concept of tragedy in Miller's plays, with particular reference to *After the Fall*. In "The Creative Experience of Arthur Miller" (Oct. 1969) Miller dismisses the identification of his plays with those of Ibsen, noting that during his apprenticeship and even after *All My Sons* he experimented with a number of theatrical styles in his plays. He also notes that, had he not written *The Crucible*, McCarthyism would not have been recorded in dramatic literature; writers of the time simply did not respond. Through a discussion of the perceived autobiographical nature of *After the Fall*, Martin leads Miller to make comments on what he expects from a play. Finally, Miller talks about the significance of his Jewishness on his play writing. In "Arthur Miller and the Meaning of Tragedy" (May 1970) Martin reviews statements on tragedy that

Miller made in earlier essays, then asks the playwright to explore those comments in reference to *After the Fall* and *The Price*.

In 1971 Rust Hills taped an extended and free-ranging conversation–about critics and reviewers, writing in progress, differences between fiction and drama, McCarthyism, writing groups and programs, and the anonymity of the writer in America–between Miller, William Styron, Inge Morath, and Rose Styron, who were neighbors in Roxbury, Connecticut. Miller compares earlier critics, who tried to illuminate a play's meaning, with current reviewers of drama's "dwindling audience": "Where you have a thriving theater, which is inexpensive, easy to get into, and is a part of the lives of the people, then the make-or-break power of the critic is minimal." Young writers, he says, especially need the encouragement that comes from writing teachers. Miller claims to have a "romantic faith in the truth," though most people have such fragmented experiences that they are not open to art. Much of today's art tries too hard–disastrously–to be relevant; "everything gets vulgarized, made more crude." Audiences today often have no sense of organic unity in a work of art, with the "new Naturalism" focusing on the surface, not the depth or center–on "surrealistic illogicality."

Josh Greenfield's 13 February 1972 interview is a testimony to Miller's devotion to the art of play writing. Miller discusses his writing habits, the absence of a desire to direct, his opinions of Kazan and Harold Clurman as directors, the vicissitudes of theatrical success, the paucity of playwrights of his generation, realism in the theater, the writing of novels, politics, writers in jail in the United States and the Soviet Union, and Miller's literary reputation. There are more personal questions as well, about "Woman's Liberation," his wife's cooking, his Mercedes 280 SEL, his trips to the city and to the theater (to see plays by Harold Pinter and "some of the black playwrights" such as Charles Gordone and Ed Bullins).

Ronald Hayman's 1973 interview in his *Playback II* offers insight into Miller's thinking on Ibsen, Brecht, and Beckett, and on a range of aspects of drama and theater. It is a narrative, incorporating and expanding Miller's comments from his earlier interview with Hayman and his essays, and adding new ones. Miller comments in particular on his regard for other playwrights. He says he originally borrowed a sense of the past from Ibsen, but he does not see Ibsen as "a basis for working now," for the contemporary theater has formally repudiated the role of the past. Though he respects Brecht, he denies his influence. He has little regard for

younger playwrights who, under the influence of Beckett and Ionesco, are all writing in a uniform style. Miller also offers his opinion of whether or not play writing can be taught and extends the discussion into commentary on the process of writing and on the task
of finding a theatrical form.

Tom Buckley (29 Aug. 1972) conducted an interview with
Miller, Harold Clurman, and others involved in the production of
The Creation of the World and Other Business. A kind of postmortem,
the interview explores reasons for the failure of Miller's only comedy. Miller discusses *Up from Paradise*, a musical version of *The Creation of the World and Other Business*, also commercially unsuccessful,
in a 17 April 1974 interview with Mel Gussow.

Robert W. Corrigan's autumn 1974 interview focuses on Miller's play writing. Though Corrigan notices a shift away from tragedy in his plays, Miller denies any deliberate change in emphasis
and reaffirms many of his earlier beliefs and principles. Miller does
agree that the level of consciousness of his characters is higher in
the later plays than in the earlier ones. He also remarks that he is
not concerned with tragic form during the writing process, nor
does he begin his play with a preconception of dramatic form.

Murray Schumach's interview, "Miller Still a 'Salesman' for a
Changing Theater" (26 June 1975), was conducted on the eve of
the 1975 revival of *Death of a Salesman*. Miller sees a coherence in
the 1975 audience, a shared sense of values that was not present in
the original audience. He discusses his involvement in the McCarthy controversy, noting that pickets forced a production of *Death of
a Salesman* in Illinois to close. Miller continues to be distressed over
American attitudes toward theater as an "isolated phenomenon"
when, for him, it is "sensitive to economic and social surroundings."

Miller returned to the University of Michigan in 1974 to talk
again with students. Published by Robert A. Martin and Richard D.
Meyer as "Arthur Miller on Plays and Playwriting" (Dec. 1976), the
session engaged a range of questions on American drama and Miller's plays. While much of the material is familiar, one student's question forced Miller onto new terrain. When pressed, the playwright
confessed he did not believe in God in a conventional sense but believed there was a level of human experience that we penetrate, partially, "at exalted moments."

Christian-Albrecht Gollub is interested in Miller's literary influences. In an interview conducted in 1975 and published in 1977,
Gollub reminds Miller that twenty years earlier he had said he

would not know who his favorite playwright was for twenty years. Though still reluctant to answer, Miller does name O'Neill and Pinter–without admitting that they influenced his own work, as did the Greeks and Shakespeare. Miller also notes that at age twenty he read "a lot of Russians," George Bernard Shaw, and, later, Sean O'Casey. Gollub and Miller also discuss the workers' theater and Clifford Odets's *Waiting for Lefty* (1937). No contemporary American playwright, Miller avers, has succeeded in attracting large audiences, though his own plays have been popular in Europe. Gollub asks questions about Miller's sense of himself as a playwright, his writing habits, how he feels when he sees his plays performed ("pained"), differences between American commercial theater and European repertory theater, his role in the theater in the 1970s, the production of *Up from Paradise*, his own theatergoing habits and those of the theatergoing public, and the task of the writer. When asked if he was an optimist, Miller characterized himself as "a dispassionate observer of the ongoing disaster of the human race."

James J. Martine's " 'All in a Boiling Soup' " (1979) is a particularly well-prepared and probing interview that recovers comments from earlier interviews and, in effect, holds Miller accountable for them. Like Gollub, Martine asks the writer about literary influences and assessments and about his reading habits. In response to his question on Pirandello, Miller admits that he did not appreciate him until recently and now considers him immensely important. Miller's measure of significant playwrights is their "relevance to their time." Miller also elaborates on earlier remarks concerning his concept of "community," both within his plays and in theater audiences. He describes an American writer's ethnic background as "part of his equipment." Martine also attempts to gauge Miller's sense of cultural change by asking whether Willy Loman would have been better off in the 1960s or today; the question becomes an invitation to Miller to talk about a decline in comradeship among people, an increase in "amorphousness." Martine follows up with a question of whether or not the "paranoid politics of McCarthyism" could happen again, to which Miller, predictably, replies in the affirmative. Martine also engages Miller in an updated discussion on the state of the theater, the role of critics, academic scholarship, his working habits, and television.

Leonard Moss's 1979 interview with Miller, published in 1980 as " 'The Absence of the Tension' " in his book on Miller, begins with a discussion of *The Price*, which Miller calls a play about "the architecture of sacrifice." It moves quickly to Miller's judgment of contemporary history, including his views on Vietnam and Czechoslovakia, his feeling that the tension between capitalism and communism is gone. When asked whether he had a "personal model in the moral world," Miller explored possibilities in particular writers but came up with no candidates. Miller goes on at length about his vision of a democratic socialism and its possibilities in America.

Though Miller's more recent work has not received critical acclaim, the interest in Miller remains, and he continues to give interviews. Studs Terkel (Sept. 1980) talked with Miller in an interview occasioned by the premiere of Miller's *The American Clock*, a play set in the Depression and inspired by Terkel's *Hard Times* (1970). The conversation is at once informative and nostalgic, seemingly composed of the reminiscences and judgments of two socially aware citizens of the 1930s. Miller's contemporary concern is with a "deep dislocation" that he feels is about to take place and, for many, has already occurred. Miller calls *The American Clock* "a story of the United States talking to itself."

James Lardner (26 Oct. 1980) met with Miller in Baltimore, where the playwright was in rehearsal for *The American Clock*. In "Arthur Miller–Back in Control at 65," the playwright speaks of authorial dominance; of the television production of *Playing for Time*, which omitted much of the script; and of screenwriting, which he was unwilling to do because he felt it necessitated a relinquishing of control. When asked to comment on contemporary playwrights he admired, Miller admitted, as he had before, that he never went to the theater very much. Miller comments on the social backdrop for *The American Clock* (the Depression) and calls the "kaleidoscopic, semidocumentary" play a "prebourgeois structure."

V. Rajakrishnan's May 1980 interview begins with the observation that Miller's more recent plays seem to move away from the social and ideological commitment of the early work into more metaphysical concerns. Though Miller agrees, he is quick to express his vision of all experience as an articulated whole. The interview comes closer than any other to encapsulating Miller's philosophical worldview. Along the way, Rajakrishnan engages Miller in commentary on Albert Camus, Jean-Paul Sartre, absurdism, and many of Miller's plays, including *After the Fall*, *Incident at Vichy*, and *The Price*.

In " 'The Will to Live' " (Sept. 1984) Steven R. Centola builds on his own assessment of Miller's work as reflective of "existential humanism." The discussion teases Miller's ideas on tragedy, masks, connectedness; and, in his characters, self-recognition and self-deception, fate and free will, and guilt. Throughout the interview, Centola persists in suggesting connections between Miller's views and Sartre's. He asks specific questions as well about *Death of a Salesman, The Price,* and *After the Fall.*

Roudané's 1983 interview, published in *Michigan Quarterly Review* in 1985, offers extended commentary on Miller's concept of the creative process. Miller speaks of the engine that drives his plays-in-the-making (one character "wrestling with his dilemma"), and of dramatic form in *All My Sons, Death of a Salesman,* and *The Crucible.* Miller explains that he composes by writing one thousand to three thousand pages, then editing and revising; he speaks as well of how the one-act *A View from the Bridge* became a two-act play. The writer also comments on changes in audience perceptions of several of his plays, attributing reactions to the historical moment. He also defends the complexity of his female characters, particularly Kate Keller and Linda Loman, then offers comments on *An Enemy of the People* and on *Incident at Vichy* as a play driven not by character but by theme. He speaks as well of the rehearsal process and concludes with a statement about what the theater today should try to accomplish. For Miller, theater should confront all people, not just one social faction.

Miller's May 1986 interview with Mark Lamos, who directed the Hartford Stage Company's revival of *The Crucible,* focuses on practical, rather than philosophical, questions. Lamos elicits Miller's comments on *The Crucible* and the Wooster Group's *L.S.D.* The two speak of a play's coherence, the "common thread running through everything." Actors and directors often reveal a thread other than the one the playwright identifies; John Malkovich's Biff, for example, helped Miller see *Death of a Salesman* as Biff's play rather than Willy's, while the production done in China refocused attention on Linda. Once again, Miller registers his concern for high theater ticket prices and his wish for a less elite audience. He speaks of the shift in theater form from symphonic orchestration to a kind of impressionistic writing that is not concerned with the impact of the past on the present. The interview concludes with Miller's remarking on the moral responsibility of the writer, which is, finally, "telling the news."

Miller's most recent interview was occasioned by his first original screenplay, *Everybody Wins,* a film scheduled for release in late 1989. In "On Film Credits List, That Miller Is Arthur" (22 Nov.

1988), Miller tells Caryn James that *Everybody Wins* came to him as a movie; hence he decided to let it be one–despite his hatred for film production (though "I love the writing"). By Miller's account, this suspense film is really about "reality and the arbitrary way we do decide it's real."

Miller's interviews have been consistently congenial and informative, providing American scholars and the theatergoing public with a portrait of a playwright who can surely claim to be the most important in post-World War II drama, if not in this century. There is no doubt that Miller, though committed to completing at least some of the half-finished plays he has begun, will be generous in granting additional interviews as well. But, finally, the most memorable and revealing of all Miller's interviews will remain the one he gave, reluctantly, in 1956, in Washington, D.C. For it was then that Miller, like many of his artistic colleagues, was called before the House Un-American Activities Committee. At center stage, Miller admitted attaching his name to protests and appeals initiated by "Red front groups" and attending several Communist party meetings, but he denied membership in the Communist party. Most importantly, he refused to name others who might have been involved, proving–as he has on numerous occasions before and since–that he is not only a playwright of conscience but a man of conscience as well.

Critical Studies: Books

The first full-length study of Arthur Miller's work was Dennis Welland's *Arthur Miller*, published in 1961. Welland establishes the format that was to become standard in Miller scholarship: an overview chapter on the dramatist, followed by a play-by-play analysis in separate chapters. The book presents brief discussions of the plays from *The Man Who Had All the Luck* and *All My Sons* ("Beginnings of Realism") through *A View from the Bridge*. Welland places Miller's work within a tradition of American literature dating back to Ralph Waldo Emerson. A concluding chapter on "The Drama, the Family and Society" acknowledges that this early study can only be a progress report and expresses confidence in Miller's ability to dramatize human complexities.

Robert Hogan's *Arthur Miller*, in the University of Minnesota "Pamphlets on American Writers" series, appeared in 1964. A forty-eight-page essay on Miller and his work, the monograph both reflects and sets the tone for Miller scholarship: Hogan thinks that the meaning and importance of Miller's work are in the tragic spirit that his plays embody. This extended essay offers a balanced assessment of the plays through *After the Fall.*

A second full-length study of Miller's work appeared in 1965. Sheila Huftel's *Arthur Miller: The Burning Glass* offers an overview chapter on Miller, followed by chapters on each dramatic work. Her coverage of plays runs from *The Man Who Had All the Luck* to *Incident at Vichy,* though *A Memory of Two Mondays,* dismissed as a minor work, receives only a few paragraphs. Huftel also includes sections on *Focus, The Misfits,* and "Miller on Playwriting," the last of which attempts to compare Miller to other playwrights, such as Brecht and Tennessee Williams. The opening chapter includes excerpts from Miller's testimony before the House Un-American Activities Committee in 1956. Throughout, Huftel is attentive to critical opinions of Miller's work and to Miller's own comments (some taken from his letters to her). Her analyses identify the plays' recurring concerns: the characters' quests for self-knowledge and their preoccupation with guilt and responsibility. An appendix provides cast lists for the New York and London premieres, and for a few other productions of the plays from *All My Sons* through *Incident at Vichy.* The only extended discussion of Miller's unfinished film script, "Bridge to a Savage World," also appears in this thorough and useful (though no longer current) study.

Huftel's book was followed by Edward Murray's, in 1967. *Arthur Miller: Dramatist* is without an overview essay; its contents include chapters on each of the plays from *All My Sons* to *Incident at Vichy,* including *A Memory of Two Mondays.* Murray provides extensive summaries of each play and offers conventional analyses of character, structure, and theme. In a brief conclusion Murray speaks to the unevenness of Miller's work and notes that the canon reflects no clear line of development.

Leonard Moss's Twayne book, *Arthur Miller,* also appeared in 1967. Moss begins with an overview that includes biographical information on Miller. Subsequent chapters deal with the early work, *Death of a Salesman,* and "Four 'Social Plays' " (*The Crucible, A View from the Bridge, A Memory of Two Mondays, The Misfits*). Moss pairs *After the Fall* and *Incident at Vichy* in a final chapter on the plays, concluding the volume with a chapter entitled "The Perspective of a Playwright." In 1980 Moss expanded the book by adding discussions of *The Price* and *The Creation of the World and Other Business,* updating the chronology, the biographical chapter, and the bibliography, and appending a 1979 interview. The book is a solid analysis that attempts to shift the focus from Miller as social playwright to Miller as psychological playwright. Moss pays particular attention to Miller's use of the language of the "common man."

Two books on Miller were published in 1970. Hayman's *Arthur Miller* follows the conventional arrangement, offering play-by-play analyses through *The Price*. An interview with Miller replaces an overview chapter; a concluding chapter assesses Miller's achievement in the context of modern European and American drama. Hayman sees Miller's social commitment as the distinguishing feature of his plays and notices the importance of the effect of the past on the present lives of Miller's characters. Though Hayman is often critical of Miller's work, the constraints of this compact volume do not allow him to do more than register his sense of Miller's weaknesses. Hayman ends the study with a catalog of stage productions and cast lists.

The second volume published in 1970 departs from the form of previous books, but its purpose is the same. Benjamin Nelson's *Arthur Miller: Portrait of a Playwright* attempts to offer a comprehensive look at the playwright's work and thought within the context of place and time. Throughout the study, which covers the plays from *The Man Who Had All the Luck* through *The Price*, Nelson makes connections between Miller's life and his dramatic art. He sees the recurring motif in Miller's work as the need for human connection. Over three hundred pages long, the book ranges freely, offering lively discussions and a balanced reading of the Miller canon.

Welland, who published the first book on Miller in 1961, returned to the playwright's work in 1979 with the publication of *Miller: A Study of His Plays*, and again in 1983 with a revised and enlarged edition of that work, titled *Miller: The Playwright*. Welland's earlier views on the earlier plays reappear here as a prologue to discussions of the plays through *The Archbishop's Ceiling* and *Fame* in the 1983 edition. The focus in both volumes is not on the place Miller occupies within an American literary tradition but on the plays themselves. Long a student of Miller's work, Welland offers brief but insightful analyses of the range of Miller's plays. The volume contains a chronology and a list of American and British premieres of Miller's plays and films.

Neil Carson's study, *Arthur Miller* (1982), in the Grove "Modern Dramatists" series is yet another play-by-play account, ending with *The Creation of the World and Other Business* and *Playing for Time*. Two biographical chapters—"The Young Playwright" and "The

World that Would Be Perfect"–precede the analyses, which begin with *The Man Who Had All the Luck* and *All My Sons*. Carson reviews previous scholarship on each play, noting particular approaches. A concluding chapter speaks to the playwright's developing vision: from a "prophet," intent on raising consciousness and transforming, to a photographer, or psychological realist. He notes as well Miller's contribution to a distinctive American dramatic idiom, his place among social dramatists, and his stature as a "religious writer," intent on saving souls.

A book that departs from the standard format is N. Bhaskara Panikkar's *Individual Morality and Social Happiness in Arthur Miller* (1982), published in New Delhi, India. Following a chapter on "Arthur Miller: The Artist as Moralist," Panikkar frames chapters by pairing "Social Tension," "Psychological Tension," "Moral Tension," and "Social Happiness" with "Individual Morality." Panikkar then explores "Dramatic Technique and the Theme of Individual Morality and Social Happiness" and, finally, "Miller and the American Moralistic Tradition." Appendices, including charts, document "The Class Basis of Miller's Characters," "Sexual Code Violations," "Morality Versus Mortality," and "Individual Morality in Miller's Non-Dramatic Works." The purpose of the book is "to relate Miller's moralistic vision to the American ideal of social happiness." Though American readers will undoubtedly be amused by this rigorous codification of morality, the book is a fascinating–and instructive–exposition of American values from a cross-cultural perspective.

A second book published in New Delhi is Santosh K. Bhatia's *Arthur Miller: Social Drama as Tragedy* (1985), which examines the concept of tragedy in six of Miller's plays: *All My Sons, Death of a Salesman, The Crucible, A View from the Bridge, After the Fall,* and *The Price.* An introduction discusses tragedy–Greek, Elizabethan, and modern–identifying five common characteristics: conflict, suffering, tragic irony, awakening, and a metaphysical dimension. Bhatia sees Miller's tragic vision as being consistently rooted in socioeconomic problems.

The most up-to-date book on Miller, in Ungar's "Literature and Life" series, is by June Schlueter and James K. Flanagan (1987), containing an opening biographical chapter by Flanagan and play analyses, through *Danger! Memory (I Can't Remember Anything* and *Clara)*, by Schlueter. A concluding chapter assesses Miller's fifty years as a playwright, crediting him not only with an unrelenting social conscience but with imaginative innovation in theatrical form. The extensive critical biography is a comprehensive account of the relationship between Miller's private and public lives and his dramatic career.

Books on Miller in the "miscellaneous" category include James Goode's *The Story of "The Misfits"* (1963), which is a detailed account of the filming of *The Misfits*; C. J. Partridge's *Death of a Salesman* (1969), a fifty-seven-page booklet written for students in British schools; and Sidney H. White's *Guide to Arthur Miller* (1970), a forty-seven-page essay in pamphlet form.

Critical Studies: Collections of Essays

Though publication of essays on Miller's work has reached the status of an industry, the dozen edited collections are, for the most part, valuable, for they provide convenient access to the critical essays and reviews that have contributed most significantly to Miller scholarship, and they offer the reader an opportunity to see patterns in that criticism. Four of these collections–Robert W. Corrigan's *Arthur Miller: A Collection of Critical Essays* (1969), James J. Martine's *Critical Essays on Arthur Miller* (1979), Robert A. Martin's *Arthur Miller: New Perspectives* (1982), and Harold Bloom's *Arthur Miller* (1987)–include essays of a general nature as well as essays on individual plays.

Five books–John D. Hurrell's *Two Modern American Tragedies* (1961), Gerald Weales's *"Death of a Salesman"* (1967), Walter J. Meserve's *The Merrill Studies in "Death of a Salesman"* (1972), Helene Wickham Koon's *Twentieth Century Interpretations of "Death of a Salesman"* (1983), and Harold Bloom's *Arthur Miller's "Death of a Salesman"* (1988)–are devoted to Miller's best-known play. As would be expected, there is some duplication among them, particularly in the most recent, Bloom's; yet collectively they offer a representative sample of criticism of the play, much of which has been concerned with the nature of tragedy.

Two of the collections–Gerald Weales's *"The Crucible"* (1971) and John H. Ferres's *Twentieth Century Interpretations of "The Crucible"* (1972)–devote themselves to *The Crucible*. A recent volume–Bloom's *Arthur Miller's "All My Sons"* (1988)–reprints essays written on *All My Sons*.

Finally, Dorothy Parker's *Essays on Modern American Drama* (1987) reprints essays on Tennessee Williams, Miller, Edward Albee, and Sam Shepard that have appeared in the journal *Modern Drama*. (Those on Miller are by Barry Gross, on *All My Sons*;

C. W. E. Bigsby, on *After the Fall;* Robert A. Martin, on *The Crucible;* and Lawrence D. Lowenthal, on *Incident at Vichy.*)

Two of the general collections, Corrigan's and Martin's, are in the Prentice-Hall "Twentieth Century Views" series. The Corrigan collection contains nine essays by Herbert Blau, Harold Clurman, Tom F. Driver, Eric Mottram, Brian Parker, M. W. Steinberg, Robert Warshow, Gerald Weales, and Raymond Williams; a chronology of important dates; and a selected bibliography. Corrigan's "Introduction: The Achievement of Arthur Miller" views Miller's achievement twenty years after he was "first catapulted to fame," following the 1947 production of *All My Sons.* Corrigan finds two distinct patterns in Miller's work, the first through *A View from the Bridge* (1957), the second through *The Misfits* (1961). Beginning with *After the Fall,* Miller's plays move from a "crisis of consciousness" to one of conscience.

Martin's *New Perspectives* collection is divided into two sections: "Overviews," by Paul Blumberg, Ruby Cohn, Orm Overland, Thomas E. Porter, Kenneth Rowe, and Weales; and "Views," by Enoch Brater, Lawrence D. Lowenthal, Walter J. Meserve, Leonard Moss, Benjamin Nelson, Stephen S. Stanton, J. L. Styan, and Weales. Of the fourteen essays, six were written especially for the collection. The goal of the volume is to record the "current state of Miller criticism and to assess his development as a playwright." Martin's introduction discusses the importance of the family unit in Miller's plays through *The American Clock.*

Bloom's 1987 collection is one of three on Miller in the "Modern Critical Views/Interpretations" series. The volume offers little that is not already conveniently available to the Miller scholar, for, while it reprints material from the 1980s, those materials are almost exclusively excerpts from books (Bigsby, Neil Carson, Moss, Dennis Welland, and Williams); moreover, it reprints essays previously reprinted (Driver, Esther Merle Jackson, Overland as well. Only two of the essays, by E. Miller Budick and Clinton W. Trowbridge, do not appear in other edited collections. In his introduction to the volume Bloom, prompted by the stage success of Miller's plays, asks if there is an "element in drama that is other than literary." He suggests that the American literary tradition, which remains Emersonian, has excluded history and drama.

Martine's *Critical Essays on Arthur Miller* (1979) is a collection of another sort. A valuable resource book that proceeds play by play, beginning with *The Man Who Had All the Luck* and concluding with *The Creation of the World and Other Business*, it includes not only essays (Bigsby, David Bronson, Arthur D. Epstein, Barry Gross, two by Irving Jacobson, Lowenthal, Martin, two by Porter, Martin Roth, Allen Shepherd, Trowbridge, Daniel Walden, and Arvin R. Wells) and an original interview (Martine) but reviews of productions as well (two by Brooks Atkinson, two by John Chapman, Alan S. Downer, two by Walter Kerr, Frederick Morgan, Lewis Nichols, John Simon, Douglas Watt, and three by Richard Watts, Jr.), offering, in effect, a critical overview of Miller's career. Martine's introduction is an excellent bibliographic essay, a survey of criticism on Miller that provides a defining context.

The earliest collection on *Death of a Salesman*, by Hurrell (1961), clearly establishes this connection. In addition to providing the texts of *Death of a Salesman* and Tennessee Williams's *A Streetcar Named Desire* (1947), it reprints essays on tragedy in the modern world–Joseph Wood Krutch's "The Tragic Fallacy," John Gassner's "Tragic Perspectives: A Sequence of Queries," and Orrin E. Klapp's "Tragedy and the American Climate of Opinion"–and on the modern American theater–Kenneth Tynan's "American Blues . . . ," Eric Bentley's "Better than Europe?," and Krutch's from " 'Modernism' in Modern Drama." The Miller section reprints two of the playwright's essays ("Tragedy and the Common Man" and "On Social Plays"); reviews and criticism by Atkinson, George Jean Nathan, Eleanor Clark, Clurman, and William J. Newman; excerpts from interviews in the form of a radio program; and an essay on *Death of a Salesman* ("Confusion and Tragedy") written for the volume by Richard J. Foster. There is also an essay by W. David Sievers on both Miller and Williams.

Weales's collection (1967), in the Viking "Text and Criticism" series, also contains the text of *Death of a Salesman*, essays by Miller ("Tragedy and the Common Man," "The *Salesman* Has a Birthday," "The American Theater," "Introduction to *Collected Plays*," and "Morality and Modern Drama"), reviews, and essays. Its purpose is to present a variety of opinions and readings of the play, from the earliest reactions in 1949 through 1963. A section on "*Salesman* in Context" reprints general essays on Miller as well as four literary analogues: Walter D. Moody's "The Know-It-All Salesman"; Eudora Welty's "Death of a Traveling Salesman"; Tennessee Williams's "The Last of My Solid Gold Watches"; and Irwin Shaw's "The Eighty-Yard Run." Weales's introduction reviews questions of genre and speaks to the critical reception of the play.

The Meserve collection (1972), in the "Merrill Studies" series, presents six essays on the reception of *Death of a Salesman*, then divides the critical essays into three categories: the play as social problem; the play as tragedy; and characters and style. Meserve's preface begins with a verse, "Who Killed Willy Loman?," in which each character–and society–in turn denies responsibility. Meserve explores the question of blame with respect to Willy's deception and death.

Koon's "Twentieth Century Interpretations" volume on *Death of a Salesman* (1983) presents ten essays, all reprinted (Bates, Field, Gordon, Kennedy, Lawrence, Oberg, Otten, Parker, Siegel, Welland). Her introduction provides an overview, touching on biography, production, character, and tragedy–concerns reflected in traditional criticism of *Death of a Salesman*.

Bloom's 1988 volume on *Death of a Salesman*, in Chelsea House's "Modern Critical Interpretations" series, duplicates, as its introduction, Bloom's introduction to his 1987 *Arthur Miller* volume and reprints three essays (Cohn, Jackson, Parker) appearing in previous collections. But it selects seven essays on the play (Aarnes, Bigsby, Brucher, Heyen, Hoeveler, Innes, Szondi)–all published since 1975–that do not appear in other collections, making this volume a valuable scholarly resource.

Weales's 1971 collection on *The Crucible*, in the Viking "Text and Criticism" series, reprints the text of that play and offers background material. There is a section on "Miller on *The Crucible*"; and another section offers general essays on Miller (Baxandall, Hunt, Weales, Wiegand). One section presents historical context essays, while another offers contemporary context essays. In his introduction, Weales urges more attention to the play's dramatic qualities rather than to its historical accuracy or its polemics. Reprinted comments, reviews, and essays do both.

Ferres's collection on *The Crucible* also offers a variety of materials. Two background essays–George L. Kittredge's "Witchcraft and the Puritans" and Earl Latham's "The Meaning of McCarthyism"– are followed by reviews (Gassner, Hayes, Kerr), interpretations (Blau, Curtis, Hill, Moss, Murray, Popkin, Welland), and viewpoints (Douglass, Ganz, Hogan, Huftel, Mottram, Steinberg), many of which are excerpts from books on Miller and a few of which appeared earlier in the general collections. The volume concludes with an additional scene, titled, for the collection, "A Private Meeting of John and Abigail." The scene appeared in a revised version of act 2 in a 1953 production. Ferres's introduction speaks to the contemporary appeal of *The Crucible*, which comments on the right of dissent, individuality, and heroism.

As with Bloom's general collection, many of the essays in his 1988 *All My Sons* volume are excerpts from books (Huftel, Moss, Schlueter, Welland—or, in the case of Bigsby, from the Miller portion of his book on American drama), and two of the essays have been collected previously (Gross, Overland). But the volume does contain an essay not previously reprinted (Yorks) and one not previously published (Centola). Also reprinted, as "The Question of Relatedness," is a portion of Miller's introduction to *Collected Plays*.

Critical Studies: Major Reviews, Articles, and Book Sections

Over the nearly fifty years of his professional play writing career, Miller has consistently attracted the attention of theater critics and, at least since the late 1950s, the academic community as well. As elder statesman of the American theater, Miller has had virtually all of his plays, from *The Man Who Had All the Luck* through *Danger! Memory*, produced in New York, and none of the productions has gone unnoticed by reviewers. Those interested in the critical reception of Miller's plays on the stage can get an overview from Bigsby's excerpts in *File on Miller*. The annual volumes of *New York Theater Critics' Reviews* offer a convenient and thorough source of reprints of reviews that appeared in New York publications.

A quick look at the secondary Miller bibliography, even though selective, suggests that the volume of critical material on Miller's work is enormous, leaving any bibliographic essayist with the task of selection. Because editors' choices for the several collections on Miller and his individual plays suggest sound principles of selection, many of the essays contained in those volumes are summarized here; however, space has prevented including summaries of all but a few of the reviews. In fact, the tendency of this essay is to prefer scholarly essays over reviews, but that tendency in no way neutralizes the recognition that the performance life of a play is a vital part of its character.

Three early essays compare Miller and Tennessee Williams. Alan S. Downer, in "Mr. Williams and Mr. Miller" (Summer 1949), insists that there are differences between the two playwrights but applauds both as serious artists who have enriched American drama. Kenneth Tynan, in "American Blues: The Plays of Arthur Miller and Tennessee Williams" (May 1954), welcomes Miller and Williams as a new generation of playwrights. Tynan had little doubt that Miller was a playwright of enormous importance and credited both dramatists with creating a powerful body of English-language drama. W. David Sievers's "Tennessee Williams and Arthur Miller," a section of his book on *Freud on Broadway* (1955), brings a psychoanalytic approach to the work of the two, focusing, in the case of Miller, on father/son relationships, particularly in *Death of a Salesman*. Miller's responses to a questionnaire submitted to him by Sievers reveal that, while the writer acknowledges connections between Freudian formulations and the psychic life of his characters, he does not feel equipped to analyze the unconscious influences that inform his plays. A decade later Ralph Willett, in "The Ideas of Miller and Williams" (1966), approached the two playwrights again, his purpose being to identify similarities between them.

Much of the criticism of Miller has centered on the concept of tragedy, since Miller himself spoke to the matter in "Tragedy and the Common Man" and since reviewers were persistent in using Aristotle's description of classical tragedy as the measure of Miller's work. Alvin Whitley, in "Arthur Miller: An Attempt at Modern Tragedy" (1953), evaluates *All My Sons* and *Death of a Salesman* in the context of Aristotle's comments and Miller's. M. W. Steinberg, in "Arthur Miller and the Idea of Modern Tragedy" (Autumn 1960), commends Miller's effort to offer a definition of modern tragedy; he examines his plays and essays–in particular "Tragedy and the Common Man"–and suggests how Miller's theatrical assumptions relate to earlier tragedy. Steinberg concludes that Miller's work fluctuates between traditional Greek and Christian concepts of tragedy, between social and individual emphases. But unlike either, it does not have a religious context.

Raymond Williams, in "The Realism of Arthur Miller" (Summer 1959), introduces the "other" generic consideration into Miller scholarship, applauding Miller for having restored social concerns to the theater–concerns that were not prominent in drama of the late 1940s. His essay examines *All My Sons, Death of a Salesman, The Crucible, A Memory of Two Mondays,* and *A View from the Bridge* not as tragedies but as dramas of social consciousness.

Tom F. Driver's piece, "Strength and Weakness in Arthur Miller" (May 1960), is a balanced assessment of Miller's achievements as a playwright. Driver examines not only the plays but Miller's introduction to the *Collected Plays* in order to determine Miller's strengths, which he determines are a "public" view of theater, which respects the audience; a concern with the social; a desire to report experience realistically; and a desire to heighten consciousness through theater. But when Driver judges Miller by the playwright's own critical standards, he finds unresolved contradictions, particularly in his reliance on the psychological even as he hopes to emphasize the social. Driver finally blames Miller's theatrical shortcomings on a limited conception of the relationship between the human being and society.

In "Arthur Miller and the Loss of Conscience" (Spring 1960) William B. Dillingham explores a central theme of Miller's plays and essays: the obligation to assume a place in a world of love and responsibility. The protagonists of Miller's plays fail in this obligation, which, in Miller's vision, provides the material for tragedy. Dillingham looks especially at *All My Sons, Death of a Salesman, The Crucible,* and *A View from the Bridge,* noticing how his protagonists both discover and lose their consciences.

In "Arthur Miller: The Strange Encounter" (Winter 1960) Henry Popkin examines *Death of a Salesman, The Crucible,* and *A View from the Bridge* as parables or fables which reflect the social and political climate of their time. He notes as well that in all three plays sex is a destructive influence, responsible for and symptomatic of his heroes' problems.

A valuable essay is Emile G. McAnany's "The Tragic Commitment: Some Notes on Arthur Miller" (May 1962), which presents, through quotation and commentary, Miller's dramatic theory. In the second section of the essay, "Pattern and Reality: Willy Loman as Tragic Hero," McAnany emphasizes the role that Willy's sense of himself as father played in his behavior and destruction. Another discussion of Miller's work as tragedy is John Prudhoe's "Arthur Miller and the Tradition of Tragedy" (Oct. 1962), which attempts to reconcile the formal demands of realism and tragedy.

Gerald Weales, in "Arthur Miller: Man and His Image" (Fall 1962), offers a reassessment of Miller's career, fifteen years after his first commercial success. Weales proposes that a profitable way of viewing the plays is through the concern, on the part of each of Miller's protagonists, with identity or name. He works through the plays from *All My Sons* to *A View from the Bridge,* showing how each protagonist must decide whether to accept or reject the image of self imposed upon him by society.

Arthur Ganz's companion essays, "The Silence of Arthur Miller" (Fall 1963) and "Arthur Miller: After the Silence" (Fall

1964), offer evaluations of Miller's career, the first through *A View from the Bridge* and *A Memory of Two Mondays*, written before his eight-year hiatus from the stage, and the second on *After the Fall*, which marked the resumption of Miller's public play-writing career in 1964. Ganz is encouraged by *After the Fall*, which he feels moves beyond the oversimplifications of the earlier plays into a more complex vision.

Three essays by Harold Clurman, conflated into "Arthur Miller's Later Plays" for the Corrigan collection, first appeared in 1964, Summer 1965, and April 1968, respectively. "Arthur Miller: Theme and Variations," prompted by Miller's comment that all his plays were, in a sense, autobiographical, reviews Miller's personal background and then examines the plays through *After the Fall* for evidence of that background. "Director's Notes: *Incident at Vichy*" is an account of Clurman's direction of that play at the ANTA-Washington Square Theater. "The Merits of Mr. Miller" explores Miller as a moralist, measuring his effectiveness in a survey of the plays through *The Price*.

Eric Mottram's 1967 essay, "Arthur Miller: The Development of a Political Dramatist in America," sees Miller's work, and particularly the plays that were then his most recent (*After the Fall* and *Incident at Vichy*), as "typical of frustrated American liberalism." After reviewing Miller's own political commitments, Mottram turns to a discussion of the plays from *The Man Who Had All the Luck* through *Incident at Vichy*, noting how Miller's hopes of connecting the individual and society were frustrated by his dramatic obsessiveness–with, for example, "law and authority, self and society"–which led to oversimplification, confusion, and, finally, "a paralysis of desperate warnings."

Clinton W. Trowbridge's interest in Miller's plays arises from the paradox of tragedy: though the hero is destroyed, the play affirms humanity. In "Arthur Miller: Between Pathos and Tragedy" (Dec. 1967) Trowbridge argues that Miller's dramatic writing displays a movement from pathos to tragedy.

Alan Stambusky continues the discussion of Miller as a tragic dramatist in "Arthur Miller: Aristotelian Canons in the Twentieth Century Drama" (1968). This close comparison of Miller's concept of tragedy to Aristotle's results in Stambusky's suggestion that Miller has misread Aristotle. Stambusky evaluates several of Miller's plays–*All My Sons, Death of a Salesman, The Crucible, A View from the Bridge, After the Fall,* and *Incident at Vichy*–in the context of both

Aristotle's description of tragedy and Miller's. Though critical of Miller's particular achievements, Stambusky concludes that Miller, more than any other American playwright, has embodied the principles and spirit of classical tragedy.

In his overview essay for the 1987 Bloom collection, excerpted from *Drama from Ibsen to Brecht* (1968) and titled, by the editor, "Arthur Miller: An Overview," Raymond Williams reviews the plays from *All My Sons* through *After the Fall*, noting Miller's experiments with several dramatic forms. He sees Miller's work as having an "independence of occasion" that contrasts with the American tradition.

Two essays published in Summer 1969 make an interesting pairing. Raymond H. Reno's "Arthur Miller and the Death of God" brings a theological perspective to Miller's work, viewing all Miller's plays since *Death of a Salesman* as "subsequent to the fall of God." Without God, the human being is responsible only to other human beings; Miller's plays reflect this doctrine of sociology. Paul Blumberg also speaks of the sociology of Miller's plays, though without Reno's sense of loss. In "Sociology and Social Literature: Work Alienation in the Plays of Arthur Miller" he discusses Miller as a social playwright who, of all modern playwrights, has the "most to say to contemporary sociologists." Blumberg distills Miller's discussions of the social play into a definition of that form as one that "demonstrates the impact of social forces" on characters, emphasizes the similarity of men, and asks how human beings should live. He then turns to the plays to cite specific instances of Miller's social concerns, and, particularly, his treatment of the theme of work alienation.

Ruby Cohn, in "The Articulate Victims of Arthur Miller" (1971), explores the idioms of Miller's characters from *All My Sons* through *The Price*. Willy Loman, for example, speaks in clichés and repetitions, even as Charley speaks in "salty proverbs" and Ben in "active epigrams." Cohn argues that the language of Miller's plays consists of "crisp dialogue," "concrete images, Jewish inflections, and rhythmic repetitions."

Morris Freedman's "The Jewishness of Arthur Miller: His Family Epic" (1971), a chapter in his *American Drama in Social Context*, explores Miller's treatment of guilt in his "family tetralogy": *All My Sons, Death of a Salesman, After the Fall,* and *The Price*. Freedman proposes that the plays may be read as commentary on the same family in different circumstances and from different perspectives and that the development of that family reflects changing middle-class American—and particularly Jewish-American—values.

Thomas E. Porter explores two recurring themes in Miller's plays: business and law. In "The Mills of the Gods: Economics and Law in the Plays of Arthur Miller" (1982) he categorizes *All My Sons, Death of a Salesman,* and *The Price* as "business plays" and *The Crucible, A View from the Bridge,* and *After the Fall* as "judicial plays." The plays in both categories reflect Miller's concern with the conflict between the ideal and the actual.

The process of play writing is the subject of Orm Overland's "The Action and Its Significance: Arthur Miller's Struggle with Dramatic Form" (Mar. 1975), as it was of Allan Seager's "The Creative Agony of Arthur Miller" (Oct. 1959). Overland sees in Miller's introduction to the *Collected Plays* a sequence recording initiative and response as the playwright reacts to critical response and looks forward to the challenge of the next play. The essay examines the implications of Miller's theories of dramatic form and his distrust of the theater. Seager's essay is an informative piece on what the creative act entails for Miller. Seager speaks of the genesis of several plays, of Miller's writing habits, the physical spaces in which he writes, the relationship Miller establishes with the performance texts of his plays. Helen McMahon's "Arthur Miller's Common Man: The Problem of the Realistic and the Mythic" (Spring 1972) assesses Miller's dramatic style, which she sees as a combination of realism, naturalism, and symbolism.

Daniel Walden, in "Miller's Roots and His Moral Dilemma: or, Continuity from Brooklyn to *Salesman*" (1979), reviews Miller's early years in Brooklyn and at the University of Michigan and his development as a writer. Walden sees a connective thread in Miller's career through *Death of a Salesman,* in the playwright's concern both for the middle American and for his own Jewish heritage.

Kenneth Rowe's "Shadows Cast Before" (1982) is a personal account of Rowe's professor/student relationship with Miller at the University of Michigan, where Miller did his play-writing apprenticeship. Rowe discusses *No Villain, They Too Arise,* and "The Grass Still Grows," calling them "The Abe Simon Family Trilogy." The essay is one of the few to deal with these early works, available only in typescript.

Scholarship focusing on individual plays has been as abundant as the more general essays. Most of the essays on *All My Sons* annotated here appear in Bloom's collection on that play. A few selections will suggest the pattern of that scholarship, which, like the more general scholarship on Miller, has been especially attentive to the question of genre.

Samuel A. Yorks, in "Joe Keller and His Sons" (Autumn 1959), proposes that Keller, "a typical product of a century devoted to ideological power conflicts," mirrors Miller's own personal and ideological conflicts. Though the play presents this struggle in the context of generational division, it may foreshadow Miller's own stand before the House Un-American Activities Committee, in which the playwright affirmed the principle of private dignity. Despite Miller's intentions, *All My Sons*, Yorks claims, affirms family, not state, loyalties.

In "The Living and the Dead in *All My Sons*" (1962) Arvin R. Wells argues that a reading of *All My Sons* from a purely sociological or psychological perspective leads to oversimplification. *All My Sons*, like other Miller plays, has a "density of texture" in which characters reflect social values and, at the same time, engage in an identity quest within the context of those values.

W. Arthur Boggs's "*Oedipus* and *All My Sons*" (Autumn 1961) explores connections between Miller's play and the play of Sophocles, and Richard L. Loughlin's "Tradition and Tragedy in *All My Sons*" (Feb. 1964) identifies connections between the Miller play and the Old Testament, Greek tragedy and epic, and the medieval morality play.

Barry Gross's essay, "*All My Sons* and the Larger Context" (Mar. 1975), argues that the Keller family inhabits the play so prominently and insistently that any other context is neutralized. Because of this the play fails in both content and form.

Steven R. Centola, in "Bad Faith in *All My Sons*" (1988), looks at each of the major characters in *All My Sons*, exploring ways in which complexities and contradictions in character result in bad-faith actions. Chief among the manifestations of bad faith is Joe Keller's refusal to accept responsibility. The essay, in essence, is an argument for the necessity of social commitment.

Not surprisingly, *Death of a Salesman* has received more critical attention than any other of Miller's plays, and it remains, even through more than forty years of criticism, the play for which he is most celebrated. A selection of essays from 1949 through 1987, arranged by decade, will suggest early and continuing reactions to the play as well as patterns in critics' perceptions.

One of the earliest commentaries is by John Gassner. In "Aspects of the Broadway Theatre" (Feb. 1949) he proposes that *Death of a Salesman* is not the masterpiece the reviewers claim. Its language is not memorable, its protagonist is not a believable tragic hero, and its dramatization of American values is oversimplified. Yet the play, he admits, is emotionally gripping; it connects with American life, and, for many reasons documented in the essay, is "a victory for modern realism."

Noticing the power of the play in the American theater, Ivor Brown, in "As London Sees Willy Loman" (28 Aug. 1949), compares New York and London responses to *Death of a Salesman*, attempting to explain why Americans appear to have been more deeply moved by Willy Loman than the British. The piece offers a broad sociological analysis of the two cultures.

Two commentators not accustomed to writing about the theater responded to *Death of a Salesman* as well. One was Daniel E. Schneider, a psychoanalyst, who, in "Play of Dreams" (Oct. 1949) (which became part of his *The Psychoanalyst and the Artist* [1950]), analyzes Willy's "flashbacks" as psychic projections, dramatizing the repressed. Schneider reads the play as the "dream of a younger, unpreferred son." A. Howard Fuller, then president of the Fuller Brush Company, also joined in the critical reaction to *Death of a Salesman*. In "A Salesman is Everybody" (May 1949) he defends the salesman as an appropriate peacetime representative of American society, a hero of modern tragedy.

Essays published in the 1950s concerned themselves with the question of responsibility, with the coherence of Miller's vision, with the Jewish character of the play, and, once again, with the play as social drama or tragedy, often through comparisons with other literary works.

George R. Kernodle, in "The Death of the Little Man" (1955-1956), attempts to fix responsibility for Willy's death. Unable to do so, he concludes that the play does not provide an answer; but he does urge that a balance between the psychological and the sociological should inform one's reading of the play.

William Wiegand's very sensible essay, "Arthur Miller and the Man Who Knows" (Winter 1957), examines *Death of a Salesman* in the context of Miller's earlier work and the "Values" the playwright supported. Taking his cue from the definition of "classic," which refers to a "coherent system," Wiegand searches for–and finds–coherence in Miller's dramatic vision.

George Ross's "*Death of a Salesman* in the Original" (Feb. 1951) was prompted by a Yiddish theater production of Miller's play, a production that led Ross to understand how thoroughly the American-Jewish experience informs the play. For Ross, a Jewish Willy Loman provides a lens of clarity for the professional and personal problems of the salesman.

Gordon W. Couchman places Willy Loman in the tradition of George F. Babbitt, the success-worshipping hero of Sinclair Lewis's novel. In "Arthur Miller's Tragedy of Babbitt" (Oct. 1955), he identifies connections, then notes differences in the times (1920s, 1940s) that produced the two literary works. Paul N. Siegel's "Willy Loman and King Lear" (Mar. 1956) explores connections between *Death of a Salesman* and *King Lear,* both plays about men whose catastrophes result from their failures to know themselves. Judah Bierman, James Hart, and Stanley Johnson ask whether Willy is the likely literary companion of Oedipus and Othello. Interested in Willy as tragic hero, they conclude, in "Arthur Miller: *Death of a Salesman*" (1958), that Willy, unlike his literary counterparts, has only "the weakness of his ignorance"; his unexamined life is not worth living. Yet the play insists that we ask essential questions about humanity.

Because so much criticism of *Death of a Salesman* hangs on the definition of tragedy, several scholars in the 1960s approach the play from this perspective. Remy G. Saisselin's "Is Tragic Drama Possible in the Twentieth Century?" (1960) begins and ends with this question. In between Saisselin explores changes in worldview from Aristotle's *Poetics* to Miller's *Death of a Salesman.* He concludes that tragic experience is still possible but asks whether or not the absurd has pre-empted modern tragedy.

George de Schweinitz looks to the Western tragic tradition for defining measures, then applies them to the play. In "*Death of a Salesman:* A Note on Epic and Tragedy" (Winter 1960) he examines the relationship between the tragic and the epic, which have common characteristics and are often mixed. De Schweinitz's analysis reveals that *Death of a Salesman* reflects elements of both traditional structures.

Richard J. Foster's "Confusion and Tragedy: The Failure of Miller's *Salesman*" (1961) examines the differences among Aristotle's, Miller's, and the critics' conceptions of tragedy. Foster concludes that *Death of a Salesman* fails in the matter of "intellectual content and order."

In *"Death of a Salesman*: Tragic Myth in the Modern Theater" (Sept. 1963) Esther Merle Jackson proposes that American dramatists, unable to avail themselves of native myths, have had to create new ways of interpreting reality. *Death of a Salesman,* she suggests, universalizes the "nature of human crises" in the United States.

Charlotte F. Otten argues that *Death of a Salesman* is more than a play about the American dream; it is a play that, like *Oedipus Rex,* dramatizes the quest for self-knowledge. In "Who Am I? . . . A Re-Investigation of Arthur Miller's *Death of a Salesman"* (Feb. 1963) she compares the two plays, connecting Willy and Oedipus, Linda and Jocasta, and Biff and Teiresias.

Lois Gordon's wide-ranging essay, *"Death of a Salesman:* An Appreciation" (1969), explores two opposing critical positions concerning the play, the social and the tragic. It then proposes a means of unifying them by viewing the play as a narrative poem and analyzing its total effect.

The decade also brought essays on less familiar topics. Sister M. Bettina, in "Willy Loman's Brother Ben: Tragic Insight in *Death of a Salesman"* (Feb. 1962), explores the possibility that Ben, rather than being a person external to Willy, is a projection of Willy's personality and a symbol of Willy's dream.

John V. Hagopian sees *Death of a Salesman* as a schizophrenic play, embodying the same divisions reflected in Miller's commentary about the play and the play itself. In *"Death of a Salesman"* (1962) he notices that one of the more serious problems with the play is that Biff, not Willy, should be viewed as the protagonist, for it is he who struggles most for understanding. Throughout, Hagopian suggests that Miller does not understand his own work.

In "The Right Dream in Miller's *Death of a Salesman"* (Oct./ May 1963-1964) Stephen A. Lawrence approaches the play through Happy, whom, he claims, we have condemned too quickly. Happy's pledge to carry on where Willy left off reflects not merely self-delusion but, more importantly, love–which Willy believes in and which makes the salesman attractive to an audience.

Guerin Bliquez turns to the neglected wife of Willy Loman, suggesting she plays an important role in her husband's "pathetic downfall." In "Linda's Role in *Death of a Salesman"* (Feb. 1968) Bliquez notes that, while Miller characterizes Linda as the stable force in the family, her prodding provides the play's impetus and direction and leads to Willy's doom.

One of the more refreshing essays on *Death of a Salesman* is Barry Gross's "Peddler and Pioneer in *Death of a Salesman*" (Feb. 1965), which discusses the play in the context of the American frontier tradition. Gross argues that Willy fails because he tries to wed the peddler and the pioneer, the contemporary Brooklyn salesman with the myth of his father. Barclay W. Bates pursues a similar approach, arguing that Willy's civilization—which "made the choice between Wall Street and Walden Pond"—is responsible for destroying him. In "The Lost Past in *Death of a Salesman*" (Sept. 1968) he notes that Willy, in his love for a preindustrial pastoral life, his dedication to the frontier spirit, and his unshakable sense of patriarchal responsibility, is an anachronism.

The way in which *Death of a Salesman* reflects the American success myth is the subject of Thomas E. Porter's "Acres of Diamonds: *Death of a Salesman*" (1969). Porter traces the history of the Horatio Alger myth, then reads *Death of a Salesman* in that context.

One of the less adulatory essays, critical of Miller's writing, is Joseph A. Hynes's "'Attention Must Be Paid. . . '" (Apr. 1962). Unlike other essays that register reservations about the play, Hynes concedes nothing. He notices improbabilities, sentimentalities, generalities, and inconsistencies in Miller's dramatic art, pointing out as well that the play cannot work as tragedy because Willy fails to know himself.

Brian Parker, by contrast, defends *Death of a Salesman* as a play that expresses American values and, in blurring the line between realism and expressionism, engages effectively in theatrical experiment. In "Point of View in Arthur Miller's *Death of a Salesman*" (Jan. 1966) he treats both the essays and the plays, claiming that Miller did not give himself sufficient credit for writing as well as he did.

Arthur K. Oberg identifies a distinctive speech in Miller's plays through *Incident at Vichy:* it is a New York idiom with a Jewish inflection. In "*Death of a Salesman* and Arthur Miller's Search for Style" (Fall 1967) Oberg discusses Miller's use of metaphor, cliché, and, finally, rhythm in *Death of a Salesman;* Oberg regards rhythm as its stylistic strength.

The set designer for *Death of a Salesman*, Jo Mielziner, provides further insight into the style of the play in "Designing a Play: *Death of a Salesman*" (1965). In her account of the evolution of the set, from September 1948 through the play's Philadelphia tryout in 1949, she describes her effort to conceive a design scheme that would allow shifts in scenes without the necessity of physical set changes.

The next decade began with reexaminations of the same questions. Sighle Kennedy, for example, in a May 1970 article, asks, "Who Killed the Salesman?" Character by character, Kennedy proposes candidates, dismissing each as the single cause of Willy's suicide and concluding that, though *Death of a Salesman* ends with a question, it is a question that audiences care about.

In " Hamartia in *Death of a Salesman*" (1972) B. S. Field, Jr., tackles the task of judging whether the final disaster is appropriate to the protagonist's "hamartia." Through examining the scenes in which Willy trains his sons, Field concludes that Willy, who has made moral eunuchs of his sons, has earned his miserable life and death.

Borrowing psychological terminology, Joel Shatzky, in "The 'Reactive Image' and Miller's *Death of a Salesman*" (Feb./Mar. 1973), proposes a pattern in modern drama of the "reactive image," a view of human behavior that privileges cultural determinism over self-determinism. The pattern involves the dramatization of the human being as a trapped victim, whose efforts to escape result in frustration, failure, and, in reaction, violence. The "reactive character" functions within a play that relies heavily on the family unit and that is infused with the playwright's prejudgment of moral issues. Shatzky applies the "reactive image" to *Death of a Salesman,* the representative American play.

Irving Jacobson explores the relationship between family dreams and success in the Miller play. In "Family Dreams in *Death of a Salesman*" (May 1975) he examines dreams of transformation, prominence, synthesis, and unity.

Christopher Innes, in "The Salesman on the Stage: A Study in the Social Influence of Drama" (Fall 1977), identifies three post-World War II plays about salesmen: O'Neill's *The Iceman Cometh* (1946), Miller's *Death of a Salesman,* and Jack Gelber's *The Connection* (1960). All three combine realistic and expressionistic techniques to examine American values of "popularity, prosperity, security, and success." This intelligent essay is divided between analysis of the plays and consideration of the question of whether or not drama can have a social impact. Innes notes that the plays anticipate the attitudes of the 1960s, which rejected the Protestant work ethic and sought alternative societies.

Diane Long Hoeveler proposes that *Death of a Salesman* may be read as *Everyman*. In *"Death of a Salesman* as Psychomachia" (Fall 1978) Hoeveler argues that Miller's technique resembles that of the morality play, in which the central character's psyche determines characters and events. The essay argues that all the play's characters are aspects of Willy's "splintered mind."

William Heyen tries to explain the disparity between the dramatic value of the play and its effect in the theater. In "Arthur Miller's *Death of a Salesman* and the American Dream" (1975), which Heyen characterizes as a "personal, impressionistic essay," Heyen touches on a number of aspects of the play and his responses to them, including the identification of Willy with Benjamin Franklin's America. After reviewing the confusion and ambiguities of the play, he admits once again that its force is in its impact: he is "hurt for Willy."

Miller's dramatic form is the subject of a number of essays published in the 1980s, among them Enoch Brater's "Miller's Realism and *Death of a Salesman*" (1982). Brater reminds his readers that, while Miller is known as a realist, a dozen of his early, unpublished plays experimented with other dramatic forms. He points to the failings of *All My Sons* as a realistic play, then applauds *Death of a Salesman* as a successful rendering of that form. Miller's realism, though, is concerned less with "what happens than why."

Giving the question of tragedy a different shape, William Aarnes, in "Tragic Form and the Possibility of Meaning in *Death of a Salesman*" (Dec. 1983), argues that, while Willy may not have the stuff of the tragic hero, Miller brings him to life through the ironic use of tragic form. Aarnes first documents the evidence for Willy as a pathetic man, then argues that "ritual-based actions" and myths (such as the Adonis myth) both expose the emptiness of Willy's life and affirm the "possibility of meaning beyond that life."

In "Memory and Dramatic Form in *Death of a Salesman*" (1987) Peter Szondi looks briefly at *All My Sons* as a play of imitation (of Ibsen), then focuses on structural innovations in *Death of a Salesman*. In the earlier play the past is represented as it emerges in memory: "of its own accord." The relationship between past and present in *Death of a Salesman* revises the relationship pursued by Ibsen and by Miller in *All My Sons*, removing the necessity of confining references to the past in dialogue. The concurrent representation of past and present, Szondi argues, establishes a new principle of dramatic form.

Richard T. Brucher is more interested in a thematic emphasis. In "Willy Loman and *The Soul of a New Machine*: Technology and the Common Man" (Dec. 1983) he provides an extended discussion of Tracy Kidder's and Miller's works, exploring societal attitudes toward technology and ways in which those attitudes are engaged in the play. Brucher suggests that *Death of a Salesman* provides a context for reading Kidder's *The Soul of a New Machine* (1981), which attempts "to bring computer technology into the American popular culture." The most important connection between the two works is the continuing effort to insist on personal identity within a technological world.

C. W. E. Bigsby feels that the success of *Death of a Salesman* over four decades and in many countries shows that it is more than a dramatization of the American dream. In *"Death of a Salesman:* In Memoriam" (1988) (an excerpt from volume 2 of his *A Critical Introduction to Twentieth-Century American Drama*) he suggests that the thematic centerpiece of the play consists of Willy's debate with himself and with an inhospitable world. Though Bigsby's analysis is not designed to argue a thesis, it is one of the more perceptive critical interpretations of the play.

With five collections of essays devoted to *Death of a Salesman,* the reader will have no difficulty finding material on the play, which, of course, is also discussed in the book-length studies of Miller.

The play that Miller has several times identified as his own favorite, *The Crucible,* first staged during the height of the McCarthy controversy, has also attracted considerable attention; and, despite Miller's insistence that the play is about the conflict "between a man's raw deeds and his conception of himself," most scholars have insisted on testing the play historically or plumbing its allegorical depths.

David Levin's "Salem Witchcraft in Recent Fiction and Drama" (Dec. 1955) identifies four novels and plays that engage the historical event. His discussion of *The Crucible* points to historical inaccuracies and oversimplification and to the "almost oppressively instructive" tone of the play: Miller lines up good and evil with a moral authority much like that he is criticizing.

Philip Walker approaches the play as dramatic allegory, not fully achieved. In "Arthur Miller's *The Crucible*: Tragedy or Allegory?" (Fall 1956) he notices how the play falls between categories of tragedy and allegory, fully satisfying the requirements of neither.

Robert Warshow's "The Liberal Conscience in *The Crucible*" (Mar. 1953) speaks of ways in which Americans have viewed the Salem witchcraft trials, noticing that Miller's approach is to connect the trials with American civil rights history. Warshow sees a special injustice in Miller's interpretation, since the Salem trials were not political and to try a person for witchcraft cannot be considered fair by modern standards. Miller simplifies and distorts to secure the analogy between accused witches and accused communists.

In "Miller's *The Crucible:* Which Witch is Which?" (Spring 1963) James W. Douglass questions the logic of Miller's categorizing as a witch anyone who "hands over his conscience to another." In the prosecution's terms, a witch is one who consorts with the Devil, and, in Miller's terms, the Devil is the prosecution itself. The greatest irony, in Douglass's opinion, is that Miller seems not to be aware of the presence of a Devil in *The Crucible*, even a Devil he has himself created.

The excerpt from Arthur Ganz's "The Silence of Arthur Miller" (Fall 1963) reprinted by Ferres argues that, in *The Crucible*, Miller does not define the enemy: the Salem judges might be sincere believers and authoritarians. Miller does, however, define heroism, which lies in self-knowledge.

Herbert Blau's essay on *The Crucible* (1964) (titled "The Whole Man and the Real Witch" in Corrigan and "No Play Is Deeper Than Its Witches" in Ferres), by contrast, sees the parallel between the witch trials and the communist hearings as worth making, and he sees value in Miller's exploration of "the handing over of one's conscience." Miller is not successful, however (as is, for example, Dostoyevski), in representing the psychology of his characters, including the interior dynamic of mass hallucination. (Blau also offers comments on his own production of *The Crucible*.)

Henry Popkin's essay on *The Crucible* (Nov. 1964) focuses on plot as the engine that drives *The Crucible*. He examines each act as "argument and incident," an "alternation of crises," turning on witchcraft. *The Crucible*, he concludes, is not a play of ideas but a play of action and suspense. The essay also notices that, in order to avoid the blameless hero, Miller assigns guilt of another sort to John Proctor: adultery rather than witchcraft.

Penelope Curtis sees *The Crucible* as a play which, while discrediting belief in evil forces, presents itself as a play about evil forces. In

"*The Crucible*" (1965), Curtis examines the people of Salem, the poetic compression of Miller's language, and the court scenes to understand the play as a portrait of a "possessed community."

Phillip G. Hill considers George Jean Nathan's criticism of *The Crucible,* defending the play against charges that it is at once "internal" and propagandistic and that it is ineffective in terms of character development and structure. In "*The Crucible*: A Structural View" (Dec. 1967) he addresses the last of these, analyzing the piece as a "well-made play" that works in the theater–his touchstone throughout.

In "Precision and Pseudo Precision in *The Crucible*" (Apr. 1967) Stephen Fender considers Miller's Salem community, challenging the view that the moral viewpoint of its population is consistent. Fender sees in the language of Salem's citizens the speech of a society "totally without moral referents." The characters of Miller's play, he argues, have no understanding of how moral abstractions translate into human action.

In "The Long Shadow of the Law: *The Crucible*" (1969) Thomas E. Porter reviews the history of the law in America and particularly the notion of a "fair trial." He then discusses this democratic ideal with respect to the play.

David M. Bergeron, in "Arthur Miller's *The Crucible* and Nathaniel Hawthorne: Some Parallels" (Jan. 1969), discusses the play in relation to Hawthorne's *The Scarlet Letter* (1850), comparing Proctor and Dimmesdale and establishing parallels in setting, characters, and themes. Another literary comparison is proposed by Jeanne-Marie A. Miller, in "Odets, Miller, and Communism" (June 1976), which considers kinships between *The Crucible* and Clifford Odets's *Till the Day I Die* (1935), both designed as warnings to the American people.

A fascinating supplement to the play is offered by Chadwick Hansen, who, in "The Metamorphosis of Tituba, or Why American Intellectuals Can't Tell an Indian Witch from a Negro" (Mar. 1974), examines the character of Tituba in literature and history.

Robert A. Martin's "Arthur Miller's *The Crucible*: Background and Sources" (Sept. 1977) comments on productions of *The Crucible* and provides considerable information on the Salem witchcraft trials. Martin's argument is that, while critics have tended to read the play as political allegory, it may be productively read as well as a play that defines the cultural and historical background of American society.

The goal of A. P. Foulkes's "Demystifying the Witch Hunt (Arthur Miller)" (1983) is not to offer an interpretation of *The Crucible* but to explore the "historical processes of communication" "with which, in its day, it was involved and which it attempted to challenge." Part of a study on *Literature and Propaganda*, the essay presents the play not as propaganda but as an attempt to demystify propaganda. Foulkes's analysis is lively and informed, though he is unable finally to assess the extent to which *The Crucible* succeeded in demystifying history. He does note, however, that the play is effective in providing a basis for resistance.

Walter J. Meserve, in *"The Crucible*: 'This Fool and I' " (1982), discusses the structure of *The Crucible* as contributing to the confusion between the wise and the foolish, noting that the action of the play is built on lies and confessions. The essay is a careful analysis of how this play works as a drama of the individual and of society.

E. Miller Budick's "History and Other Spectres in Arthur Miller's *The Crucible*" explores his use of history in the play. Budick argues that *The Crucible* is a complex consideration of Puritanism and McCarthyism which does more than merely promote a moral position; the play examines the ways in which historical consciousness and memory connect politics and tragedy. *The Crucible* reinforces the recognition that it is difficult to distinguish between spectres and witches, between the subjective and the objective.

Though *A View from the Bridge*, in both its one-act and two-act forms, was, of course, reviewed, the play has still not received the scholarly attention it deserves—as James J. Martine points out in his *Critical Essays on Arthur Miller*. The discussions in the full-length studies of Miller might be represented by Carson's treatment of the play (1987): he compares the two versions and, measuring them against Miller's aesthetics, examines the playwright's attempt to turn the one-act version into a more effective tragedy.

One of the more thorough essays on the play is by Arthur D. Epstein, who offers a close critical analysis. In "A Look at *A View from the Bridge*" (Spring 1965) Epstein describes the two-act version of *A View from the Bridge* and discusses its framing device, its characters, the concepts of tragedy and inevitability, and Rodolpho's singing of "Paper Doll" as it relates to the play's homosexual and incestuous suggestions.

The play received further attention in 1973 when Albert Rothenberg and Eugene D. Shapiro brought a special perspective to their comparison of two plays in "The Defense of Psychoanalysis in Literature: *Long Day's Journey into Night* and *A View from the Bridge.*" Another literary comparison came from Steven R. Centola, in "Compromise as Bad Faith: Arthur Miller's *A View from the Bridge* and William Inge's *Come Back, Little Sheba*" (Autumn 1986).

J. L. Styan, always interested in the theatrical life of a play, asks "Why *A View from the Bridge* Went Down Well in London: The Story of a Revision" (1982), offering a synthesis of Miller's comments on *A View from the Bridge,* textual and performance details, and audience response to assess the success of the revised version of the play in Peter Brook's London production. He concludes that "when Miller displays dramatic insight beyond mere literacy, he is irresistible."

A Memory of Two Mondays, produced in a double bill with *A View from the Bridge,* has been dismissed by many as a thin, even trivial effort. Though not much criticism on the play exists beyond the reviews, it is included in several of the full-length studies. Benjamin Nelson's "*A Memory of Two Mondays:* Remembrance and Reflection in Arthur Miller," a section from his 1970 book, treats the drama as a memory play, comparing it with Tennessee Williams's *The Glass Menagerie* (1945) and noticing its nonrealistic details.

June Schlueter's 1987 assessment of the play is respectful, even admiring. She sees in the warehouse world of "endless receiving and shipping, of tedium, of waiting, and of returning the next day to live through the routine again" connections in situation, tone, and style with Beckett's *Waiting for Godot* (1952)–and an achievement in dramatic form.

Reviews of *After the Fall,* staged eight years after *A View from the Bridge* and marking Miller's return to the commercial stage, spend much time rebuking Miller for having so shamelessly exposed his personal life on stage. Despite Miller's characterization of such a claim as "gossip," evaluation of the play, and particularly of Maggie, almost invariably looked for likenesses to Miller and Marilyn Monroe. Scholars also made the connections, though they were generally more temperate in doing so.

Leonard Moss, for example, in "Biographical and Literary Allusion in *After the Fall*" (Mar. 1966), prefers to examine Miller's propensity, throughout the canon, for "autoplagiarism," which produces not specific autobiographical allusions but recurring motifs and characters. Moss's position is that the strength of *After the Fall* is in its personal flavor. Its weakness, he proposes, is the assignment of narration to Quentin, which prevents the drama from speaking for itself.

Edward Murray agrees with Epstein's identification of the play's fault. In "Point of View in *After the Fall*" (Dec. 1966) he criticizes the play's point of view as static and repetitious, an invitation to the playwright to oversimplify and overconceptualize.

After the Fall provided scholars with the occasion to compare the earlier Miller with the later Miller and to reassess his playwriting career. C. W. E. Bigsby, for example, in "The Fall and After: Arthur Miller's Confession" (Sept. 1967), sees Quentin as an alternative version of Willy Loman, who, having met success, now must honestly assess his values.

Gerald Weales, in "Arthur Miller: Man and His Image" (Fall 1962), concludes that both *After the Fall* and *Incident at Vichy* are inferior to Miller's early work since they sacrifice action and character to argument. Weales suggests that Miller's commitment to philosophical themes has led him to make statements rather than dramas. Peter Buitenhuis's title, "Arthur Miller: The Fall from the Bridge" (Spring/Summer 1967), suggests a similar disappointment. Weales goes on, however, to propose that, when examined in terms of the search for identity, the two recent plays are consistent and continuous with the earlier canon. Allan Lewis's title, "Arthur Miller— Return to the Self " (1970), implies a similar continuity, and Clinton W. Trowbridge, in "Arthur Miller: Between Pathos and Tragedy" (Dec. 1967), implicitly suggests this connection as well, by pursuing, once again, the genre question, as does Paul T. Nolan, by renewing the comparison with Williams, in "Two Memory Plays: *The Glass Menagerie* and *After the Fall*" (1966).

An especially hospitable assessment is Allen J. Koppenhaver's "*The Fall* and After: Albert Camus and Arthur Miller" (Sept. 1966), which, like Moss's essay of the same year, pursues the connection between *After the Fall* and Camus's *The Fall* (1956). Koppenhaver praises Miller's play for its humanistic content and its theatrical form.

Though the 1970s brought diminished interest in the play, several articles explore particular aspects of it: Rolf K. Högel discusses the concept of time in "The Manipulation of Time in Miller's *After the Fall* " (1974); Irving Jacobson traces historical and literary allusions in "Christ, Pygmalion, and Hitler in *After the Fall*" (Aug. 1974); and John D. Engle treats "The Metaphor of Law in *After the Fall*" (1979).

Albert Wertheim, in "Arthur Miller: *After the Fall* and After" (1981), analyzes *After the Fall* as a "pilgrimage of modern life." The free-form set and the "dramatized interior monologue" allows the juxtaposition of a variety of moments in Quentin's mental life: a "triumph of Miller's technique." Wertheim considers subsequent plays as well, including *Incident at Vichy*, *The Price*, and, more briefly, *The Creation of the World and Other Business*. In all, he notes, Miller deals with "insight and responsibility," set against the Nazi concentration camps or the Fall.

Writing from the perspective of 1982, Stephen S. Stanton, in "Pessimism in *After the Fall*," suggests that Miller's new, pessimistic philosophy of life is expressed in this play. Stanton surveys criticism on the play and attempts to correct misconceptions. He examines the play from the perspectives of structure, language and speech, characterization, and theme.

In "The Monomyth and Arthur Miller's *After the Fall*" (1986), Centola looks for "universal" material in *After the Fall*, twenty years after critics refused to allow the play to speak to anything but Miller's private life. Using Joseph Campbell's concept of the "monomyth," he examines the movement of the play in relation to that myth's structural organization, concluding that *After the Fall* is successful in transforming the personal into the symbolic.

Richard Schechner and Theodore Hoffman's interview with Elia Kazan, "Look, There's the American Theatre" (1964), provides valuable insights into the production of *After the Fall*, as do Nancy and Richard Meyer's "Setting the Stage for Lincoln Center" (Jan. 1964) and "*After the Fall*: A View from the Director's Notebook" (1965).

Similarly, Harold Clurman's "Director's Notes: *Incident at Vichy*" (Summer 1965) offers an anatomy of the ANTA-Washington Square Theater production of that play, including early impressions and notes, characterizations, physical movements, and business.

Though *Incident at Vichy*, a play in which Jews are systematically rounded up for identification in Nazi-occupied France, brought far less critical attention than *After the Fall*–a comment that may be made of all of Miller's subsequent work–two essays in particular suggest the direction of criticism. In "Arthur Miller's *Incident at Vichy*: A Sartrean Interpretation" (Mar. 1975) Lawrence D. Lowenthal proposes that Miller's play dramatizes Jean-Paul Sartre's *Anti-Semite and Jew* (1946) and provides an example of the French philosopher's definition of the "theater of situation." Lowenthal discusses moral position as well as dramatic form. Leslie Epstein, in

"The Unhappiness of Arthur Miller" (Spring 1965) assaults Miller for the lack of understanding of the historical situation and for a failure of dramatic courage.

Three assessments of *The Price* suggest the scholarly reaction to that 1968 play. C. W. E. Bigsby, in "What Price Arthur Miller? An Analysis of *The Price*" (1970), offers a critical reading, connecting it with other Miller plays and with the work of other dramatists, including Peter Weiss. Bigsby assesses *The Price* as a "sharp improvement over his last two plays," noting that the dialogue is not pretentious (as in *After the Fall*), the manipulation not simpleminded (as in *Incident at Vichy*).

Ralph Willett also evaluates *The Price* in the context of Miller's other plays–and reevaluates his own assessment of Miller as a social playwright. In "A Note on Arthur Miller's *The Price*" (1971) Willett traces Miller's persistent concern with the individual within the family unit. He concludes that Miller is a playwright of "romantic individualism."

Gerald Weales offers a reading of *The Price* that proposes that the play relies on the audience's willingness to admit "that there may be efficacy in conversation." In "All About Talk: Arthur Miller's *The Price*" (Winter 1972) he explores his own fascination with the play, which is "the way that theme emerges in a work in which talk is both tool and subject."

Two essays on Miller's adaptation of *An Enemy of the People* (1951)–David Bronson's "*An Enemy of the People*: A Key to Arthur Miller's Art and Ethics" (Winter 1968-1969) and Einar Haugen's "Ibsen as Fellow Traveler: Arthur Miller's Adaptation of *An Enemy of the People*" (Autumn 1979)–accomplish different aims. Haugen records and evaluates Miller's deviations from Ibsen, commending Miller for his effort to restore Ibsen's relevance but stopping short of applauding the playwright's dramatic achievement. Bronson compares "master" and "disciple" with respect to the handling of dramatic elements and the task of "truth-seeking."

Miller's only comedy, *The Creation of the World and Other Business*, and the musical version, *Up from Paradise*, were not well received in New York. One of the few critical essays to appear on the play, aside from discussions in full-length studies of Miller, is Centola's "What Price Freedom? The Fall Revisited: Arthur Miller's *The Creation of the World and Other Business*" (June 1985). Centola's concern is with Miller's persistent interest in the Fall, expressed through a number of theatrical styles. For that reason, and because this is Miller's only comedy, Centola thinks the play is worth studying. His essay notices ways in which Miller reinterprets the story of Adam and Eve in order to insist that life does go on after the Fall.

The Archbishop's Ceiling has, similarly, gone virtually unnoticed by the academic community. June Schlueter, in "Power Play: Arthur Miller's *The Archbishop's Ceiling*" (Winter/Summer 1986-1987), discusses *The Archbishop's Ceiling* as one of Miller's most complex excursions into the interplay of truth and fiction. Under an Eastern European archbishop's ceiling, which may or may not conceal microphones, Miller's fictional writers become involved in a power struggle that may be read as the playwright's apology for art.

In fact, all of Miller's recent works—*The American Clock*, *Elegy for a Lady*, *Some Kind of Love Story*, and *Danger: Memory!* (Comprising *I Can't Remember Anything* and *Clara*)—have yet to receive extended critical attention. The Schlueter/Flanagan book, published in 1987, offers coverage of all the plays through that date.

Nearly fifty years after Miller's apprenticeship at the University of Michigan, his position as elder statesman of the American theater is secure. While critical opinion has already reflected the tendency for each decade to value and revalue its dramatic literature, few would diminish the major contribution Miller has made to American drama. The growing commercialization of the American theater has made it more difficult even for a playwright of Miller's stature to "succeed" on Broadway, and the elder Miller seems increasingly to devalue such success. But even in his seventies, he remains professionally (and politically) active, eager to contribute more dramatic works to his already substantial canon. In June of 1986, for example, Miller contributed a new script, *Thief*, for a benefit reading (as did David Mamet) at the Westside Arts Theater in New York. And the *New York Times* of 22 November 1988 revealed that Miller was the screenwriter for *Everybody Wins*, an original film script, to be directed by Karel Reisz, with Debra Winger and Nick Nolte in the leading roles.

Clearly Miller's new works will provide research opportunities for scholars, joining the work of the last decade to which attention still needs to be paid. But scholars interested in the early work should not, despite volumes of existing criticism, feel that these plays have been exhausted. For nearly all such scholarship has focused, with varying emphases, on conventional elements of drama such as character, structure, and theme, informed by biographical, theatrical, social, and generic considerations. As such, the full-length studies, individually and collectively, and all of the scholarly articles offer a valuable assessment of the work of a man who may well be remembered as the most important postwar playwright of this century.

But one would hope that the next generation of Miller scholarship will bring special critical perspectives to his work, shifting the emphasis from what the academic community now calls "interpretation" to what it calls "criticism." A collection that moves in that direction, forthcoming from Fairleigh Dickinson University Press, is *Feminist Rereadings of Modern American Drama*, edited by June Schlueter, which includes essays on "The Exchange of Women and Male Homosocial Desire in *Death of a Salesman* and *Another Part of the Forest*," by Gayle Austin; "Women and the American Dream in *Death of a Salesman*," by Kay Stanton; "Paper Dolls: Melodrama and Sexual Politics in Arthur Miller's Early Plays," by Jeffrey D. Mason; and "Betrayal and Blessedness–Explorations of Feminine Power in *The Crucible, A View from the Bridge*, and *After the Fall*," by Iska Alter. There are other perspectives, of course, that could bring new and exciting insights to Miller's plays.

Marsha Norman

(1947-)

Linda L. Hubert
Agnes Scott College

PRIMARY BIBLIOGRAPHY

Books

Getting Out. Garden City, N.Y.: Doubleday, 1979. Play.
Third and Oak: The Laundromat. New York: Dramatists Play Service, 1980. Play.
'night, Mother. New York: Hill & Wang, 1983. Play.
Third and Oak: The Pool Hall. New York: Dramatists Play Service, 1985. Play.
The Fortune Teller. New York: Random House, 1987. Novel.
The Holdup. New York: Dramatists Play Service, 1987. Play.
Four Plays: Getting Out, Third and Oak, The Holdup, Traveler in the Dark. New York: Theatre Communications Group, 1988.

Premiere Productions

Getting Out. Louisville, Ky., Actors Theatre of Louisville, Nov. 1977.
Third and Oak. Louisville, Ky., Actors Theatre of Louisville, Apr. 1978.
Holidays, ten playlets written by Norman, Lanford Wilson, Megan Terry, Oliver Halley, Douglas Turner Ward, Israel Horowitz, Tom Eyen, John Guare, Preston Jones, and Ray Araaha. Louisville, Ky., Actors Theatre of Louisville, Jan. 1979.
Circus Valentine. Louisville, Ky., Actors Theatre of Louisville, Feb. 1979.
'night, Mother. Cambridge, Mass., American Repertory Theater, Dec. 1982.
The Holdup. San Francisco, American Conservatory Theater, Apr. 1983.
Traveler in the Dark. Cambridge, Mass., American Repertory Theater, Feb. 1984.

Sarah and Abraham. Louisville, Ky., Actors Theatre of Louisville, June 1988.

Selected Other
It's the Willingness. "Visions," PBS, 1978. Teleplay.
Third and Oak. "Earplay," NPR, May 1979. Radio play.
In Trouble at Fifteen. NBC, Jan. 1980. Teleplay.
"Happy Birthday, Marsha . . . or, Why You Should Love Your Birthday Instead of Fear It," *Vogue,* 173 (Sept. 1983), 364. Essay.
"Sam Shepard–The Incredible Man," *Vogue,* 174 (Feb. 1984), 356-358. Essay.
"Articles of Faith, A Conversation with Lillian Hellman," *American Theatre,* 1 (May 1984), 11-15. Interview.
"Lillian Hellman's Gift to a Young Playwright," *New York Times,* 26 Aug. 1984, section 2, pp. 1, 7. Essay.
"Becoming a Writer Was Success Enough," *New York Times Book Review,* 25 Nov. 1984, p. 14. Book review of *Saroyan,* by Lawrence Lee and Barry Gifford.
"Life without Excellence Doesn't Go Anywhere, It just Wanders Around," *Ms.,* 13 (Jan. 1985), 84-117. Essay.
The Laundromat. HBO, 8, 16 Apr. 1985. Teleplay.
"Ten Golden Rules for Playwrights," *Writer,* 98 (Sept. 1985), 13, 45.
'night, Mother. Universal, 1986. Screenplay.
"TV Families," *Ms.,* 16 (July/Aug. 1987), 38, 40. Essay.
"The Role of a Lifetime," *Agnes Scott Alumnae Magazine* (Fall 1987), 9-11. Graduation address.

SECONDARY BIBLIOGRAPHY

Bibliography
Woolfe, Irmgard. "Marsha Norman." In *American Playwrights Since 1945: A Guide to Scholarship and Criticism,* ed. Philip C. Kolin. Westport, Conn.: Greenwood, forthcoming 1989.

Interviews
Betsko, Kathleen, and Rachel Koenig. "Marsha Norman." In their *Interviews with Contemporary American Women Playwrights.* New York: Beech Tree, 1987, 324-342.
Brustein, Robert. "Conversations with Marsha Norman," *Dramatists Guild Quarterly,* 21 (Autumn 1984), 9-21.

Cleage, Pearl. Interview with Marsha Norman, *Goodlife* (Nov. 1984), 13-15.

Cohen, Ron. "Marsha Norman's Journey into Night," *W.,* 22-29 Apr. 1983, p. 18.

"Five Dramatists Discuss the Value of Criticism," *Dramatists Guild Quarterly,* 21 (Spring 1984), 11-25. With Robert Anderson, A. R. Guerney, Jr., James Kirkwood, Norman, and Peter Stone.

Franklin, Rebecca. "Playwright Marsha Norman is Not a Sweet Little Thing," *Birmingham News,* 9 Sept. 1979, p. E3.

Gussow, Mel. "Women Playwrights, New Voices in the Theater," *New York Times Magazine,* 1 May 1983, pp. 22, 26, 30, 34, 38, 40.

Harmetz, Aljean. "Faith and Charity Make a Movie of a Hit Play," *New York Times,* 10 Aug. 1986, section 2, pp. 1, 21.

Klemesrud, Judy. "She Had Her Own 'Getting Out' to Do," *New York Times,* 27 May 1979, section 2, pp. 4, 19.

Lawson, Carol. "Broadway: Marsha Norman Has Two New Works Ready for Staging," *New York Times,* 11 Feb. 1983, p. C2.

Lawson. "Broadway: Two-Woman Play About Suicide Is Coming in March," *New York Times,* 18 Feb. 1983, p. C2.

Malitz, Nancy. "Marsha Norman Plays It Her Way," *USA Today,* 5 May 1983, p. D5.

Mootz, William. " 'Getting Out' Getting Ready for Playing Broadway," *Louisville Courier-Journal,* 8 Oct. 1978, p. B1.

Mootz. " ' 'night, Mother' is 'Hello, Broadway' for Marsha Norman," *Louisville Courier-Journal,* 2 Apr. 1983, p. H1.

Mootz. " ' 'night, Mother' Wins Pulitzer Prize for Marsha Norman," *Louisville Courier-Journal,* 19 Apr. 1983, p. A1.

Mootz. "Norman: Keeping Fame Under Control," *Louisville Courier-Journal,* 10 June 1979, p. C1.

Robertson, Nan. " ' 'night, Mother' Affects Its 2 Stars," *New York Times,* 13 Apr. 1983, p. C21. Interview with Kathy Bates and Anne Pitoniak.

Sanoff, Alvin P. "Tarot Cards Catch the Eye of a Master Writer," *U.S. News & World Report,* 102 (8 June 1987), 78.

Saunders, Dudley. "Dann Byck, Marsha Norman Calm Before Opening Night," *Louisville Times,* 31 Mar. 1983, p. B1.

Saunders. "Marsha Norman," *Louisville Times,* 8 Aug. 1978, p. C1.

Savran, David. "Marsha Norman." In his *In Their Own Words: Contemporary American Playwrights.* New York: Theatre Communications Group, 1988, 178-192.

Smith, Helen. " 'Getting Out' Marsha Norman Springs the Traps," *Atlanta Journal and Constitution*, 28 Mar. 1981, p. C1.

Span, Paula. "Marsha Norman's Stages of Memory," *Washington Post*, 30 Apr. 1983, p. C1.

Stahl, Linda. "Marsha Norman, The Storyteller," *Louisville Courier-Journal Magazine*, 20 May 1984, p. 4.

Stone, Elizabeth. "Playwright Marsha Norman: An Optimist Writes About Suicide, Confinement and Despair," *Ms*, 12 (July 1983), 56-59.

Stout, Kate. "Writing for the 'Least of Our Brethren,' " *Saturday Review* (Sept./Oct. 1984), 29-33.

"30 and Loving It," *Harper's Bazaar*, 116 (July 1983), 100-104.

Tremblay, Anne. "Altman Makes a Cable Film Abroad," *New York Times*, 20 Jan. 1985, section 2, p. 26.

Wallack, Allan. "The Acrid Dialogue of Imprisonment," *Newsday*, 8 May 1983.

Wohlfert-Wihlborg, Lee. "Broadway Hit about Suicide is a Source of Joy for Pulitzer-Winning Marsha Norman," *People*, 19 (16 May 1983), 55-56.

Critical Studies: Major Reviews, Articles, and Book Sections

Asahina, Robert. "The Real Stuff," *Hudson Review*, 37 (Spring 1984), 99-104.

Boyum, Joy Gould. "Movies: *'night, Mother*," Glamour, 84 (Oct. 1986), 26.

Breslauer, Jan. "A Theater of One's Own: *Feminist Theatre* by Helene Keyssar," *Theater* (Winter 1985), 89-91.

Brustein, Robert. "Don't Read This Review!," *New Republic*, 188 (2 May 1983), 25-27.

Canby, Vincent. "Film: 'Mother' and 'Otello' Play Down to Us," *New York Times*, 21 Sept. 1986, section 2, pp. 19, 26.

Chinoy, Helen Krich, and Linda Walsh Jenkins. *Women in American Theatre*. New York: Crown, 1981.

Clurman, Harold. "Theatre," *Nation*, 227 (Nov. 1978), 557.

Corliss, Richard. "Blasted Garden: *Traveler in the Dark*," *Time* (27 Feb. 1984), 101.

Denby, David. "Movies: 'Fighting Back,' " *New York*, 19 (22 Sept. 1986), 159.

Denby. "Stranger in a Strange Land: A Moviegoer at the Theater," *Atlantic Monthly* (Jan. 1985), 37-45.

DeVries, Hillary. "Marsha Norman's 'Traveler' Stumbles into a Pedantic Wilderness," *Christian Science Monitor*, 22 Feb. 1984, p. B19.

DeVries. "Once Loved, Once Spurned, A Playwright Now Returns," *Christian Science Monitor*, 8 June 1988, pp. B1, B32.

Dorsey, Tom. "Marsha Norman's Script Helped Make 'Skag' Look Like a Winner," *Louisville Courier-Journal*, 24 Jan. 1980, p. C2.

Drake, Sylvia. " 'Getting Out' in L.A.: a Flinty, Spirit-Stirring Play," *Louisville Times*, 17 Feb. 1978.

Eder, Richard. "Louisville Festival Offers 6 New Plays," *New York Times*, 16 Nov. 1977, p. C21.

Fox, Terry Curtis. "Early Work," *Village Voice*, 6 Nov. 1978, pp. 127, 129.

Gilman, Richard. "Theater," *Nation*, 236 (7 May 1983), 585-586.

Glover, William. "New Yorker Hails Louisvillian's Play," *Louisville Courier-Journal*, 24 Oct. 1978, p. B10.

Hart, Lynda. "Doing Time: Hunger for Power in Marsha Norman's Plays," *Southern Quarterly*, 25 (Spring 1987), 67-79.

Hempel, Amy. "My Mother the Clairvoyant," *New York Times Book Review*, 24 May 1987, p. 10.

Hughes, Catharine. "The Pulitzer Puzzle," *America*, 148 (7 May 1983), 361.

Kakutani, Michiko. "Books of the Times," *New York Times*, 13 May 1987, p. C23.

Kalem, T. E. "Seared Soul: *Getting Out* by Marsha Norman," *Time*, 113 (28 May 1979), 80.

Kauffmann, Stanley. "All New, All American," *New Republic*, 181 (7 July 1979), 25.

Kauffmann. "More Trick than Tragedy," *Saturday Review* (Sept./Oct. 1983), 47-48.

Kauffmann. "Stanley Kauffmann on Films, High Pressure and Low," *New Republic*, 195 (13 Oct. 1986), 26.

Kerr, Walter. "The Joy of the Unexpected," *New York Times*, 10 Apr. 1983, section 2, p. 5.

Kerr. "A Pinch of Variety Never Hurts," *New York Times*, 3 June 1979, section 2, pp. 5, 24.

Keyssar, Helene. "Success and Its Limits." In her *Feminist Theatre: An Introduction to Plays of Contemporary British and American Women*. London: Macmillan, 1984; New York: Grove, 1985.

Kramer, Mimi. "My Mother, the Psychic," *Vogue*, 177 (May 1987), 199.

Kroll, Jack. "Before and After Meet in a Girl," *Newsweek*, 93 (28 May 1979), 103.

Kroll. "End Game," *Newsweek*, 101 (3 Jan. 1983), 41-42.

Kroll. "A Modern Crisis of Faith," *Newsweek*, 103 (27 Feb. 1984), 76.

"The Laundromat," *Variety*, 10 Apr. 1985, p. 63.

Leonard, John. "In Brief: *The Laundromat*," *New York*, 18 (15 Apr. 1985), 101.

Lieberman, Susan. " *'night, Mother*," Theatre Crafts, 19 (May 1985), 22, 46, 48.

Mall, Janice. *"Fortune Teller* by Marsha Norman," *Los Angeles Times Book Review*, 21 June 1987, p. 4.

Maslin, Janet. "Film: Sissy Spacek in ' *'night, Mother*,' " *New York Times*, 12 Sept. 1986, p. C7.

McDonnell, Lisa J. "Diverse Similitude: Beth Henley and Marsha Norman," *Southern Quarterly*, 25 (Spring 1987), 95-104.

Metzger, Deena. *"Getting Out* by Marsha Norman (Mark Taper Forum)," *Ms.*, 6 (June 1978), 26-28.

Mootz, William. " 'Getting Out'–as New York Critics Saw It," *Louisville Courier-Journal*, 5 Nov. 1978, p. H14.

Murray, Timothy. "Patriarchal Panopticism, or The Seduction of a Bad Joke: *Getting Out* in Theory," *Theatre Journal*, 35 (Oct. 1983), 376-388.

" *'night, Mother*, A Shot Premise?," *Los Angeles*, 31 (May 1986), 52.

Nightingale, Benedict. "Or Not to Be," *New Statesman*, 109 (15 Mar. 1985), 36.

O'Connor, John J. "Burnett and Madigan Star in 'Laundromat,' " *New York Times*, 4 Apr. 1985, p. C18.

O'Hara, Jane. "Saturday Night, Alive, or Dead," *Macleans*, 97 (5 Nov. 1984), 52.

Oliver, Edith. "News from Off Off," *New Yorker*, 54 (6 Nov. 1978), 152-153.

Raidy, W. A. "Getting Out After Time," *Plays and Players*, 26 (July 1979), 36-37.

Rich, Frank. "Theater: ' *'night, Mother*' at Harvard," *New York Times*, 12 Jan. 1983, p. C15.

Rich. "Theater: Suicide Talk in ' *'night, Mother*,' " *New York Times*, 1 Apr. 1983, p. C3.

Saunders, Dudley. " 'Circus Valentine' Too Often Strained, Artificial," *Louisville Times*, Feb. 1979.

Saunders. " 'Getting Out' in New York," *Louisville Times*, 24 Oct. 1978, p. C1.

Simon, John. "Free, Bright, and 31," *New York*, 11 (13 Nov. 1978), 152.

Simon. "Journeys Into Night," *New York*, 16 (11 Apr. 1983), 55-58.

Simon. "Out of the Crucible," *New York*, 12 (28 May 1979), 98.

Simon. "Theater Chronicle: Kopit, Norman, and Shepard," *Hudson Review*, 32 (1979), 77-88.

Spencer, Jenny S. "Norman's *'night, Mother:* Psycho-drama of Female Identity," *Modern Drama*, 30 (Sept. 1987), 364-375.

Stone, Laurie. "Say Good Night, Jessie," *Ms.*, 15 (Oct. 1986), 20.

Weales, Gerald. "*Getting Out*: A New American Playwright," *Commonweal*, 106 (12 Oct. 1979), 559-560.

Weales. "Really 'Going On,'" *Commonweal*, 110 (17 June 1983), 370-371.

BIBLIOGRAPHICAL ESSAY

Bibliography

The bibliography in this volume and the one prepared by Irmgard Woolfe (to be published in early 1989) are the only guides to works by and about Marsha Norman. The bibliography here offered makes no claims to be definitive; perhaps with the passage of time scholars may be better able to sift through the extensive media coverage inspired by Norman's sudden metamorphosis from playwright to Pulitzer Prize winner (in 1983, for *'night, Mother*). Scholarly work on Norman is just beginning and will undoubtedly increase in scope and significance. At present brief newspaper notices must supply the bulk of critical opinion.

Interviews

Although no formal biography of Marsha Norman has been published, information about her is readily available. Her brief career has generated a substantial number of not-so-substantial newspaper and magazine interviews that reveal details of her personal and creative lives and provide forums for statements of her artistic convictions.

Several early interviews document the process of writing and producing Norman's plays. Judy Klemesrud's piece for the *New York Times* of 27 May 1979 performs that service for *Getting Out;* Paula Span (30 Apr. 1983) and Elizabeth Stone (July 1983) do the same for *'night, Mother*. The success of *'night, Mother* stimulated more probing interviews as well. The substantial article/interview by Mel

Gussow, "Women Playwrights, New Voices in the Theater" (1 May 1983), features Norman in an account that recognizes the growing influence of women playwrights (such as Beth Henley and Megan Terry) and producers in the 1970s and 1980s. The article inspired controversy among some feminist writers and critics, who apparently resented the selection of the "conservative" Norman as the apotheosis of women playwrights.

Norman is indeed often questioned about her attitude toward "women's theater" (sometimes defined as being composed of the group of activist playwrights who in 1972 founded the Women's Theater Council, which was, in Gussow's words, "designed to discover and encourage new women playwrights"). Norman typically notes her sympathies for feminist objectives, her impatience with organizations, the apolitical character of her own plays, and her dislike of being obliged to conform to any program. She told Robert Brustein (Autumn 1984) that she hopes her plays inspire other women to write: "I feel that my responsibility to my work *is* a political responsibility. When I do my work well, that's how I can help." She delights in the fact that *'night, Mother* "came along at the exact moment when a play about two women, written by a woman, could be seen as 'a human play.' " She is grateful that the appeal of the play transcends sexual distinction and that its values are human as well as female: "But it proves that what happens to women is important, that the mother-daughter relationship is as important as father-son." Her qualified expression of commitment to women's issues leads some feminists to view her as "the enemy"; she tells, Pearl Cleage (Nov. 1984) of her despair over the lukewarm reception she received when she spoke at the Women's Center at Stanford University. But her professional enthusiasm is sustained in large measure because she sees a healthy future for women in drama. She told Kathleen Betsko and Rachel Koenig (1987) of her satisfaction at the recent appearance of "significant women dramatists in significant numbers," which was "a real reflection of a change in women's attitudes towards themselves. It is a sudden understanding that they can be, and indeed are, the central characters in their own lives."

A spring 1984 discussion with fellow playwrights Robert Anderson, A. R. Guerney, Jr., James Kirkwood, and Peter Stone gave Norman the opportunity to voice her views on a persistent topic in her interviews–the shortcomings of theatrical criticism. (In the first lines of the Betsko/Koenig piece she states, "There aren't many good writers writing about the theater. That's the problem. Very few of our critics can write. And yet most people get their information about the theater from the critics, not from the theater itself.") In the discussion with the other playwrights and an audience of critics, Norman laments the limitations of practical criticism and posits an educational role for critics, urging them to do more than pronounce glib verdicts on plays. As she phrased it in the Brustein interview, "We don't need critics stamping out plays as though they were forest fires or dangerous diseases. Word of mouth is good for stamping out plays." She would have critics write about the world of theater, helping young playwrights understand "what works and what doesn't": "Ideally, one should be able to learn to write a play by reading criticism as one is growing up." Audiences should also be helped to appreciate the distinction between the written text and the production, perhaps even by the selling of play texts in theaters.

Linda Stahl's feature, "Marsha Norman, The Storyteller" (20 May 1984), is a lengthy, illustrated profile of Norman's childhood and personal life. The piece also records Norman's pained but resilient response to the "mostly savage" reviews of *Traveler in the Dark.*

The conversation with Brustein, besides revealing Norman's attitudes on women's issues and on the role of criticism in the promotion of drama, provides useful commentary by the playwright on her works. She considers her primary literary gift to be her capacity to listen, and her chief artistic objective is "to make confusion clear." She speaks about her artistic failures, referring to *Circus Valentine* and *The Holdup*, which taught her how to "close the set"–that is, to keep the characters onstage–a technique she uses more successfully in *'night, Mother.* She also speaks of two things she admires and appreciates: the American Repertory Theatre, which provided the supportive environment for the realization of *'night, Mother;* and Sam Shepard's work. The interview with Cleage underscores Norman's respect for Shepard.

The most comprehensive and most recent Norman interview is that published by Betsko and Koenig. Norman's responses in the Betsko/Koenig interview seem polished and well rehearsed; she has worked through many of her comments in previous pieces. The scope of topics is considerable: life in New York City; childhood experiences in Louisville that provided for the development of her writerly preference for solitude; personal familial relationships, perhaps responsible for her persistent mother-daughter themes of possession and control; questions of her artistic individuality in tension with the political obligations urged by so many of her colleagues in the profession; her commitment to prescriptive rules of play writing ("I'm convinced that there are absolutely unbreakable rules in the theater, and that it doesn't matter how good you are, you can't break them"); and analysis of her particular plays. Disagreeing with those who find the character Jessie's suicide defeatist, Norman argues that *'night, Mother* is "a play of nearly total triumph." Puzzled by the criticism of *Traveler in the Dark* as "too clever.... Too smart," Norman acknowledges that her risky ambition to create "a sympathetic smart person for the American stage" resulted in a talkativeness unwelcome in contemporary American theater.

Critical Studies: Major Reviews, Articles, and Book Sections

The premiere production of Marsha Norman's first play, *Getting Out*, was reviewed most notably by New York critic Richard Eder (16 Nov. 1977). Eder admired the "gritty, authentic feeling of the author for her character," but he was troubled by his perception that this split character—the "wildcat child" Arlie and the subdued and mindful woman Arlene that she became—never coalesced. He also disliked the sense in the play of "case histories" being dramatized. Apparently, the first New York production in 1978 changed his mind: still objecting to the taint of psychological textbook in its theme, he nonetheless described the language of the play as "pure, troubling life" (quoted in William Mootz, 5 Nov. 1978).

Playwright Deena Metzger (June 1978), who covered the Los Angeles production of *Getting Out* at the Mark Taper Forum, was very approving of the production, identifying a theme that would be developed in later criticism: the "essential care that women offer each other, a theme rarely if ever depicted on the stage." Sylvia Drake (17 Feb. 1978) commented that Los Angeles audiences had previously been fed large helpings of drama about prison life—but that *Getting Out* was the first to confront effectively the problems of release. She was astonished by Norman's knowledge of prisons and wondered if Norman's work with disturbed children (at Kentucky Central State Hospital in the early 1970s) gave her access to the interiors of imprisoned existence and helped her develop the tough and gutsy language she employed so convincingly in the play.

In the context of a brief plot summary, Edith Oliver (6 Nov. 1978) found the Phoenix Theatre production of *Getting Out* to be extremely effective: she was particularly responsive to the conclusion of the play and was convinced, unlike Eder, that the dual character of Arlie and Arlene indeed coalesced. In contrast, William Glover's brief and cautious review (24 Oct. 1978) found "more to admire than fault"; but he saw problems with the play's "inconclusive" ending.

More New York and national critics were interested in the play once it reached New York's Theatre de Lys in 1979. Walter Kerr (3 June 1979) was sympathetic to the characters, but he found the Job-like sufferings it so relentlessly heaped upon its double central character unconvincing and intolerable. T. E. Kalem, in *Time* (28 May 1979), commended the dramatic vitality of the play; he admired the text and the fine acting, but seemed uncomfortable with his approval: "the play is partly an index of an indecipherable malaise in the society from which it springs. . . . [and] what sort of society is it that derives comfort from putting rouge on a corpse?" But Jack Kroll, in *Newsweek* (28 May 1979), found both the play and the audience's enthusiasm for it anything but depressing: "*Getting Out* is exhilarating with the energy of truth, of compassion, of empathy, of a sincerity that becomes luminous and exciting." He noted with admiration Norman's "powerful writing."

Gerald Weales, in *Commonweal* (12 Oct. 1979), described *Getting Out* as a flawed but promising first play. His problem was with the secondary characters, such as the mother, who "come close to caricature," and with the tedious exposition of several Arlie scenes. He approved of the theatrical counterpointing of the Arlie/Arlene character and admired the effective paralleling of speeches in scenes that "indicate dramatically that what was best in Arlie–her vitality, her drive–has not been killed, cannot be killed if Arlene is to survive." Oddly, Stanley Kauffmann (7 July 1979) hated the "stale theatrical device" of doubling, which simply concealed what neither Marsha Norman nor the "raving critics" noticed: "there is no connection between the two people." His caustic objections indicted the play's director, Jon Jory, as well.

John Simon wrote enthusiastically of both New York productions. He applauded (13 Nov. 1978) the "spiny, realistic play about not exactly prepossessing people"; and by commending Norman's writing, he provided a counter to Kalem's objection that the play was too gloomy: "It is written with such a brisk, fresh, penetrating touch that sordid, brooding things take on the glow of honesty, humanity, very nearly poetry." Simon extended his admiration for the play in a substantial essay in the *Hudson Review*, honoring it as one of the three best plays of the 1979 season. The 1979 piece provided a fine analysis of specific dramatic strategems, which Simon went so far as to describe as "brilliant." His third published comment on the play (28 May 1979) lamented the ineffectuality of the play's producers, who failed to move the play to Broadway in a timely fashion. His regard for the play itself, however, was confirmed. He noted that its language was its "greatest asset": "coarse-grained, unvarnished, often hateful, sometimes fumbling for tenderness, funny yet beyond laughter . . . heartbreaking yet a stranger to tears. And always frighteningly true."

Countless presentations on Marsha Norman's work have been made during the last few years at scores of academic conferences; the initial published lecture is Timothy Murray's October 1983 piece. The title, "Patriarchal Panopticism, or The Seduction of a Bad Joke: *Getting Out* in Theory," well portrays the sense of intellectual congestion conveyed by his demandingly theoretical analysis. Far too intricate to summarize adequately or accurately here, this demanding article provides provocative probing into what the underlying structures (and strictures) of this play reveal about its characters, its author, its audience, and American culture. With reference to John Simon's review accolades, he writes, "But what, I want to ask, lies behind such a desire to turn a victim of child abuse and rape into a glowing, poetic figure? What constitutes the legitimate self that we as the theatre community might want for Arlene? And how might *Getting Out* portray not only still another victimized woman, but also a viciously uncompromising macho theatre? How might *Getting Out* reflect a theatre whose search for new profit-making images delays our admission of the public crimes committed by our playwright fathers, our own beholding, and our quest for unproblematic and idealist retorts to real, although violent, challenges of our patriarchal ideology and economy? Finally, is theatricality thus condemned? Or, in ironic contrast, does *Getting Out* produce a theatrical substitute for such a sordid world of displaced institutional responsibility?" Murray's interest in the sociological constraints revealed in theatricality leads him to ponder issues of power and authority: the play is about "the power of interpretive communities." The struggle of the female characters with their respect for the various voices of "the man" prompts Murray to analyze the various "bad" jokes of the play. These jokes and the audience laughter they provoke provide ironic evidence of Arlene's essentially problematic reintegration into the community—we are dealing with "laughing struggle[s] for power."

Reviews of Norman's second play, *Third and Oak,* were generally approving. The play has reached a national audience through its radio and television productions, although it has sparked only limited critical attention. The production in Louisville of both one-acts comprising the play under the above title was pronounced by local critics a success; John Leonard (15 Apr. 1985) raved about the Robert Altman-directed television version, titled *The Laundromat,* but John J. O'Connor (4 Apr. 1985) described it as "little more than a well-acted curiosity," valuable, primarily, because it raised the standards of the Home Box Office network. Differences between the texts of the play–the published version subtitled *The Laundromat* omits the character of Shooter, while the version subtitled *The Pool Hall* restores the character from the original stage production–will no doubt ultimately stir some scholarly attention.

Norman's first failure, *Circus Valentine,* inspired more circumspect commentary from Norman herself than from anyone else. She draws on the experience of this failure in an Agnes Scott College videotape lecture, "Time and Learning How to Fall" (30 Apr. 1984).

Norman's *The Holdup,* written before *'night, Mother,* has been produced only in regional theaters. National theater critics have been uninterested in it to this point, but the 1987 publication of the text–and a recent increase in regional productions–will, no doubt, encourage increased critical scrutiny.

The prizes that Norman's *'night, Mother* garnered are as heavy as those heaped on *Getting Out*–heavier, considering the weight of the Pulitzer. Nonetheless, reviews are divided along the critical lines first established in discussions of *Getting Out.* Simon (11 Apr. 1983) continued to praise Norman's work, Weales (17 June 1983) was circumspect and restrained, and Kauffmann (Sept./Oct 1983) again proved to be chief among hostile reviewers.

Kauffmann declared the play to be "more trick than tragedy"– "fundamentally a stunt." The fact that the character Jessie announces her decision to commit suicide is the crux of his objection: what demented delight can she possibly take in putting her mother (and presumably the audience) through ninety minutes of torment? Kauffmann is thus offended by what he sees as Norman's lack of comprehension of her character: "That grim, twisted Jessie is latent in the script, of course, or she couldn't be perceived; but Norman, deliberately or unwittingly, has chosen to present Jessie as a rustic female samurai who speaks implicitly to the residual nobility in us all."

Robert Asahina (Spring 1984) joined Kauffmann in deploring the play as gimmicky and dependent on "idiot realism" (the stage clock keeps actual time, for instance). His main criticism was that the play was boring. Richard Gilman (7 May 1983), though not entirely condemning, resisted the results of the critical "hyperbole machine" in praising the play. His reaction to Jessie's death was muted: "When the shot sounded . . . I wasn't startled, dismayed or much moved; it was all *sort of* sad, *sort of* lugubrious." He deplored the fact that Jessie did not seem to be free to make her decision: she was too encumbered by troubles. David Denby (Jan. 1985), like Kauffmann, declared the play–or at least its conclusion–to be a stunt. Jessie's escape from her "lower-middle-class kitsch prison" could be managed only by pulling the trigger–and Denby determined, like Gilman, that a more intense, more profound horror would have resulted if there were convincing evidence of tempting freedoms rejected by Jessie. As is, the play seemed "vulgarly mechanical."

Frank Rich (1 Apr. 1983) and Jack Kroll (3 Jan. 1983) set the stage for Norman's Broadway success with their glowing accounts of the American Repertory Theatre production of *'night, Mother* in Cambridge, Massachusetts. Kroll spoke, for example, of the play as "a benign explosion . . . showering us with truth, compassion and uncompromising honesty." Rich's second rave review seems impressively tuned to Norman's personal concept of her work. He focused on the differences of perception that characterized Jessie's sense of deprivation and Thelma's contentment with respect to the life they share, and he concluded that the play was "not a message play about the choice to commit suicide. It's about contemporary life and what gives it–or fails to give it–value." He understood that one result of the play was to underscore the fact that hope is concomitant with understanding–and that Norman's contribution to the theater, by bringing dignity to "forgotten and tragic American lives," was poignant and significant.

The enthusiasm of the Rich review is matched by the admittedly biased comments of American Repertory Theatre director Robert Brustein (2 May 1983). His discussion of the management of time in the play is valuable, and his insights into the motives and strategies of the two characters are keen. His error may be in linking Norman with the likes of Eugene O'Neill (his way of defining the importance he feels that the young playwright represents). The connection has been considered ludicrous by reviewers such as Gilman.

Curiously, the reviews of subsequent productions of *'night, Mother* in Los Angeles and London were not enthusiastic. An English comment by Benedict Nightingale (15 Mar. 1985) is of particular interest because it proposed that American critics tend to approve plays that "see relationships in isolation"; the British, however, insist on a context of social comment. Nightingale cited one unintentionally humorous review that characterized Jessie, who speaks of the failure of her interest in such things as rice pudding, as "a frustrated consumer, the spoiled American dependent on her material goodies." He accused Norman of suggesting in the play that "such trumpery deprivation justified the great sin of self-slaughter."

Politics of a slightly different order are the subject of Helene Keyssar's essay in her *Feminist Theatre* (1984). She provides carefully reasoned criteria by which to identify feminist playwrights. The primary notion is that new feminist playwrights go beyond recognition to transformation; that is, their characters must push past the limits of traditional discovery and self-recognition to effect change and re-ordering in the world around them. In a fine discussion of *Getting Out* (noting, incidentally, the problematic disappearance of Arlene's mother from a scene), Keyssar explains the promise of the play in terms of the friendship offered by Ruby, "the woman with few skills or resources who can survive and offer support to another with recompense." She does not see *'night, Mother* as hopeful or helpful to the promotion of societal change; she responds to Norman's inference that her play should be valued for its exploration of "secret worlds" with the observation that such "knowledge is not sufficient, and off-stage suicide does not transform society. It denies it."

A surprising counter to the reading Keyssar suggests comes from Jenny S. Spencer in "Norman's *'night, Mother*: Psycho-drama of Female Identity" (Sept. 1987). Convinced by her own experience that the nature of responses to the play depends on the sex of the playgoer, she dismisses universal themes, which she stipulates exist in the play as secondary ("of death and desire, of human dignity and human pain, of hope and existential despair"), and concentrates instead on how the play affects the viewer in gender-specific ways. The impact of the play on women viewers is potentially "more terrifying," she explains, because women identify with both mother and daughter. The male viewer takes a more objective stance outside those roles; the play may be "over-distanced for men (producing indifference)"; it is assuredly "under-distanced for women (producing pain)." She notes that the play's political effect depends on the theatrical event–how the work is performed, discussions that follow, response to reviews, and the like. Understanding that this political impact is necessarily an essential concern with feminist practice, Spencer thus implicitly works to redeem the play from those who fault it, though she acknowledges the risks of presenting a "mirror to reality in which women mis-recognize themselves in quite traditionally negative ways." Her article may not convince the fanatically fixed, but it represents both beautiful argument and faithful scholarship.

Lynda Hart's essay, "Doing Time: Hunger for Power in Marsha Norman's Plays" (Spring 1987), is a splendid treatment of feminist themes and images. Hunger–its management and its connection to motherhood–becomes a metaphor for the independence for which Norman's characters struggle in both *Getting Out* and *'night, Mother:* both plays probe "the complex interconnections . among women's searches for autonomy, their hunger, both literal and figurative, and the problems that arise from mother/daughter bonding." Hart's conclusion provides a telling question for "questing women": "can we rejoice in and grow strong through our hunger, or must we become, ourselves, the world's repast?"

One final short essay seems partly inspired by the Keyssar article described above. Lisa J. McDonnell compares the two female Pulitzer Prize-winning playwrights of the 1980s with a few deft generalizations in her essay "Diverse Similitude: Beth Henley and Marsha Norman" (Spring 1987). She remarks on the playwrights' shared gifts for storytelling (and helpfully identifies the various "stories" in their plays) and links that gift predictably to their common southern heritage. The observations about narrative technique at least provoke a reminder that Norman has earnestly avoided any marked southernness in her plays: *'night, Mother* is the ultimate expression of anonymity of place she cultivates in disregard of southern sensibility. That the teleplay of *The Laundromat* was shot on a soundstage in Paris is just one delicious irony–suggesting the universal dependability of dinginess, perhaps.

"Southern gothic humor" is the second of the shared characteristics that sharpen the distinctions between these playwrights. Henley's humor is "wild and outrageous, Norman's dry and sardonic." A third emphasis, on family connections, establishes their differences as well. Henley depicts families as useful nuisances, ultimately "sources of strength"; "Norman's tendency is to underscore the theme of 'getting out,' moving beyond familial bonds (even loving ones), to establish one's own place as a human being."

Reviews of *Traveler in the Dark*, Marsha Norman's 1984 "failure," complain about its excessive intellectualism, its unappealing protagonist, and the inappropriate acting that marked the Cambridge premiere production. Nonetheless, scholarly work on this play will surely commence now that the text has been published. There is, as Norman says, as much to learn from failure as success.

Norman's play *Sarah and Abraham* (1988), which marked her cautious return to the theater after a four-year hiatus, was presented by the Actors Theatre of Louisville in a nonreviewable production. She apparently was unwilling to risk critical hostility.

There has not been much critical excitement to date provoked by Norman's significant foray away from play writing–her 1987 novel, *The Fortune Teller*. The novel is, as reviews generally note, entertaining but artistically uncertain. Comparisons to *'night, Mother* are inevitable, particularly because of the book's handling of time. "Unity" here is one day; chapters are identified by time of day. The novel–perhaps *because* it is flawed–demands some attention.

Although feminist approaches to Norman's work clearly dominate the present critical scene, Norman's own remarks in interviews may suggest the course of future productive scrutiny. She and Helene Keyssar independently puzzle over definitions of realism; surely some good work as relates to her plays is forthcoming on that large topic. Scholars may also prove to be interested in the reactions of foreign audiences, who have different cultural attitudes toward suicide, to *'night, Mother*. Norman's film version of *'night, Mother*, largely a box-office and critical disappointment, should be studied, though its textual and other sorts of departures from the play are slight. Certainly criticism that acknowledges the formal structures (musical strategies, for example) and the classical bases of Norman's plays would be appropriate confirmation of the playwright's own values. Most of all, of course, the future of Norman criticism will depend on her future–what she writes, where it plays, who will care. Norman is an enormous talent, and still young. Certainly her bibliography will swell dependably from year to year.

David Rabe

(1940-)

Rodney Simard
California State University, San Bernardino

PRIMARY BIBLIOGRAPHY

Books

The Basic Training of Pavlo Hummel. New York: French, 1972; London: French, 1972. Play.

Sticks and Bones. New York: French, 1972; London: French, 1973. Revised edition, New York: French, 1979. Play.

The Basic Training of Pavlo Hummel and Sticks and Bones: Two Plays by David Rabe. New York: Viking, 1973. Includes an introduction by Rabe.

In the Boom Boom Room. New York: Knopf, 1975; London: French, 1975. Revised edition, New York: Grove, 1986. Play.

The Orphan. New York: French, 1975. Play.

Streamers. New York: Knopf, 1977. Play.

Hurlyburly. New York: Grove, 1985. Play.

Goose and Tomtom. New York: Grove, 1986. Play.

Premiere Productions

Sticks and Bones. Villanova, Pa., Varsey Theatre, Villanova University, 10 Feb. 1969.

The Basic Training of Pavlo Hummel. New York, Estelle R. Newman Theatre, 20 May 1971.

The Orphan. New York, Florence Sutro Anspacher Theatre, 30 Mar. 1973.

Boom Boom Room. New York, Vivian Beaumont Theatre, 8 Nov. 1973.

Burning (reading). New York, Martinson Hall, 13 Apr. 1974.

In the Boom Boom Room. New York, Florence Sutro Anspacher Theatre, 20 Nov. 1974.

Streamers. New Haven, Conn., Long Wharf Theatre, 30 Jan. 1976.

289

Goose and Tomtom. New York, Public Theatre, 6 May 1982.
Hurlyburly. Chicago, Goodman Theater, 2 Apr. 1984.

Selected Other
"Each Night You Spit in My Face," *New York Times,* 18 Mar. 1973, section 2, pp. 3, 20. Open letter to Oleg Yefremov and Andrzej Wajda of the Sovremennik Theater in Moscow, in which Rabe expresses his disapproval of an unauthorized Russian production of *Sticks and Bones.*
I'm Dancing as Fast as I Can. Paramount, 1982. Screenplay.

SECONDARY BIBLIOGRAPHY

Bibliographies
King, Kimball. "David Rabe." In his *Ten Modern American Playwrights: An Annotated Bibliography.* New York: Garland, 1982, 187-196. Primary and secondary.
Kolin, Philip C. *David Rabe: A Stage History and A Primary and Secondary Bibliography.* New York & London: Garland, 1988.

Interviews
Berkvist, Robert. "How Nichols and Rabe Shaped 'Streamers,'" *New York Times,* 25 Apr. 1976, section 2, pp. 1, 12. With Mike Nichols.
Berkvist. " 'If You Kill Somebody,' " *New York Times,* 12 Dec. 1971, section 2, pp. 3, 22.
" 'Boom Boom Room' and the Role of Women," *New York Times,* 24 Nov. 1973, p. 22. With Madeline Kahn.
Brockway, Jody. "Defining the Event for Myself," *After Dark* (Aug. 1972), 56-57.
Freedman, Samuel G. "Rabe and the War at Home," *New York Times,* 28 June 1984, p. C13.
Freedman, and Michaela Williams. "A Conversation Between Neil Simon and David Rabe: The Craft of the Playwright," *New York Times Magazine,* 26 May 1985, pp. 36-38, 52, 56-57, 60-62.
Gill, Brendan. "Talk of the Town: Rabe," *New Yorker,* 47 (20 Nov. 1971), 48-49.
Gussow, Mel. "Rabe Is Compelled 'to Keep Trying,' " *New York Times,* 12 May 1976, p. 34.
Gussow. "Second David Rabe Play to Join 'Pavlo Hummel' at Public Theater,' " *New York Times,* 3 Nov. 1971, p. 43.

Critical Studies: Major Reviews, Articles, and Book Sections

Adler, Thomas P. " 'The Blind Leading the Blind': Rabe's *Sticks and Bones* and Shakespeare's *King Lear*," *Papers on Language and Literature*, 15 (Spring 1979), 203-206.

Asahina, Robert. "The Basic Training of American Playwrights: Theater and the Vietnam War," *Theater*, 9 (Spring 1978), 30-37.

Bernstein, Samuel J. "*Sticks and Bones* by David Rabe." In his *The Strands Entwined: A New Direction in American Drama*. Boston: Northeastern University Press, 1980, 15-36.

Bigsby, C. W. E. "The Theatre of Commitment." In his *A Critical Introduction to Twentieth-Century American Drama*, volume 3: *Beyond Broadway*. Cambridge: Cambridge University Press, 1985, 291-333.

Brown, Janet. "*In the Boom Boom Room*." In her *Feminist Drama: Definition & Critical Analysis*. Metuchen, N.J. & London: Scarecrow, 1979, 37-55.

Brustein, Robert. "The Crack in the Chimney: Reflections on Contemporary American Playwriting," *Theater*, 9 (Spring 1978), 21-29.

Brustein. "Drama in the Age of Einstein," *New York Times*, 7 Aug. 1977, section 2, pp. 1, 22.

Brustein. "Theatre in the Age of Einstein: The Crack in the Chimney." In his *Critical Moments: Reflections on Theatre & Society 1973-1979*. New York: Random House, 1980, 107-123.

Cohn, Ruby. "Narrower Straits: Ribman, Rabe, Guare, Mamet." In her *New American Dramatists: 1960-1980*. New York: Grove, 1982, 27-46.

Cooper, Pamela. "David Rabe's *Sticks and Bones*: The Adventures of Ozzie and Harriet," *Modern Drama*, 29 (Dec. 1986), 613-625.

Corry, John. "Rabe Disavows the 'Goose' He Thought He Had Closed," *New York Times*, 8 May 1982, p. 17.

Fleckenstein, Joan S. Reviews of *Streamers* by David Rabe, *The Estate* by Ray Aranha, and *The Runner Stumbles* by Milan Stitt, *Educational Theatre Journal*, 28 (Oct. 1976), 408-410.

Gussow, Mel. "A Rich Crop of Writing Talent Brings New Life to the American Theatre," *New York Times*, 21 Aug. 1977, section 2, pp. 1, 17.

Gussow. "Theater: 'Goose and Tomtom' Opens," *New York Times*, 8 May 1982, p. 17.

Harrell, Barbara. "American Self-Image in David Rabe's Vietnam Trilogy," *Journal of American Culture*, 4 (1981), 95-107.

Hermann, William. "When the Battle's Lost and Won: David Rabe." In his *Understanding Contemporary American Drama.* Columbia: University of South Carolina Press, 1987, 81-124.

Hertzbach, Janet S. "The Plays of David Rabe: A World of Streamers." In *Essays in Contemporary American Drama*, ed. Hedwig Bock and Albert Wertheim. Munich: Hueber, 1981, 173-186.

Hoffman, Ted. Introduction to *Famous American Plays of the 1970s*, ed. Hoffman. New York: Dell, 1981, 9-27.

Homan, Richard L. "American Playwrights in the 1970s: Rabe and Shepard," *Critical Quarterly*, 24 (Spring 1982), 73-82.

Hughes, Catharine. "David Rabe." In her *American Playwrights, 1945-1975.* London: Pitman, 1976, 81-87.

Hughes. "New York," *Plays and Players*, 18 (Aug. 1971), 54-55, 85.

Hughes. "Part Two: The Theatre Goes to War." In her *Plays, Politics, and Polemics.* New York: Drama Book Specialists, 1973, 67-124.

Kauffmann, Stanley. "Sunshine Boys," *New Republic*, 168 (26 May 1973), 22, 33-34.

Kellman, Barnet. "David Rabe's 'The Orphan': A Peripatetic Work in Progress," *Theatre Quarterly*, 7 (Spring 1977), 72-93.

Kerr, Walter. "David Rabe's 'House' Is Not a Home," *New York Times*, 2 May 1976, section 2, p. 5.

Kerr. "He Wonders Who He Is–So Do We," *New York Times*, 30 May 1971, section 2, p. 3.

Kerr. "When Does Gore Get Gratuitous?," *New York Times*, 22 Feb. 1976, section 2, pp. 1, 7.

Kohler, Klaus. "Das 'Underground Theatre.'" In *Studien zum amerikanischen Drama nach den zweiten Weltkrieg*, by Eberhard Bruning, Kohler, and Bernhard Scheeler. Berlin: Rütten & Loening, 1977, 178-213.

Little, Stuart W. "*Sticks and Bones.*" In his *Enter Joseph Papp: In Search of a New American Theater.* New York: Coward, McCann & Geoghegan, 1974, 139-170.

Marranca, Bonnie. "David Rabe's Viet Nam Trilogy," *Canadian Theatre Review*, 14 (Spring 1977), 86-92.

Phillips, Jerrold A. "Descent Into the Abyss: The Plays of David Rabe," *West Virginia University Philological Papers*, 25 (Feb. 1979), 108-117.

Prochaska, Bob. "David Rabe," *Dramatics* (May/June 1977), 18.

Reston, James, Jr. Introduction to his *Coming to Terms: American*

Plays & the Vietnam War. New York: Theatre Communications Group, 1985, vii-xii.

Rosen, Carol. "Acting Tough in the Barracks." In her *Plays of Impasse: Contemporary Drama Set in Confining Institutions.* Princeton: Princeton University Press, 1983, 207-259.

Simard, Rodney. "David Rabe: Subjective Realist." In his *Postmodern Drama: Contemporary Playwrights in America and Britain.* Lanham, Md., New York & London: University Press of America/ American Theater Association, 1984, 117-129.

Simon, John. "Domestic Infernos," *New York,* 4 (22 Nov. 1971), 76.

Stothard, Peter. "Sticks and Bones/Streamers," *Plays and Players,* 25 (Apr. 1978), 24-25.

Weales, Gerald. "The Stage: Rampant Rabe," *Commonweal,* 96 (10 Mar. 1972), 14-15.

Werner, Craig. "Primal Screams and Nonsense Rhymes: David Rabe's Revolt," *Educational Theatre Journal,* 30 (Dec. 1978), 517-529.

BIBLIOGRAPHICAL ESSAY

Bibliographies

The bibliography in Kimball King's *Ten Modern American Playwrights* (1982) is the most useful early listing of works by and about David Rabe. King cites Rabe's primary publications through 1981 and gives a substantial annotated list of criticism and reviews. But Philip C. Kolin's *David Rabe: A Stage History and A Primary and Secondary Bibliography* (1988) supersedes King and all other early bibliographical work on Rabe. Kolin's book includes a brief biographical essay on the playwright, featuring material on his Vietnam service in 1965-1967; an account of his tenure as a staff writer for the *New Haven Register* magazine, the *Sunday Pictorial,* in 1969-1970; a lengthy stage history of Rabe's dramatic work that provides plot summaries, bibliographical information, and production information; and comprehensive primary and secondary bibliographies. The primary bibliography lists published and unpublished plays, novels, short stories, poems, prefaces and afterwords, newspaper articles, and reviews by Rabe; the secondary bibliography lists bibliographies, biographical entries, and critical studies on Rabe's work as a whole and on individual plays. The critical overviews are accompanied by extensive annotations. Kolin concludes with a helpful name and place index.

Interviews

Several interviews with David Rabe have been published, and while all are interesting and provide a range of insights, none is totally satisfactory. Perhaps because Rabe was catapulted to success so quickly and at such a young age, the early interviews treat him more like a celebrity than a serious artist; he is quoted, largely conversationally, rather than questioned, and no one challenges his observations or tries to present them as organic statements. Most interviewers are content to prompt him to biographical remarks and summaries of his plays, partially, no doubt, because of Rabe's experience in Vietnam, but partially also because the phenomenon of an Iowa-born, exceptionally young, Off-Broadway dramatic success was so novel.

Typical of early interviews is Robert Berkvist's " 'If You Kill Somebody' " (12 Dec. 1971), most important for Rabe's comment that he chose to write about the Vietnam War as a way of "defining the event for myself." Brendan Gill's "Talk of the Town: Rabe" interview (20 Nov. 1971) is a rambling collection of impressionistic and abstract observations, establishing what would become one of Rabe's favorite topics: the visceral, not intellectual, nature of his plays. He tells Gill that he is rather more the medium than the shaper of his drama, that his plays "come from deep inside." Mel Gussow (3 Nov. 1971) interviewed Rabe a few weeks earlier than did Gill, sounding a typical, early note of hyperbolic praise by quoting Rabe's producer, Joseph Papp, who asserts, "He [Rabe] is the most important writer we've ever had. . . . There's a great link between him and O'Neill. . . ."

By 1973 Rabe was giving more substantial interviews. In " 'Boom Boom Room' and the Role of Women," conducted by the cultural-news department of the *New York Times* (24 Nov. 1973), Rabe is paired with Madeline Kahn, who played Chrissy in the premiere production of Rabe's play *Boom Boom Room*, and together they address the early perception that the play was misogynistic. Rabe expresses his belief that the play's setting–a cheap Philadelphia nightclub–has distinct connections with Vietnam: both, he thinks, are places of violence and victimization. Of the protagonist, Chrissy, he says, "I think she comes out with some of the most incredible ideas I've written, in my mind, in any of the plays." On several occasions Rabe has pointed to the revised version of the play, *In the Boom Boom Room*, as the best of his works. As Rodney Simard notes in *Postmodern Drama* (1984), "He considers the play the touchstone of his canon to date, one that examines the dehumanization of the individual in a context independent of the metaphor of the war."

Rabe strikes this same note in Mel Gussow's "Rabe Is Compelled 'to Keep Trying' " (12 May 1976), asserting that *In the Boom Boom Room* "illuminates the real nature of the other plays." Unfortunately, he goes no farther and instead falls back on a discussion of his writing process, outlining how he begins with the ending and writes the play backward: "The end becomes the metaphor" that governs the drama. Robert Berkvist (25 Apr. 1976) jointly interviewed Rabe and director Mike Nichols, presenting some atypically substantial information. Noting that fear, defined as the need to bond to someone, is the impetus that propels Rabe's *Streamers*, Nichols says that the play is "about people trying to recruit others into their own reality." Rabe adds that it is "about people misunderstanding each other."

More recently, in Samuel G. Freedman's "Rabe and the War at Home" (28 June 1984), Rabe talks about the autobiographical dimension of his play *Hurlyburly* and how his plays happen through him and are beyond his control. Freedman makes two engaging points, declaring that one of Rabe's constant concerns is "the difficulty of manhood" and that one of his recurrent themes is "the loss of a moral center of life."

Rabe continues to discuss *Hurlyburly* in a more recent interview, jointly granted with Neil Simon, moderated by Freedman and Michaela Williams (26 May 1985). Rabe states that *Hurlyburly* proves that he is not just a playwright of Vietnam. He also briefly discusses the sense of competition between film and the theater. As so often before, he talks about his process of creation and the role of the unconscious, in rather abstract terms. Taken together, the collected interviews do only a little to satisfy the need for a Rabe biography.

Critical Studies: Major Reviews, Articles, and Book Sections
David Rabe has both suffered from and enjoyed the same sort of critical attention that was visited nearly a generation earlier on Edward Albee; both were quickly successful and crowned by critics as saviors of the theater, playwrights who would assume Eugene O'Neill's mantle and revitalize American drama. Also like Albee, Rabe's critical status declined after initial expectations failed to

come to fruition. When he first came to public attention in 1971, partially caught in the media net surrounding producer Joseph Papp, he had two plays being produced simultaneously by the New York Shakespeare Festival's Public Theater. An apparently boundless creative inspiration was initially confirmed in the next five years, as Rabe's *The Orphan, In the Boom Boom Room,* and *Streamers* quickly followed in premiere. Then the theatrical world waited in anticipation. Rabe's 1976 triumph, *Streamers,* was followed by an ill-fated production of *Goose and Tomtom* in 1982; the playwright disavowed the production and for the first time made disparaging public remarks about Papp, his mentor, for whom he had had nothing but praise in the past. To many critics the failure was evidence that Rabe's promise was false, that he was a brief phenomenon who could write well about only one subject, Vietnam. Concerning the production of *Hurlyburly* in 1984, critics were more moderate, willing to judge Rabe on the plays he had written rather than on expectations of what he should write. But his quick start has doubtlessly affected subsequent opinion.

Rabe's 1971 "double debut" captured a wide range of attention: critics and scholars quickly tried to take his measure. The Vietnam issue was painful and ongoing, and *The Basic Training of Pavlo Hummel* and *Sticks and Bones* spoke to the times. Rabe was one of the first playwrights who tried to transmute the Vietnam experience into art, and his presentations matched the enormity of the subject. Among the first to announce that Rabe was "very likely the best playwright yet spawned by the Vietnam war" was Catharine Hughes, in "New York" (Aug. 1971), her review of *The Basic Training of Pavlo Hummel.* She praises the play's ambitiousness and its multiple and sometimes conflicting levels of action and, like many others, excuses its weaknesses as the flaws of an initial effort. The confusions in the play are seen as evidence of Rabe's fecundity. Walter Kerr, in "He Wonders Who He Is–So Do We" (30 May 1971), strikes the same note. Kerr writes that "the play is like a current of air on a very hot night that teases us and then goes away. It lacks a discovery," and that "the odds are promising, but they seem to be without ends." This puzzled but admiring review is cast in the kind of abstract and pyrotechnic language that many used in attempting to pinpoint ideas concerning Rabe's innovative early effort.

By 1972 the critical tone concerning Rabe became more concrete and forceful, more assured in pronouncement. In "The Stage: Rampant Rabe" (10 Mar. 1972) Gerald Weales claims that

"David Rabe is plainly a phenomenon, . . . the most successful serious playwright to turn up in the American theater in recent years." He calls *Sticks and Bones* "a play which, for all its imperfections, speaks directly and movingly to its own time." Not all critics were so accepting of its flaws, however; Stanley Kauffmann led a counterreaction in "Sunshine Boys" (26 May 1973), his review of *The Orphan*, the first play Rabe staged after his 1971 successes. Kauffmann attacks the then-current trend toward critical inflation: "A new playwright of small talent is hailed by them ['professional yea-saying' critics] as a big talent, gets an inflated reputation, and then, with future work, gets deflated." Further, "That process—very sad for the writer—is beginning to happen yet once more in the case of David Rabe." He observes that the negative reaction to *The Orphan* follows a pattern (similarly manifested in Albee's career); he thinks the new play "is not much different from or worse than the work they praised; and now they have to know it." Citing a list of contemporary playwrights who had produced engaging first works, he predicts "that none of the above will write anything that is even up to the level of what he has been acclaimed for."

But in an essay in her *Plays, Politics, and Polemics* (1973) Catharine Hughes is undaunted in her enthusiasm for Rabe's work. Her criticism is among the first to examine Rabe's overall literary accomplishment seriously. Stating that *The Basic Training of Pavlo Hummel* is "one of the best, if not the best play to come out of America's Vietnam nightmare," she finds virtue in its ambiguities and complexities. Rabe, she observes, "realizes that horror and comedy, like tragedy and comedy, are seldom far apart," and that his concern with "the *why* of how men act" is more important than "one-dimensional point scoring." He "refuses to grind the axe, to present pure victims and pure monsters." Ambiguity in Rabe's drama is not a weakness, but rather a fidelity to the murkiness of contemporary existence.

In spite of the critical and popular failure of *The Orphan*, Rabe continued to be seen, along with Sam Shepard, as one of the most promising American playwrights to enter the scene since Albee. The fact that his career got an early boost under the guidance of noteworthy impresario Joseph Papp became a source of some interest. In a chapter of his *Enter Joseph Papp: In Search of a New American Theater* (1974), Stuart W. Little outlines Rabe's association with Papp during the period *Sticks and Bones* was being produced. He illuminates aspects of the controversy surrounding the broadcast of the play on television, which created a censor's debate that did much to keep Rabe in the media spotlight. Little quotes Papp on Rabe: "He's our greatest playwright today. He says things indirectly. He doesn't come right out and say it." Hughes similarly confirms Papp's and her own earlier assessments in a section of her *American Playwrights, 1945-1975* (1976), stating that Rabe is "the most significant American playwright to appear since Albee." Continuing to be one of his most firm and vocal advocates, and directly countering Kauffmann's prediction that his future work would be mediocre, she boldly asserts that "he is far too talented to go down on the records only as a prisoner of Vietnam and it requires little critical prescience to suggest that he will not."

Those who had begun to doubt Rabe's staying power were delighted with his success with *Streamers*, which seemed to belie the weaknesses of *The Orphan*. Still considered by many to be his best effort, the play was received with admiration and relief—and with caution. In her review in *Educational Theatre Journal* (Oct. 1976), Joan S. Fleckenstein takes a moderate position, observing that "*Streamers* is a slowly developing but increasingly interesting mood piece, making a sensitive statement about loneliness and camaraderie in the midst of the fear of dying." Fleckenstein goes so far as to consider *Streamers* the final installment in a Rabe war trilogy, replacing *The Orphan*. A dissenting voice regarding *Streamers* is Peter Stothard's. In his review of British productions of *Streamers* and *Sticks and Bones* (Apr. 1978), he submits that the later play "is neither the long-delayed conclusion to the trilogy nor indeed any part of it at all." Calling it "banality spiked with violence," he is, nonetheless, admiring of the earlier work, which he calls "a near-masterpiece of moral theatre."

Stothard was not alone in voicing objection to stage violence in his distaste for *Streamers*. Discussing the issue in "When Does Gore Get Gratuitous?" (22 Feb. 1976), Walter Kerr muses that many playgoers walked out on *Streamers* because the violence in the play tried to affect but only alienated. Kerr considers Rabe a legitimate and serious writer but not an effective theatrical "designer."

Like many first reviewers of the play, Kerr also puzzles over the issue of sexuality. Subsequent studies have tentatively addressed the issue, but without vigor or resolution; a thorough study of the treatment of homosexuality in Rabe's work has yet to appear. One school of thought views the homosexuality in *Streamers* metaphorically, akin to the sexual disjunctions and conflicts among the heterosexuals in *In the Boom Boom Room*; another school hesitantly suggests that gayness is the central concern of *Streamers*.

After *Streamers* moved to New York later in 1976, Kerr again reviewed the play. In "David Rabe's 'House' Is Not a Home" (2 May 1976) he softens his earlier position concerning the play's graphic violence. He probes beneath the surface, discussing war as a dramatic metaphor and voicing what has now become standard critical opinion: Rabe's dramatic world is bounded and defined by despair. Kerr's observations paved the way for more analytical approaches to Rabe's plays. In December 1978 Craig Werner published "Primal Screams and Nonsense Rhymes: David Rabe's Revolt," still one of the most useful critical essays on his canon. Observing that "a society composed of isolated individuals risks chaos," Werner contends that, in his Vietnam trilogy, Rabe "confronts the radical disunities of the American experience and attempts to forge a means of expression to overcome alienation." Developing Kerr's earlier observations, he discusses Vietnam as a symbol of aimless action and the United States Army as a metaphor of impersonal, dehumanizing systems.

Calling *The Basic Training of Pavlo Hummel* "a classic work of the American imagination," Werner asserts that one of its most vivid observations concerns the effect of the Vietnam episode on language. Werner suggests that Rabe uses language as an evasive tool, as a way of escaping, or ignoring, the isolated, fragmented quality of human existence. In *The Basic Training of Pavlo Hummel, Sticks and Bones*, and *Streamers* the characters *are* the language they use, more so than is usually inherent in the dramatic medium. Werner concludes that Rabe's vision, in spite of his expressed wish for greater human order through his use of language, "remains basically pessimistic." Earlier (Spring 1977), Barnet Kellman's "David Rabe's 'The Orphan': A Peripatetic Work in Progress" also discussed Rabe's use of language, this time as a weapon. Kellman worked with Rabe on various productions of *The Orphan*, allowing penetrating and serious evaluation of a play that was characteristically regarded as inferior. Kellman went a long way toward establishing its importance in the evolution of Rabe's aesthetic.

A series of general studies that include discussions of Rabe's work also appeared in the late 1970s, and each evinces the new level of seriousness in Rabe criticism achieved after the premiere of *Streamers*. Robert Asahina, in "The Basic Training of American Playwrights: Theater and the Vietnam War" (Spring 1978), writes that

Rabe is "the only playwright really concerned with the art of the theater rather than with the form or the content of the media," but Asahina is less than admiring of the products. In *The Basic Training of Pavlo Hummel* he finds empty characters and a static plot, and, in *Sticks and Bones*, he finds "inadequate and abstruse symbolism." Mel Gussow, in "A Rich Crop of Writing Talent Brings New Life to the American Theatre" (21 Aug. 1977), notes the great influence of Samuel Beckett, Albee, and Harold Pinter on contemporary playwrights and discusses the importance of the Vietnam War as a focal point of the newer drama. Of the young writers he surveys, he finds Lanford Wilson and Sam Shepard to be the most talented and Rabe to be "the most overtly tragic." Robert Brustein's overview, "Drama in the Age of Einstein" (7 Aug. 1977), is similar in scope to Gussow's, but more theoretical. Brustein believes that "postmodernists" such as Rabe react in their plays against the dreary horror of cause-and-effect existence and are thereby returning to a dramatization of mystery. He observes that Rabe is "most typical" of the young generation, and that he is closest to Arthur Miller in his impulses. Brustein develops these ideas further in "The Crack in the Chimney: Reflections on Contemporary American Playwriting" (Spring 1978), in which he calls Rabe "the most typical and the most highly esteemed of the younger generation playwrights." Again emphasizing Rabe's affinities to Miller, he finds too much mystery in the plays. Brustein's chapter in his *Critical Moments: Reflections on Theatre & Society 1973-1979* (1980) is essentially a conflation and reworking of these two essays.

In "Descent Into the Abyss: The Plays of David Rabe" (Feb. 1979) Jerrold A. Phillips presents what, along with the Werner essay on language, must be considered one of the most useful essays on Rabe yet to appear. Stating that in *In the Boom Boom Room* "existence is just some physical process, without any individual significance," he finds a "vision of existential nothingless as the core of all experience" in Rabe's plays and notes that their structure typically involves a character led to the recognition of this nothingness. In concluding that Rabe thinks of life primarily as a biological process, devoid of meaning, Phillips has struck an engaging and potentially rich vein of ideas applicable to Rabe. Thomas P. Adler's " 'The Blind Leading the Blind': Rabe's *Sticks and Bones* and Shakespeare's *King Lear*" (Spring 1979) discusses Rabe's indebtedness to the classic work and describes a fusion of realism and theatricalism in the modern play. A bit weak in insight and originality is Janet Brown's chapter on *In the Boom Boom Room* in her *Feminist Drama: Definition & Critical Analysis* (1979). Brown sees "a highly structured, completely inflexible patriarchy" in the play, in which all the characters "must interrelate according to limited sexual roles," and she surmises that Rabe wrote the play "as a personal attempt to empathize with the plight of woman as object." She draws from Kenneth Burke's metacritical Pentad to identify "clusters" of imagery and concludes that the play is a profoundly "deterministic dramatic statement."

Samuel J. Bernstein's chapter on *Sticks and Bones* in his *The Strands Entwined: A New Direction in American Drama* (1980) views the Rabe play as an extension of social protest "to a realm of fundamental existential perception." He considers *Sticks and Bones* "a major work of dramatic art, . . . explosive; like a poem, its verbal and theatrical images are so associatively and spontaneously presented that it resists simple, direct retelling." Ted Hoffman, in the introduction to his *Famous American Plays of the 1970s* (1981), disagrees, contending that "Rabe is not a 'protest' playwright. Neither is he an affirmer. He is mordant and paradoxical, committed, in a large scale or small, to witnessing human decomposition during a time of upheaval." Janet S. Hertzbach, in "The Plays of David Rabe: A World of Streamers" (1981), emphasizes the time element in the plays, claiming that *Streamers* is the only transcendent Rabe play. Her balanced overview of the canon offers few other original insights and concludes that, in Rabe's drama, "Men live in a world so irrational that there is no order to subvert." Similarly useful and balanced, if also unadventurous, is the chapter on Rabe and British playwright Arnold Wesker in Carol Rosen's *Plays of Impasse: Contemporary Drama Set in Confining Institutions* (1983). Rosen observes that the American is "by far the more pessimistic," and that the "reality of pain . . . is what sets Rabe's plays apart from other theatrical responses to Vietnam." She contends that the Rabe canon moves from an emphasis on military routine in the Vietnam plays "to a more profound emphasis on the hopelessness and despair of those people trapped in the world onstage, which is finally an analogue of our world."

Rabe's professional divorce from Joseph Papp, spurred by Papp's unauthorized staging of *Goose and Tomtom*, the first Rabe play produced after *Streamers*, is recounted in John Corry's "Rabe Disavows the 'Goose' He Thought He Had Closed" (8 May 1982). The controversy with Papp deflected much attention from the problems with the play itself, but it did receive generally negative reviews, such as Mel Gussow's (8 May 1982). But critical judgment concerning the play, the most recent Rabe has published (*Hurlyburly* is his most recently staged play), has yet to be fully articulated, perhaps pending revision and a successful production. Work on the body of Rabe's writings continued to be generated, however. Noting Rabe's "extraordinary use of language," Richard L. Homan, in "American Playwrights in the 1970s: Rabe and Shepard" (Spring 1982), finds in the plays a common struggle to comprehend violence and death. Commenting on his "obscenity" and "marked realism," Ruby Cohn, in a chapter in her *New American Dramatists: 1960-1980* (1982), notes that among his contemporaries, Rabe is "further from Broadway conventions in subject and form." She further contends that in *The Orphan*, "Rabe aimed at a more positive hero [than in his two earlier plays] and fell flat on his pen," and that "the whole is tedious confusion," full of "embarrassing efforts at verse." Cohn continues: "The Boom Boom Room, a sexual marketplace, is Rabe's metaphor for contemporary American civilization, where art degenerates to pandering." A monumental figure in dramatic studies, C. W. E. Bigsby, in his *A Critical Introduction to Twentieth-Century American Drama*, volume 3: *Beyond Broadway* (1985), pauses briefly in his sweep of contemporary drama to discuss Rabe: "In many ways what appears political [about Rabe's plays] is more strictly psychological; what seems social is more clearly metaphysical."

A study that further develops Craig Werner's linguistically oriented approach to Rabe is Rodney Simard's chapter in his *Postmodern Drama: Contemporary Playwrights in America and Britain* (1984). Simard sees in Rabe's plays a fusion of realism, absurdism, and epic theater. He asserts that "Rabe's dramatic vision is decidedly existential" as well as "apocalyptic," and that the plays are "contemporary moralities," each of which "suggests a framework of objective reality but dramatizes the individual perceptions of the characters on a subjective level. The 'real' action takes place within the consciousness of the individual." Like Werner in his emphasis on the importance of Rabe's uses of language, Simard claims that *The Orphan* is "a dramatization of the theory of relativity," and that, in all the plays, Rabe "cynically charts the barrenness of a postmodern existential wasteland." He concludes that Rabe's dramatic experiment with multiple layers of reality, embodied in parallel layers of linguistic systems, "turns the reader's attention away from the exteriors to the internal world of the individual, where people live in isolation despite their elaborate social structures and life is dramatized on the level of existential reality, contingent on but independent of objective reality."

Pamela Cooper, in "David Rabe's *Sticks and Bones*: The Adventures of Ozzie and Harriet" (Dec. 1986), offers an interesting reassessment: "Although the three plays [of the Vietnam trilogy] are generally respected by critics, Rabe has received comparatively little scholarly attention, perhaps because of the nature of his subject-matter." She notes of *Sticks and Bones*: "Today the play has lost the power it once drew both from the exhaustive media coverage which the war received throughout its duration, and from the climate of growing public indignation." Emphasizing the dignity and emotional impact of the Rabe plays, she observes that he presents "life as euphemism." A recent contribution to Rabe scholarship is William Hermann's Rabe chapter in his *Understanding Contemporary American Drama* (1987), which notes the playwright's "fierce and scrupulous honesty" and his position as "a punishing scourge moving through a corrupt social order." Rabe, a moralist, "has searched for the right forms of ritual theater to embody his high sense of overriding purpose." Hermann also presents an analysis of *Hurlyburly*, in which he draws attention to "the blazing vitality of its stage language." He thinks the play, which depicts the lives of a boozy, creative group of friends, functions as a logical companion to *In the Boom Boom Room*. Although designed for the general reader, Hermann's study is a valuable contribution and is probably the best introduction to Rabe's drama.

The critical establishment has been slow (after an over-enthusiastic false start) to recognize the importance and seriousness of Rabe's contribution to contemporary drama. Many published studies suggest what may and should follow in Rabe scholarship, particularly in the area of gender studies. Happily, the dramatic community has no reason not to believe that the Rabe canon today is only a foundation, and that many more provocative and challenging plays are yet to appear from a playwright whose significant position should no longer be in any serious question.

Ntozake Shange

(1948-)

Catherine Carr Lee

University of California, Davis

PRIMARY BIBLIOGRAPHY

Books

For Colored Girls Who Have Considered Suicide/When the Rainbow is Enuf. San Lorenzo, Cal.: Shameless Hussy Press, 1975; New York: Macmillan, 1976; London: Methuen, 1978. Play.

Sassafrass. Berkeley, Cal.: Shameless Hussy Press, 1977. Novella.

Nappy Edges. New York: St. Martin's, 1978. Poetry.

Three Pieces: Spell #7; A Photograph: Lovers in Motion, Boogie Woogie Landscape. New York: St. Martin's, 1981. Plays.

Sassafrass, Cypress & Indigo. New York: St. Martin's, 1982. Novel.

A Daughter's Geography. New York: St. Martin's, 1983. Poetry.

From Okra to Greens. St. Paul, Minn.: Coffee House, 1984. Poetry.

See No Evil: Prefaces, Essays & Accounts, 1976-1983. San Francisco: Momo's Press, 1984.

Betsey Brown. New York: St. Martin's, 1985. Novel.

From Okra to Greens: A Different Kinda Love Story: A Play With Music & Dance. New York: French, 1985.

Ridin' the Moon in Texas: Word Paintings. New York: St. Martin's, 1987. Poetry and prose.

Premiere Productions

For Colored Girls Who Have Considered Suicide/When the Rainbow is Enuf. New York, Studio Rivbea, 7 July 1975.

Where the Mississippi Meets the Amazon, by Shange, Thulani Nkabinda, and Jessica Hagedorn. New York, Public Theater, 18 Dec. 1977.

A Photograph: A Still Life with Shadows/A Photograph: A Study of Cruelty. New York, Public Theater, 21 Dec. 1977. Revised as *A Photograph: Lovers in Motion.* Houston, Equinox Theater, Nov. 1979.

From Okra to Greens. New York, Barnard College, Nov. 1978.

Black & White Two-Dimensional Planes. New York, Sounds-in-Motion
   Studio Works, Feb. 1979.
Spell #7. New York, Public Theater, 3 June 1979. Revised, New
   York, Public Theater, 15 July 1979.
Boogie Woogie Landscapes. New York, Symphony Space Theater, 26
   June 1979.
Mother Courage & Her Children, adapted from Bertolt Brecht's play.
   New York, Public Theater, 13 May 1980.
Three Views of Mt. Fuji. San Francisco, Lorraine Hansberry Theater,
   5 June 1987.

Selected Other
Melissa & Smith. St. Paul, Minn.: Bookslinger, 1976. Short story.
"Is not so gd to be born a girl (1) . . . Otherwise i would think it
   odd to have rape prevention month (2)," *Black Scholar,* 10 (May/
   June 1979), 28-30. Poems.
"Unrecovered Losses/Black Theatre Traditions," *Black Scholar,* 10
   (July/Aug. 1979), 7-9. Essay. Reprinted as Foreword to *Three
   Pieces,* 1981.
"Who Says Black Folks Could Sing and Dance?," *Dance Magazine,* 57
   (Aug. 1983), 78-80. Review of Dance Black America.
"Women and the Creative Process: A Panel Discussion," with Susan
   Griffin, Norma Leistiko, and Miriam Schapiro, *Mosaic,* 8 (Fall
   1984), 91-117.
Foreword to *Black Book,* photographs by Robert Mappleworth. New
   York: St. Martin's, 1986.

SECONDARY BIBLIOGRAPHY

Interviews
Betsko, Kathleen, and Rachel Koenig. "Ntozake Shange." In their *In-
   terviews with Contemporary Women Playwrights.* New York: Beech
   Tree, 1987, 365-376.
Blackwell, Henry. "An Interview with Ntozake Shange," *Black Ameri-
   can Literature Forum,* 13 (Winter 1979), 134-138.
Buckley, Tom. "The Three Stages of Ntozake Shange," *New York
   Times,* 16 Dec. 1977, p. C6.
Dong, Stella. "Ntozake Shange," *Publishers Weekly,* 227 (3 May 1985),
   74-75.
Early, James. "Interview with Ntozake Shange." In *In the Memory of
   Frances, Zora, and Lorraine: Essays and Interviews on Black Women*

and Writing, ed. Juliette Bowles. Washington, D.C.: Institute
for the Arts & the Humanities, Howard University, 1979,
23-26.

Fraser, Gerald. "Theater Finds an Incisive New Playwright," *New
York Times*, 16 June 1976, p. 27.

Gillespie, Marcia Ann. "Ntozake Shange talks with Marcia Ann
Gillespie," *Essence* (May 1985), 122.

Guthmann, Edward. "Shange's Fond Memories," *San Francisco Chronicle*, 19 June 1987, p. 87.

Levine, Jo Ann. " 'Bein' a Woman, Bein' Colored': A Black Artist
Looks at her New Success," *Christian Science Monitor*, 9 Sept.
1976, p. 23.

Lyons, Brenda. "Interview with Ntozake Shange," *Massachusetts Review*, 28 (Winter 1987), 687-696.

Shange, Ntozake. "Ntozake Shange Interviews Herself," *Ms.*, 6
(Dec. 1977), 34-35, 70-72.

Smith, Yvonne. "Ntozake Shange: A 'Colored Girl' Considers Success," *Essence* (Feb. 1982), 12-14.

"Talk of the Town," *New Yorker*, 52 (2 Aug. 1976), 17-19.

Tate, Claudia. "Ntozake Shange." In her *Black Women Writers at
Work*. New York: Continuum, 1983, 149-174.

Vallely, Jean. "Trying to Be Nice," *Time*, 108 (19 July 1976), 44.

Critical Studies: Major Reviews, Articles, and Book Sections

Bambara, Toni Cade. *"For Colored Girls*–And White Girls Too," *Ms.*,
5 (Sept. 1976), 36-38.

Baraka, Amiri. "Afro-American Literature & Class Struggle," *Black
American Literature Forum*, 14 (Spring 1980), 5-14.

Barnes, Clive. "American-style *Courage* is an Asset for Public," *New
York Post*, 14 May 1980.

Barnes. "Ntozake Shange's *For Colored Girls* Opens at Papp's
Anspacher Theater," *New York Times*, 2 June 1976, p. 44.

Bauer, Grace. Review of *Ridin' the Moon in Texas: Word Paintings*, *Library Journal*, 112 (1 May 1987), 71.

Beaufort, John. "Black Cast Electrifies Off-Broadway 'Choreopoem,' " *Christian Science Monitor*, 7 June 1979, p. 19.

Beaufort. "A Treasure-Trove of Black Talent on the New York
Stage," *Christian Science Monitor*, 19 May 1980, p. 19.

Bell, Roseann Pope. Review of *For Colored Girls Who Have Considered
Suicide/When the Rainbow is Enuf*, *Black Collegian*, 7 (May/June
1977), 48-49.

Bigsby, C. W. E. *A Critical Introduction to Twentieth-Century American Drama*, volume 3: *Beyond Broadway*. Cambridge: Cambridge University Press, 1985, 410-415, 425-426.

Brown, Beth. Review of *A Daughter's Geography*, *CLA Journal*, 29 (Mar. 1986), 378-386.

Brown, Elizabeth. "Ntozake Shange." In *Dictionary of Literary Biography*, volume 38: *Afro-American Writers After 1955: Dramatists and Prose Writers*, ed. Thadious M. Davis and Trudier Harris. Detroit: Gale Research, 1985, 240-250.

Brown, Janet. *Feminist Drama: Definition and Critical Analysis*. Metuchen, N.J.: Scarecrow, 1979, 114-132.

Calio, Louise. "A Rebirth of the Goddess in Contemporary Women Poets of the Spirit," *Studio Mystica*, 7 (Spring 1984), 50-59.

Christ, Carol P. " 'I Found God in Myself . . . & I Loved Her Fiercely': Ntozake Shange." In her *Diving Deep and Surfacing: Women Writers on Spiritual Quest*. Boston: Beacon Press, 1980, 97-120.

Christian, Barbara. "No More Buried Lives: The Theme of Lesbianism in Lorde, Naylor, Shange, Walker," *Feminist Issues*, 5 (Spring 1985), 3-20.

Cohen, Esther. "Three Sisters," *Progressive*, 28 (Jan. 1983), 56.

A Daughter's Geography, unsigned review, *Choice*, 21 (Jan. 1984), 56.

Eder, Richard. "Miss Shange's Rousing Homilies," *New York Times*, 22 July 1979, section 2, p. 3.

Eder. "Papp Proves Less is More," *New York Times*, 2 Apr. 1978, section 2, p. 1.

Eder. "Sovereign Spirit," *New York Times*, 22 Dec. 1977, p. C11.

Eder. "Stage: Miss Shange's Dramatic Poetry in *Spell #7* at Public," *New York Times*, 4 June 1979, p. C13.

Eder. "Stage: *Spell #7* by Ntozake Shange," *New York Times*, 16 July 1979, p. C12.

Fabre, Geneviève. "Ntozake Shange," *Revue Francaise des Etudes Americaines*, 10 (1980), 259-270.

Flowers, Sandra Hollin. "*Colored Girls*: Textbook for the Eighties," *Black American Literature Forum*, 15 (Summer 1981), 51-54.

Friedman, Susan Stanford. "Creativity and the Childbirth Metaphor: Gender Difference in Literary Discourse," *Feminist Studies*, 13 (Spring 1987), 49-82.

Gelman, David. "This Time Shange Casts No Spell," *Newsweek*, 94 (30 July 1979), 65.

Gilbert, Harriett. "Somewhere Over the Rainbow," *Book World–Washington Post*, 15 Oct. 1978, pp. 1, 4.

Gillespie, Patti P. "America's Women Dramatists, 1960-1980." In *Essays on Contemporary American Drama*, ed. Hedwig Bock and Albert Wertheim. Munich: Hueber, 1981, 187-206.

Gomez, Jewelle. "Black Women Heroes: Here's Reality, Where's the Fiction?," *Black Scholar*, 17 (Mar./Apr. 1986), 8-13.

Gottfried, Martin. "*Rainbow* Over Broadway," *New York Post*, 16 Sept. 1976.

Grumbach, Doris. "Ntozake Shange's Trio," *Book World–Washington Post*, 22 Aug. 1982, pp. 1-2.

Gussow, Mel. "Brecht in Old West," *New York Times*, 14 May 1980, p. C20.

Gussow. "Stage: 'Colored Girls' Evolves–Play Moves to Broadway: To Be Seen and Savored," *New York Times*, 16 Sept. 1976, p. 53.

Gussow. "3 'Satin Sisters' Spin a Poetry of Nostalgia at Stage Cabaret," *New York Times*, 19 Dec. 1977, pp. D20, D44.

Gussow. "Women Write New Chapter in the Theater," *New York Times*, 8 June 1979, p. C3.

Hajek, Friederike. "Ethnizität und Frauenemanzipation: Der afroamerikanische Roman nach den sechziger Jahren," *Weimarer Beiträge*, 31 (1983), 466-486.

Harper, Michael S. "Three Poets," *New York Times Book Review*, 21 Oct. 1979, pp. 18-21.

Hernton, Calvin. "The Sexual Mountain and Black Women Writers," *Black Scholar*, 16 (July/Aug. 1985), 2-11.

Hinerfeld, Susan Slocum. "A Poet's Crowded Colloquial Novel of Black and Poor Carolinian Women," *Los Angeles Times Book Review*, 22 Aug. 1982, p. 2.

Honey, Maureen. "A Sensibility of Struggle and Hope," *Prairie Schooner*, 58 (Winter 1984), 111-112.

Howard, Camille Cole. "Ntozake Shange: When She's Good," *San Francisco Chronicle*, 10 May 1987, review section, pp. 1, 7-9.

Isaacs, Susan. "Three Sisters," *New York Times Book Review*, 12 Sept. 1982, pp. 12-13, 16.

Kalem, T. E. "He Done Her Wrong," *Time*, 107 (14 June 1976), 74.

Karenga, M. Ron. "On Wallace's Myths: Wading Thru Troubled Waters," *Black Scholar*, 10 (May/June 1979), 36-39.

Kauffmann, Stanley. "Suite and Sour," *New Republic*, 175 (3-10 July 1976), 20.

Keller, Karl. "A Performing Playwright/Poet Who Records the Pulse of a People," *Los Angeles Times Book Review*, 29 July 1984, p. 4.

Kerr, Walter. "From Brilliance to Bewilderment to a Blunder," *New York Times*, 13 June 1976, section 2, p. 5.

Keyssar, Helene. *Feminist Theatre: An Introduction to Plays of Contemporary British and American Women.* London: Macmillan, 1984; New York: Grove, 1985, 128, 140-147, 149, 177.

Keyssar. "Locating the Rainbow: Gestures of Drama and Political Acts." In her *The Curtain and the Veil: Strategies in Black Drama.* New York: Franklin, 1981, 211-217.

Kissel, Howard. "Mother Courage," *Women's Wear Daily* (14 May 1980).

Kroll, Jack. "Women's Rites," *Newsweek*, 87 (14 June 1976), 99.

Mael, Phyllis. "A Rainbow of Voices." In *Women in American Theatre: Careers, Images, Movements*, ed. Helen Krich Chinoy and Linda Walsh Jenkins. New York: Crown, 1981, 320-324.

Malveaux, Julianne. "Political and Historical Aspects of Black Male/Female Relationships," *Black Scholar*, 10 (May/June 1979), 32-35.

Mitchell, Carolyn. " 'A Laying on of Hands': Transcending the City in Ntozake Shange's *For Colored Girls Who Have Considered Suicide When the Rainbow is Enuf.*" In *Women Writers and the City: Essays in Feminist Literary Criticism*, ed. Susan M. Squier. Knoxville: University of Tennessee Press, 1984, 230-248.

Murray, Timothy. "Screening the Camera's Eye: Black and White Confrontations of Technological Representation," *Modern Drama*, 28 (Mar. 1985), 110-124.

Nappy Edges, unsigned review, *Publishers Weekly*, 214 (31 July 1978), 83.

Nelson, Don. "Shange Casts a Powerful *Spell*," *New York Daily News*, 16 July 1979.

Ogunyemi, Chikwenye Okonjo. "Womanism: The Dynamics of the Contemporary Black Female Novel in English," *Signs*, 11 (Autumn 1985), 63-80.

Oliver, Edith. Review of *For Colored Girls*, *New Yorker*, 52 (14 June 1976), 77.

Oliver. Review of *Mother Courage and Her Children*, *New Yorker*, 56 (26 May 1980), 77.

Oliver. Review of *A Photograph: A Study of Cruelty* and *Where the Mississippi Meets the Amazon*, *New Yorker*, 54 (2 Jan. 1978), 48-49.

Oliver. Review of *Spell #7*, *New Yorker*, 55 (16 July 1979), 73.

Patraka, Vivian M. "Staging Memory: Contemporary Plays by Women," *Michigan Quarterly Review*, 26 (Winter 1987), 285-292.

Peters, Erskine. "Some Tragic Propensities of Ourselves: The Occasion of Ntozake Shange's *For Colored Girls . . . ,*" *Journal of Ethnic Studies*, 6 (Spring 1978), 79-85.

Prado, Holly. "In Verse," *Los Angeles Times Book Review*, 8 Jan. 1984, p. 9.

Rich, Frank. " 'Mother Courage' Transplanted," *New York Times*, 15 June 1980, section 2, p. 5.

Richards, Sandra L. "Conflicting Impulses in the Plays of Ntozake Shange," *Black American Literature Forum*, 17, no. 2 (1983), 73-78.

Rushing, Andrea Benton. "For Colored Girls, Suicide or Struggle," *Massachusetts Review*, 22 (Autumn 1981), 539-550.

Schindehette, Susan. Review of *Betsey Brown*, *Saturday Review*, 11-12 (May/June 1985), 74-75.

See No Evil: Prefaces, Essays & Accounts, 1976-1983, unsigned review, *Kirkus Review*, 52 (1 Mar. 1984), 252.

See No Evil: Prefaces, Essays & Accounts, 1976-1983, unsigned review, *Publishers Weekly*, 225 (16 Mar. 1984), 81.

Simon, John. "Avant-Garde and 'Taint Your Wagon,' " *New York*, 13 (26 May 1980), 79-81.

Simon. "*Enuf* Is Not Enough," *New Leader*, 59 (5 July 1976), 21-22.

Simon. "Fainting Spell," *New York*, 12 (30 July 1979), 57.

Simon. Review of *A Photograph*, *New York*, 11 (16 Jan. 1978), 58.

Staples, Robert. "The Myth of Black Macho: A Response to Angry Black Feminists," *Black Scholar*, 10 (Mar./Apr. 1979), 24-33.

Stasio, Marilyn. "Shange Casts a Mixed *Spell*," *New York Post*, 5 June 1979.

Taylor, John Russell. Review of *For Colored Girls Who Have Considered Suicide/When the Rainbow Is Enuf*, *Plays and Players*, 27 (Dec. 1979), 16-17.

Wallace, Michele. "For Colored Girls, the Rainbow is not Enough," *Village Voice*, 16 Aug. 1976, pp. 108-109.

Washington, Mary Helen. "New Lives and New Letters: Black Women Writers at the End of the Seventies," *College English*, 43 (Jan. 1981), 1-11.

Watkins, Mel. "Sexism, Racism and Black Women Writers," *New York Times Book Review*, 15 June 1986, pp. 1, 35-37.

Watt, Douglas. "Brecht's *Mother Courage* Scalped Out West," *New York Daily News*, 14 May 1980.

Watt. "Here's to the Ladies Again," *New York Daily News*, 16 Sept. 1976.

Willard, Nancy. "Life Abounding in St. Louis," *New York Times Book Review*, 12 May 1985, p. 12.

Williams, Sherley Anne. "Roots of Privilege: New Black Fiction," *Ms.*, 12 (June 1985), 69-72.

Wilson, Edwin. "The Black Experience: Two Approaches," *Wall Street Journal*, 21 Sept. 1976, p. 24.

BIBLIOGRAPHICAL ESSAY

Interviews

The earliest interviews with Ntozake Shange appeared in East Coast publications during the time Shange's play *For Colored Girls Who Have Considered Suicide/When the Rainbow is Enuf* (hereafter referred to as *For Colored Girls*) first received critical attention. With Gerald Fraser (16 June 1976) she remembers a series of suicidal bouts she suffered through in the years before she met with literary success and also comments on the "incredibly antifemale aura" of the Black Arts Movement. She speaks sensitively about the male characters in her work, "about men I have loved and I've picked," without blaming them for their difficulties. These early comments about men are especially significant in light of the criticism she later received for the supposed antimale bias of the play.

In a *New Yorker* "Talk of the Town" interview (2 Aug. 1976) Shange reminisces about her childhood, describing her early reading of Simone de Beauvoir, Herman Melville, and others. To read Faulkner she had "to pretend to be white to understand what he's saying about blacks." A darker side of her experience emerges in an interview with Jean Vallely (19 July 1976). Shange reports that she "was always what you call a nice child," but that her rage has "been there all the time." Vallely describes Shange's suicide attempts: at various times before writing *For Colored Girls* she stuck her head in a gas oven, drank Drano, slashed her wrist, overdosed on Valium, and drove her Volvo into the Pacific. She also admits her fear that *For Colored Girls* "would be criticized as 'too emotional, too colored, too female.'" With Jo Ann Levine (9 Sept. 1976) Shange talks of her family and their reactions to her work. In an interview with Tom Buckley (16 Dec. 1977) Shange acknowledges that she was

raped and suggests that rape and child molestation are more hei-
nous than murder.

The last early interview of note is a self-interview Shange composed for *Ms.* (Dec. 1977). Utilizing the nonstandard spelling and
punctuation that characterize her writing, Shange touches on
themes that she will develop more fully in later interviews: her preference for the term "colored," which she considers more inclusive
than "black"; fond memories of afternoon family variety shows she
helped stage as a child and home visits from black artists, writers,
and musicians such as Dizzy Gillespie, Chico Hamilton, Sonny Till,
and Chuck Berry; and the influence of great black writers such as
LeRoi Jones (Amiri Baraka) and Ishmael Reed on her own work.

Shange conducted her first substantial interviews with James
Early and Henry Blackwell. With Early (1979) she discusses the
need for black poets to take themselves as seriously as they do black
musicians. She complains that Western culture sees art primarily as
commodity, "when in fact, art is a way of living." The frequency of violence in her work, she says, reflects the threat of violence from all
fronts under which black women live. Shange's frustration with critics she thinks do not understand her work, a recurring theme in
later conversations, first emerges here; her responses to critics provide some of her most illuminating comments about the nature of
her work. She believes that her play *A Photograph* ran only briefly because white critics found the male protagonist, Sean David, to be
too brilliant and attractive. She points out that the more she writes,
the more her work should become clearer to people: "I don't think
it would be very clear if you had only read *Sassafrass* or only read
For Colored Girls or only saw *A Photograph.*"

In the interview with Blackwell (Winter 1979), Shange defines
her poetic aesthetic as "a very conscious effort to be concise and powerful and as illusory as possible, so that the language can, in fact,
bring you to more conclusions than the one in the poem, but that
that one conclusion can't be avoided, even though there are thou-
sands of others roaming around. And there should be wit and
grace and a movement from one image to another, so that there's
no narrowness to the body of your work." She identifies as well
what she sees as a woman's aesthetic: "those parts of reality that are
ours, those things about our bodies, the cycles of our lives that
have been ignored for centuries in all castes and classes of our people, are to be dealt with now. . . . One has to speak about things inherently female. And that is my persona. A woman."

Shange gave a brief but significant interview to Yvonne Smith (Feb. 1982), in which she mentions that she had not read the article (by Robert Staples, in *Black Scholar* [Mar./Apr. 1979]) that accused Shange and fellow black writer Michele Wallace of having an anti-black-male bias. She saw no reason to read "material that is designed to create a sense of illegitimacy in my person or my culture. . . . I know there *is* a woman's culture and that we are oppressed." Instead of responding directly to Staples's charges Shange sent *Black Scholar* two poems that dealt with rape and female genital mutilation.

The interview with Claudia Tate (1983) is one of the more comprehensive Shange has given. Concerning negative critical responses to her work, Shange says that she usually does not read critics. If she does, "I'll just be vitally damaged because what I write is an offering of myself to the world. When somebody attacks that, then they're saying I'm not alive. . . . " She used nonstandard punctuation in her novella *Sassafrass* because "if you put it down, you had to start all over again. I did not want the book to be something you could put down when it got too emotional." She finds that male and female writers differ in their sense of emotional bonding with their own work; with male writers, "there's usually an *idea* as opposed to a *reality*." With women, art and life more nearly coexist. Shange also insists in the interview on the validity of a distinct Afro-American culture, pointing out that she is not going to footnote the cultural references in her work: "Either you know us or you don't. . . . We do not have to refer continually to European art as the standard. That's absolutely absurd and racist, and I won't participate in that utter lie." The audience Shange imagines as she writes is composed of "little girls who are coming of age. I want them to know that they are not alone." Finally, Shange points out that the environment in which she writes profoundly influences her work; she also discusses the creative process, directing, and the commercialization of *For Colored Girls*. She continues to work in the theater but believes the theater business "is very sick." The stage, however, "gives my stuff what I cannot give it," in spite of the fact that black actors and artists are still confined by popular expectations and stereotypes.

In a shorter interview with Stella Dong (3 May 1985), Shange returns to the subject of her critics. She disagrees with the assessment that she is "vengeful": "I love too many people for that." Still angry, she does not feel as powerless as she did when she was younger. She is as "serious as I ever was about oppression of women and children, racism, imperialism in Latin America and Africa, apartheid," but in her work since *For Colored Girls* she has tried to examine smaller themes: "I've tried to look at the choices available to these characters." She most prefers to write poetry because of the spontaneity she feels when writing, but she enjoys the sense of power that comes from novel-writing or from directing a stage play.

Although not as wide-ranging as Tate's, two more recent conversations are useful and illuminating. In an interview with Kathleen Betsko and Rachel Koenig (1987), Shange identifies what she sees as a split between Afro-American and Anglo-Western concepts of art, suggesting that the latter "is very keen on specific disciplines as opposed to multidisciplinary approaches." Her work, faithfully Afro-American, has always been multimedia; at heart she is a performance artist. Her theater work is an "anomaly. . . . I haven't stopped writing plays–I just feel more at home in performance because that is what I started out doing." She has encountered hostile audiences only in the United States, and "if I had to say who my enemies are, I would say male chauvinists, and English-speaking nationalists who resent my work with Latin American countries and my bilingualism, and who refuse to admit they live in the Western hemisphere which is predominantly Spanish-speaking." Shange suggests that male critics have difficulty with her work because "it is impossible to enter the territory of someone you oppress with the knowledge you have as an oppressor." She also complains that "people think after *For Colored Girls* I died." Too often minority writers are accused of producing only one good work: "It's not that they fall silent, it's that they are not continuous commercial successes." She finds theater to be the weakest of the art forms in America, blaming the problem primarily on the high production costs, but also on the difficulties inherent in collaboration. Yet she enjoys directing, both her own plays and the work of other playwrights.

With Brenda Lyons (Winter 1987) Shange continues to develop many of the themes discussed in earlier interviews. She also takes up questions of sexuality, disagreeing with the critical charge that her novel *Sassafrass, Cypress & Indigo* (1982) is homophobic. Since she feels that choosing a lesbian life-style is not necessarily a solution to the problem of living in a sexist society, she wanted to point out in the novel what she saw as problems in the gay community. She also expounds on a racial theme, noting that when she used the term "colored girls" fifteen years earlier, she meant what in 1987 she would call "people of color." The first artistic/ performance group she worked with was multiracial, so she used the term "colored girls" as a "little tongue-in-cheek thing." In a more technical vein she describes plot in her fiction as "undulating" rather than linear, and while she recognizes the risks she takes by not conforming to traditional expectations of fiction, she does not believe that a work should be immediately accessible to a reader; reading is like meeting somebody new: "You can't learn somebody's personal imagery and their personal iconography that quickly." Shange is acutely concerned with the politics of language and the potential for dishonesty in language; she does not want to use the language in ways that "the powers that be" use it.

A brief interview with Edward Guthmann (19 June 1987) also deserves attention. Shange says that in her most recent work she is more forgiving of her characters, "more tolerant of frailty" than before. She discusses her play *Three Views of Mt. Fuji* (1987), in which she wanted "to look upon the role of art and sex in a creative person's life, and how passions, whether sexual or literary/artistic, can become mixed together." She comments on the difficulties in setting priorities in life; passion for a lover and passion for creative work can be very much the same, but it can be hard to decide which is more important and "who will be more faithful in the end."

Critical Studies: Major Reviews, Articles, and Book Sections

In recent years scholars have begun to treat Shange's material in an academic context: in the 1980s several significant articles and book sections focusing on her aesthetic concerns have appeared. For example, Elizabeth Brown has contributed a balanced biographical and critical overview in a volume of the *Dictionary of Literary Biography* (1985). However, much Shange commentary over the years has taken the form of theater reviews, beginning with the controversial reception of *For Colored Girls*.

Although somewhat puzzled by the form of Shange's "choreopoem"–a performance of poetry, music, and dance–New York critics were overwhelmingly positive about the June 1976 opening of *For Colored Girls* at Joseph Papp's Public Theater. Writing for the *New York Times*, Clive Barnes (2 June 1976) calls the play "a very humbling but inspiring thing for a white man to experience." Shange's writing is "tense poetic beauty. . . . beautiful, pungent, accurate." Also in the *New York Times*, Walter Kerr (13 June 1976) notes that some passages in the play are "conventional," but "it has drama hidden and boiling just beyond an apparently controlled surface." Jack Kroll, in *Newsweek* (14 June 1976), calls the performance "political in the deepest sense, but there's no dogma, no sentimentality, no grinding of false mythic axes." Edith Oliver, for the *New Yorker* (14 June 1976), praises the performance and calls it "entirely free of the rasping earnestness of most projects of this sort." T. E. Kalem, in *Time* (14 June 1976), describes "a poignant, gripping, angry and beautiful theater work"; somewhat prophetically, Kalem suggests that "black men are going to wince."

Reviewers were no less enthusiastic when the play moved to the larger Booth Theater later in 1976. Mel Gussow (16 Sept. 1976) praises "the closeness, the intimacy, and the specificity of the revelations that make the play so tangible and so poignant." Martin Gottfried, in the *New York Post* (16 Sept. 1976), calls the play "the kind the stage was created for." He notes "some lack of variety in the selection of material" but feels that "the writing is regularly beautiful and exquisite." In the *New York Daily News* Douglas Watt (16 Sept. 1976) praises the play's "overpowering impression"; while Edwin Wilson, in the *Wall Street Journal* (21 Sept. 1976), calls it "a remarkable, inspiring evening." Writing for *Ms.*, Toni Cade Bambara (Sept. 1976) describes the performance as "blisteringly funny, fragile, droll and funky, lyrical, git down stompish." She notes that although "men appear exclusively as instruments of pain, there is no venom." In the *Black Collegian* Roseann Pope Bell (May/June 1977) anticipates the later controversy when she declares that the play "is not about the oppression of Black women by Black men."

Early exceptions to this praise came from Stanley Kauffmann (3-10 July 1976) and John Simon (5 July 1976). Writing for the *New Republic*, Kauffmann calls the play "hyperdramatic and–as writing–superficial" and suggests that plays written by blacks have tended to be overrated by white critics. Simon, in the *New Leader*, proves to be one of Shange's most vitriolic critics, calling the play "pathetic nonsense"; he believes Shange appeals to guilty white consciences because she is not only black but female, and he blames white critics for praising black artists regardless of the quality of their work. John Russell Taylor, in *Plays and Players* (Dec. 1979), complains that at times the writing "all sounds as phoney as hell" but concedes that "when she relaxes . . . the result can be funny and touching, and, yes, in its spare vividness actually poetic." While praising Shange's "clarity and honesty about the black woman's vulnerability," Michele Wallace (16 Aug. 1976) finds the play's resolution—"a religious conversion to self-love"—to be simplistic.

The most troubling questions about *For Colored Girls*, however, came from black male academics. Erskine Peters, in "Some Tragic Propensities of Ourselves" (Spring 1978), criticizes the play for its hostility to black men and questions the wisdom of presenting such a negative portrayal to white audiences. He also finds that Shange's personal ideology is responsible for "the terribly warped perspective which controls the play." Robert Staples (Mar./Apr. 1979) complains that Shange does not tell "the story of why so many black men feel their manhood, more accurately their feeling of self-respect, is threatened by black women." He suspects that Shange's middle-class upbringing cuts her off from the realities of black experience, that she fails to understand that "the structural underpinnings for sexism are not the same in black society." M. Ron Karenga (May/June 1979) accuses Shange of "bitterness and one-dimensionality," and Amiri Baraka (Spring 1980) complains that she "deals in effects but not causes." In Shange's defense Julianne Malveaux (May/June 1979) insists that "a poem is not a polemic"; she believes that Shange "has presented a slice of black life, not a series of generalizations and statements about black men and women."

Other comments about *For Colored Girls* help to sustain as well as to explain the controversy. Among the most illuminating are the thoughts of Andrea Benton Rushing (Autumn 1981). Reflecting on what she felt was missing for her as a black American woman, Rushing suggests that Shange, like the women in the play, is cut off from two of the most important black cultural supports: "the extended family and the black church." She believes that Shange is removed from "black literary and political history as well." Shange's women are "as isolated and alienated as the typical, middle-class single white woman in contemporary urban America," which might account at least partially for the play's success with white audiences.

In "*Colored Girls*: Textbook for the Eighties" (Summer 1981), Sandra Hollin Flowers offers a much more positive response, believing that "Shange demonstrates a compassionate vision of black men—compassionate because though the work is not without anger, it has a certain integrity which could not exist if the author lacked a perceptive understanding of the crisis between black men and women." In its treatment of the modern black predicament Flowers enthusiastically ranks *For Colored Girls* with Ralph Ellison's *Invisible Man* and

Richard Wright's *Native Son*. Jewelle Gomez, in "Black Women Heroes: Here's Reality, Where's the Fiction?" (Mar./Apr. 1986), also defends the play, suggesting that the "real scandal for her detractors
was that most of her poems were not really about men at all. While
men may have been present, the black woman's experience was the
center at all times." Finally, Calvin Hernton, in "The Sexual Mountain and Black Women Writers" (July/Aug. 1985), and Mel Watkins, in "Sexism, Racism and Black Women Writers" (15 June
1986), provide useful discussions of the issues raised and place
Shange in a broader context.

Shange's *A Photograph* received far less attention and praise
than *For Colored Girls*. Although Edith Oliver (2 Jan. 1978) finds
that Shange's "poetic talent and passion carry the show," Richard
Eder (2 Apr. 1978) complains that "the work is forced, and finally
broken by its form." John Simon (16 Jan. 1978), predictably, declares it "exactly the same drivel" as *For Colored Girls*. However,
both Oliver and Mel Gussow (19 Dec. 1977) praise Shange's poetic
performance in *Where the Mississippi Meets the Amazon*, a recital by
Shange, Thulani Nkabinda, and Jessica Hagedorn that ran concur-
rently with *A Photograph* at New York's Public Theater beginning in
late 1977.

Shange's next major production, *Spell #7*, found unequivocal
praise from Edith Oliver (16 July 1979), Don Nelson (16 July
1979), and John Beaufort (7 June 1979). Richard Eder (4 June
1979) suggests that the workshop production was uneven, but "in
the best of the sketches, Miss Shange's wit, lyricism and fierceness
are marvelously evident." After the show's move to Broadway, Eder
(16 July 1979) finds it to be "a most lovely and powerful work"; he
is pleased that Shange removed the white woman satire, a piece
that "broke the play's quality of direct, spontaneous feeling." However, Marilyn Stasio (5 June 1979) is more ambivalent, suggesting
that the work "lacks the dramatic focus and force" of *For Colored
Girls*, while David Gelman (30 July 1979) believes Shange may yet
find a conventional framework to be more successful. Simon (30
July 1979) finds the play to be further evidence that Shange's success comes only from her status as a black woman.

Shange's Obie-winning adaptation of *Mother Courage & Her Children* also met with divided responses. Clive Barnes (14 May 1980),
John Beaufort (19 May 1980), and Mel Gussow (14 May 1980) are
highly enthusiastic; Gussow believes that Shange's version "can
stand as a considerable dramatic achievement," while Barnes de-

clares that Brecht would have approved of Shange's decision to cast the play in the American Southwest between 1866 and 1881. Edith Oliver (26 May 1980) finds it "the most telling and controlled writing . . . that Miss Shange has ever done," but she questions whether the transposition works. John Simon (26 May 1980), Frank Rich (15 June 1980), Howard Kissel (14 May 1980), and Douglas Watt (14 May 1980) agree that Shange's version distorts and misinterprets Brecht's intentions.

Not surprisingly, most of the academic attention to Shange's work has focused on *For Colored Girls*, generally attempting to place it in the context of other feminist works and to elucidate its method and feminist message. Book sections and chapters on Shange begin with Janet Brown's *Feminist Drama: Definition and Critical Analysis* (1979). An insightful reader of Shange's poetry, Brown examines the "primary associational clusters" in the poems of *For Colored Girls*. She identifies "the dirt and loneliness of cities on the sensory level, the isolation of the technological society on the abstract level, and the oppression of black women by black men on the familial level. Opposing this cluster is one that associates singing, dancing, and natural beauty on the sensory level, relationships of equality between men and women on the familial level, and a mythological, non-Christian spirituality on the abstract level." She also recognizes a pattern of symbolic action that runs through each poem as well as through the play as a whole.

In *Diving Deep and Surfacing: Women Writers on Spiritual Quest* (1980), Carol P. Christ considers the ontological questions that *For Colored Girls* raises, suggesting that the play is "a search for the meaning of the nothingness experienced and a quest for new being." Her questions about what she calls the mysticism of the title are enlightening; her discussion of Shange's nonstandard grammar is less so.

Although not available in English, Geneviève Fabre's essay, "Ntozake Shange," in *Revue Francaise des Etudes Americaines* (1980) should be noted as an early indicator of the extent of Shange's impact. Fabre discusses the evolution of *For Colored Girls* from a coffee house/bar performance work to a Broadway production, paying particular attention to its political and commercial implications. She also notes the female separatist elements in the work.

Two brief but useful discussions, from Patti P. Gillespie (1981) and Phyllis Mael (1981), place *For Colored Girls* in a contemporary context. In "A Rainbow of Voices," Mael identifies the play as "a femi-

nist variation of the archetypal journey in search of the self."
Gillespie, in "America's Women Dramatists, 1960-1980," sees
Shange as the product of three significant shifts in the patterns of
drama in the 1960s and 1970s: the emergence of noncommercial theater, black women playwrights, and feminist playwrights.

Helene Keyssar provides a more detailed analysis in "Locating
the Rainbow: Gestures of Drama and Political Acts" (1981); she emphasizes Shange's "genealogical debt to black drama" more so than
the feminist orientation. Keyssar calls the play "a vividly political
act," one that "shows the audience a place to act and helps it to recon-
sider 'what is and is not a political act' in drama." Keyssar extends
her discussion in *Feminist Theatre: An Introduction to Plays of Contemporary British and American Women* (1984). She points out that Shange's
insistence on the necessity of music and dance is rooted not only in
Afro-American experience but in traditions of feminist drama; and
she identifies Shange's "motivating image" of "combat breathing,"
an idea borrowed from Franz Fanon that Shange discusses in *See
No Evil* (1984). As Keyssar defines it, "combat breathing" is "the necessary reaction of people whose territory is occupied." Responding
to the charges of antimale bias leveled at Shange, Keyssar suggests
that the "Beau Willie Brown" episode sensitively identifies the despair of both Crystle *and* Beau Willie. One of Keyssar's most interesting contributions is her discussion of the reception of *For Colored
Girls* in England, where audiences were unable to understand the dialect and found the emphasis on racial consciousness alienating.

Readers will find a more extensive analysis of Shange's metaphor, "combat breathing," in Sandra L. Richards's "Conflicting Impulses in the Plays of Ntozake Shange" (1983). Examining both *For
Colored Girls* and *Spell #7*, Richards focuses on the "dialectic between the felt constrictions of the social order and the perceived limit-
lessness of the natural order." She finds that Shange's work dis-
turbs and provokes many of her audiences because the plays do not
reconcile the extremes of "ecstatic spirituality" and "devastating social reality."

A unique perspective on Shange's use of the cityscape comes
from Carolyn Mitchell, in " 'A Laying on of Hands': Transcending
the City in Ntozake Shange's *For Colored Girls* . . ." (1984). Given
Shange's many comments in interviews about the influence of her environment on her emotional state, and especially about her negative feelings for New York City, that other critics have not also examined closely the city as a symbol is somewhat surprising. Mitchell

looks at Shange's poetic imagery and spiritual symbolism and contrasts Shange's concept of the city with that of Paul Tillich, who
treats the city as a "centralizing and inclusive place." Shange, she
notes, inverts the idealized city of biblical, literary, and historical
thought.

C. W. E. Bigsby offers one of the more penetrating analyses
of Shange's language in *A Critical Introduction to Twentieth-Century
American Drama*, volume 3: *Beyond Broadway* (1985). He believes that
Shange is "supremely conscious of the irony of working in a language which could never be made to express a selfhood warped by
that language. . . . Her strategy, therefore, is to disassemble that language and then reconstruct it." He also notes a paradox inherent in
the play: the work is both "a lament for the forces which conspire
to limit the freedom of women" and "a lyrical celebration. . . . The
grace of movement, the polyphony of sound, the shaping of poetry
inevitably resist the threat of anarchy which she observes." The
verse inevitably "blunts the edge of her social critique."

Several critical articles include short but significant references
to Shange's dramatic work. Readers may want to consult Louise
Calio's "A Rebirth of the Goddess in Contemporary Women Poets
of the Spirit" (Spring 1984); Susan Stanford Friedman's "Creativity
and the Childbirth Metaphor: Gender Difference in Literary Discourse" (Spring 1987); and Vivian M. Patraka's "Staging Memory:
Contemporary Plays by Women" (Winter 1987). Also of interest is
Mary Helen Washington's "New Lives and New Letters: Black
Women Writers at the End of the Seventies" (Jan. 1981), an essay ad-
dressing the oversights of white feminist critics. Timothy Murray's
"Screening the Camera's Eye: Black and White Confrontations of
Technological Representation" (Mar. 1985) examines *A Photograph*
in the context of modern black drama and the media.

While Shange has been best known and most influential as a
dramatist, her poetry and prose works have drawn attention as
well. Like the theater reviews, the responses are again ambivalent,
but readers may want to consult several representative reviews for
comments on Shange's language and structure. Her poetry collection, *Nappy Edges* (1978), received responses from Harriett Gilbert
(15 Oct. 1978), Michael S. Harper (21 Oct. 1979), and *Publishers
Weekly* (31 July 1978). All three find the material uneven, noting
Shange's self-consciousness, but Harper likes the "sharp, intense vignettes," and Gilbert praises Shange's "awareness of the beauty of
sound and vision" and the "majesty of words."

Shange's first novel, *Sassafrass, Cypress & Indigo,* has likewise met with mixed reviews. Critics praise Shange's lyricism and imagery but find that the narrative does not always cohere; the writing is sometimes superficial. Representative reviews include those of Doris Grumbach (22 Aug. 1982), Susan Isaacs (12 Sept. 1982), Susan Slocum Hinerfeld (22 Aug. 1982), and Esther Cohen (Jan. 1983).

Responses to the poems in *A Daughter's Geography* (1983) are more uniformly positive. Maureen Honey (Winter 1984) reflects the general enthusiasm: "This volume delights, inspires, and enlightens. Shange's political astuteness, ear for the street, and earthiness are a rare combination and one to be savored." As Beth Brown (Mar. 1986) suggests, Shange seems to have "matured in her questioning of the male-female relationships" in this book; for other significant reviews readers should consult Holly Prado (8 Jan. 1984) and *Choice* (Jan. 1984).

Reviewers were much less favorable about Shange's next published work, *See No Evil: Prefaces, Essays & Accounts, 1976-1983. Kirkus Review* (1 Mar. 1984) calls it a collection of "slight credos and jottings," while *Publishers Weekly* (16 Mar. 1984) finds it "strident." Karl Keller (29 July 1984) is more sensitive to Shange's aims. He identifies "a couple of valuable ideas in this collection": the notion of "combat breathing" and the plea for audiences to give as much legitimacy to black writers as they do to black musicians. However, he finds that she "does not go far in exploring these two good ideas" and calls for "more of the anger, the ideas, the music."

Nancy Willard (12 May 1985) praises Shange's most recent novel, *Betsey Brown* (1985), for being "more straightforward and less idiosyncratic" than *Sassafrass, Cypress & Indigo,* and she likes Shange's "extraordinary ear for the spoken word." Susan Schindehette (May/June 1985), however, finds that "there is no glue to bind [the] elements into a flowing whole"; she believes that the novel "isn't really a novel after all. It is dramatist Shange's latest play." She points to the episodic style and suggests that Shange's language needs to be performed to be fully appreciated. Sherley Anne Williams (June 1985) raises a different issue: Shange's nonstandard dialect makes all of her characters sound alike, which diminishes the credibility of the middle- and upper-class characters.

Ridin' the Moon in Texas: Word Paintings (1987), a collection of poems and short stories, also met with varying responses. While Grace Bauer (1 May 1987) calls the writing "lively, sensuous,"

Camille Cole Howard (10 May 1987) finds it to be "an uneven book, but worth the effort."

Several articles have focused on thematic issues in *Sassafrass, Cypress & Indigo*, placing Shange in a context with other black writers. These include Barbara Christian's "No More Buried Lives: The Theme of Lesbianism in Lorde, Naylor, Shange, Walker" (Spring 1985); Chikwenye Okonjo Ogunyemi's "Womanism: The Dynamics of the Contemporary Black Female Novel in English" (Autumn 1985); and Friederike Hajek's German-language "Ethnizität und Frauenemanzipation: Der afroamerikanische Roman nach den sechziger Jahren" (1983).

Shange's creative contribution seems far from completed, but it remains to be seen in which genre she will concentrate. Commenting on her frustration with the theater, she told Betsko and Koenig that she has two plays ready for production, "but I'm not writing any more until these two go on [stage]. What's the point?" The impact of *For Colored Girls* on black and feminist drama is indisputable, but in the future we can expect closer treatments of the poetry and fiction, and readings of *For Colored Girls* will be increasingly informed by the perspectives Shange offers in her other works. As Shange pointed out in the Early interview, her intentions cannot be appreciated in fragments. The issues are much the same from one work to another: black experience in the United States, the oppression of women, the problems of the Third World. But the point of view continues to shift; each work offers a different perspective of the same vision.

Sam Shepard

(1943-)

Lynda Hart
University of Pennsylvania

PRIMARY BIBLIOGRAPHY

Books

Five Plays. Indianapolis: Bobbs-Merrill, 1967; London: Faber & Faber, 1969. Comprises *Chicago, Icarus's Mother, Red Cross, Fourteen Hundred Thousand*, and *Melodrama Play*. Republished as *Chicago and Other Plays*. New York: Urizen, 1981.

La Turista. Indianapolis: Bobbs-Merrill, 1968; London: Faber & Faber, 1969. Play.

Operation Sidewinder. Indianapolis: Bobbs-Merrill, 1970. Play.

Sam Shepard: Mad Dog Blues & Other Plays. New York: Winter House, 1972. Comprises *Mad Dog Blues, Cowboy Mouth* (by Shepard and Patti Smith), *The Rock Garden*, and *Cowboys #2*.

The Unseen Hand and Other Plays. Indianapolis: Bobbs-Merrill, 1972. Comprises *The Unseen Hand, Forensic and the Navigators, The Holy Ghostly, Back Dog Beast Bait, Shaved Splits*, and *4-H Club*.

Hawk Moon. Los Angeles: Black Sparrow, 1973. Poetry and prose.

The Tooth of Crime; and, Geography of a Horse Dreamer. New York: Grove, 1974; London: Faber & Faber, 1974. Plays.

Action and The Unseen Hand. London: Faber & Faber, 1975. Plays.

Angel City, Curse of the Starving Class & Other Plays. New York: Urizen, 1976; London: Faber & Faber, 1978. Comprises *Angel City, Curse of the Starving Class, Killer's Head, Action, Mad Dog Blues, Cowboy Mouth* (by Shepard and Smith), *The Rock Garden*, and *Cowboys #2*.

The Rolling Thunder Logbook. New York: Viking, 1977. Chronicle of Bob Dylan's Rolling Thunder Revue.

Buried Child & Seduced & Suicide in B^b. New York: Urizen, 1979. Plays.

Sam Shepard: Seven Plays. New York & Toronto: Bantam, 1981; London: Faber & Faber, 1985. Comprises *Buried Child, Curse of the Starving Class, The Tooth of Crime, La Turista, Tongues, Savage/ Love,* and *True West.*

Motel Chronicles. San Francisco: City Lights, 1982. Poetry and prose.

Fool for Love and The Sad Lament of Pecos Bill on the Eve of Killing His Wife. San Francisco: City Lights, 1983.

Fool for Love and Other Plays. New York & Toronto: Bantam, 1984. Comprises *Fool for Love, Angel City, Melodrama Play, Cowboy Mouth* (by Shepard and Smith), *Action, Suicide in B♭, Seduced,* and *Geography of a Horse Dreamer.*

A Lie of the Mind and The War in Heaven. New York: New American Library, 1986. Plays.

Premiere Productions

Cowboys. New York, Theatre Genesis, 10 Oct. 1964.

The Rock Garden. New York, Theatre Genesis, 10 Oct. 1964.

Dog. New York, La Mama Experimental Theater Club, 10 Feb. 1965.

Rocking Chair. New York, La Mama Experimental Theater Club, 10 Feb. 1965.

Up to Thursday. New York, Cherry Lane Theatre, 10 Feb. 1965.

Chicago. New York, Theatre Genesis, 16 Apr. 1965.

Icarus's Mother. New York, Caffe Cino, 16 Nov. 1965.

4-H Club. New York, Cherry Lane Theatre, 1965.

Red Cross. New York, Judson Poets' Theatre, Jan. 1966.

Fourteen Hundred Thousand. Minneapolis, Minn., Firehouse Theatre, 1966.

La Turista. New York, American Place Theatre, 4 Mar. 1967.

Melodrama Play. New York, La Mama Experimental Theater Club, 18 May 1967.

Cowboys #2. New York, Old Reliable Theatre, 12 Aug. 1967.

Forensic and the Navigators. New York, Theatre Genesis, 29 Dec. 1967.

The Holy Ghostly. New Troupe Branch, La Mama Experimental Theater Club, 1969 European and American college tour.

The Unseen Hand. New York, La Mama Experimental Theater Club, 26 Dec. 1969.

Operation Sidewinder. New York, Repertory Theatre of Lincoln Center, 12 Mar. 1970.

Shaved Splits. New York, La Mama Experimental Theater Club, 20 July 1970.

Mad Dog Blues. New York, Theatre Genesis, 4 Mar. 1971.

Cowboy Mouth, by Shepard and Patti Smith. Edinburgh, Traverse Theatre, 12 Apr. 1971; New York, American Place Theatre, 29 Apr. 1971.

Back Bog Beast Bait. New York, American Place Theatre, 29 Apr. 1971.

The Tooth of Crime. London, Open Space, 17 July 1972; Princeton, New Jersey, McCarter Theatre, 11 Nov. 1972.

Geography of a Horse Dreamer. London, Theatre Upstairs at the Royal Court, 2 Feb. 1974.

Little Ocean. London, Hampstead Theatre Club, 25 Mar. 1974.

Action. London, Theatre Upstairs at the Royal Court, 16 Sept. 1974; New York, American Place Theatre, 4 Apr. 1975.

Killer's Head. New York, American Place Theatre, 4 Apr. 1975.

Angel City. San Francisco, Magic Theatre, 2 July 1976.

Suicide in Bᵇ. New Haven, Yale Repertory Theatre, 15 Oct. 1976.

Inacoma. San Francisco, Magic Theatre, 18 Mar. 1977.

Curse of the Starving Class. London, Royal Court Theatre, Apr. 1977; New York, New York Shakespeare Festival, 2 Mar. 1978.

Buried Child. San Francisco, Magic Theatre, 27 June 1978.

Tongues. San Francisco, Magic Theatre, 1978.

Savage/Love. New York, American Place Theatre, Feb. 1979.

Seduced. New York, American Place Theatre, Feb. 1979.

True West. San Francisco, Magic Theatre, 10 July 1980.

Fool for Love. San Francisco, Magic Theatre, 8 Feb. 1983.

The Sad Lament of Pecos Bill on the Eve of Killing His Wife. New York, La Mama Experimental Theater Club, Sept. 1983.

Superstitions. New York, La Mama Experimental Theater Club, Sept. 1983.

A Lie of the Mind. New York, Promenade Theatre, 22 Nov. 1985.

Selected Other

Zabriskie Point, by Shepard, Michelangelo Antonioni, and Fred Gardner. M-G-M, 1970. Screenplay.

"Visualization, Language, and the Inner Library," *Drama Review,* 21 (Dec. 1970), 49-58. Essay. Collected in *American Dreams: The Imagination of Sam Shepard,* ed. Bonnie Marranca. See Collection of Essays.

"Autobiography," *News of the American Place Theatre*, 3 (Apr. 1971), 1-3.

"American Experimental Theatre Then and Now," *Performing Arts Journal*, 2 (Fall 1977), 13-14. Essay. Collected in Marranca. See Collection of Essays.

Paris, Texas. Road Movies, 1984. Screenplay.

Fool for Love. Cannon, 1985. Screenplay.

SECONDARY BIBLIOGRAPHY

Bibliographies and Checklists

Bigsby, C. W. E. "Theatre Checklist No. 3: Sam Shepard," *Theatrefacts*, 3 (Aug./Oct. 1974), 3-11. Primary and secondary.

Hart, Lynda. *Sam Shepard's Metaphorical Stages*. Westport, Conn.: Greenwood, 1987, 149-152. Primary and secondary.

Oumano, Ellen. *Sam Shepard: The Life and Work of an American Dreamer*. New York: St. Martin's, 1986, 163-170. Primary and secondary.

Shewey, Don. *Sam Shepard*. New York: Dell, 1985, 187-189. Primary and secondary.

Biographies

Oumano, Ellen. *Sam Shepard: The Life and Work of an American Dreamer*. New York: St. Martin's, 1986.

Shewey, Don. *Sam Shepard*. New York: Dell, 1985.

Interviews

Chubb, Kenneth. "Metaphors, Mad Dogs, and Old Time Cowboys," *Theatre Quarterly*, 4 (Aug./Oct. 1974), 3-16. Collected in Marranca. See Collection of Essays.

Coe, Robert. "The Saga of Sam Shepard," *New York Times Magazine*, 23 Nov. 1980, pp. 56-59, 118-124.

Dark, John. "The 'True West' Interviews," *West Coast Plays*, 9 (1981), 53-71.

Fay, Stephen. "Renaissance Man Rides Out of the West," *London Sunday Times Magazine*, 26 Aug. 1984, pp. 16-19.

Fay. "the silent type," *Vogue*, 175 (Feb. 1985), 213-218.

Freedman, Samuel. "Sam Shepard and the Mythic Family," *New York Times*, 1 Dec. 1985, section 2, pp. 1, 20.

Goldberg, Robert. "Sam Shepard, American Original," *Playboy*, 31 (Mar. 1984), 90, 112, 192-193.

Hamill, Pete. "The New American Hero," *New York*, 16 (5 Dec. 1983), 75-102.

Kakutani, Michiko. "Myths, Dreams, Realities–Sam Shepard's America," *New York Times*, 29 Jan. 1984, section 2, pp. 1, 26.

Kroll, Jack. "Who's That Tall Dark Stranger?," *Newsweek*, 106 (11 Nov. 1985), 68-74.

Lippman, Amy. "Rhythm and Truths: An Interview with Sam Shepard," *American Theatre*, 1, no. 1 (1984), 9-13, 40-41.

Oppenheim, Irene, and Victor Fascio. "The Most Promising Playwright in America Today is Sam Shepard," *Village Voice*, 27 Oct. 1975, pp. 80-82.

Peachment, Chris. "The Time Out Interview," *Time Out* (London), no. 731, 23-29 Aug. 1984, pp. 14-17.

VerMuelen, Michael. "Sam Shepard, Yes, Yes, Yes," *Esquire*, 93 (Feb. 1980), 79-86.

Critical Studies: Books

Auerbach, Doris. *Sam Shepard, Arthur Kopit, and the Off-Broadway Theater*. Boston: Twayne, 1982.

Hart, Lynda. *Sam Shepard's Metaphorical Stages*. Westport, Conn.: Greenwood, 1987.

Mottram, Ron. *Inner Landscapes: The Theater of Sam Shepard*. Columbia: University of Missouri Press, 1984.

Critical Studies: Collection of Essays

Marranca, Bonnie, ed. *American Dreams: The Imagination of Sam Shepard*. New York: Performing Arts Journal, 1981.

Critical Studies: Major Reviews, Articles, and Book Sections

Albee, Edward. "Theatre: Icarus's Mother," *Village Voice*, 25 Nov. 1965, p. 19.

Bachman, Charles R. "Defusion of Menace in the Plays of Sam Shepard," *Modern Drama*, 19 (Dec. 1976), 405-415.

Bank, Rosemarie K. "Self as Other: Sam Shepard's *Fool for Love* and *A Lie of the Mind*." In *Feminist Rereadings of Modern American Drama*, ed. June Schlueter. Madison, N.J.: Fairleigh Dickinson University Press, forthcoming 1989.

Barnes, Clive. "The Theater: Sam Shepard's 'The Tooth of Crime,' " *New York Times*, 12 Nov. 1973, section 2, p. 77.

Bigsby, C. W. E. *A Critical Introduction to Twentieth-Century American Drama*, volume 3: *Beyond Broadway*. Cambridge: Cambridge University Press, 1985, 221-250.

Bigsby. "Sam Shepard: Word and Image." In *Critical Angles: European Views of Contemporary American Literature*, ed. Marc Chénetier. Carbondale: Southern Illinois University Press, 1986, 208-219.

Blau, Herbert. "The American Dream in American Gothic: The Plays of Sam Shepard and Adrienne Kennedy," *Modern Drama*, 27 (Dec. 1984), 520-539.

Brustein, Robert. "Love From Two Sides of The Ocean," *New Republic*, 188 (27 June 1983), 24-25.

Callens, Johan. "Memories of the Sea in Shepard's Illinois," *Modern Drama*, 29 (Sept. 1986), 403-415.

Carroll, Dennis. "The Filmic Cut and 'Switchback' in the Plays of Sam Shepard," *Modern Drama*, 28 (Mar. 1985), 125-138.

Cima, Gay Gibson. "Shifting Perspectives: Combining Shepard and Rauschenberg," *Theatre Journal*, 38 (Mar. 1986), 67-81.

Cohn, Ruby. *New American Dramatists: 1960-1980*. New York: Grove, 1982, 171-186.

Cohn. "Sam Shepard: Today's Passionate Shepard and His Loves." In *Essays on Contemporary American Drama*, ed. Hedwick Bock and Albert Wertheim. Munich: Hueber, 1981.

Davis, Richard A. "'Get Up Outa' Your Homemade Beds': The Plays of Sam Shepard," *Players*, 47 (Oct./Nov. 1971), 12-19.

DeRose, David. "Slouching Towards Broadway: Shepard's *A Lie of the Mind*," *Theater*, 17 (Spring 1986), 69-74.

Eder, Richard. "Sam Shepard's Obsession is America," *New York Times*, 4 Mar. 1979, section 2, pp. 1, 27.

Falk, Florence. "The Role of Performance in Sam Shepard's Plays," *Theatre Journal*, 33 (May 1981), 182-198.

Feingold, Michael. "Sam Shepard, Part-time Shaman," *Village Voice*, 4 Apr. 1977, pp. 72-75.

Funke, Lewis. "Singing the Rialto Blues," *New York Times*, 5 Mar. 1967, section 2, pp. 1, 5.

Ganz, Arthur. Afterword to *Realms of the Self: Variations on a Theme in Modern Drama*. New York: New York University Press, 1980, 215-219.

Glore, John. "The Canonization of Mojo Rootforce: Sam Shepard Live at the Pantheon," *Theater*, 12 (Summer/Fall 1981), 53-65.

Gussow, Mel. "The Deeply American Roots of Sam Shepard's Plays," *New York Times*, 2 Jan. 1979, p. C7.

Gussow. "Intimate Monologues That Speak to the Mind and the Heart," *New York Times*, 19 Dec. 1979, p. 3.

Hart, Lynda. "Sam Shepard's Pornographic Visions," *Studies in the Literary Imagination*, 21 (Fall 1988), 69-82.

Hart. "Sam Shepard's Spectacle of Impossible Heterosexuality: *Fool for Love.*" In *Feminist Rereadings of Modern American Drama*, ed. Schlueter. Madison, N.J.: Fairleigh Dickinson University Press, forthcoming 1989.

Herman, William. "Geography of a Play Dreamer: Sam Shepard." In his *Understanding Contemporary American Drama.* Columbia: University of South Carolina Press, 1987, 23-80.

Kerr, Walter. "The Audience Helped Write the Play," *New York Times*, 18 Mar. 1973, section 2, p. 3.

Kerr. " 'I Am! I Am!' He Cries—But Am He?," *New York Times*, 22 Mar. 1970, section 2, pp. 1, 3.

Kerr. "Where Has Sam Shepard Led His Audience?," *New York Times*, 5 June 1983, section 2, pp. 3, 16.

Kleb, William. "Sam Shepard's *Inacoma* at the Magic Theatre," *Theater*, 9 (Fall 1977), 59-64.

Kramer, Mimi. "In Search of the Good Shepard," *New Criterion*, 2 (Oct. 1983), 51-57.

Lion, John. "Rock 'n' Roll Jesus with a Cowboy Mouth," *American Theatre*, 1 (Apr. 1984), 4-13.

Marranca, Bonnie. "Sam Shepard." In *American Playwrights: A Critical Survey*, volume 1, by Marranca and Gautam Dasgupta. New York: Drama Book Specialists, 1981.

Mazzocco, Robert. "Sam Shepard's Big Roundup," *New York Review of Books*, 32 (9 May 1985), 21-27.

McCarthy, Gerry. " 'Acting It Out': Sam Shepard's *Action*," *Modern Drama*, 24 (Mar. 1981), 1-12.

Nash, Thomas. "Sam Shepard's *Buried Child*: The Ironic Use of Folklore," *Modern Drama*, 26 (Dec. 1983), 486-491.

Nightingale, Benedict. "Even Minimal Shepard is Food for Thought," *New York Times*, 25 Sept. 1983, section 2, pp. 5, 26.

Orbison, Tucker. "Mythic Levels in Sam Shepard's *True West*," *Modern Drama*, 27 (Dec. 1984), 506-519.

Powe, Bruce W. "The Tooth of Crime: Sam Shepard's Way With Music," *Modern Drama*, 24 (Mar. 1981), 39-46.

Putzel, Stephen. "Expectation, Confutation, Revelation: Audience Complicity in the Plays of Sam Shepard," *Modern Drama*, 30 (June 1987), 147-160.

Rich, Frank. "Stage: *Fool for Love*, Sam Shepard Western," *New York Times*, 27 May 1983, p. C3.

Rich. "Stage: Shepard's *True West*," *New York Times*, 24 Dec. 1980, p. C9.

Rich. "Theater: *A Lie of the Mind* by Sam Shepard," *New York Times*, 6 Dec. 1985, p. C3.

Robertson, Nan. "The Multidimensional Sam Shepard," *New York Times*, 21 Jan. 1986, p. C15.

Rosen, Carol. "Sam Shepard's *Angel City*: A Movie for the Stage," *Modern Drama*, 22 (Mar. 1979), 39-46.

Savran, David. "Sam Shepard's Conceptual Prison: *Action* and *The Unseen Hand*," *Theatre Journal*, 36 (Mar. 1984), 57-74.

Simon, John. "Soft Centers," *New York*, 16 (13 June 1983), 76-77.

Simon. "Theater Chronicle: Kopit, Norman, and Shepard," *Hudson Review*, 32 (Spring 1979), 77-88.

Smith, Michael. "Theatre: *Cowboys* and *The Rock Garden*," *Village Voice*, 22 Oct. 1964, p. 13.

Weales, Gerald. "American Theater Watch, 1979-1980," *Georgia Review*, 34 (Fall 1980), 497-508.

Wetzsteon, Ross. "Sam Shepard: Escape Artist," *Partisan Review*, 49, no. 2 (1982), 253-261.

Wetzsteon. "A Season for All Seasons," *Village Voice*, 6 June 1977, p. 93.

Whiting, Charles G. "Inverted Chronology in Sam Shepard's *La Turista*," *Modern Drama*, 29 (Sept. 1986), 416-422.

Wilcox, Leonard. "Modernism vs. Postmodernism: Shepard's *The Tooth of Crime* and the Discourses of Popular Culture," *Modern Drama*, 30 (Dec. 1987), 560-573.

Wren, Scott Christopher. "Camp Shepard: Exploring the Geography of Character," *West Coast Plays*, no. 7 (1980), 75-106.

Zinman, Toby Silverman. "Sam Shepard and Super-realism," *Modern Drama*, 29 (Sept. 1986), 423-430.

Zinman. "Shepard Suite," *American Theatre*, 1 (Dec. 1984), 15-17.

BIBLIOGRAPHICAL ESSAY

Bibliographies and Checklists

Sam Shepard and his critics have been so prolific that to keep up with the material published by and about him is difficult. C. W. E. Bigsby (Aug./Oct. 1974) made the first attempt, with a checklist containing brief annotations of all Shepard's plays through the unpublished *Little Ocean* and a brief listing of secondary commentary. The checklist is now out of date but is still useful, especially for its descriptions of some of the earlier and lost plays. Don Shewey (1985) and Ellen Oumano (1986) include primary bibliographies in their respective studies; their secondary bibliographies are highly selective. Lynda Hart's *Sam Shepard's Metaphorical Stages* (1987) gives a listing of Shepard's stage plays and premiere production dates as well as a listing of secondary criticism. The entry in this volume provides the most comprehensive primary and secondary Shepard bibliographies compiled to date.

Biographies

The first published Shepard biography, Don Shewey's *Sam Shepard* (1985), apparently was written in recognition of the playwright's continually increasing fame as a movie star. The author seems to have interviewed everyone who knows Shepard even in passing to compile this collection of anecdotes. Although he attempts to relate the story of Shepard's life to his work, critical commentary is slight. Instead, he includes stories about Shepard that are meant to appeal to his fans, whom Shewey assumes are primarily female. At one point Shepard is described as "the thinking woman's beefcake." Shewey recounts a number of anecdotes that play up Shepard's macho image, such as the time Shepard urinated in a stage toilet during an acting workshop at the University of California at Riverside. Shewey also pays attention to what he considers to be Shepard's "aggressive heterosexuality." Many of his plays have opened at Theatre Genesis in New York and at San Francisco's Magic Theatre; Shewey claims both venues are known for their hetero-male-centeredness. The author neglects to provide footnotes, perhaps because the book's projected audience seems to be readers who are interested more in social intrigue than in literary biography.

Readers interested in scholarly biography will be more satisfied with Ellen Oumano's *Sam Shepard: The Life and Work of an American Dreamer* (1986), which is an extended survey of Shepard's career as both playwright and actor. The book, written for general and scholarly audiences alike, is a well-documented compilation of information about Shepard's life and work. As biography, it is accurate and well written and avoids sensationalism.

Interviews

Although Shepard has granted many interviews, he still has the reputation of being reluctant to speak with critics. He is indeed rather taciturn in such sessions, and he digresses frequently to discuss topics that interest him, such as cars, prizefights, and rodeos. In spite of Shepard's reputation for silence, the collected interviews offer much information about Shepard's early life and career, and they frequently include revealing comments concerning his role as an artist, the way in which he writes plays, and the purpose he believes they serve. What emerges in the interviews is the impression that Shepard does not like to talk about his work; as he clearly indicates more than once, he simply wants to be left alone to do it. As John Lion points out in his article "Rock 'n' Roll Jesus with a Cowboy Mouth" (Apr. 1984), Shepard interviews read rather like "fireside chat[s]."

One of the earliest and best Shepard interviews was given to Kenneth Chubb (Aug./Oct. 1974) for *Theatre Quarterly*. It is rich with information about Shepard's boyhood and adolescence, his early play-writing attempts, and his scanty dramatic education (the only play he recalls reading is Samuel Beckett's *Waiting for Godot*, which a "beatnik" dropped in his lap at a party). Shepard discusses the circumstances that led to the writing of *Cowboys* and *The Rock Garden*, as well as his unpublished early plays (*Up to Thursday*, *Dog*, and *Rocking Chair*). Especially interesting are Shepard's remarks on *Icarus's Mother* and *The Tooth of Crime*. Chubb includes some interesting comments on artistic direction, as Shepard announces his intention to "try a whole different way of writing now, which is very stark and not so flashy and not full of a lot of mythic figures and everything, and try to scrape it down to the bone as much as possible." Critics have frequently cited this remark as an indication of Shepard's turn toward realism in 1976, but the play *Action* more accurately reflects the new sensibility. But Shepard says that what he intends to write might be called "realism," but not the kind of "realism where husbands and wives squabble and that kind of stuff."

Irene Oppenheim and Victor Fascio's interview with Shepard (27 Oct. 1975) also offers an interesting and informative dialogue, which takes place at the Magic Theatre in San Francisco just before the opening of *Killer's Head* and *Action* there. Shepard talks about his choice of drama as a genre; his work with Michelangelo Antonioni and Fred Gardner on the screenplay for *Zabriskie Point;* source materials for his plays; his relationships with directors; his appreciation for Beckett, Bertolt Brecht, and Peter Brook; and the concept of time in his drama.

In "The Saga of Sam Shepard" (23 Nov. 1980) Robert Coe interviews the playwright in his Marin County, California, home. Shepard begins the interview in a characteristic way, with a conversation about rodeos, but Coe then leads him into a discussion of the parallels between his life and the subject matter of his plays. Coe finds it ironic that Shepard writes in many of his plays about a kind of mythological cowboy, and Shepard replies that he is not interested in the myth but "the real thing." Then they talk about Shepard's winning the Pulitzer Prize in 1979 for *Buried Child;* news of the award came "like news of a terminal illness." But the conversation soon rambles into nostalgia. He shows Coe the hawk moon he had tattooed on his hand at the suggestion of rock 'n' roll poet Patti Smith, his collaborator on *Cowboy Mouth*; and recounts his transformation from Steve Rogers, kid from Duarte, California, to Sam Shepard, the most talked-about playwright of the Off-Off-Broadway era. Coe and Shepard go to the Magic Theatre for a rehearsal of Shepard's *True West*, and Shepard comments, "that section about the Mojave was really breathing. You didn't have to do nothing but just be. It needs to be continually simplified like that." They then slip out of the rehearsal and go to San Francisco's Civic Auditorium to watch a simulcast of a boxing match between Roberto Duran and Sugar Ray Leonard. Shepard takes notes on the fight; director Robert Woodruff will use the material to coach the actors in *True West.* In "The 'True West' Interviews" (1981) John Dark reveals more about the production, in talks with Shepard, director Woodruff, and stage manager Kathryn Barcos.

Michael VerMuelen visited Shepard during a rehearsal of the Magic Theatre's production of *Suicide in B^b*. His article, "Sam Shepard, Yes, Yes, Yes" (Feb. 1980), focuses on the rehearsal for that play, but VerMuelen also tries to scan Shepard's entire career. The playwright, unfortunately, was particularly impenetrable that day, reinforcing his image as a half-innocent angel, half-sneering cowboy. The interview could have been an interesting inside look at Shepard's interactions with directors and actors, but he provides only a few offhand remarks about roller skating and about how the plays are not supposed to mean anything. He fixes his gaze into the distance instead and ignores questions from the actors and director Woodruff. At one point something provocative does come up, as Shepard asks a question about the role of the playwright in a dramatic production: "Is there really a sense of responsibility between the thing that you make and the people who come in touch with it?" He proposes no answer, but at least Shepard acknowledges that such a responsibility might exist.

Pete Hamill (5 Dec. 1983) interviewed Shepard on a set for the film *Country*. Hamill romanticizes Shepard, emphasizes his charm and his appeal to women, and describes touching moments between Shepard and coproducer Jessica Lange. Hamill paints a portrait of a sort of new American hero as he is being interviewed in his trailer—a copy of the magazine *Western Horseman* is on the sofa, a Remington 870 pump-action shotgun leans against the wall, and a bag of chewing tobacco is on a table. There is the usual large dose of biographical detail in the interview along with some discussion of Shepard's ambivalent feelings about acting. Hamill asks pertinent questions about Shepard's interest in music and how that is incorporated into the plays, as well as some dialogue about Shepard's concept of characterization and the influence of Peter Brook. At the conclusion of the interview Shepard announces his plans to write a comedy: "something funny. Like Laurel and Hardy."

Chris Peachment (23-29 Aug. 1984) hails Shepard as the "greatest U.S. playwright of his generation." The interview retraces much old terrain but yields some interesting commentary on *The Tooth of Crime*, the play many critics consider Shepard's best work. The playwright comments, "It's a failure as a play. Overall it doesn't have a totality or a cohesiveness." Shepard praises the work of the actors in the stage version of *Fool for Love*; he speaks of his admiration for Swedish dramatist August Strindberg, a playwright who was emphatically "*going through* something" when he wrote; he praises Terence Malick, who directed Shepard in the film *Days of Heaven*; and also recalls his collaboration with Wim Wenders, director of the film *Paris, Texas*, for which Shepard wrote the screenplay. Peachment's interview is particularly interesting because it reinforces the notion of Shepard as the romantic embodiment of the all-American rugged individualist.

Robert Goldberg's interview with Shepard for *Playboy* (Mar. 1984) is rambling conversation about fast cars, riding and roping cattle, his disdain for Broadway, his acting career, his ubiquitous father's anger, and his role as Chuck Yeager in the film *The Right Stuff;* the only new information here is the discussion of a projected screenplay, "Synthetic Tears."

Michiko Kakutani's 29 January 1984 interview is more focused on Shepard as playwright and actor than are other interviews given in 1984. Shepard reports that he does not consider acting to be a career but "just something I do." Theater, on the other hand, continues to fascinate him. It is an art form "where you could amalgamate all the art[s] . . . you can show film . . . you can dance, you can incorporate painting and sculpture, . . . the rules are wide open." He also discusses the shift from his early imagistic plays—"fractured and fragmented and broken" visions—to the later narrative dramas, a shift he describes as "some kind of evolution," which has to do with character and form: "Originally I was fascinated by form, by exteriors—starting from the outside and going in, with the idea that character is something shifting and that it can shift from one person to another." Also interesting in this interview are Shepard's views on the American male psyche: "You don't have to look very far to see that the American male is on a very bad trip."

Amy Lippman's (1984) interview focuses successfully on some of the plays and on the process of writing, but throughout Shepard displays a tendency to digress. Lippman asks Shepard pointed questions about the art of the dramatist: "Do you have a certain idea of what the play's ending will be? Do you consider your work to revolve around myths? What writers have influenced you? What playwrights?" Shepard is characteristically evasive, at one point answering "I don't know. What's the point?" But Lippman is a most persistent questioner and pushes Shepard. When he begins to mystify the process of writing, claiming, as he usually does, that he just "latches onto something" or "follows something that is already happening," Lippman presses, "But aren't you the playwright, controlling everything? You're creating it aren't you?" Shepard answers these questions with more questions, but Lippman's is the most successful interview; she comes closest to forcing an admission from Shepard that writing is not such a mysterious process as he would have it seem.

Jack Kroll follows Shepard on the movie set of *Fool for Love* in "Who's That Tall Dark Stranger?" (11 Nov. 1985). Like earlier interviewers Kroll cannot resist gathering as many biographical facts as Shepard is willing to reveal. Again emphasis is placed on Shepard's relationship with his father and, while no new details are revealed, Kroll does manage to elicit interesting comments on Shepard's feelings about women—in New York, in the early days, Shepard says, he "rode everything with hair." Robert Altman, director of the film, comments that Jessica Lange's presence on the set brings out Shepard's aggressiveness. Kroll interjects a sizable amount of critical commentary, rather blithely identifying Shepard as a writer who has created "the most searching explorations of family dynamics since O'Neill."

Samuel Freedman's "Sam Shepard and the Mythic Family" (1 Dec. 1985) includes excerpts from conversations with Shepard and his sister, Roxanne Rogers, who was assistant director of a production of Shepard's play *A Lie of the Mind*. Shepard's relationship with his father is again highlighted in this article, particularly his reactions to his father's then-recent death and the rage he felt as a young man in a tortured father-son relationship.

Stephen Fay (Feb. 1985) interviewed Shepard in a restaurant in Santa Fe, New Mexico. The lead-in to the interview refers to Shepard as "America's most intense, elusive sex symbol"; later on Fay refers to him as the "American West's version of Renaissance man." The photograph of the playwright that accompanies the interview shows him picking his teeth. The Shepard that emerges is "an untutored anarchist, an innocent pessimist, and besides that, a bit of a cowboy." The most interesting comments Fay elicits are about violence: "there's no need to be frightened of it. . . . I find I can use it as a vehicle for other feelings." The playwright also talks about relationships between men and women: they are "terrible and impossible." When Fay queries Shepard about what social class he belongs to, Shepard claims that he belongs to no class, that he is too independent to belong to anything but the Santa Fe polo club.

Critical Studies: Books

Shepard has received modest attention in book-length critical studies. He has been writing plays for almost twenty-five years, but recognition came to him rather late; it has only been since he began writing quasi-realistic plays in the late 1970s that critics have paid him much attention. Shepard has also resisted being produced on Broadway, a factor that has undoubtedly curtailed media attention and played a part in reducing the magnitude of critical inquiry. His critical status also has been complicated by his image as a "popular hero" and his fame as a movie actor.

Doris Auerbach's *Sam Shepard, Arthur Kopit and the Off-Broadway Theater* (1982), the first critical examination of Shepard's plays, is limited by space and format considerations mainly to plot summary. She gives more extended treatment to *The Tooth of Crime* and *Buried Child* with satisfying results. Her interesting unpublished correspondence with Shepard is included in excerpts.

The book's most important contribution to Shepard studies is the thesis that Shepard (and fellow playwright Arthur Kopit) share an Off-Broadway perspective, which both limits their ability to reach the heights of material success and tends to sustain them on the level they have reached. While Shepard has gone on to greater fame as an author of screenplays and a movie actor, the thesis probably still holds for that part of Shepard still devoted to theater.

Ron Mottram's *Inner Landscapes: The Theater of Sam Shepard* (1984) was the first full-length treatment of Shepard's work. Although Mottram leans heavily on biographical information, he does resist the attitude that Shepard is more interesting than his work. He also seeks to unsettle the assumption that Shepard's plays appeal more to the senses than the intellect and finds that Shepard's drama is most intellectually significant for its presentation of American culture. Mottram opens with a brief discussion of Shepard's early life and his emergence as a playwright with the production of *Cowboys* and *The Rock Garden* in 1964. Subsequent chapters analyze the plays of the 1960s, the plays written during Shepard's "crisis years" in England, the transitional plays of the mid 1970s, and the family trilogy: *Curse of the Starving Class*, *Buried Child*, and *True West*. Mottram draws parallels between Shepard's work and the works of Beckett and Brecht. Useful as an introductory overview of the Shepard canon, the book still sometimes takes on too much and ends up summarizing rather than explicating or analyzing. Mottram, like so many other Shepard critics, finally relies heavily on Shepard himself as a unifying thesis, finding him to be, like Walt Whitman, a writer who "sings himself " while projecting a profoundly disturbing image of American culture.

Lynda Hart's *Sam Shepard's Metaphorical Stages* (1987) focuses on ten plays that exemplify Shepard's growth and development as a playwright. Considering the plays from both literary and performance standpoints, Hart begins with *Cowboys #2* and proceeds through *A Lie of the Mind*, tracing Shepard's structural and thematic development from a self-conscious metatheatricalism to the modified realism of his most recent work. Hart finds that classifying

Shepard's plays is difficult partly because of his connections to European modernism, a link that is often overlooked in favor of an emphasis on American mythic elements. She contends that while the early plays concern subjective efforts to remake the world or to create it anew, the later plays contain social commentary that confronts what Shepard considers to be unacceptable elements in American life. Shepard's synthesis of forms is compared to such literary movements as metatheater, expressionism, postexpressionism, surrealism, absurdism, and realism. In an afterword Hart describes Shepard's film career and draws correspondences between the life of the actor and the art of the dramatist. Resources included in the book are a chronology and an appendix covering the playwright's published works and premiere performances.

Critical Studies: Collection of Essays

Bonnie Marranca's *American Dreams: The Imagination of Sam Shepard* (1981) is the only collection of scholarly articles on Shepard published to date. The book represents a wide spectrum of critical viewpoints and fulfills Marranca's intention of "opening up more rigorous dialogue on his work." Marranca's introduction, "Alphabetical Shepard: The Play of Words," raises many interesting issues which later articles develop more fully. She discusses Shepard's debt to Brecht, his concept of character, food imagery in the plays, the body and its landscapes, the use of jazz, melodramatic elements in the plays, the frontier ethic, and Shepard's oppressive view of women.

Gerald Weales's "The Transformations of Sam Shepard" opens the collection with a discussion of Shepard's recurrent structural emphasis on escape or transformation, which reflects thematic concerns such as "the invention of the self, its transformation under pressure through release, the need to escape, the threat or attraction of real or symbolic death." Jack Gelber's "The Playwright as Shaman" follows with a discussion of Shepard's plays as metaphysical "trips," quests, adventures, and narratives. They are a series of personal visions presented by a shaman, or visionary. John Lahr analyzes *Operation Sidewinder* in "Spectacle of Disintegration," emphasizing the play's "outlandish plot," which pits the world of the spirit against the material world. In "Image Shots are Blown" Robert Coe reads Shepard's "Rock Plays"–*Cowboy Mouth, Mad Dog Blues*, and *The Tooth of Crime*–finding in the latter a kind of "communal giving of spirit energy" that he thinks makes both theater and rock 'n' roll music great. The collection also contains Elizabeth Hardwick's introduction to Shepard's *La Turista*, useful particularly for its critique of the critic's role.

Michael Bloom explores Shepard's early plays in "Visions of the End." Defending Shepard against critics who find them mysterious and arbitrary, Bloom makes intelligible such nonnarrative work as *Chicago, The Rock Garden, Red Cross,* and *Operation Sidewinder,* which create apocalyptic visions that expose "the potential chaos that lurks beneath the contemporary scene." In "A Trip Through Popular Culture" George Stambolian shows how Shepard mixes and manipulates images from popular culture in *Mad Dog Blues,* as he "searches for a new mythology that will encompass all the diverse figures of our cultural history together with the social and psychological conditions they represent." In "Men Without Women" Florence Falk defines the Shepard landscape as the domain of "Male Homo Erectus"; it is an eminently masculine geography in which "any female is, perforce, marginalized." Falk's essay is clearsighted in its perception of the essentially homoerotic world that Shepard's characters inhabit, where women are merely handmaidens. Her reading is apparently so blatant that it has been overlooked by other critics until recently; she opens up the Shepard canon to a much-needed feminist analysis.

In "What Price Freedom" Stanley Kauffmann finds Shepard to be the "archetypal post-Broadway playwright," which he does not consider a promising appellation because it has given him artistic freedom only at the cost of being able to refine his art. In "Paired Existence Meets the Monster" Ren Fruitkin looks at coupling–"paired existence, the difficult act of being one-of-two, or two-as-one"–a recurring pattern in Shepard's plays but foregrounded in *Cowboys #2, Red Cross,* and *La Turista.* In these plays Fruitkin finds that mutuality is heir to disaster, that the binary model is built for destruction. Shepard's pairings contain a disastrous momentum that "is bound up with wayward, derailed creativity"–the fashioning of "monsters of mutuality."

In "Worse Than Being Homeless" William Kleb discusses the implications of Shepard's use of character role-reversal and his concept of the West, which is a highly charged idea in many of the plays. Kleb's is also an overview analysis that sets the tone for later psychoanalytic readings of Shepard. His use of Laingian ideas seems dated, but the article is important because it is the first reading of Shepard that draws parallels between the plays and his relationship with his father in a way that alludes to the Oedipal conflicts so apparent in the family plays.

Michael Earley enlarges critics' perceptions of Shepard's work by examining the plays in the broad context of the American literary tradition. Earley's article, "Of Life Immense in Passion, Pulse, and Power," finds in Shepard's drama "themes, language, and mythic preoccupations" linking him to such writers as Hawthorne, Melville, and Whitman. In "Looking a Gift Horse Dreamer in the Mouth" Ross Wetzsteon reads Shepard's *Geography of a Horse Dreamer* as an extended metaphor for the artist's own dilemma. The narrative operates symbolically as a substitute for the playwright's journey. The final critical article in the collection is Eileen Blumenthal's "Sam Shepard and Joseph Chaikin: Speaking in Tongues," which discusses the important collaboration of Shepard and Chaikin in the two monologues, *Tongues* and *Savage/Love*.

The Marranca collection also contains three pieces on "Directing the Plays": Robert Coe's interview with Robert Woodruff, who has directed most of the Shepard premieres at San Francisco's Magic Theatre; Michael Smith's director's notes for *Icarus's Mother*; and Richard Schechnar's illuminating rehearsal notes for the Performance Group's production of *The Tooth of Crime*. In a third section Joyce Aaron discusses her experience as an actress in Shepard's plays, and Gautam Dasgupta interviews Spalding Gray, who played Hoss in the Performance Group's production of *The Tooth of Crime*.

The final section, "Shepard on Shepard," contains four important documents, Kenneth Chubb's interview with the playwright and three Shepard essays. In the short piece "Time" Shepard discusses the crippling effect that pressure to produce full-length plays can have on a young playwright's creative development. In "American Experimental Theatre: Then and Now" Shepard continues this theme, emphasizing his dislike of the de facto requirement to move beyond experimental modes in writing. In "Language, Visualization and the Inner Library" Shepard describes the process of writing, reiterating his concern that a search for "new forms," which he feels is dictated by the intellectual/critical community, oppresses the mythical, mysterious nature of the creative process.

Critical Studies: Major Reviews, Articles, and Book Sections

Shepard's plays have captured the attention of theater reviewers from the beginning of his career. Michael Smith's review of *Cow-*

boys and *The Rock Garden* (22 Oct. 1964) buoyed Shepard's confidence and persuaded him to pursue his career as a playwright. While other early reviewers dismissed the plays as empty imitations of Beckett, Smith recognized that the work was "distinctly American and his own . . . provocative and genuinely original."

Edward Albee (25 Nov. 1965) acknowledges Shepard as one of the most gifted playwrights working in Off-Broadway but regretfully reports that the Caffe Cino's production of *Icarus's Mother* is "a mess." He gives Shepard some credit for enduring the inhospitable environment of American theater, which gives young playwrights no room to explore without the fear of being labeled failures. But he also suspects that the play signals "a premature crystallization of Shepard's theatre aesthetic" and thus finds its failure more serious. Even though Shepard's plays are not supposed to be about anything, Albee suspects that *Icarus's Mother* is indeed about something, but that that something is lost along with the best qualities of Shepard's work—"spontaneity and inevitability."

Lewis Funke's review of a *La Turista* production at the American Place Theatre (5 Mar. 1967) recognizes Shepard as the first playwright to accept the APT's option to exclude critics from performances. This was Shepard's first full-length production and, quoted in the review, he makes his opinion of critics clear: "If I ever got wealthy enough to produce my own plays, I'd never have them reviewed." Shepard says that *La Turista* is meant to be "a theatrical event, that's all."

Walter Kerr's review of *Operation Sidewinder* (22 Mar. 1970) derides the play for overpowering visual effects that render the language ineffectual. He also finds the production uninteresting because of its lumbersome set, boring music, and stale conventional jokes, which make it seem self-indulgent.

Clive Barnes (12 Nov. 1973) regards Shepard as "a young American playwright of pure brilliance and imaginative fantasy" in his review of *The Tooth of Crime*. Barnes recognizes a connection between the play's action and ritualistic combat between kings in Druidic societies, but Barnes misses the contemporary import of the ritual in American society, the "autorape" of Hoss's assistant, which Barnes describes as "hilarious but pointless." Not only is this scene one of the most disturbing stage enactments of rape in contemporary drama, it is clearly Hoss's fantasy that Becky acts out. It is also profoundly connected to the mythical combative structure of the play as a whole; men act out rituals of aggression while women serve as hand-maidens.

Walter Kerr (18 Mar. 1973) finds Performance Group's production of *The Tooth of Crime* intriguing but finally lacking thematic anchor. During the production the audience was free to side with either antagonist, and Kerr thinks the most interesting moment occurred when the audience moved away from Hoss to side with Crow, anticipating the direction of Shepard's play before the action suggested such a swing. The audience decided the issue, Kerr declares, in effect "writing Mr. Shepard's play for him."

Ross Wetzsteon (6 June 1977) reviewed Shepard's *Curse of the Starving Class* after it won the 1976-1977 Obie Award and described it as a Southern Californian cross between Chekhov's *The Cherry Orchard* (1904) and Erskine Caldwell's *Tobacco Road* (1932). "Subtler and less sentimental" than any of Shepard's previous work, it is a "big" play, the American masterpiece that critics and observers had been anticipating.

In "Sam Shepard, Part-time Shaman" (14 Apr. 1977) Michael Feingold reviews the 1977 McCarter Theater production of *Angel City*. He calls Shepard a virtuoso performer, merely dexterous on occasion but always satisfying. The play is compared to other "young-writer-meets-dream-factory stories," such as Nathanael West's *The Day of the Locust* (1939) and the Billy Wilder film *Sunset Boulevard* (1950), but Feingold finds in Shepard's play a different attack on the subject, a "different moral view." Feingold creates a good impression of the work: Shepard establishes a "neon-lit world of abrupt transformations, unexpected violence, and glorious, impassioned rhetoric," though he never makes it completely clear just what he thinks is distinctive about the play's moral vision.

Mel Gussow reviews *Tongues* and *Savage/Love* in "Intimate Monologues That Speak to the Mind and the Heart" (19 Dec. 1979). Gussow points out Joe Chaikin and Shepard's shared roots in Chaikin's Open Theatre and describes *Tongues* as "an exquisite piece of performance theater" and "a consolidation, a precis of the work of these two extraordinary theater artists over a span of 15 years." Gussow finds the key to both pieces in the last line of *Tongues:* "Tonight I am learning its language"–the language is that of death. Gussow's review is useful for the precision with which he describes Chaikin's performance, "one of those rare one-man performances in which a stage seems richly and densely populated." Chaikin performs with "balletic grace" as he "physicalizes his longing and his distress." Gussow's description of the evening's drama contextualizes and concretizes this rare collaboration.

Gussow's "The Deeply American Roots of Sam Shepard's Plays" (2 Jan. 1979) contributes to the legendmaking of Shepard that has become a minor industry. Gussow opens with a romantic description of Shepard's role in Terence Malick's film *Days of Heaven* (1978): "his presence . . . is so filled with authenticity that . . . he might become a western movie star–a Gary Cooper for the late 1970s." The plays recall mythic America in equally effective ways: the dead child in *Buried Child* reminds Gussow of the fantasy child in Edward Albee's *Who's Afraid of Virginia Woolf?* (1962). Both stand as symbols of the decay of moral America. *Buried Child* is set in a claustrophobic room just as is the Albee play, and the room in *Buried Child* is meant to point out that modern life is the constricted opposite of the frontier ethos of openness.

Richard Eder's "Sam Shepard's Obsession is America" (4 Mar. 1979) likewise recognizes the fundamentally American orientation of Shepard's work: "Like Thomas Wolfe, Shepard is haunted by the size and energy of his continent." Eder divides Shepard's plays into two groups: success plays and failure plays. The former group consists of plays, such as *The Tooth of Crime* and *Seduced*, that are peopled by mythical heroes; the latter group is composed of more realistic plays, such as *Curse of the Starving Class* and *Buried Child*, which Eder prefers because they emphasize the victims of the American dream. He finds *Buried Child* more satisfying than *Curse of the Starving Class* because the characters "gain more ground" and the images are better balanced. The realistic plays are more accessible, more connected to social reality. Realism entails a certain loss of control for a playwright but also promises the possibility of growth.

In "Theater Chronicle: Kopit, Norman, and Shepard" John Simon (Spring 1979) selects Arthur Kopit's *Wings*, Marsha Norman's *Getting Out*, and Shepard's *Buried Child* as the three best plays of the 1979 season. In each he finds that language is the least important element; all three playwrights have a strong sense of how to use the stage, and all three plays are in part studies of split personalities. The conclusions he draws from these commonalities are rather weak: he speculates that "the recession of the word causes the loss of a sense of a full unified selfhood"; perhaps it is the other way around. Simon is also puzzled by the play's contradictions in reference to the "buried child." He seems to want the play's "facts" to add up to something rational and wonders if the buried child is

Dodge's offspring, Tilden's son born of incest, or Vince. He finally concludes that "the tiny little white shoot" that pops out of the ground at the play's end is the buried child. But his speculations are not any more logical than the play's images; he seems to be forcing a reading that demands a unity and singularity, reducing rather than expanding the play. Gerald Weales's "American Theater Watch, 1979-1980" (Fall 1980) is quite useful for its description of Shepard's collaborations with actor Joe Chaikin, *Tongues* and *Savage/ Love*. Weales vividly re-creates the experience of these monologues, making an important contribution by summarizing plays that are not likely to be restaged.

Frank Rich (24 Dec. 1980) thinks that *True West* is "one of American theater's most precious natural resources," but he thinks that the production suffered from a lack of direction and amounted to "little more than a stand-up run-through of a text that remains to be explored." The dialogue died before it reached the audience, the actors stepped on each others' lines, entrances and scene-endings appeared arbitrary, and the farcical sequences created confusion rather than mirth. Rich's appreciation for Shepard's talents, however, shines through. Everything is blamed on the production, and Shepard remains an "awesome writer," a "true artist," a playwright whose "best works are organic creations that cannot be broken down into their constituent parts."

John Simon reviews a Shepard-directed production of *Fool for Love* in a 13 June 1983 issue of *New York*. He contends that Shepard overdirected the play into "frenzies of violence and excesses of languor," and despite the fine acting of the cast, the apt lighting and costumes, and the suitable set, the overdirection makes it disjointed. Despite moments of intelligible gallows humor, as a whole the play is "imponderable." Robert Brustein (27 June 1983), on the other hand, finds the same production "miraculous." He thinks that Shepard's work may well have made him one of America's finest directors. Each moment of the play is "rich with balletic nuances." Brustein particularly admires actress Kathy Baker's characterization of Mae: "She manages to exalt what in other hands might have been a slight, unfinished script into an elegiac myth of doomed love." Frank Rich (27 May 1983) thinks that *Fool for Love* is hardly "the fullest Shepard creation one ever hopes to encounter." But while he considers it less coherent than Shepard's other family plays and entirely dependent on performance energy, the play nevertheless attains an "extraordinary afterlife."

Walter Kerr (5 June 1983) loses patience with Shepard in his review of the Circle Repertory's production of *Fool for Love*. Kerr finds the play unintelligible to all but an irrationally enthusiastic "cult audience" that faithfully follows Shepard despite the fact that his work is "private and deliberately enigmatic." Kerr is unsure whether or not Shepard wants or knows how to "make his imagery clear and newly-illuminating"; in either case, Kerr finds the production to be arbitrary, boring, and meaningless, "one more sampling of Mr. Shepard's fondness for disconnective, dislocating 'effect.'"

Benedict Nightingale's review of *The Sad Lament of Pecos Bill on the Eve of Killing His Wife* and *Superstitions* (25 Sept. 1983) compliments Shepard for his creative courage. Nightingale finds that Shepard is willing to confront "fissures of feeling" that other writers shrink from exploring in drama; he never shys away from "ugly denouements." *The Sad Lament of Pecos Bill* is Shepard's acknowledgment of the American Bicentennial, a sort of "backhanded celebration" that contrasts the "magnificence of the myth" with reality. *Superstitions* is a pastiche of lines from Shepard's prose and poem book, *Motel Chronicles*: "glimpses of the unsettled furniture of Mr. Shepard's mind." Nightingale also discusses *Operation Sidewinder*, *Fool for Love*, *Buried Child*, and several other Shepard plays in passing, defending the position that Shepard is not just an American writer, but a "dramatist of international stature."

Frank Rich (6 Dec. 1985) is altogether transported by Shepard's *A Lie of the Mind*. He claims that it is Shepard's most romantic play and is fascinated by its wider vision of "the genetic fates we all share . . . that urge for salvation." He admires Shepard's expression of "a man's timeless destiny" but misses the play's overt misogyny. Rich thinks that Shepard's brain-damaged wife and his demented, castrating mothers are the best character roles he has created for women.

In "The Multidimensional Sam Shepard" (21 Jan. 1986) Nan Robertson discusses a Shepard-directed production of *A Lie of the Mind* with its cast. What emerges is a picture of a relaxed, bemused, intensely involved but noninterfering "laissez-faire" director, an admirable but sometimes intimidating person. What is most interesting, perhaps, is that not much tension exists between Shepard the playwright and Shepard the director. He let the script for the production develop in rehearsal.

Journal articles devoted to the work of Sam Shepard cover an extensive range of subjects and provide some of the most wide-ranging commentary available in criticism of contemporary drama. In " 'Get Up Outa' Your Homemade Beds' " (Oct./Nov. 1971) Richard A. Davis finds that Shepard is among the most talented of contemporary experimental playwrights. In a discussion of *Icarus's Mother, Red Cross, Chicago, Forensic and the Navigators,* and *Operation Sidewinder,* Shepard is, according to Davis, caught up in a "continual exploration of the same human problem," exemplified by the character of Duke, a rock singer who makes it big on the basis of one song in *Melodrama Play*: "prisoners get up out of your homemade beds." Davis finds that Shepard is unfortunately in the same predicament as Duke: stuck on one note.

In "Defusion of Menace in the Plays of Sam Shepard" (Dec. 1976) Charles R. Bachman describes the pattern of violence in Shepard's plays. Dramatic violence is menacingly introduced and then defused through avoidance or vitiated through alienating devices. Bachman traces subtle variations of this pattern through six early plays, pointing out similarities to the novels of Thomas Hardy along the way. The impulse toward communion overrides the impulse toward full-blown violence; momentum, a menacing force, is lacking. The point is that Shepard is attracted to violence but ultimately repelled by it. But Bachman also observes that violence comes closer to realization when the plays take more naturalistic forms. Since the trend in Shepard's writing is toward naturalism (or realism) Bachman concludes with the prescient speculation that incidences of violence should increase in future (post-1976) plays. The essay raises interesting questions but fails to account for the presence of such violence in the plays. A social or cultural critique rather than a discussion of technique alone would be useful here.

William Kleb discusses *Inacoma,* Shepard's first workshop production since 1968, in a Fall 1977 article. The article is interesting for its detailed account of the process of collective writing employed to develop the script, which explores "a life separate from the body–dreams, hallucinations, fantasies, altered states of consciousness–as well as the process of dying." *Inacoma* was a more or less private experience for Shepard, an investigation of the performance process, and Kleb found that it lacked verbal intensity. He found it problematic, "strangely retrograde, as if Shepard were trying to tie up loose ends from the past."

In "Sam Shepard's *Angel City*: A Movie for the Stage" (Mar. 1979) Carol Rosen describes how *Angel City* "explores the playwright's own cinematic imagination, his impulse towards a filmic vocabulary, rooted in myths about power." Power is a recurrent theme in Shepard's work, manifested in this play in the link between the ambition for power and the artist's drive. Rosen shows that *Angel City* has a structural logic, but that logic is cinematic rather than theatrical: "the play jump-cuts from one image, one metaphor to the next, as if two films were being spliced together."

Florence Falk (May 1981) defines "performance" in Shepard's plays as an exaggeration or intensification "through particular actions, deeds, or feats [of] certain latent tendencies or potentialities." The plays, she ably argues, are "structured in a series of performance rituals." She identifies three primary performance modes in Shepard's plays: role-playing, story-telling, and music-making, successfully connecting such seemingly disparate plays as *Angel City, Operation Sidewinder, The Tooth of Crime, Killer's Head,* and *Suicide in B♭*. Furthermore, through her analysis of Shepard's landscapes "of the cosmos, the nation, and the self," which all share the frontier as a common territory, she underscores the theatricality of Shepard's plays. Her article links Shepard's use of performance with social commentary and concludes that the commitment to performance is "the only glimmer of hope" in what is otherwise a blighted vision of America.

Scott Christopher Wren's "Camp Shepard: Exploring the Geography of Character" (1980) is a journal of Wren's experience in a playwriting workshop with Shepard and some twenty other writers. The article is interesting for its insider's look at Shepard's interactions with other writers; it captures Shepard in the unusual role of teacher. Shepard has the writers create monologues, which he insists must be written in the immediate present, through reliance on sensation and experience alone, employing no commentary, no metaphors, and no conscious manipulation of language. They are instructed to search for the inner voice that animates character instead of trying to define character from an outsider's perspective. Some of the monologues (later they move into writing some dialogue) that were generated in the workshop are included in the article. Wren captures Shepard in an unusual situation, in which he is acting out of a sense of responsibility to other artists. When the focus is not so much on his own creative products as it is on the process of writing, Shepard is apparently more forthcoming than he is in interviews.

Bruce W. Powe analyzes "Sam Shepard's Way With Music" in a March 1981 essay that uses several plays as examples but focuses particularly on *The Tooth of Crime*. Powe finds that Shepard often uses music to convey meaning in the plays, "to invoke in his work an aura of energy, . . . to structure and evoke the actual speech patterns of characters," to create textures that echo "distinctly American traditions and concerns," to "communicate the emotional perspective of either a character or situation, or the thematic center of a work," and to "initiate a kind of communion." Powe points out that Shepard's desire to evoke emotional, affective responses makes music a powerful vehicle of expression. One glaring error in Powe's analysis is his description of Shepard's use of rock 'n' roll, which Powe terms "rape" and defines as "seduction through the release of energy and rhythm." Shepard does use such music in his plays as an expression of forced penetration, but rape is not seduction, it is violence.

In " 'Acting It Out': Sam Shepard's *Action*" (Mar. 1981) Gerry McCarthy examines the Shepard play as a metaphor for the actor's experience "in extremis," at the moment "when he is deserted by his technique and is most acutely aware of his own identity." McCarthy compares Shepard's method to Pirandello's and Beckett's and finds Shepard more "rigorous and less ostentatious" than the former, more "impressionistic and allusive" than the latter. The striking theatricalism of the play builds into a metaphor of disintegrating society, and at the heart of the metaphor is the inability of the characters to recognize that they share "the same fundamental existential problem." McCarthy's argument that Shepard's play presents an arbitrary departure from Beckett's rationalist ordering is not altogether convincing. Also problematic is his warning not to judge Shepard on the "articulateness of his thought." McCarthy's article does, however, explain Shepard's use of theatricalism in *Action*.

In "The Canonization of Mojo Rootforce: Sam Shepard Live at the Pantheon" (Summer/Fall 1981) John Glore devotes much-needed attention to the "patina of cliches" that constitute the Shepard image, pointing out that they "cover over and smooth out the details and idiosyncrasies of his plays." Glore accurately unsettles the overemphasis in Shepard criticism on his use of a kind of emblematized man, a blend of the mysterious, aloof farmer and the James Dean-like rebel, more accurately grounding Shepard's work in the "pseudo-ritualistic theatre of the late '60s." Countering majority criticism that locates Shepard in the mainstream of the American literary tradition, Glore argues that Shepard's work owes more to Artaud's Theater of Cruelty than most critics have acknowledged. The early plays, Glore argues, are "short bursts of violent creativity, impulsive, totally unencumbered by preconceived strictures." Glore also locates another tendency in Shepard's plays: a return to classical structures, especially in *The Tooth of Crime.* Shepard's late-period "stalking of the masterpiece" is most clearly exemplified in *Curse of the Starving Class* and *Buried Child*, but Glore finds in these plays a tension between Shepard's desire to write "classics," plays that are unified, purposeful, and resolute, and an underlying aesthetic of uncertainty, "a counterforce of obfuscation and iconoclasm." Glore applauds Shepard for his resistance to resolution and his "gypsy blood," his "mojo rootforce" that "fights to keep control."

In "Sam Shepard: Escape Artist" (1982) Ross Wetzsteon warns readers that his claims for Shepard will seem hyperbolic only to those who have not understood the profound impact Shepard has made on America's younger noncommercial playwrights. Wetzsteon makes quite a few exaggerated claims. He calls Shepard, with O'Neill, one of the two greatest playwrights in the history of American theater; he declares that Shepard challenges theatrical conventions as effectively as Beckett or Brecht; and he calls *Curse of the Starving Class* an American version of *The Cherry Orchard.* Wetzsteon's enthusiasm for Shepard leads him to suggest that Shepard's inventions are altogether new visions: that his plays take up emotional rather than physical space; exist in immediate rather than continuous time; and contain spontaneous rather than coherent characters. These are apt descriptions, but they are hardly inventions created by Shepard in isolation.

In sharp contrast with the critical majority, Mimi Kramer (Oct. 1983) questions the value of Shepard's work. As she wades through the mass of criticism that valorizes Shepard's "shamanism," "totemism," and "mythology," she finds little to justify the critical acclaim that he has received. Kramer focuses on Bonnie Marranca's collection, *American Dreams: The Imagination of Sam Shepard*, finding it to be "a series of long monologues in his praise," and criticizes its failure to address the question of why Shepard deserves all the attention. Kramer calls *True West* "middlebrow family entertainment" along the lines of the television series *I Love Lucy. Fool for Love* is referred to as "a trite statement that fantasies exist." In the early plays, Kramer argues, Shepard wrote as if there were no audience at all; in the later plays he locates and controls an audience's reactions with no apparent end in mind. She concludes that "Sam Shepard has precious little to say."

Thomas Nash's "Sam Shepard's *Buried Child*: The Ironic Use of Folklore" (Dec. 1983) argues that Shepard's 1979 Pulitzer Prize-winning play is "a modern version of the central theme of Western mythology, the death and rebirth of the Corn King." In Nash's reading, the play begins realistically but moves into myth, and "dim outlines of sacrificial rituals and dying gods begin to reappear in it." He compares Shepard's play to Shirley Jackson's 1949 story, "The Lottery," both of which end in the revelation of murders that are tied to the growth of corn. Thus, the play is not realistic but ironic (as Northrop Frye defines the "ironic mode").

In "Mythic Levels in Sam Shepard's *True West*" (Dec. 1984) Tucker Orbison argues that contrary to some critical assessments, mythic elements have not disappeared from Shepard's more recent family plays. Orbison demonstrates how the concept of the West in *True West* is not of a point on the compass but of a "geographical center on a mythic map," a map recognizable as the habitat of a Natty Bumppo or a Geronimo. A second level of myth is concerned with the mystery of the artist, and Lee, of *True West*, as banal as his story may seem, is the artist who believes in the power of his narrative to mysteriously emerge from the undercurrents in life. Orbison argues further that the play dramatizes what in a Jungian construct is one of the most fundamental human myths, the archetypal hostility of two brothers. Lee, the "shadow figure," is autonomous, emotional, possessive, and linked inextricably with Austin, the ego figure who seeks psychic integration with his shadow self but can never achieve it: hence the unresolved ending, as the brothers square off against each other and the lights fade slowly to black.

In "Shepard Suite" (Dec. 1984) Toby Silverman Zinman discusses George Ferencz's production of Shepard's *Suicide in B♭*, *Back Bog Beast Bait*, and *Angel City* at La Mama Experimental Theater Club. Zinman pays particular attention to the use of music; jazz drummer Max Roach's scores for these plays have the structure and freedom of actual jazz. Ferencz directs his ensemble in a way reminiscent of the collective improvisation of jazz, which Zinman finds precisely suited to Shepard's language, a language containing the power, rhythm, and "high risk" of jazz improvisation.

In "The American Dream in American Gothic: The Plays of Sam Shepard and Adrienne Kennedy" (Dec. 1984) Herbert Blau unites two unlikely candidates through their "persistence of desire in language to overcome the failed promise" of the American dream. Unlike most American dramatists, Shepard and Kennedy do not lack richly evocative linguistic gifts. Blau celebrates the dazzling explosions of language in Shepard's monologues, his "fantastic ear for all the subcultural vernaculars of American life." In Shepard and Kennedy are voices that rescue the intellectual and verbal possibilities of the dramatic genre, he concludes.

David Savran places Shepard within "the Modernist insurgence" in "Sam Shepard's Conceptual Prison: *Action* and *The Unseen Hand*" (Mar. 1984). Savran points out that critical difficulty in writing about Shepard's plays is due to the failure to recognize the deep-seated, enacted critique of fundamental dramatic relationships already in his plays. In *Action*, the Shepard play that comes closest to deconstructing traditional modes of theatrical production, Savran finds that Shepard, ironically, preserves rather than transforms or supersedes traditional theatrical forms. The desire for escape manifested in Shepard's work is undercut by his nostalgic commitment creating a "conceptual prison." Savran locates a deep contradiction in Shepard: entrapment is ubiquitous, but the desire for escape is not eliminated by the assurance of its impossibility. Thus Savran finds Shepard in an "anxious position in the Modernist tradition." The locus for Shepard's "impossible" desire lies in the female characters, who constitute a possible escape mechanism which is suppressed due to nostalgia that is in constant tension with the desire for release into productive action.

John Lion calls Shepard "the inkblot of the 80s" in his article "Rock 'n' Roll Jesus with a Cowboy Mouth." As artistic director of the San Francisco Magic Theatre, Lion has worked closely with Shepard and offers interesting details about the process of directing a Shepard play. He primarily discusses the Magic Theatre production of *Fool for Love,* giving readers excerpts from actual dialogue with Shepard during rehearsal. What emerges is an impression of Shepard as a playwright who knows precisely what he wants to happen onstage and resists realistic staging. He also draws interesting parallels between Shepard, Elvis Presley (featured on the poster for *Fool for Love*), and Allen Ginsberg. Lion insists that Shepard merits all the attention he has received and that art cannot be held up to standards of ethics and morality. Somewhat ironically, he concludes that all of Shepard's work contains a bedrock of myth—dead myths, but myths that hold out for the possibility of Christian redemption.

Robert Mazzocco's "Sam Shepard's Big Roundup" (9 May 1985) recognizes the influence of Whitman and Kerouac in Shepard's work, but Mazzocco joins the round of voices that celebrate Shepard's break with literary tradition and the grounding of his plays in improvisation and "youth culture," an "America of Buffalo Bill and Andrew Jackson, but surely not that of Henry James or Henry Adams." He argues that *The Tooth of Crime* is the quintessential Shepard play: "one of the most original achievements in contemporary theatre." Without Shepard, Mazzocco argues, contemporary American theater would have little to offer, since Shepard is the only playwright of his generation who has created a body of work that represents a lifetime achievement from Mazzocco's perspective.

In "The Filmic Cut and 'Switchback' in the Plays of Sam Shepard" (Mar. 1985) Dennis Carroll analyzes Shepard's "most characteristic stylistic device: a sudden transition from one strand of action or frame of reference to another." Developed from the transformational strategies Shepard learned as a member of Joe Chaikin's Open Theatre, Carroll finds such maneuvering more, organic to film. Carroll observes the operation of these techniques in four phases: the most developed is the "switchback" (a term he borrows from film pioneer D. W. Griffith), which is a device "used to depict a profound schism of both identity and vision in the playwright's artist-surrogate." Carroll convincingly argues his claims with examples from the plays, but it is not clear what this analysis adds to our understanding of Shepard's work that has not been accounted for by discussion of transformations as actors' devices.

In "Inverted Chronology in Sam Shepard's *La Turista*" (Sept. 1986) Charles G. Whiting proposes an explanation for the reversed chronology of the play's two acts. Such a structural arrangement creates dramatic irony, the first example Whiting finds of Shepard's theme of "failed escape" emphasizing discontinuity, process, and open-ended "resolutions." Whiting shows that Shepard's penchant for failed resolutions is not a later development but an integral structural principle; however, he does not make much of an attempt to account for the vision that informs these aborted escapes.

In "Memories of the Sea in Shepard's *Illinois*" (Sept. 1986) Johan Callens attempts to rescue Shepard's plays from their masculine bias by arguing that a realistic critical viewpoint overlooks the underlying symbolism in the family plays. Callens's mythic reading focuses on the family relationship in *Buried Child*, which recalls an "original, mythic state of One-ness, a feminine and organic bond between man and nature." The incest in the play, however misguided, is an attempt to "make the holistic Dream come true by reestablishing the union between mother and child." Callens's discovery of a "female landscape," through incest and water and fertility symbolism, leads him to a reevaluation of the female characters in the play: Halie becomes a primal force associated with water symbols, and Shelly becomes a "catalyst in the ritual revelation of the double offense of incest and infanticide." Callens's article, ironically, reinforces rather than redresses the negative view of women in Shepard's plays. His reading of *Buried Child* calls attention to the patriarchal equation of Woman and Nature, which rests on an assumption of biological essentialism and renders women as passive receptors, interceptors, or "catalysts," as Callens would have it, of male-defined concepts.

Gay Gibson Cima (Mar. 1986) compares Shepard's plays to artist Robert Rauschenberg's "combines," which are "constructions which merged painting and sculpture in a surreal attempt to push beyond the collages of Braque and Picasso." Cima argues that Shepard's plays call for directors, actors, and audiences who can respond to the disruption of traditional ideas of framing and representation. He suggests that an understanding of Rauschenberg's art can serve as a model for correctly responding to Shepard's stage images. The desire to experience Shepard's plays as representational wholes is frustrated by the absence of closure or the ambiguity of action, even in plays as seemingly realistic as *Buried Child*. Cima makes a good argument for reading that play's two conflicting main actions, one Ibsenesque in its retrospective narrative frame, the other a surreal and unsuccessful attempt to cancel the other. The "mystery" of the two Vinces, one the buried child and the other the young grandson, is illuminated in Cima's reading of multiple aesthetics at work in the play. Cima bolsters his analysis with Shepard's own repeated assertions about avoiding psychological unity in his concept of characterization as well as testimony from directors and actors who have experienced Shepard's work. Cima convincingly demonstrates that Shepard's puzzling ambiguities are not due to carelessness or lack of talent, but are intentional constructs that place the viewer in the same position as the writer, in an active, performing role.

In "Sam Shepard and Super-realism" (Sept. 1986) Zinman compares Shepard's family plays to the super-realist art of contemporary painters such as Ralph Goings, Richard Estes, and Tom Blackwell. In both she senses movement "away from the conceptual to-ward the perceptual, away from idea toward fact and event." Zinman puzzles over Shepard's intended response to his images, lean-ing toward the theory that the images simply *are*, that they require the same suspension of judgment upon which super-realist painters insist.

David DeRose (Spring 1986) finds Shepard's *A Lie of the Mind* "surprisingly tame." He admires the play for its rich population of characters and its beautiful craftsmanship but thinks that Shepard sacrifices "mythic intensity" and "wild theatricality" to make this play more accessible to a mainstream audience. *A Lie of the Mind* pre-miered in New York at the Promenade, a theater with a Broadway ad-dress but an official Off-Broadway status; DeRose finds the play "dan-gerously close to the bright lights of Broadway."

In "Modernism vs. Postmodernism: Shepard's *The Tooth of Crime* and the Discourses of Popular Culture" (Dec. 1987) Leonard Wilcox offers a way of reading Shepard that departs from the empha-sis on "nostalgia" by conceptualizing the duel in the play not only as a dialogue between the postmodern poles of pleasure and power, but also, on an allegorical level, as a battle between modernism and postmodernism. The Hoss character affirms "a modernist ethos of ar-tistic mastery and a sense of history and tradition," while Crow, Hoss's antagonist, has no time for nostalgia and is ahistorical, "a fig-ure of immaculate surfaces at home in the postmodern world." The duel of words between the characters occurs in a space of postmodern language, where "words battle to assert mastery over a no-man's-land; where discourse approaches its object as a posses-sion to be disputed and fought over, and where identity is con-structed in language." Shepard is ambivalent concerning these two discourses, yearning for modernist nostalgia while at the same time undercutting it. Shepard's family plays may suggest a movement to-ward Hoss's side of the contest, but in *The Tooth of Crime* the victory is grim and uneasy and clearly on the side of Crow, the "master adapter."

Stephen Putzel borrows Patrice Pavis's phrase "theatrical rela-tionship" to analyze spectator reception in "Expectation, Confuta-tion, Revelation: Audience Complicity in the Plays of Sam Shepard" (June 1987). Putzel focuses on the social, ideological, and literary constructs that spectators bring to a Shepard play and posits a vari-ety of audiences that are likely to admire Shepard's work. Putzel se-lects five plays to demonstrate his positions, all having their own "historicities": *Angel City* is steeped in the world of Hollywood and American big business; *Suicide in B*^{b} "conjures with the world of Raymond Chandler novels, the seamier side of the American jazz scene, and film noir"; *Curse of the Starving Class* "presents the world of the American family and the disappearing American farm culture"; *Fool for Love* evokes the American West, the rugged individual, and romantic clichés; and *A Lie of the Mind* brings together many of these worlds, but, more important perhaps, builds a stage world "out of the mystique of Sam Shepard himself." While Putzel's descriptions of the worlds in the five plays add relatively little to Shepard criticism, his focus on the spectator and his discussion of audience reception theory make very important contributions. He shows how *Angel City* uses film and theater as framing devices, while *Suicide in B*^{b} is more self-consciously theatrical. *Fool for Love* creates a "fifth wall' that avoids naturalism; however, the then most recent production of *Curse of the Starving Class* (the 1985 Patricia Daily/Arthur Master production, directed by Robin Smith), the film version of *Fool for Love*, and *A Lie of the Mind* indicate that Shepard's success has "forged a new audience with different horizons of expectations." In these productions audience expectations are "confirmed rather than confuted, and much of the revelatory quality is lost," Putzel argues. Calling for something new in Shepard's work, Putzel regrets what he sees accurately as a trend toward stagnation, in which affluent audiences' expectations are met. Shepard has become a "star with a star's audience," and that, for Putzel, does not bode well for the American theater.

Book sections on Shepard have been written by leading American literary critics. Arthur Ganz's afterword to his *Realms of the Self: Variations on a Theme in Modern Drama* (1980) is about Shepard's play *La Turista*. Ganz links Shepard with the American literary tradition through recurrent motifs of "the self transformed, the flight from hostile reality, and the achieving of a visionary fulfillment [in *La Turista*] through the archetypally romantic union with a beneficent nature." Bonnie Marranca's chapter on Shepard in *American Playwrights: A Critical Survey* (1981) is a sound overview of the plays through *Buried Child*. Marranca avoids rigid classification of the plays, finding them highly individualistic and eclectic, containing elements of absurdism, science fiction, naturalism, rock music, and detective fiction. She locates a unifying "thematics of consciousness" in Shepard's work, "the essence of an individual's awareness of himself in the world." She also argues that Shepard's plays emphasize atmosphere over dramatic structure; they evoke shifting realities. Marranca's discussion of Shepard's drama is in concert with the critical majority in terms of his criticism of American culture. It is a persistent, obsessive critique that, nonetheless, always expresses hope for "the triumph of the human spirit." Her analysis emphasizes Shepard's concern with performance as subject matter, particularly the recurring theme of the artist's power of self-creation. Finally, though she finds Shepard to be a playwright who creates with "great bravura," she feels his accomplishments have been exaggerated. She considers him most lacking in the ability to create independent female characters and points out that in order for him to become a playwright of great stature "his presentation of women will have to undergo a transformation." Marranca is basically enthusiastic about Shepard's ability to create experience on the stage that "continues to surprise and elate us," though she warns against prematurely elevating him to the status of great American playwright.

Ruby Cohn's chapter in her *New American Dramatists: 1960-1980* (1982) categorizes Shepard's plays into three phases: the early "collages," such as *Cowboys #2* and *The Rock Garden*, which dramatize "telling caricatures of American reality"; a second phase of satiric fantasies, beginning with *La Turista*, written in preparation for Shepard's "most incisive portrait of an artist," *The Tooth of Crime*; and a third, realistic, phase that begins with *Curse of the Starving Class*, the first play of Shepard's family trilogy, which Cohn thinks may compose Shepard's "attempts at Greek tragedy." Although she finds themes repeated through all phases, Cohn argues that Shepard's plays—some of them—are most memorable for their rhythms and images. Like O'Neill both in his movement from experimental forms to realism and in his dramatization of an America "mired in sin," Cohn stops short of hailing Shepard as "the all-American playwright, as though there were virtue in speaking for a chosen people."

C. W. E. Bigsby's chapter on Shepard, in volume 3 of his *A Critical Introduction to Twentieth-Century American Drama* (1985), is an overview of Shepard's plays that is firmly in the critical mainstream. Bigsby calls Shepard the most exciting product of the Off-Off-Broadway movement, an "intuitive" creator of "animating images." His early plays elaborate single or clustered images so that reality is never singular. Music plays an important role as an "emotional trigger" in the works. The plays are said to operate "principally on a nonrational, associative level and are not best approached through rational textual analysis." Bigsby considers *Operation Sidewinder* to be the signal of an important shift in Shepard's work," as the vaguely perceived sense of menace becomes objectified and an implicit need to intervene, at the level of myth or reality, is proposed." Like many other critics, Bigsby thinks *The Tooth of Crime* is Shepard's most accomplished play. Bigsby delineates a further shift with *Curse of the Starving Class*, which initiates the series of realistic plays, but it is a realism that is "under pressure," strained "in the direction of metaphor." Bigsby's discussion of Shepard's major plays is a well-written introduction.

Bigsby also has published a chapter on Shepard in Marc Chénetier's *Critical Angles: European Views of Contemporary American Literature* (1986). Here Bigsby scans the Shepard canon, identifying recurrent images of "fractured worlds" that are pervaded by an overwhelming feeling of anxiety and paranoia. Bigsby links Shepard's work with Harold Pinter's "comedies of menace," Tennessee Williams's romantic fatalism, and Edward Albee's apocalyptic visions. He asserts that Shepard's plays are "simply not susceptible to analysis in conventional terms. They are, rather, kaleidoscopes of images and characters that can find common ground only in myth." Bigsby finds *Operation Sidewinder* to be the Shepard play that comes closest "to engaging the immediate realities of the American political system," and Bigsby regards it as something of a fluke in a body of work that otherwise is more interested in creating graphic and memorable images of the products of an unjust system than in investigating the causes of injustice. Like other critics, Bigsby ponders Shepard's persistent evocation of mystery and concludes that it is a strategy the playwright preserves out of his desire to protect it, since in mystery lies a possible source of redemption.

William Herman's chapter on Shepard in his *Understanding Contemporary American Drama* (1987) succumbs to the tendency to overestimate his work. The chapter also contains some unfortunate factual errors, and his analysis is sketchy at best. Intended as an introduction for students and "good nonacademic readers," the chapter relies heavily on Bigsby, whose work is more insightful, thorough, and interesting.

In the past decade Shepard has commanded voluminous critical attention. Much of it, however, has been in the form of paeans to his visual histrionics, and only a few critics have attempted to address the group of Shepard's plays without resorting to vagueness. After more than twenty years of secondary commentary, many critics still consider Shepard's plays extraordinarily resistant to traditional forms of exegesis. Perhaps this indicates a need to examine the plays from the perspective of nontraditional methodologies. Shepard's rise to film stardom has perhaps also daunted the response of critics to his plays. But his contribution to culture, with its peculiar blend of popularity and esotericism, is a phenomenon in the American theater that bears further analysis.

Critics have only begun to scratch the surface of Shepard's significance from materialist, cultural, and feminist perspectives. Although critics like Florence Falk and Bonnie Marranca have opened the way for dialogue about Shepard's masculine bias, there remains much work to be done in this area. Lynda Hart, in "Sam Shepard's Pornographic Visions" (Fall 1988), argues that Shepard's *A Lie of the Mind* and his screenplay *Paris, Texas* re-create the pornographic gaze of his male heroes, which is reinforced by the response of mainstream reviewers. As a feminist spectator, Hart draws attention to Shepard's ironic attempt to create female authenticity, which is in fact subverted by the representational apparatus of his later works. June Schlueter is currently editing a collection of essays, to be published in 1989 as *Feminist Rereadings of Modern American Drama*, that will contain two articles on Shepard. Lynda Hart's "Sam Shepard's Spectacle of Impossible Heterosexuality" will argue that *Fool for Love* marks a transition for Shepard into explorations of the "mystery between men and women." From a feminist perspective, Shepard's idea of this "mystery" is shrouded in an ambivalent attitude toward male violence that is repellent but seductive, often received by critics as romantic. Rosemarie K. Bank's "Self as Other: Sam Shepard's *Fool for Love* and *A Lie of the Mind*" will use Foucault's notion of the "heterotopic" to signal a shift away from binary critical constructs. In Bank's analysis Shepard's plays explore doubling and transformations of gender that challenge and confound received traditions.

Early in his career Shepard was established as a countercultural artist: this stance has remained an unspoken assumption in much of the criticism of his work. The political import of his plays has been neglected while critics have deferred to commentary that addresses his artistic achievements. As literary discourse grows increasingly attuned to the inseparability of art and politics, new ways of seeing Shepard's plays should abound.

Megan Terry
(1932-)

Karen L. Laughlin
Florida State University

PRIMARY BIBLIOGRAPHY

Books

Calm Down Mother: A Transformation for Three Women. New York: French, 1966. Play.

Viet Rock; Comings and Goings; Keep Tightly Closed in a Cool Dry Place; The Gloaming, Oh My Darling: Four Plays. New York: Simon & Schuster, 1967. Includes production notes by Terry.

The People vs. Ranchman and Ex-Miss Copper Queen on a Set of Pills. New York: French, 1968. Plays. Includes prefaces and a directing note by Terry.

Approaching Simone. New York: French, 1970. Old Westbury, N.Y.: Feminist Press, 1973. Play.

Three One-Act Plays: The Magic Realists, Sanibel and Captiva, One More Little Drinkie. New York: French, 1970.

The Tommy Allen Show. New York: French, 1971. Play.

Couplings and Groupings. New York: Pantheon, 1972. Study of American attitudes toward marriage.

Megan Terry's Home: Or Future Soap. New York: French, 1972. Play.

Babes in the Bighouse. Omaha: Omaha Magic Theatre, 1974. Play.

Henna For Endurance. Omaha: Omaha Magic Theatre, 1974. Play.

Hospital Play. Omaha: Omaha Magic Theatre, 1974. Play.

Hothouse. New York: French, 1974. Play.

Two One-Act Plays: Pro-Game and Pioneer. Holly Springs, Miss.: Ragnarok, 1975.

Willa-Willie-Bill's Dope Garden: A Meditation in One Act on Willa Cather. Birmingham, Ala.: Ragnarok, 1977. Play.

American King's English for Queens: A New Musical in Two Acts. Omaha: Omaha Magic Theatre, 1978.

100,001 Horror Stories of the Plains. Omaha: Omaha Magic Theatre, 1978. Play.

Attempted Rescue on Avenue B. Omaha: Omaha Magic Theatre, 1979. Revised as *Retro.* Omaha: Omaha Magic Theatre, 1985. Play.

Brazil Fado. Omaha: Omaha Magic Theatre, 1979. Play.

Comings and Goings. New York: French, 1980.

Fireworks. Omaha: Omaha Magic Theatre, 1980. Play.

The Trees Blew Down. Omaha: Omaha Magic Theatre, 1980. Play.

Flat in Afghanistan. Omaha: Omaha Magic Theatre, 1981. Play.

Fifteen Million Fifteen Year Olds. Omaha: Omaha Magic Theatre, 1983. Play.

High Energy Musicals from the Omaha Magic Theatre. New York: Broadway Play Publishing, 1983. Includes *Babes in the Bighouse, Running Gag,* and *American King's English for Queens.*

Molly Bailey's Traveling Family Circus: Featuring Scenes from the Life of Mother Jones. New York: Broadway Play Publishing, 1983. Play.

Two By Terry Plus One. Schulenberg, Tex.: I. E. Clark, 1984. Includes *Pro Game* and *The Pioneer.*

Goona Goona. Omaha: Omaha Magic Theatre, 1985. Play.

Kegger. Omaha: Omaha Magic Theatre, 1985. Play.

Objective Love. Omaha: Omaha Magic Theatre, 1985. Play.

Family Talk. Omaha: Omaha Magic Theatre, 1986. Revised as *Dinner's in the Blender,* 1988.

Sleazing Toward Athens. Omaha: Omaha Magic Theatre, 1986. Play.

Future Soap. Omaha: Omaha Magic Theatre, 1987. Play.

Sea of Forms, by Terry and Jo Ann Schmidman. Omaha: Omaha Magic Theatre, 1987. Play.

Premiere Productions

Beach Grass. Seattle, Wash., Cornish Theatre, 1955.

Go Out and Move the Car. Seattle, Wash., Cornish Theatre, 1955.

Seascape. Seattle, Wash., Cornish Theatre, 1955.

New York Comedy: Two. Saratoga, N. Y.: Saratoga Gallery Theatre, 1961.

Ex-Miss Copper Queen on a Set of Pills. New York, Cherry Lane Theatre, 1963.

When My Girlhood Was Still All Flowers. New York, Open Theatre, 1963.

Eat at Joe's. New York, Open Theatre at Sheridan Square Playhouse, Dec. 1963.

Calm Down Mother. New York, Open Theatre at Sheridan Square Playhouse, 29 Mar. 1965.

Keep Tightly Closed in a Cool Dry Place. New York, Open Theatre at Sheridan Square Playhouse, 29 Mar. 1965.

The Gloaming, Oh My Darling. Minneapolis, Firehouse Theatre, 1965.

Comings and Goings: A Theatre Game. New York, Open Theatre at La Mama Experimental Theatre Club, Apr. 1966.

The Magic Realists. New York, Open Theatre at La Mama Experimental Theatre Club, 1966.

Viet Rock: A Folk War Movie. New York, Open Theatre at La Mama Experimental Theatre Club, 25 May 1966.

The People vs. Ranchman. Minneapolis, Minn., Firehouse Theatre, 1967.

Changes. New York, La Mama Experimental Theatre Club, 1968.

Jack-Jack: A Trip. Minneapolis, Minn., Firehouse Theatre, Spring 1968.

The Key Is At the Bottom. Los Angeles, Cal., Mark Taper Forum Lab, 1968.

Massachusetts Trust. Waltham, Mass., Brandeis University, Aug. 1968.

The Tommy Allen Show, Los Angeles. Los Angeles, College of the Immaculate Heart, 1969.

Approaching Simone. Boston, Boston University, 25 Feb. 1970.

The Tommy Allen Show, Omaha. Omaha, Omaha Magic Theatre, 25 June 1970.

The Tommy Allen Show, New York. New York, Actors Studio, 1970.

Choose a Spot on the Floor, by Terry and Jo Ann Schmidman. Omaha, Omaha Magic Theatre, 15 June 1972.

Grooving. New York, Brooklyn Academy of Music, 1972.

Susan Peretz at the Manhattan Theatre Club. New York, New York Theatre Strategy Festival at Manhattan Theatre Club, 1973.

Thoughts, by Terry and Lamar Alford. New York, Theatre de Lys, 19 Mar. 1973.

St. Hydro Clemency; or, A Funhouse of the Lord: An Energizing Event. New York, St. Clement's Theatre, 24 May 1973.

Nightwalk, by Terry, Sam Shepard, and Jean-Claude Van Itallie. New York, Open Theatre at Theatre of St. Clements, 8 Sept. 1973.

We Can Feed Everybody Here. New York, Westbeth Feminist's Collective, Jan. 1974.

Hothouse. New York, Circle Repertory Theatre, Feb. 1974.

The Pioneer. Omaha, Omaha Magic Theatre, Spring 1974.

Babes in the Bighouse. Omaha, Omaha Magic Theatre, Fall 1974.

Pro Game. New York, Theatre Genesis, 24 Oct. 1974.

The Narco Linguini Bust. Omaha, Omaha Magic Theatre, 1974.

Molly Bailey's Traveling Family Circus: Featuring Scenes from the Life of Mother Jones. Los Angeles, Mark Taper Forum Lab, 1974.

100,001 Horror Stories of the Plains. Omaha, Omaha Magic Theatre, 1976.

Brazil Fado. Omaha, Omaha Magic Theatre, 1977.

American King's English for Queens. Omaha, Omaha Magic Theatre, Mar. 1978.

Running Gag, by Terry and Jo Ann Schmidman. Omaha, Omaha Magic Theatre, Jan. 1979.

Fireworks. Louisville, Ky., Actors Theatre of Louisville, 1979.

Attempted Rescue on Avenue B. Chicago, Chicago Theatre Strategy, Mar. 1979.

Goona Goona. Omaha, Omaha Magic Theatre, Nov. 1979.

Comings and Goings: The Musical. Omaha, Omaha Magic Theatre, Spring 1980.

Henna for Endurance. Omaha, University of Nebraska, April 1980.

Scenes From Maps. Omaha, University of Nebraska, May 1980.

Objective Love. Omaha, Omaha Magic Theatre, Dec. 1980.

Winners. Santa Barbara, Cal., Process Theatre, Spring 1981.

The Trees Blew Down. Los Angeles, The Fifth Estate, May 1981.

Kegger. Omaha, Omaha Magic Theatre, Sept. 1982.

Fifteen Million Fifteen Year Olds. Omaha, Omaha Magic Theatre, Aug. 1983.

X-Rayed-iate, by Terry and Jo Ann Schmidman. Omaha, Omaha Magic Theatre, May 1984.

Family Talk. Omaha, Omaha Magic Theatre, Apr. 1986.

Sleazing Toward Athens. Omaha, Omaha Magic Theatre, June 1986.

Sea of Forms. Omaha, Omaha Magic Theatre, Sept. 1986.

Dinner's in the Blender. Omaha, Omaha Magic Theatre, Aug. 1987.

Walking Through Walls. Omaha, Omaha Magic Theatre, 20 Nov. 1987.

Retro. Omaha, Omaha Magic Theatre, Mar. 1988.

Selected Other

The Dirt Boat. Seattle, KING, 1955. Teleplay.

Viet Rock: A Folk War Movie, Tulane Drama Review, 11 (Fall 1966), 196-227. Includes an introduction by Terry.

"Cool Is Out! Uptight Is Out!," *New York Times*, 14 Jan. 1968, p. D17. Essay.

Home: Or Future Soap. New York, WNDT, 19 Jan. 1968. Teleplay.

Sanibel and Captiva. Boston, WGBH, 1968. Radio play.

"Who Says Only Words Make Great Drama," *New York Times*, 10 Nov. 1968, section 2, pp. 1, 3. Essay.

One More Little Drinkie. PBS, 1970. Teleplay.

American Wedding Ritual Monitored/Transmitted by the Planet Jupiter. Earplay, NPR, 1972. Radio play.

Massachusetts Trust. In *The Off-Off Broadway Book*, ed. Albert Poland and Bruce Mailman. Indianapolis: Bobbs-Merrill, 1972. Play.

American Wedding Ritual Monitored/Transmitted by the Planet Jupiter, Places: *A Journal of the Theatre*, 1 (1973), 33-34. Playlet.

"Women and the Law." Omaha, PBS, 1976. Television documentary.

"American Experimental Theatre Then and Now," *Performing Arts Journal*, 2 (Fall 1977), 13-24. Includes statement by Terry.

"Two Pages A Day," *Tulane Drama Review*, 21 (Dec. 1977), 59-68. Autobiographical essay.

"Janis Joplin." In *Notable American Women: The Modern Period*, ed. Barbara Sicherman, Carol Hurd Green, Ilene Kantrov, Harriette Walker. Cambridge, Mass.: Harvard University Press, 1980, 385-387. Biographical essay.

"Omaha Magic: Playwright's Theatre," *Southwestern Review*, Fall 1980.

Katmandu, Open Places, 38/39 (Spring 1985), 78-83. Play.

SECONDARY BIBLIOGRAPHY

Bibliography

Coven, Brenda. *American Women Dramatists of the Twentieth Century: A Bibliography*. Metuchen, N.J.: Scarecrow, 1982, 201-204.

Interviews

Betsko, Kathleen, and Rachel Koenig. "Megan Terry." In their *Interviews with Contemporary Women Playwrights*. New York: Beech Tree, 1987, 377-401.

Leavitt, Dinah L. "Megan Terry." In *Women in American Theatre: Careers, Images, Movements*, ed. Helen Krich Chinoy and Linda Walsh Jenkins. New York: Crown, 1981, 285-292.

L., L. "Five Important Playwrights Talk About Theatre Without Compromise and Sexism," *Mademoiselle*, 75 (Aug. 1972), 288-289,

386-387. Interview with members of the Women's Theatre Council: Terry, Julie Bovasso, Rosalyn Drexler, Maria Irene Fornes, and Rochelle Owens.

"Making a Life in Art: Megan Terry Interviews." In *Women in American Theatre: Careers, Images, Movements*, second edition, ed. Helen Krich Chinoy and Linda Walsh Jenkins. New York: Theatre Communications Group, 1987, 328-330. Excerpts from the Leavitt interview and the Betsko and Koenig interview.

Weintraub, Rodelle. "The Center of Life: An Interview With Megan Terry." In *Fabian Feminist: Bernard Shaw and Women*, ed. Weintraub. University Park: Pennsylvania State University Press, 1977, 214-225.

Critical Studies: Major Reviews, Articles, and Book Sections

Asahina, Robert. "The Basic Training of American Playwrights: Theater and the Vietnam War," *Theater*, 9 (Spring 1978), 30-37.

Atchity, Kenneth John. "Five Plays of Protest at the Crossroads." In *To Find Something New: Studies in Contemporary Literature*, ed. Henry Grosshans. Pullman, Wash.: Washington State University Press, 1969, 4-27.

Barnes, Clive. *New York Times*, 9 March 1970, p. 43. Review of *Approaching Simone*.

Cohn, Ruby. "Actor Activated: Gelber, Horovitz, Van Itallie, Terry, Fornes." In her *New American Dramatists: 1960-1980*. New York: Grove, 1982, 47-73.

Cohn. "Camp, Cruelty, Colloquialism." In *Comic Relief: Humor in Contemporary American Literature*, ed. Sarah Blacher Cohen. Urbana: University of Illinois Press, 1978, 281-303.

Diamond, Elin. "(Theoretically) Approaching Megan Terry: Issues of Gender and Identity," *Art and Cinema*, 1 (Fall 1987), 5-7.

Feldman, Peter L. "Director's Note," *Tulane Drama Review*, 11 (Fall 1966), 197-198.

Feldman. "Notes for the Open Theatre Production," *Tulane Drama Review*, 10 (Summer 1966), 200-208.

Gillespie, Patti P. "America's Women Dramatists, 1960-1980." In *Essays on Contemporary American Drama*, ed. Hedwig Bock and Albert Wertheim. Munich: Hueber, 1981, 187-206.

Kerr, Walter. "One Succeeds, the Other Fails," *New York Times*, 27 Nov. 1966, section 2, p. 1. Review of *Viet Rock*.

Keyssar, Helene. "Megan Terry: Mother of American Feminist Drama." In her *Feminist Theatre: An Introduction to Plays of Contem-*

porary British and American Women. London: Macmillan, 1984, 53-76.

Klein, Kathleen Gregory. "Language and Meaning in Megan Terry's 1970s 'Musicals,'" *Modern Drama,* 27 (Dec. 1984), 574-583.

Kroll, Jack. "Waiting for God," *Newsweek,* 75 (19 Mar. 1970), 64. Review of *Approaching Simone.*

Mackay, Barbara. "Women on the Rocks," *Saturday Review/World,* 1 (6 Apr. 1974), 48-49. Review of *Hothouse.*

Marranca, Bonnie. "Megan Terry." In *American Playwrights: A Critical Survey,* volume 1, ed. Marranca and Gautam Dasgupta. New York: Drama Books, 1981, 183-192.

Natalle, Elizabeth. *Feminist Theatre: A Study in Persuasion.* Boston: Scarecrow, 1985.

Pasoli, Robert. *A Book on the Open Theatre.* Indianapolis: Bobbs-Merrill, 1970.

Schechner, Richard. "The Playwright as Wrighter," introduction to Terry's *Four Plays.* New York: Simon & Schuster, 1967, 7-18. In his *Public Domain: Essays on the Theatre.* Indianapolis: Bobbs-Merrill, 1969, 121-131; New York: Avon, 1969, 133-143.

Schlueter, June. "*Keep Tightly Closed in a Cool Dry Place:* Megan Terry's Transformational Drama and the Possibilities of Self," *Studies in American Drama, 1945-Present,* 2 (1987), 58-69.

"Voices of Protest," *Time,* 88 (21 Oct. 1966), 61. Review of *Viet Rock.*

Wagner, Phyllis Jane. "Introduction" and "On Megan Terry." In *Approaching Simone,* by Terry. Old Westbury, N.Y.: Feminist Press, 1973, 9-35.

Walter, Sydney S. "Notes for the Firehouse Theatre Production," *Tulane Drama Review,* 10 (Summer 1966), 208-213.

BIBLIOGRAPHICAL ESSAY

Bibliographies and Checklists

The bibliographical entry on Megan Terry in Brenda Coven's *American Women Dramatists of the Twentieth Century* (1982) provides a fairly comprehensive list of plays published or produced through 1978 but indicates as unpublished several texts which are now available. Coven's secondary bibliography consists of useful citations for fifteen reviews of early productions ranging from *Viet Rock* to *Hothouse.* Unfortunately, she cites only commonly indexed periodicals, such as *Newsweek, Time,* and *Saturday Review.* The bibliography in this volume is the most comprehensive yet compiled; but it remains for others interested in Terry's work to establish a more complete record of reviews in regional and alternative presses.

An up-to-date listing of Terry's plays in print (or available in photocopied versions) may be obtained from the Omaha Magic Theatre (1417 Farnam Street, Omaha, Neb. 68102).

Interviews

Beyond providing biographical information, primarily about her life in the theater, interviews with Terry chronicle the development of Off- and Off-Off-Broadway theater over the past twenty-five years and establish many of the themes and stylistic questions that have become central to critical studies of her work.

The earliest of these, "Five Important Playwrights Talk About Theatre Without Compromise and Sexism" (Aug. 1972), documents Terry's work with the Women's Theatre Council, founded by Terry and five others in an effort to develop the work of women playwrights and to get plays reflecting "their particular sensibility" produced. Terry's contributions to the interview are especially useful to readers interested in her role as champion of women's participation in American theater. Detailing the problems faced by women working in commercial theater, Terry underlines the need for women to take control of their own art and furnishes striking examples of how council members have done just that. Another facet of Terry's feminism is revealed in her comments on the crippling impact of sexism: "It so permeates one's whole life, if one is a woman, that it's impossible to begin to define it. All I know is, until the women's consciousness began to rise, . . . I was living like with 17% of my power. I was living like a guerrilla in this society, hiding behind men, trying to work through men."

Rodelle Weintraub's more comprehensive "The Center of Life" (1977) comes from the period after Terry joined the Omaha Magic Theatre. Published in a collection of essays on George Bernard Shaw and accompanied by annotations linking Terry's statements with Shaw's writings, the interview gives readers a glimpse of Terry's own sense of her place within the history of dramatic literature. Terry acknowledges the influence of Irish playwrights Shaw, Yeats, O'Casey, and Synge, highlighting the latter's impact in relation to her own sense of dramatic dialogue: "I *love* all the different ways Americans talk. . . . I love the variety of sounds. . . . I think of speech as music." Weintraub's interview is rich in biographical information as well, touching on Terry's childhood, educational background, and theater experiences in both Seattle and New York. Most illuminating are the playwright's remarks on the power of theater as a means to political change. Even if political theater reaches only a small segment of the population, she argues, those who do see it "usually are the shakers and movers and their ideas filter down." Discussing her own writing style, Terry divides her plays into three types: "personal plays," seen as a means of writing her way "to mental health"; "history plays" such as *Approaching Simone* and *Mollie Bailey's Traveling Family Circus: Featuring Scenes from the Life of Mother Jones;* and plays such as *Babes in the Bighouse* and *Viet Rock* demonstrating Terry's role "as a citizen." Terry's feminism is less central here than in other interviews, but her comments on the typecasting rampant in New York theater in the 1950s, on the seemingly nontraditional, nonlinear structures of the plays, and on her interest in matriarchy and women's religion will be of value to readers studying these aspects of Terry's work.

Terry's closing remark to Weintraub, that "theatre is the center of life," becomes the starting point for Dinah L. Leavitt's 1981 interview, which develops Terry's sense of the theater's religious dimension. Criticizing the materialism of Marxism, Terry reformulates her view of the theater's power, now stressing its nature as a *community* experience that offers a means of transcending individual materiality. The interview is also a valuable source of information on Terry's links with the women's movement and her views of feminist theater. Arguing vehemently against a strict feminist "party line," Terry nevertheless proudly defines herself as a feminist and defines feminist drama as "anything that gives women confidence, shows themselves to themselves, helps them to begin analyzing whether it's a positive or negative image, it's nourishing." Emphasizing women's strength, and listing the women writers who have had the greatest influence on her, Terry now sets her work apart from that of male playwrights, whose drama she sees as male-centered and affording actresses few challenging or satisfying roles. Unlike the earlier interviews, Leavitt's also includes comments about issues and techniques in individual Terry plays, including *Hothouse, Approaching Simone, Attempted Rescue on Avenue B,* and *American King's English for Queens.* Terry describes *Attempted Rescue on Avenue B,* for example, as showing "a woman coming to terms with . . . her creative power, aside from procreative power, and being able to create new products to send out into the world." Finally, Terry points to the play of children, cartoon characters, stand-up comedy, and even her grand-mother as sources of the transformation technique so central to her writing and to her work with the Open Theatre.

The most recent Terry interview, Kathleen Betsko and Rachel Koenig's "Megan Terry" (1987), is also the most extensive, present-ing Terry in her many roles as playwright, director, teacher, actress, and spokeswoman for the Omaha Magic Theatre. Terry gives the reader a useful perspective on American theater in the 1950s and 1960s as she notes both formative influences emerging from the-ater's exchange with other arts and the impact of historical events such as the assassination of John F. Kennedy. Of particular interest are Terry's reflections on how the Open Theatre and other groups "democratized the theater," reducing its dependence on European models, expanding its subject matter, and making way for an explo-sion of play-writing talent. Her often harsh words for media review-ers reveal her acerbic wit. On the subject of critical responses to the work of women playwrights, for example, she observes, "They want a fried egg. A beginning, a middle and an end, with a rising cli-max. A male orgasm." The more personal biographical information included here focuses on female role models, early power struggles with men (where Terry quickly learned "that when a woman opens her mouth there are consequences!"), and her roots in a "pioneer cul-ture" that taught her the value of work and family cooperation and offered her strong bonds with other women. While she insists that she writes "for the whole human race," and not just for other women, Terry again acknowledges the feminism of her work, not-ing, "I want to redress the balance! Men run everything." Scattered comments on Terry's plays offer valuable insights about both themes and techniques: cross-gender casting was used in *Babes in the Bighouse* because "we thought it was a clear way for men to learn how to empathize with women"; *American King's English for Queens* demonstrates how "roles and attitudes toward the self are shaped within the family by how one is spoken to"; *Brazil Fado* uses ex-cerpts from actual news reports to compare the sadomasochistic rela-tionship of an American couple with "the continuing tragedies in Central and South America." Equally revealing are Terry's thoughts on the role and place of her theater. Describing the Omaha Magic Theatre's commitment to voicing community concerns, Terry sums up the goals and message of her work in highly positive terms: "Life is possible. . . . Art is about taking action. . . . I believe in tak-ing creative action. What else is there to do?"

Critical Studies: Major Reviews, Articles, and Book Sections

As a subject for academic criticism, Megan Terry has had until very recently at least three strikes against her: her work with alternative theater in the 1960s, which initially received relatively little critical attention and where her efforts were often overshadowed by those of fellow Open Theatre playwright Jean-Claude Van Itallie; her subsequent move to the Omaha Magic Theatre, which likewise has been virtually ignored by media reviewers despite the considerable success of the theater in the midwest; and her identity as one of the many American women playwrights whose writing has generally been overlooked by the critical establishment because of its nontraditional style and subject matter.

The critical studies that have appeared differ widely in their assessment of Terry's contribution to American theater as well as in the depth and breadth of their analyses. The first, Richard Schechner's "The Playwright as Wrighter" remains one of the most laudatory and (not necessarily for that reason) one of the best discussions of her early work. Written as the preface to her 1967 play compilation, this essay testifies to Schechner's enthusiasm for the alternative theater movement in which he, too, played a central part. Not surprisingly, the director of the Performance Group praises Terry for developing a non-literary, performance-centered mode of theater, and he heralds the work of the Open Theatre as "laying the groundwork for the American theatre's future."

Schechner identifies Terry's work with transformations as the central contribution of her collaboration with the Open Theatre. Building on Peter Feldman's lucid definition of the technique—as "an improvisation in which the established realities or 'given circumstances' . . . of the scene change several times during the course of the action . . . swiftly and *almost without transition,* until the audience's dependence upon any fixed reality is called into question" (Summer 1966)—Schechner analyzes its use in three of Terry's plays. *Keep Tightly Closed in a Cool Dry Place* illustrates transformations in character and situation, which "explode a routine situation into a set of exciting theatrical images" and develop the play's "theme of entrapment, escape, torture, and exploitation" by means of associations rather than through traditional, organic development. *Comings and Goings,* "an organic piece playing out variations on the theme of male-female love relationships," changes the actors, breaking audience identification of actor and character and allowing for a sharper focus on the possibilities of the play's action.

371

The "richness" of *Viet Rock,* in Schechner's view, stems from the inter-weaving of both of these types of transformations. Schechner's assessment of *Viet Rock* as "non-political" is as controversial as his analysis of its structure is illuminating. For Schechner, the value of Terry's work lies not in its argument but in its formal innovations.

Robert Pasoli's 1970 study of the Open Theatre also offers an insider's view of her transformation plays as it traces their evolution in Open Theatre workshops and, in the case of *Viet Rock,* through subsequent productions. References to Terry scattered throughout Pasoli's *A Book on the Open Theatre* give the reader a rare glimpse of her working style and provide access to otherwise unpublished excerpts from her production notebooks. His searching analyses of *Viet Rock* and *Keep Tightly Closed in a Cool Dry Place* again emphasize Terry's development of transformation, but, in contrast with Schechner, Pasoli describes her "Brechtian concern with the curable ills of the time."

Kenneth John Atchity's 1969 study of "Five Plays of Protest at the Crossroads" takes a similar stand on Terry's politics, presenting *Viet Rock* as an example of the "theatre of protest." Atchity compares the play with four others from the same era, including Barbara Garson's *MacBird!* (1966) and Jean-Claude Van Itallie's *America Hurrah* (1967). Clearly uncomfortable with these plays' formal experimentation and often cynical tone, however, Atchity argues for a balance between technique and "poetic vision," which he comes to define as a humanistic optimism. In contrast with Walter Kerr's extremely negative review of *Viet Rock* (27 Nov. 1966), which compared the play unfavorably with *America Hurrah,* Atchity prefers Terry's play to Van Itallie's, finding it more "humanly determined." His brief analysis includes some helpful observations about the centrality of violence in Terry's early drama and about her portrayal of war as "a characteristic expression of human nature." But his traditionalist tastes come to the fore as he criticizes *Viet Rock* for its excess of emotion, its focus on one particular war rather than on a "wider-dimensioned world," and, most important, for its failure to resolve the personal and social dilemmas it presents.

Nearly ten years later, Robert Asahina attacks *Viet Rock* from the opposite side, comparing it with other plays dealing with the Vietnam War. Whereas Atchity has reservations about the literary value of Terry's "protest play," Asahina's "The Basic Training of American Playwrights: Theater and the Viet Nam War" (Spring 1978) criticizes *Viet Rock* as an example of "value-free" theater. Citing

Schechner's praise of the play's political neutrality, Asahina asserts that in 1960s theater, "the problematic link between aesthetic and political radicalism . . . was almost completely severed by the increasingly formalistic thrust of avant garde experimentation." Readers may disagree with Asahina's argument that *Viet Rock* is more concerned with the media than it is with the war itself, but all will be enlightened by the links he establishes between the formal innovations of *Viet Rock* (and other plays of the period) and "the technological modes of the rapidly emerging news media." His suggestion, for example, that the structure of *Viet Rock* more closely resembles the short "spots" of the nightly news than the cinematic cutting to which this structure is usually compared provides a new perspective on Terry's work with transformations and scenic montage.

With *Approaching Simone,* Terry finally won acceptance by media critics, as evidenced by the Obie awarded to her for the play as well as by the enthusiastic reviews of Jack Kroll (19 Mar. 1970), Clive Barnes (9 Mar. 1970), and others. The first scholarly analysis of Terry's plays to appear in the 1970s reflects this positive assessment. Phyllis Jane Wagner's "Introduction" to *Approaching Simone* (1973), is also the first to present a woman-centered perspective on her work. In her accompanying biographical note ("On Megan Terry"), Wagner highlights the centrality of feminist concerns in many of the plays that preceded *Approaching Simone,* identifying questions of identity—especially sexual identity and the destructiveness of gender roles—as basic to this early work. Her analysis of *Approaching Simone* also focuses on this theme and is enriched by insights gleaned from unpublished interviews with the playwright. Especially telling are Terry's comments on the way a male-dominated society inhibits women's personal growth, a situation which provided the impetus for her work on Simone Weil: "[Women] need to know that a woman can make it and think clearly in a womanly way. All the heroes are dead or killed or compromised, and women *need* heroes. That's why I wrote *Approaching Simone*." Noting the feminism inherent in the structure of *Simone* as well as its subject matter, Wagner applauds Terry's presentation of an internal conflict, one which gives the title character her own intrinsic value rather than bowing to traditional drama's definition of female characters primarily in their relation to men. But Wagner cannot resist expressing her disappointment with the play's resolution: Simone's passive self-sacrifice appears to Wagner as "a capitulation" to forces outside herself, which detracts from Terry's portrayal of an otherwise positive female role model.

Barbara Mackay's review article, "Women on the Rocks" (6 Apr. 1974), compares the premiere production of *Hothouse* with other Off-Broadway plays deriving from the current wave of feminism and is among the first to situate Terry's work within the burgeoning feminist theater of the 1970s. Though critical of the play's tendency toward melodrama and its presentation of alcohol and maternal love as "the only surefire remedies for heartache," Mackay praises *Hothouse* for its focus on the unique problems of women. She offers readers a thoughtful analysis of Roz as a woman whose seductive bravado masks "a pathetic, aging earth mother with no outlet for her lust or her tenderness."

Less beneficial are Ruby Cohn's two discussions of Terry's drama. The first considers the uses of "Camp, Cruelty, Colloquialism" (1978) in plays by Terry and other American playwrights of the 1960s and 1970s. Cohn's conclusion that "against the smiling grain of the American people, its contemporary playwrights have carved a drama whose humor sometimes touches on the tragic" proposes an intriguing framework for analysis. But her brief remarks on the "cumulative" humor of the rapid transformations in *Comings and Goings,* or the blending of comic and "dark values" in *Viet Rock,* remain too superficial to be of much assistance in understanding the complexities of Terry's humor.

The chapter on performance-oriented playwrights in Cohn's study of *New American Dramatists: 1960-1980* (1982) presents a slightly fuller discussion of Terry. "Actor Activated: Gelber, Horovitz, Van Itallie, Terry, Fornes" opens with a concise but informative description of the rise of Off-Off-Broadway. Subsequent comments on Terry's plays are largely descriptive and often characterized by cryptic assessments: *Viet Rock* "does not accomplish Terry's stated objective of 'getting at the essence of violence,' but it does present strong group images"; the family of *American King's English for Queens* "succeeds theatrically, if not humanistically." Cohn's overview succeeds as a general introduction to Terry's work in the 1960s and 1970s, but readers interested in in-depth analysis should look elsewhere.

As its title suggests, Patti Gillespie's article on "America's Women Dramatists, 1960-1980" (1981) places Terry's work of this period in a different context. Tracing general trends in the work of contemporary American woman playwrights, Gillespie emphasizes

Terry's involvement with the Open Theater, which Gillespie sees as providing "the most certain link between the avant garde of the 1960s and the developing feminism of the 1970s." Though she has little to say about the specifics of Terry's plays, Gillespie's article is of value in establishing Terry's pivotal role in the development of American feminist theater.

Other Terry criticism in the 1980s tends to place her work in one of the two categories sketched out by Cohn and Gillespie, with those who emphasize Terry's feminism generally offering a more positive assessment of her achievement. Bonnie Marranca's article in *American Playwrights* (1981) takes the more historical approach, looking at both male and female playwrights working in "nonmainstream" theater. Her chapter on Terry identifies contemporary American social issues as Terry's principal theme, pointing also to human (and especially women's) relationships and to the notion of dominance and submission as central to many of Terry's plays. From the standpoint of structure, Marranca, too, emphasizes the playwright's work with transformations, heralding this technique as "an important development in performance theory in the American theatre."

Marranca's observations on links between Terry's plays and their literary or historical context are especially revealing. Discussing the transformations in *Keep Tightly Closed in a Cool Dry Place,* for example, Marranca notes that this technique "reflects the modern temper. It is a notion of dramatic character that revels in action, fragmentation, and the divided self." Joining the debate over *Viet Rock*'s politics, she argues that the play "echoed the fragmentation of the times" while demonstrating the sense of political engagement shared by many theater groups performing during the Vietnam era. In judging the early transformation plays to be Terry's "most successful," however, Marranca puts forward some controversial, often extremely harsh assessments of Terry's more recent works, describing *Approaching Simone* as "a skimpy hagiography in a silly musical form" and *American King's English for Queens* as "a lackluster attempt at uniting linguistic and feminist thought." Nevertheless, Marranca offers the discerning reader perceptive analyses of both themes and techniques, making her study a useful introduction to Terry's drama.

The most extensive commentary on Terry's work to date, Helene Keyssar's chapter on "Megan Terry: Mother of American Feminist Drama" (1984), develops a much more positive view of

Terry's achievements. Keyssar outlines Terry's concerns as a feminist, praising her "precise criticism of stereotyped gender roles, [her] affirmation of women's strength, and [her] challenge to women to better use their own power." But she is most impressed by Terry's work with transformation, which, for Keyssar, is basic to the feminist dramatic aesthetic. As she traces Terry's career, Keyssar seeks to demonstrate Terry's "sustained yet never repetitive development of transformation as the central convention of feminist drama."

Though sometimes sketchy, Keyssar's comments on individual plays include excellent insights about much of Terry's work. Her analysis of *Comings and Goings,* for example, points to the play's grounding in "the rituals that structure and inform our daily lives" and clarifies the play's treatment of power and its relationship to social and gender roles. She similarly draws out the feminist dimension of *Viet Rock,* noting that play's concern with "sexism in the military" and with "the interchangeability of the weak." There are problems in Keyssar's analysis, arising principally from her sometimes loose application of the notion of transformation (she describes the title character's story of her fall from wealth to poverty in *Ex-Miss Copper Queen on a Set of Pills,* for example, as a transformation tale). But her chapter on Terry is significant in its recognition of Terry's contributions to the development of a unique, feminist dramaturgy and of her nurturing and sustaining role for other American women playwrights.

Much narrower in its focus, Elizabeth Natalle's *Feminist Theatre: A Study in Persuasion* (1985) incorporates two of Terry's plays in a rhetorical study of the persuasive strategies used by feminist theater. Her chapter on "Sexual Politics" presents *Babes in the Bighouse* as "a play that persuades by emphasizing the negative conditions of life in a women's prison" and blaming patriarchy itself for the dehumanization of the female prisoners. Her chapter on "Family Roles and Relationships," highlights the rhetorical impact of audience participation in post-performance discussions of *American King's English for Queens.* Neither analysis is especially penetrating, though readers interested in American feminist theater may find Natalle's book of interest as a point of departure.

A much more satisfying reading of these and other recent Terry plays may be found in Kathleen Gregory Klein's "Language and Meaning in Megan Terry's 1970s 'Musicals' " (Dec. 1984). Emphasizing Terry's concern with the ways language influences both individual and societal behavior, Klein contrasts Terry's plays with attacks on the communicative powers of language launched by absurdist playwrights. In Klein's view, Terry's work in the 1970s centers on "the uses made of language, action, and meaning," and she ably defends this thesis through sustained analyses of *American King's English for Queens, Babes in the Bighouse, Brazil Fado,* and *The Tommy Allen Show.* Discussing *Babes in the Bighouse,* for example, she demonstrates the use of language as a weapon, showing how the play "stresses the confusion among language, behavior, and meaning which the authority figures and prisoners manipulate." In addition to giving substantial weight to plays critics like Marranca have dismissed as trivial, Klein's article demonstrates a coherence in Terry's recent work which others have overlooked.

More recently, June Schlueter's excellent article, "*Keep Tightly Closed in a Cool Dry Place:* Megan Terry's Transformational Drama and the Possibilities of Self " (1987), looks back at the early transformation plays in an attempt to establish the significance of Terry's contribution to the development of the American theater. Developing her argument through the most lucid analysis of *Keep Tightly Closed in a Cool Dry Place* written to date, Schlueter convincingly demonstrates Terry's innovations in the creation of dramatic character, showing how the play not only changes our understanding of character but also provokes reflection on the very process of the formation of the self. Particularly enlightening are her comments on the "afterimages" left as the characters shift roles, which, she argues, "combine in a densely layered portrait that challenges the clear, sharp outlines of the realistically drawn face." Her presentation of the play's historical vignettes and allusions to popular culture as creating a "subtext for the centering situation" of the three men in their prison cell likewise helps establish the formal and thematic integrity of the play and offers a valuable model for future analyses of Terry's work. And in noting the usefulness of transformation for the feminist deconstruction of gender, Schlueter recognizes Terry's contribution to feminist theater as well as to the more general alternative theater movement.

Finally, Elin Diamond's "(Theoretically) Approaching Megan Terry: Issues of Gender and Identity" (Fall 1987) links Terry's critique of gender roles and myths with other examples of contemporary theater practice as well as with a substantial body of theoretical discourse. In a remarkably clear and concise theoretical preamble, Diamond traces the controversy over the idea of a fixed, centered self and its implications for feminists, who have had to resurrect the now questionable notion of identity in their efforts to criticize gender polarities. Drawing on both semiotics and psychoanalysis, Diamond then analyzes Terry's use of transformations and the images and gestures accompanying them to challenge the stability or continuity of identity and to demonstrate the reductiveness of the gendering process. Diamond's stimulating comments on plays ranging from *Viet Rock* to *American King's English for Queens* should convince skeptics that there is indeed something "vital and theoretically illuminating about [Terry's] method and her work."

Both the positive tone and the sophisticated critical frameworks of these most recent studies suggest that Terry's drama may finally be receiving the critical attention it deserves. While it is difficult to predict the precise direction of future research, it seems likely that scholars will continue to explore Terry's contributions in the area of feminist theater, further developing the implications of transformation and exploring the uses of this technique throughout her canon. Terry's work on contemporary social issues, from the war in *Viet Rock* to the problems of alcoholism and family violence presented in *Kegger* and *Goona Goona*, should also become the focus of critical analysis. And as Terry continues to gain recognition for her substantial contributions to the development of the American theater, plays such as *Calm Down Mother, Approaching Simone,* and *American King's English for Queens* should take their place as central texts in the corpus of American drama.

Wendy Wasserstein
(1950-)

Patricia R. Schroeder
Ursinus College

PRIMARY BIBLIOGRAPHY

Books

Uncommon Women and Others. New York: Dramatists Play Service, 1978.

Isn't It Romantic. New York: Doubleday, 1984.

Premiere Productions

Uncommon Women and Others. New York, Phoenix Theater, 1977.

Isn't It Romantic. New York, Phoenix Theater, 1981. Revised version, New York, Playwrights Horizons, 1983.

Tender Offer. New York, Playwrights Horizons, 1983.

The Man in a Case, adapted from Anton Chekhov's story as part of the production *Orchards.* New York, Lucille Lortel Theater, 1986.

The Heidi Chronicles. New York, Playwrights Horizons, Dec. 1988.

Selected Other

Uncommon Women and Others. Theater in America, PBS, 1978. Teleplay.

"The Itch to get Hitched," *Mademoiselle,* 87 (Nov. 1981), 146-147. Essay.

The Sorrows of Gin, adapted from John Cheever's story. PBS, 1981. Teleplay.

"The Newest Woman," *Esquire,* 101 (May 1984), 175-176. Review of Sara Davidson's *Friends of the Opposite Sex.*

Phil and Molly: The New Romantics, New York Times Magazine, 4 Nov. 1984, pp. 36-37, 72, 74. Play.

"Giving In to Gluttony," *Esquire,* 106 (July 1986), 60-61. Essay.

"New York Theater: Isn't It Romantic?," *New York Times,* 11 Jan. 1987, section 2, pp. 1, 28. Essay.

The Girl From Fargo: a Play, by Wasserstein and Terence McNally, *New York Times,* 8 Mar. 1987, section 2, pp. 5, 18.
"Assignment: Comedy," *New York Times Magazine,* 30 Aug. 1987, pp. 80-81, 90. Essay.
Episode of *Trying Times.* PBS, 1987.

SECONDARY BIBLIOGRAPHY

Interviews
Betsko, Kathleen, and Rachel Koenig. "Wendy Wasserstein." In their *Interviews with Contemporary American Playwrights.* New York: Beech Tree, 1987, 418-431.
"Your Thirties: The More Decade," *Harper's Bazaar,* 117 (June 1984), 146-147.

Critical Studies: Major Reviews and Articles
Barnes, Clive. "Chekhov Ambushed by Writers," *New York Post,* 23 Apr. 1986.
Barnes. " 'Isn't It Romantic': and It's Funny, Too," *New York Post,* 16 Dec. 1983.
Bayles, Martha. "Playwrights as Jokesmiths," *Wall Street Journal,* 27 Aug. 1984, p. 11.
Beaufort, John. Review of *Orchards, Christian Science Monitor,* 30 Apr. 1986, p. 24.
Beaufort. Review of Second Annual Young Playwrights Festival, *Christian Science Monitor,* 25 Apr. 1983, p. 15.
Beaufort. "A Wry Reunion," *Christian Science Monitor,* 30 Nov. 1977, p. 26.
Bennetts, Leslie. "An Uncommon Dramatist Prepares Her New Work," *New York Times,* 24 May 1981, section 2, pp. 1, 5.
Bolotin, Susan. Review of *Isn't It Romantic, Vogue,* 174 (Mar. 1984), 128.
Carlson, Susan L. "Comic Textures and Female Communities 1937-1977: Clare Boothe and Wendy Wasserstein," *Modern Drama,* 27 (Dec. 1984), 564-573.
Corliss, Richard. "Broadway's Big Endearment," *Time,* 122 (26 Dec. 1983), 80.
Drake, Sylvie. " 'Romantic': When Love Is Easier Said Than Done," *Los Angeles Times,* 31 Jan. 1984, section 6, p. 1.
Drake. "Will the Real Wendy Please Stand Up?," *Los Angeles Times,* 28 Oct. 1984, Calendar section, p. 40.

Eder, Richard. "Dramatic Wit and Wisdom Unite in 'Uncommon Women and Others,' " *New York Times*, 22 Nov. 1977, p. 48.

Gold, Sylviane. Review of *Orchards, Wall Street Journal*, 28 Apr. 1986, p. 22.

Gold. "Wendy, the Wayward Wasserstein," *Wall Street Journal*, 7 Feb. 1984, p. 30.

Goldberg, Robert. Review of *Trying Times, Wall Street Journal*, 26 Oct. 1987, p. 25.

Gussow, Mel. "New 'Romantic' by Wendy Wasserstein," *New York Times*, 16 Dec. 1983, p. C3.

Gussow. "Theater: 'Isn't It Romantic,' " *New York Times*, 15 June 1981, p. C11.

Gussow. "Theater: 'Orchards,' 7 One-Acts," *New York Times*, 23 Apr. 1986, p. 18.

Isn't It Romantic, unsigned review, *Variety*, 17 June 1981, p. 84.

"Isn't It Romantic? The Answer is an Emphatic Yes from Playwright Wendy Wasserstein," *People*, 21 (26 Mar. 1984), 77.

Kakutani, Michiko. "A Play and Its Author Mature," *New York Times*, 3 Jan. 1984, p. 20.

Kalem, T. E. "Stereotopical," *Time*, 110 (5 Dec. 1977), 111.

Kaplan, Peter W. "A break for comedy writers: they're key to TV series due August 5," *New York Times*, 13 June 1984, p. 26.

Kerr, Walter. "Are Parents Looking Better on Stage?," *New York Times*, 26 Feb. 1984, section 2, p. 7.

Kerr. "Does This Play Need a Stage?," *New York Times*, 28 June 1981, section 2, p. 3.

Kissel, Howard. " 'Isn't It Romantic,' " *Women's Wear Daily*, 16 Dec. 1983.

Newton, Edmund. "Women One Can't Forget," *New York Evening Post*, 22 Nov. 1977.

Nightingale, Benedict. "There Really Is a World beyond 'Diaper Drama,' " *New York Times*, 1 Jan. 1984, section 2, p. 14.

Oliver, Edith. "The Day Before the Fifth of July," *New Yorker*, 57 (22 June 1981), 86-87.

Oliver. "Theater: Off Broadway," *New Yorker*, 53 (5 Dec. 1977), 115. Review of *Uncommon Women and Others*.

Oliver. "Theater: Off Broadway," *New Yorker*, 59 (13 June 1983), 98. Review of *Tender Offer*.

Oliver. "Theater: Off Broadway," *New Yorker*, 59 (26 Dec. 1983), 68. Review of *Isn't It Romantic*.

"A Playwright's Choice of 'Perfect' Plays," *New York Times*, 14 Jan. 1979, section 2, p. 1.

Richards, David. "Sweet Nothings," *Washington Post*, 3 May 1985, p. C1.

Rosenfeld, Megan. "After the Revolution," *Washington Post*, 6 May 1985, p. B7.

Shales, Tom. "In the Comedy Zone," *Washington Post*, 17 Aug. 1984, p. B1.

Simon, John. "Failing the Wasserstein Test," *New York*, 14 (29 June 1981), 36-37.

Sirkin, Elliott. Review of *Isn't It Romantic, Nation*, 238 (18 Feb. 1984), 202-204.

Watt, Douglas. "Holyoke Hen Sessions," *New York Daily News*, 22 Nov. 1977.

Watt. " 'Isn't It Romantic': Sometimes," *New York Daily News*, 16 Dec. 1983.

Wilson, Edwin. "No Straight Path to Happiness?," *Wall Street Journal*, 24 July 1981, p. 21.

BIBLIOGRAPHICAL ESSAY

Interviews

Kathleen Betsko and Rachel Koenig (1987) provide the only in-depth interview with Wendy Wasserstein, although many newspaper articles include extensive quotations from the playwright. Several of Wasserstein's recurring concerns emerge in these articles as well as in her own published essays. Foremost among them is her understanding of women's changing roles in the 1980s. The conflicts that arise when women want to "have it all" (career, husband, children, friendships, self-fulfillment) provide her major literary theme. As quoted by Leslie Bennetts (24 May 1981), Wasserstein claims, "I think a woman's experience right now is about options and making choices. When you have someone making a choice, it's inherently dramatic." She also emphasizes the importance of writing so that women's voices can be heard. She told Betsko and Koenig, "Though women are often said to write 'small tragedies,' they are *our* tragedies, and therefore large, and therefore legitimate. They deserve a stage."

Wasserstein also frequently discusses the nature and function of comedy in interviews and articles. She tells Betsko and Koenig that she sees comedy as "a way to cope"; on a broader scale comedy serves as a nondidactic forum for presenting political subjects (such as the issue of women's "life choices"). Inherent to Wasserstein's comedic vision is her understanding of language; she repeatedly creates articulate characters who are unable to communicate their emotions.

Wasserstein is often asked to comment on the autobiographical elements in her work. Holly of *Uncommon Women and Others* and Janie of *Isn't It Romantic* share many of Wasserstein's personal characteristics, and Tasha Blumberg of *Isn't It Romantic* is loosely patterned on Wasserstein's mother. While acknowledging this overlap between life and art, Wasserstein has repeatedly asserted that there is as much of herself in every character she creates as there is in Holly or Janie. She tells Michiko Kakutani (3 Jan. 1984), "I believe a play is really successful when you divide yourself up into all the characters."

Critical Studies: Major Reviews and Articles

Susan L. Carlson's December 1984 essay on Wasserstein as a writer of feminist comedy is the only major journal article on the playwright to appear to date. Contrasting the female community in *Uncommon Women and Others* with that created by Clare Booth in *The Women* (1937), Carlson maintains that Wasserstein's play marks a significant departure from traditional comic models. Her comic world does not support the status quo; rather, it is a place where "women can work within a female community to challenge social roles."

Reviews of the premiere production of *Uncommon Women and Others* were usually favorable, although some had reservations. Richard Eder (22 Nov. 1977), Edmund Newton (22 Nov. 1977), and Edith Oliver (5 Dec. 1977) applauded Wasserstein's blend of clever wit and sympathy. Douglas Watt (22 Nov. 1977) and Oliver, however, noted that the play was structured as a succession of scenes and lacked a real plot. Watt's remark that Wasserstein had a genuine "way with words," coupled with his wish that she would "put them to the service of a real story," typified the predominant response.

The 1981 version of *Isn't It Romantic* opened to much less favorable reviews. Critics such as Mel Gussow (15 June 1981) and Walter Kerr (28 June 1981) saw the play as an example of unfulfilled potential, depending to a confusing extent on one-line jokes (what John Simon [29 June 1981] called "prickly cuteness" and "scattershot bitchiness"). Simon and a reviewer for *Variety* (17 June 1981) questioned the lack of conflict or direction in the play and found the ending un-convincing. Even those who enjoyed the play, such as the *Variety* re-viewer, suggested that it needed "proper pruning" and that Wasserstein was not yet "a fully adept craftswoman."

In the seven revisions of the play that led to the 1983 revival, Wasserstein solved many of the problems of the original. The care-ful cutting of superfluous jokes, the intensified focus on one charac-ter rather than on a series of interactions among many characters, and the revision of the ending were applauded by reviewers such as Gussow (16 Dec. 1983), Watt (16 Dec. 1983), Kakutani (3 Jan. 1984), Kerr (26 Feb. 1984), and Oliver (26 Dec. 1983). Kerr in partic-ular praised her elevation of the mother characters from the level of stereotype. Watt complained that even the revision was episodic and uneven; Howard Kissel (16 Dec. 1983) complained that the char-acters were clever but undeveloped; and David Richards (3 May 1985) thought that the plot lacked confrontation. Despite the prob-lems in the play, however, critics seem generally to regard Wasserstein's blend of compassion and humor as an important contri-bution to contemporary American theater.

Given the fact that only a single full-length essay has been writ-ten on Wasserstein, research opportunities abound. More work needs to be done on *Uncommon Women and Others* and *Isn't It Roman-tic*, her two most heavily reviewed plays, as well as on a subsequent work, *Tender Offer*, and *The Man in a Case*, her 1986 adaption of the Chekhov short story. Wasserstein has also written a screenplay for *Un-common Women and Others* and a teleplay of the John Cheever story "The Sorrows of Gin." Criticism should not only focus on the femi-nist and other social aspects of the work but on the technical charac-teristics by which those concerns are expressed.

Tennessee Williams
(1911-1983)

Pearl Amelia McHaney
Georgia State University

PRIMARY BIBLIOGRAPHY

Books

Battle of Angels. New York: New Directions, 1945. Play.

The Glass Menagerie: A Play. New York: Random House, 1945; London: Lehmann, 1948.

27 Wagons Full of Cotton and Other One-Act Plays. Norfolk, Conn.: New Directions, 1945; London: Grey Walls, 1947. Comprises *27 Wagons Full of Cotton: A Mississippi Delta Comedy; The Purification; The Lady of Larkspur Lotion; The Last of My Solid Gold Watches; Portrait of a Madonna; Auto-Da-Fee: A Tragedy in One Act; Lord Byron's Last Love Letter; The Strangest Kind of Romance: A Lyric Play in Four Scenes; The Long Goodbye; Hello from Bertha;* and *This Property is Condemned.* Enlarged edition, Norfolk, Conn.: New Directions, 1953. Adds *Something Wild . . . ; Talk to Me Like the Rain and Let Me Listen . . .;* and *Something Unspoken.*

You Touched Me! by Williams and Donald Windham. New York: French, 1947. Play.

A Streetcar Named Desire. New York: New Directions, 1947; London: Lehmann, 1949. Play.

One Arm and Other Stories. New York: New Directions, 1948.

American Blues: Five Short Plays. New York: Dramatists Play Service, 1948. Comprises *Moony's Kid Don't Cry; The Dark Room; The Case of the Crushed Petunias: A Lyrical Fantasy; The Long Stay Cut Short, or The Unsatisfactory Supper*; and *Ten Blocks on the Camino Real: A Fantasy.*

Summer and Smoke. New York: New Directions, 1948; London: Lehmann, 1952. Play.

The Roman Spring of Mrs. Stone. New York: New Directions, 1950. Novel.

The Rose Tattoo. New York: New Directions, 1951; London: Secker & Warburg, 1954. Play.

I Rise in Flame, Cried the Phoenix. Norfolk, Conn.: New Directions, 1951. Play.

Camino Real. Norfolk, Conn.: New Directions, 1953; London: Secker & Warburg, 1958. Play.

Hard Candy: A Book of Stories. New York: New Directions, 1954.

Cat on a Hot Tin Roof. New York: New Directions, 1955; London: Secker & Warburg, 1956. Revised edition, New York: New Directions, 1975. Play.

Lord Byron's Love Letter: Opera in One Act, music by Raffaello de Banfield. New York: G. Ricordi, 1955. Libretto.

In the Winter of Cities: Poems. Norfolk, Conn.: New Directions, 1956. Enlarged edition, Norfolk, Conn.: New Directions, 1964.

Baby Doll: The Script for the Film. New York: New Directions, 1956; London: Secker & Warburg, 1957. New York edition includes *27 Wagons Full of Cotton* and *The Long Stay Cut Short.*

Orpheus Descending, with Battle of Angels: Two Plays. New York: New Directions, 1958. Republished as *Orpheus Descending.* London: Secker & Warburg, 1958. Play.

Suddenly Last Summer. New York: New Directions, 1958. Play.

Garden District: Two Plays: Something Unspoken and Suddenly Last Summer. London: Secker & Warburg, 1959.

Sweet Bird of Youth. New York: New Directions, 1959; London: Secker & Warburg, 1961. Revised edition, New York: Dramatists Play Service, 1962. Play.

Period of Adjustment. New York: New Directions, 1960; London: Secker & Warburg, 1961. Revised edition, New York: Dramatists Play Service, 1961. Play.

Three Players of a Summer Game and Other Stories. London: Secker & Warburg, 1960.

The Night of the Iguana. New York: New Directions, 1962; London: Secker & Warburg, 1963. Revised edition, New York: Dramatists Play Service, 1963. Play.

The Eccentricities of a Nightingale and Summer and Smoke: Two Plays. New York: New Directions, 1964; Toronto: McClelland & Stewart, 1964.

Grand. New York: House of Books, 1964. Memoir.

The Milk Train Doesn't Stop Here Anymore. New York: New Directions, 1964; London: Secker & Warburg, 1964. Play.

The Knightly Quest: A Novella and Four Short Stories. New York: New Directions, 1967. Revised and enlarged as *The Knightly Quest: A Novella and Twelve Short Stories.* London: Secker & Warburg, 1968.

Kingdom of Earth (The Seven Descents of Myrtle). New York: New Directions, 1968. Revised edition, New York: Dramatists Play Service, 1969. Play.

Dragon Country: A Book of Plays. New York: New Directions, 1969; Toronto: McClelland & Stewart, 1969. Comprises *In the Bar of a Tokyo Hotel; I Rise in Flame, Cried the Phoenix; The Mutilated; I Can't Imagine Tomorrow; Confessional; The Frosted Glass Coffin; The Gnädiges Fräulein;* and *A Perfect Analysis Given by a Parrot.*

In the Bar of a Tokyo Hotel. New York: Dramatists Play Service, 1969. Play.

The Two-Character Play. New York: New Directions, 1969. Play.

Small Craft Warnings. New York: New Directions, 1972; London: Secker & Warburg. 1973. Play.

Out Cry. New York: New Directions, 1973. Play.

Eight Mortal Ladies Possessed: A Book of Stories. New York: New Directions, 1974.

Moise and the World of Reason. New York: Simon & Schuster, 1975; London: Allen, 1976. Novel.

Memoirs. Garden City, N.Y.: Doubleday, 1975; London: Allen, 1976.

Androgyne, Mon Amour: Poems. New York: New Directions, 1977.

Where I Live: Selected Essays, ed. Christine R. Day and Bob Woods. New York: New Directions, 1978.

Vieux Carré. New York: New Directions, 1979. Play.

A Lovely Sunday for Creve Coeur. New York: New Directions, 1980. Play.

Steps Must Be Gentle: A Dramatic Reading for Two Performers. New York: Targ, 1980.

It Happened the Day the Sun Rose. Los Angeles: Sylvester & Orphanos, 1981. Short story.

Clothes for a Summer Hotel: A Ghost Play. New York: New Directions, 1983. Play.

The Remarkable Rooming-house of Mme. Le Monde. New York: Albondocani Press, 1984. Play.

Stopped Rocking and Other Screenplays. New York: New Directions, 1984. Comprises *Stopped Rocking; All Gaul Is Divided; The Loss of a Teardrop Diamond;* and *One Arm.*

The Red Devil Battery Sign. New York: New Directions, 1988. Play.

Premiere Productions

Battle of Angels. Boston, Wilbur Theater, 30 Dec. 1940.

The Glass Menagerie. Chicago, Civic Theater, 26 Dec. 1944; New York, Playhouse Theater, 31 Mar. 1945.

You Touched Me. New York, Booth Theater, 25 Sept. 1945.

Summer and Smoke. Dallas, Gulf Oil Playhouse, 8 July 1947; New York, Music Box Theater, 6 Oct. 1948.

A Streetcar Named Desire. New York, Barrymore Theater, 3 Dec. 1947.

The Rose Tattoo. Chicago, Erlanger Theater, 29 Dec. 1950; New York, Martin Beck Theater, 3 Feb. 1951.

Camino Real. New York, National Theater, 19 Mar. 1953.

27 Wagons Full of Cotton. New Orleans, Tulane University, 18 Jan. 1955.

Cat on a Hot Tin Roof. New York, Morosco Theater, 24 Mar. 1955.

Orpheus Descending. New York, Martin Beck Theater, 21 Mar. 1957.

Garden District: Suddenly Last Summer and *Something Unspoken.* New York, York Playhouse, 7 Jan. 1958.

Sweet Bird of Youth. New York, Martin Beck Theater, 10 Mar. 1959.

I Rise in Flame, Cried the Phoenix. New York, Theater de Lys, 14 Apr. 1959.

Period of Adjustment. New York, Helen Hayes Theater, 10 Nov. 1960.

The Night of the Iguana. New York, Royale Theater, 28 Dec. 1961.

The Milk Train Doesn't Stop Here Anymore. New York, Morosco Theater. 16 Jan. 1963.

Slapstick Tragedy: The Gnädiges Fräulein and *The Mutilated.* New York, Longacre Theater, 22 Feb. 1966.

The Two-Character Play. London, Hampstead Theater Club, 12 Dec. 1967; New York, Quaigh Theater, 14 Aug. 1975.

The Seven Descents of Myrtle. New York, Ethel Barrymore Theater, 27 Mar. 1968.

In the Bar of a Tokyo Hotel. New York, Eastside Playhouse, 11 May 1969.

Out Cry. Chicago, Ivanhoe Theater, 8 July 1971; New York, Lyceum Theater, 1 Mar. 1973.

Small Craft Warnings. New York, Truck and Warehouse Theater, 2 Apr. 1972.

The Red Devil Battery Sign. Boston, Schubert Theater, 18 June 1975.

This Is (An Entertainment). San Francisco, Geary Theater, 20 Jan. 1976.

Eccentricities of a Nightingale. New York, Morosco Theater, 23 Nov. 1976.

Vieux Carré. New York, St. James Theater, 11 May 1977.

Tiger Tail. Atlanta, Alliance Theater, 19 Jan. 1978.

Creve Coeur. Charleston, Spoleto Festival U.S.A., 5 June 1978. Entitled *A Lovely Sunday for Creve Coeur*. New York, Hudson Guild Theater, 17 Jan. 1979.

Kirche, Kuchen und Kinder. New York, Jean Cocteau Repertory Theater, Sept. 1979.

Will Mr. Merriwether Return from Memphis? Key West, Fla., Tennessee Williams Fine Art Center, 25 Jan. 1980.

Clothes for a Summer Hotel. New York, Cort Theater, 26 Mar. 1980.

Something Cloudy, Something Clear. New York, Jean Cocteau Repertory Theatre, 25 Aug. 1981.

Selected Other

"At Liberty." In *American Scenes*, ed. William Kozlenka. New York: Day, 1941, 175-182.

"The Blessings and Mixed Blessings of Workshop Productions," *Dramatists Guild Quarterly*, 13 (Autumn 1976), 16, 23-25. Essay.

" 'I Have Written a Play for Artistic Purity,' " *New York Times*, 21 Nov. 1976, section 2, pp. 1, 5. Essay.

The Travelling Companion, Christopher Street, 5 (Nov. 1981), 32-40. Play.

Beauty is the Word; Hot Milk at Three in the Morning, Missouri Review, 7, no. 3 (1984), 186-200. Early plays.

Letters

Tennessee Williams' Letters to Donald Windham 1940-65, ed. Donald Windham. New York: Holt, Rinehart & Winston, 1977.

Collection

The Theatre of Tennessee Williams, 7 volumes. New York: New Directions, 1971-1981.

SECONDARY BIBLIOGRAPHY

Bibliographies and Checklists

Adler, Thomas P., Judith Hersch Clark, and Lyle Taylor. "Tennessee Williams in the Seventies: A Checklist," *Tennessee Williams Newsletter*, 2 (Spring 1980), 24-29. Primary and secondary.

Arnott, Catherine M. *Tennessee Williams on File*. London & New York: Methuen, 1985. Primary and secondary.

Carpenter, Charles A. "Studies of Tennessee Williams' Drama: A Selective International Bibliography: 1966-1978," *Tennessee Williams Newsletter*, 2 (Spring 1980), 11-23.

Chesler, S. Alan. "Reassessment and Assessment." In Tharpe, 1977, 848-880.

Chesler. "*A Streetcar Named Desire*: Twenty-Five Years of Criticism," *Notes on Mississippi Writers*, 7 (Fall 1974), 44-53.

Cohn, Alan M. "More Tennessee Williams in the Seventies: Additions to the Checklist and the Gunn Bibliography," *Tennessee Williams Newsletter*, 3 (Spring/Fall 1982), 46-50.

Gunn, Drewey Wayne. *Tennessee Williams: A Bibliography*. Metuchen, N.J.: Scarecrow, 1980. Primary and secondary.

Hayashi, Tetsumaro, ed. *Arthur Miller and Tennessee Williams: Research Opportunities and Dissertation Abstracts*. Jefferson, N.C.: McFarland, 1983, 61-124.

McCann, John S. *The Critical Reputation of Tennessee Williams: A Reference Guide*. Boston: G. K. Hall, 1983.

Presley, Delma Eugene. "Tennessee Williams: Twenty-Five Years of Criticism," *Bulletin of Bibliography*, 30 (Jan./Mar. 1973), 21-29.

Biographies

Choukri, Mohamed. *Tennessee Williams in Tangier*, translated by Paul Bowles. Santa Barbara: Cadmus, 1979.

Donahue, Francis. *The Dramatic World of Tennessee Williams*. New York: Ungar, 1964.

Leavitt, Richard, ed. *The World of Tennessee Williams*. New York: Putnam's, 1978.

Maxwell, Gilbert. *Tennessee Williams and Friends*. Cleveland: World, 1965.

Rader, Dotson. *Tennessee: Cry of the Heart*. Garden City, N.Y.: Doubleday, 1985.

Rasky, Harry. *Tennessee Williams: A Portrait in Laughter and Lamentation.* New York: Dodd, 1986.
Spoto, Donald. *The Kindness of Strangers: The Life of Tennessee Williams.* Boston: Little, Brown, 1985.
Steen, Mike. *A Look at Tennessee Williams.* New York: Hawthorn, 1969.
Van Antwerp, Margaret A., and Sally Johns, eds. *Dictionary of Literary Biography Documentary Series*, volume 4: *Tennessee Williams.* Detroit: Gale, 1984.
Williams, Dakin, and Shepherd Mead. *Tennessee Williams: An Intimate Biography.* New York: Arbor House, 1983.
Williams, Edwina Dakin, as told to Lucy Freeman. *Remember Me to Tom.* New York: Putnam's, 1963.
Windham, Donald. *Lost Friendships: A Memoir of Truman Capote, Tennessee Williams and Others.* New York: Morrow, 1987. Includes Windham's *As If . . . : A Personal View of Tennessee Williams.* Privately printed, 1985.

Interviews
Barron, Mark. "Newest Find on Broadway Is a Mississippi Playwright Named Tennessee Williams," *Memphis Commercial Appeal*, 24 Nov. 1940, section 1, p. 14. Collected in Devlin, 3-5.
Bilowit, Ira J. "Roundtable: Tennessee Williams, Craig Anderson, and T. E. Kalem Talk about *Creve Coeur*," *New York Theatre Review* (Mar. 1979), 14-18. Collected in Devlin, 308-317.
Brown, Cecil. "Interview with Tennessee Williams," *Partisan Review*, 45 (1978), 276-305. Collected in Devlin, 251-283.
Buckley, Tom. "Tennessee Williams Survives," *Atlantic* (Nov. 1970), 98, 100-106, 108. Collected in Devlin, 161-183.
Chandler, Charlotte. *The Ultimate Seduction.* Garden City, N.Y.: Doubleday, 1984, 317-355.
Davis, Louise. "That Baby Doll Man: Part I," *Tennessee Magazine*, 3 (Mar. 1957), 12-13, 30-31. Collected in Devlin, 43-49.
Devlin, Albert J., ed. *Conversations with Tennessee Williams.* Jackson, Miss. & London: University Press of Mississippi, 1986.
Evans, Jean. "The Life and Ideas of Tennessee Williams," *New York PM Magazine*, 6 May 1945, pp. M6-M7. Collected in Devlin, 12-19.
Fayard, Jeanne. "Meeting with Tennessee Williams." In her *Tennessee Williams.* Paris: Seghers, 1972. Translated by Marlene J. Devlin in Devlin, 208-212.

Freedley, George. "The Role of Poetry in the Modern Theater," *Theater Time*, WNYC-Radio, New York, 3 Oct. 1945. Collected in Devlin, 20-24.

Frost, David. "Will God Talk Back to a Playwright? Tennessee Williams." In his *The Americans*. New York: Stein & Day, 1970, 33-40. Collected in Devlin, 140-146.

Funke, Lewis, and John E. Booth. "Williams on Williams," *Theatre Arts*, 46 (Jan. 1962), 16-19, 72-73. Collected in Devlin, 97-106.

Gaines, Jim. "A Talk about Life and Style with Tennessee Williams," *Saturday Review* (29 Apr. 1972), 25-29. Collected in Devlin, 213-223.

Gelb, Arthur. "Williams and Kazan and the Big Walk-Out," *New York Times*, 1 May 1960, section 2, pp. 1, 3. Collected in Devlin, 64-68.

Grauerholz, James. "Orpheus Holds His Own: William Burroughs Talks with Tennessee Williams," *Village Voice*, 16 May 1977, pp. 44-45. Collected in Devlin, 299-307.

Gruen, John. "Tennessee Williams." In his *Close-Up*. New York: Viking, 1968, 86-95. Collected in Devlin, 112-123.

Hewes, Henry. "Tennessee Williams–Last of Our Solid Gold Bohemians," *Saturday Review* (28 Mar. 1953), 25-27. Collected in Devlin, 30-33.

Hicks, John. "Bard of Duncan Street: Scene Four," *Florida Magazine (Orlando Sentinel)*, 29 July 1979, pp. 18-19. Collected in Devlin, 318-324.

Inge, William. " 'Tennessee' Williams, Playwright, Author," *St. Louis Star-Times*, 11 Nov. 1944, p. 11. Collected in Devlin, 6-8.

Isaac, Dan. "Talking with Tennessee," *After Dark* (Oct. 1969), 46-50. Collected in Devlin, 134-139.

Jennings, Robert C. "*Playboy* Interview: Tennessee Williams," *Playboy*, 20 (Apr. 1973), 69-84. Collected in Devlin, 224-250.

Keith, Don Lee. "New Tennessee Williams Rises from 'Stoned Age.' " *New Orleans Times-Picayune* 18 Oct. 1970, section 3, p. 6. Collected in Devlin, 147-160.

Lewis, R. C. "A Playwright Named Tennessee," *New York Times Magazine*, 7 Dec. 1947, pp. 19, 67, 69-70. Collected in Devlin, 25-29.

Murrow, Edward R. "Interview with Tennessee Williams, Yukio Mishima, and Dilys Powell." Collected in Devlin, 69-77.

Rader, Dotson. "The Art of Theater V: Tennessee Williams," *Paris Review*, 81 (Fall 1981), 145-185. Collected in Devlin, 325-360.

Reed, Rex. "Tennessee Williams Turns Sixty," *Esquire*, 76 (Sept. 1971), 105-108, 216-223. Collected in Devlin, 184-207.

Ross, Don. "Williams in Art and Morals: An Anxious Foe of Untruth," *New York Herald-Tribune*, 3 Mar. 1957, section 4, pp. 1-2. Collected in Devlin, 38-42.

Ross. "Williams On a Hot Tin Roof," *New York Herald-Tribune*, 5 Jan. 1958, section 4, pp. 1, 7. Collected in Devlin, 50-53.

Ruas, Charles. "Tennessee Williams." In his *Conversations with American Writers*. New York: Knopf, 1985, 75-90. Collected in Devlin, 284-295.

Schmidt-Muhlisch, Lothar. " 'Life Is a Black Joke,' " *Die Welt* (West Berlin), 29 Dec. 1975, p. 13. Translated by Kathryn Wright Brady in Devlin, 296-298.

Stang, Joanne. "Williams: Twenty Years after *Glass Menagerie*," *New York Times*, 28 Mar. 1965, section 2, pp. 1, 3. Collected in Devlin, 107-111.

Terkel, Studs. "Studs Terkel Talks with Tennessee Williams." Collected in Devlin, 78-96.

Van Gelder, Robert. "Playwright with 'A Good Conceit,' " *New York Times*, 22 Apr. 1945, section 2, p. 1. Collected in Devlin, 9-11.

Wager, Walter. "Tennessee Williams." In *The Playwrights Speak*. New York: Delacorte, 1967, 213, 224-237. Collected in Devlin, 124-133.

Wallace, Mike. "Tennessee Williams." In *Mike Wallace Asks: Highlights from 46 Controversial Interviews*, ed. Charles Preston and Edward A. Hamilton. New York: Simon & Schuster, 1958, 20-23. Collected in Devlin, 54-58.

Waters, Arthur B. "Tennessee Williams: Ten Years Later," *Theater Arts* (July 1955), 72-73, 96. Collected in Devlin, 34-37.

Weatherby, W. J. "Lonely in Uptown New York," *Manchester Guardian Weekly*, 23 July 1959, p. 14. Collected in Devlin, 59-63.

Whitmore, George. "Interview: Tennessee Williams," *Gay Sunshine*, 33/34 (Summer/Fall 1977), 1-4. Collected in *Gay Sunshine Interviews*, ed. W. Leyland. San Francisco: Gay Sunshine Press, 1978, 310-325.

Critical Studies: Books

Bigsby, C. W. E. *A Critical Introduction to Twentieth Century American Drama*, volume 2: *Williams, Miller, Albee*. Cambridge: Cambridge University Press, 1984. 1-134.

Boxhill, Roger. *Tennessee Williams*. New York: St. Martin's, 1987.

Falk, Signi L. *Tennessee Williams*. Boston: Twayne, 1962. Revised, 1978.

Fedder, Norman J. *The Influence of D. H. Lawrence on Tennessee Williams*. The Hague: Mouton, 1966.

Hirsch, Foster. *A Portrait of the Artist: The Plays of Tennessee Williams*. Port Washington, N.Y.: Kennikat, 1979.

Jackson, Esther Merle. *The Broken World of Tennessee Williams*. Madison: University of Wisconsin Press, 1965.

Londre, Felicia Hardison. *Tennessee Williams*. New York: Ungar, 1979.

Nelson, Benjamin. *Tennessee Williams: The Man and His Work*. New York: Oblensky, 1961.

Phillips, Gene D. *The Films of Tennessee Williams*. East Brunswick, N.J.: Associated University Presses, 1980.

Shaland, Irene. *Tennessee Williams on the Soviet Stage*. Lanham, Md.: University Press of America, 1987.

Tischler, Nancy M. *Tennessee Williams*. Austin, Tex.: Steck-Vaughn, 1969.

Tischler. *Tennessee Williams: Rebellious Puritan*. New York: Citadel, 1961.

Weales, Gerald. *Tennessee Williams*. Minneapolis: University of Minnesota Press, 1965.

Yacowar, Maurice. *Tennessee Williams and Film*. New York: Ungar, 1977.

Critical Studies: Collections of Essays

Bloom, Harold, ed. *Tennessee Williams*. New York: Chelsea House, 1987.

Bloom, ed. *Tennessee Williams's A Streetcar Named Desire*. New York: Chelsea House, 1988.

Coulon, C., ed. *Coup de Théâtre*, 5 (Dec. 1985). Tennessee Williams issue.

Miller, Jordan Y., ed. *Twentieth Century Interpretations of A Streetcar Named Desire*. Englewood Cliffs, N.J.: Prentice-Hall, 1971.

Parker, Dorothy, ed. *Essays on Modern American Drama: Williams, Miller, Albee, and Shepard*. Toronto: University of Toronto Press, 1987.

Parker, R. B., ed. *The Glass Menagerie: A Collection of Critical Essays*. Englewood Cliffs, N.J.: Prentice-Hall, 1983.

Stanton, Stephen S., ed. *Tennessee Williams: A Collection of Critical Essays*. Englewood Cliffs, N.J.: Prentice-Hall, 1977.

Tharpe, Jac, ed. *Tennessee Williams: A Tribute.* Jackson: University Press of Mississippi, 1977.

Tharpe, ed. *Tennessee Williams: 13 Essays.* Jackson: University Press of Mississippi, 1980.

Critical Studies: Special Journals and Newsletters
Tennessee Williams Newsletter (Ann Arbor, Mich.), volumes 1-2 (Jan. 1979-Fall 1980).
Tennessee Williams Review (Boston, Mass.), volumes 3-4 (Spring 1981-Spring 1983).

Critical Studies: Major Reviews, Articles, and Book Sections
Adler, Jacob H. "Tennessee Williams' South: The Culture and the Power." In Tharpe, 1977, 30-52.

Adler. "Williams's Eight Ladies," *Southern Literary Journal*, 8 (Fall 1975), 165-169.

Adler, Thomas P. "The Dialogue of Incompletion: Language in Tennessee Williams's Later Plays," *Quarterly Journal of Speech*, 61 (Feb. 1975), 48-58. Abridged in Stanton, 74-85.

Adler. "Notes for *The Two-Character Play,*" *Tennessee Williams Review*, 3 (Spring/Fall 1982), 3-5.

Adler. "The Search for God in the Plays of Tennessee Williams," *Renascence*, 26 (Autumn 1973), 48-56. Collected in Stanton, 138-148.

Adler. "The (Un)reliability of the Narrator in *The Glass Menagerie* and *Vieux Carré,*" *Tennessee Williams Review*, 3 (Spring 1981), 6-9.

Armato, Philip M. "Tennessee Williams' Meditations on Life and Death in *Suddenly Last Summer, The Night of the Iguana,* and *The Milk Train Doesn't Stop Here Anymore.*" In Tharpe, 1977, 558-570.

Atkinson, Brooks. " 'Streetcar' Tragedy—Mr. Williams' Report on Life in New Orleans," *New York Times*, 14 Dec. 1947, section 2, p. 3. Collected in Miller, 32-34.

Atkinson. "Theatre: Early Williams," *New York Times*, 22 Nov. 1956, section 1, p. 50. Collected in R. B. Parker, 20-21.

Balachandran, K. "Tennessee Williams in India: Stagings and Scholarship," *Notes on Mississippi Writers*, 20, no. 1 (1988), 17-27.

Barranger, Milly S. "New Orleans as Theatrical Image in Plays by Tennessee Williams," *Southern Quarterly*, 23 (Winter 1985), 38-54.

Beaurline, Lester A. "*The Glass Menagerie*: From Story to Play," *Modern Drama*, 8 (Sept. 1965), 142-149. Collected in R. B. Parker, 44-52.

Bennett, Beate Hein. "Williams and European Drama: Infernalists and Forgers of Modern Myths." Collected in Tharpe, 1977, 429-459.

Bentley, Eric. *What Is Theatre? Incorporating The Dramatic Event and Other Reviews 1944-1967*. New York: Atheneum, 1968. Reviews of *Camino Real*, 74-78; *Cat on a Hot Tin Roof*, 224-231.

Berkman, Leonard. "The Tragic Downfall of Blanche du Bois," *Modern Drama*, 10 (Dec. 1967), 249-257. Collected in Bloom, 1988, 33-47.

Berkowitz, Gerald M. "Williams' 'Other Places'—A Theatrical Metaphor in the Plays." In Tharpe, 1977, 712-719.

Berlin, Normand. "Complementarity in *A Streetcar Named Desire*." In Tharpe, 1977, 97-103.

Bigsby, C. W. E. "Tennessee Williams: Streetcar to Glory." In *The Forties: Fiction, Poetry, Drama*, ed. Warren French. De Land, Fla.: Everett/Edwards, 1969, 251-258. Collected in Miller, 103-108.

Bigsby. "Valedictory." In his *A Critical Introduction to Twentieth Century American Drama*, volume 2: *Williams, Miller, Albee*. Cambridge: Cambridge University Press, 1984, 117-134. Collected in Bloom, 1987, 131-149.

Blackwell, Louise. "Tennessee Williams and the Predicament of Women," *South Atlantic Bulletin*, 35 (Mar. 1970), 9-14. Collected in Stanton, 100-106.

Blitgen, Sister M. Carol, B. V. M. "Tennessee Williams: Modern Idolator," *Renascence*, 22 (Summer 1970), 192-197.

Borny, Geoffrey. "The Two Glass Menageries: An Examination of the Effects on Meaning That Result from Directing the Reading Edition as Opposed to the Acting Edition of the Play." In *Page to Stage: Theatre as Translation*, ed. Ortrun Zuber-Skerritt. Amsterdam: Rodopi, 1984, 117-136.

Borny. "Williams and Kazan: The Creative Synthesis," *Australian Drama Studies*, 8 (1986), 33-47.

Bray, Robert. "The Burden of the Past in the Plays of Tennessee Williams." In *The Many Forms of Drama*, ed. Karelisa V. Hartigan. Lanham, Md.: University Press of America, 1985, 1-9.

Brooks, Charles B. "Williams' Comedy." In Tharpe, 1977, 720-735; in Tharpe, 1980, 173-188.

Broussard, Louis. *American Drama: Contemporary Allegory from Eugene O'Neill to Tennessee Williams.* Norman: University of Oklahoma Press, 1962, 110-118.

Brown, John Mason. "Southern Discomfort." In his *Seeing More Things.* New York & Toronto: Whittlesey House/McGraw-Hill, 1948, 266-272. Excerpted in Miller, 41-46.

Brustein, Robert. "America's New Culture Hero: Feelings without Words." In Bloom, 1988, 7-16.

Buckley, Peter. "Tennessee Williams' New Lady," *Horizon,* 23 (Apr. 1980), 66-71.

Callaghan, Barry. "Tennessee Williams and the Cocaloony Birds," *Tamarack Review,* 39 (1966), 52-58.

Campbell, Michael L. "The Theme of Persecution in Tennessee Williams' *Camino Real,*" *Notes on Mississippi Writers,* 6 (Fall 1973), 35-40.

Cardullo, Bert. "Drama of Intimacy and Tragedy of Incomprehension: *A Streetcar Named Desire* Reconsidered." In Tharpe, 1977, 137-153; in Bloom, 1988, 79-92.

Casper, Leonard. "Triangles of Transaction in Tennessee Williams." In Tharpe, 1977, 736-752; in Tharpe, 1980, 189-205.

Cate, Hollis L., and Delma E. Presley. "Beyond Stereotype: Ambiguity in Amanda Wingfield," *Notes on Mississippi Writers,* 3 (Winter 1971), 91-100.

Chesler, S. Alan. "An Interview with Eve Adamson: Artistic Director of Jean Cocteau Repertory Theatre," *Tennessee Williams Review,* 3 (Spring/Fall 1982), 38-45.

Chesler. "Orpheus Descending," *Players,* 52 (1977), 10-13.

Clark, Judith Hersch. "The Countess: Center of *This is (An Entertainment).*" In Stanton, 179-181.

Clayton, John Strother. "The Sister Figure in the Plays of Tennessee Williams," *Carolina Quarterly,* 12 (Summer 1960), 47-60. Collected in R. B. Parker, 109-119.

Cless, Downing. "Alienation and Contradiction in *Camino Real*: A Convergence of Williams and Brecht," *Theatre Journal,* 35 (Mar. 1983), 41-50.

Cluck, Nancy Anne. "Showing or Telling: Narrators in the Drama of Tennessee Williams," *American Literature,* 51 (Mar. 1979), 84-93.

Clurman, Harold. "The New Note in Tennessee Williams," *Nation,* 202 (14 Mar. 1966), 309. Collected in Stanton, 71-73.

Coakley, James. "Time and Tide on *Camino Real.*" In Tharpe, 1977, 232-236; in Bloom, 1987, 95-98.

Cohn, Ruby. "The Garrulous Grotesques of Tennessee Williams." In her *Dialogue in American Drama.* Bloomington: Indiana University Press, 1971, 97-129. Collected in Stanton, 45-66; collected in Bloom, 1987, 55-70.

Cohn. "Late Tennessee Williams," *Modern Drama,* 27 (Sept. 1984), 336-334.

Cohn. "Tribute to Wives," *Tennessee Williams Review,* 4 (Spring 1983), 12-17.

Cole, Charles W., and Carol I. Franco. "Critical Reaction to Tennessee Williams in the Mid-1960's," *Players,* 49 (Fall-Winter 1974), 18-23.

Colt, Jay Leo. "Dancing in Red Hot Shoes," *Tennessee Williams Review,* 3 (Spring/Fall 1982), 6-8.

Corrigan, Mary Ann. "Beyond Verisimilitude: Echoes of Expressionism in Williams' Plays." In Tharpe, 1977, 375-412.

Corrigan. "Memory, Dream, and Myth in the Plays of Tennessee Williams," *Renascence,* 28 (Spring 1976), 155-167.

Corrigan. "Realism and Theatricalism in *A Streetcar Named Desire,*" *Modern Drama,* 19 (Dec. 1976), 385-396. Collected in D. Parker, 27-38; collected in Bloom, 1988, 49-60.

Costello, Donald P. "Tennessee Williams' Fugitive Kind," *Modern Drama,* 15 (May 1972), 26-43. Collected in Stanton, 107-122.

Crawford, Cheryl. *One Naked Individual: My Fifty Years in the Theatre.* Indianapolis & New York: Bobbs-Merrill, 1977, 183-201.

Da Ponte, Durant. "Tennessee Williams's Gallery of Feminine Characters," *Tennessee Studies in Literature,* 10 (1965), 7-26. Excerpted in Miller, 53-56.

Davis, Joseph K. "Landscapes of the Dislocated Mind in Williams' *The Glass Menagerie.*" In Tharpe, 1977, 192-206.

Debusscher, Gilbert. "And the Sailor Turned into a Princess: New Light on the Genesis of *Sweet Bird of Youth,*" *Studies in American Drama,* 1 (1986), 25-31.

Debusscher. "French Stowaways on an American Milk Train: Williams, Cocteau, and Peyrefitte," *Modern Drama,* 25 (Sept. 1982), 399-408.

Debusscher. " 'Minting Their Separate Wills': Tennessee Williams and Hart Crane," *Modern Drama,* 26 (Dec. 1983), 455-476. Collected in Bloom, 1987, 113-130; republished as "Menagerie,

Glass, and Wine: Tennessee Williams and Hart Crane" in R. B. Parker, 31-43.

Debusscher. "Tennessee Williams' Lives of the Saints: A Playwrights' Obliquity," *Revue des Langues Vivantes*, 40 (1974), 449-456. Collected in Stanton, 149-157.

Debusscher. "Tennessee Williams's Unicorn Broken Again," *Revue Belge de Philologie et d'Histoire*, 49 (1971), 875-885.

Derounian, Kathryn Zabelle. " 'The Kingdom of Earth' and *Kingdom of Earth: (The Seven Descents of Myrtle)*: Tennessee Williams' Parody," *University of Mississippi Studies in English*, 4 (1983), 150-158.

Dervin, Daniel A. "The Spook in the Rainforest: The Incestuous Structure of Tennessee Williams' Plays," *Psychocultural Review*, 3 (1979), 153-183.

Dickinson, Hugh. "Tennessee Williams: Orpheus as Savior." In his *Myth on the Modern Stage*. Urbana: University of Illinois Press, 1969, 278-309.

Dickson, Vivienne. "*A Streetcar Named Desire*: Its Development through the Manuscripts." In Tharpe, 1977, 154-171.

Drake, Constance. "Blanche Dubois: A Re-evaluation," *Theatre Annual*, 24 (1968), 58-69.

Draya, Ren. "The Fiction of Tennessee Williams." In Tharpe, 1977, 647-662.

Durham, Frank. "Tennessee Williams: Theatre Poet in Prose," *South Atlantic Bulletin*, 36 (Mar. 1971), 3-16. Collected in R. B. Parker, 121-134.

Ehrlich, Alan. "A Streetcar Named Desire Under the Elms: A Study of Dramatic Space in *A Streetcar Named Desire* and *Desire Under the Elms*." In Tharpe, 1977, 126-136.

Embrey, Glenn. "The Subterranean World of *The Night of the Iguana*." In Tharpe, 1977, 325-340; in Tharpe, 1980, 65-80.

Fedder, Norman J. "Tennessee Williams' Dramatic Technique." In Tharpe, 1977, 795-812; in Tharpe, 1980, 229-246.

Free, William J. "Camp Elements in the Plays of Tennessee Williams," *Southern Quarterly*, 21 (Winter 1983), 16-23.

Free. "Williams in the Seventies: Directions and Discontents." In Tharpe, 1977, 815-828; in Tharpe, 1980, 247-260.

Fritscher, John J. "Some Attitudes and a Posture: Religious Metaphor and Ritual in Tennessee Williams' Query of the American God," *Modern Drama*, 13 (Sept. 1970), 201-215.

Ganz, Arthur. "The Desperate Morality of the Plays of Tennessee Williams," *American Scholar*, 31 (Spring 1962), 278-294. Collected in Stanton, 123-137; collected in Bloom, 1987, 99-111.

Georgoudaki, Catherine. "The Plays of Tennessee Williams in Greece, 1946-1983," *Notes on Mississippi Writers*, 16 (1984), 59-93.

Gillen, Francis. "Horror Shows, Inside and Outside My Skull: Theater and Life in Tennessee Williams's Two-Character Play." In his *Forms of the Fantastic: Selected Essays from the Third International Conference on the Fantastic in Literature and Film*. New York: Greenwood, 1986, 227-231.

Goldfarb, Alvin. *"Period of Adjustment* and the New Tennessee Williams." In Tharpe, 1977, 310-317.

Gresset, Michel. "Orphée sous les tropiques, ou les themes dans le théâtre recent de Tennessee Williams." In his *Le Théâtre Moderne, II: Depuis la Deuxième Guerre Mondiale*. Paris: Editions du Centre National de la Recherche Scientifique, 1967, 163-176.

Gunn, Drewey Wayne. "The Troubled Flight of Tennessee Williams' *Sweet Bird*: From Manuscript through Published Texts," *Modern Drama*, 24 (Mar. 1981), 26-35.

Gunn. "The Various Texts of Tennessee Williams's Plays," *Educational Theatre Journal*, 30 (Oct. 1978), 368-375.

Hafley, James. "Abstraction and Order in the Language of Tennessee Williams." In Tharpe, 1977, 753-762.

Hale, Allean. "Tennessee's Long Trip," *Missouri Review*, 7 (1984), 201-212.

Harwood, Britton J. "Tragedy as Habit: *A Streetcar Named Desire*." In Tharpe, 1977, 104-115.

Hays, Peter L. "Arthur Miller and Tennessee Williams," *Essays in Literature*, 4 (1977), 239-249.

Hays. "Tennessee Williams' Use of Myth in *Sweet Bird of Youth*," *Educational Theatre Journal*, 18 (Oct. 1966), 255-258.

Heilman, Robert Bechtold. *The Iceman, the Arsonist, and the Troubled Agent: Tragedy and Melodrama on the Modern Stage*. Seattle: University of Washington Press, 1973, 115-126, 138-141. Excerpt collected as "Tennessee Williams' Approach to Tragedy" in Stanton, 17-35. Excerpt collected as "The Middle Years" in Bloom, 1987, 71-83.

Heuermann, Hartmut. "Die Psychologie in Tennessee Williams' *The*

Milk Train Doesn't Stop Here Anymore," *Amerikastudien*, 19, no. 2 (1974), 266-279.

Hilfer, Anthony C., and R. Vance Ramsey. "*Baby Doll*: A Study in Comedy and Critical Awareness," *Ohio University Review*, 11 (1969), 75-88.

Holditch, W. Kenneth. "The Last Frontier of Bohemia: Tennessee Williams in New Orleans, 1938-1983." *Southern Quarterly*, 23 (Winter 1985), 1-37.

Holditch. "Surviving with Grace: Tennessee Williams Today," *Southern Review*, 15 (Summer 1979), 753-762.

Holditch. "Surviving with Grace: Tennessee Williams Tomorrow," *Southern Review*, 22 (Autumn 1986), 892-903.

Hughes, Catharine. "Tennessee Williams: 'What's Left?' " *America*, 134 (10 Jan. 1976), 10-11. Collected in Stanton, 171-173.

Hulley, Kathleen. "The Fate of the Symbolic in *A Streetcar Named Desire.*" In her *Drama and Symbolism*, Cambridge: Cambridge University Press, 1982, 89-99. Collected in Bloom, 1988, 111-122.

Hurley, Paul J. "*Suddenly Last Summer* as 'Morality Play,' " *Modern Drama*, 8 (Feb. 1966), 392-402.

Jackson, Esther Merle. "The Anti-Hero in the Plays of Tennessee Williams." In Stanton, 87-99.

Jackson. "Music and Dance as Elements of Form in the Drama of Tennessee Williams," *Revue d'histoire du théâtre*, 15 (1963), 294-301.

Jackson. "Tennessee Williams." In *American Theatre Today*, ed. Alan S. Downer. New York: Basic, 1967, 73-84.

Jackson. "Tennessee Williams' *Out Cry*: Studies in Dramatic Form at The University of Wisconsin, Madison," *Tennessee Williams Newsletter*, 2 (Fall 1980), 6-12.

Jackson. "Tennessee Williams: Poetic Consciousness in Crisis." In Tharpe, 1977, 53-72.

Jones, Betty Jean. "Tennessee Williams' *Out Cry*: Studies in Production Form at The University of Wisconsin, Madison, Part II," *Tennessee Williams Review*, 3 (Spring/Fall 1982), 9-16.

Jones, John H. "The Missing Link: The Father in *The Glass Menagerie*," *Notes on Mississippi Writers*, 20 (1988), 29-38.

Jones, Robert Emmet. "Sexual Roles in the Works of Tennessee Williams." In Tharpe, 1977, 545-557.

Kahn, Sy. "*Baby Doll*: A Comic Fable." In Tharpe, 1977, 292-309.

Kahn. "*The Red Devil Battery Sign*: A First Impression." In Stanton, 175-178.

Kahn. "*The Red Devil Battery Sign*: Williams' Götterdämmerung in Vienna." In Tharpe, 1977, 362-371.

Kahn. "Through a Glass Menagerie Darkly: The World of Tennessee Williams." In *Modern American Drama: Essays in Criticism*, ed. W. E. Taylor. De Land, Fla.: Everett/Edwards, 1968, 71-89.

Kalson, Albert E. "A Source for *Cat on a Hot Tin Roof*," *Tennessee Williams Newsletter*, 2 (Fall 1980), 21-22.

Kalson. "Tennessee Williams at the Delta Brilliant." In Tharpe, 1977, 774-794; in Tharpe, 1980, 207-227.

Kalson. "Tennessee Williams Enters *Dragon Country*," *Modern Drama*, 16 (June 1973), 61-67.

Kazan, Elia. "Notebook for *A Streetcar Named Desire*." In *Directors on Directing*, ed. Toby Cole and Helen Krich Chinoy. Indianapolis: Bobbs-Merrill, 1963, 364-379. Excerpted in Miller, 21-27.

Kernan, Alvin B. "Truth and Dramatic Mode in the Modern Theatre: Chekhov, Pirandello, and Williams," *Modern Drama*, 1 (Sept. 1958), 101-114. Excerpted in Bloom, 1987, 9-11.

King, Thomas L. "Irony and Distance in *The Glass Menagerie*," *Educational Theatre Journal*, 25 (May 1973), 207-214. Collected in R. B. Parker, 75-86; collected in Bloom, 1987, 85-94.

Kolin, Philip C. " 'Sentiment and humor in equal measure': Comic Forms in *The Rose Tattoo*." In Tharpe, 1977, 214-231.

Kramer, Victor A. "Memoirs of Self-Indictment: The Solitude of Tennessee Williams." In Tharpe, 1977, 663-675.

Larsen, June Bennett. "Tennessee Williams: Optimistic Symbolist." In Tharpe, 1977, 413-428.

Leon, Ferdinand. "Time, Fantasy, and Reality in *The Night of the Iguana*," *Modern Drama*, 11 (May 1968), 87-96.

Loney, Glen. "Tennessee Williams, the Catastrophe of Success: 'You Can't Retire from Being an Artist,' " *Performing Arts Journal*, 7 (1983), 73-87.

MacNicholas, John. "Williams's Power of the Keys." In Tharpe, 1977, 581-605; in Tharpe, 1980, 113-137.

Magid, Marion. "The Innocence of Tennessee Williams," *Commentary*, 25 (Jan. 1963), 34-43. Excerpted in Miller, 73-79.

Matthew, David C. " 'Towards Bethlehem': *Battle of Angels* and *Orpheus Descending*." In Tharpe, 1977, 172-191.

May, Charles E. "Brick Pollitt as Homo Ludens: 'Three Players of a Summer Game,' and *Cat on a Hot Tin Roof*." In Tharpe, 1977, 277-291; in Tharpe, 1980, 49-63.

Mayberry, Susan Neal. "A Study of Illusion and the Grotesque in Tennessee Williams' *Cat on a Hot Tin Roof*," *Southern Studies*, 22 (Winter 1983), 359-365.

McBride, Mary. "Prisoners of Illusion: Surrealistic Escape in *The Milk Train Doesn't Stop Here Anymore*." In Tharpe, 1977, 341-348.

McGlinn, Jeanne M. "Tennessee Williams's Women: Illusion and Reality, Sexuality and Love." In Tharpe, 1977, 510-524.

Miller, Jordan Y. "*Camino Real*." In *The Fifties: Fiction, Poetry, Drama*, ed. Warren French. De Land, Fla.: Everett/Edwards, 1970, 241-248.

Miller. "The Three Halves of Tennessee Williams' World," *Studies in the Literary Imagination*, 21 (Fall 1988), 83-95.

Moorman, Charles. "*The Night of the Iguana*: A Long Introduction, a General Essay and no Explication at All." In Tharpe, 1977, 318-324.

Moritz, Helen E. "Apparent Sophoclean Echoes in Tennessee Williams's *Night of the Iguana*," *Classical and Modern Literature*, 47 (Summer 1985), 305-314.

Munro, C. Lynn. "The Tattooed Heart and the Serpentine Eye: Morrison's Choice of Epigraph for *Sula*," *Black American Literature Forum*, 18 (Winter 1984), 150-154.

Napieralski, Edmund A. "Tennessee Williams' *The Glass Menagerie*: The Dramatic Metaphor," *Southern Quarterly*, 16 (Oct. 1977), 1-12.

Nelson, Benjamin. " 'The play is memory.' " In his *Tennessee Williams, The Man and His Work*, 98-100, 103-12. Collected in R. B. Parker, 87-95.

Niesen, George. "The Artist against the Reality in the Plays of Tennessee Williams." In Tharpe, 1977, 463-493; in Tharpe, 1980, 81-111.

Nolan, Paul T. "Two Memory Plays: *The Glass Menagerie* and *After the Fall*," *McNeese Review*, 17 (1966), 27-38. Excerpted in R. B. Parker, 144-154.

Ower, John. "Erotic Mythology in the Poetry of Tennessee Williams." In Tharpe, 1977, 609-623.

Parker, R. B. "The Circle Closed: A Psychological Reading of *The Glass Menagerie* and *The Two-Character Play*," *Modern Drama*, 28 (Dec. 1985), 517-534.

Parker. "The Composition of *The Glass Menagerie*: An Argument for Complexity," *Modern Drama*, 25 (1982), 409-422. Collected in D. Parker, 12-26; excerpted as "The Texas Drafts of *The Glass Menagerie*" in R. B. Parker, 53-61.

Pease, Donald. "Reflections on Moon Lake: Presences of the Playwright." In Tharpe, 1977, 829-847; in Tharpe, 1980, 261-279.

Peterson, William. "Williams, Kazan and the Two Cats," *New Theatre Magazine*, 7, no. 3 (1967), 14-19.

Phillips, Jerrold A. "Imagining *I Can't Imagine Tomorrow*," *Tennessee Williams Review*, 3 (Spring-Fall 1982), 27-29.

Phillips. "*Kingdom of Earth*: Some Approaches." In Tharpe, 1977, 349-353.

Pitavy, Danièle. "L'Intruse: Stratégie du Désir dans *Desire Under the Elms* et *A Streetcar Named Desire*," *Coup de Théâtre*, 3 (Dec. 1983), 17-27.

Pitavy, F. "*Cat on a Hot Tin Roof*: Le Jeu du Mot et de la Chose," *Coup de Théâtre*, 5 (Dec. 1985), 79-88.

Pitavy-Souques, D. "Au Soir de la Fête: Notes sur l'Espace dans *Cat on a Hot Tin Roof*," *Coup de Théâtre*, 5 (Dec. 1985), 45-54.

Porter, Thomas E. "The Passing of the Old South: *A Streetcar Named Desire*." In his *Myth and Modern American Drama*. Detroit: Wayne State University Press, 1969, 153-176.

Prenshaw, Peggy W. "The Paradoxical Southern World of Tennessee Williams." In Tharpe, 1977, 5-29; in Tharpe, 1980, 3-27.

Presley, Delma Eugene. "Little Acts of Grace." In Tharpe, 1977, 571-580.

Presley. "The Moral Function of Distortion in Southern Grotesque," *South Atlantic Bulletin*, 37 (May 1972), 37-46.

Presley. "The Search for Hope in the Plays of Tennessee Williams," *Mississippi Quarterly*, 25 (Winter 1971-1972), 31-43.

Presley and Hari Singh. "Epigraphs to the Plays of Tennessee Williams," *Notes on Mississippi Writers*, 3 (Spring 1970), 2-12.

Prosser, William. "Loneliness, Apparitions, and the Saving Grace of the Imagination," *Tennessee Williams Newsletter*, 2 (Fall 1980), 13-15.

Quinby, Lee. "Tennessee Williams' Hermaphroditic Symbolism in *The Rose Tattoo, Orpheus Descending, The Night of the Iguana*, and *Kingdom of Earth*," *Tennessee Williams Newsletter*, 1 (Fall 1979), 12-14.

Quintus, John Allen. "The Loss of Dear Things: Chekhov and Williams in Perspective," *English Language Notes*, 18 (Mar. 1981), 201-206.

Quirino, Leonard. "The Cards Indicate a Voyage on *A Streetcar Named Desire.*" In Tharpe, 1977, 77-96; in Tharpe, 1980, 29-48; in Bloom, 1988, 61-77.

Quirino. "Tennessee Williams' Persistent *Battle of Angels,*" *Modern Drama,* 11 (May 1968), 27-39. Collected in Bloom, 1987, 43-54.

Raifailovich, Pnina. "Tennessee Williams's South," *Southern Studies,* 23 (Summer 1984), 191-197.

Reck, Tom Stokes. "The First *Cat on a Hot Tin Roof*: Williams' 'Three Players,' " *University Review,* 34 (Mar. 1968), 187-192.

Reck. "The Short Stories of Tennessee Williams: Nucleus for His Drama," *Tennessee Studies in Literature,* 16 (1971), 141-154.

Richardson, Thomas J. "The City of Day and the City of Night: New Orleans and the Exotic Unreality of Tennessee Williams." In Tharpe, 631-646.

Riddell, Joseph N. "*A Streetcar Named Desire*–Nietzsche Descending," *Modern Drama,* 5 (Feb. 1963), 421-430. Collected in Miller, 80-89; collected in Bloom, 1987, 13-22; collected in Bloom, 1988, 21-31.

Roderick, John M. "From 'Tarantula Arms' to 'Della Robbia Blue': The Tennessee Williams Tragicomic Transit Authority." In Tharpe, 1977, 116-125; in Bloom, 1988, 93-101.

Rogoff, Gordon. "The Restless Intelligence of Tennessee Williams," *Tulane Drama Review,* 10 (Summer 1966), 78-92.

Ross, Marlon B. "The Making of Tennessee Williams: Imaging a Life of Imagination," *Southern Humanities Review,* 21 (Spring 1987), 117-131.

Rowland, James L. "Tennessee's Two Amandas," *Research Studies,* 35 (Dec. 1967), 331-340. Collected in R. B. Parker, 62-74.

Sacksteder, William. "The Three Cats: A Study in Dramatic Structure," *Drama Survey,* 5 (Winter 1966-1967), 252-266.

Scanlon, Tom. "Reactions II: Family and Psyche in Tennessee Williams." In his *Family, Drama, and American Dreams.* Westport, Conn.: Greenwood, 1978, 156-160, 166-179. Collected in R. B. Parker, 96-108.

Scheick, William J. " 'An Intercourse Not Well Designed': Talk and Touch in the Plays of Tennessee Williams." In Tharpe, 1977, 763-773.

Scheye, Thomas E. "*The Glass Menagerie*: 'It's no tragedy, Freckles.' " In Tharpe, 1977, 207-213.

Schlueter, June. "Imitating an Icon: John Erman's Remake of Tennessee Williams's *A Streetcar Named Desire*," *Modern Drama*, 28 (Mar. 1985), 139-147.

Schvey, Henry I. "Madonna at the Poker Night: Pictorial Elements in Tennessee Williams's *A Streetcar Named Desire*." In Bloom, 1988, 103-109.

Seivers, David. *Freud on Broadway: A History of Psychoanalysis and the American Drama*. New York: Hermitage House, 1955, 370-388. Excerpted in Miller, 90-93.

Simard, Rodney. "The Uses of Experience: Tennessee Williams in *Vieux Carré*," *Southern Literary Journal*, 17 (Spring 1985), 67-78.

Skei, Hans H. "The Reception and Reputation of Tennessee Williams in Norway," *Notes on Mississippi Writers*, 17, no. 2 (1985), 63-81.

Sklepowich, Edward A. "In Pursuit of the Lyric Quarry: The Image of the Homosexual in Tennessee Williams's Prose Fiction." In Tharpe, 1977, 525-544.

Skloot, Robert. "Submitting Self to Flame: The Artists's Quest in Tennessee Williams, 1935-1954," *Educational Theatre Journal*, 25 (May 1973), 199-206.

Smith, Harry W. "Tennessee Williams and Jo Mielziner: The Memory Plays," *Theatre Survey*, 23 (Nov. 1982), 223-235.

Spivey, Ted R. "Tennessee Williams: Desire and Impotence in New Orleans." In his *Revival: Southern Writers in the Modern City*. Gainesville: University of Florida Press, 1986, 122-138.

Stamper, Rexford. "*The Two-Character Play*: Psychic Individuation." In Tharpe, 1977, 354-361.

Stanton, Stephen S. "Some Thoughts about *Steps Must Be Gentle*," *Tennessee Williams Review*, 4 (Spring 1983), 48-53.

Starnes, Leland. "The Grotesque Children of *The Rose Tattoo*," *Modern Drama*, 12 (Feb. 1970), 357-369. Collected in D. Parker, 39-51.

Stauffacher, Paul K. "Designing Tennessee Williams' *Out Cry*," *Tennessee Williams Review*, 3 (Spring-Fall 1982), 17-20.

Stein, Robert B. "*The Glass Menagerie* Revisited: Catastrophe without Violence," *Western Humanities Review*, 18 (Spring 1964), 141-153. Enlarged in R. B. Parker, 135-143; revised and abridged in Stanton, 36-44.

Taubman, Howard. "Diverse, Unique Amanda," *New York Times*, 16 May 1965, section 2, p. 1. Collected in R. B. Parker, 22-25.

Taylor, William E. "Tennessee Williams: The Playwright as Poet." In Tharpe, 1977, 624-630.

Thompson, Judith J. "Symbol, Myth, and Ritual in *The Glass Menagerie, The Rose Tattoo*, and *Orpheus Descending*." In Tharpe, 1977, 679-711; in Tharpe, 1980, 139-171.

Tischler, Nancy M. "The Distorted Mirror: Tennessee Williams' Self-Portraits," *Mississippi Quarterly*, 25 (1972), 389-403. Collected in Stanton, 158-170.

Tischler. "A Gallery of Witches." In Tharpe, 1977, 494-509.

Tischler. "The South Stage Center: Hellman and Williams." In *The American South: Portrait of a Culture*, ed. Louis D. Rubin, Jr. Baton Rouge: Louisiana State University Press, 1980, 323-333.

Traubitz, Nancy Baker. "Myth as a Basis of Dramatic Structure in *Orpheus Descending*," *Modern Drama*, 19 (Mar. 1976), 57-66. Collected in D. Parker, 3-11.

Turner, Diane E. "The Mythic Vision in Tennessee Williams' *Camino Real*." In Tharpe, 1977, 237-251.

Vidal, Gore. "Selected Memoirs of the Glorious Bird and the Golden Age," *The New York Review of Books*, 5 Feb. 1976, pp. 13-18.

Von Szeliski, John T. "Tennessee Williams and the Tragedy of Sensitivity," *Western Humanities Review*, 20 (Summer 1966), 203-211. Collected in Miller, 65-72.

Vowles, Richard B. "Tennessee Williams: The World of His Imagery," *Tulane Drama Review*, 3 (Dec. 1958), 51-56.

Watson, Charles S. "The Revision of *The Glass Menagerie*: The Passing of Good Manners," *Southern Literary Journal*, 8 (Spring 1976), 74-78.

Weales, Gerald. "Tennessee Williams' Achievement in the Sixties." In his *The Jumping-Off Place: American Drama in the 1960s*. New York: Macmillan, 1969, 3-14. Collected in Stanton, 61-70.

Wiessman, Philip. "Psychopathological Characters in Current Drama: A Study of a Trio of Heroines," *American Imago*, 17 (Fall 1960), 271-288. Excerpted as "A Trio of Tennessee Williams' Heroines: The Psychology of Prostitution" in Miller, 57-64.

Willett, Ralph W. "Ideas of Miller and Williams," *Theatre Annual*, 22 (1966), 31-40.

Wolf, Morris Philip. "Casanova's Portmanteau: *Camino Real* and Recurring Communication Patterns of Tennessee Williams." In Tharpe, 1977, 252-276.

Yacowar, Maurice. "The Film Version of *The Glass Menagerie* (1950)." In R. B. Parker, 26-30.

Young, Stark. "The First Production of *The Glass Menagerie*," *New Republic*, 12 (16 Apr. 1945), 505. Collected in R. B. Parker, 15-19.

BIBLIOGRAPHICAL ESSAY

Bibliographies and Checklists

No fully descriptive bibliography of work by and about Tennessee Williams is available, but Drewey Wayne Gunn's *Tennessee Williams: A Bibliography* (1980) is nonetheless indispensable. Although it contains numerous errors and omissions (noted in George Miller's review in *Tennessee Williams Review*, 3 [Spring/Fall 1982], 51-54), Gunn's bibliography covers Williams's published plays, fiction, essays, occasional pieces, and unpublished manuscripts with thoroughness. Gunn also lists production information, reviews, interviews, biographies, and criticism, including dissertations. One of Gunn's most important contributions is his attempt to identify significant revisions of Williams's material, an onerous task considering the fact that Williams often rewrote. Gunn's primary bibliography is updated in checklists by Thomas P. Adler, Judith Hersch Clark, and Lyle Taylor (Spring 1980) and Alan M. Cohn (Spring/Fall 1982).

Catherine M. Arnott's *Tennessee Williams on File* (1985) is a handy listing of premiere and New York play productions, and television and film productions, that also contains excerpts from reviews. Plays are listed chronologically according to the probable time of composition. The book should be used cautiously for it contains several ghosts and errors: *The Bag People*, a novel said to be published in 1982, is unknown; the short story "It Happened the Day the Sun Rose" was privately printed in 1981, not as part of a short story collection by Simon and Schuster; and volumes 6 and 7 of *The Theatre of Tennessee Williams* were published in 1981, not 1976.

Delma Eugene Presley's "Tennessee Williams: Twenty-Five Years of Criticism" (Jan./Mar. 1973) is an accurate and useful listing of criticism and reviews from 1945 to 1970. Charles A. Carpenter's "Studies of Tennessee Williams' Drama: A Selective International Bibliography: 1966-1978" (Spring 1980) calls attention to the broad international criticism Williams has received. John S. McCann's *The Critical Reputation of Tennessee Williams: A Reference Guide* (1983) is the only annotated secondary bibliography available and is indispensable. Items are alphabetically listed by year through 1981 and are indexed. The best bibliographic essay available is S. Alan Chesler's "Tennessee Williams: Reassessment and Assessment" (1977), which is a discussion of major critical interpretations of Williams's *The Glass Menagerie, A Streetcar Named Desire, Cat on a Hot Tin Roof, The Night of the Iguana,* and *Suddenly Last Summer.*

Biographies

The first Williams biography, *Remember Me to Tom* (1963), is a sentimental memoir written by Williams's mother, Edwina Williams. She reprints Williams's early prize-winning poems and essays and many of his letters. Accounts of his family life, illnesses, moves, and his relationships with his sister, Rose, and his father, C. C. Williams, are also recorded. Although the book is necessarily biased and makes too many references to Williams's father's brutality and to Edwina Williams's inability to cope, it gives an interesting portrait of the playwright's youthful and apprentice years.

Gilbert Maxwell's *Tennessee Williams and Friends* (1965) is a harmless biography of Williams and Maxwell and their social acquaintances in the 1940s and 1950s. Maxwell draws heavily on Edwina Williams's book for his account of the early years. The book is most worthwhile for Maxwell's effort to explain the ambivalence and contrariness so prevalent in Williams's personality.

In *A Look at Tennessee Williams* (1969) Mike Steen collects twenty-four interviews he conducted with writers, film and play directors, producers, actors and actresses, and friends of the playwright. Each interviewee informally recounts favorite memories of Williams: his humor, his art, his forgetfulness, his kindness. One of the finest metaphors for Williams is offered by actor Michael Wilding, who says, "Tennessee is like a bullfighter. He has to work close to the horns all the time, to be so successful, and he has been so successful, writing his own poetic kind of Southern thing. And the critics expect him to be better each time. He can't be better each time. And the critics are the ones who are killing him by making him work closer to the horns." Steen's book provides a fine beginning for a needed study of the working relationships between Williams, as playwright and screenwriter, and his actors, directors and producers.

The World of Tennessee Williams (1978), edited by Richard Leavitt, is an illustrated coffee-table book presenting playbills, photographs, reviews, poems, letters, movie stills, and posters. Leavitt's collection gives an interesting chronological account of the Williams that resides in the public domain.

Volume 4 of the *Dictionary of Literary Biography Documentary Series* (1984), edited by Margaret A. Van Antwerp and Sally Johns, is devoted entirely to Williams. It is a collection of interviews, essays, critical articles, book reviews, and speeches, selected to represent Williams's entire career. There are a few errors in the dating of productions, and a 1978 biography listed as by Catharine R. Hughes does not exist, but the variety of information provided makes the volume a useful reference work.

Following William's death in February 1983 several biographies were published. The first is by Williams's brother, Dakin Williams, written with the help of Shepherd Mead. *Tennessee Williams: An Intimate Biography* (1983) is a personal account that draws too heavily on the books by Edwina Williams and Mike Steen, offering few additional insights. The next biography is even more self-indulgent. Dotson Rader's *Tennessee: Cry of the Heart* (1985) is haphazardly organized and gives the impression of being scholarly when it is really a reminiscence. Rader is often content to retell Williams's *Memoirs* from his own point of view. Although he captures much of Williams's voice, Rader concentrates on the most sensational aspects of Williams's life; his sufferings and disappointments are glorified.

In 1985 Donald Spoto published the first critical biography of Williams, *The Kindness of Strangers: The Life of Tennessee Williams*. Spoto's book is a full and accurate account that makes creative use of reports from Williams's friends and acquaintances. Although the biography is filled with facts, Spoto does not add significantly to existing critical interpretation. He gives plot summaries and details the writing and production of the plays but does not attempt to answer questions of criticism. He does make an interesting assertion that Williams had a "deep-seated hatred of homosexuality," but he does not further explore the idea. (See W. Kenneth Holditch's excellent essay-review, "Surviving with Grace: Tennessee Williams Tomorrow" [Autumn 1986], which discusses the biographies from 1963-1985, and Marlon B. Ross's "The Making of Tennessee Williams: Imaging a Life of Imagination" [Spring 1987], which is an excellent review of Rader's and Spoto's works.)

Not a critical biography, Harry Rasky's *Tennessee Williams: A Portrait in Laughter and Lamentation* (1986) attempts to give an objective but personal view of Williams in the 1970s. The book is the tale of Rasky's experiences with Williams as he was making the 1973 film documentary *Tennessee Williams' South*. Especially interesting are the discussions about the South, the Williams play *Out Cry*, and the character Quentin of *Small Craft Warnings*. Rasky reports Williams's affectionate acknowledgment of his father, whose legacy is the playwright's own wanderlust. Williams had requested Rasky to direct the Atlanta premiere of *Tiger Tail*, a drama based on the play *Baby Doll*, and Rasky also recounts that experience. Rasky intends to give an honest, sensitive portrait of Williams, using Williams's own words as often as possible, the very element missing in Spoto's fuller, more academic account.

Donald Windham's *Lost Friendships: A Memoir of Truman Capote, Tennessee Williams and Others* (1987) includes Windham's 1985 privately published memoir *As If . . . : A Personal View of Tennessee Williams*. Windham alternates between personal reminiscences and critical evaluations of plays and stories. The controlling metaphor is Williams's paradoxical blend of seriousness and humor: Williams's "kind actions were sometimes prompted by his guilt about his cruel ones." Windham concludes his pseudo-psychoanalysis by saying that "as well as becoming one with life, he [Williams] had become one against the world."

Lyle Leverich, producer and friend of Williams, is, as of 1988, writing an authorized biography; the first of two volumes is scheduled for 1989 publication by William Morrow. Leverich hopes to show how "Tennessee Williams" is an invention meant to protect the real "Tom Williams." Virginia Spenser Carr is also working on a biography of Williams. It is hoped that each of these works will combine a personal understanding and a scholarly examination of Williams and his work, so that complete pictures of the man and the artist will emerge.

Interviews

Conversations with Tennessee Williams, edited by Albert J. Devlin (1986), is an excellent gathering of the most important of Williams's interviews. Ranging from 1940, during the time Williams's first full-length production, *Battle of Angels*, was underway, to a 1981 *Paris Review* interview, the interviews in Devlin's collection represent, in effect, an autobiography that reveals much more about Williams's art and craftsmanship than the playwright's own *Memoirs*. The early interviews are mostly biographical, dealing in part with his adoption of the name "Tennessee," his southern background, his family history, and the early one-acts. Also in the early interviews are candid opinions which became characteristic of the playwright: in an interview with Mark Barron (24 Nov. 1940) Williams attests to his paradoxical need for and fear of Broadway. Speaking of *Battle of Angels*, he says, "I'm getting out of town the minute my play opens and maybe sooner. Where I'll go I don't know. Just wherever my feet take me." He was notorious for seeking early escape from the publicity he simultaneously craved and was never to settle anywhere for very long. In 1945, the year *The Glass Menagerie* premiered in New York, Jean Evans (6 May 1945) asked if he always "wrote about unhappy, trapped, hopeless people." Williams replied that "it's human valor that moves me. The one dominant theme in most of my writings, the most magnificent thing in all human nature, is valor–and endurance." In a brief interview with R. L. Lewis (7 Dec. 1947) Williams says that "the creation of character" is his primary purpose in playwriting. "I have always had a deep feeling for the mystery in life, and essentially my plays have been an effort to explore the beauty and meaning in the confusion of living." Lewis notes that Williams seemed to have "few close friends" and that he displayed "enthusiasm for travel," two aspects of his life which were firmly established by this time.

Henry Hewes (28 Mar. 1953) asks Williams to explain *Camino Real*. Williams addresses questions about the locale, the time blocks, and the symbolism, and declares, "I don't believe in using symbols *unless* they clarify." In the Louise Davis interview (Mar. 1957), the South and southernness are topics.

In "Williams and Kazan and the Big Walk-Out" Arthur Gelb (1 May 1960) lets Williams tell his side of the controversial story of the estrangement between the playwright and the director. Elia Kazan, who had already directed productions of *A Streetcar Named Desire*, *Camino Real*, *Sweet Bird of Youth*, and *Cat on a Hot Tin Roof* to rave reviews and positive criticism, had just quit the direction of *Period of Adjustment*. Gelb manages to let Williams make his apologies and also tells of Kazan's offhand remarks about the "sniping" that had been going on.

The interviews of the 1970s concentrate on Williams's personal life: his homosexuality; hospitalizations; drug abuse; and his debilitating fear of death. In addition, Williams is usually asked to justify each of his new plays. With Jim Gaines (29 Apr. 1972) he discusses *Small Craft Warnings*, but Williams sees "no reason for a writer to attempt an assessment of his own work; he's probably an unreliable judge." Williams talks about his social conscience and his political awareness, especially in relation to his play *Red Devil Battery Sign*, in a 1975 interview with Charles Ruas. Although Williams does not do the majority of the talking in Ira J. Bilowit's "Roundtable" interview (Mar. 1979), he does speak about his *A Lovely Sunday for Creve Coeur*, vehemently stating that "there is no lesbianism involved. Not even the faintest hint."

The final interview in Devlin's book is an airing of opinion on a variety of topics suggested by Dotson Rader (Fall 1981). In addition to the obvious subjects: Williams's writing habits and his attitudes concerning people in the drama profession, sex, and death, Williams talks about his most obscure play, *Clothes for a Summer Hotel*, and his most autobiographical play, *Something Cloudy, Something Clear*. Of the latter he said that the title "refers to my eyes. My left eye was cloudy then because it was developing a cataract. But my right eye was clear. It was like two sides of my nature. The side that was obsessively homosexual, compulsively interested in sexuality. And the side that in those days was gentle and understanding and contemplative."

Two interviews of importance were unavailable for inclusion in Devlin's collection. The first is a Summer/Fall 1977 interview with George Whitmore for *Gay Sunshine*. Williams asserts that he does not write for a homosexual audience because that would be too limiting. Furthermore, the importance of his work is not "sexual orientation, it's social." Williams "doesn't find it necessary" to write homosexual literature; he says, "I could express what I wanted to express through other means." But his homosexuality makes him more sensitive, and therefore a better artist. Speaking of *Out Cry*, he says he was not influenced by Pirandello; rather, he just "didn't know the borderline between reality and fantasy."

In *The Ultimate Seduction* (1984) Charlotte Chandler writes about the few days she spent interviewing Williams in Key West, Florida, in the late 1970s. About the biographical nature of his work Williams says, "Everything a writer of fiction creates has to come out of himself. What we write may develop in a heightened or exaggerated form, but it's usually something that we've experienced or observed." He talks about the self-consciousness of success, his loneliness, the shock of truth, the need for human intimacy, his bohemian lifestyle and the hypocrisy of the 1970s. Throughout his career Williams was known as an easy interview; in early sessions he chose phrases that would satisfy and delight without revealing his private life. Later interviews were more revealing. His conversations with Chandler, as she records them, are touching but self-condemning: "I have often disappointed [people]. To know me is not to love me. At best it is to tolerate me."

Critical Studies: Books

The first full-length studies of Williams's work, Benjamin Nelson's *Tennessee Williams: The Man and His Work* (1961), Signi L. Falk's *Tennessee Williams* (1962), and Nancy M. Tischler's *Tennessee Williams: Rebellious Puritan* (1961), cover the early development of Williams as a poet, short-story writer, and one-act playwright. Full-length plays through *Sweet Bird of Youth* are also discussed. Falk's book was revised in 1978 to consider Williams's work through *Memoirs*. In 1969 Tischler published a second book, *Tennessee Williams*. The value of these early works lies in their synopses of Williams's output without the emphasis on his homosexuality that came in the 1970s.

Nelson details Williams's early life as it influences his writing. After discussing the formative stages of the plays, Nelson makes references to popular critical reception more than academic evaluations. The book is especially helpful regarding early unpublished work (as of 1961) and early criticism.

Tischler concentrates on the psychological aspect of the plays in light of Williams's childhood and his psychoanalysis in the 1960s. Tischler's Williams is a romantic, burdened by his Puritan background, his overattachment to his mother, his illnesses, and his loneliness. Tischler comes closer than Nelson or Falk to the issues of the 1970s when in the conclusion, she queries of her study, "Sometimes we wonder if Williams' men aren't really women and vice versa. The characters are often Freudian case studies; their actions arise from hysterias and obsessions." Tischler concludes that Williams "lacks stability of philosophy, government, or religion." His work "contains two forces in constant conflict: flesh and spirit, reality and dreams, brutality and ideals." She makes frequent use of Williams's own descriptions and explanations of both his life and the plays, but no documentation is given.

Falk's book is a thematic discussion of Williams's characters: gentlewomen; southern wenches; desperate heroes, and deteriorating artists. In the 1978 revision she describes the plays following *Sweet Bird of Youth* as "unabashed confessions" and suggests that "what motivates this extended self-exposure, this laying open to the public of so much bitterness and suffering and his own individual lifestyle, is a question to challenge the most sympathetic doctor for tortured spirits."

A fourth book that attempts to classify Williams, considering work through *The Milk Train Doesn't Stop Here Anymore*, is Gerald Weales's *Tennessee Williams* (1965). Weales groups Williams's characters as various "fugitive kinds": artist; insane person; cripple; sexual specialist; and foreigner. He identifies basic themes, theatrical devices, and symbols common to Williams's plays. Recognizing the bond between Williams's life and work and his continual effort to write for the popular theater, Weales states, "He rewrites to find the play implicit in the original material" and "to get the audience he would like to have."

Norman J. Fedder's *The Influence of D. H. Lawrence on Tennessee Williams* (1966) is a careful study of textual parallels between Lawrence and Williams. Both writers "reflect the essential concerns of the anti-materialistic, anti-rational Romantic tradition." Fedder evaluates three Lawrencian elements evident in Williams's work: conflict between flesh and spirit; antagonism toward bourgeois civilization; and animal symbolism. The three elements are especially obvious in Williams's *I Rise in Flame, Cried the Phoenix* but can also be found in the short fiction, early poems, and several full-length dramas. *Battle of Angels* and *Orpheus Descending* are related to Lawrence's *Lady Chatterly's Lover* (1928), declares Fedder. *The Glass Menagerie* and *Sons and Lovers* (1913), he continues, are both autobiographical illustrations of domineering mothers, weak fathers, artistic sons, and aborted relationships. Fedder also closely compares Williams and Windham's *You Touched Me!* with Lawrence's short story of the same title, and considers Williams's *Summer and Smoke* to be very similar to "The Virgin and the Gypsy," a Lawrence story that Fedder says Williams listed among his reading. However, Fedder considers *Camino Real* especially weak "when one compares it with Lawrence's symbolic masterpiece on the same subject, 'St. Mawr.' "

Throughout his argument Fedder is convincing without being dogmatic. He recognizes the difficulty in comparing themes from different genres, although "Williams has written works which recapture in dramatic form the aesthetic impact of much of Lawrence's short fiction." In the final analysis, though, Fedder concludes that "Williams fails to achieve the literary stature of Lawrence." The study is interesting and believable; Fedder goes beyond mere comparison to make worthwhile analyses that help make clear Williams's interpretations of the concerns he shared with his predecessor.

The most scholarly full-length study of Williams's plays (through *The Night of the Iguana*) is Esther Merle Jackson's *The Broken World of Tennessee Williams* (1965). Concentrating on Williams's visions and his forms of dramatic technique rather than on his life, Jackson is the first academic critic to give Williams credit for developing and using a dramatic theory. She also writes about Williams's dramaturgy without reducing the plays to novelistic narratives.

Williams, Jackson writes, answers Walt Whitman's call for an American voice as he responds to the post-World War II world with theater created for performance, for the populace. Although Williams relies heavily on models of realistic/naturalistic drama, Jackson thinks that he ultimately rejects realism for romanticism. The "pattern of figuration" in his drama "is romantic in quality, especially in its preoccupation with hallucinatory levels of experience." By dramatizing the "poetic paradox" of good in evil, light in dark, body against soul, Williams "represents the struggle of man to transcend his humanity, to provide for himself a mode of reconciliation with divine purpose." *The Glass Menagerie* has little if any of an Aristotelian sense of action; instead it is a series of lyric moments in which "action is aesthetic; it is the growth of understanding." Although Williams is often accused of writing only for the kind of commercial theater found on Broadway, of not being an intellectual, of not being a reader, Jackson clearly demonstrates that his art, beyond the artist's personality, successfully dramatizes civilization's ironies.

In plays such as *A Streetcar Named Desire, Cat on a Hot Tin Roof, Summer and Smoke, The Rose Tattoo,* and *Camino Real,* Jackson thinks that Williams created "myths of modern life." She calls them "synthetic" myths, "composed after the manner of cinematic montage, from the fragments of many ethical, philosophical, social, poetic, intellectual and religious perspectives," illustrating "the image of modern man caught between opposing logics—man in search of a means of reconciliation." But, like many others, he never connected the fragments, never fully solved the "problem of modern art: the evolution of a truly effective mode of aesthetic transcendence."

Jackson argues that Williams's typical "antihero" is based on "a radical perception of new dangers for mankind" and "new modes of courage." While European dramatists use Prometheus as antecedent, Williams models his antihero after Orestes, whom Jackson defines as "an image of man concerned with his own power, responsibility, and complicity in the evil of the universe." Blanche,

Alma, Brick, Kilroy, Chance, and Val each dramatize an inner struggle of guilt and responsibility. Jackson says, "Like Hamlet, Blanche DuBois reveals her inner nature by playing out her conflicted roles."

Jackson's book also includes fine discussions of Williams's concept of plastic theater and of *Camino Real*. Although the play is not regarded as completely successful, Jackson feels it is a significant accomplishment in Williams's developing form.

A later study which considers Williams's work of the mid 1960s and 1970s is Felicia Hardison Londre's *Tennessee Williams* (1979). Though it has several limitations, most notably the absence of an innovative critical viewpoint, it offers a good chronology and covers the most important influences of Williams's life on his work. For each work, Londre gives a synopsis, some evaluative judgment and production comments, and points out connections to other works. For the full-length plays she notes television and film productions, comparing interpretations by various actresses and directors.

Much less objective is Foster Hirsch's *A Portrait of the Artist: The Plays of Tennessee Williams* (1978). Hirsch reexamines the canon, illustrating that "all–most all–the plays are homosexual fantasies." Blanche DuBois is thus "cast as an effeminate male . . . a guilt-ridden gay"; *Suddenly Last Summer* becomes Williams's "ultimate homophile fantasy"; and "no Williams play is written on the pattern of the traditional heterosexual chase." Williams, believes Hirsch, would have written his plays differently had it not been for the restrictive social milieu of the 1940s and 1950s. But Hirsch does not substantiate his assertions.

Two excellent and complementary studies of films of Williams's work have been published: *Tennessee Williams and Film*, by Maurice Yacowar (1977); and *The Films of Tennessee Williams*, by Gene D. Phillips (1980). Yacowar includes a complete filmography, listing release dates, directors, producers, screenplay writers, directors of photography, art directors, music composers, designers, movie companies, and the length and cost for each of the films. The bibliography lists articles about Williams in film journals and books not often listed in other bibliographies. The index is cross-referenced and includes both literary and technical film terms.

Yacowar's excellent opening chapter introduces the complex issue of play adaptation and film interpretation: "A good adaptation is not one that makes no changes, but one in which changes serve the intention and thrust of the original." With this measure in mind, Yacowar studies the compromises made in each Williams film. *Baby Doll* is considered the best comedic adaptation; *Boom!*, the most cinematic. *The Night of the Iguana* and *Boom!* are the "best of the Williams adaptations because in both there is the energy and freedom of original creativity." However, Yacowar believes "insensitive compromises" altered the expressionistic *The Glass Menagerie*, a memory play, into a realistic romance. The adaptation of *A Streetcar Named Desire* was much more successful, "as subtle and as powerful as the play." The film also "introduced Method acting to the mass audience and . . . assumed that there was an audience for serious, challenging cinema." *The Rose Tattoo, Period of Adjustment,* and *Sweet Bird of Youth* did not succeed as well in re-creating the original tensions of the dramas.

Phillips's equally excellent book is less evaluative than Yacowar's. Using Williams's own comments and those of directors, actresses and designers, Phillips focuses on the making of the films and critical responses to them. The study is arranged by directors, so *A Streetcar Named Desire* and *Baby Doll*, directed by Elia Kazan, are discussed in one chapter. Kazan, Phillips notes, "is one of the very few film directors who treats a screenplay with the same respect that he would give a work for the stage." Phillips also pays attention to technical problems, such as lighting, sets, casting, and film censorship. The book gives a fascinating overall view of the film industry.

Irene Shaland's *Tennessee Williams on the Soviet Stage* (1987) is an interesting study of the reception of Williams in the Soviet theater since the first production of a Williams play in 1961. Because the Russian stage held to its realistic psychological traditions after the Bolshevik Revolution, it was slow to accept the myth of the past in Williams's plays as being other than naturalistic. In many productions the sexual aspects were reduced or deleted and the religious and sociopolitical possibilities were emphasized. Critical reviews illustrate that Soviet audiences are beginning to understand Williams's work less as "an attack on American culture" than as a convincing statement of "people's eternal need for one another."

Roger Boxhill's *Tennessee Williams* (1987) begins with a very subjective biography and finds, in Williams's use of the themes of past and present, real and unreal, and temporal loss, evidence of the autobiographical in all the plays. Boxhill claims to be "concerned with the plays as theatre" and discusses "such matters as performance, character interpretation, staging, theme, context," but much of the book is plot synopsis and it is full of stereotypical characterizations. He classifies characters as either wanderers or faded belles, or both (as in the case of Hannah in *The Night of the Iguana*). The late plays (from *The Milk Train Doesn't Stop Here Anymore* to *Clothes for a Summer Hotel*) are given brief attention without serious analysis.

Critical Studies: Special Journals and Newsletters

Volumes 1 and 2 of the *Tennessee Williams Newsletter* appeared in 1979 and 1980. Volumes 3 and 4 were published under the title the *Tennessee Williams Review* from 1981 to 1983. Publication ceased after the Spring 1983 issue. The journal published criticism, book and production reviews, abstracts of articles and papers delivered at meetings, notes, queries, and news of forthcoming publications and productions. Kenneth Holditch has announced that a new *Tennessee Williams Journal* will begin publication in Fall 1988.

Critical Studies: Major Reviews, Articles, and Book Sections

Several collections gather the better articles and reviews concerning Williams and his work, presenting a variety of interpretations by literary and theater critics, producers, and directors. Williams wrote in seven distinct genres: poetry, short story, essay, one-act drama, full-length drama, novel, and screenplay. He constantly reworked material and produced versions of plays under different circumstances with diverse texts and interpretations.

Esther Merle Jackson, however, establishes a basic groundwork in her essay, "Tennessee Williams" (1967). She writes that the playwright "attempts to recover for drama its primary identity as a pre-literary form." He does so by purposefully developing a popular dramatic form for a popular audience. His language, plots, and characters all reflect the "ambiguous reality of his perception." Jackson outlines three stages of Williams's dramatic development: the personal lyricism of the early period, as in *The Glass Menagerie*; the major period of production (1945-1955), in which he extended his search for truth using mythic patterns; and his efforts, in the plays of 1958-1962, to resolve the human conflict.

In a more recent study of Tennessee Williams as a southern writer, "The Paradoxical Southern World of Tennessee Williams" (1977), Peggy W. Prenshaw recognizes Williams's impulse to escape the bonds of history even as he is caught by the paradoxes inherent to the southern life. Prenshaw discusses the effect of the past on the present in *The Glass Menagerie* and the consequences of human sexuality in the plays. Williams discusses the relationship of art and life as therapy to "distract from his self-destructiveness"; however, neither his drama nor his characters can resolve the paradoxical tension inherent in the relationship.

Although many critics take a psychological approach to Williams's work, two studies specifically apply Freudian theories. David Seivers, in his *Freud on Broadway* (1955), identifies Williams's main theme as "the central power of sex in human life." He identifies the neuroses in the characters of *The Glass Menagerie, A Streetcar Named Desire* (the "quintessence of Freudian sexual psychology"), *Summer and Smoke,* and *Camino Real.* Seivers is especially insightful using Freudian analysis for *Camino Real.* Williams's cynicism and his use of dream symbolism are said to alienate the play's audience. "Dreams," writes Seivers, "at best require interpretation—and a cosmic dream of universal degeneracy and depravity proved more than a little disturbing for playgoers." Daniel A. Dervin, in "The Spook in the Rainforest: The Incestuous Structure of Tennessee Williams' Plays" (1979), also writes about dreams, primarily in relation to *Suddenly Last Summer.* That play illustrates what "happens to a work of imagination when it is charged with the incredible condensation power of a dream."

A few textual studies of Williams's plays have appeared, but much remains to be done in this area. Tom Stokes Reck makes a good beginning survey in "The Short Stories of Tennessee Williams: Nucleus for His Drama" (1971), identifying three types of connections between short story and drama. Occasionally Williams transfers a line or an element from one work to another without regard to character or situation. In other cases a theme is used with new characters or situations. Reck briefly discusses six full-length plays which evolved directly from short stories, but his analysis is necessarily cursory and should be used only as a starting point. Drewey Wayne Gunn approaches the textual complexities of Williams's work differently. In "The Various Texts of Tennessee Williams's Plays" (Oct. 1978) Gunn argues that the revisions published by Dramatists Play Service are often superior to the reading texts from New Directions. He lists various texts and revisions, noting where textual studies have been made or begun and suggests much else that should be closely examined.

The problem of text is central in an essay by Nancy Anne Cluck, "Showing or Telling: Narrators in the Drama of Tennessee Williams" (Mar. 1979). Readers of plays, Cluck argues, often know more than audiences because Williams provides full descriptive narrations in the reading texts of his plays. Surveying the images employed by Williams the poet, philosopher, playwright, and narrator in his published stage directions and through his "disguised narrators" in *The Glass Menagerie, Cat on a Hot Tin Roof, A Streetcar Named Desire, Camino Real*, and *The Rose Tattoo*, Cluck concludes that the written plays succeed in *telling* what the stage plays *show*. She does not, however, indicate what texts she is reading, nor what differences may be present in variant texts. Nor does she take up the issue of the origin of the sets and character descriptions and stage directions, which in many cases were developed within the collaborative context of a play's evolution and production, involving directors, designers, and actors as well as the playwright.

A more "stage wise" point of view is found in "Tennessee Williams and Jo Mielziner: The Memory Plays" (Nov. 1982), by Harry W. Smith. Mielziner designed the sets for *The Glass Menagerie, A Streetcar Named Desire*, and *Summer and Smoke*. Smith believes that Williams's "vision of dramatic life most subtle in its use of human values" is perfectly defined by Mielziner's "visual definition of mood." The "translucent tissue," "the gaudy kaleidoscope" and the "intricate pattern of emotional filigree" of Mielziner's sets "thrust" the plays into the audience.

Gilbert Debusscher studies Williams from a literary point of view in " 'Minting Their Separate Wills': Tennessee Williams and Hart Crane" (Dec. 1983). Although the article does not approach the depth of Fedder's book-length study of D. H. Lawrence and Williams, Debusscher discusses the biographical and literary connections of the two, stressing the strength of Williams's identification with Crane, manifested in epigraphs, titles, and allusions to Crane in Williams's stories and plays. The character of Amanda, Debusscher argues, is drawn as much from Crane's mother as from Edwina Williams. *Steps Must Be Gentle*, an early Williams one-act, is a dialogue between the ghosts of Crane and his mother.

Williams's humor has been only briefly examined. William J. Free makes an excellent examination of the "Camp Elements in the Plays of Tennessee Williams" (Winter 1983). "Camp," as Free defines it, is "humor produced by our recognition of juxtaposed extreme incongruities." Free uses the examples he so well identifies (Stanley and Blanche, Maggie and Brick, Amanda and Laura) to illustrate that Williams's plays, through the use of the humorous device, "provide an index to the severity of the reorganization our culture is undergoing."

Critics have identified isolation, the absence of God, death, sexuality, and morality as the major themes in Williams's plays. Writing in 1962, Arthur Ganz defines the "rejection of life" as "the greatest crime" in the plays. In "The Desperate Morality of the Plays of Tennessee Williams" (Spring 1962) Ganz argues for the strength and consistency of Williams's morality. Most interesting is his discussion of the two versions of the third act of *Cat on a Hot Tin Roof*. Ganz discusses the plays according to the morality of the characters or the situations which determine the characters' actions. Finally, "condemning what he most desires to pardon, he must sometimes, in order to condemn at all, do so with ferocious violence." Delma Eugene Presley's essay, "The Search for Hope in the Plays of Tennessee Williams" (Winter 1971-1972), treats the plays of the 1960s, and she concludes that Williams is not able to resolve the conflicts of his characters and settles into sentimentality rather than authenticity. The absence of God and the awareness of death are stronger than the hopeful affirmations of the earlier successful plays, but not as convincingly dramatized.

John J. Fritscher, in "Some Attitudes and a Posture: Religious Metaphor and Ritual in Tennessee Williams' Query of the American God" (Sept. 1970), and John MacNicholas, in "Williams' Power of the Keys" (1977), consider Williams's view of God. Fritscher's essay is a psychological, biographical reading, imposing an Oedipal framework on the plays to discover Williams's dual concept of God as wrathful and loving. MacNicholas studies the "etiology of damnation" in the plays, how Williams uses the dramatic potential of damnation, and "how redemption may arise out of acute despair."

Robert Bechtold Heilman, in "Tennessee Williams' Approach to Tragedy" (collected in Stanton, 1977), is one of many critics who try to define the form of Williams's drama. It is sometimes melodramatic, sometimes seriocomic, sometimes "approaching tragedy." Although *A Streetcar Named Desire* has a tragic structure, it tends toward melodrama because Blanche is a monopathic character, not torn or divided. Conflicting emotions and problems make *Summer and Smoke* and *Cat on a Hot Tin Roof* more tragic. Heilman also studies *Slapstick Tragedy* and *In the Bar of a Tokyo Hotel*, in which the "artist is in some sense also a victim of himself," which places the play in "the realm of tragedy." Although Williams was still creating tragic characters in the 1970s and 1980s, he was not integrating them into complex tragic dramas, in Heilman's opinion.

In his "Three Halves of Tennessee Williams' World" (Fall 1988) Jordan Y. Miller explores the paradoxical choices offered to the characters in Williams's major plays. Although the plays, in which "God so often seems absent," are tragic, some hope is usually offered in the final scenes.

Several critical questions concerning texts, the use of screen projections, the form and style of the memory play, and the roles of Tom and Amanda come out of analyses of Williams's first successful play, *The Glass Menagerie*. Lester A. Beaurline makes a good examination of the four stages of the play's composition in his essay on*"The Glass Menagerie*: From Story to Play" (Sept. 1965). He evaluates the changes made from the sixteen-page story "The Portrait of a Girl in Glass" to a sixty-page one-act, to the reading version published by New Directions, and finally to the Dramatists Play Service acting version, which Beaurline calls definitive. In this version Beaurline thinks that "Williams's most successful revisions of stage directions unobstrusively change the story's matter-of-fact tone into memory." The acting version is also James L. Rowland's choice. His argument is based upon a close study of the changes in the role of Amanda. In his article, "Tennessee's Two Amandas" (Dec. 1967), he argues that in the acting version Amanda is "more conversational, more human and more realistic." R. B. Parker disagrees in his article "The Composition of *The Glass Menagerie*: An Argument for Complexity" (1982). Examining a poem, intermediate revisions, the screenplay, and television production drafts, Parker concludes that the reading text, which refers to the screen projections omitted from the stage play, "reflects more truthfully the complexity of response that can be traced throughout many drafts and rewritings of the play."

In "Two Memory Plays: *The Glass Menagerie* and *After the Fall*" (1966) Paul T. Nolan discusses the levels of consciousness dramatized in a memory play. "The new 'memory play,' unlike the dream play and expressionistic drama, is a projection of the conscious mind . . . concerned only with that action that is understood and retained in the mind of the protagonist." Nolan establishes the difference between an objective recording of the past and selective, subjective memory. This reading emphasizes the importance of Tom's role in the play, a view that Thomas L. King supports in "Irony and Distance in *The Glass Menagerie*" (May 1973). King examines

Tom's soliloquies and finds tension between sentimental nostalgia and detached irony. Tom's lines reveal humor, irony, and self-consciousness and make *The Glass Menagerie* Tennessee William's autobiographical dramatization, not Amanda's. Another article by R. B. Parker, "The Circle Closed: A Psychological Reading of *The Glass Menagerie* and *The Two-Character Play*" (Dec. 1985), continues his 1982 examination and illustrates that Tom's character is the principal interpretive problem. Tom's remembering sets the play's mood, and his narration establishes the tone. The audience sees only what the character Tom selects from his memory, which is not necessarily a reality. Parker connects the "emotional escape and introversion" of *The Glass Menagerie* with *The Two-Character Play*, which is also selective memory, a play within a play, concentrating upon a brother and sister. Both plays represent Williams's "solipsism" in his use of art to escape his "own existential self-consciousness."

Elia Kazan's "Notebook for *A Streetcar Named Desire*" (1963) has become the single most important device for interpreting *A Streetcar Named Desire*. Kazan notes with clarity each of the characters' motivations and actions. Thomas E. Porter, in "The Passing of the Old South" (1969), studies the characterization of Blanche, whom he defines as both an intruder and the heroine of the play. She creates the play's tension, reflecting Williams's own ambivalence regarding the relative values of the old South and contemporary society.

The symbolism of *A Streetcar Named Desire* has been given much critical attention. Joseph N. Riddell argues in "*A Streetcar Named Desire*–Nietzsche Descending" (Feb. 1963) that the play fails "in its overabundant intellectualism, its aspiration to say something about man and his civilization, its eclectic use and often contradictory exploitation of ideas." Nietzsche's Apollonian-Dionysian conflict is not successfully resolved in the play, for the "final scene does insinuate moral predilections while the substance of the play has obviated the moral scene for the ritualistic." The real violence, Riddell says, is in Blanche's "forced recognition of the conflicting drives within herself."

Leonard Quirino, in "The Cards Indicate a Voyage on *A Streetcar Named Desire*" (1977), thinks that Williams uses symbols and archetypes (the cards of destiny, the voyage of experience) to "create a dialectic between soul and body to depict universally significant problems such as the conflict and mutual attraction between desire and death." The play is not a sentimental, steamy melodrama, but a tragic parable of existence. "The Fate of the Symbolic in *A Streetcar*

Named Desire" (1982) by Kathleen Hulley presents a symbolic reading of the play in which "Blanche, Stella, and Stanley interchange
the positions of actor, director and audience." Theater is a semiotic
system on stage; the "stage re-presents reality, it doubles it, but it is
not it." Therefore, once the primary level of the acting is accomplished and the symbolic level of Williams's manipulation of the destructive forces is dramatized, the audience interprets and inte-
grates. "Theatre, hysteria, and commentary spring from the same
assumptions about the nature of meaning: that meaning lies beyond what is revealed and is absent from what is present."

Camino Real is "becoming the artistic equal of Williams's best
'conventional plays,'" writes Jordan Y. Miller in *"Camino Real"*
(1970), but the play must be studied in performance, not merely
read. Now that expressionism is out of style, Miller suggests that students might study the play as a dramatization of the "survival of
the human spirit which constantly refuses to accept the reality
which surrounds it." Two excellent articles concur with Miller's opinion of *Camino Real*. James Coakley, in "Time and Tide on the
Camino Real" (1977), praises the play for its form, which informs its
theme. The nonlinear, episodic movement of the drama reinforces
Williams's perception of life as fragmentary, aimless, and ambiguous. "The most serious challenge of this play is its refusal to accept
time either as sequential or as the fundamental common denomina-
tor of human affairs." In "Alienation and Contradiction in *Camino
Real*: A Convergence of Williams and Brecht" (Mar. 1983), Downing Cless demonstrates the convergence of Brecht's "epic realism"
and Williams's "poetic realism." Both playwrights present contradictions within characters, between relationships, and between individuals and society.

Elia Kazan's directing is important and a point of controversy
in the dramatic realization of *Cat on a Hot Tin Roof*. Two studies published in 1967 evaluate the play's various versions. William
Peterson, in "Williams, Kazan and the Two Cats," makes a careful
comparison of Williams's original play with the Broadway version,
which incorporated substantial revisions suggested by Kazan.
Peterson prefers the first version "because it maintains and expands
the structural devices of verbal repetition and variation, of parallel situations and characters; . . . the characters remain themselves . . .
and it maintains the theme of mendacity." William Sacksteder (Winter 1966-1967) agrees in his article "The Three Cats: A Study in Dra-

matic Structure" but also discusses and actually prefers the structure of the film version of the play.

In "Tennessee Williams' Persistent *Battle of Angels*" (May 1968) Leonard Quirino explains that both *Battle of Angels* and *Orpheus Descending* fail because each is an overly ambitious attempt "to portray what he [Williams] considers by nature indefinable, a something buried in the very nature of existence." In "*Suddenly Last Summer* as 'Morality Play'" (Feb. 1966) Paul J. Hurley also writes about a "something" that Williams was trying to dramatize. Hurley says Williams uses cannibalism and homosexuality to show Sebastian as a villain, not a hero, to dramatize that "man may be destroyed by ignoring, rather than succumbing to, the need for participation in society." What some have denigrated as sexual perversion, Hurley considers a "legitimate metaphorical device."

Peter L. Hays makes a careful examination of "Tennessee Williams' Use of Myth in *Sweet Bird of Youth*" (Oct. 1966), discussing castration and the Adonis myth. In "The Troubled Flight of Tennessee Williams's *Sweet Bird*: From Manuscript through Published Texts" (Mar. 1981) Drewey Wayne Gunn examines three successive texts for the play. Gunn thinks Kazan influenced Williams to "cheapen" his original concept "in order to achieve a more spectacular production on stage" and recommends a 1958 unpublished script as Williams's best version. Gunn's article demonstrates the excellent use of manuscript materials to respond to critics' assumptions.

Kathryn Zabelle Derounian reevaluates *Kingdom of Earth* in her article "'The Kingdom of Earth' and *Kingdom of Earth*: (*The Seven Descents of Myrtle*): Tennessee Williams' Parody" (1983). Williams uses parody first to "mock established genres" and then to "mock his own previous work." The well-written article gives Williams's play new, serious consideration. Anthony C. Hilfer and R. Vance Ramsey take reviewers and academic critics to task in their article "*Baby Doll*: A Study in Comedy and Critical Awareness" (1969), establishing the "very real achievement of the film" by discussing the deletions made in published versions and the various endings that were written for publication and production. In "Tennessee Williams and the Cocaloony Birds" (1966) Barry Callaghan argues that *The Gnädiges Fräulein* is a "captivating theatrical experience" that critics should not dismiss. The Fräulein "rises above her moral condition," as Williams "has exorcised his obsessive sense of guilt . . . She is not a helpless victim of self-hatred and repression."

Williams's late play *Vieux Carré* is applauded in Rodney Simard's "The Uses of Experience: Tennessee Williams in *Vieux Carré*" (Spring 1985). Williams uses the house of his early bohemian years in New Orleans as the protagonist in the play, which helps to objectify the play. "Williams transcends the usual uses of biography, for he does present his audience with his experience, but without artistic formulation; biography does not inform the work—it is the work." William J. Free gives an excellent accounting of some of Williams's later work in "Williams in the Seventies: Directions and Discontents" (1977). Williams, Free says, wrote plays in this period about his life, but without imagination. *Out Cry* and *Small Craft Warnings* "are failures of dramatization rather than failures of theme."

Three articles of the 1980s published after Williams's death help give an overview of the last half of his career. In "Late Tennessee Williams" (Sept. 1984) Ruby Cohn says Williams's dramatic triad of sex, South and violence, absent in the plays of the 1960s, occurs in variations in the three major plays of Williams's last decade, *The Two-Character Play* (which "may be his masterpiece"), *Vieux Carré* ("the playwright newly dramatizes the fate of art"), and *Clothes for a Summer Hotel*. The latter play asks, "What is the price of artistic creation?" The answer, according to Cohn's reading, is "human betrayal." Allean Hale identifies the affinities Williams's later plays have with Japanese Noh theater in "Tennessee's Long Trip" (1984). Discussing *In the Bar of a Tokyo Hotel* and *The Two-Character Play*, Hale shows that these "closet dramas" ask "serious questions about life and art."

Some of the best recent criticism is the chapter by C. W. E. Bigsby in his *Twentieth Century American Drama*, volume 2: *Williams, Miller, Albee* (1984). Bigsby's criticism shows the advantage of objectivity and distance. He is not influenced by popular reception or autobiographical assertions. Of Williams's early lyricism, Bigsby says it was often self-conscious poeticism, but was "equally capable of rising to genuine eloquence." *The Glass Menagerie* has a "fluidity of style that Williams came to value both as a theatrical mode and a personal strategy." Bigsby includes biographical readings of the plays but in a subtle way, allowing the plays precedence over the life. He notes that both Williams and his characters flee time. Drawing from Williams's papers deposited at the University of Texas, Bigsby quotes Williams's comments on *The Glass Menagerie, Summer and Smoke*, and *A Streetcar Named Desire*, which as "a trio seemed definitive of what I had to say in the form of long plays, which embodied a single theme, or legend, that of the delicate haunted girl who first appeared as Laura, the basic theme of the over-sensitive misfit in a world that spins with blind fury." The "personal energy" in these plays is "both a private anguish and a sense of cultural crisis," concludes Bigsby.

Bigsby finds *Camino Real* dramatically "less than convincing" through an analysis of its structure and characters. He concludes that "the freedom of its form is undercut by the coercive logic of its development. Since the characters are themselves derived from fictions, they are necessarily denied the world of possibility to which the protagonist, Kilroy, aspires. And hence much of the tension is dissipated."

Considering the critical argument concerning the third act of *Cat on a Hot Tin Roof*, Bigsby agrees with Kazan that Maggie and Big Daddy are the vital forces of the play; their energies focus the action. It is not fear of homosexuality that frightens Brick, but fear of life itself. Brick's is the "fundamental dilemma of the Williams protagonist"; that is, the "desire to resist a process which pulls him into the world of sexual and emotional maturity with its tensions, its profound ambivalences and its casual implications." Bigsby does well to limit his direct application of the biography and to let the plays speak for themselves as an expression of Williams's sensitivities and fears.

In autumn 1986, W. Kenneth Holditch reviewed the many Williams biographies published up to that time. In his article, "Surviving with Grace: Tennessee Williams Tomorrow," Holditch poses the following questions for critics to answer: "Can the best plays be considered as poetry or only as dramatic literature, and which aspect is more important? What is the true quality of the plays of the last two decades? Of what value are the other writings of Tennessee Williams–novels, short stories, poems?" Critics would do well to address these questions. New Directions plans an eighth volume of *The Theater of Tennessee Williams* which will include four full-length plays (*Vieux Carré, A Lovely Sunday for Creve Coeur, Clothes for a Summer Hotel,* and *The Red Devil Battery Sign*), and a ninth, of short plays, including *Moony's Kid Don't Cry, The Dark Room,* and *The Case of the Crushed Petunias.* New Directions is also hopeful of publishing several short plays that have been given regional production but are as yet unpublished, such as *Something Cloudy, Something Clear, Will Mr. Merriwether Return?, This Is (An Entertainment),* and *A House Not Meant to Stand.* Doubtless, as more manuscripts, letters, and playscripts become available, scholars will be better able to assess the prolific career of Tennessee Williams and to throw more light into the obscure corners of his considerable achievement.

Lanford Wilson

(1937-)

Martin J. Jacobi
Clemson University

PRIMARY BIBLIOGRAPHY

Books

Balm in Gilead and Other Plays. New York: Hill & Wang, 1965. Comprises *Balm in Gilead, Ludlow Fair,* and *Home Free!*

The Rimers of Eldritch and Other Plays. New York: Hill & Wang, 1967. Comprises *The Rimers of Eldritch, Days Ahead, This Is the Rill Speaking,* and *Wandering: A Turn.*

The Madness of Lady Bright and Home Free! London: Methuen, 1968. Plays.

The Gingham Dog. New York: Hill & Wang, 1969. Play.

Lemon Sky. New York: Hill & Wang, 1970. Play.

The Sand Castle and Three Other Plays. New York: Dramatists Play Service, 1970. Comprises *The Sand Castle, Sextet (Yes), Stoop,* and *Wandering: A Turn.*

Summer and Smoke, music by Lee Hoiby. New York: Belwin-Mills, 1972. Adapted from Tennessee Williams's play. Libretto.

The Great Nebula in Orion and Other Plays. New York: Dramatists Play Service, 1973. Comprises *The Great Nebula in Orion, The Family Continues, Victory on Mrs. Dandywine's Island,* and *Ikke, Ikke, Nye, Nye, Nye.*

The Hot l Baltimore. New York: Hill & Wang, 1973. Play.

The Mound Builders. New York: Hill & Wang, 1976. Play.

Serenading Louie. New York: Dramatists Play Service, 1976. Play.

Brontosaurus. New York: Dramatists Play Service, 1978. Play.

5th of July. New York: Hill & Wang, 1978. Play.

Talley's Folly. New York: Hill & Wang, 1979. Play.

Thymus Vulgaris. New York: Dramatists Play Service, 1982. Play.

Angels Fall. New York: Hill & Wang, 1983. Play.

Talley and Son. New York: Hill & Wang, 1986. Play.

Burn This. New York: Hill & Wang, 1987. Play.

Premiere Productions

So Long at the Fair. New York, Caffe Cino, 25 Aug. 1963.

No Trespassing. New York, Caffe Cino, 16 Jan. 1964.

Home Free. New York, Caffe Cino, 16 Jan. 1964.

The Madness of Lady Bright. New York, Caffe Cino, 19 May 1964.

Balm in Gilead. New York, La Mama Experimental Theatre Club, 20 Jan. 1965.

Ludlow Fair. New York, Caffe Cino, 1 Feb. 1965.

This is the Rill Speaking. New York, Caffe Cino, 20 July 1965.

The Sand Castle. New York, La Mama Experimental Theatre Club, 22 Sept. 1965.

Miss Williams: A Turn. New York, La Mama Experimental Theatre Club, 3 Nov. 1965.

Days Ahead. New York, Caffe Cino, 28 Dec. 1965.

Sex Is Between Two People. New York, Caffe Cino, 28 Dec. 1965.

Wandering: A Turn. New York, Caffe Cino, 10 Apr. 1966.

The Rimers of Eldritch. New York, La Mama Experimental Theatre Club, 13 July 1966.

Untitled Play. New York, Judson Poets' Theater, 26 Jan. 1968.

The Gingham Dog. Washington, D.C., Washington Theatre Club, 26 Sept. 1968.

Lemon Sky. Buffalo, N.Y., Studio Arena Theatre, 26 Mar. 1970.

Serenading Louie. Washington, D.C., Washington Theatre Club, 1 Apr. 1970.

Sextet (Yes). New York, Circle Repertory Theatre, 11 Feb. 1971.

The Great Nebula in Orion. Manchester, England, Stables Theatre Club, 18 Feb. 1971.

Ikke, Ikke, Nye, Nye, Nye. New Haven, Conn., Yale Cabaret, 13 Jan. 1972.

The Family Continues. New York, Circle Repertory Theatre, 21 May 1972.

The Hot l Baltimore. New York, Circle Repertory Theatre, 4 Feb. 1973.

The Mound Builders. New York, Circle Repertory Theatre, 2 Feb. 1975.

Brontosaurus. New York, Circle Repertory Theatre, 25 Oct. 1977.

5th of July. New York, Circle Repertory Theatre, 27 Apr. 1978. Revised as *Fifth of July.* New York, New Apollo Theatre, 5 Nov. 1980.

Talley's Folly. New York, Circle Repertory Theatre, 3 May 1979.

Thymus Vulgaris. Los Angeles, Lee Strasberg Institute, 4 Jan. 1981.

A Tale Told. New York, Circle Repertory Theatre, 11 June 1981. Revised as *Talley and Son.* New York, Circle Repertory Theatre, 22 Oct. 1985.
Angels Fall. Miami, Fla., New World Festival, 19 June 1982.
A Betrothal. London, England, Man in the Moon Theatre, 30 Sept. 1986.
Burn This. Los Angeles, Mark Taper Forum, 22 Jan. 1987.

Selected Other
Stoop. New York Television Theatre, WNET, 28 Nov. 1969. Teleplay.
The Migrants. Playhouse 90, CBS, 3 Feb. 1974. Teleplay.
Taxi. Hallmark Hall of Fame, NBC, 2 Feb. 1978. Teleplay.
"Observations of a Resident Playwright," *New York Times,* 23 Apr. 1978, section 2, p. 5. Essay.
"Meet Tom Eyen, Tom Eyen," *Horizon,* 22 (July 1979), 43-48.
Chekhov, Anton. *The Three Sisters.* New York: Dramatists Play Service, 1984. Translation.

SECONDARY BIBLIOGRAPHY

Interviews and Informal Pieces
Albright, William. "Lanford Wilson, From 'Burn' to 'Balm,' " *Houston Post,* 2 Feb. 1986, p. F3.
Allen, Jennifer. "Portrait: Lanford Wilson," *Life,* 3 (June 1980), 29-30.
Baker, Rob. "Lanford Wilson's Family Affair," *New York Daily News,* 5 June 1981, pp. M2-M3.
Barnett, Gene A. "Recreating the Magic: An Interview with Lanford Wilson," *Ball State University Forum,* 25 (Spring 1984), 57-74.
Bennetts, Leslie. "Marshall Mason Explains a New Stage," *New York Times,* 11 Oct. 1987, section 2, pp. 5, 14.
Bennetts. "Talking To . . . Lanford Wilson and Terrance McNally: On Love, Responsibility, and Sexual Obsession," *Vogue,* 178 (Feb. 1988), 216, 220.
Berkvist, Robert. "Lanford Wilson—Can He Score on Broadway?," *New York Times,* 17 Feb. 1980, section 2, pp. 1, 3.
Blau, Eleanor. "How Lanford Wilson Writes with Actors in Mind," *New York Times,* 27 Jan. 1983, p. C15.
Dace, Trish. "Plainsongs and Fancies," *Soho Weekly News,* 5 Nov. 1980, p. 20.

Flately, Guy. "Lanford is One 'L' of a Playwright," *New York Times,* 22 Apr. 1973, section 2, pp. 1, 21.

Freedman, Samuel. "Lanford Wilson Comes Home," *New York Times Magazine,* 30 Aug. 1987, pp. 28, 63-64.

Freedman. "Lanford Wilson Enjoys a Triumph over Time," *New York Times,* 26 Dec. 1985, p. C13.

Gussow, Mel. "Lanford Wilson on Broadway," *Horizon,* 23 (May 1980), 30-37.

Haller, Scott. "The Dramatic Rise of Lanford Wilson," *Saturday Review,* 8 (Aug. 1981), 26-29.

Kakutani, Michiko. "I Write the World As I See It Around Me," *New York Times,* 8 July 1984, section 2, pp. 4, 6.

Kellman, Barnet. "The American Playwright in the Seventies: Some Problems and Perspectives," *Theatre Quarterly,* 8 (Spring 1978), 45-58.

Shewey, Don. "I Hear America Talking," *Rolling Stone,* 22 July 1982, pp. 18-20.

Soric, Peggy. "Sound Catcher," *Springfield News-Leader,* 30 Jan. 1983, p. G1.

Swift, Elliott. "The Life and Times of Playwright Lanford Wilson," *Hamptons,* 11 Aug. 1983, pp. 12-13, 16.

Wallach, Allan. "Lanford Wilson," *Newsday,* 27 Apr. 1980, pp. 21-22, 26, 32-33.

Weales, Gerald. "American Theater Watch, 1979-1980," *Georgia Review,* 34 (Fall 1980), 497-508.

Wetzsteon, Ross. "The Most Populist Playwright," *New York,* 15 (8 Nov. 1982), 40-45.

Critical Studies: Books

Barnett, Gene. *Lanford Wilson.* Boston: G. K. Hall, 1987.

Busby, Mark. *Lanford Wilson.* Boise, Idaho: Boise State University Press, 1987.

Critical Studies: Major Reviews, Articles, and Book Sections

Barnes, Clive. "Brilliant Staging Can't Save Rash and Empty *Balm in Gilead,*" *New York Post,* 1 June 1984.

Barnes. "*The Gingham Dog,* Autopsy of a Marriage," *New York Times,* 24 Apr. 1969, p. 41.

Barnes. "One Hit, Circle Rep's Rep," *New York Post,* 24 Oct. 1985.

Barnes. "Stage: Immediacy Illuminates Wilson's *Lemon Sky,*" *New York Times,* 18 May 1970, p. 40.

Barnes. "Talley is no Folly," *New York Post,* 4 May 1979.

Barnes. "The Theater: Lanford Wilson's 'Hot l Baltimore,' Herald of a New Pattern," *New York Times,* 23 Mar. 1973, p. 21.

Barnes. "Wilson's *Tale* Told Brilliantly," *New York Post,* 12 June 1981.

Bigsby, C. W. E. *A Critical Introduction to Twentieth-Century American Drama,* volume 3: *Beyond Broadway.* Cambridge: Cambridge University Press, 1985, 26-28, 219, 417.

Branam, Harold. "Lanford Wilson." In *Critical Survey of Drama,* volume 5, ed. Frank N. Magill. Englewood Cliffs, N.J.: Salem, 1985, 2095-2103.

Brustein, Robert. "Two Couples," *New Republic,* 182 (5 Apr. 1980), 28. Review of *Talley's Folly.*

Clurman, Harold. "Theatre," *Nation,* 210 (1 June 1970): 668-669. Review of *Lemon Sky.*

Clurman. "Theatre," *Nation,* 216 (5 Mar. 1973), 313-314. Review of *The Hot l Baltimore.*

Clurman. "Theatre," *Nation,* 220 (15 Mar. 1975), 314-316. Review of *The Mound Builders.*

Clurman. "Theatre," *Nation,* 225 (26 Nov. 1977), 571. Review of *Brontosaurus.*

Clurman. "Theatre," *Nation,* 226 (13 May 1978), 579. Review of *5th of July.*

Clurman. "Theatre," *Nation,* 228 (26 May 1979), 609. Review of *Talley's Folly.*

Clurman. "Theatre," *Nation,* 230 (15 Mar. 1980), 316. Review of *Talley's Folly.*

Cohn, Ruby. "Broadway Bound: Simon, Kopit, McNally, Wilson." In her *New American Dramatists 1960-1980.* New York: Grove Press, 1982.

Dasgupta, Gautam. "Lanford Wilson." In *American Playwrights: A Critical Survey,* volume 1, ed. Dasgupta and Bonnie Marranca. New York: Drama Book Specialists, 1981, 27-39.

Disch, Thomas M. "Theater," *Nation,* 245 (14 Nov. 1987), 569-570. Review of *Burn This.*

Dreher, Ann Crawford. "Lanford Wilson." In *Dictionary of Literary Biography,* volume 7: *Twentieth-Century American Dramatists, Part Two: K-Z,* ed. John MacNicholas. Detroit: Gale, 1981, 350-368.

Gill, Brendan. "The Theatre," *New Yorker,* 56 (3 Mar. 1980), 62. Review of *Talley's Folly.*

Gill. "The Theatre," *New Yorker*, 56 (17 Nov. 1980), 172-173. Review of *Fifth of July*.

Gill. "The Theatre," *New Yorker*, 58 (31 Jan. 1983), 101. Review of *Angels Fall*.

Gill. "The Theatre: Breaking Up," *New Yorker*, 45 (3 May 1969), 107. Review of *The Gingham Dog*.

Gottfried, Martin. "*The Gingham Dog*," *Women's Wear Daily*, 24 Apr. 1969.

Gottfried. "*The Hot l Baltimore*," *Women's Wear Daily*, 23 Mar. 1973.

Gottfried. "*Lemon Sky*," *Women's Wear Daily*, 18 May 1970.

Gussow, Mel. "Lanford Wilson's Lonely World of Displaced Persons," *New York Times*, 15 Oct. 1987, section 2, p. 5.

Gussow. "Stage: Fiery 'Brontosaurus,' " *New York Times*, 27 Oct. 1977, p. C17.

Gussow. "Stage: 'Serenading Louie' Harks Back," *New York Times*, 6 May 1976, p. 45.

Gussow. "Stage: The Unwanted People of 'Hot l Baltimore,' " *New York Times*, 8 Feb. 1973, p. 37.

Herman, William. "Down and Out in Lebanon and New York: Lanford Wilson." In his *Understanding Contemporary American Drama*. Columbia: University of South Carolina Press, 1987, 196-271.

Hughes, Catharine. "From Taylor to Talley," *America*, 145 (18-25 July 1981), 35.

Jacobi, Martin J. "The Comic Vision of Lanford Wilson," *Studies in the Literary Imagination*, 21 (Fall 1988), 119-134.

Kane, Leslie. "The Agony of Isolation in the Drama of Anton Chekhov and Lanford Wilson," *West Virginia University Philological Papers*, 31 (1986), 20-26.

Kaufmann, Stanley. "Theater: Two One-Acters," *New York Times*, 23 Mar. 1966, p. 42. Review of *Ludlow Fair* and *The Madness of Lady Bright*.

Kerr, Walter. "The Crazies Are Good To Listen To," *New York Times*, 4 Mar. 1973, section 2, p. 3. Review of *The Hot l Baltimore*.

Kerr. "Stage: *Talley's Folly* by Lanford Wilson," *New York Times*, 21 Feb. 1980, p. C15.

Kerr. "When Best-Laid Plans Go Awry," *New York Times*, 15 Nov. 1987, section 2, pp. 5, 21. Review of *Burn This*.

Kissel, Howard. "*Fifth of July*," *Women's Wear Daily*, 6 Nov. 1980.

Kissel. *"A Tale Told,"* *Women's Wear Daily,* 12 June 1981.

Kroll, Jack. "Hope Against Hope," *Newsweek,* 96 (24 Nov. 1980), 129. Review of *Fifth of July.*

Kroll. "Love in a Folly," *Newsweek,* 95 (3 Mar. 1980), 53. Review of *Talley's Folly.*

Lewis, Theophilus. "Theatre," *America,* 116 (11 Mar. 1967), 354-355. Review of *The Rimers of Eldritch.*

Novick, Julius. "Theater," *Nation,* 231 (29 Nov. 1980), 588-589. Review of *Fifth of July.*

O'Connor, John. "The Wilson Touch," *Wall Street Journal,* 22 May 1970, p. 8. Review of *Lemon Sky.*

Oliver, Edith. "The Theatre: Off Broadway," *New Yorker,* 42 (2 Apr. 1966), 124. Review of *Ludlow Fair* and *The Madness of Lady Bright.*

Oliver. "The Theatre: Off Broadway," *New Yorker,* 43 (4 Mar. 1967), 132-133. Review of *The Rimers of Eldritch.*

Oliver. "The Theatre: Off Broadway," *New Yorker,* 46 (30 May 1970), 72. Review of *Lemon Sky.*

Oliver. "The Theatre: Off Broadway," *New Yorker,* 49 (31 Mar. 1973), 77. Review of *The Hot l Baltimore.*

Oliver. "The Theatre: Off Broadway," *New Yorker,* 50 (17 Feb. 1975), 84-85. Review of *The Mound Builders.*

Oliver. "The Theatre: Off Broadway," *New Yorker,* 52 (17 May 1976), 124-125. Review of *Serenading Louie.*

Oliver. "The Theatre: Off Broadway," *New Yorker,* 54 (8 May 1978), 90. Review of *5th of July.*

Oliver. "The Theatre: Off Broadway," *New Yorker,* 55 (14 May 1979), 81-82. Review of *Talley's Folly.*

Oliver. "The Theatre: Off Broadway," *New Yorker,* 57 (22 June 1981), 86-87. Review of *A Tale Told.*

Oliver. "The Theatre: Off Broadway," *New Yorker,* 58 (1 Nov. 1982), 134-135. Review of *Angels Fall.*

Oliver. "The Theatre: Off Broadway," *New Yorker,* 60 (11 June 1984), 112-113. Review of *Balm in Gilead.*

Oliver. "The Theatre: Off Broadway," *New Yorker,* 61 (23 Dec. 1985), 80-81. Review of *Lemon Sky.*

Oliver. "The Theatre: Off Broadway," *New Yorker,* 63 (26 Oct. 1987), 130. Review of *Burn This.*

Parolli, Robert. "The Courtship of John Malkovich," *Nation,* 202 (4 Apr. 1966), 403-404. Review of *This Is the Rill Speaking.*

Paul, John Steven. " 'Who Are You? Who Are We?': Two Questions Raised in Lanford Wilson's *Talley's Folly*," *Cresset* (Sept. 1980), 25-27.

Rich, Frank. "Play: *Angels Fall*, Lanford Wilson's Apocalypse," *New York Times*, 18 Oct. 1982, p. C15.

Rich. "Stage: *Burn This*, by Lanford Wilson," *New York Times*, 15 Oct. 1987, p. C23.

Rich. "Stage: *Fifth of July*, Talleys 33 Years Later," *New York Times*, 6 Nov. 1980, p. C19.

Rich. "Stage: *Serenading*, by Lanford Wilson," *New York Times*, 3 Feb. 1984, p. C3.

Rich. "Stage: *A Tale Told*, Part 3 of Talley Family Story," *New York Times*, 12 June 1981, p. C3.

Rich. "Theatre: Wilson's *Mound Builders*," *New York Times*, 1 Feb. 1986, p. 17.

Sainer, Arthur. "Lanford Wilson." In *Contemporary Dramatists*, ed. James Vinson. New York: St. Martin's, 1973, 830-833.

Schvey, Henry. "Images of the Past in the Plays of Lanford Wilson." In *Essays on Contemporary American Drama*, ed. Hedwig Bock and Albert Wertheim. Munich: Huebler, 1981, 225-240.

Sheed, Wilfrid. "The Stage," *Commonweal*, 84 (29 Apr. 1966), 82. Reviews of *Ludlow Fair* and *The Madness of Lady Bright*.

Simon, John. "All in the Family," *New York*, 14 (21 June 1981), 46-47. Review of *A Tale Told*.

Simon. "Demirep," *New York*, 18 (4 Nov. 1985), 64. Review of *Talley and Son*.

Simon. "Folie à Deux," *New York*, 12 (21 May 1979), 76. Review of *Talley's Folly*.

Simon. "Houses Divided," *New York*, 19 (6 Jan. 1986), 53. Review of *Lemon Sky*.

Simon. "Ideals Lost—And Found," *New York*, 16 (7 Feb. 1983), 58. Review of *Angels Fall*.

Simon. "Likable but Unlikely Transplant," *New York*, 11 (15 May 1978), 77-78. Review of *5th of July*.

Simon. "Mating Dance," *New York*, 20 (26 Oct. 1987), 168-169. Review of *Burn This*.

Simon. "The 'Me' You Must Get to Know," *New York*, 3 (1 June 1970), 75. Review of *Lemon Sky*.

Simon. "A Physician in the House," *New York*, 17 (11 June 1984), 72-73. Review of *Balm in Gilead*.

Simon. "Playing with Fire," *New York,* 17 (13 Feb. 1984), 68-69. Review of *Serenading Louie.*

Simon. "Rum Deals, Two with Coke," *New York,* 19 (10 Feb. 1986), 56. Review of *The Mound Builders.*

Simon. "Timon of Dublin," *New York,* 13 (17 Nov. 1980), 65. Review of *Fifth of July.*

Simon. "Too Much Heat? Too Much Brain?," *New York,* 15 (1 Nov. 1982), 79. Review of *Angels Fall.*

Simon. "Under the Flag," *Newsweek,* 65 (22 Feb. 1965), 93.

Watt, Douglas. "Confidences Shared in Close Confines," *New York Daily News,* 18 Oct. 1982. Review of *Angels Fall.*

Watt. "It's No Place to Live, But It's Worth a Visit," *New York Daily News,* 23 Mar. 1973. Review of *The Hot l Baltimore.*

Watts, Richard, Jr. "Picture of a Doomed Marriage," *New York Post,* 24 Apr. 1969. Review of *The Gingham Dog.*

Watts. "The Visit to California," *New York Post,* 18 May 1970. Review of *Lemon Sky.*

Weales, Gerald. "*Angels Fall:* Epistle of Peter to New Mexico," *Commonweal,* 109 (17 Dec. 1982), 690-691.

Weales. "Flawed and Fascinating," *Commonweal,* 108 (11 Sept. 1981), 500-502. Review of *A Tale Told.*

Weales. "Stage: *Talley's Folly:* Lanford Wilson as Cyclist," *Commonweal,* 107 (23 Feb. 1980), 182-183.

Weales. "Theater," *Commonweal* (28 June 1975), 360-361. Review of *The Hot l Baltimore.*

Wilson, Edwin. "Hot and Bothered: Malkovich on Fire," *Wall Street Journal,* 21 Oct. 1987, 34. Review of *Burn This.*

Witham, Barry. "Images of America: Wilson, Weller, and Horovitz," *Theatre Journal,* 34 (May 1982), 223-232.

BIBLIOGRAPHICAL ESSAY

Interviews and Informal Pieces

A good deal of the standard biographical information on Lanford Wilson appears in interviews. In "Lanford is One 'L' of a Playwright" (22 Apr. 1973) Guy Flately asks the playwright if all the perverted losers in his plays suggest a shambles of a childhood; Wilson then discusses his parents' divorce and remarriages and his moves to San Diego, Chicago, and New York. He says of *The Hot l Baltimore* that it is not simply about perverted losers but about "losers who refuse to lose." Jennifer Allen (June 1980) recounts Wilson's decision to write more positive plays: "I wrote a tragedy called *Serenading Louie*, about a man who kills his family, which was staged in Washington in 1970. I used to stand in the lobby and watch people come out of the theater, rush to the water fountain and take a tranquilizer. I didn't want to do that to an audience. I decided I had to find something more positive to say. So I made *Hot l Baltimore* a comedy." Of the Talley plays, Wilson says that "I wanted to get out of New York, to write about America, and that's the America I know," although Samuel Freedman (26 Dec. 1985) quotes Wilson as saying that the Missouri plays have been only a sideline to his major dramatic concerns.

In Robert Berkvist's interview (17 Feb. 1980) Wilson claims that he is more comfortable working with Marshall Mason and the repertory company at New York's Circle Repertory Theatre than he could ever be working on Broadway, and in fact prefers the arrangement to potentially lucrative Broadway success. Berkvist also offers standard biographical data, emphasizing Wilson's discussion of the dismantling of the culture he had observed in the razed buildings of San Diego, Chicago, and New York; the playwright claims to have put his feelings about this dismantling into his plays, asking "What are we losing and what is it doing to us?" Mel Gussow's "Lanford Wilson on Broadway" (May 1980) is perhaps the most positive interview/article on the dramatist; Gussow approves not only of the way in which the playwright presents his themes through his characterizations but also of the themes themselves. Wilson says of his plays that "they're all the same! They all deal with someone preserving something from the past," and he implies a biographical connection in his description of Wilson's slow restoration of his Sags Harbor home. Gussow also notes David Mamet's claim that Wilson is the contemporary playwright he most admires.

Gene A. Barnett's interview, "Recreating the Magic" (Spring 1984), which serves as groundwork for his later Twayne book, offers the information that viewing Arthur Miller's *Death of a Salesman* (1949) was one of Wilson's first and most powerful goads toward play writing, that his playing of Tom in Tennessee Williams's *The Glass Menagerie* (1945) while in high school was another, and that his viewing of Eugene Ionesco's *The Lesson* (1957) was a third. Barnett also relates that Wilson is somewhat unhappy with *The Madness of Lady Bright* being seen as the "first homosexual play," since in the then-current climate homosexuality was viewed disparagingly; Wilson also talks about biographical connections to *The Hot l*

Baltimore (Wilson, like the Girl, is a "railroad freak") and to *Angels Fall* (whose message of finding peace in useful work is a belief Wilson has said he also holds).

Michiko Kakutani (8 July 1984) emphasizes in his conversation with Wilson the playwright's ability to capture the speech rhythms of those around him. According to Wilson, Fick's monologue at the end of act 1 of *Balm in Gilead* was spoken verbatim to him on the street. Wilson also discusses his strong religious upbringing, which leads him to regard his plays as "Baptist sermons" that raise the question, "why are we behaving this way?" Also offered is a reason why the playwright turned from the tragic, dark visions of the early plays to the more positive emphases of the later ones, a reason that differs from the standard tale about the lobby after the performance of *Serenading Louie;* he tells Kakutani that producer Joseph Cino's suicide was an event which "showed me things I didn't want to know, what I didn't want to think about . . . and led me to ask, 'what positive things can I dwell on,' because the negative things were doing me in."

A few more of these informal articles deserve attention. In interviews with Leslie Bennetts (11 Oct. 1987) and Samuel Freedman (30 Aug. 1987) Wilson primarily discusses *Burn This,* yet each also offers something fuller. Bennetts reports that the playwright compares *Burn This* to Tennessee Williams's *A Streetcar Named Desire* (1947); Wilson also states that "the play is not about a monster snuffing at the window. It's about the monster within. And that's the territory I consider dangerous." In Freedman's interview Wilson says that the Talley plays were only "a side trip that took me away from the line of my work," and that his writing, at a standstill in the early 1980s, did not begin again until he had seen Albert Innaurato's *Gemini* (1977), David Mamet's *Glengarry Glen Ross* (1984), and David Robe's *Hurlyburly* (1985) and recovered his ear for city dialect and his ability to discomfit audiences. Certainly the monologue delivered by Pale in act 1 of *Burn This* is quite similar to the one delivered by Ricky Roma at the end of the first act of *Glengarry Glen Ross;* and the suggestion that a goal of the playwright is to discomfit audiences seems to give the lie to his statements about the effects that the audience of *Serenading Louie* and the suicide of Cino had on him.

In "The Most Populist Playwright" (8 Nov. 1982) Ross Wetzsteon makes an observation that helps one understand the mixed reactions about plot and theme Wilson has always received:

"While other socially conscious playwrights scorn American values as corrupt," Wetzsteon notes, "Wilson mourns their corruption–a crucial distinction to audiences far more willing to weep at elegies than to applaud manifestos." That is to say, Wilson does not have the bitterness and cynicism exhibited by many modern American dramatists and seemingly required of them by many critics. The clarification that Wetzsteon's distinction provides is most clearly evident when attention is turned to the conflicting evaluations of Wilson's reviewers.

Critical Studies: Books

At present only two short books have been written about Wilson, both published in 1987. Gene Barnett's *Lanford Wilson* is a 170-page volume in the Twayne's United States Authors Series, with an opening biographical chapter and an annotated bibliography and index. Covering the playwright's work through *Angels Fall*, its principal aim, as Barnett writes in the preface, is "to present an overall view of all the playwright's œuvre and in that presentation to convey some idea of the dramaturgy involved–the themes, characters, structure, and dramatic and literary techniques and devices." Barnett emphasizes the lyricism of the plays, arguing that "any discussion of his plays eventually must touch on his love of language and the effectiveness with which he uses it." Quite accurately, Barnett notes that Wilson can create a rounded character with only a few lines of dialogue, and that the lack of strong plot lines is oftentimes more than balanced by the poetry of the speech rhythms.

The plays' themes are analyzed by means of a chronological progression, including attention to the unpublished material. According to Barnett, Wilson's intertwined themes are "particularly applicable to America and Americans, but they achieve universality through their timelessness": they include a series of conflicts–the old and durable versus the new and sterile; community and meaningful occupations versus disengagement and rootlessness; friendship and love versus lack of commitment and joyless adulteries. Wilson usually avoids overtly political themes (with exceptions being the racial conflict in *The Gingham Dog*, the aftermath of the Vietnam era in *Fifth of July*, and nuclear accidents in *Angels Fall*), preferring instead to let such issues arise out of more broadly humanistic concerns in the works. His characters come from both his rural Missouri background and his urban experiences, and they range from the small-town teenagers of *The Rimers of Eldritch* to big-city pimps, prostitutes, and drug dealers. Common to all is the treatment given them by the playwright: whether they are the upper-class over-achievers in *Serenading Louie,* the lower-class denizens in the all-night café of *Balm in Gilead,* or the many and varied characters in be-tween, Wilson is less concerned to castigate their flaws than he is to present them—flaws and all—compassionately. As Barnett says of *Balm in Gilead,* and could as easily have said of *The Hot l Baltimore* and other plays, "the playwright's presentation of the characters' courage and persistence in confronting low life suggests that even such people as these have his respect." Barnett notes that "it is fre-quently claimed that his [Wilson's] plays do not have villains in the usual sense of the term," and while in fact there are villains—such as Calvin Talley and the citizens in Eldritch—in general the observa-tion is accurate.

As regards the plays' structures, Barnett reiterates another com-mon observation, that they oftentimes lack a strong or even discern-able plot line. Such plays as *Balm in Gilead, The Hot l Baltimore,* and *Fifth of July* are less plot-driven than they are character and language-driven. However, Barnett's comments about style and technique are somewhat confusing. He notes that Wilson "is a traditional writer who is at his best with straightforward realism . . . [yet] typically American in his urge toward experimentation and in his opti-mism." More accurately, one can say that through the years Wilson has moved from impressionism and a pessimistic naturalism to a guarded yet optimistic realism, and from technical experimenta-tions to more standard approaches. As Barnett observes, Wilson has experimented in his early works with layered dialogue, with char-acters directly addressing audiences, with repeating scenes for ef-fect, and with disrupted chronology.

Finally, Barnett's *Lanford Wilson* is useful for its identification of the influences on the playwright: "He liked the best of what he was exposed to in the late 1940s and early 1950s—Arthur Miller, Ten-nessee Williams, Thornton Wilder, and (to some degree) William Inge and Lillian Hellman. From Miller and Williams, he learned the uses of memory in dramatic structure, as well as the possibilities of free-flowing time. From Williams, he learned how to address his audience directly. Thornton Wilder's work demonstrated the play-wright's freedom to throw 'time to the winds.' Inge, himself a mid-westerner, reminds the young Wilson of the rich possibilities of mid-western settings and characters. Wilson's Talleys of *Talley and Son* owe something to Hellman's foxlike Hubbards (also perhaps to Miller's Keller family of *All My Sons*). Wilson's principal foreign influence, apparent in a work like *Fifth of July*– is probably Chekhov (of whom he is very fond), especially his poetic style and evocative texture." Also mentioned are William Saroyan's *The Time of Your Life* (1939), Eugene O'Neill's *The Iceman Cometh* (1946), and Maxim Gorky's *The Lower Depths* (1902), for their influence especially on *Balm in Gilead* and *The Hot l Baltimore*.

The other monograph, Mark Busby's *Lanford Wilson* (1987), is a fifty-two-page publication in the Boise State University Press's Western Writers Series. Obviously, it does not offer as thorough an overview as does Barnett's book, but it is still valuable as an introduction to Wilson's work. Except for its lack of formal chapter divisions, the structure of Busby's book is similar to Barnett's. It opens with biographical material that adds little new information to what had already been published about the playwright's early years; however, it does tie Wilson's personal history to the themes of generational conflict and a concern for the past that surface repeatedly in his drama. After the biographical sketch, Busby creates for his reader the pamphlet's biggest problem. A plethora of organizational strategies are offered and partially developed, so that the direction of the book is hard to follow. First he notes that Wilson has had a "seven-phase career"; he sketches in the phases but then drops this pattern to say that "any discussion of Wilson's plays can be easily organized around the settings he uses: "California, the Midwest, New Mexico, and the East." He discusses the California plays and early plays of the Midwest but then switches his strategy once more, writing that "one of the primary differences between Wilson's early plays and most of his later ones is the change from the harshly pessimistic and critical outlook of *The Rimers of Eldritch* to a more upbeat, positive approach." With this statement he takes up the major works from *The Hot l Baltimore* to *Angels Fall*. The seven-stage chronological overview aside, the shift from the geographical to the emotional classifications indicates the critical thinness of each approach. The Midwest provides the context for perhaps Wilson's most pessimistic play, *The Rimers of Eldritch*, and also for the most clearly and strongly optimistic play, *Talley's Folly*, while the East is the setting for the pessimistic *Balm in Gilead* as well as the optimistic *The Hot l Baltimore*. The truth of the matter is that Wilson's developing œuvre follows neither pattern well. It is more accurate to say that his early plays present a pessimistic naturalism, and that his later plays, after *Serenading Louie*, become more realistic and therefore less pessimistic, with the realism portraying sometimes the comic, sometimes the tragic, and sometimes a middle ground.

Busby identifies the themes noted by Barnett: "the importance of place, the past, work, and family"; an ambivalence toward traditional values; and the importance of communication. Of some interest also is his use of Leo Marx's *The Machine in the Garden* (1964) to make the point that Wilson celebrates "the pastoral rather than the primitive ideal." This distinction helps clarify Wilson's emphasis on society, tradition, and communication over the Modernist emphasis on individualism, dislocation, and inarticulateness, and also his thematic development from naturalism to realism. However, despite Barnett's claims that any analysis of Wilson must include a discussion of his dialogue, Busby does little more than touch on the poetic nature of Wilson's language. He does mention influences, including those mentioned by Barnett and also adding Dylan Thomas and Robert Sherwood, as he numbers among the dramatist's "artistic forebears" Willa Cather, William Faulkner, and Eudora Welty. He also discusses Wilson's "repertory approach," by which he means the playwright's reliance on actors' and even audiences' feedback in revising his plays' drafts, noting that "throughout his career, Wilson has made a practice of revising his works after they have opened."

Critical Studies: Major Reviews, Articles, and Book Sections

As is true of the book-length studies of Wilson, there is a paucity of critical essays and book chapters, and most of these are overview essays.

Ann Crawford Dreher's essay (1981) is the longest of the overviews and is quite informative through *War in Lebanon*, the early version of what later premiered as *A Tale Told* and was finally staged and published as *Talley's Folly*. She discusses Wilson's major themes and the significance of his structural and stylistic experiments, refers to the quality of his language, and offers as influences and comparisons not only Williams, Thomas, and Thornton Wilder but also Gorky and Jack Gelber. The essay by Arthur Sainer in James Vinson's *Contemporary Dramatists* (1973) offers a somewhat earlier analysis, in which Sainer states that "evil events and evil forces seem almost nonexistent" in the plays–a point later repeated by Barnett and others–and calls the playwright's relationship to his characters "one of tender observer"–a description repeated by numerous later critics. Sainer's statement about Wilson's tenderness toward his characters is reasonable even in light of the later plays, but his statement that no evil exists in the worlds of *The Madness of Lady Bright, Balm in Gilead,* and *The Rimers of Eldritch* overstates the case. It may be, in *The Madness of Lady Bright,* or even in *Balm in Gilead,* for instance, that there is no agent of evil, but both plays show a society which destroys people; *The Rimers of Eldritch,* furthermore, not only presents an evil society but also evil citizens.

Gautam Dasgupta, in another overview (1981), describes the early plays straightforwardly and neutrally; *The Rimers of Eldritch* is praised as a play that "pulled together the poetic and dramatic to create . . . a built-in dramatic tension" and is contrasted thereby with the diffuse character-driven earlier plays such as *Balm in Gilead* and *This is the Rill Speaking.* However, Dasgupta is never so laudatory again, saying of *The Gingham Dog* that "paperback psychology and sociology account for a lot of the soul searching on the part of Vincent and Gloria, and it all boils down to very little in the final analysis"; saying of *The Mound Builders* that its "abstruse structure" confuses and that its dialogue lacks "poetry and sincerity"; and saying of *5th of July* that its characters practice "anarchy of language and deed without a backbone." Dasgupta reads *5th of July* and *The Hot l Baltimore* as extremely pessimistic, a reading which appears to be unique to him, and he selects as the worst play Wilson's favorite—*The Mound Builders.*

Henry Schvey's "Images of the Past in the Plays of Lanford Wilson" (1981) is another overview, but one which offers an analysis of "the essential thematic unity in Wilson's work from *The Hot l Baltimore* to *Talley's Folly.*" Throughout this analysis are brief yet insightful remarks on individual plays. For instance, *The Hot l Baltimore* is considered to be similar to *The Iceman Cometh,* but also different: "While O'Neill concentrates on the unfortunate necessity of illusions and pipe dreams as a means of survival for the inhabitants of Harry Hope's saloon, Wilson stresses the importance of hope among his lost souls." Furthermore, says Schvey, Wilson destroys any chance of dramatic tension through his "insufficiently critical attitude" toward the characters and their "unreasonable faith" in the future. Likewise, Chekhov's *The Cherry Orchard* (1904) is considered clearly superior to *The Hot l Baltimore;* Chekhov's characters also hope for the future, but, unlike Wilson's, their hopes are balanced by the reader's awareness that "the characters exist in a world where hope is not always enough." Schvey compares *5th of July* with *The Hot l Baltimore,* arguing that the final plea for commitment in

5th of July is echoed by the dance in the hotel lobby; *5th of July* is the better-crafted work, though, since Ken is "so much more convincingly drawn than any of the hopeful outcasts of the earlier play."

The most recent of the overviews, Harold Branam's 1985 essay in Frank N. Magill's *Critical Survey of Drama*, contains some acute observations. It describes a similarity among the early, longer works: they "tend to be uneven, diffuse, almost plotless, with the subject matter providing the main interest. . . . *The Hot l Baltimore* . . . illustrates the format on which Wilson has relied (in lieu of plot) with repeated success–an updating of the old parlor or weekend drama which brings together a group of disparate characters in an interesting setting (usually threatened, usually around a holiday) and allows them to interact." Branam recounts the important themes, emphasizing Wilson's interest in family, and he ends by wondering if the playwright's movement "from a prophetic to a priestly stance, from the Old Testament vision of punishment toward the New Testament vision of love," suggests that he is developing a religious solution to the recurring thematic conflicts.

In "Broadway Bound: Simon, Kopit, McNally, Wilson," chapter 2 of *New American Dramatists 1960-1980* (1982), Ruby Cohn offers a series of plot summaries of Wilson's plays through *Talley's Folly*. Of particular interest is the comparison of Lady Bright with Tennessee Williams's Blanche Dubois and the observation that *The Rimers of Eldritch* "dramatizes evil in the town of Eldritch, with a suspense that is rare for Wilson"; the rare suspense had also been observed by Dasgupta, while the presence of evil had already been denied by Sainer. Unfortunately, Cohn does not develop her observations in any depth. William Herman's chapter in his *Understanding Contemporary American Drama*, "Down and Out in Lebanon and New York" (1987), is limited to analyses of five plays, *Balm in Gilead, The Rimers of Eldritch,* and the three Talley plays, and it offers little new information; Herman's most significant contribution is in noting that Wilson complicates his picture of the American family by introducing strong and important characters who are alien to the traditional American clan–characters such as the homosexual Jed Jenkins of *Fifth of July* and the Jewish Matt of *Talley's Folly*.

Barry Witham's discussion of Wilson's work in "Images of America: Wilson, Weller, and Horovitz" (May 1982) is limited to two pages on *5th of July*, about which he says that "the author's vision is not a hopeless one. Wilson's America is ultimately a garden, a place where things can still be cultivated, renewed, and reborn."

John Steven Paul (Sept. 1980) limits his analysis to *Talley's Folly,* although he attempts to develop a larger context. "The greatest American plays," Paul asserts, "the most durable and performable, are those in which the playwright began with a character and asked him or her not What will you do now? or What do you think? but, simply, Who Are You? . . . The play presenting a single fascinating character was joined by the melting pot play, a form apparently unique in world drama, in which one location, often a restaurant, a tavern, or a streetcorner, serves as a microcosm for American society." He includes in this genre *The Iceman Cometh,* Frank Capra's film *You Can't Take It With You* (1938), William Inge's *Bus Stop* (1955), Williams's *Small Craft Warnings* (1972), and *The Hot l Baltimore.* (Paul's description of the genre is echoed by Branam.)

Martin J. Jacobi's "The Comic Vision of Lanford Wilson" (Fall 1988), addresses charges made by reviewers that the playwright is overly sentimental. Jacobi argues that the later plays, beginning with *The Hot l Baltimore* but especially with *5th of July* and *Talley's Folly,* harmonize two interests that repeatedly appear in opposition in earlier plays: first, a sympathetic depiction of the traditions and values that shape society; and, second, compassionate portrayals of misfits and outcasts, people not sympathetic to their society. The playwright thus moves from earlier pessimistic views of outsiders who might have saved themselves from destruction but did not, to optimistic views of individuals who challenge societal prejudices but still find acceptable places within society. Thus Wilson moves from pathos and incipient tragedy to true comedy.

Reviews of Wilson's premieres and revivals constitute the bulk of published material on the playwright. As is often the case with reviews, some of those listed in the bibliography do little more than describe the plot, scene, and characters of the play considered. However, some include astute observations and criticisms that deserve development in extended critical essays. A few reviewers have covered many of Wilson's plays and so have rather fully developed their criticisms concerning the playwright's themes and style.

Reviewing *Ludlow Fair* and *The Madness of Lady Bright,* Edith Oliver (2 Apr. 1966) called Wilson's work "almost worthless–there are no characters, there is no drama," and all is pervaded by a "shameless, old-fashioned mawkishness." She has repeatedly criticized Wilson for his synthetic plots and characters and his sentimentality and has gotten so specific as to point out the superiority of Edward Albee in writing about marital discord (17 May 1976). She has said of the revival of *Balm in Gilead* that "it does indicate, time after time, the various directions in which Mr. Wilson would be moving in the years to come, and that is the most interesting thing about it," and of *Burn This* that it is half again too long because of its foul language (26 Oct. 1987). With the exception of *Burn This* she has approved of Wilson's later work more than the earlier, even though she has never been unstinting in her criticism.

Gerald Weales has also reviewed many of Wilson's plays and, like Oliver, finds a good deal to dislike. Reviewing *The Hot l Baltimore,* he writes that, "except for Leonard Melfi, Lanford Wilson has always struck me as the schmaltziest of the up-from-off-off-Broadway playwrights"; he also notes that the plays which the Circle Rep produces invariably return to "old fashioned realism and a healthy respect for stereotypes and–I'm sorry–sentiment" (28 June 1975). These criticisms of sentimentality and realism, while seemingly incongruous, are echoed by Oliver and others. Weales makes two observations that might well be expanded in scholarly investigations. When speaking of *Angels Fall,* he notes that Wilson has an old-fashioned view of female vocations–as lovers, wives, and mothers. He points out that the novelist of *The Mound Builders* and the heiress of *Fifth of July* are "much closer to despair than the wives, widows, mothers with whom they share stage space" (17 Dec. 1982), and while the despair of Mary and Gabrielle in *Serenading Louie* and of Netta Talley at the conclusion of *Talley and Son* at least qualify this observation, there seems much truth in his point.

Weales also makes a good point concerning the first two Talley plays (23 Feb. 1980). He thinks they both have the look of happy endings, yet the family, in *Fifth of July,* made up of "a gallery of spiritual, intellectual, physical failures," suggests otherwise. *Talley's Folly* ends with the promise of a "marriage of two sterilities"; in life this might be acceptable, but "on the stage, where images carry conventional audience expectations, it is at best cold comfort." It is unclear how Weales would fit these observations into his belief in Wilson's schmaltziness, and in fact his suggestions concerning this less-than-schmaltzy play writing bear more attention.

Harold Clurman has offered a more positive reading of Wilson in his reviews, and it is a reading that comes close to countering Weales's complaint about Wilson's propensity for realism: "Realism, which certain theater connoisseurs are constantly assuring us has shot its bolt, still has much to offer–especially in the United States. The fashionable denial of realism's worth often seems to me an eva-sion." Oftentimes, he continues, a denial of realism–whether for purposes of a pessimistic naturalism or an optimistic romance–is less a philosophical stance than an emotional response against society– that is, less artistic than neurotic (5 Mar. 1973). He appreciates Wilson's realism much more than the "chromatic demonology which a number of Wilson's contemporaries derive from certain European models" (1 June 1970) and is thankful that the playwright has "overcome the tendencies which have confined a good number of dramatists of his generation to a narrow emotional range and to structural devices of limited creative yield" (15 Mar. 1980). It might be fair to say that Clurman's perspective on Wilson differs from Weales's along the lines of Wetzsteon's differentiation between playwrights who mourn the loss of American values and those who simply scorn them: surely, the presentation of "demonic" characters and events will less likely earn the charge of "sentimentalist" than would the presentation of an elegiac tone or of characters who are sympathetic and even positive.

John Simon also reviews Wilson's plays from a generally positive perspective, although he does find faults. Of *5th of July* he notes (15 May 1978) that even though the play has affinities with Chekhov's *The Cherry Orchard, Uncle Vanya,* and *The Three Sisters,* "climates of thought and feeling have a way of emerging skewed from a later sensibility"; he expands this observation on artistic imitation by saying that Chekhov had "intimations of a collapsing empire and a social order heading for bloody extinction while *5th* is concerned only with the end of feeble political and sexual protests." Something is "gravely amiss" in *Serenading Louie,* yet it also contains a line about which Simon writes, "I can't think of any other living American playwright who could have written a line this subtle and penetrating, this pregnant and this painful, in such utterly simple, denuded language" (13 Feb. 1984). Of *Angels Fall,* he says simply that it is the best American play on Broadway that season (7 Feb. 1983), and of the revival of *Balm in Gilead* that his artistry illustrates "the difference between routine competence and art, between a play accosting life and life itself trapped in a play" (11 June 1984).

A Tale Told is less entertaining than *Fifth of July* and less enchanting than *Talley's Folly,* Simon argues in his review of what was later to become *Talley and Son,* but it is "more imposing, more commanding of respect, than either of its predecessors" (21 June 1981). What Simon finds to approve is not just the realism so problematic to Weales, but also the craft with which Wilson has produced the well-made play—an aspect of Wilson's work that has drawn attention also from Brendan Gill (17 Nov. 1980; 31 Jan. 1983).

Simon also finds the time to evaluate modern dramatists in his reviews. He considers the two best contemporary playwrights to be Sam Shepard and Wilson—"the heir to Williams—and Wilson is better if less original, since he is more literate, more disciplined, more humane." In a 26 October 1987 review Simon writes, "Lanford Wilson seems to me at present our soundest, most satisfying dramatist. He is more disciplined and dependable than Sam Shepard; more various and productive than Tina Howe, Marsha Norman, David Rabe; less autobiographically obsessed than any number of others; and far less quirky, mean-spirited, puny than David Mamet. . . . To people who want eccentricity or mania from their playwrights, he may seem a bit bland; to those who value comprehensiveness, comprehension, and compassion, his pre-eminence is perspicuous."

A number of other reviewers of Wilson's plays are clearly to be counted among his supporters. Of *Lemon Sky* Martin Gottfried writes that it is "awesomely complicated" yet excellently handled, and that Wilson is "one of the very most talented writers in all the American theatre" (18 May 1970); John O'Connor remarks that with this play Wilson has become "one of America's most accomplished and significant playwrights" (22 May 1970); Richard Watts, Jr., sees it as "brilliantly acted and well staged, and probably a better play than the production shows" (18 May 1970). Other reviews generally favorable to Wilson include those of Clive Barnes and Mel Gussow, while reviewers taking a relatively neutral stance include Gill, Walter Kerr, and Frank Rich.

Reviews of two plays in particular deserve specific attention because of critical observations that are developed. *Fifth of July* has received a great deal of attention from reviewers, who are interested in its vision of the American dream and its portrayal of community and human relationships. Despite some disparaging comparisons with Chekhov's drama, the thematic development Wilson shares with Chekhov is seen to be the source of this play's power. Howard Kissel observes of Jed's activities that "the garden is new, which is fitting for an American *The Cherry Orchard*. What the characters learn, which seems almost un-American, is that "the garden should be cultivated rather than abandoned in the quest for something new" (6 Nov. 1980). Frank Rich sees in the play a blending of Chekhov and Mark Twain and calls it a vision of Wilson's "morning-after Independence Day dream of a democratic America—a community with room for everyone, an enlightened place where the best ideals can bloom" (6 Nov. 1980). And Julius Novick states that "Lanford Wilson is sensitive to the genuine idealism, the shallowness and triviality, and eventual disillusionment of the 1960s radicalism. But his play is all the more attractive, more authentic even, because it comes to no conclusion about The Sixties" (29 Nov. 1980). It seems fair to say that this play is Wilson's most respected work; as Jack Kroll writes, "If Lanford Wilson's *Talley's Folly* won the Pulitzer Prize, as it did, then his *Fifth of July* deserves at least the Nobel" (24 Nov. 1980).

Wilson's latest play, *Burn This,* has also generated some interesting observations. It seems as if it can stand as rebuttal to those criticisms that Wilson is too sentimental or that his realism is ineffectual. Thomas M. Disch thinks it a "great" play, part comedy and part tragedy. What makes the play serious, he argues, "is that the lovers lock into their final clinch with such dismay and regret that they might as well have entered a suicide pact as become lovers" (14 Nov. 1987); Gussow views the play in similar fashion, noting that Wilson "exposes deep, uncauterized emotional wounds—and offers no salve," and that while Pale and Anna come together at the end, "it would be precipitous to think of that as a happy ending. There is no guarantee of durability in this relationship" (15 Oct. 1987).

Wilson has said that the title *Burn This* refers to a phrase a writer attaches to a painfully private letter (Freedman, 30 Aug. 1987), and Gussow asserts that the secret to be "burned" is that Larry, Anna's homosexual roommate, "is destined to be a watcher on the sidelines, at most a voyeur, but not someone who can realize his own passions. In a sense, that charge becomes self-descriptive of the plight of the objective artist, the playwright, who is condemned to be an observer and not an actor." A similar observation is made by Edwin Wilson, who says that when the playwright has Anna take Pale as her lover, he suggests that art is not enough, that homosexuality is incomplete, that a woman like Anna is really fleeing from her true nature with homosexual roommates (21 Oct. 1987). Frank Rich combines these two observations when he asserts that "in a play in which no pair of lovers—whether homosexual or heterosexual—has ever lived together, Larry's voyeurism and disconnectedness seem to say more about the playwright's feelings on loss and longing than the showier romance at center stage" (15 Oct. 1987). In short, the consensus building on the theme of this play seems to be that the artist can create a community but cannot join it, and that the creativity requires sexual sterility.

The emerging consensus regarding *Burn This* can bear additional critical attention, not only for the sake of a fuller understanding of the play but also of the role of sexual nonconformity in Wilson's œuvre. He is generally credited with the first "homosexual play" (*The Madness of Lady Bright*), and while he agrees with Wilfrid Sheed (29 Apr. 1966) that "it ceases to be of fundamental importance that the focus is homosexual," Wilson nonetheless often employs homosexuality and lesbianism, incest, sterility, and prostitution as the means of developing the subject of "human loneliness, abandonment, and cyclic betrayal." Sexual nonconformity plays so large a role in the plays that it would certainly sustain an extended analysis. A feminist scholar might want to expand upon Weales's comments concerning Wilson's treatment of women and investigate whether or not the playwright does reinforce traditional perceptions of women's occupations. On another topic altogether, Wilson's religious imagery would also sustain extended critical attention. Branam and others have remarked on the religious imagery, Wilson himself has alluded to his interest in it, and works like *Balm in Gilead* and *Angels Fall* are obvious as starting places.

Certainly attention to Wilson's stylistic excellencies would be well rewarded. The lyrical quality of his prose is probably the subject of most frequent comment by critics and reviewers, and even those who otherwise find the playwright unsatisfactory laud this aspect of the plays. For some it is the center of their interest, replacing character and plot as the hallmark of his work, and for others it is the means by which characters are quickly and convincingly developed. Wilson's stylistic experiments—with overlapping dialogue, repeated action, and the like—could be included here or could form the basis of a separate analysis. And, one might attempt to answer the question of why the playwright has increasingly moved from impressionism and stylistic experimentation toward the conventional, well-made play.

A biographical or psychological critic should explore the relationship of Wilson's life to his plays. The playwright tells Ross Wetzsteon (8 Nov. 1982) that "a friend of mine once told me that in all my work I'm either trying to put my family back together again or to create a new one. I guess he was right." As other examples, there have been repeated comparisons drawn between his early life and *Lemon Sky*, a good deal of his Missouri upbringing is undoubtedly in the Talley plays, and he has remarked to Don Shewey (22 July 1982) that the activities of the male prostitutes in *Balm in Gilead* are based in part on his personal experiences in Chicago and New York. One might also consider more fully the literary influences. Wilson has expressed his appreciation of Tennessee Williams and Anton Chekhov, for example, and it would be useful to know to what extent his plays reflect his readings of Saroyan, Miller, Gorky, and others and to what extent comparisons between these writers and Wilson are coincidental.

Other research opportunities abound. Regardless of which ones get attention, it seems clear that Wilson has established himself as an important figure in American drama and one worthy of much more scholarship than has yet been produced.

Cumulative Indexes

Cumulative Index to Authors

Cumulative Index to Critics

Fuller, A. Howard   3:255
Funke, Lewis   3:230, 343
Gabbard, Lucina P.   3:33, 39
Gado, Frank   1:58, 360, 361
Gaillard, Dawson F.   1:340
Gaines, Jim   3:412
Gale, Steven H.   3:157
Gallagher, Brian   2:323
Galloway, David D.   1:116, 139, 374, 378
Galvin, Brendan   2:296, 297, 440
Gangewere, R. J.   2:289, 301, 304
Ganz, Arthur   3:250, 262, 357, 422
Gardner, John   1:68, 173, 175, 179, 180, 182, 186
Garis, Robert   1:66
Garrett, George   1:177, 178, 180
Garrigue, Jean   2:29
Gassner, John   3:246, 255
Gaukroger, Doug   1:208
Gayle, Addison, Jr.   1:34
Gealy, Marcia   1:285
Géfin, Laszlo K.   2:267
Geismar, Maxwell   1:127
Gelb, Arthur   3:412
Gelb, Barbara   1:202; 3:232
Gelb, Phillip   3:231
Gelber, Jack   3:340
Gelman, David   3:319
Gelmis, Joseph   1:241
Gelpi, Albert   2:194, 198
Gendron, Dennis   2:111, 114
George, Diana Hume   2:318, 319, 320, 328, 329, 332
Gerard, Albert   1:31
Gerlach, John   1:189, 190
Gersham, James T.   1:74
Gerson, Steven M.   1:130
Gerst, Angela   1:59
Gerstenberger, Donna   2:212
Gervais, Ronald J.   1:286

Giannetti, Louis D.   1:332
Giantvalley, Scott   3:26, 27, 36, 46
Gibson, Donald B.   1:37
Gilbert, Harriett   3:322
Gilbert, Sandra M.   2:194, 199
Gilbert, Susan   1:190
Gilder, Joshua   1:171, 184
Gill, Brendan   3:33, 165, 168, 294, 451
Gillespie, Gerald   1:78
Gillespie, Patti P.   3:320, 374
Gillikin, Dure Jo   2:142
Gilman, Richard   1:255; 2:186, 194; 3:285
Gindin, James   1:150
Giolman, Richard   3:36
Girgus, Sam B.   1:286
Giroux, Robert   2:47
Gitenstein, Barbara   1:152
Givner, Joan   1:295
Glancy, Eileen K.   2:84, 85
Glaser-Wohrer, Evelyn   1:58, 65, 66
Glenn, Eunice   1:410
Glick, Nathan   2:145
Glore, John   3:350
Glover, Albert   2:245
Glover, William   3:28, 281
Goeller, Allison Deming   1:419
Gold, Dale   1:204
Goldberg, Maxwell H.   2:231, 232
Goldberg, Robert   3:336
Golden, Daniel   1:155
Goldensohn, Lorrie   2:64, 65
Golding, Alan   2:265
Goldman, L. H.   1:123, 124, 126, 137, 140, 142, 148, 150
Goldman, Mark   1:282
Goldsmith, Arnold L.   1:285
Gollin, Rita K.   1:290
Gollub, Christian-Albrecht   3:236
Gomez, Jewelle   3:319